American Journalism

To McKenna, Delaney, Matthew, and Garrett

American Journalism

History, Principles, Practices

Edited by W. David Sloan
and Lisa Mullikin Parcell

McFarland & Company, Inc., Publishers

Jefferson, North Carolina, and London

Library of Congress Cataloguing-in-Publication Data

American journalism : history, principles, practices / edited by
W. David Sloan and Lisa Mullikin Parcell.
p.   cm.
Includes bibliographical references and index.
ISBN 0-7864-1371-9 (softcover : 50# alkaline paper) ∞
1. Journalism—United States.   I. Sloan, W. David
(William David), 1947–   II. Parcell, Lisa Mullikin.
PN4853.A48   2002
071'.3—dc21   2001008468

British Library cataloguing data are available

Cover art ©2002 PicturesNow.com

Manufactured in the United States of America

McFarland & Company, Inc., Publishers
Box 611, Jefferson, North Carolina 28640
www.mcfarlandpub.com

Contents

Preface: Journalism's Memory

This book is intended to help journalists and students appreciate their profession better. It does that by recounting the history of the most important principles and practices in the field. As memory is to an individual, so history is to a profession. Without knowing one's past, a person has an incomplete knowledge. Likewise, without knowledge of journalism's background, neither working journalists nor students can have a full regard of the career they have chosen.

Often, we in journalism take for granted the ideas we hold and the customs we have adopted. Yet, every one of them has come about through a long period of development. Every principle and practice of present-day journalism has undergone change a number of times. Nothing that we do is the same as it was when it began. Knowing about the nature of journalism's ideas and customs throughout history enlarges our understanding of what we do today. Without such knowledge, we find it difficult to understand why we do things as we do and, as a result, are limited in our ability to assess what we do or to improve how we do it.

Each chapter herein was written specifically for this book and provides an overview history of an important part of the field. In many instances, the chapters are the first such survey histories on the topic. Since space limits the amount of detail that can be included, each chapter necessarily provides only the highlights. To assist readers who wish to explore a topic further, each chapter includes a bibliography of suggested readings about a variety of historical aspects of the chapter's topic.

The editors and authors hope that readers will come away from this book with a much greater awareness of what journalists and journalism are doing today and a deepened respect for the important roles they play.

1

The Purposes of Journalism
Julie Hedgepeth Williams

There was yet another rumor in circulation. Again, someone had planted a scandal about the royal family, or maybe there was a charge against the conduct of ministers or judges. There was sure to be a sex scandal attached to the whole thing or maybe allegations of governmental malfeasance. People were only too happy to believe these rumors, although anyone with half a thought in his head would realize that at least some of them had to be false.

You might think the scene was this year, in the supermarket checkout lane, but instead it was 1690, in Boston, the most intellectually vigorous city in the American colonies. There had been a press in Massachusetts since 1638 and almost everyone could read—and how they did read! The local press turned out tract after tract of Puritan religious fare; and every ship that visited the harbor brought books, pamphlets, and newspapers from the Old World to the New. Newspapers arrived via ship, too, including the *London Gazette,* the *Athenian Mercury* from London, a Dutch *Mercury* from Holland, and various other titles. Americans read these faithfully. They had no local newspaper, however, to tackle American news as a primary focus.

But in 1690, an experiment was about to take place. Benjamin Harris was putting to press an American newspaper, not a European one. It was called *Publick Occurrences, Both Forreign and Domestick,* and as far as Harris was concerned, this one would do much to solve American troubles. America was, of course, ruled by the English monarchy. So it should theoretically have been sufficient for Americans to read English newspapers. But there was something lacking in that plan, something American. Local issues got short shrift in the urbane European press. Harris would consequently focus on local troubles.

Those troubles happened to be related to the monarchy, but they were American in nature. England's Catholic King James had been ousted in 1688, and in 1689, Protestants William and Mary had taken over the throne. In America, various colonial officials were losing their jobs (one was even hanged) in the political unrest associated with the change in the monarchy, and all of this was excellent grist for the rumor mill. The rumor mill, as Harris saw it, was turning out nothing but garbage these days. Although a healthy oral culture supported truths told by word of mouth, rumors by their nature got magnified in their retelling, especially if they seemed fantastic. The cure for such false rumors, Harris thought, would be *Publick Occurrences.*

In his first (and, as it turned out, his last) edition of *Publick Occurrences,* editor Harris offered a prospectus that sketched out the purposes and policies of his newspaper. He focused on the need for a "Faithful Relation" of events. Harris told readers he would be a good reporter: he would ask well-regarded, credible citizens to write articles for his paper. These citizens' credible reports, in turn, would have the effect of "... Curing, *or at least the* Charming *of that* Spirit of Lying, *which prevails amongst us....*"[1]

That wasn't the end of it. The editor went on to make a threat to the rumormongers who spread falsehoods all over the colony. *Publick Occurrences* would print the names of liars who originated the outrageous rumors. Harris commented, *"It is Suppos'd that none will dislike this Proposal, but such as intend to be guilty of so villainous a Crime."* In both cases, Harris was obviously trying to bring reality into focus.

In Puritan Massachusetts, it was also important that the newspaper report "occurrences" (as the title suggested), which today we might call "news events." In that first and only issue of Harris' newspaper, the "occurrences" included such things as colonists Indians had kidnapped, the cancellation of an invasion into French Canada, a disastrous fire, an outbreak of smallpox. The point of such reporting, as the prospectus emphasized, was to remind people that God was at work in the colony. Presumably bad news would show the Almighty's displeasure. Good occurrences were a blessing from God. In other words, the newspaper would be a vehicle for readers to understand God's commentary on the local scene. Thus it was imperative to have the truth about local occurrences made plain.

To Benjamin Harris, *Publick Occurrences* would aid the Domestick scene far more than the Forreign. It would ultimately make American matters plain, giving the truth and correcting lies. It would set up the reality of America for all readers to see. What was real in rumor-filled 1690? *Publick Occurrences* would let you know.

Publick Occurrences failed after one issue when authorities banned it, apparently due to reports in the paper on a sex scandal in the French royal family and allegations of malfeasance in the leadership of Indian allies.[2] But ever after, the American press would strive to do as Benjamin Harris had done. Like Benjamin Harris, the press realized it held reality in its hands. It could present truth as it was. As various men and women of the press realized the great power of presenting truth, some of them concluded that the press could—and should—also create reality as it ought to be. Harris wanted to publish truth as it was with accurate reporting. But his chief goal in doing so was to force a better reality to the surface—

to build a colony on truth by putting a stop to lies.

That dual role that America's first newspaperman had envisioned became, indeed, a basic issue for the press across time. The press had a purpose of publishing the truth. Should that truth be what was literally there? Or should it construct a reality that Americans presumably needed to achieve? The desire to publish truth has been in the press from the very start. The basic question in that endeavor, however, is as old as humanity itself. What is truth?

For some editors, truth was a nitty-gritty, day-to-day reflection of reality, of what *was*. Editor Thomas Whitmarsh in 1732 South Carolina sought his readers as writers so that they might communicate the straight facts about everything from the growing of hemp[3] to the cure of smallpox.[4]

Other colonial editors, however, saw the truth issue differently. Rather than reflecting the community at large, they quite deliberately tried to mold a reality that was meant to be. In New York, where factions had divided local politics for decades, the faction out of power in 1733 hired an immigrant named John Peter Zenger to publish a newspaper as their voice. In that publication, they continuously lampooned the governor of the colony, whom they claimed was negligent in the defense of the colony.[5] The faction was certainly trying to direct public opinion against the governor and, in that way, foment some sort of change in New York politics. They were sculpting reality in New York. The faction that backed Zenger assumed the press had power—and used it to create a reality that needed to be, in the publishers' opinion. They deliberately did not give two sides of every story. There was only one side, the right side, the true reality that imperfect mankind *should* be trying to grasp.

Such stubbornness was replayed as the American colonies stumbled toward war with Britain. Editors indeed used their press to take charge of truth itself, trying to sculpt reality as it should be. They urged in their pages that the truth be brought into focus. Why would anyone, they reasoned, support things that were self-evidently false? Pro-American printer John Holt wrote in his *New-York Journal* that it was his duty to publish *only* what was morally correct. "In short, I have endeavored to propagate such political Principles ... as I shall always freely risk my Life to defend," he explained.[6]

On the other side, James Rivington, a Loyalist New York editor, saw freedom of the press as the freedom for any reader to publish opinions about any topic—even though pro–American Patriot factions were pressuring him to publish their ideas only. Thus, he said, "TRUE SONS OF LIBERTY" would print impartially. Rivington promised to print anything submitted to his *Gazetteer,* "whether of the Whig or Tory flavor."[7] He was trying to protect Loyalist ideas by giving them a forum, of course, but nevertheless, he was arguing that the power of the truth lay in reflecting the entire portrait of America in a grand and accurate balance. The press was to show absolute reality.

Even Loyalist editors found out, however, that there was no way to maintain that stance. As political and military pressures increased, eventually everyone had to take sides. All editors had to persuade readers as to the reality that was correct. Editors published very slanted battle coverage to boost their particular side. When the British took Philadelphia during the Revolution, Loyalist Rivington sang the blessings of the conquerors. "The fine appearance of the soldiery, the strictness of their discipline, the politeness of the officers, and the orderly behavior of the whole body," he reported, "immediately dispelled every apprehension of the inhabitants, kindled joy in the countenances of the well affected, and gave the most convincing refutation of the scandalous falsehoods which evil and designing men had long been spreading to terrify the peaceable and innocent."[8]

Meanwhile, the Green brothers, Patriot editors in Connecticut, portrayed the British soldiers as brutes. In the Greens' reports on the battles for Philadelphia, British soldiers barged into every house near the battlefield, pulled their light artillery into people's bedrooms, and fired out the windows into stubble and hay. That cowardly means created lots of smoke, which forced Americans to retreat rather than fire willy-nilly into the smoke and maybe into their own troops.[9]

The net effect of such reporting was, of course, that the absolute truth was lost. No one knew which account of the battle was correct—and Revolutionary War–era editors didn't care. To them, truth was not a fixed fact. Truth was open to interpretation. The truth had to be *made* true. Truth was based on perception, and the *correct* perception was all-encompassing.

Thus, shortly after the war began, a faction-oriented press was well-established. It carried over easily throughout the Revolution and into the next period of the press, which historians have named the "party press" era. A new nation was forming. No one knew if a republic could really work, but here were the Americans who had fought and won the long battle to give it a good try. It was probably inevitable that parties formed to try to steer the raw nation into certain channels. Thomas Jefferson wanted a weak central government and power in the states. Alexander Hamilton wanted a strong federal government, with relatively weak states. These two powerful men wound up as George Washington's advisors, and almost immediately parties began to coalesce around them. It seemed natural to these new parties that the press use its power and its factional tendencies as tools in the work to build the country's political system—to create the great truth that seemed to be within the grasp of the new nation, if only they could get the word out.

Thus, in the party press era, parties vied for public attention and favor by hiring editors and newspapers to tout reality as it *ought* to be. They discussed one party as right, the other as wrong. They urged voters to the polls, not just for the patriotic duty of voting, but specifically to elect the man chosen as the darling of the newspaper. Editors were on the payroll of parties, and this was well-known and accepted. "WHIGS of NEW-YORK!" one New York newspaper exhorted its readers, "is it desirable that J. PHILLIPS PHOENIX shall be our next Mayor, with a WHIG COUNCIL? If Yea, just say the word! To be victorious now, we have but to will it!... Three days, only, bring us to the Election. BE READY!"[10]

A Raleigh, North Carolina, paper published extensive, intricate details of business in the U.S. Senate and U.S. House of Representatives and took front-page space to publish a letter decrying a detractor of James Madison. "Your opposition to Mr. Madison, previously to his late election, was marked by an intemperate personal hostility. In the gratification of your spleen you violated every rule of decorum, and forfeited much of your pretension to the character of a gentlemen," the writer huffed. He added with a sigh of relief, however, "But you failed in your attempt to crush him and only rendered yourself ridiculous."[11]

Although there were wins and losses in every editor's column, in the end the party press achieved what it had thought it should do. It had sculpted the reality of the new nation. In the aggregate, it did much to establish parties and gave roots to a political system that thrived on the checks and balances inherent in a multiparty concept of politics. The party press helped that effort go grass-roots, to involve ordinary readers into the fierce loyalty of the party system. Ultimately, then, the media of the day helped create the reality of American politics. They took the republic of the Founding Fathers' dreams and helped mold a political system from it into a reality that stands pretty much intact today. There were other forces at work, to be sure, but the press had a hand in making the party system a fixture of daily life in the nation. It created that truth by *trying* to create it, by deliberately molding reality as it seemed right. The press of the party era was no passive reflection. It was deliberate in its will to create truth.

While newspaper advocates were working the minds and hearts of the people toward sympathy with various political parties in much of the young nation, starting in 1833 an unexpected twist was taking place in the press of New York City—a twist that by most counts turned very few heads outside of that city ... at first. In the end, though, that new "penny press" set up strong standards for portraying reality in all its dirty detail. Eventually the press across the nation would begin to mimic that concept of reality as gospel. This new press movement would help answer the question, "What is truth?" by insisting that the truth was even in dirt and squalor and ignorance, not just in lofty party ideals.

In New York in 1833, printer Benjamin Day founded the *Sun,* a newspaper that he hoped would make him some money during a particularly rough time for his print shop. There had been an epidemic of cholera, and everyone who could afford to had left town. That left little business for his press, and Day thought perhaps a newspaper would bring in some cash. Day decided he would try some ideas that were new to him. First of all, he would try to sell the *Sun* for just a penny a copy. As early as 1769 this had been tried in America without success,[12] for newspapers customarily were bought a year at a time by subscription. But perhaps this time Day was thinking of the masses of immigrants pouring into New York City in recent years. They were too poor to flee the epidemic. So there they were as potential customers. They were also too poor to subscribe a year at a time, but Day figured that just about everyone had a penny in his pocket and might spare it on a day-to-day basis. Thus he began the penny press, in part to meet his own economic needs but also to meet the economic reality of his presumed audience.

For such a paper truly to work, there would have to be one final ingredient, which Day got quickly: He hired George Wisner as a reporter. Wisner already worked for another newspaper in town, reporting court news.[13] When Wisner moved to the *Sun,* which was cheap enough for the rabble of the town to afford, suddenly the court news was an attractive commodity. Wisner didn't bother with high-profile court cases involving the elite. Instead, he went to the daily police court in New York, where the ordinary drunkards, thieves, and wife-beaters were all tried. He put these people in the paper. For example, he recorded the court appearance of John Dolly, who "was so very drunk last night that he imagined himself to be in his own native Lun'on." Wisner used Dolly's dialect in reporting the story. "'Your vorship,' said John. 'What?' said the magistrate.—'Vy, I vas so fatigued last night that my ead haked—I urt my eel on the sidewalk—and fell down. I say, you vorship, will you let me go um?'" Dolly was fined $1.[14]

Likewise, Wisner recorded the sad story of Tommy Williams, a boy who was caught stealing cakes to feed to himself and his friends, who were pretending to be actors. Wisner recorded the exchange between the magistrate and the child:

> Magistrate. You little rogue, don't you know you are on the high road to ruin?
> Pris. I didn't mean any hurt—(crying)....
> Magistrate. Well, Tommy, did you ever personate any other character but that of Othello?
> Prisoner. (Wiping his eyes.) No sir, but aunt Susy says how if I does well in Othellur, she's goin' to learn me to play comedy. (Laughter [in the court].)
> The magistrate said he was willing to be lenient..., and if Jackson [the victim] would forgive the prisoner, he should be discharged. The complainant was unfavorable, and poor little Tommy was committed.[15]

Wisner's police column hit home with the readers. Sales skyrocketed. Benjamin Day's paper was a success, largely because it reflected a greater reality. Since the Revolution, the press had been cast primarily for those interested in political matters—and naturally, therefore, the primary audience were the movers and shakers of society, the elite who had a chance at being most directly affected by political decisions. True, the ordinary people had gained a grass-roots sort of interest, but the wealthy had a more tenacious interest. News had been priced pretty much for them, too, and it had never particularly focused on news of the masses. The *Sun*, however, for the first time, was a paper that actually reflected the whole strata of New York society, focusing on and appealing to the people who had never been included before. The *Sun* was reflecting New York as it was, with all its grit and sweat, at a price the gritty and sweaty could afford.

It worked. Newspapers around the city began to imitate the *Sun*. Horace Greeley, for instance, founded the *New York Tribune* as a penny paper in hopes of getting his Whig political party message before a wider audience. He soon dropped the Whig format. The *New York Times* was born as a penny paper, hoping to cash in on the new format. James Gordon Bennett founded the *New York Herald*, quickly setting himself up as the arbiter of the ultimate

reality. He saw the press as something of a journalistic savior of mankind, with himself as the messiah. He knew Truth! He bore Reality to the reader! Bennett's personal philosophy was that "[a]n editor must always be with the people—think with them—feel with them—and he need fear nothing, he will always be right...."[16] As he bragged in his *Herald*, "This is the age of the Daily Press, inspired with the accumulated wisdom of past ages, enriched with the spoils of history, and looking forward to a millennium of a thousand years, the happiest and most splendid ever yet known in the measured span of eternity!"[17]

An interesting outgrowth of the penny press' self-image was the idea that objectivity was part of truth. While parties controlled the traditional dailies in New York, Bennett proclaimed that a true media messiah was of no party, was not on the payroll of any faction. "Formerly no man could read unless he had $10 to spare for a paper," Bennett wrote. "Now with a cent in his left pocket, and a quid of tobacco in his cheek, he can purchase more intelligence, truth and wit, than is contained in such papers as the dull Courier & Enquirer, or the stupid Times for three months." In fact, he said, the *Courier & Enquirer* and the *Times* cared less about helping readers than about currying the favor of business concerns. "All these large papers are in the hands of stock-jobbers. None are free as the mountain wind but the small dailies. We are the fellows that will tell the truth."[18]

Although Bennett was by no means free of personal prejudice, he at least proclaimed that the true press, the press that would save the world, did not look through a party's glasses. The eyes of the press were clear, seeing all sides and thereby coming to truth. Across time, the mainstream press eventually adopted the penny press' philosophy. It became popular to think of objectivity as a requirement of telling the truth, of portraying reality. It became essential to reach various strata of society by telling them that they, too, were part of reality by including them as subjects of the news and as consumers of the news. But the wholesale adoption of that concept of reality would be some time in coming. Other forces were at work on the press.

Just as the widely reflective press of the colonial times had given way to a partisan Revolutionary press, it was impossible to avoid the compulsion to shape truth as the Civil War approached. The press, just beginning to feel the penny papers' new sense of reflecting reality as a whole picture, again shifted to shaping reality—to propounding reality as it ought to be—as the nation fell apart over slavery and related economic issues. An active antislavery press was growing. Founded specifically to arouse people to the antislavery cause, these newspapers decried stodgy thinking and openly discussed slavery as immoral. At first these anti-slavery writers seemed unusually fanatical. However, as the Civil War erupted, that strong type of stand became more typical. The ordinary press took on, once more, a party stance in the hopes of influencing the nation's reality.

The issues of union and slavery were so inflammatory, so critical in the shape of the nation, that it was impossible not to take sides. *The Crisis,* a pro–Southern newspaper published in the unlikely locale of Columbus, Ohio, applauded churches that had refused to let abolitionists preach. "... [S]o insulting, overbearing and unchristian have [pro-abolition preachers] become that they impudently, where they have the power, suspend Gospel Preachers for preaching Christ instead of their political John Brown," *The Crisis* complained. "Members of churches have been insulted and expelled because they dared to suggest that it was doing violence to the Gospel of the Prince of Peace to make the Sabbath a day of electioneering from the pulpit...."[19]

The supporters of the North were just as passionate in their press. "*God bless you for the high and noble patriotism and loyalty of your sheet!* "a Union soldier wrote to *Harper's Weekly.* "Oh, that those cowards at the North who desire 'peace at any price' could be fired with one spark of the high and self-sacrificing spirit that animates the army! We who risk most and suffer most by the war desire *no peace till every black and crime-stained traitor heart is crushed in the dust, and every seed of future treason and rebellion annihilated.*"[20]

In the South, newspapers in occupied territory fled town to town, state to state, rather than acquiesce to Northern conquerors. A Vicksburg, Mississippi, paper published on wallpaper when it ran out of regular paper. The word had to get out to bolster the truth, as editors fervently believed truth to be. Northerners likewise had to be defended by publication as well as by gun, for publication was the important public record of thought. Reality, as it ought to be, had to be shaped and maintained in the public mind. There could be no turning from the press' duty to mold reality as it ought to be, never giving in to the doom at hand.

While earlier it had taken from the time of the Revolution to the arrival of the penny newspaper for the press to leave behind an advocacy role and gain a sense of reflecting reality as it was, the press bounced back to a reflecting position much more quickly after the Civil War. By the end of the war, techniques had been perfected whereby large and fancy illustrations could be published in magazines or newspapers at a relatively small cost. It was a woodcut process, which had long been used in the press, but the high cost of woodcuts was prohibitive until Frank Leslie and others like him pioneered a faster, cheaper method of reproducing pictures in the press. The press era starting around the time of the Civil War and for some decades to follow was noteworthy for its headfirst, deep dive into the world of the visual image. It was the beginning of a revolution in media that would lead to all 120-plus television channels of today, bringing with it a similar persona: Now news events could be shown and described by picture instead of by a thousand (or fewer) words. Hand-in-hand with that, ordinary events or non-events could be shown by picture.

With the development of the illustration, the press again became the reflector of truth— at least, as long as truth could be drawn into a picture. The press took up a goal of depicting the world at large in its accurate glory. Sumptuously illustrated travelogues, for instance, were popular in the press of post–Civil War America. Readers could marvel at places they'd never go and otherwise would never have seen. They could also see fashions that were popular in New York or Paris. Readers could see news events depicted, too, and they could look at realistic pictures of human suffering and human joys. It was a great reflection of the world in a way that had never been possible before. This open-eyed reflection process was democratic. It captured kings and commoners alike in illustrations, making both pauper and king come alive to viewers. *Harper's* showed a happy woman receiving a Valentine from a gentleman and a few pages later showed pictures of starving, bone-thin babies in an ill-provided foster home.[21] An issue of *Frank Leslie's Illustrated Newspaper* featured scenes of soldiers in Turkey dancing to celebrate an armistice; a ferryboat accident in Ireland; traveling merchants among Australian aborigines; a charity drive in Russia; and a procession of African chieftains and their slaves. These ran alongside pictures from all parts of the United States, including scenes from the nation's exciting Centennial Exposition in Philadelphia.[22]

The pictures were all sanitized to a degree, for these were works of art and not photographs. But once more, as had been pioneered in the colonial press and re-engineered by the *Sun,* the press again sought to reflect the world in a broad mirror, and even if the pictures were a little cleaned up, they tapped into the strong human sense of vision to connect people with the great world as it was. Thus, they reflected the world in a great and enjoyable but passively truthful mirror.

As had been common in press history, however, the purposes of the press were destined to shift again. After the media mastered the art of the truth in the visual, it seemed that editors and writers chafed with the desire to make truth more true to a bigger vision. Thus the press entered a long period in which it was known for trying very forcefully and colorfully to shape reality as it should be. As the 19th century drew to a close, William Randolph Hearst was the rising star in the newspaper world, striving to become king of the newspaper hill. Ultimately, in a bid to repeat James Gordon Bennett's role as something of a journalistic savior, Hearst created a reality that left its mark on people around the globe for years to come: He helped bring about the Spanish-American War. Hearst, owner of the *New York Journal,* himself took credit for the Spanish-American

War of 1898, repeatedly calling it "the Journal's War."[23] He went to Cuba for the war, joyful about what he had accomplished. His reporter James Creelman actually formulated a battle plan and led the charge on a Spanish fort, with Hearst taking the story down for him and sending it on to the wire. Creelman was injured in the battle, but Hearst overlooked that. "I'm sorry you're hurt," he bubbled, "but wasn't it a splendid fight?"[24] By instigating the war and personally having a part of it, Hearst succeeded in his very public attempt to create reality, to shape the world around him, to boot Spain out of the hemisphere and to make America an empire by winning Spain's holdings abroad. Via "the Journal's War," America acquired colonial possessions, most notably the Philippines. Truly, Hearst held reality in his hands, making America a world power.

If Hearst went too far in leading the nation into battle, the next great movement in journalism tried to create truth in a wholly different way. As the 20th century dawned, the most important movement in journalism (reflecting similar concerns in the nation as a whole) was the reform movement. Dubbed "muckrakers" by a disgruntled Theodore Roosevelt, reporters such as Ida Tarbell and Lincoln Steffens spent months and even years researching and then exposing the evils of society in multi-installment magazine articles. It was, in a way, *Publick Occurrences* reincarnated in the early 20th century. *Publick Occurrences* had sought to undo malicious lies by telling the truth in 1690. The best muckraking pieces were, in like manner, all billed as true history, a straight reflection of life as it was. Articles were careful to point out the provable evils and ills of big business, big government, big religion, and other institutions, supporting their claims with documented facts. The hallmark of the good muckrakers was careful attention to accuracy and detail.

Ida Tarbell took more than a year to research the history of Standard Oil, which became the first famous muckraking piece. In fact, as she recalled, she didn't discover the proof of some of the most shocking practices of Standard Oil until the articles were already being published month by month. Although she found numerous complaints from independent oil producers, claiming that the giant Standard Oil Company had interfered with their oil shipments and pressured potential buyers to cancel orders in favor of orders from Standard, she did not automatically believe them. As she put it, she had to take into account the suspicion competitors had of one another. After some time, however, she found the proof that she had awaited. A teenage office worker, burning records for Standard Oil, began noticing the name of his Sunday School teacher in the papers he burned. The teacher was an independent oil refiner. "It was not long before he saw to his distress that the concern for which he was working was getting from the railroad offices of the town full information about every shipment that his friend was making," Tarbell recalled later. "Moreover, [the boy found] that the office was writing to its representative in the territory to which the independent oil was going, 'Stop that shipment—get that trade.'" The anxious teenager saved out the evidence and gave it to a friend, who had been reading Tarbell's *McClure's* series. He turned the documents over to her.[25] For Tarbell, it was imperative to have proof before she could believe and then publish information that had long been rumored.[26]

Similarly, Lincoln Steffens, another famous muckraker, brought together stories that were already known in exposing governmental corruption in Minneapolis. "The exposure of Minneapolis was all over; the main facts had been running scrappily as news in the papers for a year. My job was to collect and combine the news serial into one digested, complete review," he recalled later.[27] Top muckrakers such as Steffens and Tarbell saw their job more as historian than as an exposer of ills. Their role was to bring together the known facts in a meaningful way. In turn they firmly believed that such an accurate history of a topic would help bring about legitimate demand for reform, built on a bedrock of truth and not of speculation. It was a bold attempt to shape reality in the way the journalists thought it should be—by showing truth as it already was. If they accurately reflected evil, society would rightly demand change. In that way, muckraking would

fulfill the role foreseen for journalism in 1690 in *Publick Occurrences* by both reflecting and shaping reality.

Muckraking as an all-encompassing movement largely died out in the 1910s, and the themes of shaping reality by simultaneously reflecting it seemed to die with it. World War I brought a repeat of one-sided press coverage, which historically seemed to be a necessity in wartime. Once more, as had happened in the Revolutionary War and the Civil War, the media in general offered a consensus-like support of the American cause in the war. An Alabama newspaper, for instance, reported during World War I of a rally against the Germans that an attorney named Godbey conducted. "Mr. Godbey's analysis of the Hun mind and his damnable intrigues to destroy civilization was the most masterful and convincing effort ever made her[e]," the writer proclaimed. "[H]e referred to the fact that Germans were the only people who had ever set hate to music. He declared that the Hun's hymn of hate would rise up to dam[n] him when, possibly future generations would forget his rape and murder of innocent women and children."[28] Again, there was an attempt to paint reality very starkly against the enemy and very much for the allies, as Hearst had done in "the Journal's War."

But the media were on the brink of a new era. By the 1920s, radio began taking its place in the world of media. It had the effect of bringing people together via the airwaves, of somehow reflecting the truth and then beckoning listeners to conform to it. Radio suddenly offered all people a connection to the world at large. Rural people could tune into popular music, popular dramas, popular quiz shows. No one need be isolated any more, at least as far as entertainment went. Whatever they heard in New York, they could also hear in Kansas, as long as they had a radio. Ironically, this democratizing effort at reaching all society (much as the *Sun* had done a hundred years or so earlier) began the shaping of society that has brought debates about broadcasting ever since. The broadcasting system would one day be cursed for leveling regional differences by promoting one style of speech as clearest, one type of music as the most popular, one type of politician as the most smooth-voiced or (when TV added pictures to the mix) as the most handsome and thus the most vote-worthy. The effect was a portrayal of society in one "typical" image.

That molding of society via broadcasting was largely unplanned in the 1920s and 1930s, but World War II again brought a deliberate media attempt to mold public opinion, to create reality as it ought to be. As in all previous wars, the media felt a need to support the right cause, the good one. As it always had done in wartime, the press had to choose clinical neutrality or an opinion, and it chose opinion. Battles were reported faithfully, but there was a distinct attempt to sharpen the difference between ally and enemy.

Interestingly, however, the era also saw devoted use of media that purported to reflect the world as it was. One of the latest technological advances in the media, which enjoyed great use in the war, was the newsreel. Television technology was in its infancy, but movies had been playing, along with newsreels, for some years. The moving picture brought a new wrinkle. Now a person did not have to be newsworthy or even need to speak on an issue. Just by passing by the camera at a certain time, he *was* the news. It was a reflection of the public at large in a hitherto unknown scale. The newsreel could capture people and their everyday actions in a whole different scope than could a traditional print news story.

World War II newsreels put out by Castle Films, for example, showed crying children and anxious parents ducking into ditches to avoid bombs in France; grass-skirted Ethiopian soldiers in a pathetic, barefoot retreat from Italian invaders; women calmly entering a Parisian bomb shelter; and American soldiers marching smartly and crisply on the training ground. The goal seemed to be to draw in the ordinary refugee, the everyday soldier, alongside the more notable people, for the newsreels also showed Australian leaders mapping strategy and captured Axis leaders on trial. It was an elevation of the common man alongside presidents and generals.[29] The developing technology of the newsreel certainly brought a sense of wide, unblinking reflection of the world.

And yet, those same newsreels, heirs historically to all past war coverage, were adamantly patriotic. They reinforced pro–American opinion on the movie screens and maybe in the hearts and minds of audiences in movie theaters everywhere. Castle newsreels were congratulatory when the camera caught an Italian pilot in a downed aircraft throwing up his hands in surrender. They showcased the clever American/Australian attack on the Japanese fleet in the Bismarck Sea with a detailed map explaining strategy. They glorified America as "the nation that [had] taught the world to fly" and now was training its best and brightest in aerial warfare.[30] It was a strange twist of purpose and scope for the media. On the surface, the media reflected people as they actually were. But the all-encompassing mirror of the camera lens was under the dictatorship of the editor. The Second World War's media manipulated those clear-eyed shots into patriotic reality only, a vital boost to the war effort that few questioned then or now. The media combined the faithful reflection of reality with the deliberate orchestration of reality in reporting World War II.

In the post–World War II era, the major media development was television, whose phenomenal appeal and seemingly unbounded technological advancements keep us tied to our televisions today for both traditional news and unending entertainment. The same questions of truth have plagued television as they have plagued media across centuries. Television, like newsreels, had the opportunity to portray truth as it rolled by, to be the mirror of even the most ordinary man and woman in the street. And yet television could also be conceived of as the all-encompassing theater with a neatly staged play at hand. The play could purport to be true to life, but in the end it might really be a scripted picture of life.

To what degree, then, does television reflect truth or shape it? The question has constantly come up since television took the media world by storm. Believing as humans do that "if you can see it, it's so," TV-watching humankind has frequently been lulled into thinking television was the ultimate mirror ... and then been shocked to discover that the mirror was more limited than anyone had ever imagined. Thanks to television, watchers could see the horror of Vietnam. TV mirrored so grossly and so accurately the body counts and disappointments of battle that over time newspeople ignored the traditional patriotic themes so consistently a part of all past war coverage. The media grew heady with the power of making the war true by showing the dark reality of it, while the military complained loudly that the media failed to show the truth of just causes, the reality of devoted fighting men, and the true deficiencies of communism. Whereas the media of the past had created a patriotic truth supportive of an ultimate truth, the media of Vietnam were decried for too realistic a definition of truth. Death and disappointment were true, but so was patriotic duty. The camera did not lie, critics said, but perhaps its focus and angle did.

No matter what the critics complained about, by the latter part of the 20th century traditional news media operated on the philosophy that reality ought to be reflected objectively, with all sides having their say. To reporters and editors from all media, this form of truth was the gospel. Without such a philosophy, they believed, they would not be taken seriously and therefore could not possibly succeed. Indeed, as media owners demanded firmer profits in the 1980s and 1990s, closing unprofitable outlets, survivors clung ever more tenaciously to the idea that all reporting had to be fair and objective, balancing all sides. In spite of the fact that bottom-line worries sometimes led to change and experimentation in some industries, in the news industry such demands sent writers scurrying to the fundamentals that the penny press espoused—to the objective truth as a bedrock. Objectivity would reflect everyone and would favor no one. As an example, the *Christian Science Monitor* recently reported the arrival of McDonald's in Brazilian slums. The article balanced both sides. "Although her meat and shrimp empanadas have always sold well, Edina Nascimento is worried about the arrival of a McDonald's nearby," the newspaper reported. "She knows that next to Happy Meals, her pastries would look decidedly sad." On the other hand, a 13-year-old named Dimitri da Silva, licking a McDonald's ice cream cone, told the *Monitor*, "I used to buy ice

cream down the road, but they weren't as good. These ones are expensive but worth it."[31] That type of balanced quoting sounds natural and journalistically typical to readers of today, but it was certainly not always the case.

By century's end, mankind was perhaps no closer to answering the old question, "What is truth?" The traditional media, however, were firmly convinced that "truth" meant "the world as it is." Party interpretation, factional alliances, and even old-fashioned patriotism seemed to be relics of the journalistic past. To most editors, the only way to create a successful newspaper was to make a concerted, almost sacred, effort to reflect the world in its full array of opinions, ethnicity, agreements, disagreements, and so on. The only opportunity to offer suggestions for shaping that world came in the editorial section, a rather hallowed ground reserved mainly for the seasoned veterans. Reporters had to remain neutral. Truth, after all, was in their hands.

Selected Readings

Gleason, Timothy W. "Legal Advocacy and the First Amendment: Elisha Hanson's Attempt to Create First Amendment Protection for the Business of the Press." *American Journalism* 3 (1986): 195–206.

Hudson, Frederic. *Journalism in the United States from 1690 to 1872.* 1873; reprint, New York: Haskell House, 1968. See especially Chapter XXVII, "The New York Herald," 428–55, and XXVIII, "More of the New York Herald," 456–90.

Knightley, Phillip. *The First Casualty: From Crimea to Vietnam, the War Correspondent as Hero, Propagandist, and Myth Maker.* New York: Harcourt Brace Jovanovich, 1975.

Procter, Ben. *William Randolph Hearst: The Early Years, 1863–1910.* New York: Oxford University Press, 1998.

Sloan, Wm. David. "Examining the 'Dark Ages' Concept: The Federalist-Republican Press as a Model." *Journal of Communication Inquiry* 2 (1982): 105–19.

Tarbell, Ida M. *All in the Day's Work: An Autobiography.* New York: Macmillan, 1939.

Thomas, Isaiah. *The History of Printing in America, with a Biography of Printers and an Account of Newspapers.* 1810. 2nd edition, Marcus A. McCorison, ed. New York: Weathervane Books, 1970.

Notes

1. *Publick Occurrences, Both Forreign and Domestick* (Boston, Mass.), 25 September 1690.

2. This information was given by two early colonists. See diary entry of 25 September 1690 by Samuel Sewall in M. Halsey Thomas, ed., *The Diary of Samuel Sewall, 1674–*

1729, vol. 1 (New York: Farrar, Straus, and Giroux: 1973), 267. See also Cotton Mather to John Cotton, 17 October 1690, in Kenneth Silverman, comp., *Selected Letters of Cotton Mather* (Baton Rouge: Louisiana State University Press, 1971), 27–28.

3. *The South-Carolina Gazette* (Charleston), 15 January 1732.

4. Ibid., 18 March 1732.

5. *The New-York Weekly Journal*, 17 and 24 December 1733, for example.

6. *New-York Journal*, 18 August 1774.

7. *Rivington's New-York Gazetteer*, 22 April 1773.

8. Ibid., 8 November 1777.

9. *Connecticut Journal* (New Haven), 15 October 1777.

10. *New York Tribune*, 10 April 1841. This paper shortly became a famous neutral newspaper, but it did start life as a party paper.

11. "Political," *The Star* (Raleigh, N.C.), 15 February 1810, 1–2. See pages 2–3 for Senate and House proceedings.

12. *The Penny Post* (Philadelphia), 13 January, 1769.

13. *New York Sun*, 9 September 1833.

14. "Police Office," in ibid., 5 April 1834, 2.

15. Ibid. In the original, the material in parentheses was in brackets.

16. *The Courier & Enquirer* (New York City), 12 November 1831. Bennett left this newspaper to found his famous *Herald*.

17. *New York Herald*, 16 May 1835.

18. Ibid.

19. "A New Church Movement," *The Crisis* (Columbus, Ohio), 16 December 1863, 1.

20. Letter in "Peace Through Victory," *Harper's Weekly* 8 (24 September 1864), 1.

21. Picture titled "Arrival of the Country Postman on St. Valentine's Morning," and picture titled "Discovery of Three Half-Starved Alms-House Children…" in *Harper's Weekly* 3 (19 February 1859): 113 and 116 respectively.

22. "The Pictorial Spirit of the Illustrated European Press," *Frank Leslie's Illustrated Newspaper* 43 (18 November 1876), 172. See, in that same issue, "American Journalism," 173, for pictures from the Exposition, as well as random pictures on pages 173 and 181.

23. "How Do You Like the Journal's War?" *New York Morning Journal*, 9 and 10 May 1898, articles starting on front pages.

24. Creelman later recounted the incident as quoted. He is quoted in W. David Sloan, Julie K. Hedgepeth, Patricia C. Place, and Kevin Stoker, *The Great Reporters: An Anthology of News Writing at Its Best* (Northport, Ala.: Vision Press, 1992), 26, 31.

25. Ida M. Tarbell, *All in the Day's Work: An Autobiography* (New York: Macmillan, 1939), 225–26.

26. Ibid., 225.

27. Lincoln Steffens, *The Autobiography of Lincoln Steffens* (New York: Literary Guild, 1931), 374.

28. "Patriotic Mass Meeting Sunday Largely Attended; Godbey is Orator," *Albany-Decatur Daily* (Albany and Decatur, Ala.), 8 July 1918, 1.

29. These and others mentioned in the text were the subjects of various Castle Films newsreels that covered World War II and that were distributed in both home and theater versions and in both silent and "talkie" versions.

30. The quoted material is from a silent version of a Castle Film, for home use, whose overall title is "Battle of Bismarck Sea," although the quoted material was not related to the Battle of Bismarck Sea.

31. Andrew Downie, "McXperiment: serving billions in the slums?" *Christian Science Monitor* (Boston, Mass.) 26 February 2000, 1, 10.

2

Politics and Partisanship

FORD RISLEY

Just 15 days before George Washington took the presidential oath of office, the first issue of the *Gazette of the United States* came off the press in a small newspaper office in New York. The timing was no accident. A supporter of the emerging Federalist Party, editor John Fenno had approached Federalist leaders earlier in the year about starting a newspaper in the new nation's capital, New York City. Fenno, an experienced journalist, knew that he would need financial support from the Federalists to successfully publish a paper. He apparently got the assurances he needed because on April 15, 1789, he launched his four-page paper.

Fenno declared that the *Gazette* would be an outspoken supporter of the new administration. His newspaper would "hold up the people's own government in a favorable light" and "impress just ideas of its administration by exhibiting FACTS."[1] He gave Federalist leaders, including John Adams, Alexander Hamilton, and Rufus King space in the paper to write political essays. In return, Treasury Secretary Hamilton made sure that the *Gazette* received government printing jobs. When the federal government moved to Philadelphia in 1790, Fenno moved the *Gazette* there as well.

The *Gazette*'s relationship with the Federalist party was not unusual. By the end of the century, more than a dozen newspapers would have financial arrangements with the country's political parties. During America's first century, newspapers were openly partisan and, in many respects, were partners in governing the nation. Editors had been major supporters in

America's drive for independence, and political leaders turned to them for support as the new government took shape. In return, party leaders gave their newspaper supporters lucrative contracts to print government documents. The relationship, which lasted until the late 19th century, served both groups—and also served the country. A partisan press kept the electorate informed and helped newspapers gain a financial foothold in their communities. By the 20th century, a more independent and objective press did not have to rely on government patronage, although it would still maintain a great interest in politics.

Beginning with the *Boston News-Letter*, American newspapers had always emphasized politics. But the Stamp Act of 1765 led colonial newspapers to take an active, partisan role in politics. The Stamp Act, levied on all printed material and legal documents produced in the colonies, was the first direct tax the British Parliament imposed. Colonial editors used their papers to oppose the tax and organize public resistance, including a boycott of British goods sold in the colonies. Opposition to the Stamp Act, which Parliament repealed a year later, gave newspaper printers confidence in their political influence with readers. During the next nine years, they continued to play an active partisan role in the continuing arguments over taxation. In fact, newspapers found it increasingly difficult to remain neutral. Although some Tory papers supported the British, most journals sided with the colonists.[2]

Some of the most active political papers were found in Boston. Benjamin Edes published the *Boston Gazette*, a radical newspaper that became one of the most influential and widely read in the colonies. Sam Adams, a leader of the Sons of Liberty, wrote hundreds of political essays for the *Gazette*, arguing that Parliament was overstepping its authority over the colonies. When tensions grew and erupted with the Boston Massacre in 1770, the *Gazette* printed a story expressing outrage at the actions of British troops. Paul Revere's woodcut of the five colonists the British troops killed during the fighting accompanied the account.[3] During the Revolutionary War, which began in 1776, newspapers maintained their partisan roles with colonial journals trying to boost American morale by emphasizing the importance of fighting. Isaiah Thomas, publisher of the *Massachusetts Spy*, wrote, "Let us not busy ourselves now about our private internal affairs, but with the utmost care and caution, attend to the grand American controversy, and assist her in her earnest struggle in support of her natural rights and freedom."

In the new nation that emerged from the war, partisanship remained the hallmark of newspapers. The press served as an important forum for debate, particularly during deliberations over the ratification of the U.S. Constitution. Supporters of the Constitution and a strong central government, known as the Federalists, made their arguments known in the *Federalist Papers*, which were first printed in newspapers throughout the new states. "Nothing is more certain than the indispensable necessity of government; and it is equally undeniable that whenever and however it is instituted, the people must cede to it some of their natural rights, in order to vest it with requisite power," John Jay wrote in one installment of the *Federalist Papers*.[4] The group opposing a strong federal government, known as the Anti-Federalists, used newspaper essays such as "Centinel" to argue on behalf of a Bill of Rights. Typical was the following "Centinel" essay: "Friends, Countrymen and Fellow Citizens: Permit one of yourselves to put you in mind of certain liberties and privileges secured to you by the constitution of this commonwealth, and to beg your serious attention to his uninterested opinion and upon the plan of fed-

eral government submitted to your consideration, before you surrender these great and valuable privileges up forever."[5]

By the time George Washington was elected president, the political antagonism between the Federalists and Anti-Federalists was boiling over. So it was not surprising that both of the country's emerging political parties turned to newspapers to help spread their message and attract followers. To counteract the influence of Fenno's *Gazette of the United States*, the Anti-Federalists persuaded the well-known writer Philip Freneau to move to Philadelphia and start another paper, the *National Gazette*. To help him get established, Secretary of State Thomas Jefferson gave him the Department of State's printing contract. Freneau attacked Federalist policies, including the Bank of the United States, and made fun of the aristocratic airs of its leaders, such as Hamilton. Jefferson later remarked that "[Freneau's] paper has saved our constitution which is galloping fast into monarchy."[6]

Fenno's and Freneau's papers were not the only partisan journals. Other editors with an interest in politics lined up behind the Federalists and Anti-Federalists hoping to become party spokesmen and receive government patronage. Benjamin Franklin Bache, the grandson of Benjamin Franklin, began publishing the *Aurora* in Philadelphia in 1790. One of his most popular targets was President Washington. Reacting to Washington's farewell address, Bache wrote: "If ever a nation was debauched by a man, the American nation has been debauched by Washington. If ever a nation has suffered from the improper influence of a man, the American nation has suffered from the influence of Washington. If ever a nation was deceived by a man, the American nation has been deceived by Washington."[7] William Cobbett, publisher of *Porcupine's Gazette*, matched Bache's stinging criticisms of the Federalists. Upon founding the *Gazette*, he proclaimed, "Professions of impartiality I shall make none." He argued that any editor who "does not exercise his own judgment, either in admitting or rejecting what is sent to him is a poor passive fool and not an editor."[8]

The government's need to publish official

acts and documents helped political factions support newspapers. Congress took the first step in 1789 by authorizing the Secretary of State to select newspapers in which to publish copies of the laws and resolutions that Congress passed. The practice gained popularity, was expanded, and eventually spread to the state and local level. The government turned to newspapers because the press, in many respects, was regarded as part of the political system. After all, the First Amendment to the Constitution safeguarded freedom of the press, making the press the only business specifically protected by law. Newspapers also benefited from other privileges including reduced postage rates and free exchanges. Moreover, government did not tax newspapers. In many respects, they came to be regarded not strictly as a private business, but as a public service.[9]

By 1800 the nation's capital had moved to Washington, D.C., and it became common for the presidential administration to have an official newspaper in the city. In an era before the interview or press conference, the official administration paper was the means by which the president spoke to the nation. In some cases, he sent correspondence to the editor, which was printed in the newspaper with little editing. In others, the president and editor met regularly, with the editor later writing editorials expressing the president's views. The administration paper also printed executive orders and presidential statements such as the State of the Union address. The country's newspaper exchange system aided the influence of the administration editors. If any two editors mutually exchanged papers, they could mail their papers free of charge, thus providing administration papers with a circulation far beyond Washington.[10]

The leading administration paper for some 25 years was the *National Intelligencer*, which Samuel Harrison Smith founded in 1800. He had won the friendship of Jefferson, the president-elect, and was committed to the ideals of the Republican Party. He expressed his support for the Jefferson administration when he wrote in 1807, "[The editor] conscientiously believes the existing administration have uprightly and wisely discharged their du-

ties. He is, therefore, the friend of that administration, and whatever new dangers may environ them, from the injustice of foreign powers, or from internal machinations, he shall view in the light of new motives to exertion."[11] Smith eventually sold the *National Intelligencer* to Joseph Gales, Jr., who, with his partner, William Seaton, continued the paper's support for the Republican party. The paper was one of President James Madison's biggest supporters during the War of 1812. In return, it received administration support.[12]

During the second party system, which saw the rise of the Democrats and Whigs, political parties battled just as intensively and continued using newspapers to reach voters. After he lost the disputed 1824 presidential election, Andrew Jackson made newspapers one of the key components of his Democratic organization. He found sympathetic editors such as Amos Kendall of the *Argus of Western America*, Duff Green of the *United States Telegraph*, and Francis P. Blair of the *Washington Globe* who helped him win the White House four years later. In many respects press partisanship reached its peak during the eight years of the Jackson administration as he rewarded press supporters not only with government contracts but political office as well. He appointed some 50 journalists to positions in his administration, including making Kendall a member of his "Kitchen Cabinet," an informal group of advisers that, in many respects, had more influence on executive policy than the official Cabinet.[13]

Although Jacksonian Democrats made great use of their newspapers allies, the Whigs also had lots of friends in the press. In fact, they were supported by a network of newspapers larger than that of the Democrats. Some of the most vocal Whig papers published in small communities. They included Samuel Bowles' *Springfield* (Mass.) *Republican* and Thurlow Weed's *Albany* (N.Y.) *Evening Journal*. Weed, in fact, was one of the leaders of the Whig party; and the *Evening Journal*, in many respects, became the national spokesman for the party.

In the battle for national office, the Democrats and Whigs also utilized a new election technique, the campaign newspaper. Jackson had proven the success of the campaign paper during the 1828 election, and other presidential candidates quickly followed suit. Over the next 30 years, hundreds of campaign papers began publishing, not just in Washington, D.C., but in virtually all the states. They went by such names as the *Jacksonian, Old Soldier, Coon Hunter, Clay Bugle,* and *Campaign Dealer.* Their editors saw them as a "muster," their contents "ammunition," and their readers as a "great army of volunteers" to help their candidate win office.[14] The most successful campaign paper was the *Log Cabin,* published by Horace Greeley on behalf of William Henry Harrison during the 1840 presidential campaign. Making extensive use of engravings, songs, and cartoons, Greeley effectively contrasted the aristocratic incumbent, Martin Van Buren, with the simple, patriotic war hero, Harrison. The latter won the election.

Congressmen had always had far more difficulty using the press than the president did. The majority party had been able to exert an influence by awarding printing contracts to key Washington papers. But the hundreds of Congress members could not manage the press in the same way that a single president could. Thus, a senator might find his speech described by a friendly reporter as "full of marrow and grit, and enunciated with a courage which did one's heart good to hear. No mealy mouthed phrases ... but strong and stirring old English, that had the ring of true metal." Another paper might describe the same senator as having "...a soft, catlike step; a keen, snaky eye; a look and address now bold and audacious, and then cringing and deprecatory; his whole air and mien suggesting a subdued combination of Judas Iscariot with Uriah Heep."[15]

By the 1830s, the newspaper landscape was beginning to change. The advent of the penny press introduced major changes to the way newspapers conducted business. Led by such papers as the *New York Sun* and *New York Herald,* newspapers in major cities sought out advertising and circulation, instead of political patronage, as the primary source of revenue. Whereas the party papers emphasized political and business news, the penny papers focused on

general-interest news.[16] Yet most newspapers remained vigorously partisan, and that partisanship was reflected in the growing debate over the future of slavery in the United States.

Abolitionists recognized that the press could be a powerful ally in their fight against slavery. Among the earliest antislavery publications was the *Genius of Universal Emancipation,* founded by Benjamin Lundy in 1821. Often referred to as "the little paper with the great name," the *Genius* was uncompromising in its criticism of slavery and provoked widespread hostility. Lundy later hired an experienced journalist, William Lloyd Garrison, to help him publish the *Genius.* Garrison was an even more fiery critic of slavery and called for immediate emancipation of all slaves. He and Lundy soon parted company, and in 1831 Garrison started his own abolitionist newspaper, the *Liberator,* in Boston. Blacks in America, he declared in the first issue, were as entitled to "life, liberty, and the pursuit of happiness" just the same as whites. Of his determination to see slavery ended, he wrote: "I will be as harsh as truth, and as uncompromising as justice. On this subject, I do not wish to think, to speak, or write, with moderation.... I am in earnest—I will not equivocate—I will not excuse—I will not retreat a single inch—AND I WILL BE HEARD."[17]

The small number of black-owned newspapers were openly partisan in their support for abolition. Most of them struggled financially and were short-lived. The best-known black publication was the *North Star,* published by Frederick Douglass. An escaped slave, he had gained fame as an abolitionist speaker. He recognized that a newspaper could spread his message and founded the *North Star* in 1847. "The objective of the North Star," a prospectus announced, "will be to attack slavery in all its forms and aspects; advocate universal emancipation; exact the standard of public morality; promote the moral and intellectual improvement of the colored people; and to hasten the day of freedom to our three million enslaved fellow-countrymen."[18]

In the South, which depended heavily on slavery for its agricultural economy, many newspapers reacted aggressively to the increasing calls for emancipation. The South had fewer and smaller newspapers than the North, but most were devoted supporters of the region's way of life. In fact, the sectional papers of the South were similar to partisan papers in that both could be emotional regarding threats to their interests and policies. However, these southern sectional papers differed from partisan papers in that they focused almost exclusively on sectionalism in public life, discovered their mission in defending the South rather than in winning public office, and spoke for a state or region instead of a political party.[19] Even the South's handful of penny papers, which declared themselves independent of political parties, could not stay out of the debate.[20]

Particularly outspoken were the so-called "Fire-Eaters," who defended slavery and attacked abolitionists at every opportunity. The dean of southern fire-eaters was Robert Barnwell Rhett, editor of the *Charleston Mercury*. As the debate over slavery grew increasingly intense during the 1850s, he and a growing number of southern editors called for the South to declare its independence and secede from the United States. "The South must control her own destinies or perish," the *Mercury* declared.[21] The election of President Abraham Lincoln, an outspoken critic of slavery, in 1860 emboldened more southern newspapers to call for secession. "*We have but three months in which to work*," stressed the *Athens* (Ga.) *Southern Banner*. "On the 4th of March, 1861, we are either *slaves in the Union or freemen out of it*. Let true men and Georgians decide for themselves."[22]

The year 1860 marked a turning point in the government's relationship with the press. The Government Printing Office was established that year amid growing concerns about the cost and effectiveness of newspapers printing the federal government's documents. President-elect Lincoln also made it clear that he did not want an official journal and instead would deal with the press in his own shrewd way. The institution of a newspaper as the official presidential organ was over.[23]

Lincoln understood the importance of public opinion, and toward that end he cultivated his relationship with the press. Lacking an official journal, he regularly met with a group of correspondents, expressing his opinions and encouraging them to share their views regarding the war. He also made it a habit to visit the telegraph office in Washington to get the first news of major battles. He used the Associated Press when he wanted to make his official statements and speeches public. When he delivered his now-famous Gettysburg Address in 1863, he gave a copy to an AP reporter. At one point during the war, he remarked, "The press has no better friend than I am—no one who is more ready to acknowledge its tremendous power for both good and evil." Steeped in the tradition of partisanship, many editors, including James Gordon Bennett of the *New York Herald*, Horace Greeley of the *New York Tribune*, and Henry Raymond of the *New York Times*, did not hesitate to criticize Lincoln or his wartime policies when they believed it was warranted. Greeley wrote one of the most famous editorials of the war, "The Prayer of Twenty Millions," as a personal appeal to the President to free the slaves. The most vocal critics of Lincoln were so-called "Copperhead" editors, who supported the South and believed the war should not be fought.[24]

As the Civil War ended, an independent press clearly was on the rise. Party papers would never monopolize debate to the extent they had, although they would continue to play prominent roles. It was not that party leaders did not want an official organ. "A party without an outspoken fearless advocate and defender, in short an '*organ*' will so 'go where the woodbine twineth,'" one Democrat wrote another in 1874. "*We should start a news paper at once*." And most newspapers were more than glad to get funding from any source they could, even far away. John Forsyth, editor of the *Mobile* (Ala.) *Register* appealed to Democratic friends in New York for financial support. Yet, as one historian of the period has noted, "the parties found that organs were not easily kept in tune."[25]

Newspapers learned that independence from party domination was good for business. News increasingly became the selling point for newspapers in the big cities. This focus on a different type of news could be seen in the nation's capital, where the role of the Washington reporter was growing in importance. To compete successfully with their rivals, major metropolitan papers could not rely on news from the wire services. They needed their own correspondents, journalism veterans eager to uncover stories no one else had. In an era rife with political corruption and scandal at all levels of government, reporters on "Newspaper Row" did their best to uncover the stories. Some observers argued that this focus on exposure overlooked the many honest and hardworking bureaucrats in government. Moreover, the competition to outdo one's rivals pushed some reporters beyond the bounds of responsibility. The worst political correspondents did not separate fact and rumor, often printing stories overheard in back rooms without verifying the information.[26]

Political leaders began to recognize they would have to take a more active role in managing the news. Office holders began feeding reporters information not readily available in the hopes of influencing the direction of a story. When that failed, some officials sought to "buy" reporters with gifts or part-time jobs in government. The most egregious example was that of Uriah Hunt Painter of the *Philadelphia Inquirer*, who became a paid lobbyist for several interests.[27] But other reporters were outraged by the practices that some political reporters engaged in. "Pickaway," the *Cincinnati Enquirer*'s correspondent in Indianapolis, was offered a gold watch by state house clerks and a box of cigars from a legislator. He declined them both and wrote about the bribes in his paper.[28]

By the end of the 19th century, politicians could no longer count on the press to provide automatic support. In fact, journalists increasingly saw themselves as watchdogs over government. Whereas journalists in the past mixed news with opinion, favoring politicians and parties whom they supported, increasingly they viewed the two as separate, a concept that became known as "objectivity." The goal of objectivity led journalists to adopt news-gathering techniques such as interviewing, using documents, and going beyond what they saw or heard at an event such as a speech or meeting. The press still had a great interest in politics, but the focus was now on how those in government could serve the public interest.

At the turn of the century, reform-minded journalists, led by the so-called "muckrakers," revealed stories of graft and corruption in all levels of government. Perhaps the best example of reform journalism focusing on problems in government was "The Shame of Cities," a series of magazine articles by Lincoln Steffens, detailing corruption in cities such as Minneapolis, Philadelphia, and Chicago. Steffens concluded that the shame of the cities was the shamelessness of citizens. In most cities, he found that "corruption was not merely political; it was financial, commercial, [and] social...." Leading citizens and business owners often were involved with politicians in stealing from government, he reported.[29]

Facing an increasingly critical press, some in government recognized they would need to be more aggressive in trying to manage the news. Gifford Pinchot, chief of the U.S. Forest Service from 1898 to 1910, created what is believed to be the first official press bureau. Its staff published hundreds of pamphlets, reports, and press bulletins publicizing the Forest Service's work. By 1912, other federal agencies had press agents, including the Post Office and the Department of State. Pinchot also advised President Theodore Roosevelt, another politician who recognized the importance of having good relations with the press. As governor of New York, he had courted the press by holding twice-a-day meetings with reporters in the state capital. During his two terms in the White House, he gave reporters unprecedented access, setting up a pressroom close to the Oval Office and regularly inviting reporters into his office for question-and-answer sessions. However, like former presidents, Roosevelt also became frustrated with the news media. He labeled reform-minded reporters "muckrakers" because he believed they focused too much of their work on the problems in society.[30]

Although the news media became increasingly independent and forced political leaders to turn to other means to influence the press, political allegiances did not disappear entirely. One of the best-known editors of the early 20th century, William Allen White of the *Emporia* (Kan.) *Gazette*, gained a national reputation as a spokesman for the grassroots Republican Midwest.[31] In many cases, the allegiances of a newspaper tended to reflect the dominant party in a state or region. Thus papers in the East and South tended to be more Democratic, while those in the Midwest and West sided more with the Republicans. Most major newspapers also continued the practice of endorsing political candidates, especially those running for president. The two publishing giants of the early 20th century, Joseph Pulitzer and William Randolph Hearst, had a great interest in politics. Hearst, in particular, saw himself as president-maker, lining up support for or opposition to candidates from the chain of newspapers he had put together across the country.[32]

Critics charged that the strong editorial support given to some candidates showed that newspapers remained partisan, despite their claims of independence. Despite his wide support among the electorate, President Franklin Roosevelt increasingly fell out of favor with editors, leading some critics to claim that the press was conservative and out of step with the times. Press opposition also forced Roosevelt to look to other means to communicate with the public and turn to a new invention, the radio. With radio, he could circumvent the press and speak directly to the public. He started "fireside chats," radio addresses to the nation that allowed him to show his warmth and charisma, while explaining his programs. Roosevelt's administration, in fact, was an astute observer of the press, recognizing how it could help shape news coverage. Roosevelt met with journalists more than any other president, holding almost 1,000 press conferences during his 12 years in office. He also appointed the first designated presidential press secretary, Stephen T. Early, a former journalist who established a coordinated bureaucracy in the White House to deal with the news media.[33]

News management became even more institutionalized after World War II. The Eisenhower Administration created the White House Office of Communications. Later presidents expanded it. Following the lead of the president and Congress, a growing number of elected officials at the state and local level hired press secretaries or entire offices devoted to dealing with the press. President John F. Kennedy showed the power of television as a public relations tool, especially the televised press conference. In the 1960s, the Vietnam War significantly changed the relationship between politics and the press. During the administration of President Lyndon Johnson, many members of the national press increasingly distrusted the veracity of information the administration provided about the war and other issues. The term "credibility gap" became popular in describing the news management style of the Johnson Administration.

In this growing atmosphere of distrust, critics increasingly charged that many members of the news media had become too liberal. The administration of President Richard Nixon, in particular, viewed the press with great suspicion. The administration's point man on the subject, Vice President Spiro Agnew, argued that the television networks and the so-called "Eastern establishment press," in particular, were guilty of "querulous criticism." In one memorable speech, he called the press "nattering nabobs of negativism." By the time the *Washington Post's* Watergate investigation brought down Nixon, many were describing the government and press as "adversaries."[34]

The *Post's* Watergate reporting was a clear indication of how the relationship between the press and politics had changed over two centuries. Two groups that had been political partners now often viewed one another with suspicion and distrust. By the end of the 20th century, a largely independent press still had a great interest in politics, but it was more in politics as a news story, reported objectively and free of partisanship. Political parties and interest groups turned to other means to spread their message, especially television political advertising. With advertising, politicians—not journalists—decided the content of their message.

Selected Readings

Baldasty, Gerald J. "The Press and Politics in the Age of Jackson." *Journalism Monographs* 89 (1984).

Bryan, Carter R. "Negro Journalism Before Emancipation." *Journalism Monographs* 25 (1969).

Casey, Ralph D. "Scripps-Howard Newspapers in the 1928 Presidential Campaign." *Journalism Quarterly* 7 (1930): 207–31.

Clark, E. Culpepper. "Francis Warrington Dawson: The New South Revisited." *American Journalism* 3 (1986): 5–23.

Davis, Harold E. "'A Brave and Beautiful City': Henry Grady and the New South." *American Journalism* 5 (1988): 131–44.

Ford, Edwin H. "Colonial Pamphleteers." *Journalism Quarterly* 13 (1936): 24–36.

Graham, Thomas. "Charles H. Jones: Florida's Gilded Age Editor-Politician." *Florida Historical Quarterly* 59 (July 1980): 1–23.

Graham, Thomas. "Charles H. Jones: Spokesman for the Western Idea." *Missouri Historical Review* 75 (April 1981): 294–315.

Hofstadter, Richard. "William Leggett, Spokesman of Jacksonian Democracy." *Political Science Quarterly* 58 (1950): 581–94.

Hofstetter, C. Richard. "News Bias in the 1972 Campaign: A Cross-Media Comparison." *Journalism Monographs* 58 (November 1978).

Humphrey, Carol Sue. *The Press of the Young Republic.* Westport, Conn.: Greenwood Press, 1996.

Knudson, Jerry W. "Political Journalism in the Age of Jefferson." *Journalism History* 1 (1974): 20–23.

Levermore, Charles H. "The Rise of Metropolitan Journalism, 1800–1840." *American Historical Review* 6 (1901): 446–65.

Majors, William R. *Editorial Wild Oats: Edward Ward Carmack and Tennessee Politics.* Macon, Ga.: Mercer University Press, 1984.

Osthaus, Carl R. *Partisans of the Southern Press: Editorial Spokesmen of the Nineteenth Century.* Lexington: University Press of Kentucky, 1994.

Rivers, William L. *The Adversaries: Politics and the Press.* Boston: Beacon Press, 1970.

Robinson, Elwyn B. "The *Public Ledger:* An Independent Newspaper." *Pennsylvania Magazine of History and Biography* 64 (1940): 43–55.

Sloan, W. David. "The Early Party Press: The Newspaper Role in American Politics, 1788–1812." *Journalism History* 9 (Spring 1982): 18–24.

Sloan, W. David. "The Party Press, 1783–1833." Chap. 5 in W. David Sloan and James D. Startt, eds., *The Media in America: A History,* 5th ed. Northport, Ala.: Vision Press, 2002.

Smith, Culver H. *The Press, Politics and Patronage: The American Government's Use of Newspapers, 1789–1875.* Athens: University of Georgia Press, 1977.

Steirer, William F., Jr. "A Study in Prudence: Philadelphia's 'Revolutionary' Journalists." *Journalism History* 3 (1976): 16–19.

Summers, Mark Wahlgren. *The Press Gang: Newspapers and Politics, 1865–1878.* Chapel Hill: University of North Carolina Press, 1994.

Ward, Hiley. "The Media and Political Values: Image-Building in the 1840 Log Cabin Campaign." Chap. 7 in W. David Sloan and James D. Startt, eds., *The Significance of the Media in American History.* Northport, Ala.: Vision Press, 1994.

Notes

1. *Gazette of the United States,* 27 April 1791.

2. See, generally, Arthur M. Schlesinger, *Prelude to Independence: The Newspaper War on Britain, 1764–1776* (New York: Alfred A. Knopf, 1958).

3. *Boston Gazette,* 28 May 1780.

4. *Federalist Papers,* No. 2.

5. *Independent Gazetteer,* 7 October 1787.

6. "Jefferson to Washington," quoted in Worthington C. Ford et al., eds., *Journals of the Continental Congress 1774–1789* (Washington, D.C.: U.S. Government Printing Office), 231. For a general account of the partisanship of the period, see W. David Sloan, "The Party Press, 1783–1833," chapter 5 in W. David Sloan and James D. Startt, eds., *The Media in America: A History,* 5th ed. (Northport, Ala.: Vision Press, 2002).

7. *Aurora,* 23 December 1796.

8. *Porcupine's Gazette,* 5 March 1797.

9. Culver H. Smith, *The Press, Politics and Patronage: The American Government's Use of Newspapers, 1789–1895* (Athens: University of Georgia Press, 1967), 11.

10. See, generally, Richard B. Kielbowicz, *News in the Mail: The Press, Post Office and Public Information, 1700–1860s* (New York: Greenwood, 1989).

11. *National Intelligencer,* 7 September 1807.

12. William E. Ames, *A History of the National Intelligencer* (Chapel Hill: University of North Carolina Press, 1972).

13. Gerald J. Baldasty, "The Washington D.C., Political Press in the Age of Jackson," *Journalism History* 10 (1983): 50–71.

14. *Clay Bugle* (Harrisburg, Pa.), 18 July 1844.

15. Quoted in William L. Rivers, *The Adversaries: Politics and the Press* (Boston: Beacon Press, 1970), 12–13.

16. James L. Crouthamel, *Bennett's New York Herald and the Rise of the Popular Press* (Syracuse: Syracuse University Press, 1989).

17. *Liberator,* 1 January 1831.

18. Quoted in Carter R. Bryan, "Negro Journalism Before Emancipation," *Journalism Monographs* 25 (1969): 19.

19. Carl R. Osthaus, *Partisans of the Southern Press: Editorial Spokesmen of the Nineteenth Century* (Lexington: University Press of Kentucky, 1994), 91–92.

20. Ford Risley, "The Savannah Morning News as Penny Paper: Independent, but Hardly Neutral," *American Journalism* 16 (1999): 21–38.

21. Quoted in Osthaus, *Partisans of the Southern Press,* 86.

22. *Athens Southern Banner,* 6 December 1860. For more on the role of the southern press during the secession crisis, see Donald E. Reynolds, *Editors Make War* (Nashville: Vanderbilt University Press, 1966).

23. Smith, *The Press, Politics, and Patronage,* 228–35.

24. See, generally, Robert S. Harper, *Lincoln and the Press* (New York: McGraw-Hill, 1951).

25. Mark Wahlgren Summers, *The Press Gang: Newspapers and Politics, 1865–1878* (Chapel Hill: University of North Carolina Press, 1994), 43–75.

26. Ibid., 80–94.

27. Donald A. Ritchie, *Press Gallery: Congress and the Washington Correspondents* (Cambridge: Harvard University Press, 1991), 92–112.

28. *Cincinnati Enquirer*, 1, 4, 19 February 1875.

29. Lincoln Steffens, *The Shame of the Cities* (New York: McClure, Phillips, 1904), 14.

30. Rodger Streitmatter, "Theodore Roosevelt: Public Relations Pioneer," *American Journalism* 7 (1990): 96–113.

31. Sally Foreman Griffith, *Home Town News: Wil-liam Allen White and the "Emporia Gazette"* (New York: Oxford University Press, 1989).

32. W. A. Swanberg, *Citizen Hearst* (New York: Charles Scribner's, 1961).

33. See, generally, Betty Houchin Winfield, *FDR and the News Media* (New York: Columbia University Press, 1994).

34. Rivers, *The Adversaries*, 7–48.

3

The Press and Government

Paulette D. Kilmer

The press and the government have often been adversaries in recent years, and yet they share the mission of instilling within the public a sense of civic responsibility. Through the Civil War, they mostly worked together. However, resentment of industrialists during the Gilded Age (1865–1914), suspicion of the expanding bureaucracy of Franklin Roosevelt's administration (1933–1945), frustration in the 1960s first during the civil rights movement and later with the Vietnam War, and disgust with the Watergate scandal (early 1970s) drove a wedge of mutual mistrust between them.

In the colonial era, some newspapers tended to support those in power, while others backed the opposition factions. The government, through its licensing power, could determine who was allowed to publish. Some governors considered printers a threat to their power. Indeed, the crown's emissary in Virginia, William Berkeley, declared in 1671:

> I thank God, there are no free schools nor printing [in Virginia], and I hope we shall not have these hundreds of years; for learning has brought disobedience, and heresy, and sects in to the world, and printing has divulged them, and libels against the best government. God keep us from both![1]

Despite the concern of such officials as Virginia's Berkeley, popular resentment toward such power restrained the government's exercise of its power.

Benjamin Harris did not obtain permission before launching the colonies' first newspaper, *Publick Occurrences, Both Forreign and Domestick* in 1690. His experiences illustrate how prior restraint defined the relationship between the press and the government. He started the paper to support the Puritan's objective of accurately describing crises confronting the local government. Harris was forced to cease publication after the first issue. An item about the French king's affair with his daughter-in-law and Harris' account of military failures in battles with the French and their Indian allies in Canada offended the authorities.

In contrast to Harris, John Campbell obeyed that law when he started the first continuous newspaper in the colonies on April 24, 1704, the *Boston News-Letter*. He believed his duties as postmaster required him to provide a channel for the unpopular governor to speak to the people. Puritan leader Cotton Mather said the paper was dull, but Campbell's uncritical coverage of the crown's representatives probably also alienated readers. At any rate, he barely managed to stay in business. Campbell conspicuously declared that the *News-Letter* was "Printed by Authority."

Ironically, both Harris, who opposed the King's representatives, and Campbell, who supported them, struggled as newspaper proprietors because of their relationship with the government. The authorities squelched *Publick Occurrences* after one issue. Campbell was allowed to print, but his allegiance to his friends in power inspired him to fill many columns with boring—sometimes politically unpalatable—copy that cost him readers.

Once newspapers increased in number, governors controlled few editors. Licensing authority expired in 1730. Yet, many were printers who relied upon subsidies, including postmaster appointments. By the mid–1700s most colonies had launched newspapers. Their printers supplied the government with legal forms and books as well as a means of circulating decrees over vast areas.

Even after licensing had ended, some printers faced the threat of reprisals if they displeased officials. For example, John Peter Zenger spent 10 months in jail in 1735 for criticizing the autocratic governor of the Colony of New York. The jury refused to find Zenger guilty and, thus, sowed the seeds for truth as a defense in libel cases. Although the decision itself did not change colonial law, it revealed smoldering differences of opinion that would erupt into the demand for independence roughly four decades later.

A major issue of contention between colonists and the British government—therein also between the press and the king—was taxation. The infamous Stamp Act of 1765 required colonists to pay duties on all paper goods and dice. Of course, these fees riled and united the printers, whose profits were directly tapped. Indeed, some had to close their shops. The publisher of the *American Chronicle* of Boston went so far as to write an obituary for his newspaper.[2]

Economic concerns and declarations of the rights of British subjects quickly melded into an unstoppable force led by the furious editors. They inspired citizens to refuse the stamps, riot, burn the offensive slips of paper, threaten official distributors, and stop exporting goods to British merchants and manufacturers. The act was repealed in 1766, but the split between the crown and the press had widened visibly.

During the years leading to the Revolutionary War, newspapers either supported the Patriots, those favoring independence, or Tories, those loyal to the British. Patriot printer, inventor, and statesman Benjamin Franklin contributed letters and items about the volatile political situation. In January of 1770, he sent the *Public Advertiser* three fables. In the first cautionary tale, cows resort to milking themselves to avoid starving when the farmer destroys their hay. The moral warned that unless the Mother Country repealed all excessive taxes, the colonies would sustain themselves with their exports instead of enriching Britain. The second parable about a sassy cat who taught an arrogant eagle a lesson in the power of tenacity reminded readers of the Patriots' grievances. The third described a lion cub eventually growing strong enough to box the ears of a mastiff that had repeatedly tormented it, just as the strong-arm tactics of the British government were provoking resentment that one day might erupt into violence in America.

From the beginning, John Adams, a leader of the Patriot movement, mobilized the angry citizenry via printed materials. In a letter that newspapers printed, he declared: "If the mobs were at first the sinews, the Press and the Committees were the nerves of the Revolution...." As the *Pennsylvania Evening Post* expressed it, "The least shock in any part is, by the most powerful and sympathetic affection, instantly felt throughout the whole continent."[3]

THE NATION-BUILDING PRESS

After the Revolutionary War, two factions competed for power: the Federalists, who supported a strong central government, and the Republicans, who championed individual and states' rights. The newspapers and the government faced the challenge of building a united citizenry.

Political parties sponsored newspapers in this early national period (1789–1831) to champion their cause. Editors and politicians became partners in molding public opinion. Just as the Patriots and Tories had vilified each other, the first American political parties also denounced opponents. Parties chose editors who believed that their faction was pure and all others vile. A newspaper's relationship to the government depended on which party was in power. If the president were a Federalist, then Federalist editors supported him, and Republicans opposed him. One Federalist editor,

Benjamin Russell, concluded that William Cobbett served a vital purpose—hunting Jacobinic (French sympathizing) Republican foxes, skunks, and serpents.[4] Republicans countered by denouncing the aristocratic aims of the Federalists, whom they called the "enemy of representative government," and by promising to protect American citizens from "their [Federalist] diabolical designs."[5] A close relationship existed between parties and papers, and opposition of the press to the government resulted, not from a pervasive adversary relationship between the two, but from partisanship of individual newspapers.

Despite partisan differences, both politicians and party papers agreed on fundamental principles, such as the supremacy of the Constitution and the democratic nature of the nation's political system. Thus, they called upon citizens to embrace a shared code of honor to guide the new government as it evolved into a world power. Therein, a symbiosis emerged between these party organs and the government. The government depended upon newspapers to plant within citizens a pride in nationalism that flowered during the War of 1812. People respected the press as their mirror of the world. Newspapers and government jointly generated political life.

The close relationship between parties and newspapers was enhanced by officials' authority to award printing jobs to newspapers. This patronage system persisted from 1789 to 1875. The most coveted position was postmaster. Postmasters sent papers free to their subscribers and benefited from seeing information first. Furthermore, they confiscated opposition sheets and delayed delivery to their competitors. The patronage system help unite the states by forging a link between citizens and government via local newspapers that explained how broad issues affected particular communities. Thus, subsidies sparked interest in national politics as an extension of local realities.[6] But the party press eventually faded away with the rise of advertising as a financial base for newspapers. Facing increased criticism of the patronage system for the press, Congress stopped hiring newspapers as printers when the Government Printing Office opened in 1860.

SECRECY IN THE HOUSE DIVIDED

In 1833, Benjamin Day launched the first successful daily for readers with modest income who delighted in buying cakes and sundries from street vendors for a cent. His *New York Sun* cost a penny and fit right into the raucous outdoor market. He counted on street sales to attract advertisers and, thus, liberate him from patronage. He filled his paper with ads, court items, disasters, unusual incidents, and human-interest briefs about ordinary people. Although Day and others who soon established penny papers did not consider themselves cogs in the government apparatus, still the new cheap dailies played a vital role in the political process. The *Sun* and the popular newspapers that followed it no longer were attached to parties, but they continued to advocate partisan views. They were autonomous from the government, but as a general rule they supported government policies that agreed with their views. Although now divorced from officialdom, they nevertheless continued to believe that the government and the press shared the same goal: the good of the nation.

On the eve of the Civil War, the press—including even the partisan newspapers—had begun the slow process of weaning away from patronage. This change in financing allowed newspapers to become independent from those who had supported them in exchange for favorable coverage. The shift in editorial stance occurred when northern dailies and weeklies started to sell ads based on circulation to pay their bills. During the Civil War, except for a few penny papers, in the South political parties subsidized editors. There, editors believed it was their duty to support the goals of the government and try to boost morale.

The war did, however, intensify a particularly thorny dimension in the relationship between the press and the government—secrecy. Victory would determine whether one nation indivisible prevailed or two separate countries emerged. Revealing ticklish incidents, disclosing secret maps, or questioning official policies might prove fatal. That problem was particularly noticeable in the North. Suddenly, the tug-of-war between the press' role as the eyes and ears of the community clashed with the government's need to ensure national security and public well-being. In the North, military censors and editors often clashed. Both the Union and the Confederacy tried to censor reporters with mixed results.[7]

A GROWING INDEPENDENCE

The House Divided imagery that Lincoln coined during his debates with Stephen Douglas while running for president provides an enduring metaphor of the relationship between the press and the government in the era following the Civil War. These giant public servants worked together building a sense of common destiny within the populace as the nation expanded from the East to the West Coast and expanded its role around the globe. By the late 1870s, newspapers had switched their financial base from party coffers to advertising based on circulation. Nevertheless, many trumpeted their party's goals on editorial pages, and for some news provided an avenue for parading partisan expectations. The post–Civil War period saw a rapidly increasing independence in the press. Metropolitan newspapers continued to grow in size and to rely more and more on circulation and advertising, rather than patronage, for income. Editors for the most part believed they should continue to support parties but believed they should be free to give their own opinions. Among nearly all, there was agreement that the press should support the government.

In the first years of the 20th century, although the press and the government often shared a commitment to reform that reflected the concerns of the citizenry, politicians and journalists frequently disagreed on whom to blame and how to adjust the system. By 1900, the Progressive party had grown out of a grassroots' demand for change. A few journalists began to think of their job in ideological terms, believing the primary purpose of the press was

to crusade for liberal social and economic causes, to fight on the side of the masses of common, working people against the entrenched interests in American business and government. Although officials at all levels participated in eliminating corruption, many resented the relentless spotlight of press coverage on poverty, big business, and consumer welfare. A group of magazine writers took the lead in exposing wrongdoing and injustice. Ida Tarbell wrote a devastating history of Standard Oil, Lincoln Steffens revealed municipal fraud in major cities, and Upton Sinclair told the unsanitary story of the Chicago meat-packing industry. Sometimes, the government responded to such crusades with new laws: the Hepburn Act (1906) to regulate railroads, the Pure Food and Drug Act (1907), and the Mann Act (1909) to protect women from interstate prostitution rings. Frequently, however, politicians as well as industrialists recoiled from the fiery attacks. President Theodore Roosevelt called these journalists muckrakers. Like the character in John Bunyan's *Pilgrim's Progress*, they were too busy stirring up the filth to gaze upon the stars.[8] His metaphor shows that exposés of suffering, misbehavior, and inequity irritated even politicians who expressed ideals similar to the muckrakers' values.

Nevertheless, two crises in the 20th century demonstrated that however often the media and power brokers might disagree on policies, they always shared a commitment to the national welfare. The first crisis was World War I. In 1914, before the United States entered the war, President Woodrow Wilson proposed establishing a publicity bureau to coordinate all information about the government. "The real trouble," he explained, "is that newspapers get the real facts but do not find them to their taste and do not use them as given them, and in some of the newspaper offices news is deliberately invented."[9] Three years later, in 1917, to unite a polarized public, he partly implemented his press-bureau idea by establishing the Committee on Public Information (CPI) with newspaper veteran George Creel at the helm.

Creel knew that to engage the multitude in the psychological as well as material war with the Central powers, he needed the help of editors. Newsreels as well as the *Ladies Home Journal* (the semi-official magazine of the CPI's home-front crusades) and other periodicals also supported Wilson's fight to "make the world safe for democracy." Creel relied heavily upon weeklies and dailies. His committee produced more than 6,000 news releases, more than 50 pamphlets, thousands of ads to fill donated space in newspapers and periodicals, the daily *Official Bulletin*, and scores of pictures and posters. Metropolitan dailies ran complete CPI pamphlets. Creel estimated that he mailed 75 million detailed explanations of wartime issues. State organizations and individuals also reprinted thousands of these publications.[10] For the most part, the mainstream press backed the CPI's campaigns and leaked very little information to the enemy.

FDR AND THE PRESS — A BATTLE OF IDEOLOGY?

Between 1933 and 1945, President Franklin Roosevelt fought an internal war, the Great Depression, as well as World War II. He brilliantly managed news (sometimes more than necessary) and made use of new communication technology (including radio and newsreels) as well as the print media. He was the first to campaign for the presidency in an automobile, and he rode in an airplane to accept the nomination at the Chicago Convention in 1932. He was the first president to address the public over the radio. In his first "fireside chats," he reassured listeners that the economy would get better. Later, he explained what was going on in the war.

Washington correspondents became so chummy with him that they became, as one correspondent quipped, "united in holy newslock" with Roosevelt, who adroitly steered them toward stories he wanted reported.[11] Reporters emphasized his flamboyant, energetic style rather than his lame legs. His permanent paralysis from polio prompted him to seek feedback through his wife, Eleanor Roosevelt, as well as from advisors and the media. The First Lady wrote a column, gave speeches, and visited many communities to assess New Deal programs.

Roosevelt, like many presidents, was leery of the watchdog function of the press and used his charm, speaking ability, intelligence, and understanding of issues to supply journalists with a steady flow of information dispensed twice weekly at press conferences. Unlike the televised gatherings of today, the reporters were not allowed to quote FDR. He explained policies and answered questions on an off-the-record or deep-background basis. His press secretary distributed mimeographed handouts that correspondents could cite. Roosevelt also hired news writers to prepare press releases for various wings of the Executive Department, a practice that continues today.

In the numerous new agencies that Roosevelt's New Deal established lay the seeds for much of today's press' antagonistic attitude toward government. To attempt to promote proposed policies, the agencies set up public relations arms to provide the press with information. While much of the information was useful, the purpose of much of it seemed to be to promote administration goals and policies and to create a positive image for officials. In later years, such efforts would increase. They expanded at a rapid pace during World War II. Journalists for the most part accepted the need to support war aims and even the need for secrecy in the interest of national security. Following the war, however, government PR efforts continued unabated, and journalists became increasingly skeptical of government claims that information should be classified and kept secret.

Slowly, some journalists in the 1930s were coming to consider the press as an institution whose purpose was to scrutinize the activities of other institutions such as government and big business in order to protect the public. They perceived the press as a watchdog over government. A severe liberal critic of business interests in the press, George Seldes argued that journalism was "subject to the control of an oligarchy of big money and big business which is trying to destroy the foundations upon which free government is built."[12] The press, he declared, always sided with authority, no matter how corrupt.

Although FDR and the press, for the most

part, respected one another, the President's desire to shape the facts that the public received and the journalists' need for autonomy occasionally clashed. While many correspondents and reporters liked FDR, publishers did not, especially by his second term. The issues that divided them arose from ideology—differences in attitudes toward labor, poverty, and taxes. Corporate leaders—including publishers—opposed New Deal promises to end child labor, give workers the right to strike, and provide jobs for the unemployed through government service. Not only had many newspapers become corporations, but they also relied upon children to sell their papers often under abusive conditions.[13]

Speaking to the Gridiron Club in Washington, D.C., in 1936, Roosevelt joked about the ideological differences that shaped journalists' interpretations of his record during his re-election campaign. "In a great serial which ran for several months in the papers, one of the characters bore the name of Franklin D. Roosevelt...," Roosevelt joked. "He combined the worst features of Ivan the Terrible, Machiavelli, Judas Iscariot, Henry VIII ... and Jesse James. He was engaged in a plot to wreck the American Constitution, to poison the Supreme Court, to demolish capitalism, to destroy old age security, to get us into war, and to assassinate all the men in the United States who had red hair or as newspapers claimed the rank of Colonel—in short to blot from the face of the earth the United States as we have known it."[14]

Despite the campaigns against him in such powerful dailies as the *Chicago Tribune*, Roosevelt won four elections, two of them with little newspaper support. The editorial views, however, did not reflect public sentiment. He won by a landslide in 1932 and a 62 per cent majority in 1936. Even in 1940, with most large newspapers opposing him, he took 55 per cent of the vote.

News as a Weapon— World War II

The bombing of Pearl Harbor on December 7, 1941, united editors and government officials at all levels in the quest to enroll average Americans in the home-front battle against complacency. This time around, secrecy was easier to enforce because of the increase of agencies during the New Deal—each with its own public-relations department that could suppress as well as tailor information. Political leaders, newspaper editors, and radio commentators alike stressed that grassroots support produced high morale among the fighting forces abroad. During World War II, newspapers praised citizens for conserving paper, metal, wheat, and meat as well as gasoline and other essentials. People of all ages listened on their radios to breaking news in Europe and the Pacific. Despite political differences, journalists and entertainers in all the mass media promoted the government's cause of defeating the Axis.

Just a few weeks before the decimation of the U.S. fleet at Pearl Harbor, George Creel, the director of the CPI in World War I, had called on Americans to recognize the intimate, inseparable relationship between morale and propaganda. "The 'war will' of the civilian population is a nation's second line," he argued, "and 'war will,' particularly in a democracy, depends upon the degree to which people can be made to consecrate and concentrate body, soul, and spirit in the supreme effort of service and sacrifice, giving complete assent to the truth that all business is the nation's business and every task a common task for a single purpose."[15]

By the end of World War II, journalists began challenging government policies. Simultaneously, critics started questioning the judgment and ethics of the press. For example, a magazine columnist denounced "pompously overwritten tripe" and exotically expressed dispatches from abroad. He praised war correspondents for being "honest, factual, lucid" and, therein, ensuring "the best informed home front in history."[16] The *Richmond Times-Dispatch* suggested that editorial pages kindled doubt because the publishers' emphasis had shifted from public service to making money. Often cluttering pages with "junk," such as "rousing appeals for the observance of National Cheese week," these dailies had degenerated into "vapid handbills" reflecting the publishers' "weird view of society" and rippling with "greed, arrogance, and hypocrisy."[17]

As critics examined the propaganda that had united the nation against the Axis, they blamed journalists for hiding information. The tension between the government and the press, especially the military, heightened as prospects for peace materialized. In May of 1945, *Commonweal* reproached reporters for not explaining the genuine need for secrecy, which in wartime was as inevitable as gravity. "Secrecy is only bad," it editorialized, "when it is used as a means to hide and protect dishonesty, as a means to withhold the facts necessary for making judgments, as a means to commit people to a line of action of which they are ignorant."[18]

PRESS AND GOVERNMENT HUNT WITCHES

The 20th century had witnessed a growing professionalization of journalism, and one of the most marked changes that it brought about was the press's relationship with government. Whereas the press prior to World War II generally was neutral toward or supportive of government, the period after the war saw a swing toward a neutral-to-antagonistic attitude. Journalists were beginning to adopt an institutionalized, professionalized view of themselves as the "watchdogs" of government. They grew increasingly liberal and critical toward government and other institutions such as business and religion. The changing journalistic attitude grew out of episodes such as Senator Joseph McCarthy's attacks on communism in the early 1950s, the civil rights movement of the mid–1950s to mid–1960s, the Vietnam War, and the Watergate political scandal. In all of these episodes, the "press" found itself critical of the government power structure.

In the Cold War that followed World War II, the press for the most part continued to share the government's agenda. For example, although most reporters regarded Senator Joseph McCarthy a liar, many nevertheless repeated his accusations of Communist infiltration of the government, media, and military without giving the accused a fair chance to respond. McCarthy manipulated the Washington correspondents, but most overlooked that bothersome fact because they shared his concern that Communists had taken over vital American institutions. "If Joe McCarthy is a political monster," wrote reporters Jack Anderson and Ronald May, "then the press has been his Dr. Frankenstein."[19] Nevertheless, some newspapers, including the *Christian Science Monitor* and *Milwaukee Journal*, defied McCarthy.[20] Edward R. Murrow exposed his obsession with Red spies on the CBS documentary series *See it Now*. On December 2, 1954, after the televised Army/McCarthy hearings, the Senate censured McCarthy for behaving unethically.

With time, the McCarthy episode helped to increase journalists' skepticism about the government. They became less willing to accept views simply because they came from officials. That skepticism eventually would verge on cynicism, with the prevailing journalistic view that officials could not be trusted precisely because they were officials.

Like the McCarthy episode, the civil rights movement in the 1960s also encouraged a widening gulf between the government and the press. African Americans' demand for equality often strained the relationship between the press and the government at the grassroots level. Some state governments had established Jim Crow laws that denied blacks their rights until the U.S. Supreme Court declared these laws unconstitutional in the mid–1950s. Many local governments continued, however, to treat African Americans as second-class citizens. However, at the federal level, journalists and government officials frequently shared the same goals, and much of the reporting and editorializing of liberal journalists reflected an ideology in tune with federal efforts aimed at ending official discrimination. State and local officials resented what they considered federal intrusion into state business and blamed the media for exacerbating the problems.

VIETNAM AND WATERGATE

Press skepticism toward the government that had originated years earlier came to a head during the Vietnam War and reached full flower during the Watergate scandal. Frequently, politicians blamed the media for bad news. Both Presidents Lyndon Johnson and Richard Nixon believed television was a culprit for declining popular support during the Vietnam conflict. One explanation for the United States losing that war to this day remains the televised scenes of death and destruction. Some scholars have demonstrated that media coverage was, indeed, erroneous, making it appear as if the United States were losing the war when, in fact, it was not. Another erroneous image was that the North Vietnam and Viet Cong were superior soldiers and strategists. The press, according to Peter Braestrup, for example, misrepresented most aspects of the Tet offensive of 1968, which failed to achieve most of North Vietnam's and the Viet Cong's objectives. The press, however, pictured it as a major disaster for United States policy and as an indication that North Vietnam and the Viet Cong could mount a major offensive. The press' misrepresentation, Braestrup claimed, grew out of its adversary role toward the government.[21]

However, others have argued that, in reality, the media mostly cooperated with the government. They claim that the courageous, dedicated, and intelligent correspondents, ultimately, were more paper soldiers than crusading antiwar, antigovernment crusaders. The Kennedy administration realized that restricting information had caused negative coverage in the early 1960s. It corrected that mistake, and by the peak of American involvement in the Johnson and Nixon administrations, the press colluded with the government. The Johnson administration, by "packaging and distributing that information," Clarence R. Wyatt has argued, "...influenced significantly the picture of the war. For the most direct and intense period of American involvement in Vietnam, then, the interests of the press and the government complemented each other much more than they conflicted."[22]

President Nixon, who withdrew troops from Vietnam in the early 1970s, became so obsessed with punishing the media that he drew up an enemies list. Of course, many journalists made that roster. Writing for the American Civil Liberties Union, Fred Powledge said that the Nixon administration engineered restraint of the press. Eventually, all three branches of the government participated in Nixon's vendetta. To whittle away the credibility of the Fourth Estate, Vice President Spiro T. Agnew called the Washington correspondents a pack of "nattering nabobs of negativism." He made veiled threats to revoke television-station licenses. The Nixon staff also rewarded cooperative reporters and withheld information from doubting Thomases. Nixon held 39 press conferences in six years, in an attempt to bypass the Washington press corps by speaking directly to the public via television. His desire to get even with those he believed had hurt his public image drove him to surround himself with advisors who accepted his agenda of burglaries, secret payments, smear campaigns against political opponents, and perjury.[23]

However, even in the 1970s heyday of journalistic glory during Watergate (the break-in at the Democratic National Headquarters)—leading to four Pulitzer Prizes, other awards, a best-selling book by the two ace reporters who stuck with the story (Carl Bernstein and Bob Woodward), and a movie starring Robert Redford and Dustin Hoffman, as well as increases in enrollment at journalism schools—the public blamed the media and not Nixon for the problems. (For accounts of press coverage of Watergate, see chapters 20 and 22.)The *Wall Street Journal* pointed out, "While the press is on a jag of self-satisfaction and self-congratulations, there is an unhappily large number of Americans who aren't overjoyed by the Watergate exposures—in fact, they're annoyed, angry, and hostile."[24] One citizen told *Time* magazine in November of 1973, "They [Congress and the press] are like sharks. When they smell blood, they go mad." In that same article, naysayers denounced the liberal press for inciting a "lynch-mob mentality"—"persecuting the President and tearing up the country." Like Barry Goldwater, they believed the media engaged in "incessant nitpicking" and "treason."[25]

Although Nixon diehards and conservatives blamed the press for the crisis, the owner of the *Washington Post*, Katharine Graham, argued that the messenger becomes synonymous with the unpopular message. "…[W]hat has finally given Watergate such scope and momentum," she declared, "has not been the press but the ultimate determination of responsible people to make our system of justice work. What has sustained and enlarged the scandal has not been the press, but the facts which emerged and the way those involved have reacted to each new disclosure."[26]

The impact that Vietnam and Watergate had on the relationship between the press and government was considerable. Journalists came to accept press opposition to government as a professional standard. They tended to believe that the proper role of the press was to serve as a watchdog or adversary of government. Some went so far as to argue that one of the government's paramount designs was to control information, silence the press, and deceive the public. Opposing the press in many situations, they argued, was the government, which often was reactionary and repressive. One of the government's primary aims, they claimed, was to muzzle the press. Officials realized that the press presented a barrier to their accomplishing their objectives, for it always was attempting to bring to public view what officials were trying to conceal. In such a situation, journalists declared, the press was required to act as an adversary and a watchdog of the government, aggressively protect its rights under the First Amendment, improve its investigative practices in order to uncover official wrongdoing, and remain constantly vigilant, ready to sound the alarm should government demagogues take any action to endanger American liberty.

Journalism professor William Rivers exemplified journalists' concept of an antagonistic relationship between government and the news media in his book *The Adversaries: Politics and the Press*, published in 1970. He argued that the press should exercise a vigorous adversary role against what he called the governmental-industrial-military-educational complex, for the only proper relationship between the press and government should be an antagonistic one. "The only way for a reporter to look at an official," he wrote, "is skeptically."[27] Although he disclaimed that the press' attitude should be a hostile one, he argued that there should be tension and contention between journalists and officials such as exists between opposing lawyers, rather than an amiable relationship. Believing that the governmental-industrial-military-educational complex was responsible for most of society's ills, Rivers claimed that government tried to control information through both dissemination and suppression for its own self-interest and the benefit of the establishment. It was therefore up to journalists to provide balance to the situation and thereby make the American democratic society work.

William E. Porter's *Assault on the Media: The Nixon Years*, published in 1976, expressed the prevailing view among journalists about President Nixon's attitude toward the press. Nixon, he argued, viewed the press with hostility and waged a deliberate campaign to "intimidate, harass, regulate and damage" the news media. Although the press approached Nixon with similar antagonism, Nixon's continuing battle with the media posed a great threat to freedom of the press. As a result of widespread criticism of the press that Nixon's attacks encouraged, newspapers, Porter lamented, began running more conservative material, the media grew more willing to correct errors, local television stations began to stand up to the liberal networks, local government bodies and officials became more prone to be secretive in their meetings and records, and the watchdog role of the press came to be viewed more suspiciously. All these changes, Porter said, helped point out the "frailty" of press freedom when it is subjected to a full-scale attack by a strong public official, even when that official is corrupt and has little true concern for the public interest.[28]

The post Watergate-Vietnam quandary for both the government and the media has been the loss of public confidence. The 2000 presidential election of Republican George W. Bush after several weeks of haggling with Democrat Al Gore over votes in Florida indicates that dire distrust between the press and the government cripples both. "The press," Associated Press reporter Wes Gallagher declared, "cannot remain free without the proper functioning of the government, the judicial branch, and private institutions in a democracy. The press also is an institution. All rise and fall together."[29]

Although politicians resent the vigilant press because it prevents them from steering public opinion, citizens do not trust either the government or the Fourth Estate unless the media remains independent enough to criticize power brokers. Otherwise, the public suspects that corporations, bureaucrats, or corrupt editors are manipulating information to serve their villainous purposes. In the end, both the press and government must be accountable to the people and can only fulfill that obligation by balancing respect with healthy skepticism of each other.

Selected Readings

Ames, William E. "Federal Patronage and the Washington D.C. Press." *Journalism Quarterly* 9 (1972): 22–30.

Aronson, James. *The Press and the Cold War.* Indianapolis: Bobbs-Merrill, 1970.

Hanson, Lawrence. *Government and the Press: 1695–1763.* New York: Oxford University Press, 1936.

Marbut, Frederick B. "Decline of the Official Press in Washington." *Journalism Quarterly* 33 (1956): 335–41.

Porter, William. E. *Assault on the Media: The Nixon Years.* Ann Arbor: University of Michigan Press, 1976.

Prince, Carl E. "The Federalist Party and the Creation of a Court Press, 1789–1801." *Journalism Quarterly* (1976): 238–41.

Smith, Culver. *The Press, Politics, and Patronage: The American Government's Use of Newspapers, 1789–1875.* Athens: University of Georgia Press, 1977.

Stewart, Donald H. "The Press and Political Corruption during the Federalist Administrations." *Political Science Quarterly* 67 (1959): 426–46.

Yodelis, Mary Ann. "Who Paid the Piper? Publishing Economics in Boston, 1763–1775." *Journalism Monographs* 38 (1975).

Notes

1. William W. Hening, ed., *The Statutes at Large: Being a Collection of All the Laws of Virginia*, II (Richmond, 1809–1823), 517, quoted in W. David Sloan and Julie Hedgepeth Williams, *The Early American Press, 1690–1783* (Westport, Conn.: Greenwood Press, 1994), 98.

2. *Boston Gazette*, 31 October 1765.

3. *Pennsylvania Evening Post* quoted in Robert Cecil, "Oligarchy and Mob Rule in the American Revolution," *History Today* 13:3 (1963): 204.

4. W. David Sloan, "The Early Party Press: The Newspaper Role in American Politics, 1788–1812," *Journalism History* 9:1 (1982): 21.

5. *Kennebunk Freeman's Friend*, 21 August 1805; Mathew Carey to Jefferson, 24 April 1802, Jefferson papers, Library of Congress.

6. Culver Smith, *The Press, Politics, and Patronage: the American Government's Use of Newspapers, 1789–1875* (Athens: University of Georgia Press, 1977), 248.

7. For insights into the newspapers and the government during the Civil War, see J. Cutler Andrews' two books, *The South Reports the Civil War* (Princeton, New Jersey: Princeton University Press, 1970) and *The North Reports the Civil War* (Pittsburgh: University of Pittsburgh, 1955).

8. Judson A. Grenier, "Muckraking and the Muckrakers: An Historical Definition," *Journalism Quarterly* 37 (1960): 552–58. Teddy Roosevelt attacked the reformers after David Graham Phillips' series in *Cosmopolitan* had accused Roosevelt's friend, Sen. Chauncey Depew, of taking bribes.

9. Ray Stannard Baker, *Woodrow Wilson: Life and Papers* (New York: Scribner's, 1931), 234. See especially "Wilson and the Newspaper Press," 228–35.

10. George Creel, "Propaganda and Morale," *American Journal of Sociology* 47:3 (November 1941): 346, 349.

11. Betty Houchin Winfield, *FDR and the News Media* (Urbana: University of Illinois Press, 1990) explains how Roosevelt used newspaper polls.

12. George Seldes, *Freedom of the Press* (Indianapolis: Bobbs-Merrill, 1935).

13. Gary Dean Best, *The Critical Press and the New Deal: The President versus Presidential Power, 1933–1938* (Westport, Conn.: Praeger, 1993).

14. Franklin D. Roosevelt, speech at the Gridiron Club in Washington, D.C., 21 December 1936, in Grace Tully, *F.D.R. My Boss* (New York: Scribner's, 1949), 220.

15. Creel, "Propaganda and Morale," 340.

16. Ralph Chapman, "Strictly Personal—Dateline Devilment," *Saturday Review of Literature*, 2 February 1946, 13.

17. Virginius Dabney, "What's Wrong with Newspaper Editorials? A Noticeable Shift in Emphasis from Public Service to 'Property,'" *Saturday Review of Literature*, 24 February 1945, 8.

18. "Confidence and the Press," *Commonweal*, 25 May 1945, 133.

19. Jack Anderson and Ronald May, *McCarthy, the Man, the Senator, the Ism* (Boston: Beacon, 1952).

20. See Lawrence N. Strout, *Covering McCarthyism: How the* Christian Science Monitor *Handled Joseph R. McCarthy 1950–1954* (Westport, Conn.: Greenwood, 1999).

21. See, for example, Peter Braestrup, *Big Story: How the American Press and Television Reported and Interpreted the Crisis of Tet 1968 in Vietnam and Washington* (Boulder, Colo.: Westview, 1977).

22. Clarence R. Wyatt, *Paper Soldiers: The American Press and the Vietnam War* (New York: Norton, 1993), 217. Also see Daniel C. Hallin, *The Uncensored War: The Media and Vietnam* (New York: Oxford University Press, 1986).

Kathleen J. Turner, *Lyndon Johnson's Dual War: Vietnam and the Press* (Chicago: University of Chicago Press, 1985), vii, notes that Johnson addressed the public more than 200 times in press conferences, comments, and TV speeches.

23. Louis Liebovich, *The Press and the Modern Presidency: Myths and Mindsets from Kennedy to Clinton* (Westport, Conn.: Praeger, 1998), 79.

24. Alan Otten, quoted in "Washington Report: Post-Watergate Reconstruction—Media," *Commonweal* (18 October 1974), 55.

25. "Main Street Revisited: Changing Views on Watergate," *Time* (12 November 1973), 30; Goldwater is quoted in "Covering Watergate: Success and Backlash," *Time* (8 July 1974) 68.

26. Katharine Graham, "A Vigilant Press: Its Job to Inform," *Vital Speeches of the Day* 40:15 (15 May 1974): 462.

27. William Rivers, *The Adversaries: Politics and the Press* (Boston: 1970), 273.

28. William E. Porter, *Assault on the Media: The Nixon Years* (Ann Arbor: University of Michigan Press, 1976).

29. Wes Gallagher, AP reporter, quoted in James Boylan, "Newspeople," *The Wilson Quarterly/Special Issue* (1982): 85.

4

Concepts of News

NORMA GREEN

One of the peculiar traits [of the public] is the insatiable appetite which exists in all classes of people in this country for news. It is thirst so universal that it has given rise to a general and habitual form of salutation on the meeting of friends and strangers of "What's the news?"—Nathan Hale, publisher of *Boston Daily Advertiser*, 1817[1]

Anyone who has studied journalism or worked in a newsroom of a U.S. media outlet has been exposed to a series of concepts to gauge what constitutes news that the public craves. Usually the list of criteria, codified in newswriting and reporting textbooks, includes the characteristics of timeliness, proximity, prominence, conflict, impact, human interest, and novelty. These are the generally agreed-upon values that help determine what gets published or broadcast. They guide the writers, reporters, editors, producers, photographers, and even editorial cartoonists in deciding what information is newsworthy and how it will be presented. But where did these ideas come from? This chapter addresses the evolution and development of news concepts in the United States from the colonial period of the 17th century through the 20th century.

TIMELINESS

In our modern world where time is measured in nanoseconds and news is continuously updated from all over the globe 24 hours a day, it is difficult to imagine an earlier era when information was not available on demand but rather was constrained by geographical boundaries. It is no coincidence that coastal cities were the first in the New World to sustain newspapers. Clocks were of little consequence to early American printers who were as dependent on the oceanic tides, seasonal winds, and weather as were the ships that provided their main source of news and printing supplies. Printing was a family business with no extra hands and legs available to chase down information. Most colonial printers waited for the news to come to them in the form of people stopping in their shop with news tidbits as well as foreign newspapers and correspondence delivered by mail.

The *American Weekly Mercury*, begun in 1719 near Philadelphia's harbor as the first newspaper in Pennsylvania, typified the lag between the initial report of an occurrence elsewhere and its publication in the colonies. News from Europe took up to three months to reach Philadelphia. Then, once published in the *Mercury*, it took another ten days to eight weeks to reach the other colonies.[2] Of the three components of timeliness, recency (recent disclosure), immediacy, and currency,[3] colonial printers cared most about the latter two. For them, immediacy (little delay before publication) became important only after a ship was sighted. But currency, meaning relevance to current concerns, mattered the most.

More than 300 years ago, business leaders in the British colonies along the Eastern seaboard would gather in coffeehouses and taverns at the wharves to exchange information. Proprietors and postmen soon realized that they could profit as intermediaries to the news thirsty. They discovered these merchants, traders, and bankers were willing to pay money to be among the first to hear about the latest vessel coming into the harbor, its cargo, and what the captain, crew, and passengers knew about other ports, especially the homeland. Oral news was the quickest way to slack the thirst for information but was limited by the memory of the messenger and the audience. A hardier way to satisfy yet sustain the news hunger was producing more detailed and retrievable accounts in handwritten or printed forms.

The most enterprising news pioneers such as Boston's Henry Ingraham Blake and Samuel Topliff, Jr., and New York City's John Lang impatiently scanned the horizon for incoming ships. Then they rowed out to meet them, gathered information through personal interviews and foreign newspapers brought from abroad, and then rushed back to share it in written form. They treated this information as a commodity like the beverages the businessmen bought as they awaited the latest word. With little domestic manufacturing, traders paid for imported goods in advance or upon delivery and then depended on a timely sale of merchandise to recover their costs and turn a profit. Information these news brokers obtained on delays, tariffs, shortages, or a surplus of goods was critical to the colonial economy.

Blake, who started the *New England Paladium* in 1793, was said to race from ship back to shore singing as he typeset copy relying on his memory and notes he scribbled on his cuffs and his fingernails.[4] By 1811, for an annual $10 subscription, patrons of Boston's Exchange Coffeehouse could read *Mr. Topliff's Private Marine Journals* in handwritten ledgers. Initially, using flag and ball signaling from a lighthouse and a crew of rowers ready to meet ships, he relayed news orally. Later he hired scribes and produced news books, then sent dispatches to local newspapers and eventually sold stories to publishers in Philadelphia and New York. Apparently not content to wait for news from Boston, Lang, who published the *New York Gazette* in the early 1800s, had his servants row him into the harbor and back to his office where he furtively got vital news composed, printed, and delivered to subscribers before it was entered on the coffee-house news books.

Aaron Smith Willington of the *Charleston (S.C.) Courier* made one of the most ambitious efforts. He scooped northern newspapers on the Treaty of Ghent, the U.S. diplomatic victory against Great Britain ending the War of 1812. He engaged a ship from Spain to Cuba and on to Florida where the news was then carried on horseback through Georgia and on to South Carolina well ahead of a New York–bound British ship. Later Willington's protégé, James Gordon Bennett, would heighten the importance of timeliness at the *New York Herald*, one of the early penny newspapers designed to lure the urban masses to the news habit, by offering a source a $500 bonus for every hour European news arrived at his newsroom in advance of its competitors.[5]

The penny press, fueled by advertising revenue and street sales, was part of a continuous cycle of urban commerce dating from the 1830s. Editors such as Benjamin Day of the *New York Sun* and Horace Greeley of the *New York Tribune* tried to attract and keep the readers that advertisers wanted. They attempted to build a news habit among impulse buyers with multiple daily editions that updated the front page with fresh headlines, episodic stories, and often new illustrations throughout the day. Bennett adopted the strategies of earlier English publications in his selection of news items that resounded with recency: "battles and crimes gathered a group of readers; advertised products took their money."[6] Retail establishments, like department stores and food stores, depended on a rapid turnover of their stock through newspapers that announced their latest merchandise and special sales in ads framed by compelling news stories. Newspaper owners bought high speed presses capable of churning out thousands of pages an hour, and searched for ways to woo more readers and differentiate themselves from other newspapers. They all touted timeliness.

Spurred by such rivalry, newspaper publishers used animals including horses and homing pigeons, the latter with tiny messages strapped to their legs, to supplement human and mechanical speed in delivering the news across the miles. Horses were attached in teams to stagecoaches or ridden by lone messengers especially by business papers aimed at the rising mercantile class of Americans, such as the *New York Journal of Commerce* that competed with general papers for readership. It set up an elaborate horse and pony express that met boats that hauled the mail bags off ships coming into harbor and then raced to eager editors and typesetters in their newspaper office. Such devotion to timeliness became a sporting event complete with wagers from onlookers gathered outside printing offices to see which rider would arrive first. Horses also helped spread the news across great stretches of the interior. They delivered the mail that provided the newspaper content for news-hungry editors and later carried the finished product to news-hungry subscribers. The *Missouri Gazette*, which Joseph Charless established in St. Louis in 1813, was the first English language newspaper west of the Mississippi. With no initial competition, its frequency varied, as it was contingent on mail delivery that took anywhere from two to three weeks within the Midwest, six to eight weeks from the East Coast and up to three months from Europe.[7] The Overland Mail, a 2,800-mile stagecoach line started in 1858 between Memphis and St. Louis in the East and Los Angeles and San Francisco in the West, was the most ambitious communication project that the U.S. Government subsidized to better link the country.[8] Soon it and the more famous Pony Express between Missouri and California were displaced by a news vehicle that needed no feeding or rest.

With the completion of the transcontinental telegraph in 1861, eyewitness information from an event could be transmitted across the country within minutes, not days or weeks. Five years later, the laying of the first successful trans–Atlantic cable across the ocean floor meant that North American publications were no longer dependent on transportation for communication with Europe. As a journalist of the era explained, "It gives you the news before the circumstances have had the time to

alter. The press is enabled to lay it fresh before the reader like steak hot from the gridiron, instead of being cooled and rendered flavourless by a slow journey from a distant kitchen. A battle is fought three thousand miles away and we have the particulars while they are taking the wounded to the hospital."[9] The telegraph, with its promise of nearly instantaneous transmission (albeit in code), was credited with spurring cooperation among newspapers. The Associated Press was formed as a means to share wire service expenses and still get distant information the quickest. Later, telephones, typewriters, and automobiles would further speed the newspaper reporting and writing process.

Radio news began to dilute newspaper dominance during the 1920s but by no means diminished the public hunger for timely news. Its ability to instantly update news usurped the urgency of newspaper extra editions. Many major newspapers eventually joined forces with broadcast outlets and had news staffs write for print and electronic media. By 1980, the ABC, NBC, and CBS television networks, whose news departments had enjoyed primacy for twenty years, found themselves having to compete with an upstart company. Turner Broadcasting, a coaxial cable television company, created Cable News Network (CNN) in 1980 to give subscribers news at any hour they wanted it, not just when networks traditionally scheduled it. With the 1991 U.S. Desert Storm offensive in the Persian Gulf War, CNN surpassed the traditional Big Three networks in "real time" coverage of the conflict between the United States and Iraq. Much like Civil War correspondents who monopolized telegraph lines to keep them open, CNN was the only network with continuous satellite feed from the Middle East. It offered immediacy like no previous war coverage had.

In the 1990s, with about one-third of U.S. households equipped with computers, news outlets experimented with online versions of their publications and programs. Today, several traditional media companies encompassing all aspects of news from books, newspapers, magazines, television, and radio to documentary films are merging with computer, satellite, fiber optic, and telephone providers to create a new infrastructure to deliver continuous news to subscribers. While timeliness is important, it is not the only essential factor in attracting and sustaining news hunger. Often the more local the story the better.

PROXIMITY

The geographical closeness of an event to a news audience is often the way news decisions of today are prioritized. A local story might take precedence over a national or international incident. Take the example of the Michigan newspaper, the *Alpena Echo*, that in the mid–1800s canceled its telegraph subscription citing the then new technology's local irrelevance: "...it could not tell why the telegraph company caused it to be sent a full account of a flood in Shanghai, a massacre in Calcutta, a sailor fight in Bombay, hard frost in Siberia, a missionary banquet in Madagascar, the price of kangaroo leather from Borneo, and a lot of nice cheerful news from the Archipelagoes,—and not a line about the Muskegon fire" in its home state.[10]

But this need for a local angle was not always a news priority. Local news was not valued as much as foreign news, particularly in colonial times. It was not considered worth writing about items that everyone already knew and had discussed. Covering international stories also was considered safer. Printers were not willing to risk losing their license or money on a publication they could not sell. It was safer for a colonial printer who had invested much time and effort in a mechanical press to stick with faraway news than risk censorship, confiscation of equipment, embargo of supplies, jail, or banishment for a story that displeased officials. Government-sanctioned pamphlets and broadsides, which predated newspapers in the British colonies, contained accounts of European wars and natural phenomena like a 1669 volcanic eruption of Mt. Etna in Italy.[11] That may partially explain why Benjamin Harris, who in 1690 established *Publick Occurrences, Both Forreign and Domestick*, considered to be the first native newspaper, might have thought it safer to lead in his title with news from abroad as well.

A shift to more localized stories came about as early as 1810.[12] In the decades after the War for Independence, the new nation turned inward to domestic affairs. Censorship lessened, the frontier opened to settlers, and reliance on foreign sources diminished amidst deteriorating relations with England and France that led to ship seizures, blockades, and embargoes even before the War of 1812. U.S. editors determined that there was plenty to cover right outside the print shop door. Between 1820 and 1860, domestic news increased, especially stories within the city of publication, thus taking over the role of a town crier to a much bigger audience.

A content analysis of American daily and nondaily newspapers in decades of the early 19th century preceding the Civil War indicated that foreign news declined from 28 per cent to 18 per cent as distant homelands faded in importance while local and state news increased with the growth of communities and nationalism.[13] Town meetings were a natural place to begin coverage of local issues. Soon editors were deluged with requests to cover all sorts of planned local activities.

Despite the abundance of potential local stories, selecting what to publish and still stay in business was tricky. Some frontier printers were pressured by local boosters, real estate speculators, and railroad companies who, through their advertising clout, wanted only positive local stories. Those who were hard-pressed often found it easier to print news that happened outside the community. Some rural editors, with few reporters and a large pass-along readership, found enough wire service and syndicated stories about state and national government to keep their product fresh in isolated communities. A study of Minnesota country weeklies from 1860 to 1929 found localized content increased only after 1900, surmising that earlier papers, consumed with Congress and issues of national significance, ignored local events as trivial in comparison. Only after the start of the 20th century did those newspapers begin devoting an average of two-fifths of their locally produced news space to short items about local people.[14]

Today, community newspapers and radio

as well as cable access public affairs programming cover the type of neighborhood news often missing in metropolitan newspapers and network news broadcasts: in-depth coverage of local institutions such as schools, government, religious organizations, civic, and charitable groups. They detail birthdays, weddings, anniversaries, deaths, sports, arts, and social gatherings. Colonial printer Timothy Green in his *Connecticut Gazette* of 1764 was a pioneer of this type story, that most deemed unimportant or too intimate for public sharing.[15] While few readers actually attended the weddings of the rich and famous, they were still hungry for glimpses into their lives.

PROMINENCE

Names make the news, especially those attached to people recognized for their wealth, beauty, intelligence, lineage, performance as an actor or athlete, or public standing as a politician, clergy, or physician, for instance. People who gain their fame by virtue of their birth or merit are singled out as worthy news subjects. In the United States, founded by people who were escaping European monarchies, a fascination with royalty has remained strong.

In the first and only issue of *Publick Occurrences* in 1690, Benjamin Harris printed a gossip item about the French king and his son: "France is in much trouble (and fear) not only with us but also with his Son, who has revolted against him lately and has great reason if reports be true, that the Father used to lie with the Son's Wife."[16] Over a century later, Isaiah Thomas chronicled the death of French Queen Marie Antoinette on the front page of his *Massachusetts Spy*.[17] By the late 1800s, U.S. newspapers routinely covered the marriages of newly wealthy Americans to titled European aristocracy. During one September in 1997, two world-famous women were buried: 38-year-old Lady Diana Spencer, the former Princess of Wales and ex-wife of British Crown heir apparent, and 88-year-old Mother Teresa, a Catholic nun from Macedonia who dedicated her life to the impoverished of India. News editors seemed to have no difficulty deciding who

deserved more coverage. For years before her death, Diana's face on the cover of a U.S. magazine was guaranteed to boost newsstand sales.

Politicians and government officials also have been deemed newsworthy. In 1733 an opposition political party enlisted German-born printer John Peter Zenger to publish *New York Weekly Journal* with the express purpose of criticizing the new governor, Morris Cosby, whom the opponents deemed greedy and corrupt. As a result of anti–Cosby articles, Zenger was tried in 1735 for seditious libel but was acquitted. Later, another German immigrant, Thomas Nast, would take up his artistic pen and ink to create damning editorial cartoons in *Harper's Magazine*, an illustrated weekly. Between 1869 and 1871, he portrayed the corruption in New York City's Tammany Hall, a political club that Democratic party "Boss" William Tweed ran. As a direct result of Nast's drawings, along with a *New York Times* investigation, the citizenry voted the Tweed Ring out of power.

By the 1920s, prominence meant not only politicians but also motion picture actors who became stars thanks to loyal fans and studio publicity. Newspapers and radio commentators began to cover these screen stars as news figures. Later, radio and television news as well as theatrical newsreels recorded performances that helped catapult local athletes into national heroes. By the 1960s, even those who reported the news on television had become stars to be covered in media beats by newspapers and magazines particularly. Walter Cronkite, who anchored the *CBS Evening News* for 19 years, was named to a list of best-dressed men in America and quipped that the award was based solely on what he wore from the waist up, as that was all the camera ever showed. In 1994 network news executives made the decision to interrupt regular Friday night prime time programming to broadcast live aerial views of a vehicle containing former athlete-turned-actor, O.J. Simpson, being pursued by Los Angeles police. The fact that the well-known figure was threatening to kill himself coupled with the availability of competing news helicopters hastened the unprecedented national coverage. Simpson was later tried and found innocent in the murder of his former wife and another man.

A century before Simpson's trial, the Sunday magazines of Joseph Pulitzer's *New York World* and William Randolph Hearst's *New York Journal* were designed for mass readership, including thousands of struggling new immigrants. The publishers tapped into the reverse snobbery of their readers who enjoyed reading about the human failings of the rich and famous. The society news content of the Manhattan newspapers, pioneered by Bennett's *New York Herald* in the late 1830s, influenced the news judgments of country newspapers.[18] Even in the hinterlands, it seemed readers wanted to live vicariously next door to the Astors and the Vanderbilts on New York's Fifth Avenue.

In the first decade of the 20th century, a new genre of investigative news reporting that President Theodore Roosevelt termed "muckraking" grew up around exposing the world of the privileged one-tenth of the population who owned nine-tenths of the wealth.[19] Prominent companies, some virtual monopolies, such as Standard Oil Company and their founders were the subjects of long magazine articles aimed at middle class readers. The reports pointed out the close relationships between big businesses and government. The intent was to bring about political reform by calling attention to corporate disparities and corruption. Pointing out differences is a familiar and successful approach in American news selection and evaluation.

CONFLICT

Division among people based on political ideologies, religious beliefs, socio-economic class, race, ethnicity, age, and gender has been a driving principle of U.S. news since colonial times. Differing viewpoints fueled the American Revolution. Essays, articles, and even political cartoons in the partisan press were designed to influence public opinion by building a persuasive case for one side or the other. Colonists were forced to decide whether they would take up the cause of Patriots fighting for independence or remain Loyalists to the British Crown. For the colonial printer, dependent on

government sanctions, such stories often were constrained and even clandestine. Pamphlets such as Thomas Paine's *Common Sense*, a treatise that blamed King George directly for colonial injustices, were passed from pocket to pocket and slipped under doors at night. After the physical clashes of the war subsided, partisan news continued as the young nation worked out its opposing political party ideologies in the pages of the press, at polling places, and the halls of Congress.

Reporting on court cases provided a built-in conflict between the differing prosecution and defense positions at the same trial. *New York Herald* editor James Gordon Bennett appreciated the drama of legal clashes as well as sporting events. His newspaper, which routinely covered horse racing and yachting regattas, later turned to prizefighting. In 1860, an American boxer beat an Englishman in what was billed as the fight of the century and afforded coverage equal to the nominees for the next president of the United States.

Most of the nation's news editors had to await dispatches of the Mexican War of 1846, far removed from the action. The Civil War provided the first real opportunity for news publications to send hundreds of reporters and sketch artists to the battlefront without leaving the country. Hearst valued conflict enough to send a news team to Cuba in 1899 to cover the insurrection and wait out what eventually became the Spanish American War. He was accused of war mongering in his attempt to scoop his rival Pulitzer and boost circulation. The 20th century saw American correspondents report on war from all over the world. In addition, they covered domestic strife manifest in labor strikes and boycotts, race riots, demonstrations for and against women's suffrage, civil rights, gay rights, abortions, and U.S. aid or participation in wars.

In 1925, newspaper reporters and early radio newscasters were on hand when scientific and religious precepts clashed in a Dayton, Tennessee, courtroom. The Scopes trial centered on the rights of a public school teacher to teach evolution versus creation interpretation of human life. The teacher was found guilty and fined. News stories played up the different ideological arguments inherent in the legal case—beliefs based on unquestioning faith and theory derived from systematic knowledge.

Even today, news stories covering seemingly eternal conflicts including age against youth, society against the individual, men against women, the living against the dead, and men against the gods[20] may miss the key significance for news audiences—what is the direct consequence to them? Does it hit them in the wallet or is it a threat to their health and safety? These issues command attention.

IMPACT

As the new democracy struggled to take shape in the late 1700s, journalists grappled with their role in covering it and explaining implications of federal actions to its citizenry. Philip Morin Freneau moved to Philadelphia, then the capital, to start the *National Gazette* as a voice of opposition to the Federalist administration's favored *Gazette of the United States*. He badgered Congress to allow all news representatives to cover its proceedings for the first time. In 1789, the House of Representatives opened its meetings to the press, but the Senate refused until five years later. In an unrelenting campaign, Freneau decried the obstinate body, arguing that "secrecy in your representative is a worm that will prey and fatten upon the vitals of liberty."[21] Having won that battle to cover government proceedings, the challenge remained for later White House, Congressional, and Supreme Court correspondents as well as statehouse and city hall reporters to sort through daily activities on their watch and make sense of it all for Americans each day. When they weighed various story possibilities, they determined how particular news impacted national security, economic stability, health, and safety issues, for instance. Sometimes the consequences were not immediately clear.

In an era when reporters did not shadow presidents everywhere they went, correspondent Mary Leader was said to have walked 15 miles in wintry weather to get to the 1863 Gettysburg, Pennsylvania, Civil War cemetery

dedication and report Abraham's Lincoln's expression of grief for soldiers and their principled sacrifice. Her first person account for the *Hanover Spectator* was among the earliest to realize the speech's greatness and its significance for a wounded nation. A few years later, newspaper editors would cover what a minister of the era considered the first post–Civil War event to rally the nation to action.[22] In the fall of 1871, what might at first glance have seemed a fairly local news event, a fire in Chicago, became a national story not only because of its magnitude but also the city's crucial role in the nation's economy through its prominence in rail and water transportation. Granted, the fire caused $200 million damage, killed 300 people, left about one-third of city's population homeless, and destroyed 2,100 acres of prime property. But it was not the only fire to ever strike a metropolitan area. There were other fires in Wisconsin and Michigan the same day. So what made that fire so special? One news historian argued that the fire became a barometer for a nervous new nation and reminded the country of its interdependence.[23] The global cycle of fires, floods, hurricanes, earthquakes, tidal waves, tornadoes, blizzards, heat waves, droughts, and famines reminded us of our vulnerability. No matter how distant the disaster or local the plight, poignant photographs and stirring news reports of the heroism routinely moved Americans to give generously to relief efforts.

HUMAN INTEREST

The ability of a news story to seize its audience with laughter, tears, fear, or suspense, is a strength of television. It combines sights and sounds with powerful words to manipulate feeling. But long before TV, newspapers painted word pictures that made people react. Human interest was a main focus of publications dating back to the colonial period. The *New-England Courant*, the fourth newspaper to be published in Boston, printed a news prospectus in 1723 that summed up its human interest approach in a competitive marketplace: "…the main Design of this Weekly will be to entertain the Town with the most comical and diverting incidents of Human Life, which in so large a Place as Boston will not fail of a universal Exemplification. Nor shall we be wanting to fill up these Papers with a grateful interspersion of more serious Morrals, which may be drawn from the most ludicrous and odd parts of Human Life."[24]

By the 19th century, New York City had surpassed Boston in population and human interest journalism taken to its extreme form—sensationalism. It started with the penny press newspapers sold on street corners to the masses and continued with the circulation wars between Joseph Pulitzer's *World* and William Randolph Hearst's *Journal*.

While George Wisner of the *New York Sun* was the first penny press editor to admit, in 1833, that "We newspaper people thrive best on the calamities of others,"[25] Bennett perfected the titillating formula. His *New York Herald*, started in 1835, routinely covered unusual deaths and accidents ranging from suicides, murders, and decapitations to riots and animal hunts as well as contemporary and historical executions around the world. Perhaps the apex of the *Herald's* human interest stories was its long-running, rather lascivious coverage of the 1836 Robinson-Jewett murder case. The *Herald* gave extensive coverage of the trial of a wealthy client of a prostitute who was charged with her murder. Not content to leave this story to his reporters or the police, Bennett conducted his own investigation and visited the crime scene several times, anticipating the kind of fresh, provocative details his readers loved to gossip about.[26] What had once only been whispered was soon appearing on front pages of newspapers openly hawked in public places.

The sensational content of Pulitzer's *New York World* of the 1890s was typical of the trend to broaden the scope of the human interest story to disclose what had been previously considered private scandals, playing up rumors and backroom chatter.[27] A century later, prurient news peaked in 1998—a year that started with President William Jefferson Clinton's denial of an affair with a White House intern and later retraction, amidst DNA evidence and other intimate revelations, and ended with his impeachment trial.

In 1927 Charles Lindbergh became a national hero when he piloted an airplane solo and nonstop across the Atlantic Ocean. When his firstborn son was kidnapped out of his crib and found murdered in 1932, he and his wife became objects of pity, thanks in part to the continuous tearjerker stories created by a group of reporters dubbed sob sisters, covering the investigation and subsequent murder trial. Journalism of the genteel it was not. News stories were valued for their emotional appeal and unusualness as much as their world significance.[28]

NOVELTY

Anything out of the ordinary may be newsworthy. Like sideshows at carnivals, news audiences are attracted to the unusual, the bizarre, and the supernatural. Amidst all the serious news about debt, disease, and destruction, readers and viewers and listeners desire diversions. These are usually short items, easily digested by those needing a break. Colonial editors appreciated this need for something that interrupted the routine and sought out such items from the foreign newspapers they read and reprinted. For example, Elizabeth Timothy's *South Carolina Gazette*, contained an article in the March 24, 1739, issue excerpted from a London paper about "the remarkable clause in the Will of Mr. Lilly Deceas'd, late one of his Majesty's Apothecaries" who left all his estate, read and personal, to his servant Elizabeth Miller, "conditionally, that she take care of his little dear Harlequin Dog Senesino."[29]

Landlocked readers were captivated about news of long-distance swimmers and feats of daring by mountain climbers and later astronauts. Joseph Pulitzer tapped into the desires of armchair travelers by sending one of his reporters, Elizabeth Cochrane (known as Nellie Bly), around the world during 1889–1890. Readers followed her daily dispatches from Europe to Asia and cheered when she bested the fictitious Jules Verne epic of 80 days by eight days, six hours, and 11 minutes. Her trip was such a novelty that newspapers devised a game for readers to clip and save as a way to re-live the journey. Earlier Pulitzer had rallied New Yorkers to contribute $100,000 worth of pennies to give the Statue of Liberty a proper pedestal. Hearst tried to lure readers to an archeological discovery with the headline, "Most Colossal Animal Ever on Earth Just Found Out West," making it sound like a brontosaurus might still be roaming the earth.[30] Such P.T. Barnum–like promotions reflected Hearst's childlike marvel in all things big and noisy.[31] Both Pulitzer and Hearst, among other publishers, covered and contributed to the spectacle of daily life. Today radio and TV newscasts often end with a "bright," a story or picture, often about an animal, that is humor-ous and offers a respite from the grim roundup of previous stories.

CONCLUSION

Today, Americans once again gather at coffeehouses to share information. As they log on in cybercafes, the legacy of pioneer printers and editors, reporters, photographers, and car-toonists is still traceable in the sites they select. The American hunger for news has not abated. It satisfies the basic human instinct to monitor the world, no matter how big or small it is thought to be. News gives us awareness, assur-ance, and entertainment. Nowadays, news se-lection often takes various media formats into consideration. Television news is geared to vi-sual impact—photography and artist's sketches—while newspapers lean to the unusual and local, and magazines to prominence and entertain-ment. Internet news sites, a hybrid of print and broadcast, strive for brevity—short paragraphs of text often accompanied by easy to digest soundbites and photographs. However, deep down, there are more similarities than differ-ences in news story selection and play by all media due to commonly held professional stan-dards and journalism training. After more than 300 years of waxing and waning priorities, American news decisions hinge on the elements of timeliness, proximity, prominence, conflict, impact, human interest, and novelty roughly correlating to the "when, where, who, what, how, and why" questions that journalists con-tinually confront.

Selected Readings

Avery, Donald R. "American Over European Community? Newspaper Content Changes, 1808–1812." *Journalism Quarterly* 63 (1986): 311–14.

Avery, Donald R. "The Emerging American Newspaper: Discovering the Home Front." *American Journalism* 1:2 (1984): 51–66.

Bartow, Edith Merwin. *News and These United States*. New York: Funk & Wagnalls, 1952.

Brooker-Gross, Susan R. "Timeliness: Interpretations from a Sample of 19th Century Newspapers." *Journalism Quarterly* 59 (1981): 594–98.

Crouthamel, James L. *Bennett's New York Herald and the Rise of the Popular Press*. Especially Chap. 2 "Sensation-alism and the Newspaper Revolution," 19–42. Syracuse, N.Y.: Syracuse University Press, 1989.

Hester, Al, Susan Parker Humes, and Christopher Bickers. "Foreign News in Colonial North American Newspapers, 1764–1775." *Journalism Quarterly* 57 (1980): 18–22, 44.

Ogan, Christine, et. al. "The Changing Front Page of the New York *Times*, 1900–1970." *Journalism Quarterly* 52 (1975): 340–44.

Russo, David J. "The Origins of Local News in the U.S. Country Press, 1840s–1870s." *Journalism Monographs* 65 (1980).

Shaw, Donald Lewis. "At the Crossroads: Change and Continuity in American Press News, 1820–1860." *Journalism History* 8 (1981): 38–50.

Stephens, Mitchell. *A History of News*. Fort Worth, Tex.: Harcourt Brace, 1997.

Notes

1. Editor and nephew of the patriot hanged as a spy during the American Revolution as quoted in Edith Merwin Bartow, *News and These United States* (New York: Funk and Wagnalls, 1952), 119.

2. Anna J. DeArmond, *Andrew Bradford—Colonial Journalist* (Newark: University of Delaware Press, 1949), 60–61.

3. Categories devised by Bernard Roshco, *Newsmaking* (Chicago: University of Chicago Press, 1975), 11.

4. James Melvin Lee, *History of American Journal-ism* (Garden City, N.Y.: Garden City Publishing, 1923), 154–55.

5. Tom Standage, *The Victorian Internet: The Re-markable Story of the Telegraph and the Nineteenth Century On-line Pioneers* (New York: Berkley Books, 1999), 148.

6. Mitchell Stephens, *A History of News* (Fort Worth, Tex.: Harcourt Brace College Publishers, 1997), 164.

7. David Dary, *Red Blood and Black Ink: Journalism in the Old West* (Lawrence: University Press of Kansas, 1998), 128.

8. Richard R. John, *Spreading the News: The American Postal System from Franklin to Morse* (Cambridge: Harvard University Press, 1995), 99.

9. Anonymous journalist quoted in Standage, *Victorian Internet*, 153.

10. *Alpena Echo*, n.d., quoted in ibid., 163.

11. Matthias A. Shaaber, "Forerunners of the Newspaper in America," *Journalism Quarterly* 11:3 (1934): 345.

12. Donald R. Avery, "The Emerging American Newspaper: Discovering the Home Front," *American Journalism* 1:2 (Winter 1984): 62–64.

13. Donald Lewis Shaw, "At the Crossroads: Change and Continuity in American Press News 1820–1860," *Journalism History* 8 (Summer 1981): 43.

14. Irene Barnes Taeuber, "Changes in the Content and Presentation of Reading Material in Minnesota Weekly Newspapers, 1860–1929," *Journalism Quarterly* 9 (1932): 289.

15. Bartow, *News and These United States*, 64.

16. *Publick Occurrences*, 25 September 1690.

17. "Last Moments of the Late Queen of France, From a London Paper," *Thomas's Massachusetts Spy: Or, the Worcester Gazette*, 13 February 1794.

18. James L. Crouthamel, *Bennett's New York Herald and the Rise of the Popular Press* (Syracuse, N.Y.: Syracuse University Press, 1989), 39.

19. Arthur and Lila Weinberg, eds., *The Muckrakers* (New York: Simon & Schuster, 1961), xii.

20. Writer George Steiner quoted in Melvin Mencher, *News Reporting and Writing*, 5th ed. (Dubuque, Iowa: William C. Brown Publishers, 1991), 60.

21. Philip Freneau, "To the Freemen of America," *National Gazette*, 13 February 1793, reprinted in W. David Sloan, Cheryl S. Wray, and C. Joanne Sloan, *Great Editorials*, 2nd ed. (Northport, Ala.: Vision Press, 1997), 52.

22. Unitarian minister Henry W. Bellows, "Lessons from the Ashes of Chicago," *Liberal Christian*, 21 October 1871.

23. John J. Pauly, "The Great Chicago Fire as a National Event," *American Quarterly* 36 (1984): 668–83.

24. *New-England Courant*, 11 February 1723.

25. *New York Sun*, 5 September 1833.

26. Helen MacGill Hughes, *News and the Human Interest Story* (New York: Transaction Press, 1981), 197.

27. George Juergens, *Joseph Pulitzer and the New York World* (Princeton, N.J.: Princeton University Press, 1966), viii.

28. Stephens, *A History of News*, 117.

29. *South Carolina Gazette*, 24 March 1739.

30. *New York Journal*, 11 December 1898.

31. W. A. Swanberg, *Citizen Hearst: A Biography of William Randolph Hearst* (New York: Charles Scribner's Sons, 1961), 163.

5

Ethics

JOHN D. KEELER, WILLIAM BROWN, AND DOUGLAS TARPLEY

"Professional integrity is the cornerstone to a journalist's credibility," states the preamble of the most recent code of ethics that the respected Society of Professional Journalists adopted in 1996. According to the code, integrity is accomplished by (1) being "honest, fair and courageous in gathering, reporting and interpreting information," (2) minimizing harm by treating "sources, subjects and colleagues as human beings deserving respect," (3) acting independently by being "free of obligation to any interest other than the public's right to know," and (4) being "accountable to readers, listeners, viewers and each other."

These fundamental ideals have been debated and defined by American journalists and inserted in professional codes of ethics since the beginning of the 20th century. However, since the colonial era, both those who have created and consumed journalistic fare have struggled with ethical issues related to the profession. Their concerns have been influenced by prevalent political, economic, social, religious, and technological conditions characterizing the specific historical era in which they lived. This essay traces the development of journalism ethics in the United States through a number of key periods in journalism history.

THE COLONIAL ERA

Colonial newspapers were small enterprises usually published by printers who viewed them as part of a diversified trade rather than as a professional endeavor and who seldom left their printing facilities to look for stories or investigate events. Restricted by cumbersome printing presses, shortages of paper and ink, and worn-out type, they were generally, according to our tastes today, aesthetically dull compilations of highly digested news with low circulation, inconspicuous advertising, and readers who were often lax in paying for their subscriptions. Publishers were often dependent on various types of government or private printing contracts or grants to maintain solvency.

Yet even the first colonial newspaper, *Publick Occurrences, Both Forreign and Domestick*, printed in Boston on September 25, 1690, triggered debate about journalistic independence when its publisher, Benjamin Harris, promised to painstakingly report events, be careful in dealing with sources, print retractions if reporting mistakes were made, and take steps toward "Curing, or at least the Charming of that Spirit of Lying, which prevails amongst us, wherefore nothing shall be entered, but what we have reason to believe is true."[1] The colonial governing council ordered the paper to suspend publication after one issue because Harris had not received approval before printing.

The next colonial newspaper to emerge, postmaster John Campbell's *Boston News-Letter*, first published in 1704, duly noted below its masthead that it was "Published by Authority," yet it was characterized by Campbell's precise efforts to attribute sources, minimize editorial content, and accurately present a "true account" of foreign and domestic news and "prevent a great many false reports of the same."[2]

The *Boston Gazette*, established in 1719 by Campbell's successor as postmaster, William Brooker, followed this pattern. However, it was James Franklin's *New-England Courant* in 1721 that increased the intensity of public discourse about the fundamental responsibilities of the press. Franklin and his backers used the *Courant* to oppose the *Gazette* and *News-Letter*. Supporters of the Church of England, they fueled an ongoing war of words with Reverend Increase Mather and other Puritans. They also regularly criticized colonial government authorities, who eventually arrested and temporarily imprisoned Franklin.

Controversy surrounding the *Courant* and newspapers modeled after it raised basic journalistic ethical issues. Could the press have a partisan flavor, or should it remain neutral in its perspective? Should newspapers be accountable to special interests, governmental authorities, or the reading public generally? These publications, with their liberal use of pen names, biased letters, essays, and verse, evoked questions about honesty, fairness, and accuracy in reporting and interpreting news. They also fostered debate about the propriety of editorial content that personally attacked and mocked public figures, political, social and religious institutions, and competing newspaper editors or contributors.

Debate over these issues escalated in 1733 when a faction opposed to New York Governor William Cosby backed printer John Peter Zenger in starting the *New York Weekly Journal*. Leaders of the faction used it as a platform for discussion of basic rights such as press liberty, trial by jury, and more widespread participation in governmental affairs. Although Zenger was arrested, imprisoned, and tried, the eloquent arguments of defense lawyer Andrew Hamilton led to his acquittal. The outcome established the arguments that truth should be allowed as a defense in libel cases and that juries should have the authority to determine matters of libel. It also led to greater acceptance of the idea that the press could be critical of public figures and institutions.

Although many colonial newspapers became concerned with matters of truth and impartiality, most were strong proponents of particular perspectives on any issue. Their opinions were often rooted in the worldviews of the religious dissidents and separatists who settled in colonial America. Indeed, God, biblical principles, and morals frequently were integrated into news stories, essays, and other newspaper content and questions about newspaper ideals were debated on the basis of the reality and authority of God and Scriptural truths.

Press resistance to the Stamp Act enacted by the British Parliament in 1765 marked the beginning of the revolutionary period of the colonial press lasting until 1783. Less fearful of government retribution, printers increasingly expressed their opinions on political and social issues editorially. Viewing themselves as more principled, they became advocates or opponents of independence from Great Britain. Newspapers such as the *Massachusetts Gazette* and the *Boston Gazette* became vehicles for political debate and espousal of American freedom.

Royalist newspapers such as the *Boston News-Letter*, *Boston Chronicle*, and James Rivington's *New-York Gazetteer* were published with the encouragement and protection of British authorities. Despite the vagaries of war and public or official attacks against them, they faithfully tried to record the major events of the period and the war itself. However, most newspapers seemed to have minimal concern for standards such as impartiality and fairness and engaged in ethically questionable practices such as name-calling, particularly within editorial content.

THE PARTY PRESS

By the early 1800s newspapers increased in size, circulation, frequency of publication, advertising space, and revenue. Yet many newspapers were still financially dependent on party backers for subscribers, advertising, discounted postal rates, printing contracts, government positions, legal aid, and articles and letters to be published in the newspapers themselves. As a result, during debate over the adoption of the United States Constitution, they increasingly replaced the pamphlet as a primary avenue for partisan political expression. Libelous, scandalous, personal editorial attacks on public figures and rival newspaper editors overshadowed efforts to record news and events less subjectively. In addition, specialized workers, who functioned solely in editorial positions, gradually usurped the editorial duties of printers.

Partisanship was most obvious in battles between the *Gazette of the United States*, founded in 1789 by the Federalist party as the first federal government party organ with John Fenno as its editor, and the *National Gazette*, established by Philip Freneau with Secretary of State Thomas Jefferson as its principal backer. Despite this contentious atmosphere, many newspapers openly advocated a free press. Some such as Benjamin Russell's *Massachusetts Centinel and Republican Journal* and Noah Webster's popular *American Minerva* tried to report news truthfully and factually and even remain impartial.

However, in the wake of the Federalist party's failed attempt to use the Alien and Sedition Acts (1798) to squash inflammatory anti–Federalist newspapers, Joseph Dennie, editor of the *Farmer's Weekly Museum* of Walpole, New Hampshire, expressed the general observations of many when he characterized many American newspapers as "destitute of news … wit and originality" and filled with "plagiarisms, mawkishness, dreariness, and gross folly."[3]

Although before and during the War of 1812 partisan journalism intensified, some newspapers again tried to serve as standard bearers. The Federalist *New York Evening Post* was created to "diffuse among the people correct information of all interesting subjects; to inculcate just principles in religion, morals and politics; and to cultivate a taste for sound literature."[4] The *Journal of Commerce*, a New York City daily, refused to accept advertising for objectionable medical products and lotteries. It sought to integrate news with religion

and morality and avoid "party and personal politics" and "angry altercations which they always excite."[5] The *Weekly Reader*, established in Baltimore in 1811 and edited by Hezekiah Niles, became renowned for accuracy and fairness. By pursuing such policies, newspapers like these contributed greatly to discussion about the ethical aspects of journalistic ventures.

THE PENNY PRESS

The 1830s brought a period of change in the growth, influence, character, and purpose of the press. Objective reporting became more valued than editorial opinion and personal biases. Readers began to demand news stories that presented all sides of an issue and content that met their personal needs. These changes were stimulated by industrial growth, the development of larger cities, and technological innovations including improved steam-driven printing presses. Greater advertising revenues, literacy rates and leisure time also encouraged them. This caused editors increasingly to view newspapers in commercial rather than political party terms.

In this climate, "penny" newspapers such as the *New York Transcript, Philadelphia Public Ledger, Boston Daily Times, Baltimore Sun*, Benjamin Day's *New York Sun*, and James Gordon Bennett's *New York Herald* attained high circulation, advertising revenues, and mass appeal. They utilized carriers and street sales to achieve this. Their newspaper content focused on court proceedings, police news, and human-interest stories. Proclaiming themselves politically independent and accountable to their readers, they also exposed scandals, criticized institutions, and took positions on a variety of social issues of the day.

Ethical concerns during the penny press era centered on the deleterious effects on American morality and learning caused by sensationalism, inaccuracy, and tastelessness in news and advertising content. There was equal apprehension about attacks on public figures and rival newspapers, although this was usually confined to the editorial pages, and violation of personal privacy. In their ambitious pursuit of profits, larger audiences, and more advertising, penny papers contained stories of vice, scandals, crime, and other unseemly behavior, often dealing with ordinary people rather than public figures. Notable examples include controversy about the sensationalism of prostitute Helen Jewett's murder trial in the mid–1830s by New York, Boston, and Philadelphia newspapers and uproar over Bennett's reporting and editorializing in the *New York Herald* and his ongoing conflicts with the *New York Tribune's* Horace Greeley during the 1840s.

GROWTH OF AN INDEPENDENT PRESS AND CALLS FOR REFORM

By the 1850s newspapers had become an essential part of life in the various states and territories of the time. News brokerages began to grow as significant influences on news content. Interest and debate in ethical issues related to journalism increased accordingly. In 1860, Lambert Wilmer, an experienced journalist, published the first book solely devoted to criticism of the press in which he concluded that it had misused its power, having "no just pretensions" to infringe upon the "rights and liberties of the American people."[6]

Both the pre–Civil War period and the volatile reconstruction period that followed the war provided ample opportunity for partisan journalism characterized primarily by editorial pages that contained personal attacks on public figures and competing newspapers or their editors. However, during the Civil War the press gained new public stature as a primary source of information as many newspapers recognized it was their ethical duty to painstakingly strive for accuracy in reporting news, events, and facts about the conflict that often directly involved readers' relatives and friends.

Greater circulation and advertising revenues, use of the telegraph, improved printing presses, and other technological advancements stimulated further commercial growth of the post–Civil War press leading to less dependence on special interest groups. Public opin-

ion about the value of independent thinking and reporting also led to less direct affiliation of newspapers with political parties.

Journalists began to organize and debate the purposes, nature, requirements, and ethical considerations of their profession.[7] Whitelaw Reid, who followed Horace Greeley as editor of the *New York Tribune*, called for a "representative news," free from the influence of advertising interests, that acknowledged that "newspapers print what people want." However, he emphasized that journalists should pay as much attention to news that would educate the reader such as the "greatest advancement made in physical science" as they did to accidents, crime, and less edifying news.[8] William Cullen Bryant, editor of the *New York Evening Post*, declared that a newspaper needed "careful attention as to its accuracy, and an equal careful avoidance of indecent details, and attacks on private character, and intrusions into private life." Exaggerations also should be avoided and all news and editorial material should be "fair and just, and look to the common good" and not be "false in taste or exceptionable morals."[9] The *New York Evening Post's* Parke Godwin believed editors should be "intellectual men," "firm and independent," characterized by a "just and Christian spirit," who "better relinquish their profession forever than sacrifice to it their integrity."[10]

Reform efforts of various newspapers also invigorated the trend toward professionalism and ethical standards. Most notable were the persistent, joint efforts of the *New York Times* and *Harper's Weekly* cartoonist Thomas Nast to expose the graft and corruption associated with New York City's "Boss" Tweed and his Ring. In 1871, the *Times* issued a special supplement exposing the ring's many frauds, including its control over many dozens of newspapers that involved among other things acceptance of paid advertising disguised as news. About the same time, the *St. Louis Democrat* exposed the Whiskey Ring, an organized defrauding of the government that misdirected revenue taxes from distillers. During the same period there were a number of attempts to establish religious daily newspapers such as the *Boston Evening News* and the *New York Daily Witness*.

They tried to provide news while maintaining a religious character and avoiding advertising for liquor, theaters, lotteries, and other products or services that readers might find objectionable.

Industrialization of the press during the last quarter of the 19th century brought about unethical business practices. The ownership of publications often was hidden, circulation figures were falsified, and advertising camouflaged as news was common. Critics accused the press of not only over zealously seeking profits but outright corruption. Journalists still were criticized for sensationalism, invasion of privacy, trivializing the news, and lack of thoroughness in reporting. Some critics also thought journalists had a limited understanding of various professional fields and subject matters including arts and literature. Yet many practices that might be ethically questionable today were not addressed. For example, in 1875 Ansel Kellogg introduced the "boiler plate," pre-etched printing plates that contained news, features, and columns and enabled newspaper editors to graft this material into their local newspapers without attributing it to distant reporters and editors. By 1886, Kellogg's Chicago Newspaper Union, the Western Newspaper Union, and the New York Newspaper Union were providing approximately one-third of all weekly newspapers material by this means without its supplier being revealed.[11]

NEW JOURNALISM

In the 1880s a "new journalism" was introduced, primarily by Joseph Pulitzer through his *St. Louis Post-Dispatch* and later the *New York World*. It was a journalism that concentrated on the masses rather than classes and principles rather than partisanship, according to Pulitzer.[12] It featured spirited daily news, a vigorous editorial style, crusades for civic betterment and humanitarian causes, entertaining features about daily urban life, and scoops on rival newspapers. Gossip, news tidbits, and a disregard for social customs also characterized it. Sensational headlines, liberal use of illustrations and pictures, and later color highlighted

its design. Coupled with further industrialization of the press, the development of modern advertising, and growth of urban areas and cultures, this new journalism contributed greatly to an increase in total circulation of newspapers. Essentially Pulitzer revived the sensationalism that had characterized earlier penny papers but did so with a more acceptable style and professionalism. Pulitzer told his editors to "always tell the truth, always take the humane and moral side, always remember that right feeling is the vital spark of strong writing and that publicity, *publicity*, PUBLICITY, is the greatest moral factor and force in our public life."[13]

Newspapers in various cities throughout the United States duplicated Pulitzer's model of journalism. This journalistic style did draw critics but was defended by others like the *New York Tribune's* Whitelaw Reid, who stated that "whatever their faults, your community chooses to sustain them" and newspapers should print "what they think they have reason to believe the largest numbers desire."[14] Perhaps Pulitzer's style of journalism's most ardent and well-respected critic was E. L. Godkin, editor of the prestigious *Nation* and later the *New York Evening Post*. After observing and criticizing the abuses of the "new journalism" for many years, he concluded that, "Even if the papers are clean and decent, they are fit only for the nursery."[15] The *Nation* featured Godkin's artful, humorous editorials, insistence on journalistic independence and the pursuit of truth, and the highest ideals for public figures and journalists alike. It served as an enduring ethical compass for editors and leaders who regularly read it.

THE YELLOW PRESS

During the 1890s, discussion of ethics centered on even higher levels of sensationalism. This was the result of William Randolph Hearst's adaptation of "new journalism" to the *San Francisco Examiner* and the *New York Morning Journal*, his highly competitive circulation war with Pulitzer's *New York World*, and other newspapers that followed this formula for success.

The "yellow press" was criticized for its obsession with crime, sex, catastrophes, questionable scientific discoveries, gossip, and trial by newspaper rather than jury. It was charged with overemphasizing sports, comics, and trivia. The common practices of using stories that were untrue, fake photographs, and provocative headlines also were questioned. The press' role in instigating the Spanish-American War and its inaccurate and sensationalized reporting of it were particularly controversial. In some critics' eyes, President McKinley's assassination was the fault of Hearst's incessant berating of the President. As editor of the *New York Evening Post*, Godkin summarized that "a yellow journal office is probably the nearest approach, in atmosphere, to hell, existing in any Christian state."[16]

About the turn of the century, a period described by press critic Will Irwin as "a time of transition for the country and journalism,"[17] calls for press reform increased. There was not only a concern that truth and accuracy had been lost but that powerful people like William Randolph Hearst and E. W. Scripps would control the press through the newspaper chains they were developing. Higher classes were critical of newspapers for pandering to and perpetuating working class values, presenting trivial and tasteless news, lowering moral standards, and stimulating class hatreds rather than educating and cultivating their audiences. Critics of the time were in general agreement that news should be separated from opinion and privacy should be protected. Business and news functions of newspapers should be divided, they contended. In addition, journalists should be well educated and of high moral integrity.

THE BEGINNINGS AND GROWTH OF PROFESSIONALISM

During the first decade of the 20th century, there were numerous public declarations to legally restrict the press, but fears of loss of press and speech freedom tempered this discussion. A number of states passed laws to address invasion of privacy issues or regulate the press in other ways. Some attempted to enforce honesty in advertising, and others briefly tried to license journalists.

Amid this general debate, concerns about ethical abuses and solutions formally became part of the journalist's world through the development of professional journalism codes. Movement toward formal journalism ethics began as early as the 1860s when the *Philadelphia Public Ledger* introduced "24 Rules," stressing accuracy and fairness during the Civil War. The word "ethics" first appeared in an 1889 essay on press criticism by W. S. Lilly titled "The Ethics of Journalism." About the same time, *The Journalist* (1884–1907) and its successor, *Editor & Publisher*, begun in 1901, served as vehicles through which journalists could discuss issues related to their profession and supported ethical codes, establishing journalism schools, and the creation of professional associations.[18] The first school of journalism was opened at the University of Missouri in 1908. The Columbia University School of Journalism was established in 1912 with $2 million from Joseph Pulitzer, who insisted that ethics should be at the center of all instruction.

In 1910, the Kansas Editorial Association officially adopted the first code of ethics for journalists, written by William E. Miller. The document dealt with ethical issues both on the business and editorial sides of newspaper operations. In the 1920s journalism codes of ethics were created and adopted in other states, including Missouri and Texas in 1921, South Dakota and Oregon in 1922, Massachusetts and Washington in 1923, and Iowa and New Jersey in 1924. Moreover, during this decade a number of newspapers created and adopted codes of ethics for their own publications, among them the *Seattle Times*, *Brooklyn Eagle*, *Springfield Republican*, *Sacramento Bee*, and *Kansas City Journal-Post*. The development of these codes was in part stimulated by concern about the success and possible negative long-term consequences of federal government efforts, headed by Edward Bernays, to use the press as a propaganda vehicle during the World War I period.

These codes typically stressed truth when reporting as a primary canon. Journalists were to be competent and thorough in their professional duties. They were to avoid editorializing, conflicts of interest, and advertising disguised as news or editorials. They were to fulfill their responsibility to ensure an informed public and thereby strengthen self-government. Several codes addressed kindness, mercy, and "service" to the public. Most contained some type of preamble and general internal comments that expressed some fundamental purposes of the press in American culture, reflecting a traditional libertarian press theory.

National journalism organizations were formed during this time period and formally addressed professional ethics as well. In 1922, the American Society of Newspaper Editors (ASNE) was organized under the leadership of Casper S. Yost of the *St. Louis Globe-Democrat* to deal with "common problems and the promotion of their professional ideals," as its constitution stated. The same year, at its first annual meeting, ASNE adopted a code of ethics called *Canons of Journalism*. Early ASNE meetings focused much time and energy on questions of ethics. Specifically, a bitter dispute originated about the group's authority to expel one member, Fred G. Bonfils of the *Denver Post*, who stood accused of blackmailing oil millionaire Harry Sinclair in connection with the Teapot Dome scandal. At one point a vote on expulsion was taken, but the action was rescinded and the editor was allowed to resign. Later the organization clarified its position, declaring that it did not intend to serve as a policing organization. In 1926, ASNE members voted for voluntary compliance to the organization's code.

Another major journalism professional organization, The Society of Professional Journalists (SPJ), was founded in 1909 as Sigma Delta Chi (SDX). Its first code of ethics, adopted in 1926, was "borrowed" from the ASNE and served as forerunner to the SPJ's own code written in 1973 and revised in 1984, 1987, and 1996. As these codes evolved, they stressed a number of key values: (1) giving audiences two dimensions of information—the facts and an understanding or "interpretation" of those facts (straight news stories were to present the facts, free from opinion; in-depth articles, investigative pieces, editorials, commentary and columns should give the audience some sense of what the facts mean); (2) helping audiences make intelligent and informed decisions as citizens as well as in their personal lives, including letting them know how their social institutions were operating and whether they were operating in an open manner; and (3) serving as a marketplace for the distribution of goods and services.

The national codes also identified various principles upon which journalists should stand. First, the ASNE's 1926 decision to make compliance to the codes voluntary and rely on public disapproval rather than formal enforcement became the standard for later codes. Second, there was a commitment to objectivity. Journalism historians have suggested a number of explanations of why objective news reporting developed and became a codified principle. Some attribute this to the growth of wire services like the Associated Press that required reporters to make their writing seem unbiased, since it would appear in newspapers with differing political positions. Others trace the beginnings of objective reporting to criticism of community leaders during the excesses of "yellow journalism." Still others suggest that it evolved as journalists imitated the scientific method during the first part of the 20th century. The ASNE's 1922 guideline said simply, "Sound practice makes clear between reports and expressions of opinion" and added, "News reports should be free from opinion or bias of any kind." The standard of objectivity continued to be debated and was addressed in subsequent journalism codes. By the late 1920s and on into the 1930s, 1940s, and beyond, it generally became a professional ethical norm.

Listed at the top of early and subsequent ASNE, SPJ, and other codes has been a commitment to truth telling. The codes also have made independence from political, social, and economic influences a core concept. Specifically, this has included admonitions against accepting gifts, free or reduced travel, outside employment, certain financial investments, political activity, participation in civic activity, or outside speaking engagements. Related principles stated in the first ASNE code and embraced thereafter include avoiding the appearance of impropriety or conflict of interest, being cautious in granting confidentiality to news sources but honoring it once promised, and respecting "right of privacy," although this term was not used in the initial ASNE code. Journalists also were encouraged to offer the right of reply when material critical of a person is published, pursue accuracy, impartiality and fairness, and run retractions. They were challenged to responsibly discuss, question, and confront the government and other social institutions engaged in the public's business and act as "servants of the public."

While creation, development, and application of professional codes highlighted the history of journalism ethics in the first three decades of the 20th century, there were other significant influences on the ethics of the profession. In 1924 Nelson Crawford of Kansas State University published the first textbook on newspaper ethics in the United States, *The Ethics of Journalism*. In 1929 "the journalist's journalist," Walter Lippmann, published *A Preface to Morals*, arguing that foundational to sound professional practice and a vibrant society was both an informed mind and a vibrant conscience. In 1934, in response to growth and legal and ethical issues in the radio industry, Congress passed the Communication Act that established the Federal Communications Commission (FCC). It has been charged with licensing but not censoring radio and later television broadcasters and ensuring that they operated "in the public interest, convenience, and necessity."

By the advent of World War II, professional codes or canons of journalism were a matter of public record and professional debate. Alarm and response to Nazi propaganda tactics influenced discussion about journalism ethics during and after the war. Press freedom from government interference became even more appreciated and valued. Thus in the years following World War II, the National Press Photographers Association, National Conference of Editorial Writers, and other journalism organizations adopted ethical codes modeled after previously developed professional codes.

THE RISE OF SOCIAL RESPONSIBILITY

Perhaps the most important event affecting journalism ethics during this period was the formation of the nine-member Commission on the Freedom of the Press by Robert M. Hutchins in 1944. Hutchins, president of the University of Chicago, was asked by *Time* editor-in-chief Henry R. Luce to evaluate press freedom in light of the emerging powerful media systems that had developed at the end of the war. At the same time, media critics were attacking the norm of an obsessively objective press that devalued the importance of intervention, social reform, and creativity. The Hutchins Commission report, *A Free and Responsible Press*, published in 1947, provided a framework for discussing media ethics during the next several decades. The report emphasized the need for (1) truthful accounts within a proper context, (2) public forums to solicit feedback and criticism, (3) representation for the various cultural groups within society, (4) a focus on social goals and values, and (5) public access to knowledge and information.

The Hutchins Commission report led to the publication of several books and monographs related to the report that were read and studied by many hundreds of students enrolled in journalism schools, especially during the late 1940s and 1950s. By the beginning of World War II, more than 120 journalism schools, departments, and academic programs had been established in the United States. The growth of journalism as an academic field formalized the study of journalism ethics.

During the 1950s the growth of broadcast journalism added a new dimension to ethical issues faced by journalists. The Federal Communication Commission had ruled in 1949 that the airways are public property that should be made accessible to many different viewpoints. While fairness and balance in news reporting had already been a fundamental doctrine in most journalists' codes, it now had the regulatory and enforcement backing of the FCC. The National Association of Broadcasters (NAB) established a Code Authority in 1960 to handle complaints of violations, intending to increase self-regulation of broadcasters and stave off government intrusion.

In the late 1960s journalists were scrutinized for the reporting of race riots in Detroit, Newark, New Jersey, and other American cities. A formal commission appointed by President Lyndon Johnson and headed by Governor Otto Kerner of Illinois extensively studied the news coverage and issued a published report in 1968. The Kerner Commission Report concluded that news coverage of the race riots was balanced and factual, despite a tendency toward sensationalism and a severe lack of African-American journalists covering the riots. The report raised awareness of the critical need for recruiting, educating, and promoting more minorities in the profession, especially news executives, as an ethical issue.

Several important academic works that dealt with journalism ethics also were published during the 1960s, including Gerald Edwards' *The Social Responsibility of the Press*, Kyle Haselden's *Morality and the Mass Media*, and a revised edition of William Rivers' and Wilbur Schramm's *Responsibility in Mass Communication*. Surprisingly, despite a keen interest in journalism ethics and numerous publications on the subject during the 1920s and early 1930s, these three works were the first major texts dealing with journalism ethics published from then until 1968.[19]

THE WATERGATE ERA

It was not until the monumental events of the Watergate scandal of 1973 that led to the resignation of President Richard Nixon that a sustained resurgence in attention to journalism ethics and revision of ethical codes reemerged. *Washington Post* reporters Bob Woodward and Carl Bernstein influenced journalists by maintaining high ethical standards through careful research and making sure the information in their Watergate stories was verified by a second source. Yet Watergate unearthed issues of corruption and competing values that brought to light complexities faced by journalists in an increasingly technological world. Journalists

began to recognize that in order to credibly expose unethical behavior in the institution of government, journalists themselves had to act ethically. The renewed focus on journalism ethics in the 1970s resulted in a number of new and influential books on the subject and stimulated further growth in ethics instruction and curricula in American higher.

In 1973 the National News Council was formed. It was the product of a grassroots movement that had led to the creation of press councils in various communities across the United States in the 1950s and 1960s. A cross-section of people, including media representatives, usually served on these councils. They typically debated the role of media in their communities, the relationship between press freedom and social responsibility, and investigated complaints about media unethical behavior. The National News Council performed the same basic functions on a national scale. Although it contributed to awareness and debate about journalism ethics, considerable media antagonism toward it, a lack of enforcement powers, and insufficient public support led to its demise in 1984.

The 1980s marked an era in the field of journalism in the United States where international concerns became an important focus. The McBride Commission for the Study of Communication Problems, appointed by the United Nations Educational, Scientific, and Cultural Organization (UNESCO) in 1976, published an important report in 1980, *Many Voices; One World: Communication and Society, Today and Tomorrow*. It and a number of international media ethics conferences that followed addressed ethical issues regarding communication rights, the conglomeration and control of mass media by a few western nations, and the technological reality that ethics increasingly needed to be viewed in terms of an interdependent global news media.

RECENT TRENDS

A number of significant journalism ethics publications emerged in the 1980s, including the quarterly *Journal of Mass Media Ethics*, the newsletter *Media Ethics*, and *Communication Ethics and Global Change*. During the 1990s more than a dozen significant books on media ethics were published.

The Radio-Television News Directors (RTNDA) adopted its code of ethics in 1987. The code stressed avoidance of sensationalism, unlabeled opinion, and misleading or deceptive news, audio or video materials. People were not to be identified "by race, creed, nationality or prior status" unless this was relevant to what was being presented. Avoiding conflicts of interests, respecting privacy, confidentiality of sources, and securing permission to transmit the materials of others were other standards included in the code. In addition, many other professional journalists' organizations revised their ethical codes during the 1980s and 1990s. While these codes varied in specific language, length and application, they continued to be built around core values that had been debated or encoded in the past.

Considerable debate in the 1990s concentrated on the issue of enforcing such codes. Many news executives feared that written ethical codes might be used against them in court. In addition, individual news organizations preferred to have termination of employees who violated ethical codes remain an internal matter. There was some concern that this would ultimately lead to a journalism profession regulated by laws and legal processes rather than ethical guidelines.

In the 1990s, more than at any time in American journalism history, journalists had at their disposal academic preparation that focused on journalism ethics, numerous ethics books, materials and other resources, and well conceived and defined ethical codes. Yet another concern among journalists and critics of the profession was whether many journalists had the personal integrity to apply their understanding of journalism ethics consistently. Journalists often regarded ethical codes as overly vague, impractical, static, generalized, restrictive, unenforceable, or public relations ploys. Critics pointed out that news organizations must instill a culture for ethical journalism in which ethical guidelines and behavior were an outgrowth of sound, well-communicated, and consistently applied organizational values.

Today, journalists are wrestling with ethical issues emerging from a communication technology-dominated American culture in which the lines of delineation between legitimate news and entertainment are being increasingly blurred. Sensationalism rivaling anything that characterized past journalism eras is prevalent in much journalistic fare. It is a culture in which media celebrities, including celebrity journalists, are cleverly created, marketed, and revered by audiences. In addition, a new type of journalist who concentrates on reporting celebrity news has emerged. A great deal of "news" is being derived from "reality" programs, call-in talk shows, and news greatly tailored to narrow audiences in an increasingly fragmented media environment. Ethical issues related to an increasingly diverse culture in the United States have become a focal point. At the same time, the quickly growing and evolving Internet and other technological advancements are further creating a global climate within which journalism ethics has to be considered. The Internet and other applications of newer communication technologies also are changing the nature of communication and some of the practices of journalism and empowering individuals and organizations in new ways.

As journalists debate new ethical issues in this changing media environment, the relevance of current ethical codes that were the product of hundreds of years of debate about the purposes and ethics of journalism are being considered. Yet it seems certain that as standards are modified to address new issues and adapt to this changing environment, they will have to rest on fundamental ideals that have been discussed and defined in the past and have served as the essential framework for journalism codes of ethics since they were first developed: truth in reporting, minimizing harm in dealing with others, impartiality, and accountability.

Selected Readings

Christians, Clifford G. "Fifty Years of Scholarship in Media Ethics." *Journal of Communication* (Autumn 1977), 19–29.

Cronin, Mary M. "Trade Press Roles in Promoting Journalistic Professionalism, 1884–1917." *Journal of Mass Media Ethics* 4 (1988): 227–38.

Ferré, John P. "The Dubious Heritage of Media Ethics: Cause-and-Effect Criticism in the 1890s." *American Journalism* 5 (1988): 191–203.

Garcia, Hazel-Dicken. *Journalistic Standards in the Nineteenth-Century America*. Madison: University of Wisconsin Press, 1989.

Lawson, Linda. *Truth in Publishing: Federal Regulation of the Press' Business Practices, 1880–1912*. Carbondale: Southern Illinois University Press, 1993.

McIntire, Jerilyn S. "The Hutchins Commission's Search for a Moral Framework." *Journalism History* 6 (1979): 54–57, 63.

Wood, Barry R., "Denver Newspaper Publishers and Teapot Dome." *Essays and Monographs in Colorado History* 1(1983): 25–37.

Notes

1. *Publick Occurrences, Both Forreign and Domestick*, 25 September 1690, 1.

2. *Boston News-Letter*, 2–9 April 1705.

3. *Farmer's Museum, or Lay Preacher's Gazette*, 15 April 1799.

4. *New York Evening Post*, 16 November 1801.

5. *Journal of Commerce*, 6 September 1827.

6. Lambert Wilmer, *Our Press Gang* (Philadelphia: J. T. Lloyd, 1860), 71.

7. Stephen A. Banning, "The Professionalization of Journalism: A Nineteenth-Century Beginning," *Journalism History* 24 (1998–1999): 157–63.

8. Interview with Whitelaw Reid, quoted in F. Wingate, ed., *Views and Interviews of Journalists* (New York: Arno Press and The New York Times, 1875), 26, 30, 35.

9. Interview with William Cullen Bryant, quoted in Wingate, ibid., 49–51.

10. Interview with Parke Godwin, quoted in Wingate, ibid., 222–26.

11. Eugene C. Harter, *Boilerplating America: The Hidden Newspaper* (Lanham, Md.: University Press of America, 1991).

12. Don C. Seitz, *Joseph Pulitzer; His Life and Letters* (New York, 1924), 101–02.

13. *New York World*, 29 December 1895.

14. Whitelaw Reid, "Journalistic Duties and Opportunities," *American* (1901): 317.

15. *The Nation*, 7 May 1896, 356.

16. *New York Evening Post*, 14 March 1898.

17. Will Irwin, "The Press Agent, His Rise and Decline," *Collier's* 72 (8 December 1911): 25.

18. Mary M. Cronin, "Trade Press Roles in Promoting Journalistic Professionalism, 1884–1917," *Journal of Mass Media Ethics* 4 (1988): 227–38.

19. Clifford G. Christians, "50 Years of Scholarship in Media Ethics," *Journal of Communication* (Autumn, 1977): 19–29.

6

Press Criticism

LINDA J. LUMSDEN

If beating up an editor counts, press criticism in the United States goes back at least as far as the day in 1797 when John Ward Fenno caned Benjamin Franklin Bache in the streets of Philadelphia. Anti-Federalist Bache had incensed Fenno, son of the editor of the Federalists' *Gazette of the United States*, when Bache wrote in his *Aurora* that George Washington had debauched the nation.

Confrontations such as the Fenno-Bache brawl made it easy for printer Isaiah Thomas to find a less pugilistic press critic for his *History of Printing in America* in 1810. "[T]oo many of our gazettes," he quoted a Rev. Miller, "are in the hands of persons destitute at once of the urbanity of gentlemen, the information of scholars, and the principles of virtue."[1] The parade of press critics who followed the reverend over the next two centuries have largely agreed—finding a fount of faults with the press as a cultural and an economic institution. Four broad recurring themes have punctuated more than two centuries of American press criticism: the dangers of sensationalism and inaccuracies, democracy's dependence upon a free press, the social responsibility of the press, and the detrimental influence of capitalism upon newspaper economics. Systematic, organized, and institutionalized press criticism, however, is a product of the 20th century.

Because the early American press was avidly partisan, ideology formed the basis of 18th-century criticism. Newspapers' point of view primarily concerned critics, mainly citizens debating the news in coffee houses. In a broad sense, British governors exercised a primitive yet institutionalized form of criticism by banning offensive publications or jailing their publishers, the fate suffered in 1722 by James Franklin of the *New England Courant*.

Nonetheless, the inherently obstreperous American press continued to defy the British and became the principle agent in percolating colonial alienation from England. The colonial gentry in mid-century criticized the increasingly radical colonial newspapers as rabble-rousers that stirred up the masses. As revolutionary fervor crystallized in the 1760s, loyalists complained that patriot publishers such as Sam Adams irresponsibly quashed all discussion of legitimate concerns raised by those who hesitated to sever ties with their mother country. A more serious Tory charge was that the "Journal of Occurrences," an anonymous diary published in radical newspapers in 1768–69, falsified reports of alleged brutality by the British, claims that ignited the American Revolution. Despite their fiery rhetoric about liberty, in fact, the radicals only supported freedom of expression for those who agreed with them. They harassed Tory publishers such as James Rivington, hanging him in effigy, raiding his shop, and destroying his type. Radical patriot-journalists of the period, epitomized by *Massachusetts Spy* publisher Isaiah Thomas, were propagandists who literally warred against their critics.

In the early years of the Republic, the press grew even more partisan as Americans wrestled with how to sustain a viable democracy. Because the press served as the primary instrument for creating the two-party system, press criticism was virtually indistinguishable from political persuasion. Editors, politicians, and readers agreed a newspaper existed primarily to function as the mouthpiece of a party. So no critics' eyebrows rose when Alexander Hamilton among other Federalists in 1789 founded and subsidized the *Gazette of the United States*, or leading Republicans James Madison and Thomas Jefferson helped create the *National Gazette* in 1791.

In fact, critics knocked newspapers they deemed insufficiently partisan as spineless, untrustworthy, and derelict in their duty to sway public opinion. Disdainful editors, for instance, ridiculed Samuel Harrison Smith's *National Intelligencer* as "Mr. Silky Smith's National Smoothing Plane" because of its relatively impartial reportage. Readers accepted, even applauded, the press' scurrilous style and personal invective. The vitriol rained upon Republicans by the Federalist *Porcupine's Gazette*, however, proved too vicious even for its supporters, who called upon publisher William Cobbett to soften his attacks. Cobbett eventually joined a number of publishers who found themselves in the courtroom, an alternative forum for press criticism. Savaged subjects of partisan journalism frequently sought redress through libel suits. Cobbett fled the country rather than pay a $5,000 judgment against him. The aptly titled *Wasp* was one of several newspapers forced to shut down because it lost a libel suit. Given the highly politicized function of the press, perhaps it was inevitable that the federal government emerged as the most draconian of press critics. Barely had the ink dried on the first sentence of the Bill of Rights guaranteeing a free press than the Sedition Act of 1798 criminalized criticism of government. The Federalists used the law as a tool to silence their Republican critics in the press, who endured jail or fines before Jefferson let the reviled act lapse.

Following the rise of the penny press in the 1830s, the change in the nature of news also changed the nature of criticism. Journalism moved from political tracts toward timely and racy accounts of crime, humor, gossip, and even hoaxes. The middle-class worried sensationalism corrupted public morality. Church and business leaders joined forces with the self-interested editorial elite in the "Moral War of 1840" against the irreverent James Gordon Bennett, whose *New York Herald* lavished especially florid coverage upon scandal. Bennett not so coincidentally also delighted in goading Wall Street and religion. They organized an unsuccessful boycott of the *Herald* and railed against Bennett from both editorial pages and pulpits.

As newspapers evolved into a mass medium, new critics viewed the sheer ubiquity of the press in itself as an agent of social evil. They believed coverage of crime and scandal nurtured both social ills. Men of letters emerged as curmudgeonly press critics. James Fenimore Cooper devoted nearly a decade to suing newspapers that he charged were full of damaging lies. Charles Dickens inveighed with damning observations about corrupt journalists in *American Notes*, an account of his 1842 tour. As indicated by the title of the first book of press criticism, *Our Press Gang: or, A Complete Exposition of the Corruptness and Crimes of the American Newspapers*, by Lambert A. Wilmer in 1859, none of these polemics qualified as thoughtful critiques.

Articles examining press practices began appearing in intellectual magazines after the Civil War, beginning in 1866 with the appointment of master essayist E. L. Godkin as editor of the fledgling *Nation* magazine. The aristocratic intellectual blamed newspapers for creating "a society of ignoramuses each of whom thinks he is a Solon."[2] Other magazines such as *Arena*, *Century*, and *Forum* followed the *Nation's* lead into newspaper criticism. Many of those critiques reverberated with condemnation of the sensational yellow journalism that tinged the 1890s. Godkin decried the detrimental effect upon democracy of a "venal and silly" press that beget a "puerile habit of mind," concerns echoed by *Atlantic Monthly*, *Forum*, and other magazines.[3] Academia, another blossoming profession, lent scientific credence to these charges. Social psychologist Delos F. Wilcox in 1900, for example, undertook possibly the first content analysis of newspapers to conclude that yellow journalism damaged society. Wilcox also identified the second recurring theme of press criticism, the social responsibility of the press. He wrote, "Responsibility must attach to this public function."[4]

Scholars such as Wilcox contributed to press criticism because they were outsiders, in contrast to most critics who were products of the city room. Scrutinizing the press through new prisms, they realized more quickly than journalists that the press is a product and not just a producer of culture. As early as 1909, James Edward Rogers concluded in a book-length study of city newspapers that their sensationalism and commercialism simply reflected the character of the American people. Journalism professor Willard Grosvenor Bleyer's *Main Currents in the History of American Journalism* in 1927 excused the 19th-century press on similar grounds. Sociologist Alfred McClung Lee in his case study of the role of newspapers in American life in 1937 concurred that the press is no better or worse than the society it covers.[5]

Journalists in the late 19th century gradually began to acquire a sense of themselves as professionals with standards to uphold—or raise—perhaps in reaction to some of this criticism. They launched the *Journalist* in 1884 in New York and founded the National Editorial Association in 1885. The first journalism school opened at the University of Missouri in 1908. Joseph Pulitzer atoned for his yellow journalism with a $2 million donation to found the Columbia University School of Journalism, which opened in 1912. In 1909, the first book on journalism ethics appeared, and journalism students at DePauw University organized Sigma Delta Chi, precursor of the Society of Professional Journalists. It published *Quill* in 1912, the same year that journalists conducted the first National Newspaper Conference to discuss industry problems.

That conference may have been spurred by a landmark 15-part series in 1911 by Will Irwin for *Collier's* magazine. "The American Newspaper: A Study of Journalism in Its Relation to the Public" framed the press as a public service. "I had no precedents to go by," Irwin wrote later. "Journalism was still finding itself."[6] The muckraking reporter applied his skills during visits to publishers, editors, and reporters across the country. He concluded that the power of the press sat in its news columns, rather than its editorials, because of the power of what a half century later would be defined as agenda setting.

Progressive-era reformism informed Irwin's approach. Newspapers, at their zenith of influence in the 1910s, surely would improve once someone pointed out their shortcomings to them. For Irwin, journalism's biggest handicap in its search for truth originated outside of the newsroom: the invidious influence of advertising. Journalistic improprieties such as the occasional stealing of a photograph of a deceased loved one from a family mantle likewise disgusted Irwin. Otherwise, the accomplished reporter strained to educate the public about the loftier mission of his much-maligned craft. "The newspaper, or some force like it, must daily inform [the public] of things which are shocking and unpleasant in order that democracy, in its slow, wobbling motion upward, may perceive and correct," Irwin wrote.[7] His assertion that democracy depends upon a viable press is the third thread of 20th-century press criticism.

The decade closed with a dark assessment of newspaper motives by radical muckraker and novelist Upton Sinclair. He charged that journalism had sold its soul to capitalism in *The Brass Check*. The title refers to the token brothel patrons used to buy prostitutes' services. "The Brass Check is the price of your shame—," the author addressed readers, "you who take the fair body of truth and sell it in the marketplace, who betray the virgin hopes of mankind into the loathsome brothel of Big Business."[8] Sinclair's was neither the first nor last denunciation of newspaper economics, the fourth and final recurring theme of modern press criticism.

Such diatribes became supplanted in the 1920s by more thoughtful and better documented press criticism in both magazines and books. Press criticism proliferated in periodicals in the first half of the century. One scholar counted 506 articles of press criticism published in consumer magazines from 1900 through 1939.[9]

The intellectual contributions of Walter

Lippmann raised press criticism to new intellectual heights. The astute political columnist used his reporter's tools to scrutinize his own profession. For example, he and a partner examined more than three thousand *New York Times* articles in 1920 to dissect the newspaper's inept and misleading coverage of the Russian Revolution. Lippmann also called for newspaper ethics codes, along with *New York Post* editor and newspaper-publisher-turned-critic Oswald Garrison Villard. Virtually the first task of the fledgling American Society of Newspaper Editors, in fact, was to adopt seven voluntary Canons of Journalism in 1923: sincerity, truthfulness, accuracy, impartiality, fair play, decency, and independence. By 2000, more than three dozen newspaper organizations had enacted ethics codes. Lippmann's most important contribution, however, was that he navigated new ground as a theorist of the function of the press in several influential books such as *Liberty and the News* in 1920 and *Public Opinion* in 1922. His conceptualizations charted the territory for analysis of the press as a social institution. Further theoretical analysis followed the founding in 1933 of *Journalism Quarterly*, the first academic journal on the subject.

The distinction of providing the first sustained attempt to critique the American press belongs to Robert Benchley of the *New Yorker*. Editor Harold Ross had commissioned occasional pieces of press criticism from the magazine's genesis in 1925. Within two years, "The Wayward Press" appeared exclusively beneath the byline of "Guy Fawkes," Benchley's pseudonym. The magazine's theater critic and a humorist with experience as a freelance writer, editor, and public relations practitioner, Benchley wrote more than 70 "Wayward Press" columns over the next 12 years. He focused on poor writing, inaccurate reporting, public relations puffery, ethics, and the malign influence upon the news of advertising and government propaganda. He spoke for the nation in 1932 when he wrote that the press' nauseating coverage earned it the title of "General Goat and Villain" of the Lindbergh baby kidnapping.[10] During stints as a press agent including chief of publicity for the Aircraft Board, Benchley developed radar for detecting public relations spin in news stories. Unlike his rather humorless predecessors, his droll wit and graceful writing cooled his sting.[11]

The same could be said of his successor, Abbott Joseph Liebling, who spiced his columns with caustic dollops after he revived "The Wayward Press" in 1945. Pithy A. J. Liebling's quiver of similes enlivened his criticism. Characterizing ebullient coverage of the 1948 Progressive Party presidential convention, he wrote, "Epithets that had been stored up for the occasion popped like wine for a plain daughter's wedding."[12] He delighted in deflating pomposity, especially that of the publishers and heads of encroaching newspaper chains whom he reviled as venal and unduly influenced by advertising. One headline he predicted never would appear was, "Publisher Admits He May Have Been Wrong."

In another column, he puckishly took literally a pronouncement by a *Chicago Tribune* reporter that the slimness of New York periodicals proved their inferiority. He set out with a scale to apply this surefire method of measuring quality to a variety of periodicals, discovering that the Chicago telephone directory weighed twice as much as two Sunday *Tribunes*. Liebling's greatest shortcoming may have been that he ignored the broadcast media he disdained. His fixation upon newspapers was one reason his nostalgic tonics for the press began to lose relevance toward the last of the 82 "Wayward Press" columns published before his death in 1963.[13]

During the Depression, newspaper publishers experienced near universal condemnation as greedy and hypocritical capitalists. The government, the public, and members of journalism's lower echelons charged that publishers blocked New Deal reforms because of their own financial interests. It may have been easy for publishers to dismiss as sour grapes charges—made in 1939 by former newspaperman Harold Ickes, then Secretary of the Interior—that newspapers represented the upper classes rather than ordinary people because Franklin Roosevelt was Ickes' boss. They could not so easily shrug off criticism from revered William Allen White of the *Emporia* (Kan.) *Gazette*, the quintessential journalist of the people. The same year that Ickes' *America's House of Lords* appeared, White took the podium as newly installed president of the American Society of Newspaper Editors to chastise his colleagues for allowing the editorial side of the industry to become subordinate to its business side.[14] Both men repeated charges that had been meticulously assembled throughout the decade by the publishers' most persistent critic, former ace foreign correspondent George Seldes.

The century's most famous press critic, Seldes also was its longest lived. Born in 1890, the one-time World War I reporter for the *Chicago Tribune* served in his 104 years as the link between 20th-century press critics. They ranged back to Irwin, whom Seldes said inspired him, and forward to post–Watergate columnists such as Nat Hentoff, who acknowledged their debt to Seldes. The Communist leadership kicked him out of Moscow, and Benito Mussolini booted him out of Rome. After covering the Loyalists in the Spanish Civil War, Seldes returned to the United States during the Depression and trained his sights upon American newspaper publishers—more familiar in the scrappy Seldes' lexicon as "moral slaves whose minds are paralyzed by the specter of profits."[15] The newspaper industry was just one more illegal trust to him. He coined a new pejorative phrase for publishers in *Lords of the Press* (1938), in which he excoriated the American Newspaper Publishers Association for exploiting child labor, ambushing the newspaper guild, and brandishing the First Amendment to avoid taxes and regulation. More than any other person, Seldes made press criticism important.

Libertarian Seldes bristled at the conservative tone of much of mainstream journalism. "If the Associated Press had reported the Boston Tea Party," he wrote in *Freedom of the Press*, "it would probably have been an indignant story of Reds defying authority and destroying private property."[16] That quip is about as light as the iconoclastic idealist got, which set Seldes apart from the urbane *New Yorker* critics. Balancing his heavy-handedness, however, was the meticulous documentation that scaffolded his scathing indictments. To demonstrate how publishers abused the First Amendment, for instance, he detailed 29 charges of law violations against a dozen newspapers. His greatest contribution to press criticism probably was *In fact: An Antidote for Falsehood in the Daily Press* (the "f" was intentionally lower case), a four-page weekly he published from 1940 to 1950. Among those he inspired was I. F. Stone. Seldes gave him tips on how to make ends meet when in 1953 Stone launched *I. F. Stone's Weekly*, which performed Seldes-style intellectual vivisection upon congressional politics.

World War II temporarily silenced the clamor for press reform. But even before the bullets stopped, scholars embarked in 1944 upon a unique, privately sponsored inquiry into the power of the press. The findings of the Commission on Freedom of the Press remain significant for several reasons: They emphasized the social responsibility of the press, called upon the press rather than government to regulate itself, and expanded the definition of the press to the electronic media. Most importantly, they have shaped the media's steps toward self-improvement ever since the March 26, 1947, release of the committee report, *A Free and Responsible Press*.

Thirteen academic heavyweights comprised the commission mainly funded by $200,000 from magazine magnate Henry Luce. He named as its chair his friend Robert M. Hutchins, chancellor of the University of Chicago. The Hutchins Commission named five responsibilities of the press: to provide a truthful, comprehensive, and intelligent account of the day's events in a context that gives them meaning; to regard themselves as a common carrier and forum for the exchange of comment and criticism; to project a representative picture of the constituent groups in society; to present and clarify the goals and values of the society; and to provide full access to the day's intelligence.

Although those responsibilities resonate today, at the time many journalists' reactions were lukewarm at best, not in least because no journalists sat on the commission. The commission further alienated its subjects by closing its proceedings, which included interviews and testimony from some 300 people. Most chilling to journalists, however, was that *A Free and Responsible Press* hinted at possible future governmental regulation if newspapers failed to assume their social responsibility. "They are great concentrations of private power," the report said of newspapers. "If they are irresponsible, not even the First Amendment will protect their freedom from governmental control."[17]

Following on the heels of respected lawyer Morris L. Ernst's *The First Freedom*, another blast at the unaccountability of the press lords, the Hutchins Commission report forced the journalistic establishment to wake up to the fact that it had better begin cleaning house. A surprising number of journalist/critics already had proposed government regulation to improve press performance. The field was so smarmy in 1912 that even *Editor & Publisher* advocated licensing journalists to keep out riffraff. Irwin in 1911 called for mandatory retractions. So did Sinclair, who also suggested a law requiring that all stories be approved by their principal subjects before publication. Lippmann supported both of these proposals. (Today, 31 states have mandatory retraction statutes.) William Allen White at mid-century even called for criminalizing publication of details of violent crime. Others, including Seldes and Liebling, advocated an endowed press. None appeared, probably because, as Irwin and Sinclair feared, whoever endowed the newspaper inevitably would control its contents.

After the Hutchins report appeared, journalists scurried to organize their own institutions for self improvement. The American Press Institute opened its doors in 1946, followed the next February by *Nieman Reports*, the nation's first journalism review. The National Council of Editorial Writers organized in July 1947, and that October the Associated Press Managing Editors presented their first written critique of Associated Press service. Sigma Delta Chi drafted an ethics code in 1948. By 1949, *Editor & Publisher* had even sponsored a panel discussion on how American newspapers could improve themselves. ASNE at mid-century formed a Committee on Responsibility, adopting the key word of the Hutchins Commission report, which advocated more

press criticism. The newly formed Association for Education in Journalism also launched a Committee on Professional Freedom and Responsibility. The American Society of Editors established a committee to discuss the need for newspapers to critique and improve themselves. While no concrete reforms materialized, these developments indicate that the Hutchins Commission motivated the industry finally to take a hard look at itself.[18]

The commission's decision to include broadcast media proved timely, as television within the decade began to push newspapers off their pedestal as the preeminent news medium. The electronic media also delved into criticizing the press, first on the weekly radio show, "CBS Views the Press," in 1947, and later on its televised successor, "WCBS-TV Views the Press," in the late 1950s and early 1960s. TV news earned legitimacy after Edward R. Murrow on CBS's "See It Now" challenged master media manipulator Sen. Joseph McCarthy. Most newspapers and the wire services, critics largely agreed, had dropped the ball on exposing McCarthyism as a communist witch hunt. Most passively reported his groundless accusations, so it fell to Murrow—on TV— to expose McCarthy as a bullying emperor without clothes. TV news soon, however, found itself on the receiving end of critiques as press criticism morphed into media criticism. Criticism of broadcast news began to appear in trade publications such as Variety and consumer magazines such as *TV Guide* and on TV programs such as CBS's *Eye on the Press*. Broadcast news also fell under the purview of TV columnists such as John Carmody of the *Washington Post* and John J. O'Connor of the *New York Times*.

The power for good or bad of television images that beamed war and riots into the nation's living rooms became obvious during the political and social upheaval of the 1960s. Some scholars trace the genesis of the civil rights movement to powerful TV images of dogs and hoses turned upon peaceful protesters against segregation in the South. On the other hand, government-sponsored commissions such as the National Advisory Commission on Civil Disorders (Kerner Commission) in 1968 partially blamed the media for exacerbating race riots while ignoring black communities in general. TV reports eventually may have forced the public to question the morality of the Vietnam War, but in 1965, Morley Safer's footage of Marines torching a Vietnamese village earned more enmity for the CBS reporter than for the military. Disbelieving viewers charged that Safer faked the footage, and his boss Frank Stanton got an earful of Lyndon Johnson's profane press criticism when the president awoke him with a pre-dawn call to complain that "your boys shat on the American flag."[19]

Johnson's crude comment is indicative of the hurricane force with which the federal government flew at the media in the following decade of dissent. Harassing the media became Nixon administration policy. The administration also promoted the relatively new term "the media" to remove the press from its venerable tradition as the voice of the people.[20] In 1971, the White House imposed prior restraint upon an American newspaper for the first time in history by blocking the *New York Times* from printing the Pentagon Papers for 15 days. The White House also sicced upon the media Vice President Spiro Agnew, whose alliterative speeches protested the "small and un-elected elite" that he charged controlled American news.[21] The assault failed to quash the *Washington Post's* revelations about the Watergate scandal that forced Nixon to resign in 1974. Although the saga of the *Post's* Watergate exposé has assumed almost mythological significance for journalists, a number of contemporaries criticized the investigation as partisan and irresponsible. And the investigation's legacy of digging for dirt has been blamed for breeding journalistic cynicism that became the biggest bane of many critics in the 1990s.

The defiant atmosphere of the 1960s may have helped spur more self-scrutiny within the press. Several insider journals joined the Society of Professional Journalists' venerable *Quill* in the evening shade of the century, beginning with *Columbia Journalism Review* (1961–); the counter-cultural *More* (1971–78); and *Washington Journalism Review*, now *American Journalism Review* (1977–). General interest magazines also formalized press criticism, such as *Newsweek's* semi-regular "Newswatch" column. David Shaw, who went on to win a Pulitzer Prize in 1991, was named media critic for the *Los Angeles Times* in 1974. Shaggy counter-culture city weeklies that shot up like Microsoft stocks in the 1980s buzzed like horse flies around their Clydesdale-sized daily competitors, partially filling a void in coverage of one of any community's most influential institutions.

Industry institutes devoted to critiquing and improving journalism sprouted like crocuses in spring in the post–Watergate years. The Poynter Institute founded in 1975 began hosting a spectrum of classes and seminars for mid-career journalists as well as cub student reporters to promote excellence and integrity in journalism. The Freedom Forum Media Studies Center in New York City opened in 1985 to research press issues and publish the results in monographs and its *Media Studies Journal*. Women and minorities also organized to monitor mainstream media. Donna Allen launched the "Media Report to Women" newsletter in 1972. The National Organization of Black Journalists organized in 1975, followed by the Asian American Journalism Association (1981–), National Association of Hispanic Journalists (1984–), and Native American Journalism Association. All four cosponsored Unity 1994 and Unity 1999, conventions dedicated to addressing diversity in news media hiring and coverage. They also dove into cyberspace alongside numerous on-line grassroots media watchdog groups when they joined with the National Lesbian and Gay Journalists Association and San Francisco State University to launch the NewsWatch web site (www.newswatch.org). Outside the industry, other watchdog organizations that critique news media include the conservative Accuracy in Media (1969–) and the left-leaning Fairness and Accuracy in Reporting (1986–), which today delivers criticism via web sites, newsletters, and radio shows.

Such organizations forced newspapers to be more responsive to complaints. Hawaii established a press council in 1969, a generation after the Hutchins Commission had recommended creation of an independent news council to monitor press performance and improve standards. The Minnesota Press Council followed in 1971. Most news organizations, however, rejected press councils as an invitation to censorship. After five years of increasingly antagonistic relations with the Nixon administration, for instance, ASNE in 1973 voted against officially favoring press councils. A national news council that opened that year failed to win support from the journalistic establishment and shut down in 1984. A more popular reform than councils for dealing with reader complaints was the hiring of ombudsmen to improve relations between newspapers and readers. The *Louisville Courier-Journal* appointed the first ombudsman in 1967. In 1999, the Organization of Newspaper Ombudsmen counted 170 members.

Newspapers provided critics plentiful fodder. The decade's most memorable journalistic gaffe occurred when the *Washington Post* returned the 1981 Pulitzer Prize for feature writing that reporter Janet Cooke had pocketed for her saga of an eight-year-old heroin addict. She admitted she made it up. The Cooke scandal serves as a convenient fault line between a generation in which the news media, despite critics, did succeed as a watchdog over government and a subsequent period when the media's credibility declined. Articles analyzing press performance proliferated. In 1999, an online search found 883 references to articles analyzing journalistic ethics, 218 on media criticism, and 64 on press criticism over the past 20 years. A perusal of these articles shows that many of the problems that bothered their authors' predecessors remain unsolved. Ironically, Spiro Agnew resurfaces as a prescient press critic. Less catchy perhaps than his alliterative slap at TV's "nattering nabobs of negativism," Agnew's denunciations of the alleged elitism of media stars, instant analysis by TV journalists, and mushrooming media mergers topped the list of concerns of many late-century media critics.

The power to censor by media behemoths drew much fire. Ben H. Bagdikian's denunciation of media conglomeration revived concerns first raised by Will Irwin during the initial newspaper mergers of the 1910s. Bagdikian,

dean emeritus of the University of California at Berkeley journalism school and author of several books of media criticism, demonstrated how corporate stakes have skyrocketed in his widely read *The Media Monopoly* (1983). He argued that burgeoning corporate chains degrade journalism, cause conflicts of interest, and reduce its mission from public service to piling up profits.

By the 1990s, media criticism had become standard fare on the media menu. Newspaper critics Kurtz and Shaw were joined on television by shows such as CNN's "Reliable Sources." Magazines continued to proffer highbrow analysis in features and columns such as the "Annals of Communication" by Ken Auletta in the *New Yorker*. The splashiest new entry was *Brill's Content* magazine created by *Court TV* founder Steve Brill in 1998. His $27 million investment banked upon a consumer audience intrigued by how media determine and disseminate news. *Brill's* demonstrated the Internet's potential to expand media criticism with its online, interactive media complaint board that the magazine touted as the first national "media dispute forum." Online media writers such *Salon's* James Poniewozik offered a withering, witty new perspective on what Internet cognoscenti condescend to as the dinosaur media.

New media may have multiplied, but much criticism at the finale of the 20th century echoed complaints raised during its prologue. Lippmann's pronouncement in 1920 that, "There is everywhere an increasingly angry disillusionment about the press, a growing sense of being baffled and misled," was as applicable to yellow journalism in the 1890s as to the tabloidization of news in the 1990s.[22] "Tabloidization" replaced yellow journalism as the exemplar of bad journalism. "More or less respectable news programs are succumbing to the subjects and techniques of the gossip shows," the *New York Times* opined in 1994. "[T]elevision journalists are chasing ratings."[23] The soap opera of the televised O. J. Simpson murder trial in 1995 illustrated this point, a circus foreshadowed in 1954 by the Sam Shepard murder trial, one of the first in which cameras were allowed in the courtroom.

New issues also confronted critics in the 1990s. The dark side of the World Wide Web's egalitarianism raised the concern that hyperspace made it too easy to spread rumors and mistakes not only by a disquieting new breed of online "parajournalists" such as Matt Drudge but also by eminent organizations such as the *Dallas Morning News*. Howard Kurtz of the *Washington Post*, the decade's most prominent critic, led a chorus that lamented the confluence between journalism and entertainment. "The culture of news," he wrote in a high-octane style indicative of media's accelerating pace during the decade, "once the strait-laced, buttoned-down preserve of Walter Cronkite and Huntley-Brinkley, has merged with the relentlessly glitzy world of entertainment, producing one great, roaring Oprahfied ooze of headlines and hype."[24] One rivulet of this ooze that annoyed critics was the dubious influence of celebrity reporters-turned-pundits who pontificated on fractious TV shows such as *The McLaughlin Group*. Journalists' new celebrity also contributed to new charges of arrogance and elitism that many critics blamed for survey results that showed mounting public disgust with media. James Fallows added another damning dimension to press criticism in *Breaking the News: How the Media Undermine American Democracy* (1996), when he charged that pervasive cynicism is the news media's most destructive fault. A 1995 poll by the Times Mirror Center for The People & The Press, for instance, found 71 per cent of respondents believed the media get in the way of helping society solve its problems.[25]

Journalism scholar Jay Rosen tried to stop this cynical cycle by moving from criticism into activism. The New York University professor proselytized throughout the 1990s for "public journalism" (also called civic journalism). It encourages news media to re-engage readers and viewers by helping their communities recognize and solve their problems. "Unless citizens can be re-engaged in public life," Rosen warned, "journalism will have no future."[26] Dozens of organizations experimented with public-journalism techniques such as media-sponsored community forums in the 1990s. The Pew Center for Charitable Trusts' $4.8 million Project for Excellence in Journalism (www.journalism.org) launched in 1996 spawned the Committee of Concerned Journalists, books, a web site, an online investigation series on newspapers, and forums across the nation on the future of journalism. Although controversial, public journalism represented for critics such as Rosen and Fallows the profession's most promising avenue toward salvation as it entered the 21st century.

Salvation is not too strong a word. By the beginning of the new millennium, media critics' computers were on the verge of crashing from an overload of metaphors for how low journalism had sunk. "On our eternally downward-trending graphs," James Poniewozik wrote, "'post-O. J.' means 'after everything was shot to hell.'"[27] Congress toyed in 1997 with laws limiting photojournalists after Princess Diana died fleeing from paparazzi. Critics blasted coverage of the Clinton sex scandal in 1998–99 because of reporters' rampant reliance upon rumor and unnamed sources and their obsession with salacious details. *Rolling Stone* publisher Jann Wenner contended coverage of the Clinton scandal "brought journalism to a new low."[28] The head of the Freedom Forum predicted that public disenchantment with the news media would spell the end of the First Amendment as we know it by 2050.[29]

Reviewing 100 years of press criticism in 1999, James Boylan, the first editor of *Columbia Journalism Review*, acknowledged it is difficult to attribute any reforms to press criticism.[30] Liebling once wrote that the longer he criticized the press, "the more it disimproved."[31] Other critics, however, have been more optimistic. Lippmann explained in the 1920s that the press is as important a public institution as churches, schools, and government. So press criticism is as important as criticism of those institutions. A half century later, journalism educator James Carey described the function of press criticism as an antidote to censorship by government and corruption by the media's own power and illusions.[32] "Because we shouldn't be accountable to government," explains press critic Jonathan Alter, "we have no choice but to be accountable to each other."[33] Les Brown, author of a history of press criticism, likewise labeled the practice the best defense against censorship. "The First Amendment is not the [press'] vital refuge—the goodwill of society is," he observed, echoing a similar observation by Alexander Hamilton two centuries earlier.[34] Marion Tuttle Marzolf titled her 1991 analysis of press criticism *Civilizing Voices* because the "dynamic dialogue forced by the critics" exerted a civilizing influence that made the 20th-century press more responsible and professional.[35]

What separates today's critics from their self-styled predecessors in the 19th century is that the early critics viewed the press as an external influence upon society. Today's critics realize that the press is as inseparable from society as the nervous system is from the human body. The key contribution of press criticism as it evolved in the last century into a sustained and systematic analysis is its recognition of the news media's integral role as a social institution.

Selected Readings

Blanchard, Margaret A. "The Hutchins Commission, the Press, and the Responsibility Concept." *Journalism Monographs* 49 (1977).

Blanchard, Margaret A. "Press Criticism and National Reform Movements: The Progressive Era and the New Deal." *Journalism History* 5 (Summer 1978): 33–37, 54.

Brown, Les. *The Reluctant Reformation: On Criticizing the Press in America*. New York: David McKay Co., 1974.

Burd, Gene. "The Newspaper Critic and His Critics: George Seldes and Press Criticism." *Southwestern Mass Communication Journal* 1 (1985): 43–61.

Goldstein, Tom, ed. *Killing the Messenger: 100 Years of Media Criticism*. New York: Columbia University Press, 1989.

Hudson, Robert V. "Will Irwin's Pioneering Criticism of the Press." *Journalism Quarterly* 47 (1970): 263–71.

Kurtz, Howard. *Media Circus: The Trouble with America's Newspapers*. New York: Times Books, 1993.

Liebling, A. J. *The Wayward Pressman*. Garden City, N. Y.: Doubleday & Co., 1947.

Marzolf, Marion Tuttle. *Civilizing Voices: American Press Criticism 1880–1950*. New York: Longman, 1991.

Midura, Edmund M. "A. J. Liebling: The Wayward Pressman as Critic." *Journalism Monographs* 33 (1974).

Sloan, Wm. David, and Emily Erickson Hoff, eds. *Contemporary Media Issues*. Northport, Ala.: Vision Press, 1998.

Notes

1. Isaiah Thomas, *The History of Printing in America* (1810), 2nd ed., Marcus A. McCorison, ed. (New York: Weathervane Books, 1970), 18.

2. E. L. Godkin, "Chromo-Civilization," reprinted in Wm. David Sloan, Cheryl J. Sloan, and Cheryl S. Wray, eds., *Great Editorials: Masterpieces of Opinion Writing*, 2nd ed. (Northport, Ala.: Vision Press, 1997), 125.

3. Quoted in Willard G. Bleyer, *Main Currents in the History of American Journalism* (Boston: Houghton-Mifflin, 1927), 287.

4. Delos F. Wilcox, "The American Newspaper: A Study in Social Psychology," *Annals of the American Academy of Political and Social Science* 16 (July 1900): 90.

5. James Edward Rogers, *The American Newspaper* (Chicago: University of Chicago Press, 1909); Bleyer, *Main Currents in the History of American Journalism*; and Alfred McClung Lee, *The Daily Newspaper in America* (New York: Macmillan, 1937).

6. See Will Irwin, *The Making of a Reporter* (New York: G. P. Putnam's Sons, 1942), 164–69.

7. "All the News That's Fit to Print," *The American Newspaper: A Series First Appearing in Collier's, January–July 1911* (Ames: Iowa State University Press, 1969), 46.

8. Upton Sinclair, *The Brass Check* (Pasadena, Calif.: privately published, 1919), 436.

9. See Linda Weiner Hausman, "Criticism of the Press in U.S. Periodicals, 1900–1939: An Annotated Bibliography," *Journalism Monographs* 4 (Minneapolis: Association for Education in Journalism, 1967).

10. Robert Benchley, "The Third-and-a-Half Estate," *The New Yorker* 8 (May 7, 1932): 41.

11. See Stanley L. Harrison, "'The Wayward Press' Revisited: The Contributions of Robert Benchley," *Journalism History* 19:1 (1993): 19–27.

12. A. J. Liebling, "Hot and Heated," *The New Yorker* 24 (August 14, 1948), 79.

13. See Gene Burd, "The Newspaper Critic and His Critics: George Seldes and Press Criticism," *Southwestern Mass Communication Journal* 1 (1985): 43–61.

14. Margaret Blanchard, "Press Criticism and National Reform Movements: The Progressive Era and the New Deal," *Journalism History* 5 (Summer 1978): 54.

15. George Seldes, *Lords of the Press* (New York: Julian Messner, 1938), 19.

16. George Seldes, *Freedom of the Press* (Indianapolis: Bobbs-Merrill Co., 1935), 191.

17. Commission on Freedom of the Press, *A Free and Responsible Press* (Chicago: University of Chicago Press, 1947), 80.

18. See Margaret A. Blanchard, "The Hutchins Commission, The Press and the Responsibility Concept," *Journalism Monographs* 49 (1977): 1–59.

19. Quoted in David Halberstam, *The Powers That Be* (New York: Alfred A. Knopf, 1979), 489.

20. Michael Schudson, *The Power of News* (Cambridge: Harvard University Press, 1995).

21. Les Brown, *The Reluctant Reformation: On Criticizing the Press in America* (New York: David McKay Co., 1974), 47.

22. Walter Lippmann, *Liberty and the News* (New York: Harcourt, Brace and Howe, 1920), 75–76.

23. Quoted in Joe Saltzman, "Tabloid Hysteria," *USA Today* magazine, May 1994, 21.

24. Howard Kurtz, *Hot Air: All Talk, All the Time* (New York: Times Books, 1996), 15–16.

25. "The Media's Message," *U. S. News & World Report*, January 9, 1995, 45.

26. Jay Rosen, "The Media is the Mess," *Nation*, February 5, 1996, 25.

27. James Poniewozik, "Riding shotgun," www.salon.com, June 17, 1999, accessed September 8, 1999.

28. John W. English, "U.S.A.: Was It a New Low?" *IPI Report* (Fourth Quarter 1998): 5.

29. Remarks by Charles Overby, May 4, 1999, Samford University, supplied by the Freedom Forum.

30. James Boylan, "Gnats Chasing an Elephant," *Media Studies Journal* (Spring-Summer 1999): 106–11.

31. A. J. Liebling, *The Sweet Science* (New York: Viking Press, 1956), 6.

32. James W. Carey, "Journalism and Criticism: The Case of an Undeveloped Profession," *Review of Politics* 36 (April 1974): 227–49.

33. Jonathan Alter, "New Questions—That's What Media Critics Need," *Media Studies Journal* 9 (Spring 1995): 23.

34. Brown, *The Reluctant Reformation*, 97.

35. Marion Tuttle Marzolf, *Civilizing Voices: American Press Criticism 1880–1950* (New York: Longman, 1991), 2.

7

Characteristics of Journalists

JIM UPSHAW

Mainstream America always has been uneasy with its journalists. Journalist-humorist Ambrose Bierce wrote in 1878: "I am quite serious in the statement that nobody in the United States has ever been hanged for killing a journalist; public opinion will not permit it...."[1]

Bierce's ironic words hinted at a wonder that lingers in society still: Who the hell are they, these journalists, these invaders of privacy, these screeching exploiters of a liberty they may not deserve?

Every era's news workers have sustained criticism. The American journalist needs no license to intrude and indeed is under orders to do so. Consumers often perceive gall, arrogance, error, and low motives—in journalists, not in their subjects.

News professionals write a great deal but only rarely seem to reveal their true inner nature. This can result from a lack of introspection, from modesty, from self-protection, or from journalists' timeless tendency to keep their subjects, not their own personalities, up front. In any case, the result is a gap in our knowledge of qualities that can distinguish journalists from the rest of us—a gap this chapter will address.

A QUIET BEGINNING

The journalist was absent from the early landscape of colonial America. New England settlers who had time to read—and had been taught to, which was less than probable—could burrow into books carried from home, scratch for English newspapers at the public-house, or seek news from passengers on arriving ships.

News work started in the callused hands of printers who had emigrated for reasons other than news. Some at first seemed ill suited for their historic role. These first workers to bring the colonist locally printed news of the world outside were a far cry from today's white-collar journalists. They were steeped in manual labor.

Most entered their craft in childhood, becoming "printer's devils," a job so nicknamed because it was dirty and unpleasant. The "devil" was indentured by his family to the printer as early as age seven. Living with an employer-mentor until adulthood—often in appalling conditions—the apprentice developed the skills and acumen needed to survive on his own.

The average journeyman printer in the new colonies probably would not have left England without a push. He lived on private work and, if he could win them, royal appointments to spread the royal word. A constant threat of prison and poverty if he violated rules or lost favor assured the printer of both humility and suspense. Why, then, should he leave England to seek more of both—in a raw place, among a rude people low in literacy and governed by the same King?

But there was work in America: The Crown needed published regulations and proclamations to govern its restless settlements, and was prodding printers toward the colonies. Moreover, the Puritans of Massachusetts, waging cultural war on the Anglicans, needed to generate books and sermons. So the migration got under way.

The historian Robert Harlan found colonial printers mostly white, male, Anglo-Saxon, and Protestant[2]—like the colonists they had joined. The most successful also shared ambition, flexibility, and the fortitude to flourish in an alien land. Other characteristics—political passion, resistance to authority, and a "sense of history"—were not endemic. Printers were businessmen.

When the first American newspaper appeared in Boston on September 25, 1690, its printer, Richard Pierce, escaped the brunt of official reaction. Instead it landed on an unprinterly, sharp-penned English journalist, Benjamin Harris, who supported independence for Massachusetts and wrote the contents of the paper, *Publick Occurrences, Both Forreign and Domestick*.

Harris had been imprisoned in England for flouting press restrictions. Now he was supporting Massachusetts' Puritans in their opposition to the Crown. Colonial administrators instantly shut the paper down.[3] The next newspaper was as different as its author was. John Campbell, Massachusetts postmaster, decided to publish tidings that crossed his desk, but less in journalistic fervor than out of a desire to sell news to enrich the postal treasury. He launched the *Boston News-Letter* in 1704 and maintained it rather placidly for 18 years.

HOTHEADS AND PATRIOTS

By the early 1700s, printers had become pivotal figures. Their publications brought colonists their only views of life outside the home, farm, or village. Printers became trapped in tense settings as colonial unrest grew. Sometimes gingerly, sometimes brashly, they became part of social change, a risky process that sometimes made early print shops rather similar to modern newsrooms.

Printing still was done arduously by hand, with many coordinated steps needed to produce a single impression on the page. It was a hard, tedious, filthy craft. Still, while more comfortable with type cases than with political theories, printers like Harris' associate Pierce influenced politics with their work. And demand for news and opinion transformed some printers into more authoritative printer-editors.

Rivalries sprang up, and figures emerged who matched Benjamin Harris in journalistic gumption. Notable was hotheaded James Franklin with his *New-England Courant* (and precocious brother-apprentice Benjamin, who slipped his own writings into the paper).[4] James would be jailed for satirizing the government. John Peter Zenger founded the *New York Weekly Journal* and entered combat with William Bradford's *New-York Gazette*. Soon enough, Ben Franklin was flexing his *Pennsylvania Gazette*. He was Boston-born, and most of his peers were also American natives. But newspapers in German also aided the patriot cause. Zenger embodied journalistic grit in his 1735 trial (and acquittal) for "seditious libel" against the British governor. When James Franklin evaded a ban by printing under Ben's name, he prefigured recent "underground" papers.

The Stamp Act of 1765 threatened printer-editors with heavy new costs, and they revolted, refusing to publish or trumpeting their anger in print. Patterns were emerging. From the first printers through the politically conscious (and politically sponsored) printer-editors, a set of characteristics had been taking shape. Newspapermen had created social power for words; words drew responses; and, gradually, people most capable of confronting those responses were filling the new profession's roles. Journalists knew they might be mobbed, beaten, or worse for any perceived affront. More rarely they might be socially rewarded for publishing popular messages. They knew to be tactful toward patrons, lively in writing and editing, vigilant, stubborn, and wary of presumptive authority. They were staking out ground and inventing a vivid public persona.

"Patriot" papers squabbled in print with "Royalist" printer-editors, sometimes spurring readers to respond not just verbally but physically. A mob in 1775, angry at James Rivington's anti-revolutionary stand, entered his New York newspaper office "and in about three-quarters of an hour brought off the principal part of his types...."[5] Printer-editors often faced jail, and, while not truly independent, risked much to rupture old patterns of control. That they succeeded is evidenced by the American Revolution, partly traceable to the reporting of facts about life under England's thumb.

Soon enough, the printer-editor's task would be split in two as journalism evolved further. A new journalist generally free of printing duties, and specializing in editorial content, would emerge to invent modern news—and to take much of the heat for it.

DRIVING THE CONTENT

Imagine Ben Bradlee, the *Washington Post* editor of Watergate days, in a shop apron, printing his own paper—and wince: the image explodes. The historical cord linking printer to editor is virtually extinct except in the smallest newspapers. News workers long ago diverged into career tracks based on workers' personalities, talents, attitudes, and intellectual range.

Newspapers in the post–Revolution era eventually made clear the importance of the specialized editor. Only he, freed from technical burdens, could organize facts and ideas, steer a prudent but effective course, absorb resulting criticism—and turn it into still more news. He could mine history and politics rather than metal, wood and ink. His education and social graces would open the way to broad fields of information and organizational support. He would stand strategically much closer to ruling elites (and a slowly emerging middle class) than the printer could. The prototype of this new journalist arrived in 1789, when John Fenno started a Federalist paper as a writer and editor. Historians consider him the first such real specialist to run an American newspaper.[6]

Cities soon would support many newspapers large and rich enough to require the leadership of editors. They had to pursue not just news but advertising. Their voices often were muted by this concern and by their continuing dependence on political parties. A public notice from future dictionary-maker Noah

Webster, launching the *American Minerva* in 1793, suggested the editor's typical tightrope: Free governments depended on "a general diffusion of knowledge," he wrote, promising to keep his newspaper "chaste and impartial"; but he covered his bets by pledging that the paper would be "the Friend of Government."[7]

Newspapers continued in this way until the 1830s, when editor Benjamin Day began to create mass audiences that gradually would permit papers to shed their political sponsors. Day, a seasoned printer at 23, had a grander vision than did most other journeymen. Seizing a fellow printer's idea, he opened the *New York Sun* and put papers on sale for a penny apiece.

The "penny press" drew droves of unschooled readers whose tastes demanded "human interest" news. James Gordon Bennett of the *New York Herald* already understood news as stories. His bent for the lurid and his attacks on rivals gave his paper a sensational image and large circulation. When Bennett the showman took on Day the opportunist, both profited.

Day published hundreds of inventive reports. His *Sun* went so far as to concoct "moon-dwelling bat people" for one story. Journalists were not yet subject to a rigorous ideology of truth-telling, and editors encouraged them to entertain readers. In the early and mid–19th century big-city press, vivid storytelling was most highly valued.

COUNTRY STYLE

Elsewhere, rural editors departed from the urban pattern. They often were their own reporters, covering people they met in post offices or feed stores. Their news was intimate but their papers ran lean on meager small-town advertising. Unable to subsist on journalism alone, many editors practiced law or politics on the side—which required them to balance news obligations against their material concerns.

Some editors made papers profitable through protean efforts. One such editor was Fred Nutting, editor and owner of the *Albany* (Ore.) *Democrat*. At first, he reported stories, wrote them, helped handset the type and operate the press, and distributed copies of the paper.[8] The boss who did it all could also be hard on subordinates. Owner-editor C. S. Jackson of the *East Oregonian* once scolded a manager about printers he had hired: "You have put in too many rattle-brained fellows, who cared nothing for the paper, nothing for the work they were called on (to) do."[9] Technicians also were easy targets. S. H. Hammond of the *Albany* (N. Y.) *State Register* complained: "Oh, compositors! Oh, proof-readers! And you, oh, printers' devils! … when you merely print *on* for *or*, as in a late paper of ours, a shrewd reader may discover the error; but when you drop whole words, containing the heart of a paragraph, I can scarcely express my astonishment."[10]

By the dawn of the 20th century, newspaper editors were building a self-stereotype on their penchant for running things their way. One journalist would recall of *San Francisco Chronicle* city editor Horace R. Hudson: "He would not permit the word 'drunk' for drunken man to go into the paper. He made us write 'in the street' for 'on the street,' and 'at a corner of Pine Street and Van Ness Avenue' instead of 'at the corner,' which a reporter will do nine times out of ten."[11]

By 1900, according to one study, key measures of the social ascent of editors were shooting upward: The number of editors whose fathers had been businessmen, not farmers; the number who had completed college, and the number who had started work as young adults rather than as poor children indentured to printers. These were older men than those who ran newsrooms in 1875.[12] If this tended to sever the modern editor from the hard-scrabble roots of many earlier American leaders, it also permitted him to lay claim credibly to good taste, grand goals and probity. The veteran New York editor Charles A. Dana told Union College students that an editor's staying power "is in the character, and people believe in him, because they are sure he does not mean to say anything that is not so."[13] Horace Greeley of the *New York Tribune* claimed "a love of truth for the truth's sake"[14] (even though Greeley, among other dubious moves, sent abolitionists to

"cover" strife over slavery in Kansas and write wildly distorted reports).

Henry J. Raymond of the *New York Times*, once a printer's devil, summarized his paper's visible hauteur: "We do not mean to write as if we were in a passion, unless that shall really be the case; and we shall make it a point to get in a passion as rarely as possible."[15] Such avowals by editors were common but soon would be affected by another historic splintering of the news trade. Another specialist was moving to center stage—the embodiment, perhaps, of the journalistic impulse.

Just as the editor often escaped composing-room duty, this new figure would be spared the torments of policy. His job was to capture the raw elements of news that might test readers' deepest views of the human condition. He could leave the office, scour the slums and salons, accost strangers, browbeat officials, unearth fugitives, follow cops through bloody boudoirs, and bring back stories like gleaming gifts of gold.

CHASING—AND INVENTING

Our enduring images of the reporter, coattails flying or brow furrowed over a creaky typewriter,[16] are less than two centuries old. Paul Revere shouted the news across the colonial countryside, but no one in those days was hired only to gather it. If early editors sometimes left the newsroom to seek information, they did not employ "leg men."[17]

By the early 19th century, however, the British were dispatching war correspondents abroad. By the 1820s some American papers were sending journalists to Washington. Most full-time field reporting emerged later, from the penny papers of the 1830s and the shifting social earth in which they germinated. Reporters had to be literate, available, and a bit hungry—had to write colorfully and endure marginal working conditions without complaint.

A previously jobless printer, George Wisner, first haunted police courts for the *New York Sun* (later becoming its editor). The *Herald's* Bennett assigned the "worldly"

William Attree to cover crime in time for the sensational murder of prostitute Helen Jewett and other scandals. Reporter Richard Adams Locke gave *Sun* readers the "great moon hoax" of 1835, claiming an astronomer had found creatures on the moon, some bat-like and others of "a spherical form, which rolled with great velocity across the pebbly beach...."[18]

Hoaxes showed that reporting could not only inform but surprise. But they were too good to be true, and Edwin L. Godkin, editor of *The Nation*, later bemoaned some reporters' values and the influences behind them. "Now, we do not mean to say that there are no honest, painstaking, scrupulous and accurate men employed as reporters and correspondents by the daily press," he wrote. "This would be a ridiculous calumny. But we do say that the number of such men is smaller by far than it need be or ought to be; and that the reason is that such men are not generally and systematically encouraged for their honesty and accuracy."[19]

As reporters became popularizers of a spreading America, they worked long hours for little money (except at big papers), limning tragedy and fluff, swerving from crime to trade to politics. They often wrote chronologically—no inverted pyramid yet—filling many columns before a "lede" appeared.

INGREDIENTS OF
A REPORTER

This work suited the enterprising and verbally adept. Reporter George Cary Eggleston recalled reading compulsively as a child, hiding his novels from a stern father and displaying "a skeptical, inquiring tendency of mind which distressed those responsible for me."[20] Endurance and courage helped, too. The Civil War reportedly drew a hundred reporters just to cover the Union side. Many traveled for months amid the dust and blood of combat. Future *St. Louis Globe-Democrat* editor Joseph "Little Mack" McCullagh was both a general's aide and a working war correspondent (a fusion unthinkable today). He proved ingenious at ferreting out military news and often is credited with the first formal newspaper interview.

The noted New York editor Charles Dana believed he knew what made a good reporter—that some aptitude for the eccentric trade might be discerned from what a man read. "If he takes up the newspaper and turns to the political part of the paper, and is interested in that," he declared, "why that is a good symptom of his intellectual tendencies; but if, instead of that, he takes up a magazine and sits down to read a love story, you can not make a newspaper man out of him."[21]

Some love-story devotees probably became newspapermen anyway. The burgeoning business had room for many types. Aggressive, often intrusive, focused, practical, effete, callous or empathic, intense, polished or grubby, given to haste and error, ignorant or erudite—with these and other characteristics, reporters helped to build a national consciousness.

The smallest rural papers, many in the untamed West, sent forth reporters of varying talents and propensities. Best known was Samuel Clemens—Mark Twain—who, like others on that wildest frontier, often failed to harness details of his stories to facts. Early on, Clemens embellished straight news with humor and anecdote for the famous *Virginia City* (Nev.) *Territorial Enterprise*. By the time he reached the San Francisco papers in the 1860s, his fancies and ruminations had rendered most of his journalism decidedly personal—a trait that would sell many books for him.

Reporting made newspapers vibrant and essential. In the Midwest, free-lancer Frederick Lockley defended embattled American Indians in his dispatches from Kansas. *New York Times*-man Roger Conant joined a shipload of young women sailing to the West Coast to find husbands.[22] The aristocratic Richard Harding Davis brought good looks and sharp eyes—like Twain, he also wrote fiction—to his worldwide reporting.

Journalism of lasting impact came from a grittier well-born warrior, Lincoln Steffens. This cause-driven "muckraker" penetrated social problems, and, as city editor of New York's *Commercial-Advertiser*, he hired college-educated reporters who thought as he did. Steffens wrote for the common man, as did Ida Tarbell, who exposed great social crimes.

Their work, with that of the slum-crawling Jacob Riis, reflected and supported reform impulses in American politics as the 20th century swung into gear. It also, for some, suggested identification with the oppressed, for most journalists' hours were long and their pay poor.[23]

A New Crucible

Modernization, fed on the fruits of the Industrial Revolution, placed heavy strains on the flexibility of the journalist. It brought post–1900 America widespread electric power, news through radio speakers, vast public appetites for news as global wars took their toll, television with its staggering social effects, and more leisure time in which to consume or ponder all of the above. To journalism would come richer specialization, the rise of journalism schools, a need for efficient routines to handle complex production, and new fortunes as papers grew and merged.

One of the century's first blockbuster events—the 1906 San Francisco earthquake and fire—left the *San Francisco Bulletin* virtually homeless and showed that professionalism would keep the news flowing. Reporter Herbert C. Thompson wrote in his diary with an eerie calm: "One evening on a Saturday I walked through the ruins of the cold storage and ice plant on Sansome Street near the north end of Telegraph Hill. We would take the freight elevator to the roof and there, in a temporary shed up on the top, were our editorial and composing rooms...."[24]

By now, reporters across the country shared many attitudes. With its sanctioned "outsider" status but also increasing stability, journalism moved toward craft uniformity. Arthur Krock, winner of four Pulitzer prizes, found as a rookie at the *Louisville* (Ky.) *Herald* that top-flight reporters often blended knowledge with innate abilities that probably were more important. "I decided," he later explained, "that, though industriousness, personality and the art of striking presentation of the news were indispensable in attaining senior status, these reporters had three intangible assets without which their product would have been routine: knowing the right questions and the right people to ask them of, and having a 'nose for news.' Since the latter is congenital and an instinct, a reporter has it or he hasn't."[25]

Others noticed commonalities among journalists that transcended geography. In 1910, editor Philip Littell wrote home to his wife: "In youth I supposed a great gulf between newspapermen in New York and the same in Milwaukee. No such thing. The specimens I've met in the press office and the press club are the same essentially, with the same way of looking at things."[26]

One common characteristic was pride in a freewheeling professional heritage, warts and all. The muckrakers' sympathy for social causes spread to many others—some of whom lost all neutrality. After the *Seattle Post-Intelligencer* sent Lella Secor to cover a roving "peace ship" during World War I, she soon bonded thoroughly with the delegates. Secor branded journalists aboard as "the press representatives who are so scurrilous and vicious that I have entirely severed all connection with them...."[27]

At another extreme were journalists who didn't mind cutting ethical corners. Future playwright Ben Hecht was said to have carried burglary tools in case he needed more help than sources would willingly grant. Reporter Jimmy Kilgallen wrote admiringly of a rival who posed as owner of the ocean liner *Morro Castle* to get a scoop on a fire aboard that killed 134.[28]

Building an Image

The construction of personalities had long been a feature of newsroom life. At its shallow end, one's image could turn on drinking, which could animate or destroy a news worker and sometimes managed both. At the *Chicago Inter-Ocean*, declared one reporter, "It was mere routine for the head of the copy desk to go down every evening to 'The Sewer,' a charming basement saloon next door, and sort out the copyreaders able to stand on their feet."[29] But retired *Herald Tribune* city editor Stanley Walker claimed that, by the 1930s, "habitual drunkards, along with an array of other misfits, have been driven out, and they have been replaced, for the most part, by younger, better educated and more enterprising men."[30]

As a second world war and internationalization turned American eyes abroad, some journalists nurtured and expanded their reputations for swashbuckling. Pilot-correspondent Larry Rue enjoyed recounting his perils. On various assignments, he recounted, "I was ambushed with the advance guard of the Prince Andrew Division.... I was the target of machine guns.... I traversed Russia from the Black and Caspian seas to Petrograd, without passports, or permissions of any kind, an achievement which the *Chicago Tribune* described as 'an unsurpassed feat in adventurous journalism'...."[31]

The widest stages in the news trade—particularly at the New York papers—attracted its most aggressive personalities and encouraged bravura work. Many brought not only confidence but also fine intellectual tools. Stanley Walker looked back on recent hires and marveled: "The fledglings often flabbergast their elders with their erudition—a scholarly but lively sense of words, a sound background in history and economics, the ability to translate or even to speak two or three foreign languages, a comprehensive knowledge of literature, and sometimes a definite expertness in art and music."[32]

Of course, even those gifts might not win a woman a job on the paper. Helen Kirkpatrick Milbank recalled knowing Latin and French but having to move to Geneva before winning her stripes as a *Herald Tribune* stringer.[33]

Walker, of course, wanted not just erudition but doggedness and horse sense. His paper found them all in Homer Bigart and Marguerite Higgins, who in covering World War II had no more bitter rivals for scoops than one another. That war also drew empathy for the foot soldier from the unrivaled Ernie Pyle. His reports from the trenches—until he was killed on a Pacific island—touched millions back home and taught young reporters how to write.

Journalists at mid-century were valued for traditional strengths such as Pyle's. The yellow press was decades past, and the excesses of the tabloid–TV age were yet to emerge. In fact, when a top editor wrote an open letter to the archetypal budding journalist of the 1950s, his ideas seemed almost stuffy. "Journalism is a profession for gentlemen...," he declared. "Not all in it are gentlemen. There are greedy, dishonorable, selfish stinkers in journalism, as in all lines. But it is a business that calls for gentlemen; and among the many hundreds whom I know in this business, most of them are gentlemen."[34]

Radio had elbowed its way into news. It surpassed newspapers' claims to immediacy and drama, and was fashioning a form of journalist uniquely suited to the "air." Talented newspaper and wire-service reporters soon filled radio roles. Edward R. Murrow, with rural and middle-class roots, would become their champion and model. He could be moody, overbearing, deeply negative, remote. But his reporting and commentary struck at America's vulnerabilities and drew on its strengths, as no journalist had.[35]

Murrow's work did much to establish radio and television as carriers of powerful news. Other journalists—mere individuals, delivering their findings to huge audiences—developed impact through the thunderous events of the 1950s and 1960s: the McCarthy purge of communists known and imagined, the assassination of President Kennedy, and the civil rights movement. The war in Vietnam put young David Halberstam of the *New York Times* in journalism's first rank, and Bob Woodward and Carl Bernstein rode their doggedness, talent, and energy to a Pulitzer prize for covering (actually, uncovering) the Nixon Watergate conspiracy.

These journalists worked across a canvas immeasurably larger than those of the colonial printers and even the penny-press editors. TV proved it could electrify the modern nation in an instant: Murrow skewering Sen. McCarthy for his hunts for Communists, NBC reporter John Chancellor being ejected from a political convention, CBS correspondent Morley Safer showing troops using cigarette lighters to destroy a thatched-hut village in Vietnam. Broadcast news made some people stars.

To journalism, now celebrated anew as a catalyst to democracy, came waves of ambitious, altruistic men and women. News in the 1970s was paying more[36] and experimenting more than in earlier, quieter times. Inflamed by the murder-for-hire of an Arizona journalist, investigative reporters organized nationally and made strides against fraud and corruption. Meanwhile, big money—often a danger sign for journalists—swung toward television correspondents and anchors such as Tom Brokaw, Dan Rather, and Leslie Stahl. Their images grew as TV came to fill most people's news diets.

But this renaissance was short-lived, sapped in part by its own reliance on journalists as stars. By the 1980s, newsworkers with traditional rules and routines were losing ground. Facing competitive strains and the impatience of new owners, stations and networks soon reduced investigative reporting, eliminated much "process" coverage, and generally made news less challenging and more entertaining. Hard-news veterans unable or unwilling to adapt were put out to pasture. Newspapers, too, facing similar changes by the 1990s, pursued celebrity and consumerism and often demoted weightier but less viscerally stimulating news.

Yet, journalism traditions always had included both the tawdry and the triumphal, the greedy and the grand. In recent years, new journalists were arriving for work generally better educated and more polished than their forebears were decades earlier. If this disconnected many from the "Front Page" tradition, it linked them back through time to the Davises, Bradlees and Milbanks; and it helped this new cohort move smoothly into a computerized age of urban change, increased immigration to the United States, media concentration, and global terrorism.

Reporters for major papers used computers to mine stories that the pavement-pounding diggers of yore could not have imagined. Legwork remained essential. Journalists were killed or wounded in pursuit of news or went to jail rather than reveal sources. Reporters and editors eager to "make a difference" seemed outnumbered by realists who would settle for "softer" news. But some kept struggling to push substantive investigations and to keep public-service topics up front.

Observant rookies could find elders who recalled and romanticized smoky or drafty newsrooms, who grumbled that the latest aces had been born—and would stay—soft and suburban, and who displayed the classic traits. Those traits included skepticism, a "sense" of history, tenacity, courage, aversion to being scooped, commitment to public service, willingness to wield the Constitution like a fiery sword, and a unique inclination to charge across police lines.[37]

In some, under modern pressure, these traits melded into cynicism. Journalists who always had directed distrust toward public figures were aiming it now at their own employers. The political reporter Lou Cannon spotted the tendency back in 1977, noting that much cynicism resulted from "this rather naïve expectation that newspapers will respond, as a few of them do, to a higher ethic than the profit motive."[38]

Some newer journalists would accept this readily. Older hands could turn for solace to the history of a trade in which Benjamin Harris set a daring precedent, Ben Day opened news to the masses, Tarbell and Steffens changed the country's self-image, Murrow rocked the complacent, and Woodward and Bernstein pitted a President against the Constitution. These iconic events helped build a mythos in which generations of journalists thrived, certain of their strategic value to American life.

Strategic—but enduring forever? No one knew. What counted for many, it seemed, was that their craft gave back more than it took, emotionally if not materially. Some early figures wrote news just to survive, and few recent practitioners seemed likely to have sought out journalism for its comforts. Indeed, if a single characteristic can be traced through the history of journalism, it probably is a complex, ineffable, obdurate love of the craft.

Researchers rarely target this emotion. Journalists, avoiding maudlin self-disclosure (another trait), even more rarely state it plainly. So the words of a contributing editor to *The New Republic*, addressing journalism students in 1958, are unusually revealing. "If I had millions," he said, "I know that I would still be fevered by desire to write the perfect news story. I know well enough that I shall never do it, nor even come within many miles of it, not if I outlived Methuselah; but I am addicted to the hopeless effort as firmly as a drunkard to his bottle, and through that addiction I have gained the means of sustaining life."[39]

Selected Readings

Banning, Stephen A. "The Professionalization of Journalism: A Nineteenth Century Beginning." *Journalism History* 24 (1998–1999), 157–63.

Dary, David. *Red Blood & Black Ink: Journalism in the Old West.* New York: Knopf, dist. by Random House, 1998.

Dicken-Garcia, Hazel. *Journalistic Standards in Nineteenth-Century America.* Madison: University of Wisconsin Press, 1989.

Fedler, Fred. *Lessons from the Past: Journalists' Lives and Work, 1850–1950.* Prospects Heights, Ill.: Waveland Press, 2000.

Fine, Barnett. *A Giant of the Press.* New York: Editor & Publisher Library, 1933.

Hart, Jack R. "Horatio Alger in the Newsroom: Social Origins of American Editors." *Journalism Quarterly* 53 (1976): 14–20.

Humphrey, Carol Sue. "Producers of the 'Popular Engine': New England's Revolutionary Newspaper Printers." *American Journalism* 4 (1987): 97–117.

Lancaster, Paul. *Gentleman of the Press: The Life and Times of an Early Reporter, Julian Ralph, of the Sun.* Syracuse, N. Y.: Syracuse University Press, 1992.

Lubow, Arthur. *The Reporter Who Would Be King: A Biography of Richard Harding Davis.* New York: Maxwell Macmillan International, 1992.

Sloan, Wm. David, and Julie Hedgepeth Williams. *The Early American Press, 1690–1783.* Westport, Conn.: Greenwood Press, 1994.

Smythe, Ted Curtis. "The Reporter, 1880–1900. Working Conditions and Their Influence on News." *Journalism History* 7 (1980): 1–10.

Weigle, Clifford F. "The Young Scripps Editor: Keystone of E. W.'s 'System.'" *Journalism Quarterly* 41 (1964): 360–66.

Wroth, Lawrence C. *The Colonial Printer.* Portland, Me.: Southworth-Anthoensen Press, 1938.

Notes

1. Ambrose Bierce, *San Francisco Argonaut,* 3 August 1878.

2. Robert D. Harlan, "The Colonial Printer: Two Views." Paper read at Clark Library Seminar on Intellectual Freedom, University of California, Los Angeles, June 19, 1976, 28.

3. Not that Harris went into hiding; his career continued but in a manner far less disturbing to the Crown, and two years later he became the Massachusetts colony's official printer. For details of *Publick Occurrences'* origins and Harris' colonial role, see Wm. David Sloan, "Chaos, Polemics and America's First Newspaper," *Journalism Quarterly* 70 (1992) 666–81.

4. The deception of printer-editor James by his brother-apprentice began when, according to Ben, "writing an anonymous Paper I put it in at Night under the Door of the Printing House. It was found in the Morning and communicated to his Writing Friends....They read it, commented on it in my Hearing, and I had the exquisite Pleasure, of finding it met with their Approbation...." Following publication of that item, Ben similarly—furtively—submitted several more. See Benjamin Franklin, *The Autobiography* (New York: Modern Library, 1944), 23–26.

5. *Pennsylvania Journal,* November 1775, in Richard Wheeler, *Voices of 1776* (New York: Crowell, 1972), 91–92.

6. See, for example, Wm. David Sloan and James D. Startt, eds., *The Media in America: A History,* 4th ed. (Northport, Ala.: Vision Press, 1999), 66–74.

7. *American Minerva,* 9 December 1793.

8. "Democrat-Herald History Covers 91 Years," *Albany Democrat-Herald,* 12 December 1950 (Progress edition), 9.

9. C. S. Jackson, July 24, 1903, personal papers, Oregon Collection, University of Oregon Library.

10. S. H. Hammond, *Country Margins, or Rambles of a Journalist* (New York: J. C. Derby, 1855), 121.

11. Bailey Millard, "Men and Mileposts—Met along the Rugged Roadway of My Life" (undated column), personal papers, Oregon Collection, University of Oregon Library.

12. Jack R. Hart, "Horatio Alger in the Newsroom: Social Origins of American Editors," *Journalism Quarterly* 53 (1976): 14–20.

13. Charles A. Dana, October 13, 1893, in *The Art of Newspaper Making: Three Lectures* (New York: D. Appleton, 1895).

14. Horace Greeley, *New-York Tribune,* 27 February 1868.

15. Henry J. Raymond, *New-York Daily Times,* 18 September 1851.

16. An ancient writing machine.

17. This sobriquet suggested action, speed, and power and was a source of pride for generations of reporters who earned more excitement than money. The immodest Dean Jennings used "Leg Man" as the title of his memoir (Hollywood: George Palmer Putnam, Inc., 1940), written in a hard-bitten cop-novel style.

18. *New York Sun,* 25–28 August 1835.

19. Edwin L. Godkin, "Opinion-Moulding," *The Nation* 9, 12 August 1869, 126–27.

20. George Cary Eggleston, *Recollections of a Varied Life* (New York: Henry Holt, 1910), 22.

21. Dana, *The Art of Newspaper Making,* 41.

22. Roger Conant, *Mercer's Belles: The Journal of a Reporter,* ed. Lenna A. Deutsch (Pullman: Washington State University Press, 1992).

23. Late 19th-century salaries in large cities ranged from $10 a week or less for a reporter in Boston, Baltimore or Washington to as much as $60 for a reporter in New York. (See Ted Curtis Smythe, "The Reporter, 1880–1900: Working Conditions and Their Influence on the News," *Journalism History* 7 [Spring 1980]: 2.) That $10 in Boston was equivalent to about $186 in today's dollars; but the princely New York $60 would amount to more than $1,120 today, or about $58,000 annually. (Source: *Historical Statistics of the United States,* U. S. Government Printing Office, 1975.)

24. Herbert C. Thompson, diary note, 1907, manuscripts collection, Knight Memorial Library, University of Oregon.

25. Arthur Krock, *Myself When Young: Growing Up in the 1890s* (Boston: Little, Brown, 1973), 121.

26. Philip Littell, letter to Frances Littell, January 3, 1910, personal papers, Oregon Collection, University of Oregon Library. See also Robert J. Casey, *Such Interesting People* (Indianapolis: Bobbs-Merrill, 1943), 30.

27. Lella Secor, letter to family, 10 January 1916, in *Lella Secor: A Diary in Letters 1915–1922*, ed. Barbara Moench Florence (New York: Burt Franklin & Co., 1978), 25.

28. James L. Kilgallen, *It's a Great Life: My 50 Years as a Newspaperman* (International News Service, reprinted from articles in *Editor & Publisher*, 1956), 7.

29. Casey, *Such Interesting People*, 57.

30. Stanley Walker, *City Editor* (New York: Frederick A. Stokes Co., 1934), 39.

31. Larry Rue, *I Fly for News* (New York: Albert and Charles Boni, Inc., 1932), 88.

32. Walker, *City Editor*, 40.

33. Interviews with Helen Kirkpatrick Milbank, recorded by Anne S. Kasper for the Washington Press Club Foundation as part of its oral history project, "Women in Journalism" (April 3–5, 1990), 12–16.

34. John H. Sorrells, *A Letter to a Young Man* (Cincinnati: E. W. Scripps Co., 1948), 11–12.

35. For details of Murrow's life, career and influence, see Edward R. Murrow, *In Search of Light: The Broadcasts of Edward R. Murrow, 1938–1961*, ed. Edward J. Bliss (New York: Knopf, 1967); Alexander Kendrick, *Prime Time: The Life of Edward R. Murrow* (Boston: Little, Brown, 1969); A.M. Sperber, *Murrow: His Life and Times* (New York: Freundlich Books, 1986); and Stanley Cloud and Lynne Olson, *The Murrow Boys: Pioneers on the Front Lines of Broadcast Journalism* (Boston: Houghton Mifflin, 1996).

36. Not that pay was a dominant concern to everyone. Surveys of more than 1,400 journalists showed satisfied workers ranking pay lowest as a happiness factor. Job security, autonomy, and their organizations' editorial policies ranked far higher — probably reflecting tensions over credibility and "downsizing." But news staffers who were dissatisfied placed substantial blame on their salaries. See G. Cleveland Wilhoit and David Weaver, "U. S. Journalists at Work, 1971–1992," paper presented to convention of Association for Education in Journalism and Mass Communication, August 1994, Atlanta, Ga., 25–37.

37. An examination of personality in 173 journalists found most to be more extroverted than the general population and no less neurotic, that is, anxious, emotional, insecure, or moody. See John Henningham, "The Journalist's Personality: An Exploratory Study," *Journalism & Mass Communication Quarterly* 74:3 (1997), 615–24.

38. Lou Cannon, *Reporting: An Inside View* (Sacramento: California Journal Press, 1977), 27.

39. Gerald W. Johnson, "Personality Journalism," Twelfth Annual Newspaper Guild-School of Journalism Memorial Lecture, University of Minnesota, October 30, 1958, 5.

8

Training and Education of Journalists

JOSEPH A. MIRANDO

Journalism is a relative newcomer to the typical curriculum offered at modern colleges and universities. Unlike the traditions of the ministry, law, and medicine that have long relied on educated individuals with years of formal study, the lessons of journalism developed in a largely haphazard manner initially through the experiences of town criers, wandering bards, and balladeers, and, in America from the 1600s until the 20th century, of printers, postmasters, partisan editors, and Bohemian writers. Even though language study formed the core of the classical liberal education from its very inception during the Middle Ages, prior to the 1900s American journalists were most likely to learn how to read and write while being trained how to set type, make paper, and run a press in the print shops that employed them as "printer's devils."

Classes in journalism did not appear for the first time in American colleges until the late 1800s, and whole departments and schools of journalism did not become commonplace until the middle 1900s. In the latter part of the 20th century, just as the term "J-major" became widely familiar on college campuses, departments and schools expanded to include a mass communication approach. In this way, journalism has continued to have at least the perception of still being the newcomer in academe as compared to the senior status usually afforded to other academic disciplines such as English and history.

The history of journalism education in America has been shaped by its constant struggle for credibility. Because of journalism's early strong identification with the printing trade, college was not the place where one learned how to become a journalist. Higher education was initially reserved for the rich and professional classes, and most early American journalists often got their start in journalism while serving a term of indentured servitude in a print shop. After the Civil War, innovative educators expanded their curriculums to devote more attention to areas of business and manufacturing that were having a tremendous impact on society, and journalism as part of this movement began as a set of scattered courses and sporadic lectures by adjunct instructors and guest speakers. During the late 1800s, journalism education remained limited because an attitude developed chiefly among publishers and leading journalists that journalism was better learned as events unfolded on the job rather than in the controlled environment of a classroom.

During the first half of the 20th century, press associations and news media companies helped journalism schools grow with endowments and large scale hiring of journalism graduates. But the attitude that the newsroom, not the classroom, was the proper place for learning journalism continues to persist mainly among reporters and editors. In the latter half of the 20th century journalism changed radically as rapid change in technology took place, news budgets tightened, and public confidence in the media waned. Still striving for acceptance, journalism educators struggled to keep up with these new trends by following the pace set by the industry instead of taking the lead.

THE PRINTER-JOURNALIST

Formal classroom-oriented learning in journalism was of little value during the 1700s and much of the 1800s because of the structure of both the media and higher education.

Few people living during this era could afford to support themselves solely by gathering information, writing, and editing. These were considered to be talents rather than skills, and they were more likely to be used primarily by politicians and ministers. One whose primary occupation was journalism was constantly involved in the painstaking work of printing and was rarely, if ever, referred to as a journalist. The most outward reminder of this condition is embodied in the name of the concept of "freedom of the press." Freedom to practice journalism is the implied meaning today, but at the Constitutional Convention of 1787-1788 this term would have had little meaning. The same influence is present in the printing terms that would come to describe many of the writing forms and methods that future journalism students would have to learn, such as scoop, slug, lead, sidebar, headline, and byline. These terms gave journalism strong identification as a trade rather than a profession, and such an identity was supported by a perceived need for an apprenticeship period. In order to learn the trade properly, the prospective printer-journalist firmly understood that time and space dictated how much or how little could be written and that an efficient publishing operation relied on assembly-line techniques. Such lessons were state of the art in journalism and are still today, but they were in conflict with the traditional values of the academy and still seen today as anti-intellectual.

Any student who had a career motive in attending college in early America was most likely preparing to enter the ministry or to become a lawyer or physician. The typical college curriculum was restricted to the liberal arts, and studies took place in an atmosphere similar to the traditional British boarding school. In this setting, the ancient Greek philosophy that gaining knowledge was good within itself prevailed. Rather than emphasize that students gain proficiency in a technical area, early educators were concerned with instilling in their pupils a set of values that would provide them with a sense of respect—morality, refinement, maturity, and responsibility.

Higher education offered journalists the possibility to earn a sense of respect and, along the way, raise up the field of journalism to the status of a profession. This line of reasoning is still used to justify the existence of schools of journalism and mass communication. The argument was a strong one especially after the Morrill Land Grant Act of 1862 made available thousands of acres of land for the founding of colleges that would provide training in a variety of practical subjects.

The earliest attempts at offering education in journalism involved a print shop approach. In 1834 Duff Green, partisan editor of the *United States Telegraph*, announced plans to establish the Washington Institute, a school in which students would attend classes in languages and arts and work in his print shop, but the school was never established. The first course in journalism to appear in a college curriculum was set up in 1869 at Washington and Lee University as part of a program of scholarships offered to printers in the South. Recipients received free tuition to combine classroom lessons with work in the composing room of the local newspaper under the supervision of a college faculty member.

Land-grant colleges, mainly in the Midwest, used the support of state press associations to develop many of the earliest journalism courses. Kansas State College offered a course in printing in 1873. The University of Missouri set up a course in news writing in 1878 and another course called "Materials of Journalism" in 1884. Other public colleges in the Midwest that joined the movement to start journalism courses included Iowa State University (1892), Indiana University (1893), University of Kansas (1894), University of

Michigan (1895), and the University of Nebraska (1898).

Private colleges, particularly Ivy League
institutions, also embraced journalism and employed innovative approaches. In 1871 Yale
offered students the opportunity to study and
discuss journalistic trends in literature and history on a regular schedule. The first degree in
journalism was offered by another Ivy League
school, Cornell University in 1875. The University of Pennsylvania developed the first organized curriculum in journalism in 1893. The
courses it offered included journalism history,
law and management, reporting and editing,
current topics, and special lectures by visiting
journalists.

As reflected by the first journalism textbooks, many of the most basic practices involved in reporting and news writing methods
that modern students of mass communication
strive to master were well established by the
late 1800s and became staples of early journalism education. The first journalism students
studied the inverted pyramid style of writing
instead of the time-honored narrative that was
used in other classes and dominated earlier
newspaper writing. They received training in
practices associated with what is known today
as objective reporting—factualness based on
observable phenomena and newsworthiness
based on an audience's interests rather than the
writer's interests. One of the most noted textbooks from this era was Edwin Shuman's *Steps
into Journalism*. Initially published by a correspondence school in 1894, it was still in circulation in the 1920s. Earlier popular journalism
textbooks were based on a series of articles
reprinted from the trade journal *The Journalist*,
the forerunner of the modern *Editor & Publisher* magazine. These included *Writing for the
Press* (1886) by Robert Luce, *The Ladder of
Journalism* (1889) by Thomas Campbell-Cope-
land, and *The Blue Pencil and How to Avoid It*
(1890) by Alexander G. Nevins.

THE PULITZER ENDOWMENT

By the dawn of the 20th century, journalism education in America was viewed as little more than a passing campus fad. During the
late 1800s such leading journalists as Horace
Greeley, Edwin Godkin, and Charles Dana
were on record as making harsh statements
firmly against the promotion of journalism education. Years after Lee's death, Washington
and Lee University officials even dismissed the
notion that they had ever taught journalism,
pointing out that it was offered only as a general direction for students and not an officially
prescribed course carrying academic credit.[1] In
1892 Columbia University formally rejected a
proposal to add journalism to its curriculum,
winning approval among journalists and gaining a perception as a champion of classical
studies.

But the time was ripe for journalism education to become much more than a fad.
Outspoken leaders of 19th century journalism
like Greeley were deceased. In addition, the educational theories of John Dewey and William
James were in vogue, and the emphasis in academia was rapidly shifting from a focus on the
goals of the institution to the goals of individual students. Despite the ridicule of established
reporters and editors, journalism education
could already count on a strong base of interest
among students. Memoirs of journalists of the
late 1800s contain abundant references to college students flooding newspaper offices with
job applications. All that was required was a
strong show of support from the new generation of leaders of the media industry and higher
education.

In 1903 Joseph Pulitzer set in motion a
series of events that raised journalism education
from just an idea to a full-fledged movement.
Pulitzer directed his personal secretary, Dr.
George W. Hosmer, to author a pamphlet titled "The Making of a Journalist; Why a Technical and a Professional School Is Needed."
Pulitzer instructed Hosmer to present the pamphlet to Harvard University President Charles
Eliot and new Columbia University President
Nicholas Murray Butler to ask each man if he
found the pamphlet's main idea acceptable and
to inform each that an anonymous friend was
interested in making a large donation to establish a school of journalism on his campus. Both
presidents gave their enthusiastic support. Eliot

wrote a note responding to Hosmer that included an outline for a curriculum that offered courses in newspaper management, production, law, ethics, history, and writing. However, Butler had already presented the idea to Columbia's Board of Trustees, who gave approval to establishing a school of journalism just eight days before Eliot could respond to Hosmer's inquiry.

The news that Columbia University was to establish a school of journalism created a sensation in a front page story in Pulitzer's *New York World*. The sheer size of Pulitzer's donation was incredible. Based on a steady rate of inflation, $2 million in 1903 dollars would have had the buying power today of well over a quarter-billion dollars.

The sense of legitimacy Pulitzer's gift gave journalism education was priceless. Columbia officials acknowledged in an article in the *New York World* that their school of journalism would be on equal footing with the university's schools of law, medicine, engineering, architecture, and teaching. Despite his yellow journalism war with William Randolph Hearst, Pulitzer was considered the top journalist of his day, and for good measure Columbia trustees allowed him to nominate a board of advisors that included two more prominent publishers to endorse the undertaking, Greeley's successor at the *New York Tribune*, Whitelaw Reid, and the *Chicago Daily News'* Victor F. Lawson. Harvard, America's leading university, had weighed in with its response from Eliot, who had led the institution since 1869. Butler was also distinguished in his own right with the publication of a book, *The Meaning of Education*, in 1898; and before the school of journalism would open in 1912, he would lure both Dewey and James to Columbia and run for vice president of the United States. For good measure Pulitzer also added to the board of advisors Cornell University President Andrew White, who had established the first degree in journalism.

Editorials in major newspapers and magazines across the country generally applauded Pulitzer's actions. Editors critical of the endowment recognized it as at least a praiseworthy gesture while expressing doubt that the school would improve the skills of journalists. A year after Hosmer wrote his pamphlet, Pulitzer defended his proposal in an article in the *North American Review*. "I wish to begin a movement," he wrote, "that will raise journalism to the rank of a learned profession, growing in the respect of the community as other professions far less to the public interests have grown."[2]

Columbia's School of Journalism did not open until after Pulitzer's death, but the effect of the endowment was profound. The National Editorial Association used the occasion of its meeting at the famous 1904 St. Louis World's Fair to announce its support of the endowment. The first school of journalism separate from any other academic unit on a college campus was established in 1908 at the University of Missouri. By the time the Columbia School of Journalism did open in 1912, seven colleges had set up whole departments of journalism and three had separate schools of journalism.

TECHNICAL/VOCATIONAL JOURNALISM

Journalism education grew rapidly during the early 20th century. By the time Columbia's school of journalism opened 31 colleges had at least one course in journalism. By 1918 a government monograph by James Melvin Lee showed that 91 colleges had courses in journalism, and 26 were offering enough coursework for students to earn a major in journalism. By 1926 the number of colleges offering journalism courses had risen to 230, and 50 were offering majors in journalism. By 1936, despite tight financial conditions brought on by the Great Depression, 532 colleges had courses in journalism. According to *Journalism Quarterly*, about 1,000 college students earned bachelor's degrees in journalism between 1909 and 1918, rising to 5,000 graduates between 1918 and 1928 and to about 14,000 between 1928 and 1938. Faculty members teaching journalism numbered about 172 by 1917, 426 by 1929 and 894 by 1936.[3]

During this time faculty and students established alumni support groups and professional associations still alive today that strengthened journalism's place in higher education. Three nationally prominent journalism student organizations were all founded in 1909—the Society of Professional Journalists (originally Sigma Delta Chi at DePauw University), Women in Communications, Inc. (originally Theta Sigma Phi at the University of Washington), and the Society for Collegiate Journalists (originally Pi Delta Epsilon at Syracuse University). The national honor society for journalism students, Kappa Tau Alpha, was founded in 1910 at the University of Missouri. The main organization for faculty, the Association for Education in Journalism and Mass Communication, was founded as the American Association of Teachers of Journalism in 1912 (later known as the Association for Education in Journalism). The Accrediting Council on Education in Journalism and Mass Communications and the Association of Schools of Journalism and Mass Communication both have their roots in the 1916 establishment of the American Association of Schools and Departments of Journalism.

Industry support continued to build for journalism education. By the 1920s press associations in 35 states made the promotion of journalism education a goal of their member newspapers. The McCormick and Patterson families, prominent in Chicago area journalism, endowed the Medill School of Journalism at Northwestern University, which opened in 1921, and in 1924 William J. Murphy of the *Minneapolis Tribune* endowed a school of journalism at the University of Minnesota. In 1925, in an address to journalism teachers that was widely reprinted, H. L. Mencken, a leading figure in American literary criticism and well-known for his witty social commentary, refrained from heaping ridicule on journalism education and instead credited schools with improving the standards of news reporters.[4]

The trademark of journalism education in the early 20th century was an emphasis on technical matters. The typical journalism school of the 1910s, '20s, and '30s offered a selection of courses in history, ethics, or law, but devoted most attention to reporting, writing, and editing. Some schools included courses in a broad mass media context such as manage-

ment, circulation, printing, advertising, publicity, and broadcasting, but the focus was news-editorial study designed to prepare reporters for newsroom work. For a school to become a member of the American Association of Schools and Departments of Journalism, majors were required to devote about a half or more of all their journalism courses to reporting, news writing, copy reading, editing, and editorial writing.

The technical approach led to a strict vocational emphasis. Regardless of whether they were college graduates, former reporters and editors were considered the most capable instructors, and plenty of working journalists taught classes part time or supervised students' work through special arrangements with local newspapers. Classrooms contained typewriters, and students were required to bang out stories directly on the keyboard instead of preparing rough drafts and neat outlines in their best handwriting as they learned in freshman English. Journalism students were frequently expected to put in time on the campus newspaper or at the university news bureau, and many found correspondent work for a local or out-of-town daily paper.

The technical/vocational efforts of Columbia, Northwestern, and Missouri in particular became often identified initially as models for other schools.

Columbia strove to follow the stipulations of Pulitzer's will closely. The first two directors of the school (Talcott Williams and John Cunliffe) were prominent senior newsmen who avoided the business aspects of journalism and required students to use the city of New York as their reporting beat. In 1931 Carl Ackerman, an alumnus of the school, became director, and four years later he abolished the undergraduate journalism major, set up a new admissions policy requiring students to have a bachelor's degree, and limited the curriculum to graduate study. Today Columbia restricts classes to the master's and doctoral levels.

Northwestern gained fame under its first director, Harry F. Harrington, for requiring students to take assignments directly from the city desks of Chicago daily newspapers and for employing a faculty made up of dozens of

Chicago journalists teaching part time. In the late 1930s under Director Kenneth Olson, Northwestern students began concentrating their journalism courses in the fourth year to earn a bachelor's degree and in a fifth year to earn a Master of Science in journalism. In the coming years Medill retained the hands-on approach and expanded it into a prominent Washington reporting program and a strong magazine curriculum that took advantage of Chicago's geographic market advantages.

The most popular way to teach journalism during the early 20th century was to closely align classes with the publishing operation of a campus or community newspaper. The ideal was to not only offer training in reporting and editing, but to advance a socialization process focusing on the reality of working in a newsroom. The leading proponent of this method and its founder was Walter Williams, who developed this procedure in its most advanced form by establishing a daily newspaper on the University of Missouri campus. With its own fully-equipped newsroom, printing press, photography labs, wire services, and hundreds of student reporters, the *Missourian* gave blanket coverage to the nearby town of Columbia and became the model all other student newspapers would strive to become.

The spirit of the technical/vocational model is composed of practicality, relevance, and glamour that still lures students to major in journalism. Few other classes at a typical college can offer students opportunities to hear their own teachers give first-hand accounts of history-making events, to rub elbows with decision-makers, and to have their names printed in bold print above an article that will be read and talked about by thousands of people. When the first two textbooks ever solely authored by journalism professors appeared in 1911, both were built on this approach—*The Practice of Journalism* by Walter Williams and Frank Martin and *The Writing of News* by Charles Ross. The most prominent textbook of this kind was by Medill journalism professor Curtis MacDougall and originally appeared in 1928 as *Brown and White*, was revised as *A College Course in Reporting for Beginners* in 1932, was revised again as *Interpretative Report-*

ing in 1938, went through eight more editions, and was still in use in journalism schools in the late 1980s.

Though it was intended to win favor with working journalists, the technical/vocational approach came under severe criticism. It is dependent on the media industry for guidance and thus is subject to how well-defined industry standards are. Because of widespread disagreement over just what is good journalism, memoirs of journalism school graduates contain substantial references to having to learn harsh lessons on the job that their professors never taught them and having to dismiss other lessons they were taught in J-school. Ex-journalists who became professors were free to pass on practices they had learned during their own careers, regardless of how valid they were. Textbooks written by former journalists resting on their laurels stressed stories of the "good old days."

Economist Thorstein Veblen argued that similar problems plagued many academic disciplines because colleges were becoming organized like corporations and trusts. In his 1918 book, *The Higher Learning in America,* he held that colleges, like businesses, were forced to be concerned with money matters and the appearance of greatness rather than with learning and scholarship.

The technical/vocational model was also subject to abuse in the conduct of classes. Vernon Nash's 1938 dissertation alleged that many college administrations approved journalism curricula that were little more than students being required to do publicity work for the college in the disguise of student newspapers and campus news services.[5] Albert Sutton's 1940 study found that one-third of all journalism classes nationwide were taught by someone with no credentials in journalism, and two of every three schools offering journalism had no laboratory facilities or library holdings in journalism.[6] The AASDJ stood accused of elitism and turf protection in formulating its standards of accreditation, and in 1944 a rival organization, the American Society of Journalism School Administrators, was formed by journalism schools denied membership in the AASDJ. The American Newspaper Guild, which opposed professional status for journalists to help them gain collective bargaining power, looked upon journalism education as nothing more than a way to produce college-subsidized cub reporters.

Criticism of journalism education never eased up throughout the 20th century, actually becoming in the words of Everette Dennis, a "hallowed tradition" by itself for journalists who continue to like to "snort and snarl at journalism schools." ABC News *Nightline* anchor Ted Koppel's modern criticism was just as biting as Greeley's and Godkin's when he told a student audience, "Journalism schools are an absolute and total waste of time. You cannot replicate true journalism—genuine pressure—in an academic setting."[7]

SOCIAL SCIENCE AND MASS COMMUNICATION

The mid–20th century amounted to a watershed in the history of journalism education.

For decades working journalists had argued that the best journalism school was a newspaper office, and during this period even leaders of education agreed. In his 1928 Oxford speeches and his 1930 book *Universities: American, English, German*, Rhodes lecturer Abraham Flexner argued that journalism lessons were "a few practical tricks and adjustments that an educated or clever youth would rapidly pick up 'on the job.'"[8] The American Society of Newspaper Editors, a strong past advocate of journalism education, arrived at the same conclusion in 1930 when it asserted that techniques can be taught in the office and recommended that journalism curriculums be devoted to liberal education. In *The Higher Learning in America*, a book that went through six printings between 1936 and 1945, University of Chicago President Robert M. Hutchins sounded very much like an old-fashioned reporter when he argued, "All there is to journalism can be learned through a good (general) education and newspaper work."[9] The most stinging indictment of journalism education came from the Hutchins Commission on Freedom of the Press. In its 1947 report, the Commission, made up of Hutchins and 10 noted professors from a variety of fields, alleged that journalism schools did not accept an obligation to serve as independent critics of the press, were not training students to be competent judges of public affairs, and did not recognize that a mass communication revolution was taking place in society. "The kind of training a journalist needs most today," the commission argued, "is not training in the tricks and machinery of the trade."[10]

Unlike outspoken journalists who would go so far as to issue a periodic call for the abolishment of journalism education, Flexner, Hutchins, and the Hutchins Commission attacked the technical/ vocational model and called for broad study of the mass media and their relationship to society—an aspect that gained approval by a growing number of journalism professors. In 1939, with most schools placing emphasis on a technical/vocational approach, fewer than 50 of the nation's 1,000 college journalism teachers held a Ph. D. and more than 100 had no college degree at all. However, after 1940 journalism schools rapidly began hiring more professors with a doctorate, and most of these individuals earned their terminal degrees in interdisciplinary programs that included journalism within programs in sociology, political science, and economics. Sutton found in 1940 that technical courses dominated most curriculums, but courses entitled, "Public Opinion" and "Social Influences of the Press" were on the rise. During the 1940s James Herring found rapid expansion of social science study, and courses in "Mass Communication and Society," broadcasting, and public relations were being created at twice the rate of any other journalism class.

Journalism's professional literature also experienced similar changes. *Journalism Quarterly*, founded in 1924 as a scholarly journal for teachers, was originally composed of essays, convention addresses, and proceedings similar to *Editor & Publisher* and the ASNE annual report, *Problems of Journalism*. By the 1950s *Journalism Quarterly* was publishing articles on a broad range of media topics and was making wide use of quantitative data. In the 1960s another research journal, *Journalism Monographs*, was established, and new magazines devoted to critical analysis of the media, such as the *Columbia Journalism Review*, appeared.

Among textbooks, the work of Chilton Bush of Stanford University rose to prominence. He authored *Newspaper Reporting of Public Affairs*, published in 1929 and revised in 1940 and 1951, as a guide to understanding complex issues involving city and state government, courts, and police with a minimum of technical journalism lessons. In 1954 he authored *The Art of News Communication*, a reporting book that made extensive use of communication theory and social science research. In 1965 and 1970 he combined the public affairs and social science approaches in two editions of *Newswriting and Reporting Public Affairs*.

The origin of the mass communication/social science approach to journalism education can be traced to the work of Willard G. Bleyer of the University of Wisconsin. He was one of the first to act on Pulitzer's proposals by founding Wisconsin's journalism program in 1905, but unlike his contemporaries, who were former noteworthy editors, he held a Ph.D. in English.

Unlike Columbia, Missouri, and Northwestern, Wisconsin under Bleyer offered journalism courses in marketing methods, educational publicity, printing, management, psychological principles of advertising, and the relation of the press to the public. At his insistence, convention sessions of the American Association of Teachers of Journalism were devoted to scholarly research. When graduate study in journalism began at Wisconsin, Bleyer emphasized social science technique rather than news writing technique. His master's students pioneered content analysis method, and in 1929 he created a Ph.D. program in which students would major in a social science area and earn a minor in journalism.

Bleyer's top students who came through the Wisconsin Ph.D. minor eventually became deans and directors of leading journalism schools and worked to further the mass communication/social science approach. After studying under Bleyer, Bush moved the jour-

nalism program at Stanford from the English Department to the School of Social Science, added courses titled "Geographical Aspects of Journalism" and "Sociological Aspects of Journalism," and created degree programs in social science journalism. By 1948 Bush's program was called an Institute of Journalistic Studies, and later it became the Department of Communication with an Institute of Communication Research. The first student to graduate under Bleyer with the Ph.D. minor was Ralph Casey, who took over the journalism department of the University of Minnesota and built a curriculum based on courses in contemporary political, social, and economic affairs. By 1945 he was providing training in "the communications field," and by 1966 Minnesota became a school of journalism and mass communication. He hired another Bleyer student, Ralph Nafziger, who established a communication research division at Minnesota and then returned to Wisconsin in 1949 as director of the School of Journalism and rejuvenated a program that lost its social science approach after Bleyer's death in 1935. Two Bleyer students, Lawrence Murphy and Frederick Seibert, led the rise of the University of Illinois, which became a College of Journalism and Communication in 1957 with an Institute of Communications Research.

While Bleyer and his students were the catalysts, Wilbur Schramm and his students provided the leadership and the research that gave communication study its modern prominence. Like Bleyer, Schramm had a Ph.D. in English and limited experience in journalism. As director of the University of Iowa School of Journalism, he de-emphasized skills courses in writing and editing, replaced them with courses in sociology, political science, and economics and added a doctoral program in mass communication. From the 1940s to the 1970s he worked with Bleyer students to strengthen communication programs and research centers at Stanford and Illinois.

While the technical/vocational approach was intended to give journalism education a sense of acceptance and legitimacy among the media industry, the social science/mass communication approach gave journalism education a sense of academic legitimacy and potential for leadership. Instead of copying industry standards, journalism educators relied on their own backgrounds to formulate their own theories and principles and develop their own successors.

By the 1980s more than half of all journalism programs listed in the annual *Journalism Educator* directory were connected to schools or departments of communication. But this development came at a cost. Some journalism departments changed their names to "communication" merely as a fashion statement and did little to adjust their curricula. At the same time departments of speech expanded their scope by changing names to communication but offered little or no study in journalism. Research findings also came into question. Researchers developed complicated diagrams of communication models and mountains of data that were impressive to fellow researchers but seemed confusing and of little value to journalists.

THE WOODSTEIN ERA

During the 1940s and 1950s America's college students demonstrated for the first time that they were losing interest in studying journalism. After the number of journalism majors hit 6,000 in 1938, according to *Journalism Quarterly*, enrollment fell for five straight years.[11] The decline appeared to be a brief setback connected to America's military buildup and entry into World War II, because enrollments rose again each year from 1944 to 1948, reaching 16,000 nationwide. But college enrollments nationwide were tumbling because military veterans were now rapidly graduating and low birthrates during the 1930s meant fewer new students. Journalism enrollment fell again from 1949 to 1953, showed slight gains in 1954 and 1955, then declined four of the next five years.

Amazingly, the situation changed almost overnight. From 1961 to 1979 journalism enrollments rose nearly 500 per cent. The old 1948 peak of 16,000 was passed by 1965, more than doubling to 33,000 by 1970 and more than doubling again to 71,000 by 1979. In 1970

Paul Peterson of Ohio State University found that about one half of all colleges nationwide offered a journalism course and about one-fifth offered an undergraduate major in journalism.

The most common explanation for the rise was known as the "Woodstein" phenomenon, a label made popular by Ben Bagdikian in his critique of journalism education for *The Atlantic* magazine in 1977. According to Bagdikian and other critics, students had flocked to journalism schools because they were inspired by the glamour, prestige, and intrigue of investigative reporting. During the 1960s investigative reporters such as Jack Anderson, Seymour Hersh, and Clark Mollenhoff, and new journalists such as Tom Wolfe and Truman Capote received a level of acclaim never afforded to crusading journalists and muckrakers of past eras. The biggest fame of all was reserved in the 1970s for Bob Woodward and Carl Bernstein, two young reporters at the *Washington Post* whose investigative work on the Watergate scandal eventually led to the resignation of President Richard Nixon, as well as a book, *All the President's Men*, and a movie by the same name.

Investigative reporting did became a popular course in most journalism schools, and Woodward's and Bernstein's popularity on the campus speaking circuit was proof that students were inspired. But the rush to journalism schools also took place because of a variety of converging trends. The baby boom generation, children born during the late 1940s, 1950s, and early 1960s, had reached college age, and enrollments nationwide in all disciplines were rising. Journalism was popular among students engaging in protests and activism, and the perception that the media were the adversary of government was consistent with "anti-establishment" thinking. At the same time curriculum reformers' main criticism of higher education was that it was not "relevant" to modern life. Journalism, with its emphasis on practical job skills, was a notable exception. Job skills were an important commodity to parents of baby boomers who were reared at a time when jobs were scarce during the Great Depression. Overall, universities during this era worked toward becoming centers of egalitarianism and cultural diversity. Operating as a "multiversity," a college could justify offering courses based largely on market demand, and in this environment student consumers were clearly choosing journalism.

AT A CROSSROADS

The dawn of the 21st century marked another period of transition for journalism education in America.

Enrollment growth was slower during the 1980s and 1990s but continued upward, rising to more than 150,000 today at the nation's 450 schools and departments of journalism and mass communication. Much of the growth was mainly due to a rise in interest in advertising, public relations, and communication studies as traditional "J-Schools" transformed themselves into "C-Schools." Journalism majors are still the largest segment of the enrollment, but they make up only about one-fourth of journalism school student bodies, and this number also includes schools and departments that have combined the study of traditional print journalism with broadcast to form all-purpose journalism or news-editorial curriculums.

The main trend during the 1980s and 1990s was toward finding ways to integrate both technique and theory in the journalism curriculum. In 1982 the Association for Education in Journalism, formerly known as the American Association of Teachers of Journalism, changed its name to the modern Association for Education in Journalism and Mass Communication. In 1984 the American Association of Schools and Departments of Journalism merged with the American Society of Journalism School Administrators to form the Association for Schools of Journalism and Mass Communications. David Weaver and G. Cleveland Wilhoit's studies of U.S. news people, *The American Journalist*, found that the typical modern journalism school was still offering courses in reporting or editing-related subjects in addition to courses in specialty areas such as history, law, ethics, magazine, photojournalism, radio, television, public relations, or advertising.[12]

Accreditation controversies that have plagued journalism education since 1910s continued to be a problem. A longtime standard for accredited schools was to require journalism students to devote at least 75 per cent of their coursework to liberal arts ("75–25 rule"). Constant disagreement over what courses constitute the liberal arts led educators to adjust the standard in 1989 to 75 per cent of all coursework in a 120-hour major to be non-journalism courses and a little more than half of all courses to be in traditional liberal arts subjects ("90–65 rule"). In the 1990s, the AEJMC discussed replacing the accrediting system with a new format to draw class distinctions among elite journalism schools and programs that satisfied minimum accreditation standards.

As the year 2000 approached, educators used the occasion to study the direction their field was taking and to make recommendations on the future shape of journalism education. In 1984 a task force of educators issued the Oregon Report, which criticized schools for serving merely as handmaidens to industry and by offering sequences of courses that prepare students for specific jobs in journalism. The report endorsed a "generic journalism" approach that would stress communication competence in basic writing and editing courses, emphasize a media-wide context rather than a newspaper focus in conceptual courses like law or history, and create professional modules linked to careers in a variety of media fields. In 1994 the AEJMC's Vision 2000 Task Force built on the Oregon Report and went further, recommending that universities add a mass communications and society course to their core curriculums required of all students on campus regardless of major.

Today, schools of journalism and mass communication appear to be headed for another transformation. Instead of a mass communication revolution, an information revolution is taking place with the development of the Internet as a wide-ranging social force, the merging of a broad range of media companies, attention to niche and small group concerns, the rapid changeover of computer technology, and the phenomenon of information overload. On college campuses, educators have had to deal with a nationwide call for accountability, skyrocketing student debt, and a new generation of students who tend to be more affluent and more computer savvy, but whose scores on standardized tests show a decline in basic writing skills and cultural knowledge. Facing these influences, journalism education seems fated to continue its historic pattern of having to redefine itself and seek credibility.

Selected Readings

Asher, Brad. "The Professional Vision: Conflicts Over Journalism Education, 1900–1950." *American Journalism* 11 (Fall 1994): 304–320.

Beasley, Maurine. "Women in Journalism Education: The Formative Period, 1908–1930." *Journalism History* 13 (1986): 10–18.

Bradshaw, James Stanford. "Mrs. Rayne's School of Journalism." *Journalism Quarterly* 60 (1983): 513–17, 579.

Bronstein, Carolyn, and Stephen Vaughn. "Willard G. Bleyer and the Relevance of Journalism Education." *Journalism Monographs* 166 (June 1998).

Dickson, Tom. *Mass Media Education in Transition*. Mahwah, N. J.: Lawrence Erlbaum Associates, 2000.

Emery, Edwin, and Joseph P. McKerns. "AEJMC: 75 Years in the Making: A History of Organizing for Journalism and Mass Communication Education in the United States." *Journalism Monographs* 104 (1987).

Medsger, Betty. *Winds of Change: Challenges Confronting Journalism Education*. Arlington, Va.: Freedom Forum, 1996.

O'Dell, DeForest. *The History of Journalism Education in the United States*. New York: Teachers College, Columbia University, 1935.

Reed, Perley I. "The Rise of ASJSA." *Journalism Educator* 3, 1 (1958): 10–18.

Rogers, Everett M., and Steven H. Chaffee. "Communication and Journalism from 'Daddy' Bleyer to Wilbur Schramm: A Palimpsest." *Journalism Monographs* 148 (December 1994).

Rucker, Frank W. *Walter Williams*. Columbia: Missourian Publishing Association, 1964.

Rush, Ramona R. "Patterson, Grindstead and Hostetter: Pioneer Journalism Educators." *Journalism History* 1 (1974): 129–32.

Sloan, Wm. David, ed. *Makers of the Media Mind: Journalism Educators and Their Ideas*. Hillsdale, N.J.: Lawrence Erlbaum Associates, 1990.

Sutton, Albert A. *Education for Journalism in the United States from Its Beginning to 1940*. Evanston, Ill.: Northwestern University, 1945.

Wilcox, Walter. "Historical Trends in Journalism Education." *Journalism Educator* 14, 3 (1959): 2–7, 32.

Williams, Sara Lockwood. *Twenty Years of Journalism: A History of the School of Journalism of the University of Missouri, Columbia, Missouri, U.S.A.*. Columbia: Missourian Publishing Co., 1929.

Notes

1. Charles F. Wingate, *Views and Interviews on Journalism* (New York: Patterson, 1875), 360.

2. Joseph Pulitzer, "The College of Journalism," *North American Review* 178 (May 1904): 649, 657.

3. Vernon Nash, "Educating for Journalism," unpublished Ed.D. dissertation, Columbia University, 1938: 22.

4. H. L. Mencken, "Reflections on Journalism," *Journalism Bulletin* 2 (1925): 3–5.

5. Nash, "Educating for Journalism," 23.

6. Albert Alton Sutton, *Educating for Journalism in the United States from Its Beginning to 1940* (Evanston, Ill.: Northwestern University, 1945), 100–01, 103, 104.

7. Everette E. Dennis, "Whatever Happened to Marse Robert's Dream?" *Gannett Center Journal* 2 (Spring 1988), 4–5.

8. Abraham Flexner, *Universities: American, English, German* (New York: Oxford University, 1930), 160, 161.

9. Robert M. Hutchins, *The Higher Learning in America* (New Haven, Conn.: Yale University, 1936), 56.

10. Commission on Freedom of the Press, *A Free and Responsible Press* (Chicago: University Press, 1947), 77.

11. Douglass W. Miller, comp. "News Notes," *Journalism Quarterly* 15–19 (1938–1943).

12. David H. Weaver and Cleveland G. Wilhoit, *The American Journalist*, 2nd ed. (Bloomington: Indiana University Press, 1991), 44–45.

9

Women in Journalism

CAROLYN KITCH

In 1936, when she wrote the first book-length history of women in American journalism, Ishbel Ross—a reporter herself—also commented on the working conditions of her own female colleagues. "A number throughout the country can point to front-page streamers, stories leading the paper, a heavy play on the big assignments of the day," she wrote. But these "front-page girls," she noted, had "not revolutionized the status of their colleagues. They are remarkable only because they are the exceptions.... [T]he highest compliment to which the deluded creatures respond is the city editor's acknowledgment that their work is just like a man's ... for they are all aware that no right-minded editor wants the so-called woman's touch in the news."[1]

The concerns Ross raised more than 60 years ago remain central issues for women in journalism, among both professionals and historians: To what extent does the success of a small number of high-profile individuals represent the progress of women as a professional group? And what is "the woman's touch in the news"—a softening of news, or an expansion of what news is and does? This chapter explores how these questions have repeatedly surfaced in the lives of American female journalists over the past two and a half centuries.

PRINTING, POLITICS, AND PROPONENTS OF CAUSES

Women were among the printers of colonial newspapers, working alongside their fathers and husbands, and often later inheriting and running these businesses on their own. (Indeed, such circumstances were typical not only during the 18th century but throughout the 19th century as well: most women who were accepted in the business tended to be widows, deserted wives, or impoverished daughters who turned to journalism to support their families.) Among the most prominent were Elizabeth Timothy in South Carolina and Mary Katherine Goddard in Maryland. Goddard ran Baltimore's first newspaper, the *Baltimore Journal*, during the Revolutionary War and in 1777 printed the first copies of the Declaration of Independence issued to the colonies.

By the Jacksonian era, a few women were joining the growing ranks of newspaper reporters as well. Margaret Fuller, best known today for her women's rights treatise *Woman in the Nineteenth Century*, was a European correspondent for the *New York Tribune* during the 1840s. She also edited *The Dial*, the New England literary magazine whose contributors included Ralph Waldo Emerson and Henry David Thoreau. Entering journalism at age 55 after her husband died and his family disinherited her, Anne Royall wrote about federal fraud, from postal scams to the government's theft of Indian lands, in her Washington newspapers *Paul Pry* and *The Huntress* during the 1830s and '40s. Later in the century, Mary Clemmer Ames, a former Civil War nurse, covered Congress from Washington for the *New York Independent* and the *Brooklyn Daily Union*, and Kate Field founded her own newspaper, *Kate Field's Washington*.

More common in 19th-century women's newspaper work, however, were themes related to social and political causes. Women's involvement in the abolition, temperance, and suffrage campaigns inspired many of them to begin periodicals about these subjects. Jane Swisshelm published an anti-slavery newspaper in Minnesota after doing so in her native Pittsburgh. Amelia Bloomer (now remembered for her wearing of pants) started a temperance newspaper, *The Lily*, in 1849, and four years later Paulina Wright Davis launched the first women's-rights newspaper, *The Una*. The years after the Civil War yielded two more important publications, Elizabeth Cady Stanton and Susan B. Anthony's radical newspaper, *The Revolution*, and Lucy Stone's more conservative suffrage publication, *The Woman's Journal*. In the 1890s South, Ida B. Wells, who had been born a slave, campaigned against lynching in the *Memphis Free Speech*, an African-American newspaper of which she was part owner.

"Scribbling Women"

Other female journalists of the 19th century included social causes among a variety of topics they covered as newspaper columnists. The presence of their work in the pages of major publications signaled the growing importance of female newspaper readers during an era when rising literacy, a growing middle class, and industrialization changed the patterns of women's lives. Yet the style of these journalists' writing—conversational, passionate, sentimental, scolding—that earned them loyal followings (similar to the style of female novelists of this era, including Harriet Beecher Stowe) also earned scorn from critics and, later, historians. At the time, writer Nathaniel Hawthorne dismissed them as a pack of "scribbling women."

One of Hawthorne's chief targets was the first American (female or male) to work as a newspaper columnist in the modern sense— someone paid a salary to write a regular, signed opinion piece. Sara Willis Parton, who assumed the pen name "Fanny Fern," wrote in what she herself called "pop-gun prose" for the weekly

New York Ledger from the 1850s through '70s on subjects including suffrage, women's educational and professional opportunities, dress reform, the plight of prostitutes, the inequities of marriage, and the problems of the poor. She was direct in making her points, as in this 1857 column on domestic abuse: "[T]here are aggravated cases for which the law provides no remedy…. [I]n such cases, let a woman who has the self-sustaining power quietly take her fate in her own hands, and right herself. Of course she will be misjudged and abused. It is for her to choose whether she can better bear this at hands from which she has a rightful claim for love and protection, or from a nine-days-wonder-loving public."[2]

Parton was one of several newspaperwomen who wrote under alliterative and "floral" pseudonyms. Others were "Penelope Penfeather" (Sally Joy White), a staff reporter for the *Boston Post* and *Boston Herald*, and "Grace Greenwood" (Sara J. Lippincott), who covered Washington politics for three decades. Writing for the *New York Times* in 1877, Greenwood described politicians' reaction to her interest in government corruption: "I have been sharply rebuked by my brothers, as an indiscreet sister—'speaking out in meeting,' and revealing the secrets of the vestry, the deacons, the elders, and holy men generally…. I confess I prefer serving up a spicy hash of Southern Democratic sentiment to concocting a pudding, and pricking with my pen 'the bubble reputation' of political charlatans to puncturing innocent muslin with my needle."[3]

Journalism for Female Audiences

A similar pen name, "Jennie June," was the professional signature of Jane Cunningham Croly, who is mentioned in history books as a "first" in a number of categories. During a career that spanned 40 years, she established the first women's club in the 1870s and the first women's press club a decade later, she was the first female journalist to syndicate her writing, and she was the first woman to teach college journalism. But her most lasting contribution to journalism was her creation of the first newspaper "women's pages" for the *New York Daily World* in 1894. This part of the paper provided a place to discuss women's interests, increased the number of women reading newspapers, and provided career opportunities for female journalists. Soon the *World's* competitor, the *New York Evening Journal*, was publishing a women's page edited by Marie Manning (who wrote the first romance-advice column under the pseudonym "Beatrice Fairfax").

The subject matter of newspaper women's pages mirrored the content of one of the most important magazines of the 19th century, *Godey's Lady's Book*, which Croly herself briefly edited in the 1880s. Women's magazines were not new when the widowed Sarah Josepha Hale took the reigns of this one in the 1830s: during the century's first half, more than 25 such publications existed, including fashion titles edited by Ellen Curtis Demorest and her husband, William. But none was as influential as *Godey's*, which reached 150,000 readers in the 1850s. During her 40-year tenure, Hale promoted women's education and financial independence, and, as a fashion magazine, *Godey's* pioneered advances in the printing of illustrations.

Godey's did not survive into the 20th century, but it left an important legacy. Thanks to its technological contributions, later 19th-century publications such as *Frank Leslie's Illustrated Newspaper* and his stable of magazines, including *Leslie's Popular Monthly*, were able to make artwork a central part of their offerings. (The *Leslie's* magazine empire, close to ruin at the time of its founder's death in 1880, was salvaged and run for more than two decades by his widow, Miriam Folline Squier Leslie. When she died in 1914, she left her fortune to the women's suffrage campaign.) The upscale *Godey's* also created a model for the 1883 launch of what is arguably the most influential magazine of the early 20th century, *The Ladies' Home Journal*. It set in place the modern revenue structure for the magazine industry (based on advertising, in turn based on circulation) and by 1903 reached a million readers a month.

Though their chief editors were primarily men, the mass-circulation women's magazines begun in the late 19th century employed women to write their advice columns and service articles on home care, fashion, and society, just as newspapers did. Among *The Ladies' Home Journal's* regular female contributors was Gertrude Bustill Mossell, a prominent Philadelphia African American who wrote the "Woman's Department" column for the *New York Freeman*, the nation's leading African-American newspaper. The household-departments editor of the *Woman's Home Companion*, Gertrude Battles Lane, went on to become its editor-in-chief for several decades. These magazines also showcased the work of female writers and artists—the fiction of Kathleen Norris, Mary Roberts Rinehart, Mary Heaton Vorse, Sarah Orne Jewett, and Edna Ferber and the illustrations of Alice Barber Stephens and Jessie Willcox Smith.

In the opening years of the 20th century, the major women's magazines focused on issues that affected the well-being of women and children, including public health standards, education, tenement living conditions, and child labor. This journalism, now characterized by historians as "municipal housekeeping," was based on the Progressive-era idea that women's domestic values would clean up corruption in public life. *The Ladies' Home Journal* campaigned against patent medicine and in favor of pure-food legislation. *Good Housekeeping* and *Woman's Home Companion* published articles by feminist activists Rheta Childe Dorr, Jane Addams, and Florence Kelley. Two other women's magazines of the era, the *Delineator* and the *Pictorial Review,* championed women's suffrage, the latter also covering birth control.

STUNT REPORTERS AND SOB SISTERS

At the same time women were writing about domestic matters, newspapers began to employ them to create another kind of journalism: tales of social abuse and crime that boosted newspaper circulations in the era of Hearst and Pulitzer. Pulitzer's *New York World,* the paper that employed "Jennie June" to write its women's page, also hired "Nellie Bly." Bly, whose real name was Elizabeth Cochrane, became the first internationally-famous female journalist with her round-the-world race in 1890, beating a female reporter from a rival Hearst paper. But she had already done distinguished work, going undercover to report on factory working conditions, the treatment of women in jail, the recruitment of prostitutes, and life in an insane asylum. Hearst's counterpart to Nellie Bly was "Annie Laurie" (Winifred Black), and as circulation wars escalated, newspapers hired other women to get stories by assuming disguises. Posing as homeless girls, sweatshop workers, or hospital patients, these reporters revealed dark facts of urban life in prose filled with emotion or outrage. They came to be known as "stunt reporters." In the same era, a number of male newspaper and magazine writers did essentially the same thing—Lincoln Steffens, for instance, explored the underside of American cities in his passionate "Shame of the Cities" series for McClure's magazine—but were called "muckrakers." One woman who achieved the muckraker designation was Ida Tarbell, whose exposé of John D. Rockefeller's Standard Oil company was serialized in McClure's in 1902 and 1903. Neither her writing style nor her choice of subjects was "feminine." Like novelist Willa Cather, who served as managing editor of McClure's during the century's first decade, Tarbell considered herself one of the boys and opposed women's suffrage.

Other female journalists did write (indeed, were employed to write) as women—that is, with feeling and sympathy, usually for victims of crime. The four most famous were Winifred Black, Ada Patterson, Nixola Greeley-Smith, and Elizabeth Meriwether Gilmer ("Dorothy Dix," better known for her later work as a newspaper advice columnist). When they covered the sensational 1907 murder trial of Harry K. Thaw—accused of killing architect Stanford White, the former lover of Thaw's wife, popular actress Evelyn Nesbit—these reporters told the story as a moral drama, comparing Nesbit to "a flower that has been beaten down into the ground and despoiled of its beauty by a storm." A male newspaper reporter also covering the trial ridiculed them as "sob sisters," and the term soon came to mean female journalists who sympathized with their subjects. Dorothy Dix countered: "It is only the women whose eyes have been washed clear with tears who get the broad vision that makes them little sisters to all the world."[4]

FROM "FRONT-PAGE GIRLS" TO "ELEANOR'S GIRLS"

Just as women were employed to perform "stunts" and to "sob" to gain readers, they were hired to cover sensational crimes during the Jazz Age, which also saw the debut of a new kind of newspaper, the tabloid. Called "front-page girls," these reporters included Ishbel Ross, who covered the Hall-Mills murder case (a New Jersey choir director and his lover, supposedly slain by his enraged wife) and the Lindbergh baby kidnapping for the New York Herald Tribune; Grace Robinson, who covered the Ruth Snyder trial for the New York Daily News; Dorothy Ann Harrison of the Philadelphia Record, who received tips from that city's gangsters; and Mildred Gilman, a New York Journal reporter who specialized in digging up the details of scandalous crimes. Gilman also did story "stunts" such as descending to the bottom of a river in a diving suit. She fictionalized her experiences in a novel, made into a movie, titled Sob Sisters.

The value of "the woman's angle" was stressed in journalism career guides of the era. Ethel Brazelton, who taught "Journalism for Women" at Northwestern University's Medill School of Journalism during the 1920s, listed the qualities of a good reporter and then noted, "When to the suggested faculties the reporter adds the indefinable something called 'personality'—the ability, largely compounded of sympathy and understanding, to put himself in the place of another—reportorial work becomes excellent. It is because of the added value of such reporting that the woman reporter, the woman writer, endowed by nature with certain distinctive and valuable qualities and capabilities, is in the field to stay."[5] Between 1900 and 1930, the number of women in journalism grew from 2,000 to nearly 15,000. At a 1924 University of Missouri symposium on "Women and the Newspaper," Nebraska newspaper editor Marie Weekes explained the broader reasons for women's acceptance in the field: "A decade ago it was rare to find a woman in public life with the exception of school teachers.... The World War [I] and granting of equal suffrage changed all that and women are now being recognized as leaders in business, politics, the professions. In none of these is there more opportunity for women than in journalism."[6]

The truth was that American women's opportunities in journalism (and other fields) alternately expanded and contracted over the next two decades, depending on what was happening to American men. Women's numbers in the profession remained stagnant during the Depression, when many of their jobs were cut so that men could work. Still, a few women were nationally prominent in journalism during these years. *New York Times* foreign correspondent Anne O'Hare McCormick became the first woman to win the Pulitzer Prize in 1937. Two years later, *Time* magazine named Dorothy Thompson, a syndicated newspaper and magazine political columnist, one of the two most influential women in America, along with Eleanor Roosevelt.

It was Eleanor Roosevelt herself who perhaps did the most to advance the careers of women in journalism during the 1930s and early '40s. The First Lady declared that her press conferences could be covered by women only, and since she often made news on her own, every media outlet with a Washington bureau had to hire a woman. "The newspaper women have profited enormously by her attitude toward them," reported Ishbel Ross. "They have gained prestige, and their usefulness to their papers and press services has increased, not to mention the personal satisfaction they feel at having fireside standing in the White House."[7] Such reporters, who became known as "Eleanor's girls," included Bess Furman of the Associated Press, Kathleen McLaughlin and Genevieve Forbes Herrick of the *Chicago Tribune*, Ruby Black of the United Press, Dorothy Dorcas of the International News Service, and Emma Bugbee of the *New York Herald Tribune*. Bugbee, who reported on the suffrage campaign early in her career, worked for that paper for 56 years and covered Mrs. Roosevelt for 34 years.

WOMEN COVER WAR

World War II again provided opportunity for female journalists, 127 of whom were credentialed to cover the war itself. Peggy Hull, who had covered World War I from Europe, reported the Second World War from the Pacific for the *Cleveland Plain Dealer*. Other newspaper journalists included Doris Fleeson for the *New York Daily News*, Ruth Cowan for the Associated Press, and Marguerite Higgins for the *New York Herald Tribune*. Higgins, who not only covered but participated in the May 1945 liberation of the Dachau concentration camp, later would win the Pulitzer Prize for her coverage of the Korean War.

New York Times columnist Anne O'Hare McCormick interviewed Hitler, Mussolini, Stalin, and Churchill, yet also interpreted the conflict in terms of ordinary people. She began a 1945 column by referring to another journalist who had seen "a woman emerge from a cellar and, though her house was a ruin, proceed to sweep away the dust and rubble that covered the doorstep." She used this image to explain the position of European women at the end of the war: "everywhere, before the monster bulldozers arrive to clear paths for the armies through the debris left by the bombers, women instinctively seize their brooms in this futile, age-old gesture of cleaning up the mess the men have made.... [T]here are more women than men in Europe, widows of soldiers, widows of hostages, widows of the last war, and they are bound to try."[8]

Other wartime reporters worked for magazines and the new medium of radio. Margaret Bourke-White, one of *Life* magazine's original staff photographers, flew on bombing raids and photographed concentration-camp prisoners. *Collier's* magazine published war correspondence by Martha Gellhorn. Now remembered as one of Ernest Hemingway's wives, she had a career that extended from the Spanish Civil War to Vietnam. NBC radio carried reports from Helen Hiett in Europe and Irene Corbally Kuhn in the Pacific. From Europe, Mary Marvin Breckinridge made the first radio-news broadcast by a woman on CBS, which also employed Elizabeth Wason and Sigrid Schultz, who headed the *Chicago Tribune's* Berlin bureau.

POST-WAR YEARS AND THE GROWTH OF BROADCASTING

When men returned home at war's end, many female journalists lost their jobs or were demoted. Helen Thomas, who had been hired by United Press Radio because of the wartime shortage of male reporters, was put on the graveyard shift in its Washington bureau. By the early 1960s she was covering the White House along with Sarah McLendon. Thomas went on to become the first female president of the White House Correspondents Association and officer of the National Press Club. Known as the "Dean" of the White House Press Corps, she continued to report on this beat until her retirement in 2000.

Doris Fleeson also covered Washington politics, before the war for the *New York Daily News* and after it as a syndicated columnist, and in 1951 *Time* magazine named her one of the best newspaper reporters in Washington. Fleeson served as a role model for Mary McGrory, a *Washington Star* reporter who covered the McCarthy hearings in the 1950s and later, as a syndicated columnist herself, won a Pulitzer Prize for her commentary on Watergate. Some women reported on post-war politics from abroad, including foreign correspondents Flora Lewis, Marguerite Higgins, and Georgie Anne Geyer.

After the war, most women who were on the air had entertainment shows. One of the most popular was Mary Margaret McBride's *The Martha Deane Show* (her pseudonym)—a celebrity-interview program targeted toward

women—that began at New York's WOR in 1934 and lasted two decades. Women who wanted to broadcast news were told that their voices were not authoritative enough.

One exception was Pauline Fredericks, who in 1948 became the first woman to report network-television news. When Nancy Dickerson became CBS's first female Washington correspondent in 1960, she was cautioned by a male executive "not to giggle on the air." She went on to become a political commentator for NBC. Marlene Sanders joined ABC in 1964 to do a daily newscast called "Marlene Sanders and News with the Woman's Touch," and the same year she became the first woman to anchor a network evening news program. As late as 1970, however, NBC News President Reuven Frank told *Newsweek* that "audiences are less prepared to accept news from a woman's voice than from a man's." No woman had a regular weeknight-evening news-anchor spot until 1976, when Barbara Walters became the nation's highest-paid broadcaster by signing a $1 million contract with ABC.

CIVIL RIGHTS AND SOCIAL DISCONTENT

The civil-rights movement of the 1950s and '60s inspired white American feminists and would provide the legal basis for some female journalists' actions against employers in the 1970s. For African-American women, however, the era was one more chapter in a continuing struggle to be admitted to and taken seriously in the journalism profession.

A number of women had worked in the African-American press in the 19th and early 20th centuries. One was Marvel Cooke, who wrote for the NAACP magazine *The Crisis* under W. E. B. DuBois and then the black New York paper *The Amsterdam News*. For that paper, she covered the 1939 Lincoln Memorial concert by Marian Anderson, who had been barred by the Daughters of the American Revolution from performing in Constitution Hall. The African-American opera singer, Cooke wrote, "stood in quiet, majestic dignity on the steps of the white marble memorial to the emancipator ... and raised her glorious voice in stirring protest to the un–American attitude of the D. A. R."[9] Cooke became the first female African American to work on a mainstream newspaper, a liberal New York publication called the *Daily Compass*. To get her first story, she borrowed the tactics of the white "stunt reporters" before her and posed as a cleaning woman hired per day, a job she compared to slavery.

Charlayne Hunter-Gault was already famous, having been one of the first two African-American students to integrate the University of Georgia, when she began her career at *The New Yorker* magazine. She moved into broadcast journalism in Washington, became a reporter for the *New York Times*, and then returned to broadcast, winning two Emmy Awards and a Peabody Award for her work on PBS's *MacNeil-Lehrer Report*. Other African-American women who broke the color barrier in national news media during the 1960s were Dorothy Gilliam at the *Washington Post*, where she later became a columnist, and ABC News reporter Carole Simpson, who would lead female reporters' demands for equity in assignments two decades later.

White female journalists were attacked when they supported the protest movements of the '60s. When Hazel Brannon Smith, editor-owner of the *Lexington* (Miss.) *Advertiser*, used her newspaper to crusade for racial equality, her life was threatened. For this work, she became the first woman to win the Pulitzer Prize for editorial writing. ABC News's Marlene Sanders received snide letters for her coverage of the anti-war movement. One viewer wrote, "What a joke was the sob-sister act of Marlene Sanders on the news last night as she tried to put on a tear jerker for the poor dear Columbia University student who got his head bloodied...."[10]

The Vietnam War itself provided opportunities for newswomen. Some of the 267 American women credentialed to cover the war were veteran foreign correspondents, including Georgie Anne Geyer and Marguerite Higgins, who died of an illness she contracted there. After working for more than a decade on the women's page of the *New York Times*, Gloria Emerson was assigned to cover the war for that newspaper. Liz Trotta, NBC's first full-time female foreign correspondent, served three tours of duty and wrote a book about the experience.[11] It was in Vietnam that a female journalist, photographer Dickey Chappelle, was killed in combat.

FEMINISTS CHALLENGE TRADITIONS

In 1972, a new kind of women's magazine called *Ms.* was launched by a group of feminists and edited by Gloria Steinem. Because of its refusal to provide "complementary copy" for advertisers' products, it struggled for financial solvency, eventually becoming advertising-free. *Ms.* was the most visible of some 560 feminist periodicals begun in the late 1960s and early '70s. Most positioned themselves against the mass-circulation women's magazines, which had been the target of magazine writer Betty Friedan's 1963 book, *The Feminine Mystique*. They also dismissed newspaper women's pages—with their traditional coverage of the "four F's," food, fashion, family, and furnishings—as demeaning to women.

In fact, during the 1960s, several women's-page editors had used their sections as a way of covering social issues that were not getting as much coverage in national or metro pages. At the *Detroit Free Press*, Dorothy Jurney covered pregnancy among poor black teenagers and women's involvement in autoworkers' unions. Marj Paxson of the *Houston Post*, Vivian Castleberry of the *Dallas Times Herald*, and Marie Anderson of the *Miami Herald* covered child care, poverty issues, birth control, abortion, and the women's movement in their women's pages. Charlotte Curtis (who went on to be the first woman to edit the paper's op-ed page) used the *New York Times*' women's pages to satirize society leaders even while faithfully covering them—*Time* magazine called her "the sociologist on the society beat"—and wrote about the civil rights movement.[12]

Critics countered that all news was

"women's news" and that, even if women's pages covered important topics, those topics (especially the women's movement itself) were seen as less newsworthy when they were ghettoized in a separate section. By 1969, women's pages were being transformed into "style" sections, using the models set by the *Los Angeles Times* and the *Washington Post*. Although those two particular papers' sections pioneered quality feature writing, a more common result of this change was an increase in entertainment coverage at the expense of women's issues, without those issues being picked up by other sections of the paper. Meanwhile, the women who had been editing the sections were fired or demoted. One of them was Marj Paxson, who remembered, "the activists wanted the movement news off our pages, and in their eyes, we women's editors were traitors. When editors responded by changing women's sections to general interest feature sections, women's editors paid the price. We were not considered capable of directing this new kind of feature section. That was man's work."[13]

While such traditional jobs disappeared, women in print and broadcast media fought for the chance to get the high-visibility assignments and positions they had long been denied, and to get paid what their male colleagues were earning. In 1971, after 18 years of appeals, women in the Washington press corps were admitted to the National Press Club and were no longer confined to the balcony when covering events there. And during that decade, female employees filed and won class-action lawsuits against the Associated Press, the *New York Times*, *Washington Post*, *Newsweek*, *Reader's Digest*, and NBC. These gains created opportunities, most visibly in television, for journalists such as Jessica Savitch, Leslie Stahl, Andrea Mitchell, and Diane Sawyer. At the *New York Times* itself, Soma Golden became national editor, Maureen Dowd became a Washington political correspondent (and later columnist), and Anna Quindlen began a meteoric rise from metro reporter to op-ed columnist.

WOMEN AT THE TOP

For nearly the last quarter of the 20th century, American journalism schools turned out more female than male graduates, yet at its end, men still dominated the profession's top spots on both the editorial and business sides. In the mid–1990s, one in every three front-page newspaper bylines was a woman's, and one in five newsroom managers was female. In broadcasting, one in seven top network correspondents was female, as was one in 10 general managers or station managers, and no woman headed a national broadcasting or cable network.[14]

Even rarer were female owners of journalistic media. There were only a few such people throughout American history, all coming to their positions through birth or marriage. Like Miriam Leslie, Eliza Holbrook Nicholson (known as "Pearl Rivers") was advised to declare bankruptcy when her first husband died in 1876 and she inherited his business. Instead, she saved the *New Orleans Picayune*, the South's largest daily newspaper. Although her husband, *New York Herald Tribune* owner Ogden Reid, was still alive, Helen Rogers Reid was a force in that paper's management during the 1930s, advancing the careers of Dorothy Thompson and Marguerite Higgins. Eleanor "Cissy" Patterson, born into the Medill family that founded the *Chicago Tribune*, used inherited money to buy one of the Hearst papers, the *Washington Herald*, and ran it herself. Patterson went undercover, dressed in rags, to report on homelessness, she featured subjects of interest to female readers, she hired female editors, and she encouraged young women to enter the profession. In 1940, her niece, Alicia Patterson, founded the Long Island newspaper *Newsday*.

When *Washington Post* owner Eugene Meyer died, the paper passed not to his daughter Katharine, but to her husband, Phil Graham, despite his mental instability. Only after his 1963 suicide did she become its publisher—and soon took a risk by publishing Bob Woodward and Carl Bernstein's reports on Watergate. Graham felt that real progress for women in journalism could be made only collectively. She told a group of businessmen in 1970: "Management can't meet the challenge of discrimination against women by just promoting one or two women to highly visible jobs while the rest of the corporate structure remains a male preserve."[15]

FAMILIAR THEMES FOR A NEW MILLENNIUM

History supports Graham's suggestion. Collective changes were at least as important as women's individual successes in changing the professional landscape for women in 20th-century journalism. And while women moved onto beats once reserved for male reporters, they also changed the definition of journalism to include women's lives and concerns. After *New York Times* reporter Anna Quindlen won the 1992 Pulitzer Prize—not for front-page reporting, but for commentary about family life written for the Metro section—she acknowledged that her achievement was a legacy of the 1978 women's lawsuit against the newspaper. Quindlen was also following in the footsteps of 1980 Pulitzer winner Ellen Goodman, a *Boston Globe* columnist whose feminist vignettes located the political in the personal.

In the early 1990s, after two decades of declining newspaper readership among women, women's pages made a comeback in several major dailies, a move supported by some feminist editors and by the female Vice President for News of the Scripps Howard newspaper chain.[16] In 1999, Barbara Walters, who 23 years earlier had made history as the first woman to be paid as well as her male colleagues, was still a top earner, prestige intact, doing sympathetic televised interviews with people involved in sensational stories, much in the style of Dorothy Dix or Mildred Gilman.

These women and issues were not the end of the story, but merely the latest examples of the complexity of women's roles and goals in journalism. The questions Ishbel Ross raised in 1936 about "the woman's touch" and women's workplace status in journalism are still matters of debate today.

Selected Readings

Abramson, Phyllis Leslie. *Sob Sister Journalism.* Westport, Conn.: Greenwood Press, 1990.

Baker, Ira. L. "Elizabeth Timothy: America's First Woman Editor." *Journalism Quarterly* 54 (1977): 280–85.

Beasley, Maurine H., and Sheila J. Gibbons. *Taking their Place: A Documentary History of Women and Journalism.* Washington: American University Press, 1993.

Belford, Barbara. *Brilliant Bylines: A Biographical Anthology of Notable Newspaperwomen in America.* New York: Columbia University Press, 1986.

Bennion, Sherilyn Cox. "Woman Suffrage Papers of the West, 1869–1914." *American Journalism* 3 (1986): 125–41.

Brown, Charles B. "A Woman's Odyssey: The War Correspondence of Anna Benjamin." *Journalism Quarterly* 46 (1969): 522–30.

Chudacoff, Nancy Fisher. "Woman in the News 1762–1770—Sarah Updike Goddard." *Rhode Island History* 32–33 (Fall 1973): 98–105.

Collins, Jean E. *She Was There: Stories of Pioneering Women Journalists.* New York: J. Messner, 1980.

Demeter, Richard L. *Primer, Presses and Composing Sticks: Women Printers of the Colonial Period.* Hicksville, N. Y.: Exposition Press, 1979.

Endres, Kathleen L. "The Symbiotic Relationship of Eleanor Roosevelt and the Press: The Pre-War Years." *Midwest Communications Research Journal* 2 (1979): 57–65.

Endres, Kathleen. "Jane Grey Swisshelm: 19th Century Journalist and Feminist." *Journalism History* 2 (1975): 128–32.

Henry, Susan. "Colonial Woman Printer as Prototype: Toward a Model for the Study of Minorities." *Journalism History* 3 (1976): 20–24.

List, Karen. "The Media and the Depiction of Women: The Role of Women in the New Republic." Chap. 6 in Wm. David Sloan and James D. Startt, eds., *The Significance of the Media in American History.* Northport, Ala.: Vision Press, 1994.

Marzolf, Marion. *Up from the Footnote: A History of Women Journalists.* New York: Hastings House, 1977.

Mills, Kay. *A Place in the News: From the Women's Pages to the Front Page.* New York: Columbia University Press, 1990.

Oldham, Ellen M. "Early Women Printers of America." *Boston Public Library Quarterly Journal* 10 (January 1958): 6–26; (April 1958): 78–92; (July 1958): 141–53.

Robertson, Nan. *The Girls in the Balcony: Women, Men and The New York Times.* New York: 1992.

Ross, Ishbel. *Ladies of the Press.* 1936; reprint ed., New York: Arno Press, 1974.

Sanders, Marlene, and Marcia Rock. *Waiting for Prime Time: The Women of Television News.* Urbana and Chicago: University of Illinois Press, 1994.

Schilpp, Madelon Golden, and Sharon M. Murphy. *Great Women of the Press.* Carbondale: Southern Illinois University Press, 1983.

Sebba, Anne. *Battling for News: The Rise of the Woman Reporter.* London: Hodder & Stoughton, 1993.

Smith, Henry Ladd. "The Beauteous Jennie June: Pioneer Woman Journalist." *Journalism Quarterly* 40 (1963): 169–74.

Streitmatter, Rodger. *Raising Her Voice: African-American Women Journalists Who Changed History.* Lexington: University Press of Kentucky, 1994.

Zuckerman, Mary Ellen. *A History of Popular Women's Magazines in the United States, 1792– 1995.* Westport, Conn.: Greenwood Press, 1998.

Notes

1. Ishbel Ross, *Ladies of the Press* (1936; reprint ed., New York: Arno Press, 1974), 7–8, 12–13.

2. Fanny Fern, *Ruth Hall and Other Writings*, ed. Joyce Warren (New Brunswick, N.J.: Rutgers University Press, 1986), 294.

3. Grace Greenwood, quoted in Maurine H. Beasley and Sheila J. Gibbons, *Taking Their Place: A Documentary History of Women and Journalism* (Washington: American University Press, 1993), 98.

4. Dorothy Dix, *New York Journal*, 26 January 1907.

5. Ethel M. Colson Brazelton, *Writing and Editing for Women* (New York: Funk & Wagnalls, 1927), 3. In "Construction of Gender in Newsreporting Textbooks, 1890–1990," *Journalism Monographs* 135 (October 1992), Linda Steiner notes that of nine journalism textbooks solely authored by women, seven were published between 1926 and 1936, the time when "women's journalism" became a part of journalism-school curricula; six of them stressed this type of work (12).

6. Mrs. Marie Weekes, "Journalism as a Career for Women," *The University of Missouri Bulletin: Women and the Newspaper* 25, no. 26 (10 September 1924): 12.

7. Ross, *Ladies of the Press*, 322.

8. Anne O'Hare McCormick, "Abroad: Bulldozer and the Woman with a Broom," *New York Times*, 28 March 1945.

9. Marvel Cooke, "New Laurels for Marian Anderson," *The Amsterdam News*, 5 April 1939, 1.

10. Marlene Sanders, quoted in Marlene Sanders and Marcia Rock, *Waiting for Prime Time: The Women of Tele-vision News* (Urbana: University of Illinois Press, 1988), 102.

11. Liz Trotta, *Fighting for Air: In the Trenches with Television News* (New York: Simon and Schuster, 1991).

12. "Sociologist on the Society Beat," *Time*, 19 February, 1965, 51, cited in Marilyn S. Greenwald, *A Woman of the Times: Journalism, Feminism, and the Career of Charlotte Curtis* (Athens: Ohio University Press, 1999), 77.

13. "Marjorie Paxson" [interview], quoted in Judith G. Clabes, ed., *New Guardians of the Press: Selected Profiles of America's Women Newspaper Editors* (Indianapolis: R. J. Berg & Co., 1983), 125.

14. Junior Bridge, "Diversity's Slide," *Quill*, April 1997, 46; Jean Otto, "A Matter of Opinion," *Media Studies Journal: The Media and Women Without Apology* 7, nos. 1–2 (Winter/Spring 1993), 158; Junior Bridge, "The Changing News Agenda: New Beats for Men," *Women, Men and Media Report* (1997), n. p.; Elizabeth A. Rathbun, "Woman's Work Still Excludes Top Jobs," *Broadcasting & Cable*, 3 August 1998, 22, 24.

15. Katharine Graham, quoted in Marion Marzolf, *Up from the Footnote: A History of Women Journalists* (New York: Hastings House, 1977), 114.

16. Colleen Dishon, a former women's-page editor of the previous era and a self-defined feminist, was the first to reinstitute women's pages (called "Womanews") at a major daily, the *Chicago Tribune*, in 1991. The following year, Susan Miller, vice-president for news of Scripps Howard Newspapers, noted the decline in female readership and called the abolished women's section "a strength that newspapers have lost" ("Opportunities Squandered—Newspapers and Women's News," *Media Studies Journal: The Media and Women Without Apology*, 174).

10

Publishers

FRED BLEVENS

For much of American history, publishers have played a critical role in politics, social change, and community building. They have come from all kinds of ethnic and socioeconomic backgrounds, parlaying their smarts and work ethic into successful careers and often becoming publishers by paths considered unconventional in other industries. They have started as printer apprentices as young as seven; farm kids seeking success in the big city; heirs endowed with millions to invest; revolutionaries seeking independence; and business people skilled at controlling a property for an off-site owner.

From colonial times to the millennium, thousands of young men and women have aspired to own and publish their own newspaper. Some, like William Randolph Hearst, wanted it before spending a single day in the newsroom or backshop. Others, like Joseph Pulitzer, came up through the ranks. Some, like the handful of successful colonial publishers, came across it as a side business for their printing or bookstore operations. A few postmasters found publishing to be a logical—and profitable—extension of their primary business. Others, like revolutionary printers and abolitionist publishers, rolled out papers for a specific cause. Most publishers in history, however, achieved varying levels of success with diverse combinations of determination, ability, entrepreneurial spirit, and business acumen.

There is no established pattern, no accepted norm for a career path leading to the publisher's office. In the more than 300 years of American newspaper publishing, the oppor-

tunities to become a publisher have expanded and constricted in an industry that grew beyond bounds, then contracted in a long march toward consolidation. As each year passes, the only unregulated monopoly industry in the country becomes more homogenous and more concentrated in fewer and fewer hands. Enmeshed in this gloomy, depressing picture, however, is a long and rich history of newspaper publishing in America. From bootstrap successes to empires built on family largesse, newspaper publishers have been—and remain—some of the most fascinating characters in the nation's history.

A few publishers emerged as exemplars in each of three eras of newspaper publishing evolution in the 18th century, development in the 19th century, and maturation-consolidation in the 20th century.

EVOLUTION, REVOLUTION, AND CONSTITUTION

The first publishers in the New World established the foundation of American newspapers by using the newspaper trade to extend their roles as postmasters, booksellers, and printers. Many started very young, taking printer apprenticeships in their pre- or early-teens, and often starting their own newspapers in their late teens or early 20s. Several of the most successful were endowed by printer legacies and/or by family fortunes. During the first 100 years, news developed as a commodity, although it usually took a position behind profit and views on social issues rooted in spiritual or political conflicts.

Benjamin Harris, recognized as the nation's first newspaper publisher with only one issue of *Publick Occurrences* in September 1690, was a British recalcitrant who fled his homeland for Boston in 1686 after numerous publishing clashes with the Crown. He was an Anabaptist, Whig, and veteran London publisher whose strong convictions on social issues and separation of church and state prompted several government raids on his print shop and a prosecution that pushed him to relocate in America. A highly regarded book merchant and widely read author of children's books, he arrived in Boston in 1688, successfully launching a bookstore and coffeehouse known for catering to women and the city's elite class. In Britain as well as the colonies, starting a newspaper was a way for Harris to expand his publishing business while expressing his deep-seated opposition to Catholicism and Anglicans.

The Harris model of newspapering in the colonies was well ahead of its time. Closed by opposition colonial rule, his paper had no immediate successors. Fourteen years later, John Campbell founded the *Boston News-Letter*, the country's first continuously operating paper. Unlike Harris, who sought to make money on doctrine, Campbell, an Anglican, was two years into his term as Boston postmaster, a position he assumed upon the death of his brother. Campbell, however, was the first of a long line of publisher-postmasters in the colonial period. Although not particularly skilled in journalism, he was the first to mass produce a handmade newsletter as a newspaper, sell ads to generate revenue, and take advantage of the free posting privileges afforded a postmaster.

Allied with an unpopular administration and unable to produce inspired content, Campbell lost his postmaster position in 1719 to William Brooker. Incensed by Campbell's refusal to give up the paper, Brooker started his own, the *Boston Gazette*, which, as the official organ of the colonial administration, went into competition against Campbell's *News-Letter*, sparking the nation's first newspaper war. Brooker's paper passed through four more

postmasters before becoming a true printer's paper in 1739, while Campbell continued operating the *News-Letter* until 1722, when he handed over control to his friend, printer, and close associate Bartholomew Green.

By the early 1720s, colonial newspaper publishing was on the rise, having branched from Boston to New York and Philadelphia. By mid-century, with few exceptions, startup publishers increasingly were coming from printer-bookseller ranks, launching newspapers to leverage postmaster and colonial printer appointments.

James Franklin's *New England Courant* in August 1721 was the first continuously operating venture without initial postmaster support. Franklin, a printer sprung from the ranks of lengthy apprenticeship, had been producing Brooker's *Gazette* in its first year. He took over the *Courant* from its founders, Anglican rector John Checkley and physician William Douglass, after four issues. A mouthpiece for Anglican attacks on Puritanism and Cotton Mather's smallpox inoculation campaign, it folded after five years of inspired political bickering.[1]

As newspapering spread through the colonies, it also took on a sense of family with names such as Bradford and Franklin. Some of the most prominent early publishers were printer proprietors who served apprenticeships under their fathers or brothers. In Philadelphia, Benjamin Franklin set up shop after learning the trade from brother James. Andrew Bradford did the same after apprenticing at his father's print shop in New York. He founded the *American Weekly Mercury* in 1719 and became Philadelphia's postmaster, a great advantage that Franklin stole when he purchased the *Pennsylvania Gazette* in 1729. Bradford's paper survived nicely, however, providing a stake for Bradford to reap sizable returns in land and minerals.

The Bradfords and Franklins also shared some common familial benefits. The Bradford family was involved in printing and bookselling for four generations on all sides of the family and both sides of the Atlantic. The family had amassed remarkable wealth, allying with the likes of William Penn to establish a network and bankroll that nearly guaranteed success on

American soil. The Franklins, two of America's most noted and respected early journalists, were not so pure in the blood of journalism, but they, too, had sprung from landed folk in Britain. Father Josiah Franklin fathered 17 children by two wives but managed to help his sons financially when they needed a pound or two in their many publishing ventures. Within a few decades, newspaper publishing in America was emerging from a sideline for booksellers and postmasters to a primary business for printers trained in the trade.[2]

As reading levels increased and political structures coalesced during the first half of the 18th century, publishers assumed an important part in rallying the colonies toward independence from Britain. Just as early publishers aligned themselves with religious doctrines of Puritans and Anglicans, revolutionary publishers had to choose between Patriots, some of whom became violently intolerant, and Tories, the traditional pro–British party. While the core of publishing slowly changed to one of revolutionary cause, the trend toward printer-publishers picked up momentum and new, energetic talent brought competition to the established guard.

William Bradford, Andrew's father, lost his eight-year monopoly in New York in 1733, when John Peter Zenger, a struggling, young immigrant printer from Germany, challenged his *Gazette.* Zenger founded the *New York Weekly Journal* with backing from investors opposed to Governor William Cosby. Ironically, Zenger apprenticed under Bradford, Cosby's official colonial printer, for eight years, a term that concluded when Zenger was only 19.

Historians long have argued the importance of the press in the years leading up to and including the Revolutionary War. Most, however, have agreed that publishers were important players in the political maneuvering and positioning of the country against Britain. Although leaders of the charge again were printers and booksellers, they effectively were split from postmasters and official government printers who had to maintain allegiance to colonial rule. Not surprisingly, Boston saw an increase in upstart printers anxious to challenge the Crown, a development that portended great change in the publisher's traditional role. They were led by Benjamin Edes and John Gill, who in 1755 purchased the *Boston Gazette*, William Brooker's long-running postmaster paper. Edes, a member of the Loyal Nine and the Sons of Liberty, and Gill were printers by trade who had made money on the Stamp Act before adjusting to public sentiment and instigating revolution. Other independent, anti–Crown publishers followed, building a revolutionary crescendo of Patriot propaganda that peaked during the war. Printer Isaiah Thomas, indentured as an apprentice at age seven, founded the *Massachusetts Spy,* which carried some of the most powerful accounts of war and incendiary calls to action.

Although being an independent, revolutionary publisher offered excitement and the opportunity to make a difference, it did not promote profit or longevity. Most revolutionary publishers credited with advancing the Patriot cause died in poverty. At the height of the revolution, there were 70 papers being published, almost double the number at the beginning. By the end, there were only 35, and more than half of the upstart war papers died in the interim.

The alignment of political philosophies remained rigid in the post-revolutionary period but it was a time in which publishers began to realize the economic forces that would transform publishing into a profit-centered industry. Such an environment saw remarkable growth in newspapering from the East Coast to the far reaches of the frontier (roughly the western edge of what we now know as the Midwest). The number of papers increased from 50 in 1786 to 1,200 in 1833, a phenomenal growth period fueled by lucrative government printing contracts and other partisan political largesse that compensated nicely for meager advertising revenue. For most of these 50 or so years, publishers primarily depended on sponsoring parties—Federalists and Republicans—and steep subscription rates.

During the partisan period, the purpose of publishing was to win converts, keep the faithful, and attack the other side. In several cases, the political parties were the publishers. In others, individuals endeared themselves to political power players to garner lucrative government business. Either way, publishers were increasingly coming from the ranks of politics, law, and education, just to name a few. There were noteworthy examples of journeymen printers, but knowing printing mechanics no longer was the prerequisite to owning or operating a paper. Those who rose to become publishers also were having less financial difficulty than were the upstart publishers from the hard-scrabble days in the colonies.

William Cobbett, for example, was a British subject who fled to America in 1793 to escape the heat of the French Revolution. He intended to start a school, a natural extension of his career as a tutor, but he went to work instead for pamphleteer Thomas Bradford in Philadelphia to cover Congress. He founded the *Political Censor*, a monthly, in March 1796, replacing it the next year with *Porcupine's Gazette*, a four-page daily whose primary purpose was to serve President John Adams.[3] Benjamin Russell, publisher of the Federalist *Massachusetts Centinel* in 1784, had apprenticed under Isaiah Thomas and then supervised the apprenticeship of John Fenno, who founded the *Gazette of the United States*, the mouthpiece of the Federalist party. Noah Webster founded the Federalist *Commercial Advertiser* and *Spectator* with no apprenticeship training and only after draining his farmer family's coffers to earn a degree from Yale.

Webster, who also married into a wealthy family, was not the only silver spoon case—or opportunist—during the period. Anti-Federalist publisher Benjamin Franklin Bache, who founded the *Aurora* in Philadelphia, apprenticed comfortably in Europe and the States under Benjamin Franklin, his wealthy and connected grandfather. Samuel Harrison Smith was awarded the bachelor's and master's from Penn before using a couple of early, ill-fated publishing ventures to earn Thomas Jefferson's invitation to publish the *National Gazette*, the Republican mouthpiece in the new capital of Washington.[4] Duff Green parlayed a government-surveying contract into lucrative land speculation in Missouri and then turned a fortune in a variety of St. Louis businesses, including the *St. Louis Enquirer*. In 1824, on in-

vitation of Andrew Jackson, he sold the *Enquirer* and moved to Washington to buy the party-funded *United States Telegraph* and fiercely oppose the re-election of John Quincy Adams, a position he would reverse in the years leading to the Civil War.

These men were among the most influential—and wealthiest—publishers of the young nation. Famine accompanied feast, however, and as years marched on, successful publishers—even those under subsidy of the post office, colonial endorsement, or party affiliation—were forced to realize the importance of good business as well as good journalism. Half the more than 1,000 newspapers founded before 1821 died within two years.

DEVELOPMENT OF PUBLISHING AS BIG BUSINESS

Although newspaper circulations jumped considerably, readership was homogenous during the first two decades of the 19th century. Papers were expensive at six pennies and were distributed only through subscriptions to readers who could afford them or appreciate their ponderous and often partisan content.

All that changed in the 1830s, however, in a quick succession of events that, like the early years of American newspapers, got off to a rocky start. On January 1, 1833, Horace Greeley launched the *New York Morning Post*, a disastrous and short-lived financial venture whose first issue came the day after a devastating blizzard. Greeley, a poor and self-educated Vermont farm boy who apprenticed at age 15, and investor Horatio David Sheppard, a medical doctor, were testing Sheppard's street-vendor theory that drastically reducing prices would convince readers they were getting a paper almost free.

Sheppard's dream materialized successfully eight months later with Benjamin Day, a printer who completed a six-year apprenticeship at age 20 and then founded the *New York Sun* three years later with meager personal savings. About a third of Day's first issue on

September 3, 1833, contained advertising, much of it copied from other papers, and it sold for one penny. James Gordon Bennett, a British seminary dropout who wandered around the states in various newspaper writing jobs, published the first issue of the *New York Herald* on May 6, 1835. Horace Greeley returned in 1841 with the *New York Tribune*, the third of the major penny papers.

In 1851, the *Times* entered the market as the fourth major penny paper in New York City. Founded by George Jones and Henry Raymond, a hustling 30-year-old journalist who started his career working for Greeley, the *Times* was intent on capturing a quieter and conservative audience. Raymond, whose father mortgaged the family farm to send his son through the University of Vermont, did no formal apprenticeship in journalism, though he wrote regularly for newspapers and magazines. He bounced between writing, teaching, and aspirations of higher education, all the while advancing a Republican political career. He formed a partnership with Jones, an Albany banker who had worked for Greeley on the business side. Under their arrangement, Jones and fellow Albany banker Edward B. Wesley staked $40,000 to Raymond, who would serve as editor and receive half the number of shares claimed by Wesley and Raymond. The paper had a startup circulation of 10,000, rising to 24,000 after one year, but it was not generating enough revenue to make a profit. Jones had become ill. So Wesley closed his bank business and moved to the *Times* offices in Manhattan, where he, as 40 per cent investor, used his business acumen to make the paper profitable. Although the paper lost momentum after Raymond's death, falling deeply into a $1,000-a-day debt, the modern publisher model—ownership shares distributed among partners of editors, publishers, and investors—survived through the next century.[5]

In the second half of the 19th century, publishers transformed their newspapers into finely tuned businesses, placing an increasing emphasis on their commercial role in their communities and the nation. Shifting demographics, specifically increased foreign immigration and rapid movement toward the Pacific

coast, brought new circulation opportunities. The industrialization and commercialization of urban centers produced revenue opportunities through advertising. News earned its now common position as more important than editorials, and publishers (often the primary owners) found a great source of capitalization in the stock market. Smart and successful publishers entering this rapidly changing landscape were those who shed the last vestiges of partisanship.

Such radical changes in publishing sometimes required new blood in old veins. The proprietors who once were pioneers—Raymond, Greeley, Bennett—were dying off figuratively and literally, leaving their papers to a younger, more sophisticated class of owners and bosses. The challenge for this new breed was not in disseminating views and promoting causes but in capturing more revenue than the rest of the field. This stage in the maturation of the American press was fueled by a convergence of publishing roles and spheres that previously had not been tied together—and that remain inextricably connected today. The informational role in news and advertising formed the symbiotic relationship that drove phenomenal growth. Between 1860 and 1880, the number of daily newspapers increased from 387 to 971 with total circulation rising from about 1.5 million to more than 3.5 million. By the turn of the century, nearly 2,000 daily newspapers were in operation, with almost half of those starting up during the final two decades.

Leading the new generation of publishers was a young journalist from St. Louis, Joseph Pulitzer, who bought the failing *New York World* in 1883 and promptly re-energized concepts that Day, Bennett, and Greeley had developed. Often called the father of "new journalism," he had fled his native Hungary after his widowed mother married a man Pulitzer could not tolerate. He brought with him a fine education and the spoils of sophistication (but not the cash) wrought by several generations of family wealth.

For more than 15 years, Pulitzer owned the New York market, taking stands popular with the underclasses and spearheading campaigns to raise funds for community improvement projects.[6] In 1895, however, William Randolph Hearst, who openly idolized the frail and aging Pulitzer, entered the market. Like Pulitzer, who honed his style as publisher of the *St. Louis Post-Dispatch*, Hearst came from the smaller, more provincial *San Francisco Examiner*, a paper his father gave him several years after Randolph's expulsion from Harvard. While waiting for his father's gift, he had gone to work for Pulitzer in New York, specifically to adapt Pulitzer's methods for San Francisco and, later, to use against his mentor in New York. Armed with a fortune of $7.5 million from his mother, Phoebe Apperson Hearst, and with Pulitzer in poor health, Hearst bought the failing *New York Journal* that Pulitzer's brother Albert once owned.

The quiet but redeeming late-century development of the 1890s occurred when Adolph Ochs, also coming from the outside, bought and rejuvenated the failing *New York Times* in 1896. He had little formal education and was the son of German immigrants of little means. He started throwing newspapers at a young age in Knoxville, Tennessee, and then rehabilitated the *Chattanooga Times* at age 20.[7]

Consolidation: Publishers as Iconic Businessmen

The end of the century and beginning of the next also saw the emergence of chain ownership and the beginning of a shift from on-site, personal publishers to iconic businessmen controlling vast holdings. Hearst, Ochs, and Pulitzer, already revolutionaries in their outsider successes in New York, would establish publishing empires that remain today. They would be joined by a new set of entrepreneurs. E. W. Scripps, an Illinois farm boy whose family here and in England had been in newspaper publishing for years, developed the modern chain model. By the time he joined his half-brother's *Detroit Advertiser and Tribune* in the composing and pressroom in 1872, the family name was associated with several newspaper properties. By the turn of the century, Scripps

and his family controlled a group of papers in Cleveland, St. Louis, Cincinnati, Covington (Ky.), Detroit, San Diego, Los Angeles, Kansas City, Seattle, and Akron.[8]

During this period, Harry Chandler, a New England farm boy forced west by poor health, was getting his start in the *Los Angeles Times* circulation department, working under founder Harrison Gray Otis, his soon-to-be father-in-law. Chandler was a logical successor to Otis because both shared the spirit of boosterism, conservative politics, and anti-union sentiment credited with helping develop sleepy Southern California into a major business, social, and political region. In a few decades, his West Coast start would result in the Times-Mirror Corporation, a media giant.[9]

Frank Gannett, a New York farm boy who developed circulation innovations with paper routes in his early teens, was starting his empire in 1900 as city editor of the *Ithaca News*. A newsboy and entrepreneurial hustler from a humble family, he turned from his news duties early on to develop business practices that would maximize profits and efficiency and revolutionize the business of newspapering. Eventually, he owned scores of papers in one of the country's largest chains.

S. I. Newhouse, who started ferrying papers as a youngster in New York, teamed with his brothers and sisters to launch Newhouse Newspapers from the *Staten Island Advance* in 1922. Unlike Gannett, Newhouse spent little time in news, preferring instead to earn a law degree, which he used very little, and to manage the business side. By the time he died in 1979, he had built the nation's second-largest chain, second only to Gannett Newspapers.[10]

John Knight, the son of *Akron Beacon-Journal* publisher Charles Knight, joined his father's paper in 1920 and was named managing editor five years later. In 1933, the elder Knight died, leaving his son with a paper with Depression losses made worse by a town almost solely dependent on automobile tires. Despite the odds, the young Knight saved the paper from bankruptcy and then went about amassing newspaper properties in Detroit, Miami, and Philadelphia, to name just three. The chain merged with Ridder newspapers in 1974, forming what is now Knight-Ridder, a group known for quality journalism and winning Pulitzer Prizes.

These dramatic developments forced the publishing role to change, primarily by ending the end of the popular editor-and-publisher (usually primary owner) era and beginning today's arrangement of corporate landlords and tenant or caretaker publishers. In an industry destined to constrict, the publisher's new role was right in line with the prevailing business trends of the century. Newspapers, like all industries, would "merge" and consolidate at a steady rate, primarily because market economies dictate efficiency and higher margins. Interestingly, most of the media barons who aggressively sought consolidation forbade their executives from using the term "chain." Newhouse, Knight, Scripps, and Gannett were adamant that their papers were "groups" or "families."

This new breed of publishers also had to contend with emerging forms of mass media. Although advertising had been (and remains today) an important partner with newspapers since penny press days, radio and television became the dominant mediums and primary competitors for ad dollars proliferating in tandem with the capitalist economy. As the number of newspapers decreased, so did their share of advertising.

The indicative trend that occurred in the first half of the 20th century was the sharp decrease in competitive newspaper markets. At the end of the 19th century, competitive markets outnumbered non-competitive ones by nearly 200. By 1915, the gap had closed to near even. Between World Wars I and II, competing markets dwindled from an all-time high of about 650 to a low of 117. During the same period, monopoly markets increased from a little more than 450 to nearly 1,300. By 1945, the total number of papers had decreased to less than 1,800.

The inter-war period did not signal the end or a crippling of the industry. Market correction, driven by mergers, buyouts, and consolidations, was occurring in nearly all sectors of the economy. Newspaper owners and publishers were finding their proper position in the overall marketplace as well as the diversifying industry of mass communication. Those who survived were the aggressive corporate giants. Through merger, Hearst was responsible for the closure of 16 papers between 1918 and 1928. Scripps claimed 15 more between 1923 and 1935. Chain growth went from eight groups controlling 27 newspapers in 1900 to 63 owning 328 dailies in 1935 (more than 40 per cent of total daily readership). In 2000, chains controlled more than 80 per cent of national circulation.

One of the biggest challenges facing publishers during the last half of the 20th century was the conversion of afternoon and all-day papers to morning delivery. Through most of American history, afternoon papers had been a dominant force, servicing a labor-intensive constituency that worked early hours, leaving time for casual reading later in the day. As the economy shifted to a service orientation—and, therefore, later work shifts—readers had time in the morning and none later in the day. Afternoon and evening papers also had difficulty competing with the rise of evening television news, which at least gave the appearance of being fresher than the newspaper produced earlier in the day. The changing economic landscape also came to bear on metro papers trying to distribute from downtown plants hemmed in by afternoon rush-hour traffic.

Perhaps most important, however, was the change in the fundamental position of publisher. Instead of being powerful and influential, popular or unpopular on-site owners and community players, publishers evolved into chief executives for off-site owners. That did not mean that these men (and most were and are men) were not concerned about community, politics, and social issues, but their jobs depended (and still depend) on returning margins sufficient to meet demands of the home office. Being a publisher during the 20th century became a job whose stake was in a good salary, loyalty, and business sense rather than in hopes of gaining and/or maintaining ownership in the newspaper property. The position of the publisher/owner/editor that developed during the first 200 years was split three ways— the distant owner (and, usually, the stockholders), the local publisher (always picked by the home office), and the chief news executive (usually picked by the home office).

With the shifting of duties and responsibilities that mergers and consolidations brought on, local publishers primarily came from the business side of newspapers. They seldom earned recognizable names in journalistic circles, though their chief news executives often did. In the Gannett chain today, for example, publishers are responsible for nightly electronic fund transfers to the home office in Rochester, New York. At Gannett as well as other chains, breaking the annual budget for normal operations usually earns immediate dismissal and newspaper policies are consistent, if not identical, from paper to paper. Armed with corporate manuals and standardized reporting requirements, the modern newspaper publisher must supervise annual operating budgets from a half million to hundreds of millions of dollars. They direct personnel departments with responsibility over a workforce ranging from one or two to thousands of employees.

DÉJÀ VU ON THE NEW FRONTIER

Publishing newspapers always has been and always will be a unique job. Unique because it demands that one person balance his or her allegiances to the informational, social, political, and commercial roles of newspapering. Unique because it has survived, even thrived, long after great minds predicted its demise. Whether it survives through the 21st century will depend on how it addresses its newest role in information technology.

In this, the fifth role since inception on American soil, newspaper publishers are planning and debating an industry destined for more consolidation, more interaction, and more Earth-friendly operations. No longer can they be comfortable in supervising single properties, worrying whether revenue and profit margins satisfy the home office in some distant city. Today, their publishing roles are expanding to the Internet and to cross-media part-

nerships that are melding the traditional information channels into a digitized, one-wire-per-home world.

Like their postmaster counterparts two centuries ago and the Pulitzer types at the turn of the last, traditional publishers are being challenged by a new breed of young, spirited entrepreneurs. These upstarts, armed with browsers and finely honed computer acumen, are using the World Wide Web as the new medium of democratization, the First Amendment, and, of course, free enterprise. News publishing, once considered the exclusive domain of those who could afford a press, is as simple as reporting and writing a story, then hitting a few keystrokes to put it up for the world to see—in much greater numbers than ever was or will be possible with a traditional press.

As we have seen, newspaper publishers have compromised with or accommodated nearly every challenge they have faced during the past 300 years. They still preside over the only industry capable of putting a different product on your porch or doorstep each day nearly every day of the year. Even with such a remarkable and collective record of accomplishment, they know information technology offers the biggest and most unpredictable challenge.

Selected Readings

Cebula, James E. *James M. Cox: Journalist and Politician.* New York: Garland, 1985.

Cochran, Negley. *E. W. Scripps.* New York: Harcourt Brace Jovanovich, 1933.

Darrach, Henry. *Bradford Family, 1660–1906.* Philadelphia, 1906.

Fine, Barnett. *A Giant of the Press.* New York: Editor & Publisher Library, 1933.

Fonzi, Gaeton. *Annenberg: A Biography of Power.* New York: Weybright & Talley, 1970.

Franklin, Benjamin IV, ed. *Boston Printers, Publishers, and Booksellers: 1640–1800.* Boston: G. K. Hall, 1980.

Johnson, G. W. *An Honorable Titan: A Biographical Study of Adolph S. Ochs.* Westport, Conn.: Greenwood Press, 1970.

Leapman, Michael. *Arrogant Aussie: The Rupert Murdoch Story.* Secaucus, N. J.: Lyle Stuart, 1985.

Moore, John W. *Printers, Publishing, and Editing: 1420–1886.* New York: Burt Franklin, 1968.

Pulliam, Russell. *Publisher: Gene Pulliam, Last of the Newspaper Titans.* Ottawa, Ill.: Jameson, 1984.

Seitz, Don. *The James Gordon Bennetts.* Indianapolis: Bobbs-Merrill, 1928.

Seldes, George. *Lords of the Press.* New York: Julian Messner, 1938.

Swanberg, W. A. *Citizen Hearst.* New York: Charles Scribner's & Sons, 1961.

Swanberg, W. A. *Pulitzer and the New York World.* Princeton: Princeton University Press, 1966.

Swanson, Walter S. J. *The Thin Gold Watch, A Personal History of the Newspaper Copleys.* New York: Macmillan, 1964.

Thomas, Dana L. *The Media Moguls.* New York: Putnam: 1981.

Waldrop, Frank C. *McCormick of Chicago.* Englewood Cliffs, N.J.: Prentice Hall, 1966.

Notes

1. Clarence S. Brigham, "James Franklin and the Beginnings of Printing in Rhode Island," *Massachusetts Historical Society Proceedings* 65 (March 1936): 536–44.

2. See Henry Darrach, *Bradford Family, 1660–1906* (Philadelphia: 1906).

3. William Cobbett, *The Autobiography of William Cobbett: The Progress of a Plough-boy to a Seat in Parliament,* William Reitzel, ed. (London: Faber & Faber, 1947).

4. William E. Ames, *A History of the National Intelligencer* (Chapel Hill: University of North Carolina Press, 1972).

5. See Meyer Berger, *The Story of the New York Times* (New York: Simon & Schuster, 1951); and Elmer Davis, *History of the New York Times* (New York: New York Times, 1921).

6. W. A. Swanberg, *Pulitzer and the New York World* (Princeton: Princeton University Press, 1966).

7. H. E. Salisbury, *Without Fear or Favor: The New York Times and Its Times* (New York: Times Books, 1980).

8. Negley D. Cochran, *E. W. Scripps* (New York: Harcourt, Brace, 1933).

9. Robert Gottlieb and Irene Wolt, *Thinking Big: The Story of the Los Angeles Times, Its Publishers and Their Influence on Southern California* (New York: Putnam's, 1977).

10. Richard H. Meeker, *Newspaperman: S. I. Newhouse and the Business of News* (New Haven and New York: Ticknor & Fields, 1983).

11

Economics, Business, and Financial Motivations

DANE S. CLAUSSEN

An apocryphal story told for decades has a wise or boorish older man asking a journalism student or a young journalist, "What is the first responsibility of the press?" The budding journalist, pleased with his answer, replies, "To print the truth!" To which the curmudgeon responds, "No, the first responsibility of the press is to make a profit, so that it can afford to print the truth." Here a young journalist has his eyes opened to journalism as a business. The story implies that newspapers with low or no profits probably will not print what their consciences dictate, if that content might result in losing advertisers or subscribers and that the most profitable newspapers will publish on principle because they can afford to. The first implication generally has been accurate. But the second one has been accurate only some of the time, and today less so than ever.

Studying the relative financial and other motivations of American publishers is not easy, because hundreds of sympathetic, if not glowing, biographies, autobiographies, and histories have been written about less than admirable publishers. For example, Alden Blethen, owner of the *Seattle Times* from 1896 to 1915, was corrupted by politicians, often publicly drunk, and involved in numerous political and business scandals.[1] Yet his son, Clarance Brettun Blethen, consistently portrayed him as a progressive reformer and professional journalist who, among other feats, "Almost single-handed[ly] ... stopped gambling and regulated the saloons" of Seattle.[2] In Blethen's case, and in many others, we must look at what publishers did (and didn't do) rather than focusing solely on their words, and the words of their friends, family, and uncritical admirers.

Fighting for a cause or disseminating truth has usually been subordinate to other goals: making money, winning an election or otherwise influencing government, promoting a religion, or boosting egos of reporters and editors.[3] The profit motive should be no surprise. America has always had both a capitalistic economy and culture, and few individuals who have started mass media companies were independently wealthy first. Publishers eat first, and worry about politics, religion, social conditions, and culture mostly later.

PRINTERS, THE COLONIAL PRESS, AND THE AMERICAN REVOLUTION

The precursor to American newspapers, Increase Mather's 1689 *The Present State of New-English Affairs*, announced, "This is published to prevent false reports." The first real American paper, *Publick Occurrences, Both Foreign and Domestick*, made a similar claim. This was a noble goal, of course, but printing was neither cheap nor easy, and it seems unlikely that a colonist would rush to a press simply because he wanted to publish a "correction." Rather, colonial publications had to be worth the money by attracting the "right kind" of colonists for business and religious reasons.

In the early 17th century, printers continued to publish religious and political materials, but printing grew quickly because printers willing to publish either no political news or that acceptable to the government could make money. The *Boston News-Letter's* first issue in 1704 offered government-approved content; the second added advertising. Most early newspapers specifically announced their interest in publishing advertising.

The second major reason why printing became a business enterprise, not a political or religious endeavor, was experienced printers' immigration to America from Britain. After an English licensing law expired in 1694, London's printing business became highly competitive, forcing many printers to work elsewhere. In America, an English printer could and would make a living, a poor income being better than none at all. The supposedly successful 1748–1766 printing partnership of Benjamin Franklin and David Hall had gross revenues of £28,266 for printing, stationery, books, and publishing the *Pennsylvania Gazette*. This equals only about 20 per cent of what a successful printer in London would have grossed from printing alone. Many other American printers grossed only 70 to 80 per cent of what Franklin and Hall did. Many had one or more non-printing sources of income, but in their core business, a newspaper was the way to increase revenue. Three-quarters of American printers between 1700 and 1765 started papers. The newspaper "industry" went from three in 1720 to 22 in 1760. The *News-Letter*, the colonies' first successful paper, was started by a Boston postmaster/bookseller, but by 1750, printers controlled all three of Boston's papers.

Franklin and Hall made almost 60 per cent of their money with their newspaper, but they were unusual in having 2,500 to 3,000 subscribers in the 1760s when the average paper had about 600. No wonder Hall exaggerated, telling Franklin that "our Gazette spreads more generally than all the other Papers put together on the Continent."[4] Printing also developed into a family business—such as among the Franklins, Bradfords, and others—one that a family wouldn't stay in unless it were more profitable and less risky than alternatives.

By the mid–1700s, the newspaper business' future for the next 250 years already had been foreshadowed. In 1728, Samuel Keimer rushed to start his paper *The Universal Instructor in All Arts and Sciences: And Pennsylvania Gazette*, to grab subscription and advertising revenue before Franklin could start a paper. Franklin schemed to ruin Keimer, bought the paper cheaply, and started packing it with ads.[5] He was wealthy enough by 1750 to retire at 42. In 1741, the *Boston Journal* merged with the *Boston Gazette* to form the *Gazette and Journal*. Printing news from other papers and little local news, as was the custom, also was cheap. That practice foreshadowed later heavy uses of syndicated material.

The Stamp Act of 1765 was the catalyst for the motto "No taxation without representation," proclaimed by politicians and the press alike. But printers were fighting to stay in business as much as for principle, for the Act "threatened a great diminution" of their profits, which printers were "remarkable for the[ir] attention to."[6] Before and during the American Revolution, several newspapers planned to maximize revenues by attempting to stay neutral, but the public wouldn't let them. Economic motives also are apparent among printers such as *New York Mercury* publisher Hugh Gaine, who was bribed into supporting the British[7] or *Pennsylvania Evening Post* publisher Benjamin Towne, who also switched to British allegiance so that he could stay in business in Philadelphia. The editors changed their allegiances two times or more for profit, not principle. However, most of the 33 papers started during the Revolutionary War (18 of which died by the war's end) were started for political rather than economic reasons.

THE PARTY PRESS, 1783–1833

Between 1783 and 1833, the number of U.S. newspapers jumped from 35 to about

1,200. It was American media's most political period, during which the press shaped government and politics, and government and politics dominated the press' development. That the press was sincerely interested in politics is beyond doubt. Papers vigorously published articles about every election and national issue; and the press' growth was not due primarily to the growing population, economy, or number of printers. But if anything, the press' intensely political nature, combined with the growth of government and business, freed up most publishers from economics. They received the overwhelming majority of revenues, in amounts they couldn't control (as contrasted with publishers' efforts for advertising or circulation revenue from the public), from government or political parties. Publishers on an election's winning side didn't need to worry unless he angered his patrons. Those who lost their patronage saw their incomes plummet, and many folded. The *National Gazette*, despite 1,300 subscribers, ceased two weeks after its editor, Philip Freneau, lost his government clerkship and a State Department printing contract. New York City's *American Minerva* survived the loss of its Federalist backers around 1800 only by changing from covering politics to covering business.

Advertising revenues varied widely but weren't high. Papers also could not depend on diverse readers' paid subscriptions—weeklies' annual subscriptions cost $1 to $2, and dailies cost about $8. Most Americans couldn't afford a newspaper subscription at least until well into the 19th century, and tens of thousands of readers paid for their subscriptions by barter (particularly before the Civil War). In 1845, the *Memphis Commercial Appeal* announced that it could be paid with anything that the publisher could use in his home.[8] Many simply never paid. A New York editor working for Alexander Hamilton's *New York Post* told him in 1805 that less than 1 per cent of subscribers paid on time and 30 per cent never paid at all.[9] In the 1820s and 1830s, "subscribers" owed each of the two of the largest papers in the United States, Philadelphia's *Aurora* and Washington's *United States Telegraph*, as much as $80,000 at any given moment. That amount was double

what other large newspapers would earn from subscriptions in a year. Religious, farming, and other specialized newspapers apparently were especially hard hit by deadbeat readers.[10] By 1841, even a British magazine concluded: "probably in no other country where newspapers exist do the subscribers trouble themselves less about finding the means of paying their newspaper subscriptions when due, than they do in the United States."[11]

But almost all papers were doing job printing, and aid from political parties and government officials came in the form of loans and gifts of money to buy equipment and supplies or to fund early losses, printing contracts, government appointments (to postmaster or another post), help with obtaining subscriptions and distributing papers, and free news-editorial content.

Elsewhere in the country, as it grew, the number of newspapers increased faster than the number of towns that could support them, but would-be publishers rushed to get printing, legal notices, and other income in new towns. Editors were shameless boosters, believing that what was good for the town was good for the paper, and vice versa.[12] Of course, this was particularly true for editors enticed to a town by marketing-oriented business owners. Most continued to publish little local news, preferring to fill their pages with innocuous text from exchange papers and government documents. Certainly many frontier editors would not have braved moving equipment overland, unreliable deliveries of supplies and their own newspapers, diseases, native Americans, and often unpredictable government services unless they foresaw sufficient rewards.

THE PRESS IN ANTEBELLUM AMERICA, 1833–1861

Historians disagree about whether the penny press, the mass circulation one-cent newspapers pioneered by the *New York Morning Post* and *New York Sun* in 1833, was founded because of new journalistic ideas, increasing literacy, better technology, or a larger middle class that could advertise and subscribe. In any case, the often-cited notion that these papers started as an almost noble vehicle of new journalism for the masses or as a grand experiment (rather than for profit) is incomplete at best, and generally misleading. *Post* founder Dr. Horatio D. Sheppard was a young dentist with no background in printing or publishing and little interest in politics or religion. He launched the *Post* as quickly as possible, with little capital and no marketing, to beat potential competitors.

Horace Greeley, who was to found the *New York Tribune* in 1841 and run for president in 1872, worked for Sheppard, but even he admitted to no larger purpose. Young and broke, he reluctantly took the job only after Sheppard had attracted Greeley's best friend, Francis V. Story.[13] The *Post* died, as did Story soon afterwards (while bathing in the East River near Brooklyn), but cheap papers didn't. Later that year, Benjamin Day, an experienced compositor and printer, started the *New York Sun*, which included sensational and human interest-oriented news and plenty of advertising. His first issue promised to publish, "at a price within the means of everyone, all the news of the day, and at the same time afford an advantageous medium for advertising," but he didn't keep his promise about the news. The paper's profits grew quickly; but in 1838, Day, then only 28 years old, sold the paper for about $40,000, when profits declined a little due to the 1837 depression and two new competitors.[14] The paper in fact survived for about a century.

James Gordon Bennett in 1835 started the penny *New York Herald*. It generally avoided politics, published news rather than essays and editorials, and was brash, even scandalous. He seems to have been a misanthrope. Journalist Henry Villard, after meeting him, noted his "hard, cold, utterly selfish nature," and his "inability to appreciate high and noble aims." The paper used socially impolite words, such as "leg" rather than "limb," and bitterly attacked organized religion. In 1872, the *Tribune* concluded about the *Herald's* founding, "The paper immediately became disreputable and soon became popular. It offended all parties

and all creeds."[15] Equally important, Bennett required subscribers to pay in advance, published "Personals" ads, required advertisers to change their ads every day, and competed ruthlessly for news and subscribers, if not also advertisers. The bulk of revenues began shifting from readers to advertisers with penny papers.

Outside of New York, many newspapers continued to receive party and government support. Long-time *New York Herald* writer and historian Frederic Hudson wrote that through the 1840s a "journal of any respectability" had to obtain "pecuniary aid of party,"[16] and the *Philadelphia Public Ledger* noted in 1856 that "[t]he greater portion of the press of this country is, at the present time, nothing more than the vehicle of partisan intemperance."[17] Moreover, the more important advertisers were to newspapers, and the more competition newspapers had (which was intense in many cities from the 1830s until the 1920s), the more advertisers began to exercise direct and indirect influence on content. Advertisers' power was described and criticized at length as early as 1841[18] and 1859[19] and was one of Upton Sinclair's major complaints in his 1919 *Brass Check*. Readers found advertisements disguised as news, and blatant admissions of advertising's importance. As early as 1866, *Harper's New Monthly Magazine* ordered: "I. To Merchants: (1) Advertise. (2) Advertise liberally. (3) Advertise conspicuously. II. To the People at Large: (1) Read the Advertisements. (2) Study them, and verily they shall be for your profit."[20]

THE GILDED AGE

Newspapers carried little advertising until after the Civil War. Subscriptions and single copy sales composed the overwhelming majority of a publisher's income, and publishers still supplemented that with job printing and their other traditional income sources. Publishers had always weighed the effect of a predictably unpopular story or editorial, and usually only a few subscribers would cancel. Advertisers were not as forgiving. Hundreds and then thousands of publications battled for regional and national advertising dollars. In the 1830s, advertising might account for only 20 per cent of revenue, but that increased to about 44 per cent by 1879 and to about 55 per cent by 1900. (Today advertising creates 70–80 per cent of newspaper revenue, and it varies more widely for magazines.) The September 1894 *Fame* magazine noted—still true today—that readers "barely pay for the cost of the white paper" and publications had to cater to advertisers' interests.

Post-war publishers both chose and were forced by competition and increased equipment costs to manage their companies and the industry on a "business-like basis." In this, they were similar to other industries. The 1830s market economy had bloomed into today's modern economy before World War I. Advertising, labor unions, monopolies and resulting anti-trust laws, communication and transportation systems, even the income tax would emerge during this period. Publishing benefited from the telephone, Linotype, cheaper newsprint, syndicated content (through mailed printing plates or partially pre-printed papers), printing and then the professionalization of journalism through education, professional associations and trade publications. Today's newspaper is sometimes traced to William Rockhill Nelson, who started the *Kansas City Star* in 1880, and bought the *Kansas City Times* in 1901. He was a giant (figuratively and literally) of the late 19th- and early 20th-century journalism but was the first important publisher without a writing or printing background. He had entered the industry in 1879 in Fort Wayne, Indiana, after working as a lawyer and building contractor. While he was an important crusader for reform and growth, it should not be forgotten that he arrived in Kansas City by cold, business calculation. After researching cities nationwide, he chose three finalists and, from those three, decided he had the best chance of being successful in Kansas City.[21]

Today's newspapers are characterized primarily by groups, or chains, and an early chain-builder was Edward Willis Scripps and his family. Scripps' three older siblings founded the *Detroit Evening News* in 1873, with E. W. receiving a single share of stock because incorporation required five stockholders (the fifth was John S. Sweeney, their cousin). That single share of stock formed the basis for what became Scripps-McRae League, then Scripps-Howard and then E. W. Scripps Co. again. He was primarily an entrepreneur, more interested in starting businesses[22] than in writing, editing, or influencing politicians despite (or perhaps because of) working as the *Evening News'* city editor. In 1878, he got day-to-day operational control of a new Scripps family paper, the *Cleveland Penny Press*, but he was no happier as editor than as city editor. But being forced by his siblings to cut expenses by 25 per cent to begin making profits awakened him to management as a challenge, even a game. He was bored with daily operations in Cleveland within a year and, when the Scrippses started the *St. Louis Chronicle* in 1880—again with E. W. as editor—he was bored again in five months. He wrote his brother George, "I am not pleased with this slow pokey life of waiting for the paper to pay."[23] About the Cleveland paper, he wrote his sister that "it was never started for the purpose of accomplishing a great good," and that he took over the *Cincinnati Post* "to establish the paper on a self-supporting basis ... and cause it to make enough money to yield me an income of between five and six thousand a year."[24]

Scripps was what today is called a "visionary" executive with a "big picture." He wanted control of all four family papers, and in 1887 (at age 33), he made it, although his impatience with detail soon prompted him to give day-to-day management responsibilities to Milton McRae. Eventually, Scripps owned dozens of newspapers, the Newspaper Enterprise Association syndicate, the United Press Associations wire service, and other holdings. He developed modern newspaper management, with its performance-based budgets, its circulation marketing, and its strategic plans. It was only after he became successful at the newspaper game, using profits only as a scorecard and as raw material for the game's next round, that he became interested in journalism and political and social causes. But he would claim to always have been a crusader.

Scripps published the working class'

newspapers, but he targeted those readers in large part because others ignored them, not because he was full of sympathy for the poor.[25] He built his empire quickly, particularly after 1895 by taking on partners—usually the editor and business manager—who together held 49 per cent of a newspaper's stock. But he paid stock-holding employees less and forced them to sell their shares when the newspaper became profitable. He knew that the papers would become more profitable more quickly with stock-holding. He supported organized labor, but paid his own employees poorly. He became and stayed wealthy while believing that wealth ruins a person's character.[26] Through trusts, he saddled his son, his grandchildren, and his great-grandchildren with control of his company, as if to play a cruel prank from the grave. And besides endowing the Scripps Institution of Oceanography and Miami University's Foundation for Population Research, he was not generous to charities. Despite his dislike of advertising,[27] he didn't try an adless newspaper until 1911. Even though his Chicago *Day Book* finally had become profitable (he also could have afforded an unprofitable paper), he killed it in 1917. His business philosophies are summarized by his prioritization of three directions he gave at his 1908 retirement: (1) make money, (2) obey the Ten Commandments, and (3) serve the workingman. These were not entirely consistent with his early career's refrain: "God damn the rich and God help the poor."[28]

Another giant of the period, William Randolph Hearst, was not a talented businessman. He was given his first paper, the *San Francisco Examiner*, and much of his later success in New York City competing against Pulitzer's *World* was due to building on Pulitzer's innovations. Hearst overextended himself and during the Great Depression was on the verge of bankruptcy. He sold real estate, radio stations, and part of his art collection, plus killed unprofitable newspapers to survive. He always had been more interested in politics than in profits, but he didn't want to lose money.[29]

A third giant of the period, Joseph Pulitzer, started in journalism in 1867 at a German-language newspaper and ended up owning the *St. Louis Post-Dispatch* (1878) and the *New York World* (1883). He is given credit for having revolutionized American journalism during his career by adding sports news, what used to be called "women's news," cartoons, and other common parts of today's papers. The longer he ran the *World*, the more he crusaded for the poor. His last 10 years are admired for his journalistic integrity and public service. But like Scripps, Pulitzer had not always been primarily motivated by public service through journalism. He dabbled in law and politics for six years in the 1870s, after cashing out of the German-language paper and a small daily he briefly owned for a total of $50,000. He re-entered the business only in 1878 when he bought the *St. Louis Dispatch* in a bankruptcy auction for $2,500 and was able to immediately merge it with the *Post*. By 1882, the *Post-Dispatch* was netting $45,000 per year. In New York, Pulitzer crusaded against government corruption, business fraud, and urban life's special problems. But earlier in St. Louis, he was concerned with the problems of the middle class and small businessmen, such as attacking monopoly businesses or vice (which concerned the middle class far more than the working class).

The period's "giants" are recalled because of their exceptional nature. Elsewhere, individuals who, like William Rockhill Nelson, were neither journalists nor printers by trade jumped into the business to profit from dramatic increases in advertising and population (driven largely by immigration). So many dailies were founded in the late 19th and early 20th centuries that their number reached its peak in 1915 and has been declining since.

Moreover, modern journalism ethics were not balancing the scramble for profits. If large city publishers were assumed to be more independent than those in small towns, the case of Alden Blethen is instructive. He prostituted first his *Minneapolis Tribune* and, after he sold it, the *Seattle Times* as well.[30] For example, in exchange for $5,000, the *Times*—then edited by Blethen—supported the senatorial candidacy of Watson Squire. Squire himself paid $3,000, and Blethen, his son Joseph, and their partner Otis Moore used the $5,000 to buy the newspaper! Blethen, doing nothing for the money other than editorializing for Squire, claimed he had not sold the paper's endorsement. He claimed:

> The contract under which I borrowed three thousand dollars of you in the winter of 1897 was a mutual contract and there were therefore mutual obligations. You wanted the support of *The Times* both locally, editorially, and specially from Olympia where the contest for United States Senator was going on…. Moreover to have accepted a right-out cash proposition of even the amount of money which I received from you and have the same liquidated by the kindly work I did for you would have been a direct sale of the editorial influence of the paper, whatever it is-and I have never made such a trade in my life.[31]

Journalism on the country's western frontier has been romanticized for the public by such books as David Fridtjof Halaas' *Boom Town Newspapers*, which argues that frontier newspapers were most concerned with improving day-to-day life in their circulation areas, and Robert F. Karolevitz's *Newspapering in the Old West*, which describes newspapering as an adventure or game. Western editors did serve their readers. They published news from far away, maybe even from a local's home town, they published news and advertising for far-flung residents in sparsely populated areas, and often they provided miners, farmers and saloonkeepers with their only reading matter. But Barbara Cloud concludes in her *Business of Newspapers on the Western Frontier* that the region's editors ultimately served others primarily to serve themselves. An apparently typical editor said in 1878, "In these degenerate days newspapers are run, not for glory, but for money. It is purely and strictly a matter of business."[32] Publishing in settled farming areas often was avoided because less cash was available there than in mining towns. And working for better day-to-day living was not necessarily a high priority in mining towns, when papers' readers and advertisers were more interested in saloons, prostitution, and other non-"family values."

Printers often settled where they were assured of obtaining government contracts for legal advertising or job printing, or where they were sure they could obtain real estate ads from railroads and others. Many western newspapers were packed with stories of cheap, fertile land; booming gold and silver mines; cooperative Indians; and small towns that boasted many of the same attractions as San Francisco. These newspapers were largely intended to be subscribed to by Easterners with money to invest, not local residents. Hundreds of printers-cum-editors moved to small towns in which they knew few if any people and to which they had no allegiance. If that town wasn't profitable for them, they would simply move to another one. Editors sought markets with good economies and/or in which they would have a monopoly position, so many towns that needed a newspaper had none while other towns that needed only one paper might have two or three—at least for a while. Most newspapers couldn't make it, but even among papers making a small profit, it was not unusual for an editor-printer to quit the business and become a miner, realtor, government official, or something else if that other line of work were more lucrative.[33]

MODERN MEDIA IN THE 20TH CENTURY

In the 1980s and 1990s, newspaper chains began selling many newspapers individually or in small groups to other chains. Some were swapped with others so that chains could form "clusters" of papers near each other, but others were sold by chains requiring high profit margins to other chains satisfied with lower margins. The first publisher to treat newspapers as cards in a poker game was Frank Munsey. Starting with a namesake magazine in 1889, he was rich enough within 10 years to plan a centrally-managed newspaper chain that would improve upon even Scripps' management.[34] He became notorious for buying, merging, and killing off newspapers. (See chapter 12 for an account of Munsey's newspaper mergers.)

Although many journalists' opposed such profit-minded publishers, Munsey's approach typified modern trends in journalism. Twentieth-century mass media would be the most mercenary of all. The advertising and public relations industries were booming by World War I. Newspapers had started publishing so many commercial messages disguised as news content, calling them "reading notices," that postal regulations restricted them in second-class mail in 1912. By the 1890s, a successful metro daily could be making hundreds of thousands of dollars per year in profits. While Pulitzer seemed content to manage only two newspapers (in St. Louis and New York), other publishers sought to extend their empires. Six newspaper chains had been formed by 1890, eight by 1900, 63 by 1935, and 109 by 1960. Many independent publishers received offers they couldn't refuse, other family-owned operations didn't have enough income or capital to survive the Great Depression on their own, still others were finding second- or third-generation family members not interested in the business. Particularly as newspapers became so valuable in the 1960s and later decades, families were forced to sell their newspaper to pay inheritance taxes.[35] Most of them hadn't done smart tax planning, and all of them found their newspapers going up in value faster than they could adjust to.

Of today's well-known names in publishing, most have been primarily interested in making money rather than achieving political, religious, or public service goals. The Newhouse family, for instance, has stayed out of politics. While the Knight family was known for publishing high-quality papers, the Ridder family was not. Starting in the 1990s, Ridder family values have trumped those of the Knights. Publishers such as James H. Ottaway (whose chain is now part of Dow Jones & Co.) and Alfred W. Lee (Lee Enterprises) claimed that their top priority was publishing the highest-quality newspapers they could[36] even when neither did so.

Frank Gannett started his career in the 1890s at the *Syracuse Herald* and became part-owner of the *Elmira Telegram* in 1906. He kept a low profile nationally while slowly building his chain. His name was first famous in 1929, when federal government investigations revealed that International Paper had invested more than $10 million in newspapers. The newsprint supplier had helped Gannett buy four. He again was nationally prominent in 1940, when he unsuccessfully ran for the Republican presidential nomination. Having given his common stock to the Gannett Foundation (now Freedom Forum), he sold preferred stock to finance his campaign. He died in 1957 and was succeeded by Paul Miller and then Allen H. Neuharth. The preferred stock was eventually convertible to common stock, and thus was Gannett Co. managed and owned by non-family members.

Beginning in the 1960s, to raise capital and/or avoid or delay taxes, chains started going public, first Dow Jones & Co., then Times-Mirror and, in 1967, Gannett Co. The New York Times Co., Washington Post Co., Dow Jones & Co., and Times-Mirror stock offerings were set up so that family owners retained working control of their companies. At companies such as Gannett, Lee, and (Chicago) Tribune Co., family owners were no longer involved in day-to-day management or already were minority owners.

Whether chains generally improve newspapers they buy is disputed. Then editor/publisher/owner Loren Ghiglione concluded in the early 1980s that chains' record was mixed. Media sociologist David Pearce Demers argues that many stereotypes of modern "corporatized" newspapers (including privately-owned ones)— such as an inability or unwillingness to take strong stands on local issues—are not true.[37]

In any case, publicly held media are under constant pressure to increase earnings every year, if not every quarter. Media already are among the most profitable U.S. businesses. Other companies net 3 or 5 or even 8 per cent while media earn 15 to 25 per cent. During the 1990s, many diversified media companies didn't buy newspapers because Wall Street and sometimes Main Street regarded them as archaic, with limited growth possibilities. Media firms concentrated on their broadcasting, database, and wire service operations, and eventually the Internet. But in the late 1990s, many companies sold their cable TV holdings, and the New York Times Co. boldly defied Wall Street by paying more than a billion dollars for the *Boston Globe*.

Tribune Co. is an example of companies increasingly oriented toward profits and less toward journalism. It owned eight dailies in 1982, and its subsequent decisions to shut down or sell four of them and pass on buying scores of others suggested that the company was quietly exiting print. Its decision in 2000 to buy the Times Mirror Co. surprised industry and Wall Street insiders. James D. Squires, former editor of Tribune Co.'s *Orlando Sentinel* and *Chicago Tribune*, has pointed out that Tribune Co. annual reports often never mention the journalistic quality of its products. But he gives Gannett Co. and its former chairman Neuharth credit for providing to the newspaper industry and Wall Street an economic model for today's newspapers. Neuharth took Gannett public, made dozens of acquisitions, launched *USA Today*, increased profits for 85 consecutive quarters, and published mediocre journalism. The *Wall Street Transcript* noted, "Gannett's management lives, breathes and sleeps profits and would trade profits over Pulitzer Prizes any day."[38]

By the 1990s, media were sharply curtailing their often expensive and litigation-prone investigative reporting teams. For the first time, media started settling libel suits out of court rather than fight if settling was safer or less expensive.[39] Celebrities and scandal crowded out solid reporting of government and business. Small- to medium-sized daily newspapers began experiencing difficulty hiring entry-level reporters, as journalism graduates eschewed low salaries and a supposedly archaic industry. Public confidence in journalism was low,[40] but media companies were doing little about it.

Conclusion

Over 300 years, the primary motivation of media entrepreneurs shifted as the country's culture, politics, and economy either allowed or required. The earliest editors-publishers were craftsmen at printing and retailers. During the American Revolution, many printers took a side without concern for the consequences, but others' actions suggest they were more interested in staying in business than politics.

During the party press period, editor-publishers were highly political, and sincerely so. Newspapers were aimed at the society's elite, but subscriptions often were not paid for and advertising was still a small revenue source. Thus government and party support was the difference between making a living or not, and other than making a political affiliation, revenues were mostly beyond an editor's control.

As the "democratic market" developed by the 1830s, almost all media became primarily motivated by profit and have remained so ever since. The increasing control—by individuals and by public stockholders—of newspapers by non-journalists in the 20th century has intensified this.

Selected Readings

Altschull, J. Herbert. *Agents of Power: The Role of the News Media in Public Affairs.* New York: Longman, 1984

Ames, William E. "Samuel Harrison Smith Founds the *National Intelligencer*." *Journalism Quarterly* 42 (1965): 389–96.

Baldasty, Gerald J. *E. W. Scripps and the Business of Newspapers.* Urbana and Chicago: University of Illinois Press, 1999.

Baldasty, Gerald J. *The Commercialization of News in the Nineteenth Century.* Madison: University of Wisconsin Press, 1992.

Botein, Stephen. "'Meer Mechanics' and an Open Press: The Business and Political Strategies of Colonial American Printers." *Perspectives in American History* 9: 127–225.

Cloud, Barbara. *The Business of Newspapers on the Western Frontier.* Reno and Las Vegas: University of Nevada Press, 1992.

Dickerson, Oliver Morton. "British Control of American Newspapers on the Eve of the Revolution." *New England Quarterly* (1951): 453–68.

Parker, Peter J. "The Philadelphia Printer: A Study of an 18th Century Businessman." *Business History Review* 40 (Spring 1966): 24–46.

Robinson, Elwyn Burns. "The Dynamics of American Journalism from 1787 to 1865." *Pennsylvania Magazine of History and Biography* 61 (1937): 435–45.

Teeter, Dwight L. "John Dunlap: The Political Economy of a Printer's Success." *Journalism Quarterly* 52 (1975): 3–8, 55.

Thornton, Mary Lindsay. "Public Printing in North Carolina, 1749–1815." *North Carolina Historical Review* 21 (July 1944): 181–202.

Udell, Jon G. *Economic Trends in the Daily Newspaper Business, 1946 to 1970.* Madison, Wis.: American Newspaper Publishers Association, 1970.

Notes

1. Sharon A. Boswell and Lorraine McConaghy, *Raise Hell and Sell Newspapers: Alden J. Blethen and The Seattle Times* (Pullman: Washington State University Press, 1996).

2. Clarance Brettun Blethen, "Alden," unpublished manuscript.

3. Former Gannett Co. Chairman Allen H. Neuharth's wanted his peers' respect. See James D. Squires, *Read All About It! The Corporate Takeover of America's Newspapers* (New York: Times Books, 1993), 53–54, 56.

4. Hall to Franklin, September 6, 1765, *Franklin Papers*, XII: 255–59.

5. Benjamin Franklin, *The Autobiography of Benjamin Franklin* (New Haven, Conn.: Yale University Press, 1964), 120, 126.

6. David Ramsay, *The History of the American Revolution* (Philadelphia: Isaac Collins, 1785), I, 61–62.

7. Isaiah Thomas, *The History of Printing in America* (Albany, N.Y.: J. Munsell, 1874), II, 123.

8. *The Commercial Appeal, 1840–1865* (Memphis, Tenn.: Author, n.d.), 4.

9. Allan Nevins, *The Evening Post: A Century of Journalism* (New York: Boni and Liveright, 1922), 93.

10. Delbert L. Demaree, *The American Agricultural Press, 1819–1860* (New York: Columbia University Press, 1941), 118, 376–85; and Thomas C. Leonard, *News for All: America's Coming of Age with the Press* (New York: Oxford University Press, 1995), 38–41.

11. *Knight's Penny Magazine*, 10 June 1841 (v. 10, new series v. 1), 243.

12. Barbara Cloud, *The Business of Newspapers on the Western Frontier* (Reno, Nev.: University of Nevada Press, 1992), 23–32, 36–37, 123, 153–54.

13. Horace Greeley, *Recollections of a Busy Life* (New York: J. B. Ford & Co., 1868), 91–97.

14. Frank M. O'Brien, *The Story of the Sun, New York: 1833–1918* (New York: D. Appleton & Co., 1918), 128.

15. Richard Kluger, *The Paper: The Life and Death of the New York Herald Tribune* (New York: Knopf, 1986), 100; and *New York Tribune*, 3 June 1872, 1.

16. Frederic Hudson, *Journalism in the United States from 1690 to 1872* (New York: Harper & Brothers, 1873), 410–11.

17. *Philadelphia Public Ledger*, 2 September 1856.

18. See generally James Silk Buckingham, *America, Historical, Statistic, and Descriptive* (New York: Fisher, 1841), especially at 402.

19. Lambert A. Wilmer, *Our Press Gang; or a Complete Exposition of the Corruption and Crimes of American Newspapers* (Philadelphia: J. T. Lloyd, 1859), 70–71, 151–53, 160, 348–49.

20. *Harper's New Monthly Magazine*, November 1866, 789.

21. Edwin Emery, *History of the American Newspaper Publishers Association* (1950; reprinted., Westport, Conn.: Greenwood Press, Publishers, 1950); and Staff of the *Kansas City Star*, *William Rockhill Nelson: The Story of a Man, a Newspaper and a City* (Cambridge, Mass.: Riverside Press [printer], 1915), 15.

22. E. W. Scripps to John Vandercook, March 12, 1902, Letterbooks, "Miramar," Calif.

23. Gerald J. Baldasty, *E. W. Scripps and the Business of Newspapers* (Urbana and Chicago: University of Illinois Press, 1999), 11–12; and E. W. Scripps to George Scripps, January 21, 1881, E. W. Scripps Correspondence Collection, Alden Library, Ohio University, subseries 1.2, box 1, folder 3.

24. E. W. Scripps to Annie Scripps, November 23, 1878, Scripps correspondence, subseries 1.2, box 1, folder 1; and Scripps, "Autobiography" papers, series 4, box 11, p. 354.

25. "I was not really deeply moved by sympathy for the poor and the unfortunate." See Charles R. McCabe, ed., *Damned Old Crank: A Self-Portrait of E. W. Scripps* (New York: Harper & Brothers Publishers, 1951), 135.

26. McCabe, *Damned Old Crank*, 109–12.

27. E. W. Scripps to Robert F. Paine, March 14, 1900, Letterbooks, "Miramar," Calif.

28. E. W. Scripps, *I Protest: Selected Disquisitions of E. W. Scripps*, ed. Oliver Knight (Madison: University of Wisconsin Press, 1966), 80, 83.

29. W. A. Swanberg, *Citizen Hearst: A Biography of William Randolph Hearst* (New York: Charles Scribner's Sons, 1961), 173–82.

30. Boswell and McConaghy, *Raise Hell and Sell Newspapers*, 112, 115, 148, 153–54.

31. Alden J. Blethen to Watson C. Squire, 18 October 1904, Watson C. Squire papers, Manuscripts and University Archives, University of Washington Libraries.

32. *Idaho Avalanche*, 28 September 1878.

33. Cloud, *The Business of Newspapers on the Western Frontier*, 15, 23–31, 36–37, 66–67, 79–82, 101, 153–55, 185–88.

34. *Editor & Publisher*, 26 December 1925, 8.

35. James N. Dertouzos and Kenneth E. Thorpe, *Newspaper Groups: Economies of Scale, Tax Laws, and Merger Incentives* (Santa Monica, Calif.: Rand Corporation, 1982).

36. Eugene Joseph Brown, quoted in Charles A. King, *Ottaway Newspapers: The First 50 Years* (Campbell Hall, N.Y.: Ottaway Newspapers, Inc., 1986), 23–24; and "Colleagues and Associates," *The Lee Papers: A Saga of Midwestern Journalism* (Kewaunee, Ill.: Star-Courier Press, 1947), 407–08.

37. Loren Ghiglione, ed., *The Buying and Selling of America's Newspapers* (Indianapolis: Ind.: R. J. Berg & Co., 1984), xi–xii; and David Pearce Demers, *The Menace of the Corporate Newspaper: Fact or Fiction* (Ames: Iowa State University Press, 1996).

38. Al Neuharth, *Confessions of an S.O.B.* (New York: Doubleday, 1989); and James D. Squires, *Read All About It! The Corporate Takeover of America's Newspapers* (New York: Times Books, 1993), 56.

39. Bruce W. Sanford, *Don't Shoot the Messenger: How Our Growing Hatred of the Media Threatens Free Speech for All of Us* (New York: Free Press, 1999), 1–8.

40. *Quill*, September 1999, 9–30.

12

Mergers, Chains, Monopoly, and Competition

JIM MCPHERSON

A recent list of the top 100 newspapers in the United States showed that exactly 30 had at least two names—names such as the *News & Observer*, the *Spokesman-Review*, the *Telegram & Gazette*, the *Star-Tribune*, the *Democrat & Chronicle*, the *Post-Intelligencer*, the *Sun-Sentinel*, the *Press-Enterprise*, and the *Times-Picayune*.[1] Most, if not all, earned their hyphens or ampersands in the same way—through consolidation of what had been two or more newspapers. Many of the single-name publications also had absorbed one or more competitors over the years. In addition, almost all of those "top 100" belong to newspaper chains.

"In Consolidation there is Strength and Profit."[2] Those words, from a pre–World War I trade advertisement boasting about the consolidation of two morning newspapers in Scranton, Pennsylvania, fairly well summarize the feelings of many of those in journalism throughout its history. In a variety of ways, one significant trend has been for journalism "producers"—first newspapers and later other news media—to join together in a manner that increases profits while reducing the number of journalistic voices. Deregulation regarding monopolistic media practices (including the Telecommunications Act of 1996) and a trend toward media mega-mergers that began in the 1980s (and that continued unabated through the end of the 20th century) brought increased attention to the subject, and, for some, might indicate that the trend is relatively new. Some histories suggest that it began with the rise of

well-known newspaper chains in the 19th century. Passage in 1970 of the Newspaper Preservation Act to "save" failing newspapers in two-newspaper cities formally let competing newspapers combine their resources (while often merely postponing the closure of one newspaper), but the joint operating agreements allowed by the act were, in fact, nothing new. Newspapers have been combining resources, and/or driving out weaker competitors, since before the American Revolution.[3]

The debate about whether "bigness" is positive or, in the words of a 1960s trade publication, "bad ... or merely inevitable,"[4] probably has lasted as long as the trend toward consolidation. Those critical of the trend typically believe that more editorial voices lead to a wider diversity of knowledge and opinion, and therefore a more informed citizenry. Those critics also often believe that the nature of competition makes for better journalism, as reporters and their employers vie to be first and best at providing the news. They would argue that a newspaper without direct competition has less incentive to perform in a way that benefits the most readers. On the other hand, others would argue that a newspaper that is not forced to devote resources to a circulation battle can actually better serve readers, giving them more of what they need as well as simply what they want. Some point out that one-newspaper cities typically have more than one television competitor and that the newspaper is most likely to carry meaningful political news, while television news is more likely to carry fleeting sensationalistic images of little relevance to most viewers' lives. Academic studies and history show that both sides—those who argue that increasing concentration harms journalistic quality and diversity, and those who argue that such concentration provides benefits to citizens as well as media moguls—may in various instances be right. The point of this chapter is not to debate those issues, however, but simply to trace the evolution.[5]

In some respects, newspapers have always cooperated with one another. The earliest American newspapers largely were made up of "news" taken from newspapers that came via ship from England and other locales. James Gordon Bennett, later to become famous for his penny press innovations, spent part of his early journalism career translating stories from Cuban newspapers for the *Charleston Courier*. Early news accounts were not protected by copyright, and publishers frequently took stories directly from other publications—sometimes citing the original source, sometimes not. In addition, printers exchanged news and newspapers, and sometimes even collected subscriptions for newspapers printed by others. Later, of course, newspapers formed and/or joined coalitions to procure and share news, first using clipper ships and other forms of transportation, then later the telegraph. The Associated Press, formed in the mid–1800s, became the most successful of those joint ventures, drawing complaints about its "monopoly" early in the 20th century.[6]

In fact, businessmen of all types long have noticed that, in one form or another, "in consolidation there is strength and profit." Journalists have been no exception. While they were not formal chains controlled by one man or one corporation, networks of printers—the first newspaper publishers—were common in Colonial America. Benjamin Franklin had one such network of printers, whom he helped provide with capital and resources. Established printers trained others through an apprentice system, and naturally many of those printers stayed in contact, helping one another during difficult periods. Family connections also created many early networks. In addition to the fact that nat-

ural networks evolved through the apprenticeship system and family ties, newspaper printers came together to deal with common problems such as taxes, regulation of prices, and shortages of equipment, paper, and news. Those sorts of ties are not surprising, of course. Competitors in any industry tend to pull together to face outside threats or to promote their own good, and that has been true of publishers throughout history. Trade organizations provide one example of that cooperation. Also, early issues of newspaper trade journals demonstrated how interest groups might be narrowed further, commonly carrying advertisements that named every newspaper within a state or region, so that advertisers might reach them more easily.

Newspaper mergers, some forms of chains, and the strategic elimination of competitors also occurred even in early America. Benjamin Towne's *Pennsylvania Evening Post and Daily Advertiser,* which became the nation's first daily newspaper in 1783, soon faced competition from John Dunlap's *Pennsylvania Packet and Daily Advertiser.* In truth, the two men had been battling each other with various publications for several years, with Dunlap usually producing the better and more popular product. He successfully fought off several competitors over a period of more than 20 years, and Philadelphia was, at times, a one-newspaper city. But his relationship with printer David Claypoole was more interesting, perhaps, than his competitive battles. Claypoole worked for Dunlap for years but then "left" him in 1791 to start an afternoon paper (the *Packet* came out in the mornings) that competed directly with another afternoon daily. Dunlap may have financed Claypoole's *Mail* and allowed him to use the *Packet* office for five months after entering the competition. During that period, the two printers might be said to have been maintaining the first daily newspaper joint operating agreement, nearly 200 years before the adoption of the Newspaper Preservation Act (discussed in more detail later in this chapter). Claypoole rejoined the *Packet* in 1793 as Dunlap's partner, purchasing the newspaper from him two years later. He later changed the name and then eventually had his paper absorbed by a competitor.

Some party newspapers of the late 1700s and early 1800s might be characterized as "chain" papers, in the sense that they promoted common ideas from people outside of the newspaper office, while receiving significant funding from a common source. Though a party paper might be established in a number of ways, typically by a fervent individual who happened to believe in the politics he promoted, the parties themselves helped establish and fund many newspapers to spread the political influence of the party, and to counter newspapers already established by the other party. Still, after finding qualified partisan printers, the parties apparently exercised little or no direct editorial control—nor did they need to do so. The existence of competing parties also promoted the existence of competing newspapers. In fact, the various forms of cooperation between newspapers did not prevent readers in increasing numbers of cities from enjoying the luxury of choosing between two (or more) publications.

As the party press declined and news became increasingly commercialized with the penny press of the 1830s, one might see the rise of chains as inevitable. Now newspapers were giving readers what they wanted as much as what editors thought they needed. The need to draw increasing numbers of readers and advertisers meant, in effect, that the newspaper had become a product. Like the producer of shoes or blankets or pickles, the publisher now sought—indeed, now needed—to sell as much of his product as possible. Not surprisingly, the tools and methods of other industries increasingly made their way into journalism. At first, these methods seemed to be good for the consumer in terms of competitive choice, as newspapers tried new ways to attract an ever-expanding readership.

As newspapers spread across the young nation, some concentration of ownership became more obvious. Networks or chains provided the means to start new publications, sometimes in competition with existing papers. While a newspaper struggled to gain its footing, the other paper or papers in the group could provide financial help. In other cases, two newspapers in nearby communities might be profitable—through the sharing of presses and type—when neither could have survived alone. Still other networks involved newspapers in various communities owned by members of the same family, a trend similar to that seen earlier with New England newspapers. Joint operating agreements also appeared in a variety of forms. For example, some Democratic and Republican newspapers shared buildings, published on alternate days, and circulated papers to one another's subscribers. In another agreement, two Wisconsin newspapers shared publication, with one printing on odd-numbered pages and the other on even-numbered pages.[7]

Some family-owned groupings of newspapers would seem to qualify as chains, and some individuals, including media baron Joseph Pulitzer, had previously owned more than one newspaper at a time. Still, the Scripps-McCrae League of Newspapers, established by Edward W. Scripps in 1895, commonly is viewed as the first true newspaper chain. Even the Scripps family had owned multiple newspapers since before 1880, but at least three things differentiated the Scripps-McCrae League from other, earlier chains. First, the League perhaps was the first in which one person or group oversaw operations of the entire group, rather than primarily focusing on one newspaper. Second, a corporate structure assured that the four newspapers initially in the chain—the *Cleveland Press, St. Louis Chronicle, Cincinnati Post,* and *Kentucky Post*—and those that came later would in some circumstances be treated as a unit, rather than as individual publications. And third, that same structure helped ensure that the chain would last much longer than any of its founders. It need not die out with the Scripps family. In fact, an expanded version of it survives today. In 1897, the Scripps-McCrae Press Association, later called United Press, became the first news agency established in connection with a newspaper chain. Four years later, Scripps started a newspaper syndicate to provide his chain and other newspapers with news, features, pictures, and cartoons, the first syndicate connected to a chain. With the combination of the Scripps-

McCrae group and another West Coast group, his chain controlled more than 20 newspapers by 1914.

Unlike many later chains, the Scripps style was to start new newspapers by loaning money to industrious young men, typically in mid-sized cities, rather than buying existing papers. Because some of those cities already had newspapers, the arrival of a Scripps newspaper might actually enhance competition. Samuel Irving Newhouse, founder of what by 1950 became one of the three largest chains (the chains of Scripps and William Randolph Hearst being the others), was among the many chain builders who followed the other model, buying up weak newspapers, cutting costs, and sometimes merging two papers. Like Scripps, though, he tended to leave editorial matters to local editors.

While Scripps may get credit for starting the chain movement, Hearst and Frank Munsey quickly became the symbols of the "evils" of chains. Fresh from the New York battles with Pulitzer that gave yellow journalism its name, Hearst (who later served as the model for the movie *Citizen Kane,* which he tried to squelch) used his chain to promote his political ideals and his own political ambitions, making enemies in the process. One critic wrote during World War II, "William Randolph Hearst has lived too long.... [A]t eighty years of age he has lived so long that he has seen a considerable change in his great newspaper enterprises and their once great influence."[8] The Hearst name may have lost much of its power, but by then, of course, chains were a fact of life in America. During the lifetime of Hearst—who once referred to himself as "rather a confirmed consolidationist"[9]—the chain included radio stations, magazines, two wire services, a newspaper features syndicate, and a newsreel company. Later, book publishers, television stations, and cable companies joined the mix. Some other chain builders, including John Knight (founder of part of what would become the Knight-Ridder chain), also used their expanding editorial bases to promote their own political ambitions. For others, if not most, the chain was (or became) strictly business.

And while Hearst might be said to have "lived too long," the same could not be said of many of the newspapers purchased by Frank Munsey, called the "grand executioner of newspapers" and the "destroyer of dailies." He treated his newspapers like he did his supermarkets, buying up competitors, consolidating papers, and killing off the weak. In fact, most of the newspapers he bought were eliminated or merged into other papers. He bought the old *New York Daily News* and *Washington Times* in 1901, the *Boston Journal* in 1902, and the *Baltimore Evening News* in 1908, but killed or sold them all by 1917. In a dizzying effort to boost profits, he had bought the *New York Press* in 1912; and when he also bought the *New York Sun* and *Evening Sun* in 1916, he merged the *Press* into the *Sun*. In 1920, he bought the *New York Herald* (and its Paris edition) and the *Telegram*, merged the *Sun* into the *Herald*, and gave its evening edition the *Sun* name. In 1923, he bought and killed the *New York Globe* only for its Associated Press membership; and in 1924 he bought the *New York Mail* and promptly merged it into the *Telegram*. That year, he also sold the *Herald* to the *Tribune*, creating the *New York Herald Tribune*—which would survive until 1966. His five New York newspapers became one. Upon his death, famous Kansas editor William Allen White wrote, "Munsey contributed to the journalism of his day the talent of a meat-packer, the morals of a money changer, and the manners of an undertaker. He and his kind have about succeeded in transforming a once-noble profession into an 8 per cent security."[10]

Still, some might argue that Munsey's "kind"—those who bought and operated journalism properties more for business reasons than because of journalistic ideals—were becoming the norm in America, but that his personality made Munsey easy to hate and therefore to blame. For example, the Hearst chain purchased 14 newspapers from 1918 to 1929 just to eliminate competition, while relative chain newcomer Gannett—which by the end of the 20th century would evolve into the nation's largest newspaper chain and the publisher of *USA Today*—did the same with eight newspapers. Trade journals reported consolidations and chain purchases matter-of-factly, no doubt in recognition of the power of the chains.

Not surprisingly, early consolidation and merger activity for newspapers coincided with similar activity in other businesses, though it changed somewhat over time. At first, newspaper chains mostly stuck to purchasing other newspapers (with few exceptions, such as the Scripps chain forming United Press and a features syndicate). Over time they branched out into other areas, sometimes adding forests and/or paper mills to help guarantee paper supplies. By 1920, the number of chains had expanded to 31, up from 13 just 10 years before. During the same period, the number of independent daily newspapers dropped from 2,140 to 1,889. That latter trend would continue every decade from then on, falling to 409 in 1990. The number of chains increased each decade until 1970, then began to fall as chains consolidated or swallowed one another. Meanwhile, the percentage of group-owned dailies went from 2.8 per cent in 1910 to 16 per cent in 1930, passing the 50 per cent mark by 1970 and hitting nearly 75 per cent by 1990.[11] Weekly newspapers followed similar trends, though in many cases were involved in relatively small regional chains (as have been some suburban dailies).

Competition involving chains might lead to the death of a newspaper in a number of ways. As noted, a publisher sometimes killed one paper to strengthen another of his publications. A group of newspaper publishers might even join together to purchase and close a competitor, something that happened in New York and Pittsburgh. Interestingly, sometimes chain owners also voluntarily closed papers to help their competitors. An owner would kill his newspaper in one city to leave the field open for a competitor, who would repay the favor by closing a newspaper in another city. Each then would have control of one city's readers without facing the costs of a head-to-head fight.

The reasons for newspaper deaths perhaps mattered less than the effect. Decreasing competition meant fewer options for readers. In the 1870s, for example, every American town that had a daily newspaper had at least one direct daily or weekly competitor, and the number of cities with dailies was increasing. In 1910, there were 2,200 daily newspapers in America. By that same year, however—even though the number of cities with dailies continued to increase for some time afterward—the number of cities with competing publications began to drop. That trend has not stopped, despite the fact that overall newspaper circulation has risen in each decade. In short, more and more readers are reading fewer and fewer newspapers.

In an activity that somewhat corresponded with early chain activities, though that perhaps was less detrimental to readers, competitors also formed what Scripps termed as "combinations" for such activities as setting prices and establishing exclusive delivery zones. In fact, every Scripps daily was involved in some sort of combination by 1900—three decades before the first formal joint operating agreement and 70 years before passage of the Newspaper Preservation Act.[12]

In 1920 commercial radio arrived, bringing both new competition and new opportunities for consolidation. One of the first noteworthy broadcasts involved an agreement between the *Pittsburgh Post* and KDKA to allow the radio station to report 1920 presidential election results, and many newspapers treated the coming of radio and radio stations as the news events they were. Still, many newspaper publishers feared the new medium, refusing to carry broadcast schedules in their newspapers and fighting to keep broadcasters from carrying news. The Associated Press warned its members in 1922 that releasing news for broadcast purposes violated AP bylaws. Soon, however, publishers themselves saw the financial possibilities of the new medium and began buying stations of their own. The first decade of radio saw battles, promoted largely by those publishers and news organizations that did not own radio stations. The American Newspaper Publishers Association kept trying to force radio out of the news business until 1940. By that time, newspapers at least partly owned just over 30 per cent of American radio stations, with a controlling share in more than 80 per cent of those stations. Even as early as 1931, five years after the National Broadcasting Company took to the airwaves as the first national network, newspapers were involved in the ownership of about 11 per cent of the 612 stations on the air.[13] Though some refused to carry radio program schedules, other newspapers did—including the *San Francisco Chronicle,* a rival of Hearst's *Examiner,* which ran schedules for Hearst's KUO radio as early as 1923.[14] "Of course there is some competition between broadcasting and publishing," stated one early book about radio, "but newspapers, realizing that broadcasting would take place whether they engaged in it or not, have quite sagaciously taken part so as to steer the new art along lines which would not interfere with the stability of their own field."[15]

From a journalism perspective, radio (and later television) differed from newspapers in at least two important ways. First, it was—and has been throughout its history—primarily an entertainment medium. Newspaper publishers who entered the business often intended to broadcast news, and many believed that hearing radio news would actually make people more likely to buy newspapers from which they could get more detail. As two authors argued in 1930, "Newspapers do not undertake public betterment because it is public betterment, necessarily, but because it means gaining the public's good will, support, and subscriptions."[16] For example, in 1933, the Hearst corporation announced that it would launch a series of musical-dramatic transcription programs "over a large list of selected stations with the avowed purpose of boosting the circulations of each of the 17 papers." Programs would be selected "by local Hearst editors and advertising managers."[17] That exemplified the difference between the two media—and no publisher who added a radio station to his chain of newspapers could realistically claim that news values came before business values. As NBC argued in 1935, "All broadcasting is predicated upon entertainment," even if entertainment broadcasting was a "professional occupation," from which amateurs should be excluded: "Any attempted reform which takes broadcasting facilities away from *professional* control and hands them over to *non-professional* control is a menace to good broadcasting and to the development and enlargement and educational and cultural development of the listening audience." (emphasis in original)[18]

Another important way in which radio differed significantly from newspapers is that its development depended on corporations. Profitable existing corporations (with World War I help from the federal government) were needed to provide the capital to get radio off the ground. Not surprisingly, those corporations immediately looked to expand into networks—to, in effect, form chains from the outset. Following a natural corporate path, they also tried to gain as much control as possible. Fearing what monopolies might do to the news, government regulators stepped in fairly soon to limit the number of stations an individual could own, and established a "duopoly" rule, meaning that two stations within a city could not be operated by one manager. One person also was not to be allowed to control a city's only newspapers and its only radio station. But there were exceptions even early on, such as the publisher/station manager of the *Stamford* (Conn.) *Advocate* and station WSRR, whom the Federal Communication Commission determined was "pursuing a vigorous policy of competition" between his two businesses, while facing overlapping competition from larger nearby cities. The case led a newspaper trade publication to come up with the seemingly contradictory headline, "Monopoly Allowed But With Competition."[19] The government struggled with what made an "allowable" monopoly for most of the 20th century, generally easing restrictions throughout the period so that, by 1999, 46 states and the District of Columbia had broadcast stations that shared ownership with print media publishers, many in the same cities. For example, the ABC, CBS, and NBC stations in Spokane, Washington, all were owned by companies that also produced daily newspapers—including the only daily in Spokane. The CBS affiliate provided local newscasts for the UPN and WB affiliates.[20] Other cities had similar "competitors" providing news.

The arrival of television in the 1940s actually brought less competitive friction than radio had. Radio networks quickly became television networks, and those in radio and/or newspapers wasted no time in trying to take financial advantage of the new medium.

"Newspapers and television ... television and newspapers ... they go together like headlines and deadlines, like news and pix," wrote a newspaper trade journal columnist in 1948, as television was taking off. "Each time the postman rings, he brings [news] releases which show the growing activity of publishers in the exciting—and expensive—new medium." The same article would note, "One of the hottest topics of the day 'in the trade' is the race among the networks to sign up newspaper–TVs as affiliates."[21] The *New York Times,* the *Los Angeles Times,* and newspapers throughout the nation were among the early applicants for television licenses, and those companies already involved with television actively sought newspaper partnerships. *Editor & Publisher* noted overtures from ABC in 1947: "'Maybe,' he said, 'newspapers will run their own stations; or maybe we'll arrange a deal between newspapers and our television stations'.... [The ABC official] was a little indefinite for publication. But television is a little indefinite about many things these days."[22] Even before the end of World War II, General Electric officials and staff members of the *New York Herald-Tribune* showed off television's capabilities to about 200 members of the American Newspaper Publishers Association.[23]

Besides their forays into other media, newspapers continued to combine operations and/or to be swallowed by chains. Joint operating agreements flourished, especially in the 1950s, and the number of one-newspaper cities continued to grow. While some in journalism found that troubling, others did not. "Does the man in the newsroom know that virtually his entire profession is given over to local monopolies?" asked one trade publication writer in 1965. "There is room for one [daily] in every town, but not two."[24] By 1977, chains controlled more than 70 per cent of American daily newspaper circulation, and about 60 per cent of the country's daily newspapers. In just the previous year, four large chains had acquired six smaller ones, and in that year, the American Society of Newspaper Editors addressed the issue. Gannett president Allen Neuharth noted that the "great majority" of the remaining American two-newspaper cities had morning and afternoon newspapers owned by one company, or had two papers involved in a joint operating agreement, but no overall consensus was reached about the question in the title of the session: "The Growing Concentration of Newspaper Ownership—Good or Bad?"[25] Nine years later the organization broached the subject with more alarm, as the percentage of daily circulation controlled by chains hit 75 per cent. A securities analyst at the convention offered perhaps the best analysis: "It comes as no surprise to me that there is a lot of concentration of ownership in the newspaper industry. It has been happening to every other line of business in this century. I am only surprised that it has taken so long or that it shocks anybody, if it still does, because it has been happening everywhere."[26] The trend would continue, making clear that the 1970 Newspaper Protection Act had done little to actually save competition between newspapers.

The act, supported by the American Newspaper Publishers Association, was intended to protect the weaker newspaper in two-newspaper towns by allowing the two publications to combine advertising, management, and printing resources while maintaining separate editorial staffs. The act gave joint operating agreements (JOAs) new legal protection and guidelines, but they were, in fact, nothing new. A 1933 union of the *Albuquerque* (New Mexico) *Journal* and the *Albuquerque Tribune,* in which the two newspapers combined all except their editorial operations, is generally considered to be the first true JOA. Similar combinations popped up in three other cities in the 1930s, four in the 1940s, eight in the 1950s, and four in the 1960s, before the federal government challenged a 1965 agreement to renew a 1940 JOA in Tucson, Arizona. The U.S. Supreme Court upheld the challenge in 1969, but Congress passed the Newspaper Preservation Act the following year. Two cities then became JOA sites in the 1970s, and three in the 1980s. The newspapers involved in a JOA decide when it will expire. There was a total of 13 such agreements in existence in late 1999—including the one that started it all, in Albuquerque, and the one in Tucson—down from a one-time high of 28 in the late 1970s. In most cases, the second newspaper had folded, and some critics said the Newspaper Preservation Act actually hastened some of the closures. Regardless, the trend was clear—most metropolitan dailies would, for the foreseeable future, face no significant direct competition from other dailies. Something else that might limit editorial diversity of an area is a trend identified in the 1990s for some chains to swap newspapers, so that each could achieve geographic dominance in one area. Today, at least 22 states—including California and Texas—have a single company controlling at least one-fifth of all the dailies in the state.[27]

That did not mean they faced no competition. For one thing, the late 1960s and early 1970s gave birth to another journalistic phenomenon in America besides the Newspaper Preservation Act—the alternative newspaper. Hundreds of such publications were started and most quickly fizzled, but some hung on to serve as established weekly purveyors of local and political news, entertainment, and/or recreational options. Some formed chains of their own, or were swallowed by existing chains. Today, three chains have more than 120 weekly papers each.[28] Metropolitan dailies also faced competition from suburban dailies and weeklies, along with radio, television, and a variety of Internet options. The age of great dailies led by journalistic titans battling in a great American city is over, ending as the power of chains increased. Most readers must make do with one daily. On the other hand, most readers probably always did—at one time, however, more of those readers had the opportunity to choose which daily it would be.

Selected Readings

Adams, Edward E. "Chain Growth and Merger Waves: A Macroeconomic Historical Perspective on Press Consolidation." *Journalism and Mass Communication Quarterly* 72 (1995) 376–89.

Britt, George. *Forty Years, Forty Millions: The Career of Frank A. Munsey*. New York: Farrar and Rinehart, 1935.

Dyer, Carolyn Stewart. "Economic Dependence and Concentration of Ownership Among Antebellum Wisconsin Newspapers." *Journalism History* 7 (1980): 42–46.

Evans, James F. "Clover Leaf: The Good Luck Chain, 1899–1933." *Journalism Quarterly* 46 (1969): 482–91.

Frasca, Ralph. "Benjamin Franklin's Printing Network." *American Journalism* 5 (1988): 145–58.

King, Marion Reynold. "One Link in the First Newspaper Chain, the South Carolina Gazette." *Journalism Quarterly* 9 (1932): 257–68.

Knights, Peter R. "'Competition' in the U.S. Daily Newspaper Industry, 1865–68." *Journalism Quarterly* 45 (1968): 473–80.

Kreigh, Andrew. *Spiked: How Chain Management Corrupted America's Oldest Newspaper*. Old Saybrook, Conn.: Peregrine, 1987.

Lee Papers, The: A Saga of Midwestern Journalism. Kewanee, Ill.: Star-Courier Press, 1947.

Michael, Rudolph D. "History and Criticism of Press-Radio Relationships." *Journalism Quarterly* 15 (1938): 178–84, 220.

Murphy, Lawrence W. "John Dunlap's 'Packet' and Its Competitors." *Journalism Quarterly* 28 (1951): 58–62.

Neurath, Paul. "One-Publisher Communities: Factors Influencing Trend." *Journalism Quarterly* 21 (1944): 230–42.

Nixon, Raymond B. "Trends in Daily Newspaper Ownership Since 1945." *Journalism Quarterly* 31 (1954): 3–14.

Nixon, Raymond B., and Jean Ward. "Trends in Newspaper Ownership and Inter-Media Competition." *Journalism Quarterly* 28 (1961): 3–14.

Peterson, Wilbur. "Loss in Country Weekly Newspapers Heavy in 1950s." *Journalism Quarterly* 38 (1961): 15–24.

Pilgrim, Tim. "Newspapers as Natural Monopolies: Some Historical Considerations." *Journalism History* 18 (1992): 3–10.

Ray, Royal H. "Economic Forces as Factors in Daily Newspaper Concentration." *Journalism Quarterly* 29 (1952): 31–42.

Rosse, James N. "The Decline of Direct Newspaper Competition." *Journal of Communication* 30, 2 (1980): 65–71.

Sage, Joseph. *Three to Zero: The Story of the Birth and Death of the World Journal Tribune*. New York: American Newspaper Publishers Association, 1967.

Scheiber, Thomas J. "The Newspaper Chain of W. B. Harris." *Journalism Quarterly* 28 (1951): 219–24.

Sim, John Cameron. "19th Century Applications of Suburban Newspaper Concepts." *Journalism Quarterly* (1975): 627–31.

Sterling, Christopher H. "Trends in Daily Newspaper and Broadcast Ownership, 1922–70." *Journalism Quarterly* 52 (1975): 247–56, 320.

Swanson, Walter S. J. *The Thin Gold Watch, A Personal History of the Newspaper Copleys*. New York: Macmillan, 1964.

Villard, Oswald Garrison. *The Disappearing Daily: Chapters in American Newspaper Evolution*. New York: Knopf, 1944.

Williamson, Samuel T. *Imprint of a Publisher: The Story of Frank Gannett and His Newspapers*. New York: McBride, 1948.

Weinfeld, William. "The Growth of Daily Newspaper Chains in the U.S.: 1923, 1926–1935." *Journalism Quarterly* 13 (1936): 357–80.

Notes

1. Audit Bureau of Circulation Reports for period ending September 30, 1999.

2. Advertisement for Harwell, Cannon & McCarthy Newspaper and Magazine Properties, *The Fourth Estate*, 29 May 1915, 10.

3. This refers, of course, to commercial journalism, not to forms of journalism controlled by governments – forms which tend naturally to be monopolistic.

4. William Sexton, "Bigness – bad for newspapers or merely inevitable?" *Quill,* October 1967.

5. The argument has been waged through both industry and academic sources. For a good variety of detailed discussion of the pros and cons of consolidation, see Robert G. Picard, Maxwell E. McCombs, James P. Winter and Stephen Lacy, eds., *Press Concentration and Monopoly: New Perspectives on Newspaper Ownership and Operation* (Norwood, N.J.: Ablex, 1988); John C. Busterna and Robert G. Picard, *Joint Operating Agreements: The Newspaper Preservation Act and its Application* (Norwood, N.J.: Ablex, 1993); David Pearce Demers, *The Menace of the Corporate Newspaper: Fact or Fiction?* (Ames, Iowa: Iowa State University, 1996); Doug Underwood, *When MBAs Rule the Newsroom: How the Marketers and Managers are Reshaping Today's Media* (New York: Columbia University, 1993); and, most famously, Ben Bagdikian, *The Media Monopoly* (Boston: Beacon, 1983), which has had five subsequent editions. The most recent of those maintains that the number of companies that control American mass media dropped from fifty in 1983 to just six in 2000.

6. Upton Sinclair, *The Brass Check: A Study of American Journalism,* rev. ed. (Gerard, Kan.: Haldeman Julius, 1919).

7. Carolyn Stewart Dyer, "Economic Dependence and Concentration of Ownership Among Antebellum Wisconsin Newspapers," *Journalism History* 7 (1980): 42–46.

8. Oswald Garrison Villard, *The Disappearing Daily: Chapters in American Newspaper Evolution* (1944; reprint ed., New York: Books for Libraries Press reprint, 1969), 197.

9. *Editor and Publisher,* 3 July 1937, 6.

10. William Allen White, *Emporia Gazette,* 23 December 1925.

11. Figures are from a variety of sources.

12. Edward E. Adams, "Secret Combinations and Collusive Agreements: The Scripps Newspaper Empire and the Early Roots of Joint Operating Agreements," *Journalism and Mass Communication Quarterly* 73 (1996): 195–205.

13. Paul H. Wagner, "The Evolution of Newspaper Interest in Radio," *Journalism Quarterly* 23 (1946): 182–88.

14. "Radio Broadcast Program Today," *San Francisco Chronicle,* 1 January 1923.

15. Alfred N. Goldsmith and Austin C. Lescarboura, *This Thing Called Broadcasting* (New York: Henry Holt and Company, 1930), 71.

16. Ibid.

17. "Hearst Papers Sponsor World's Disk Programs to Aid Local Circulation," *Broadcasting,* 1 January 1933, 13.

18. National Broadcasting Company, "Final Basic Principle," in *Broadcasting to All Homes,* Vol. 1 (New York: National Broadcasting Company, 1935), 67.

19. Jerry Walker, "Monopoly Allowed But With Competition," *Editor & Publisher,* 1 January 1946, 52.

20. *Broadcasting and Cable Yearbook,* 1999.

21. Jerry Walker, "News in Television, Newspapers In News," *Editor & Publisher,* 1 March 1948, 48.

22. Jerry Walker, "Newspaper Alliance Sought for Television," *Editor & Publisher,* 22 March 1947, 48.

23. "Herald Tribune Staff Gives Television Show," *Editor & Publisher,* 6 May 1944, 26.

24. Victor Jose, "Do Newspapermen Really Want Competition?" *Quill,* August 1965, 21.

25. "The Growing Concentration of Newspaper Ownership—Good or Bad?" *Problems of Journalism: Proceedings of the 1977 Convention of the American Society of Newspaper Editors,* 1977.

26. John Morton, as part of a panel, "Merger and Acquisition Frenzy in the News Business: Where Will It All End? *Proceedings of the 1986 Convention of the American Society of Newspaper Editors,* 1986.

27. Jack Bass, "Newspaper Monopoly," *American Journalism Review,* July/August 1999, 64–86.

28. Buzz Bissinger, "Feeling the Heat," *American Journalism Review* (December 1999): 48–65.

13

Freedom of the Press

MARGARET A. BLANCHARD

We hold these truths to be self-evident; that all men are created equal; that they are endowed by their creator with certain unalienable rights; that among these are life, liberty, and the pursuit of happiness....

In 1776, when these words of Thomas Jefferson topped the Declaration of Independence, colonists in what would soon become the United States already assumed that they possessed an unalienable right to liberty. Indeed, colonists had been practicing various unalienable liberties since setting foot in the New World more than a century earlier. One of the most important rights in terms of the upcoming revolution was liberty of the press—and the colonists had assumed that they had had a right to a free press at least since the early part of the 18th century when newspapers first appeared.

The British colonists in the New World had no document guaranteeing them the right to print their opinions. Even those Britons who stayed at home had no such guarantee, for the English "constitution" was largely an unwritten document and provided no list of rights or privileges. But the English had long assumed a "God-given" right to express their views, a right later scholars would call a "natural right," a right that a person enjoyed because of where the person was born.

In addition to their innate belief in their right to speak and print, however, the British also brought to the New World the tradition of suppressing material that disagreed with the official view of politics or religion. Thus, when Benjamin Harris published the first edition of his newspaper, *Publick Occurrences, Both For-reign and Domestick*, in Boston in 1690, he faced an irate colonial government that stopped the publication from continuing because Harris had failed to obtain permission from the colonial governor to publish the paper. The colonial governor was relying on British tradition of the time of licensing newspapers. The license was granted after officials had read and approved the material to be included in the newspaper. Governors were authorized by the crown to exercise this prior restraint on publication content in the colonies through 1730, even though the king no longer had power to license newspapers in England after 1695. In fact, the first permanent newspaper in the American colonies, the *Boston News-Letter*, appeared in 1704 bearing the line "published by authority," meaning it had survived governmental inspection.

For years thereafter, colonial governors continued to believe that they had the authority to stop publications that they disapproved of while colonial printers continued to believe that they had the right to print whatever they wanted. The battle ended in courtrooms numerous times, and if the printer lost (which he often did), he simply picked up his press and types and went to another colony to practice his craft. The itinerancy of printers and the power of governors ended in 1735 with the trial of John Peter Zenger for seditious libel in New York.

Zenger was the printer for a dissident faction of New York politicians who had set him up in business by creating the *New-York Weekly Journal* as the voice of opposition to the established government. The dissidents wrote the paper's contents—anonymously, of course—leaving Zenger to end up in jail charged with seditious libel. In one of the most important trials of the colonial period, Pennsylvania lawyer Andrew Hamilton argued for the right to criticize those who govern. As he told the jury in a highly emotional statement urging them to acquit Zenger, "Every man who prefers freedom to a life of slavery will bless and honor you as men who have baffled the attempt of tyranny; and by an impartial and uncorrupt verdict, have laid a noble foundation for securing to ourselves, our posterity, and our neighbors that to which nature and the laws of our country have given us a right—the liberty—both of exposing arbitrary power (in these parts of the world, at least) by speaking and writing truth."[1]

When the jury brought in a not guilty verdict, it was really declaring that Zenger had not printed the offensive pieces. Everyone knew that Zenger indeed had been the printer, but the verdict was the only way the jurors could release the printer from custody. News of Zenger's acquittal quickly reached the other colonies, and as the tempestuous days of the 1760s neared, the royal governors were unable to convict patriot printers on charges of libeling the King's government. Although there was still no written guarantee of press freedom, most Americans agreed with Andrew Hamilton that "nature and the laws of our country have given us a right ... [of] speaking and writing truth."

Revolutionary America brought new interpretations of that natural right, for patriot propagandists, with the printers agreeing, felt that they had a "right" to manipulate the truth in order to achieve an end of even greater importance—independence. Basically untrue stories of British atrocities were distributed in order to build colonial hatred of British soldiers, governors, and the monarch. Other stories—such as that of the Battle of Lexington and Concord—were so badly twisted by both

sides that no one can say with certainty what actually happened. Loyalist printers were persecuted physically; their shops and equipment were destroyed; they were driven penniless from the new American states—all in the name of the "right" of independence. Although the patriot leaders might well believe in a "natural right" to criticize individuals and institutions, it clearly was a limited right. Only patriots and their supporters were allowed to exercise it. No one debated the logic or the correctness of denying "natural rights" to opponents of independence. It was, after all, a war, and initiative in the concomitant war for the minds of men goes to those who seized it—in this case to the patriot leaders.

After the Revolution, however, the leaders of the new nation seemingly lost faith in their God-given rights. Faced with a recent history in which basic liberties such as those forbidding the housing of armies in their homes and the right to fair trials had been easily abrogated, the new leaders began to seek written guarantees to protect their fundamental freedoms. After witnessing the ineffectiveness of the Continental Congress under the Articles of Confederation, political leaders met secretly in Philadelphia in 1787 to draft a new charter. The Constitution that emerged carried no guarantees for fundamental liberties, although a vague protection for the press—"the liberty of the Press shall be inviolably preserved"—had been proposed and soundly defeated.[2]

After much debate, over the quality of proposed civil liberties, the Constitution was ratified—on the condition that it would be amended to protect fundamental freedoms. James Madison, a representative from Virginia, assumed the task of drafting these amendments and shepherding them through a Congress far more interested in establishing the federal bureaucracy. Because of his efforts, Madison is recognized as the Father of the Bill of Rights.

He suggested two amendments dealing with freedom of the press, one of which focused directly on the topic: "The people shall not be deprived or abridged of their right to speak, to write, or to publish their sentiments; and the freedom of the press, as one of the great bulwarks of liberty, shall be inviolable." His second proposal, "No State shall violate the equal rights of conscience, or of the freedom of the press, or the trial by jury in criminal cases," reflected the tendency to group different rights together.[3] After minimal debate, Madison's proposals were revised through compromise between the House and the Senate. What emerged was the now familiar First Amendment: "Congress shall make no law respecting an establishment of religion, or prohibiting the free exercise thereof; or abridging the freedom of speech, or of the press; or the right of the people peaceably to assemble, and to petition the Government for a redress of grievances."

Records of debates are almost non-existent, leaving the interpretation of the language to later generations. What is clear from the drafting of the Bill of Rights, however, is that Congress did not intend the primacy given to the First Amendment today. When the original Bill of Rights went out for ratification in 1791, today's First Amendment was third on the list—after proposals altering congressional apportionment and regulating congressional pay raises, both of which were rejected. The latter proposal was ratified in the late 20th century.

Testing the limits of the First Amendment began almost immediately. At best, the framers of the Bill of Rights could agree that freedom of the press meant no prior restraint; beyond that limited concurrence lay vast differences. The first test area focused on national security issues, for under President John Adams the nation grew worried that it would soon be at war with France. As war fears, which later proved unfounded, grew, concern about so-called French partisans within the United Stated kept pace. Supporters of the French Revolution included Thomas Jefferson and his backers who found the democratic ideals advocated in France appealing. They continued their support as the French Revolution grew bloody and as President Adams' fears increased substantially.

By 1798, the Adams administration was endorsing a series of laws know collectively as the Alien and Sedition Acts, which were designed to deport dangerous adherents of the French cause and to allow the suppression of supporters of French ideas in the United States. The Sedition Act, the primary weapon against Jeffersonian editors, was all-encompassing, punishing anyone who "shall write, print, utter or publish" any "false, scandalous and malicious writing" about the government, the Congress, or the president "with intent to defame said government, or to bring them, or either of them, into contempt or disrepute; or to excite against them, the hatred of the good people of the United States, or to stir up sedition within the United States, or to excite any unlawful combinations therein, for opposing or resisting any law of the United States," or any presidential act enforcing such laws, or "to aid, encourage, or abet any hostile designs or any foreign national against the United States, their people or government."[4]

Proposing such a limitation on freedom of the press just seven years after the ratification of the Bill of Rights caused some concern, but the Federalists, Adams' supporters, were quick to note that national security was at stake. As Harrison Gray Otis of Massachusetts pointed out in the House of Representatives, "Every independent Government has a right to preserve and defend itself against injuries and outrages which endanger its existence." Freedom of the press "is nothing more than the liberty of writing, publishing, and speaking one's thoughts, under the condition of being answerable to the injured party, whether it shall be Government or an individual, for false, malicious, and seditious expressions, whether spoken or written." The Sedition Act, he said, would simply punish "licentiousness and sedition" and would not be a prior restraint on the press, which was forbidden.[5]

Comments such as Otis' brought rejoinders about the importance of freedom of the press, especially as a presidential election loomed in 1800. Even Madison participated in the debate, as his Virginia Resolutions questioned whether freedom from prior restraint was sufficient to protect a truly free press: "A law inflicting penalties on printed publications would have a similar effect with a law authorizing a previous restraint on them. It would seem a mockery to say that no laws should be passed preventing publications from being

made, but that laws might be passed for punishing them in case they should be made."[6]
Madison favored such freedom of the press,
even if it led to abuses: "Some degree of abuse
is inseparable from the proper use of every
thing, and in no instance is this more true than
in that of the press." Thus, he said, "It is better to leave a few of its noxious branches to
their luxuriant growth, than, by pruning them
away, to injure the vigour of those yielding the
proper fruits." Indeed, he continued, "to the
press alone, chequered as it is with abuses, the
world is indebted for all of the triumphs which
have been gained by reason and humanity over
error and oppression."[7]

Madison's hopes that the press would be
left alone to do its job went unfulfilled. Overall,
25 people were arrested under the Sedition Act;
14 were indicted; 11 trials were held; and 10 convictions were announced, eight of which related to newspapers. A First Amendment challenge was never raised against the Sedition Act,
and many 20th-century scholars believed the
acts would have been upheld given the composition of the U.S. Supreme Court and the
state of legal understanding at the time. Despite
this robust effort to suppress his supporters,
Jefferson was elected president in 1800, and he
freed those still in jail because of Sedition Act
convictions. Madison's dream of a free press
left to operate in a way that would allow secure
the "triumphs which have been gained by reason and humanity over error and oppression"
was postponed for three decades.

The slavery controversy that percolated to
the top of national affairs in the 1830s tested the
limits of that generation's understanding of
freedom of the press to bring about social
change. Coming close on the heels of the circulation of an incendiary pamphlet calling for
a violent revolution of the slaves, *Appeal to the
Colored Citizens of the World* by David Walker,
and the beginning of a sharply worded abolitionist newspaper, *The Liberator* by William
Lloyd Garrison, the American Anti-Slavery
Society entered the fray in 1835. One of its activities touched directly upon the developing
understanding of freedom of the press.

The Society's first campaign sent copies
of antislavery publications through the mails

to Southern opinion leaders. The pamphlets
depicted the great Southern plantations not as
places of culture and refinement but as sites of
abuse and mistreatment of slaves. Southerners
were incensed, charging that the Anti-Slavery
Society was trying to incite a slave revolt, despite the fact that no publications were mailed
to slaves. In 1835, residents of Charleston,
South Carolina, broke into the post office,
confiscated the pamphlets, and destroyed them
in a public burning. Rather than trying to rein
Southern protesters, Postmaster General Amos
Kendall, himself a Southerner, tried to convince the abolitionists to stop the mailings.
Group leaders refused to "surrender any of the
rights or privileges" that American citizens had
to use the mails,[8] rights and privileges grounded
primarily in natural rights rather than constitutional provisions.

As the mail controversy worsened, Congress became involved, for Southerners sought
legal protection for their postmasters, seeking
a law to allow states to keep incendiary publications out of their borders. The debate gave
the Anti-Slavery Society a perfect opportunity
to offer to send its publications to Congress for
its inspection. The pamphlets, the Society said,
stressed the group's opposition to violence.
Although Congress rejected the offer, the Anti-
Slavery Society capitalized on the situation by
publishing a pamphlet pledging its membership "never intend[s] to surrender the liberty of
speech, or of the press, or of conscience—blessings we have inherited from our fathers, and,
which we mean, so far as we are able, to transmit unimpaired to our children."[9]

Efforts to allow the interception of anti-
slavery material before it reached its destination
angered some journalists of the period who attacked the measure in print. The *Dayton*
(Ohio) *Republican*, for example, charged, "The
next step will be to stop the circulation of all
antimasonic papers, then those that opposed
to the administration. This done, and censorship fairly established, we will become the *white*
slaves of the masters of the black slaves of the
South."[10] The Southern proposals failed, and a
law requiring postmasters to deliver all mail
was enacted substituted.

Anti-Slavery Society members had claimed

no First Amendment privileges, for the state of law did not allow reliance on the Bill of Rights at that time, but the appeal the abolitionists had made to the "blessings we have inherited from our fathers" was successful in winning support from some newspapers of the day. The murder of Elijah Lovejoy, an abolitionist preacher and printer, in Alton, Illinois, in 1837 as he defended his press won still additional journalists to the support of abolition. The *New York Evening Post*, for example, commented, "The right to discuss freely and openly, by speech, by press, by the pen, all political questions, and to examine and animadvert upon all political institutions, is a right as clear and certain, so interwoven with our other liberties, so necessary, in fact, to their existence, that without it we must fall at once into despotism and anarchy."[11]

Again, the defense of "liberty" springs forth in this discussion, much as the discussion of "liberty" was used in the early discussions of freedom of the press. Once more, however, the "liberty" involved is based on a rather vague belief rather than on actual legal or constitutional guarantees.

Perhaps no event in a nation's history tests its commitment to freedom of the press—both in terms of natural and constitutional rights—as does war. During the Mexican War, for example, President James K. Polk found himself regularly condemned on the front pages of newspapers for his ineptitude in conducting the war. Complementing this offense, the newspapers regularly praised generals of the opposing political party with presidential ambitions and revealed Polk's secret diplomatic negotiations. Articles in opposition newspapers such as the *National Intelligencer* "against their own government and in favour of the enemy, have done more to prevent a peace than all the armies of the enemy," Polk fumed in his diary. Indeed, he commented, "there are persons in Washington, among them the editors of the National Intelligencer, who would have been ready and willing to have despatched a courier to Mexico to discourage the government of that weak and distracted country from entering upon negotiations for peace."[12]

Polk failed in his efforts to stop news leaks about the war, even though he personally interrogated a lowly clerk in the State Department about his alleged complicity in revealing information to the press. Congress did little better when it imprisoned a reporter for the *New York Herald* in an effort to discover who was responsible for the unauthorized leak of the Treaty of Guadeloupe Hidalgo, which ended the war. Kept under house arrest in the Capitol building, the reporter was daily brought before the House in an effort to force disclosure of his source. Unable to stand on the yet uninterpreted First Amendment, the reporter refused to reveal his sources based on the code of honor that existed among reporters not to reveal the names of individuals who had confidentially provided information for publication. Although years later, journalists would try to claim this right under the First Amendment, calling it journalist's privilege, in 1848 the basis of the right again was amorphous.

Abraham Lincoln faced many of the same self-made definitions of liberty of the press during the Civil War as Northern newspaper editors undertook to advise the Union armies on their battle plans, print exhaustive casualty lists, discuss fortifications around major Northern cities, promote the immediate emancipation of the slaves in the South, and send journalists to cover the war who criticized his generals. Journalists had the right to decide how to cover the war without government interference, editors would remind the president. Tired of repeated difficulties with journalists, the War Department dusted off the 57th article of war, which allowed military commanders to limit correspondence, including newspaper articles, about the war.

Although that action was virtually useless during the Civil War, the government's attempts to regulate what went out over the telegraph, although uneven and designed only to restrict what was sent from Washington, D.C., were somewhat more successful. When the press appealed such censorship to Congress, a special committee, while noting the importance of a free telegraph to the press, agreed that information about the military or naval affairs of the country could be reasonably withheld "from the press and public in order that it may not reach the enemy."[13] A precedent for the restriction of press access to information in wartime was taking shape that would withstand efforts to overthrow it in future years.

The military's distrust of the press was also taking shape in these years. As General William T. Sherman wrote, "These newspaper correspondents hanging on about the skirts of our army reveal all plans, and are worth a hundred thousand men to the enemy."[14] Perhaps such derogatory comments could be expected from the only general to actually court-martial a reporter because of his work, but within his 1863 tirade is the belief that surfaced again in later wars. Liberty of the press, it seems, whether a natural or constitutional right would encounter substantial difficulties during wartime.

Although freedom of the press began more as a natural right in this country than a legal one, its status slowly changed. In large part, the changes were due to an increasing perception of the need to punish the "licentiousness," or abuse, of freedom of the press. In part, the changes came from an ongoing effort to codify much of American experience so that redress for grievances could be found within the court system. One thing was clear early, however: the abuse of the press surely was to be guarded against and stopped whenever possible. A Pennsylvania jurist, for example, writing in 1788 explained the state constitutional guarantee of freedom of the press "is amply secured by permitting every man to publish his opinions." But, he continued, "the peace and dignity of society" required an inquiry into the "motives of such publications ... to distinguish between those which are meant for use and reformation, and with an eye solely to the public good, and those which are intended merely to delude and defame." When publications belonged in the latter category, a judge was allowed to impose punishment because it was "impossible that any good government should afford protection and impunity" to such affronts to society.[15] Indeed, the Alien and Sedition Acts of 1798 were based on the notion that the Jeffersonians were abusing the freedom of the press by trying to incite discontent among the people.

The concern over abuse of freedom of the press found its way into early state constitutions, such as this one from New York, which underlined the judge's view by stating, "Every citizen may freely speak, write, and publish his sentiments on all subjects, being responsible for the abuse of that right."[16] Even interpretations of the First Amendment contained such cautionary language as shown by U.S. Supreme Court Justice Joseph Story's commentary in the early 19th century: "That this amendment [the First Amendment] was intended to secure to every citizen the absolute right to speak, or write, or print, whatever he might please, without any responsibility, public or private therefor, is a supposition too wild to be indulged by any rational man."[17] The press, therefore, was the target of numerous libel suits in the 19th and 20th centuries.

The notion that the press deserved some protection because of the role it played in American society was slow in coming. One of its first advocates was Judge Thomas Cooley, a leading legal interpreter, who wanted to add the public's expectations of the press to the freedom-and-responsibility equation that had been so dominant. He wrote at mid-century, "The public demand[s] and expect[s] accounts of every important meeting, of every important trial, and of all events which have a bearing upon trade and business, or upon political affairs. It is impossible that these shall be given in all cases without matters being mentioned derogatory to individuals." Because of this expectation, Cooley wondered if it might not be possible to "protect the publisher when giving in good faith such items of news as would be proper, if true, to spread before the public, and which he gives in the regular course of his employment, in pursuance of a public demand, and without any negligence, as they come from him from the usual and legitimate sources, which he has reason to rely upon; at the same time leaving him liable when he makes his columns the vehicle of private gossip, detraction, and malice."[18]

Although it took some time for courts to adopt Cooley's views, it was clear that newspaper attorneys appreciated the commentator's opinions, for they began to plead the watchdog role of the press—the responsibility of the press to keep an eye on government for average citizens—in their defenses to libel actions.

Another consistent legal problem facing the newspapers of the day was the contempt of court citation. Reporters and editors would find themselves brought before irate judges for articles on pending cases, for articles that harmed the dignity of the court, and for criticisms of judicial personages. In other words, almost any comment upon a court case that offended the sitting judge might land a reporter in trouble. Some courts began to move away from a wide-ranging contempt power and to limit actions to those reports that affected a pending case. "Judicial officers, like other public servants, must answer for their official actions before the chancery of public opinion," a Nebraska court wrote in 1900. "They must make good their claims to popular esteem by excellence and virtue, by faithful and efficient service, and by righteous conduct."[19] That opinion remained in the minority for many decades.

Indeed, protecting reputation ran through both libel and contempt cases in American courts before the U.S. Supreme Court became involved in such issues. Reputation was the foundation of a third legal problem thrust upon the press before the turn of the 20th century: the invasion of privacy. In 1890, Samuel D. Warren and Louis D. Brandeis, a pair of Boston lawyers, sought a right of privacy to protect individuals from intrusions by the press that did not violate existing libel law. Although the exact motivation for their work is murky, Warren and Brandeis denounced "instantaneous photographs and newspaper enterprise [that] have invaded the sacred precincts of private and domestic life." In their view, "The press is overstepping in every direction the obvious bounds of propriety and of decency. Gossip is no longer the resource of the idle and of the vicious, but has become a trade, which is pursued with industry as well as effrontery." Newspapers, in order "to satisfy a prurient taste … spread broadcast in the columns of the daily papers" intimate details of private lives. "Column upon column is filled with idle gossip, which can only be procured by intrusion upon the domestic circle."[20] The lawyers' plea

rose quickly to legislative notice, and measures to protect privacy soon were enacted.

The press, critics argued, had changed substantially over the years. It was positioning itself as an institution in American life deserving of special consideration in the legal system; it was an economic force; and sometimes it could misbehave and adversely affect reputation and privacy. Society in general likewise became more complicated, the nation became one of laws affecting every part of American life. Included among the laws designed to make society move more smoothly were measures dealing with libel, contempt, and privacy. For decades, these matters were adjudicated on the state court level, with the preference in decisions often going against the newspaper in order to protect the overall good of society. But conditions were about to change.

Another war led members of Congress to respond to a number of perceived threats to the nation's security by enacting a series of laws forbidding criticism of certain parts of the government or of various aspects of the war effort. World War I legal cases developed because Congress had passed legislation directly limiting some forms of press activity.[21] Although the United States Supreme Court endorsed the right of Congress to make such restrictive laws in time of war, the First Amendment played an important role in decision making.

By 1925, the First Amendment had been made applicable to the states and their laws.[22] Ostensibly the Supreme Court justices had opened the way for reviewing a variety of state court actions dealing with press-related legislation on First Amendment grounds although they did not begin such adjudication immediately. By the 1930s, the Supreme Court was deeply involved in First Amendment cases, although most of the justices' efforts involved the right of speech or of political or religious dissidents to publish their views. The possible threat of state laws on libel, for instance, seemed non-existent for the first few decades of the High Court's First Amendment adjudication as the justices reached only the age-old issue of prior restraint, which they outlawed in 1931.[23]

The first state court press decisions to feel

the sting of Supreme Court review and rever-
sal dealt with contempt of court.[24] The tide
began to turn on contempt cases in the 1940s,
when the justices ultimately determined that
comments were to be allowed on pending court
cases without the newspaper publisher standing in jeopardy of contempt charges. As Justice
Hugo Black wrote in *Bridges v. California*, "The
assumption that respect for the judiciary can be
won by shielding judges from published criticism wrongly appraises the character of American public opinion.... [A]n enforced silence
... would probably engender resentment, suspicion, and contempt much more than it
would enhance respect."[25]

The application of the First Amendment
to cases involving potential violations of state
libel laws began in 1964, when a Supreme
Court eager to encourage the Northern press to
support the civil rights movement ruled on the
libel case of *New York Times v. Sullivan*. The
case involved an editorial advertisement that
criticized the way in which L. B. Sullivan, one
of three elected commissioners of Montgomery, Alabama, behaved in a civil rights demon-
stration. Justice William Brennan made the
civil rights aspect of the case clear when he
wrote, "Thus we consider this case against the
background of a profound national commitment to the principle that debate on public issues should be uninhibited, robust, and wide-
open, and that it may well include vehement,
caustic, and sometimes unpleasantly sharp attacks on government and public officials." To
this end, he said, "The constitutional guarantees require, we think, a federal rule that pro-
hibits a public official from recovering damages for a defamatory falsehood relating to his
official conduct unless he proves that the statement was made with 'actual malice'—that is,
with knowledge that it was false or with reckless disregard of whether it was false or not."[26]

After the Court heard *New York Times v.
Sullivan*, it embarked on a number of other
First Amendment cases involving the press,
moving into free press-fair trial issues[27] as well
as those involving journalist's privilege[28] and
prior restraint in cases involving national security.[29] With each case, the justices ventured into
uncharted territory in terms of the First Amend-

ment. Indeed some of their decisions led to
charges of "judicial activism" being leveled
against a Court considered too liberal by some,
especially as the justices began reviewing decisions in such areas as obscenity[30] and regulation
of the motion pictures,[31] which they found representatives of the "press." The issue was one of
whether the Court should use a conservative
standard in evaluating claims to protection
under the press clause of the First Amendment
or whether the justices were free to adjust the
meaning the "the press" to suit changing times
and media forms. The conservatives argued
that the justices should be restricted to an understanding of the First Amendment as known
at the time that it was written—in James
Madison's era. This position, known broadly as
the original intent doctrine, could likely limit
constitutional press protection to political reportage in traditional newspapers.

Arguments that definitions of "press" be
limited to those known in the late 18th century,
however, seem to lose ground every time the
justices hear a case involving a new medium,
such as the Internet,[32] and use the First
Amendment as a base for their decision. Even
if the medium involved did not meet traditional definitions of the "press," members of
the Court seemed to accept the idea that
Americans had the natural right to spread their
ideas abroad via whatever medium might be
available. Perhaps Thomas Jefferson was on target when he wrote in 1776 that Americans "are
endowed by their creator with certain unalienable rights," including the write to speak and
write freely.

Selected Readings

Anderson, David A. "The Origins of the Press Clause."
    UCLA Law Review 30 (February 1983): 455–537.
Baldasty, Gerald J. "Toward an Understanding of the First
    Amendment: Boston Newspapers, 1782–1791." *Journalism
    History* 3 (1976): 25–30, 32.
Blanchard, Margaret A. "Filling in the Void: Speech and
    Press in State Courts Prior to Gitlow." In *The First
    Amendment Reconsidered*, ed. Bill F. Chamberlin and
    Charlene Brown, 14–59. New York: Longman, 1982.
Blanchard, Margaret A. *Revolutionary Sparks: Freedom of
    Expression in Modern America*. New York, 1992.
Bowles, Dorothy. "Newspaper Support for Free Expression
    in Times of Alarm, 1920 and 1940." *Journalism Quarterly*
    54 (1977): 271–79.

Brant, Irving. *The Bill of Rights: Its Origin and Meaning.* Indianapolis: Bobbs-Merrill, 1965.

Carroll, Thomas F. "The Evolution of the Theory of Freedom of Speech and of the Press." *Georgetown Law Journal* 11 (November 1922): 27–48.

Cobb-Reiley, Linda. "Not an Empty Box With Beautiful Words On It: The First Amendment in Progressive Era Scholarship." *Journalism Quarterly* (Spring 1992): 37–47.

Dickerson, Donna Lee. *The Course of Tolerance: Freedom of the Press in Nineteenth-Century America.* Westport, Conn.: Greenwood, 1990.

Gill, John. *Tide without Turning: Elijah P. Lovejoy and Freedom of the Press.* Boston: Beacon, 1958.

Gleason, Timothy W. "19th-Century Legal Practice and Freedom of the Press: An Introduction to Unfamiliar Terrain." *Journalism History* 14 (1987): 26–33.

Humphrey, Carol Sue. "'That Bulwark of Our Liberty': Massachusetts Printers and the Issue of a Free Press, 1783–1788." *Journalism History* 14 (1987): 34–38.

Humphrey, Carol Sue. "Greater Distance = Declining Interest: Massachusetts Printers and Protections for a Free Press, 1783–1791." *American Journalism* 9:3–4 (1992): 12–9.

Kalven, Harry, Jr. *A Worthy Tradition: Freedom of Speech in America.* New York: Harper & Row, 1988.

Leder, Lawrence H. "The Role of Newspapers in Early America: 'In Defense of Their Own Liberty.'" *Huntington Library Quarterly* 30 (November 1966): 1–16.

Levy, Leonard W. *Emergence of a Free Press.* New York: Oxford University Press, 1985.

Lofton, John. *The Press as Guardian of the First Amendment.* Columbia: University of South Carolina, 1980.

Nye, Russel B. *Fettered Freedom: Civil Liberties and the Slavery Crisis: 1830–1860.* East Lansing: Michigan State University Press, 1963; reprint, Urbana: University of Illinois Press, 1972.

Price, Warren C. "Reflections on the Trial of John Peter Zenger." *Journalism Quarterly* 32 (1955): 161–68.

Rivera, Clark. "Ideals, Interests and Civil Liberty: The Colonial Press and Freedom, 1735–76." *Journalism Quarterly* 55 (1978): 47–53, 124.

Rosenberg, Norman L. *Protecting the Best Men: An Interpretive History of the Law of Libel.* Chapel Hill: University of North Carolina Press, 1986.

Rutland, Robert Allen. *The Birth of the Bill of Rights, 1776–1791.* Chapel Hill: University of North Carolina Press, 1955.

Siebert, Frederick S. *Freedom of the Press in England, 1476–1776.* Urbana: University of Illinois Press, 1952.

Sloan, Wm. David, and Thomas A. Schwartz. "Historians and Freedom of the Press, 1690–1801: Libertarian or Limited?" *American Journalism* 5 (1988): 159–78.

Sloan, Wm. David. "The Party Press and Freedom of the Press, 1798–1808." *American Journalism* 4 (1987): 82–96.

Smith, James Morton. *Freedom's Fetters: The Alien and Sedition Laws and American Civil Liberties.* Ithaca, N.Y.: Cornell University Press, 1956; Cornell Paperbacks, 1966.

Smith, Jeffery A. *Printers and Press Freedom.* New York: Oxford University Press, 1988.

Teeter, Dwight L. "Press Freedom and the Public Printing: Pennsylvania, 1775–83." *Journalism Quarterly* 45 (1968): 445–51.

Terwillings, W. Bird. "William Goddard, Victory for Freedom of the Press." *Maryland History Magazine* 36 (June 1941): 139–49.

Van Alstyne, William W. *Interpretations of the First Amendment.* Durham, N.C.: Duke University Press, 1984.

Yodelis, Mary Ann. "Boston's First Major Newspaper War: A 'Great Awakening' of Freedom." *Journalism Quarterly* 51 (1974): 207–12.

Notes

1. James Alexander, *A Brief Narrative of the Case and Trial of John Peter Zenger*, Stanley N. Katz, ed. (Cambridge, Mass.: Harvard University Press, 1963), 99.

2. Federal Convention, 1787, quoted in Bernard Schwartz, *The Bill of Rights: A Documentary History*, 2 vols. (New York: Chelsea House Publishers in association with McGraw Hill, 1971), I: 439. The vote was seven states against, four states in favor, and one state (Rhode Island) evenly divided and thus not voting.

3. U.S. Congress, House, *Annals of Congress*, 1st Cong., 1st sess., 1: 434, 435.

4. *Statutes at Large*, 1: 596–97.

5. U.S. Congress, House, *Annals of Congress*, 5th Cong. 2nd sess., 8: 2146, 2148, and 2149.

6. "Report on the Resolutions, 1799–1800," in *The Writings of James Madison*, ed. Galliard Hunt (New York: G. P. Putnam's Sons, 1906), 6:386.

7. Ibid., 6:389.

8. Quoted in W. Sherman Savage, "Abolitionist Literature in the Mails, 1835–1836," *Journal of Negro History* 13 (1928): 164.

9. Quoted in Russel B. Nye, *Fettered Freedom: Civil Liberties and the Slavery Controversy, 1830–1860 Covering the Mexican War, the Acquisition of Oregon, and the Conquest of California and the Southwest* (East Lansing: Michigan State University Press, 1963; reprint, Urbana: University of Illinois Press, 1972), 75 (page citations to the reprint edition).

10. Quoted in John Lofton, *The Press as Guardian of the First Amendment* (Columbia: University of South Carolina Press, 1980), 86–87 (emphasis in the original).

11. *Cincinnati Philanthropist*, 12 December 1837, quoted in Nye, *Fettered Freedom...*, 151.

12. *Polk, The Diary of a President, 1845–1849*, 16 April 1847, ed. Allan Nevins (London: Longmans, Green, 1952), 218.

13. Congress, House, Committee on the Judiciary, Telegraph Censorship, 37th Cong., 2nd sess., 20 March 1862, 14.

14. William T. Sherman to John Sherman, 12 February 1863, in *The Sherman Letters: Correspondence between General and Senator Sherman from 1837 to 1891*, ed. Rachel Sherman Thorndike (New York: Charles Scribner's Sons, 1894), 190.

15. *Republica v. Oswald*, 1 Dall. (Pa.) 319, 325 (1788).

16. New York, Constitution of 1821, in Francis Newton Thorpe, comp. and ed., *The Federal and State Constitutions, Colonial Charters, and Other Organic Laws of the States, Territories, and Colonies, Now or Heretofore Forming the United States of America*, 7 vols. (Washington, D.C.: Government Printing Office, 1909), 5:2648.

17. Joseph Story, *Commentaries on the Constitution of the United States*, 2nd ed., 2 vols. (Boston: Little Brown, 1851), 2:597.

18. Thomas M. Cooley, *A Treatise on the Constitutional Limitations Which Rest upon the Legislative Power of the States of the American Union*, 2nd ed. (Boston: Little Brown, 1871), 454–455.

19. *State v. Bee Publishing Co.*, 60 Neb. 282, 296 (1900).

20. Samuel D. Warren and Louis D. Brandeis, "The Right to Privacy," *Harvard Law Review* 4 (1890): 195–96.

21. See, for example, *Schenck v. United States*, 249 U.S. 47 (1918) and *Abrams v. United States*, 250 U.S. 616 (1919).

22. See, for example, *Gitlow v. New York*, 268 U.S. 652 (1925).

23. *Near v. Minnesota*, 283 U.S. 697 (1931).

24. The Supreme Court had dealt with contempt of court issues earlier in the Twentieth Century, with the decisions generally supporting state and lower federal court rulings against the press. See, for example, *Toledo Newspaper Co. v. United States*, 247 U.S. 402 (1918).

25. *Bridges v. California*, 314 U.S. 252, 270–71 (1941).

26. *New York Times Co. v. Sullivan*, 376 U.S. 254, 170, 279–80 (1964).

27. This line of cases begins with *Sheppard v. Maxwell*, 384 U.S. 333 (1966).

28. *Branzburg v. Hayes*, 408 U.S. 665 (1972).

29. *New York Times v. United States*, 403 U.S. 713 (1971).

30. This line of cases begins with *Roth v. United States*, 354 U.S. 476 (1957).

31. *Burstyn v. Wilson*, 343 U.S. 495 (1952).

32. *Reno v. American Civil Liberties Union*, 521 U.S. 844 (1997).

14

Press Rights and Laws

GREG LISBY

The history of press rights and laws in America is the history of continuing efforts to balance the freedom of the press with the rights of others. The story has been one of continual expansion of press freedom. Although occasional setbacks have occurred, the broad sweep of time shows an ever-expanding area of the freedom of journalists and publishers to do what they want to do. Thus, in virtually every major area of law regulating the press—from prior restraint, to defamation, to obscenity, to confidentiality, to freedom of information, with the exception of privacy—today sees greater freedom for the press than it has enjoyed at any earlier time.

However, the general right of freedom of speech and of the press guaranteed by the First Amendment to the Constitution remained largely undefined and amorphous throughout the 19th century and well into the next. In part this was a technological limitation: the First Amendment was understood to protect only the print media simply because that's what the amendment said. Its lofty language appeared deceptively simple on its face. Plus, there was no other kind of mass medium throughout that period.

In part, however, this lack of definition was also because it was not until the 20th century that the U.S. Supreme Court became active in interpreting the press clause of the First Amendment. The Court's declaration in *Marbury v. Madison* that it was to be the final authority for determining "what the law is" in the newly formed country,[1] while establishing the supremacy of the federal judiciary, failed to provide any guidance in the area of press regulation for more than a century. Congress and state legislatures attempted to determine the parameters of "freedom of the press" alone. The results were at best inconsistent. For example, press freedom clauses were included in the state constitutions of nine of the 13 original colonies.[2] Press rights languished or, at worst, suffered on both the federal and state level as a result.

One early example was Congressional enactment of the Sedition Act of 1798, which punished any writing or expression that was contemptuous of the government, Congress, or the president.[3] Though supposedly passed in response to the threat of war with France, historians agree that it was in reality nothing more than a thinly disguised attempt to contain press criticism of John Adams' presidency.[4] Another in 1804, during Thomas Jefferson's presidency, was the conviction of journalist Harry Croswell in New York state for criminal libel. His appeal established the rule that truth could be used as a defense against a charge of criminal libel, as was first contended during the John Peter Zenger trial of 1735, yet did not conclude that the crime of libel, prosecuted by government—as opposed to a civil lawsuit alleging libel—was contrary to the fundamental tenets of democracy.[5]

In part this was because American practices differed from constitutional ideals. For example, states in the antebellum South passed laws prohibiting abolitionist literature;[6] and after the Civil War, Congress outlawed opposition to Reconstruction and jailed journalists

135

who criticized military rule over the former states of the Confederacy.[7]

Thus, an understanding of the history of press rights and laws in America is a recognition of the delicate balance the Constitution attempts to preserve between public rights and private rights, between openness and secrecy, between the tyranny of the majority and the tyranny of the minority, between the free flow of information and the restrictions on that flow for private profit.

PRIOR RESTRAINTS

Historically, however, if the First Amendment was understood to have any original meaning, it was as a narrow prohibition against prior restraints.[8] Including licensing of newspapers by the government, such censorship was routinely practiced by the British in the American colonies during the early colonial era. William Brooker's *Boston Gazette* in 1718, for example, carried the notation that it was "published by authority." But the danger posed by prior restraints was that the fear of censorship could also create a "chilling effect" where journalistic vigor would be replaced with timidity. Early American journalists and constitutional scholars agreed that the First Amendment, at its core, prohibited prior restraints.

The Supreme Court's first passing reference to the amendment's press clause reiterated this understanding. The purpose of the First Amendment, Justice Oliver Wendell Holmes noted, was "'to prevent all such previous restraints upon publications as had been practiced by other governments,' [but not to] prevent the subsequent punishment of such as may be deemed contrary to the public welfare."[9] Within a generation, however, Holmes himself would acknowledge that this prohibition was not absolute. In *Schenck v. United States*, he recognized that prior restraints were acceptable in times of war when "the words used are used in such circumstances and are of such a nature as to create a clear and present danger that they will bring about the substantive evils that Congress has a right to prevent."[10]

The existence of one exception to the pro-hibition against prior restraints naturally raised the question regarding the possible existence of others. The state of Minnesota, for example, enacted a statute forbidding publication of "malicious, scandalous, and defamatory" newspapers if they were determined by a court to be a "public nuisance." The first newspaper to be so labeled was Jay M. Near's *Saturday Press*. Hardly a bulwark of journalistic excellence, the paper offered its readers a strange concoction of hatred, bile, and righteousness.[11] Along with Near's anti–Semitic propaganda were accusations and revelations of police and governmental corruption. Fearing for the public safety, authorities shut down the newspaper. Near was told he could continue to publish his newspaper if it did not include any "malicious, scandalous, and defamatory" material. Instead, he challenged the statute in court.

Near finally won; and the U.S. Supreme Court overturned the statute, which Chief Justice Charles Evans Hughes termed "the essence of censorship." However, Hughes—writing for a badly divided court—acknowledged that several types of prior restraints are acceptable, further undermining the previously generally accepted understanding of press rights. He began by discussing the wartime exception: "No one would question but that a government might prevent actual obstruction to its recruiting service or the publication of the sailing dates of transports or the number and location of troops. On similar grounds, the primary requirements of decency may be enforced against obscene publications. The security of the community life may be protected against incitements to acts of violence and the overthrow by force of orderly government."[12]

More recently, the court hurriedly examined the government's claim of national security as a justification for prior restraint. In 1971, the *New York Times*, followed by the *Washington Post*, began publishing a series of articles on American involvement in Southeast Asia, based on a classified history of the Vietnam conflict, stolen by a disgruntled former government employee and given to the newspapers.[13] The government immediately sought an injunction to stop the newspapers from continuing to publish the articles, and the newspapers requested and received an immediate hearing. Because the "Pentagon Papers" did not pose a directly immediate danger to the nation, the Supreme Court two weeks later reiterated its rule that "any system of prior restraints on expression comes to this court bearing a heavy presumption against its constitutional validity" and upheld the newspapers' right to publish the secret materials.[14] Yet the problem of prior restraint remained. The papers were restrained for two weeks by the judicial review process. Today it is still unclear whether the prohibition against prior restraints includes such delays, or whether the courts should be held to the same standard prohibiting prior restraints as are the other branches of government.

DEFAMATION

The constitutional protection of libel has had a short but tumultuous history. A type of defamation, libel is published or broadcast false information that damages a person's reputation. Owing to its harmful and false nature—and to the balance between public and private interests the Constitution seeks to achieve—libel has, throughout most of American legal history, been denied constitutional protection. The government may seek a remedy for defamation through a charge of criminal libel or the person injured may seek monetary damages through a lawsuit for civil libel. Whether or not the government acted, even in the United States, historically depended in large measure upon the power and importance of the individual involved.[15] Defamation's authoritarian, English roots required the protection of the monarchy and its ministers, the nation's "best men." With the growing attainment of social equality in 20th century America came the corresponding decline in the number of criminal libel suits. The nation's "best men" could protect themselves through civil libel suits, just like everyone else. However, neither type of libel was ever thought to be constitutionally protected—not until 1964, when the Supreme Court ruled in *New York Times v. Sullivan*.[16]

In that civil libel case, the balance shifted in favor of public scrutiny of the actions of public officials, such as the Montgomery, Alabama, city commissioner charged with oversight of the police department. Before a public official could collect damages for defamatory criticism of his official conduct, the U.S. Supreme Court ruled, he must prove the statements were made with actual malice—that the journalist either knew they were false or acted in such a reckless fashion that the journalist should have known they were false. In the years following, defamation's place within the protective purview of the First Amendment has become an increasingly onerous one, as problems both definitional and practical have plagued the tenuous balance between individual reputation and press freedom.

Perhaps as important as the outcome of the Sullivan case were the circumstances surrounding it. At issue was a paid advertisement appearing in the March 29, 1960, edition of the *New York Times*. Titled "Heed Their Rising Voices," the advertisement's text documented a "wave of terror" meant to squelch the civil rights movement in the South. Ostensibly, the libel suit filed by Commissioner Luther Sullivan hinged upon two factors. One of these, that the advertisement contained factual—though, arguably, insignificant—inaccuracies, meant that the *Times* could not use the common law defense of truth in response. The other was the claim that the advertisement's references to the police and to "Southern violators" referred to (and therefore defamed) Sullivan himself, even though the text did not mention him by name. On the basis of these allegations, Sullivan prevailed in the Montgomery trial court and again, on appeal, in the Alabama Supreme Court. The result was the largest libel judgment in Alabama history.[17]

But the facts of the case seemed to demand a different ruling. For example, the Alabama property of four African-American ministers whose names were listed on the advertisement without their permission was seized by the court pending the outcome of the case. The civil rights movement of the era did indeed have legitimate complaints against southern law enforcement officials' response to their protests for equal rights. The damages assessed were unprecedented. Thus, to an extent, the Alabama rulings were not so much a remedy for Sullivan as they were a warning of what could happen to others if they dared speak out.

Though the lawsuit is inexorably entwined with the civil rights movement—it could even be argued that the U.S. Supreme Court finally acted as it did so as not to reverse the progress made through a decade of school desegregation rulings—the court's decision in *Sullivan* turned on the broader question of whether a public official is entitled to damages for defamatory falsehoods associated with his official conduct. The result was the court's formulation of the "actual malice" standard, which places the burden of proof upon the official to show that the disputed statement was made with knowledge that it was false or with reckless disregard of that falsity. Such a high standard of proof was intended to facilitate public discussion by the "citizen-critic" about the conduct and performance of public officials.

Three years later, in *Curtis Publishing Co. v. Butts/Associated Press v. Walker*,[18] the issue was more ambiguous: should a college football coach and a retired Army general be held to the same libel standard as public officials? Neither public officials nor purely private citizens, the Supreme Court concluded that Wally Butts and Edwin Walker occupied a murky niche as "public figures"—who also must prove actual malice before collecting damages for defamation. Public figures, according to the court, are those whose fame or prominence in public affairs engenders significant public interest in their activities.

The standard to be met by private citizens, however, entailed a considerable amount of grappling. A 1971 decision held that the subject under discussion, if it was an "issue of public interest," was more germane than the status of the discussants.[19] Thus, even a private citizen would have to meet the "actual malice" test, if such a person were involved in a matter of general or public concern. However, three years later, the U.S. Supreme Court appeared to back away from the subject matter test and again embrace the public/private person distinction. In *Gertz v. Robert Welch, Inc.*, Elmer Gertz, an

attorney for a family suing police for the wrongful death of their son, sued *American Opinion* magazine for contending that he was a "Communist-fronter."[20]

The question was whether Gertz would be required to prove that the falsehoods were published with actual malice since he was neither a public official nor a public figure, only a private individual. The Supreme Court recognized that private individuals, unlike public figures, do not voluntarily enter the arena of public discussion and, additionally, that their "private" status accords them fewer opportunities to refute defamatory falsehoods than opportunities available to more well-known public figures. On this basis, the court decided that private individuals should be required to meet the less exacting standard of negligence, defined as the duty of care reasonable persons owe others.

Although *Sullivan* and its progeny were meant to give the press more breathing room for discussion of public issues, they have also had other, unintended consequences. One is a spike in the perception of the press as an arrogant, cavalier institution that can harm the relatively helpless with impunity. Since *Sullivan*, merely proving that a published statement is false is no longer adequate, as it was under the common law. This has led to charges, justifiable or not, that the press has become more zealous in its reporting and less scrupulous in its fact-checking.

Even more vexing problems have plagued the public/private distinction, the necessary prerequisite for determining the standard of proof required in libel suits. The public/private standard has proven to be a subjective dichotomy. As the very notion of "publicness" is constantly renegotiated, the courts must decide on an *ad hoc* basis who is public and who is not.

Consider the libel case of Richard Jewell, the security guard on duty during the 1996 Centennial Olympic Park bombing in Atlanta. Originally, he was hailed as a hero for his discovery of the bomb. Four days later, after giving 11 press interviews, he was a suspect. Although later cleared, he sued the *Atlanta Journal-Constitution* in January 1997, claiming that its coverage depicted him as probably guilty of the crime. In October 1999, the trial court determined that he was a public figure, based on his voluntary press appearances after the bombing. Whether he was really involved in the discussion of an issue of public interest or was more like Elmer Gertz, just performing the duties of his job in public, is as yet unsettled. Press coverage of supposedly private lives continually blurs an already indistinct line, as the hazy public/private dichotomy has grown more and more nebulous. One court, for example, has concluded that "defining a public figure is like trying to nail a jellyfish to the wall."[21]

PRIVACY

Like the law of defamation, the law of privacy attempts to reconcile competing values— "the right to be let alone" and the public's "right to know." This equilibrium is also frequently shifting, due to the necessarily ambiguous distinction between the public and private spheres. Despite Samuel Warren and Louis Brandeis' call for a more fully articulated recognition of privacy as a legal right, the history of privacy jurisprudence has been more of a piecemeal process than a sweeping one.[22] Left to the discretion of the states, the legal right to privacy has evolved primarily through the enactment of state statutes and the judicial recognition of privacy rights under the common law. This dichotomy, this sense of fragmentation, pervades our understanding of the right of privacy itself: a general, encompassing comprehension of privacy as a constitutional right has been undermined by the many, specific privacy protections provided in particular situations. Privacy scholar William Prosser has categorized privacy as four related, yet distinct private wrongs, "tied together by the common name, but otherwise [having] almost nothing in common"—intrusion into one's physical solitude, the public disclosure of embarrassing private facts, the placing of someone in a false light in the public eye, and the unauthorized use of one's likeness for commercial purposes.[23]

Seven years after Prosser's delineation of the four areas of privacy and two years after the Supreme Court recognized a constitutional right of privacy,[24] the court significantly tightened the standard necessary to win a privacy claim against the press in *Time, Inc. v. Hill*.[25] There the court required a balancing of the importance of public information against private sensitivities in light of the newly formulated *Sullivan* test in the area of defamation.

In 1952, three escaped convicts held the James Hill family hostage in their home for several days. One of the prisoners was apprehended shortly afterwards. The two others were killed after an intense standoff with police. Though no physical harm came to the Hills, the family soon moved to another state and refused to speak of the incident. A year later, Joseph Hayes' novel, *The Desperate Hours*, was published. Though the novel bore a superficial resemblance of the Hills' experiences, the fictional Hilliard family was cruelly and violently treated by their captors. The book was subsequently adapted as a play.

Hill brought the lawsuit against *Life* magazine when, in an article about the opening of the play, it transported the actors to the house in which the Hills had been held hostage and had them re-enact scenes from the play. The magazine described the play as a "re-enactment" of the Hills' ordeal, despite Hayes' assertion that the play's theme was only tangentially linked to the family's experience. In what was a surreal photo spread, illustrations of the play's more violent scenes were staged at the very site of the original incident.[26] On the basis of this sensationalized reintroduction of his family into the public spotlight, Hill sued for false light invasion of privacy.

Lower court rulings for Hill were reversed by the U.S. Supreme Court, which concluded that because the Hills were public figures, although involuntary ones, they had to prove the magazine acted with "actual malice" before they could collect damages for the invasion of their privacy. In other words, if a topic is "newsworthy," generally one's right of privacy is forfeit. This has resulted in another murky area of the law in which privacy protection can be capricious—victims of sexual violence, for example, may or may not be named in the press, depending upon the newsworthiness of the incident. And, as the Internet creates a new realm of communication, the potential for invasive behavior is equally as vast. Although technological advances have made information availability more egalitarian, they have also raised troubling new questions about the extent of the right of privacy, including whether technological innovations have eviscerated the right today.

OBSCENITY

The questions raised by defamation and privacy are not nearly as vexing as those raised by obscenity. Because obscenity is not and never has been constitutionally protected, the question of what is and is not obscene is of crucial importance. Unfortunately, it is also one of the most difficult ones to answer. For example, shortly after the ratification of the First Amendment in 1791, Massachusetts made it a crime to devise "any filthy, obscene, or profane song," yet never defined exactly what that was. Similar shortcomings could have been found in federal and state statutes across the legal landscape until the early 20th century when courts began their own definitional attempts. Yet, despite years of effort, Justice Potter Stewart was not wrong when he admitted in 1964 that though he could not define what types of hardcore pornography he felt to be legally obscene, he knew it when he saw it.[27] This definitional difficulty is at least partly the result of the social equality all persons and racial groups began to enjoy in the 20th century—coupled with America's national advocacy of cultural and ethnic diversity. Arguably, if all forms of expression are equal and valued by some group, then no particular type of expression is completely without merit and obscene.

Generally, however, obscene material is sexual in nature, involving offensive depictions of sexual activity. In contrast, indecency—which has received limited constitutional protection[28]—involves the offensive depiction of body parts and functions. Determining exactly how offensive a sexually oriented depiction must be to be legally obscene has been an exercise in frustration for the U.S. Supreme

Court. Although guidelines for identifying obscenity have emerged from its rulings, the future of obscenity law holds the promise of continued uncertainty.

The Supreme Court first attempted to formulate a definition of obscenity that would square with the Constitution in 1957, in the landmark case of *Roth v. United States/Alberts v. California*.[29] In the *Roth* test, as it has become known, material would be considered obscene if, "to the average person applying contemporary community standards, the dominant theme of the material taken as a whole appeals to the prurient interest."[30] The court created a small exception to that rule in *Stanley v. Georgia*, concluding that the right of privacy protected the possession of obscene material in one's home.[31] If the First Amendment means anything at all, Justice Thurgood Marshall wrote, "it means that a State has no business telling a man, sitting alone in his own house, what books he may read or what films he may watch."[32]

The most troublesome part of *Roth* was the "contemporary community standards" test. The Supreme Court did not define its scope in *Roth*. In *Jacobellis v. Ohio*, it stated that the community standard would be a national one.[33] It reconsidered that holding in *Miller v. California* and concluded that the community standard should be a state one.[34] Reformulating the *Roth* test, the court held that the basic guidelines for defining obscenity must be "whether 'the average person, applying contemporary community standards' would find that the work, taken as a whole, appeals to the prurient interest; whether the work depicts or describes, in a patently offensive way, sexual conduct specifically defined by the applicable state law; and whether the work, taken as a whole, lacks serious literary, artistic, political, or scientific value."[35]

Obscenity, thus redefined, still remains without constitutional protection, though it could be argued that nobody today knows it when he or she sees it. All the tests have been criticized as both too elastic, with no consistency from one decision to the next, and too rigid, allowing courts to ride roughshod over free expression. The challenge for the future will be determining the parameters and boundaries of communities with the advent of the Internet. Historically, all law is geographically based. Obscene material, once it finds its way onto the Internet, creates more definitional problems with determining what community standards legally are in cyberspace.

JOURNALISTIC PRIVILEGE AND SHIELD LAWS

One conflict journalists have not won in court has been the debate over whether they are allowed to keep sources confidential and enjoy a "journalistic privilege" against testifying. Throughout much of the 19th century, the right to keep sources confidential appeared to be "a settled principle."[36] However, in 1972, the U.S. Supreme Court ruled that the First Amendment contained no such protection, no exemption for journalists from the duty of all American citizens to testify when lawfully called upon.[37] Yet because the court left the door open for legislative action, about two-thirds of the states today have enacted state shield laws that protect the anonymity of journalists' sources in certain specifically defined circumstances.

FREEDOM OF INFORMATION

As the Industrial Revolution transformed the American landscape in the 19th century, it also ushered in an era of unprecedented complexity. The rapid growth of cities and the swelling populations that flooded them led to the need for management apart from America's formerly agrarian culture. Traditional government was ill-equipped to solve the specialized problems arising from massive urbanization. To adapt, Congress and the states established expert boards and bureaus in the early part of the 20th century to deal with problems unique to a newly industrialized society—specialists to deal with specialized situations. These administrative agencies include the Federal Communications Commission, the Food and Drug Administration, and a host of other now-familiar acronyms, such as the IRS.

Less well-understood is the structure and function of such agencies. Separate and distinct from elected government, these agencies exercise considerable autonomy in their regulatory functions. Such independence streamlines the administrative process, allowing experts to exercise binding regulatory authority over specialized matters without the same responsibility to the electorate that the executive and legislative branches of government have. In fact, an administrative agency is very much a government unto itself. Within a single agency are the combined purposes of the three branches of government: a legislative function (to make regulations), an executive function (to enforce regulations), and a judicial function (to interpret regulations and determine when they have been violated).

Because agency members are appointed and not responsible by election to any set of constituents, administrative agencies have historically tended to be insular and closed to public accountability. In response to these trends, Congress enacted the Freedom of Information Act of 1966, which opened to the public vast numbers of records generated by administrative agencies.[38] In 1976, Congress enacted the Government in the Sunshine Act, which requires some 50 administrative agencies to open their meetings to the public.[39] Though a remarkable step toward government candor, neither act is without exceptions for national security, administrative documents, trade secrets, law enforcement records and meetings, and the like.

A frequent charge, leveled most often by journalists, is that administrative agencies violate the spirit if not the letter of the laws by withholding information not for some legitimate reason—such as the "clearly unwarranted invasion of personal privacy" exemption—but out of an excessive desire for secrecy to protect agency missteps, mistakes, and malfeasance. Determining the balance between openness and privacy is rarely a simple task, but in cases where emotionally-charged records or meetings are also ones of the greatest public interest, the extent of openness directly correlates with public trust in government.

One such case that illustrates acutely the difficult balance of openness and privacy involves the worst disaster in the history of space exploration—the explosion and crash of the space shuttle *Challenger* during lift-off on January 28, 1986, in which all seven astronauts aboard died. Some six weeks after the disaster, the National Aeronautic & Space Administration recovered from the wreckage a tape recording that spanned the 73 seconds from lift-off to explosion and included the astronauts' voices, as well as various background noises. In response to a written request filed under the Freedom of Information Act, NASA submitted a written transcript of the recording to the *New York Times*, but denied the newspaper's request for a copy of the tape itself, citing Exemption 6 of the Freedom of Information Act, which exempts from disclosure "personnel and medical files and similar files the disclosure of which would constitute a clearly unwarranted invasion of personal privacy."

The *Times* sued to have the tape released claiming that the enormity of the disaster and the potential for a cover-up of responsibility for the explosion required that all available information be made public. The courts had to decide if the tape recording was a "similar file" exempt from disclosure under Exemption 6 of the Freedom of Information Act. Ultimately, the courts decided that it was and rejected the argument that the aural quality of the tape provided new insights with regard to NASA's culpability in the accident. More importantly, the courts decided that the privacy interests were simply too important to warrant the tapes' release. The astronauts' families, the courts determined, would suffer unnecessarily from the disclosure—not only would they be subjected to the inevitable press scrutiny, but they would also be forced to hear the last words spoken by the doomed astronauts again and again.

However, the lack of agreement and inconsistency of the four rulings is also troubling and illustrates the difficult balancing act required.[40] While the release of important NASA documents was a necessary step toward restoring public trust in government, the protection of the privacy rights of the families of the *Challenger* astronauts was also important. Ten years later, there was no still consensus whether the release of the official transcript was sufficient.

CONCLUSION

The history of press rights and laws in America is the history of an unfinished experiment, one that may never be finished. If indeed, as Justice Oliver Wendell Holmes wrote in *Abrams v. United States*, "the best test of truth is the power of the thought to get itself accepted in the competition of the market,"[41] more governmental openness and more information are always better than less. Judge Learned Hand agreed that "right conclusions are more likely to be gathered out of a multitude of tongues, than through any kind of authoritative selection."[42] That is the hypothesis the American experiment is testing. Yet because no one can stop and restart the experiment at will, it is that ideal, delicate balance between public rights and private rights, between openness and secrecy, between the tyranny of the majority and the tyranny of the minority that the First Amendment still seeks.

Selected Readings

Adler, Renate. *Reckless Disregard: Westmoreland v. CBS et al.; Sharon v. Time.* New York: Knopf, 1986.

Blanchard, Margaret A. "The Fifth-Amendment Privilege of Newsman George Burdick." *Journalism Quarterly* 55 (1978): 39–46, 67.

Bliss, Robert M. "Development of Fair Comment as a Defense to Libel." *Journalism Quarterly* 44 (1967): 627–37.

Dan, Uri. *Blood Libel: The Inside Story of General Ariel Sharon's History-Making Suit Against Time Magazine.* New York: Simon and Schuster, 1987.

Friendly, Fred W. *Minnesota Rag: The Dramatic Story of the Landmark Supreme Court Case That Gave New Meaning to Freedom of the Press.* New York: Random House, 1981.

Gleason, Timothy W. "The Libel Climate of the Late Nineteenth Century: A Survey of Libel Litigation, 1884–1899." *Journalism Quarterly* 70 (Winter 1993): 893–906.

Gordon, David. "The 1896 Maryland Shield Law: The American Roots of Evidentiary Privilege for Newsmen." *Journalism Monographs* 22 (1972).

Kaminiski, Thomas H. "Congress, Correspondents and Confidentiality in the 19th Century: A Preliminary Study." *Journalism History* 4 (1976): 83–87, 92.

Kennedy, Sheila S. *Free Expression in America: A Documentary History.* Westport, Conn.: Greenwood Press, 1999.

Koval, James J. "Beyond the First Amendment: Impact of the Other Amendments on the Press." *Media History Digest* 7, 2 (1987): 54–60.

Levy, Leonard W. *Legacy of Suppression.* Cambridge, Mass.: Harvard University Press, 1960.

Lewis, Anthony. *Make No Law: The Sullivan Case and the First Amendment.* New York: Random House, 1991.

Neilson, Winthrop, and Frances Neilson. *Verdict for the Doctor.* New York: Hastings House, 1958.

Nelson, Harold L., ed.. *Freedom of the Press from Hamilton to the Warren Court.* Indianapolis: Bobbs-Merrill, 1967.

Pember, Don E. *Privacy and the Press.* Seattle: University of Washington Press, 1972.

Pilgrim, Tim A. "Privacy and American Journalism: An Economic Connection." *Journalism History* 14 (1987): 18–24.

Rosenberg, Norman L. *Protecting the Best Men: An Interpretive History of the Law of Libel.* Chapel Hill: University of North Carolina Press, 1985.

Scheidenhelm, Richard. "James Fenimore Cooper and the Law of Libel in New York." *American Journalism* 4 (1987): 19–29.

Ungar, Sanford J. *The Papers and the Papers: An Account of the Legal and Political Battle over the Pentagon Papers.* New York: E. P. Dutton, 1972.

Notes

1. 5 U.S. Reports 137 (1803), at 177.

2. The constitutions of Connecticut, New Jersey, New York, and Rhode Island did not include a commitment to freedom of the press in those states.

3. 1 Statutes at Large 596 (1798).

4. See Allan Nevins and Henry S. Commager, *A Short History of the United States* (New York: Alfred Knopf, 1968); Max Frankel, "Democracy in Infancy," *New York Times Magazine,* 23 January 2000, 17–18.

5. See Kyu H. Youm, "The Impact of *People v. Croswell* on Libel Law," *Journalism Monographs* 113 (June 1989); Warren C. Price, "Reflections on the Trial of John Peter Zenger," *Journalism Quarterly* 32 (1955): 161–68.

6. See Donald E. Lively, *The Constitution and Race* (New York: Praeger, 1992).

7. *Ex Parte McCardle,* 74 U.S. Reports 506 (1869).

8. See Leonard W. Levy, *Legacy of Suppression* (Cambridge, Mass.: Harvard University Press, 1960).

9. *Commonwealth v. Blanding,* 20 Massachusetts Reports 304 (1825), at 313, quoted in *Patterson v. Colorado,* 205 U.S. Reports 454 (1907), at 462.

10. 249 U.S. Reports 47 (1919), at 52.

11. See Fred W. Friendly, *Minnesota Rag: The Dramatic Story of the Landmark Supreme Court Case that Gave New Meaning to Freedom of the Press* (New York: Random House, 1981).

12. *Near v. Minnesota,* 283 U.S. Reports 697 (1931), at 716.

13. See Sanford J. Ungar, *The Papers and the Papers: An Account of the Legal and Political Battle over the Pentagon Papers* (New York: E. P. Dutton, 1972).

14. *Bantam Books v. Sullivan,* 372 U.S. Reports 58 (1963), at 70, quoted in *New York Times v. U.S.,* 403 U.S. Reports 713 (1971), at 713.

15. See Norman L. Rosenberg, *Protecting the Best Men: An Interpretive History of the Law of Libel* (Chapel Hill: University of North Carolina Press, 1985).

16. 376 U.S. Reports 254.

17. Anthony Lewis, "Annals of Law: The Sullivan Case," *The New Yorker,* 5 November 1984, 55. See also, Anthony Lewis, *Make No Law: The Sullivan Case and the First Amendment* (New York: Random House, 1991).

18. 388 U.S. Reports 130 (1967).

19. *Rosenbloom v. Metromedia,* 403 U.S. Reports 29 (1971).

20. 418 U.S. Reports 323 (1974).

21. *Rosanova v. Playboy Enterprises,* 411 Federal Supplement 440 (Southern District of Georgia, 1976), at 443.

22. Samuel Warren and Louis Brandeis, "The Right to Privacy," *Harvard Law Review* 4 (1890): 193–220.

23. William Prosser, "Privacy," *California Law Review* 48 (1960): 389.

24. *Griswold v. Connecticut,* 381 U.S. Reports 479 (1965).

25. 385 U.S. Reports 374 (1967).

26. See Leonard Garment, "Annals of Law: The Hill Case," *The New Yorker,* 17 April 1989, 90.

27. Stewart, concurring, in *Jacobellis v. Ohio,* 378 U.S. Reports 184 (1964), at 197.

28. *Federal Communications Commission v. Pacifica Foundation,* 438 U.S. Reports 726 (1978).

29. 354 U.S. Reports 476 (1957).

30. Ibid., 489.

31. 394 U.S. Reports 557 (1969).

32. Ibid., 565.

33. 378 U.S. Reports 184 (1964).

34. 413 U.S. Reports 15 (1973).

35. Ibid., 24. Citations in original omitted.

36. Thomas H. Kaminiski, "Congress, Correspondents and Confidentiality in the 19th Century: A Preliminary Study," *Journalism History* 4 (1976): 83.

37. *Branzburg v. Hayes,* 408 U.S. Reports 665 (1972).

38. 5 United States Code § 552.

39. 5 United States Code § 522(b).

40. *New York Times v. NASA,* 679 Federal Supplement 33 (District of Columbia District Court, 1987); *New York Times v. NASA,* 852 Federal Reporter (2nd ed.) 602 (District of Columbia Circuit appellate court, 1988); *New York Times v. NASA,* 920 Federal Reporter (2nd ed.) 1002 (District of Columbia Circuit appellate court, 1990); *New York Times v. NASA,* 782 Federal Supplement 628 (District of Columbia District Court, 1991).

41. Holmes, dissenting, in *Abrams v. U.S.,* 250 U.S. Reports 616 (1919), at 630.

42. *U.S. v. Associated Press,* 52 Federal Supplement 362 (Southern District of New York, 1943), 372.

15

News Gathering

MICHAEL A. LONGINOW

Joseph Pulitzer, as a young reporter, was a magnet for ridicule. He worked too much—staying on the streets and in the office day and night with seemingly no sleep. He dressed oddly, often forgetting to strap his collar on before going out. His bulbous eyes, beak nose, protruding ears, and gaping jaw commanded little respect, and his German accent did not endear him to some—particularly in St. Louis in the late 1860s. But Joey Pulitzer could find news. Pulitzer had learned to ask tough questions through hard experience—some of it from the perspective of a Union Army mule-tender prior to his reporting career.[1] His entry onto the *Westliche Post's* staff came after being bilked out of money by a sugar-plantation labor agent. Pulitzer's write-up of that event so impressed an editor of that German-language newspaper that it got Pulitzer a newsroom job offer. But the young man's drive got frequent tests. Competing journalists taunted him mercilessly, at times sending him off on false tips. Pulitzer was not deterred. He had a thirst for information that made him restless in pursuit.[2] Pulitzer, like another dogged reporter named James Gordon Bennett, Sr.—both later to become nationally-known publishers—saw their role as one of telling the hard stories of life. "I have seen human depravity to the core," Bennett would say, and he made it his job, as a reporter, to describe "the deep guilt that is encrusting over society."[3]

Emergence of reporting in the United States grew out of just such a thirst and hunger for life's descriptions—a grasping for facts, even if marginally reliable—which nourished a democracy built on publicly-informed appetite. But in its early stages, as well as in its more refined moments, news gathering could look reckless, unsettling—like Pulitzer, Bennett, or hundreds of others like them. The engines of news gathering and news storytelling would eventually become overwhelming. The very consumption of news, in some forms, would take on an appearance not of cultural nourishment, but of excess. Reporting today raises more questions than answers about the future of information gathering within a democracy.

NEWS GATHERING AND A NATIONAL IDENTITY

Those gathering news in the 18th century were those with access to more-or-less official voices. Eighteenth-century news, quite often, arose from reports of privileged travelers—in verbal or written form. Though by modern standards they might appear haphazard, "correspondent" reports on news pages had an underlying logic. The *Boston Gazette*, in 1720, noted that "by our letters from the West Indies we have an Account that the Pirates continue to be very numerous there, and to do incredible damages to trade by taking, plundering and destroying the ships of all nations without distinction that come their way,"[4] Eighteenth-century news readers sought out the "intelligence" of powerbrokers, for they were generally powerbrokers themselves. Printer/publishers gave them what they needed, ranging from merchant crisis details to the texts of speeches by colonial leaders. When Thomas Fleet, in Boston, took over as publisher of the *Weekly Rehearsal*—later to be known as the *Evening Post*—he not only reprinted London news, but "settled a Correspondence" both in large towns as well as in "the country" across New England. From these, he invited news reports on "any thing new or curious, whether in the Way of News or Speculation, worthy of public view." His correspondents got a free subscription.[5]

But finding news could be a problem. Publishing it could be even more difficult. Publishers found news nonetheless, braving criticism from authorities as well as fellow community members. Noah Webster, a contributor and editor of the *Connecticut Courant*, took the pen name Honorius to ease his exposure to "derision of meanness, the snarling of petulance, and the attacks of malevolence" from readers.[6] Despite such antagonism, publishers were not above seeking out—or fabricating—details of land-owners' relationships with slaves. Political reports were fervent, but at times drew upon bad habits from British journalistic forebears: among them, a haphazard approach to recording official discourse. Early American press news of official meetings reported hours of proceedings without notes—a trend begun, no doubt, when journalist notepads were banned in some American statehouses.[7] But when a clear official word needed to go out, public officials knew how to make a news gatherer's job easy. When President George Washington, in September 1796, wanted to announce he was stepping away from public office, he summoned D. C. Claypoole, publisher of *Claypoole's American Daily Advertiser*, for an interview.[8]

Publishers had an appetite for foreign news—nearly all of it reprinted. Newspapers got much of their news from other newspapers during this century. And the news that was reprinted generally had a political angle. This followed a pattern seen in English news gathering that, through the 1700s, was a means of staking political territory. Factual content in American newspapers of this era aimed at molding opinion—angled, as it was, by the

writing of the politically-connected. Such politically-savvy printers as James and Benjamin Franklin found ways of making certain their readers got news about English documents the printers deemed important, like the Stamp Act, and such events as the war with Spain in 1739 and the Gordon riots in 1780. But because printers doubled as editor/publishers—often in addition to several other occupations—the time to gather news was scarce. The reprinting of English news or opinion, or letters of opinion by prominent leaders grew as a journalistic tradition as much out of convenience as by political design. But gathering reprinted news by ship was far from convenient.

Printers gathered news from published cargo as well as ships' crews. This made mishaps at sea and glitches in sailing schedules a common news-gathering hurdle. Reports from across the Atlantic were commonly delayed by many weeks or months. Printers gladly snapped up British and European news pages when they arrived, but also drew on newsworthy recollections of sea captains from coffeehouses along the coast. In England, news collection in coastal drinking establishments had been a natural. Not only did sea captains gather there, so did prominent business leaders. In fact, the mail was often delivered in or near British coffeehouses through the 1680s. Boston had two such coffeehouses by 1700—among them the London Coffee House, owned by Benjamin Harris, publisher of one of the colonies' first newspapers. But not all publishers were content to wait for news to take a seat over coffee. Henry Ingraham Blake, editor of the *New England Paladium*, became known as the father of modern reporting for his habit of clambering into boats and rowing out to meet incoming ships. Upon hearing the latest, he would rush back to his printing office and set type for news pages from scribbled notes on his shirt cuffs, fingernails, or from memory. Such rowboat reporting would become common among American news publishers in ensuing years.[9]

What little speed there was in news gathering and reprint-collection by mail in the colonial era owed much not only to sea power but to horsepower—the latter ridden, for better or worse, by postriders. Among the best was Peter Mumford. Laden with mail bags, Mumford, in 1773 could cover 80 miles in 26 hours—with horse-changes in three cities. Riders like Mumford could have moved even faster had they not taken time in each city to confer with the local printer about news up and down the circuit. In one way the stop-overs made sense: postmasters were the printers in many colonial towns. The *Kentucke Gazette*, founded in 1787, opened seven years before the Lexington settlement had a post office. In absence of regular mail routes, and no doubt to gain access to outlying news, the editor set up a rudimentary postal drop in his office before mail routes began. In this way, news could come his direction all the more readily.[10] Such informal gathering of news became an underlying foundation of journalism lasting many decades.

AMERICAN NEWS FOR NEW AMERICANS

News in America after 1800 was more American, began coming more often in the local mail, and told stories of an expanding American experience in newly-settled regions. Greater amounts of news in 19th-century mailboxes—especially publishers' boxes—resulted in part from the Post Office Act of 1793. This was a law that made the sharing of newspapers between editors a free exchange. Nearly overnight, a practice known as "scissors and pastepot" journalism put out-of-town news into local hot-lead as soon as a pony rider and his bag arrived.

Meanwhile, reporting had been growing as an art and craft and would become a market force. Editors found that advertisers paid well to be part of a publication whose reporters plunged into towns and cities to gather breaking news. By the mid–1830s, New York newspapers had correspondents in Washington, Philadelphia, Boston, Canada, Jamaica, and Key West, and city newsroom staffs were growing in size as well.[11]

The Civil War, and the news-gathering

innovations that came with it, made that conflict a watershed in reporting. Most noteworthy among Civil War reporting tools was the telegraph. It was the wire dispatches from battle fronts that made wartime decision-making instantaneous rather than delayed by days or weeks. Telegraph operators used a code that Samuel F. B. Morse designed with long and short clicks, or "dots" and "dashes," that could tap out 25 to 30 words a minute. Officials, as well as army commanders, suddenly had less time to think before acting and saw repercussions of their actions more quickly than ever before. On May 24, 1844, the *New York Evening Post* called Morse "the magician at the end of the line" who had helped the newspaper capture details of George M. Dallas as Vice President.[12] But the telegraph's magic could make life rough for the magicians. Some of the first prisoners of Civil War battles were commonly telegraph operators.[13]

Civil war reporters were a hardy, reckless group, not only sneaking on and off trains, but dodging capture in battle. They survived by a combination of physical agility and persistence in tough conditions, most of the time. In one instance, however, a reporter recalled scribbling out a news story atop a marble table on a Mississippi riverboat.[14]

Though a few Confederate newspapers drew war news from the letters of soldiers,[15] military officials generally took a love-hate stance toward reporters, seen, as one example, in the correspondence of Ulysses S. Grant. In a derisive quip in 1861, he wrote, "My regiment has been reported cut to pieces once that I know of, and I don't know but oftner, whilst a gun has not been fired by us." Later that year, he would write another family member that "some of the papers have got hold of my orders by some means or other and published them. I do not know how it is. I do not let newspaper correspondents come about me." Yet Grant was too shrewd to totally avoid the latest news reports. He even passed some along to military colleagues—though he added, in one case, "for what it's worth." William Tecumseh Sherman was known to plant intentionally vague or false reports with battle reporters.[16] Reporters' perseverance against such resistance became a kind of legend in itself. And the competition among reporters to outdo each other in getting stories against all odds grew steadily.

By the 1870s, reporters were earning their way from place to place among the nation's top news staffs by exposing crime—and well-known criminals—at high levels. When O. K. Bovard handed a story of street-car contract bribes to an editor at the *St. Louis Star*, it was summarily rejected. But Bovard immediately took it across town to the *Post-Dispatch*, where a news editor asked, "What do you want for it?" Bovard replied, "You can have it if you'll give me a job." He got the job. Although city officials named in his story escaped indictment, his reporting stirred newspapers and voters across the city.[17]

Pursuit of news at all costs—and at great personal peril—owes much to publisher James Gordon Bennett and his son. The elder Bennett, founder of the *New York Herald*, introduced a sensationalism to reporting that startled readers but drew them back again and again to his popular penny paper. Eager attention to news was unheard of among sedate newspapers of his day, resulting in low subscription rates and equally low advertiser attention. "Get out of my way, ye drivelling editors and drivelling politicians," Bennett was known to bellow. His newsroom tactics and squinting scowl would eventually make him known as both champion of the poor and marauding press baron. Though he had reporting and editing experience, his start as an independent publisher began on a board laid over two flour barrels in a basement office. From there, he introduced stock-market reporting, socialite-tattling, jokes, and fashion notes. His newspaper's police blotter reports would gain wide attention when, in 1836, he took on police detective techniques to find and describe the body and crime-scene in a well-known prostitute's murder. Bennett's record of his dialogue with the brothel keeper introduced a new vividness to the journalistic interview that would become a lasting innovation.[18]

Reporters working for James Gordon Bennett, Jr.—building on his father's bent toward the sensational—set a precedent for sensory-detailed reporting, scoops, beats, creative headlines, and condensed text. The younger Bennett also became known for creation of news—from sponsored races of yachts and balloons to expeditions of reporters to far-off regions. His reporters were not averse to paying handsomely for interviews or for starting mini-wars just to report on them. Henry Stanley's plunge through interior Africa to find the missionary-explorer David Livingstone was a notable example.[19] Bennett's *Herald*, in the 1860s, reported relatively little about sports but did make space for details of "pugilism" involving "spring-heeled" fighters with bloodied faces—along with speculation as to winnings for the event's promoters.

Indeed, sports had so become part of American cultural life by the late 19th century it was, in its more sensational forms, considered news. (See chapter 21 for an account of the history of sports reporting.) The Associated Press, on June 8, 1889, used the telegraph to bring readers highlights of a 75-round, bare-knuckle fight between John L. Sullivan and Jake Kilrain. News of the two-hour-16-minute bout in the Mississippi backwoods had to be tossed, piece-by-piece, in hollowed-out balls over the heads of spectators to waiting couriers—who then raced by train to a New Orleans telegraph office to sent the reports to their competing newspapers.[20]

Meanwhile, news interviewing innovations that the Bennetts and other publishers pioneered had been growing in refinement over the century. By the late 1890s, reporters like Lincoln Steffens were using these face-to-face encounters to draw amazing statements from sources. William Randolph Hearst called Steffens "the best interviewer he had ever encountered," and a fellow journalist observed that people entering a room with Steffens would break eye contact lest they be drawn into saying something they'd later regret.[21]

Interviews weren't the only part of reporters' tool boxes in the 19th century. Surveys, increasingly, were used for compiling trend stories. One of the earliest attempts at survey-driven news collection appeared in North Carolina in 1810.[22]

But regardless of tools or methods, the common trait of reporting was shoe-leather. A reporter worth his salt simply took to the streets earlier and longer than his competitors to find news details first, or get them better. If it took an extra set of carrier pigeons or a ride on a freight train, reporters did what was needed. Ironically, though, some reporters' tendency to prefer convention to innovation made for grudging acceptance of some news-gathering tools that could have speeded their work. Two of these were the telephone and typewriter.

One of the first uses of the telephone was to send news of an Alexander Graham Bell lecture from his laboratory to newspaper offices in 1877. By the 1880s, telephones helped create two new journalistic job descriptions: "leg men," who got the information, and "rewrite men," who wrote reporters' phoned dispatches into stories. Yet despite the telephone's massive potential for speedy interaction with sources, it lacked wide acceptance for news gathering until well after 1880.

Part of the lag was weak marketing, but a larger barrier was the telegraph's massive cultural appeal—along with force of habit—in news-gathering practice. The telegraph left a printed record of one's interaction with another; the telephone did not. And the telegraph, by the 1870s, had ready-made cables connecting continent to continent around the globe. Telephones would lack this type of support for many years. The typewriter came into common use in 1884 out of concern for quick, legible news copy to hike daily wire-fed wordage: for United Press, over 17,000 words a day. Speed was crucial. The AP in Chicago, for example, was paying $100,000 a year for rental of a telegraph line to New York in the 1880s.[23]

If reporters were slow to accept some news-gathering innovations, they were slower to adopt cooperative news gathering—given the precedent of competitive advantage in reporting news. (See chapter 16 for an account of the history of cooperative news gathering.) Wire news was perhaps the strongest example of this. Since telegraph lines could take only one message at a time, line-hogging was common. One operator—perhaps with embellishment—recalled reporters bent on deadline advantage showing up at the telegraph office door with Bible in hand and, as a stalling tactic, dispatch-

ing Genesis 1:1 and continuing through Deuteronomy before something appropriately newsworthy could be inserted.[24] Telegraph line domination effectively ended in the mid–1840s with passage of the "Fifteen Minute Rule." By this, telegraph operators were to allow reporters only a quarter-hour of time, opening the line to slower competitors.[25] The Associated Press, formed in 1848 and followed in 1881 by United Press, crafted telegraph technology to the reporting needs of newspapers in both small towns and urban centers.

A slower trend in news gathering, though every bit as influential as the telegraph, was the trend toward the visual. Pictures had been part of news gathering since before the Civil War with news artists perched on hilltops sketching out battle lines, noting moves of key commanders, and counting the dead. Big-box cameras rumbled on horse-drawn wagons out to battlefields and pioneer camps through the 19th century, producing vivid pictorial news reports. Fletcher Harper, youngest brother in a well-known publishing family, began *Harper's Weekly* in 1857 and by its eighth issue was running advertisements seeking "sketches or photographic pictures of striking scenes, important events, and leading men" from anywhere in the world. He promised to pay well.[26] News illustrations using engravings could be found fairly commonly by 1850, but the first printing-press photo by halftone—of a shantytown—appeared in New York in 1880.[27] Within three decades, news gathering aimed at accompanying illustration or photos would move from journalistic novelty to widespread expectation in the nation's larger publications. (See chapter 35 for an account of the history of photojournalism.)

The end of the 19th century, with its glutted city streets, belching smokestacks, and teeming ghettos helped produce the deep inquiry by journalists known as "investigative reporting." (See chapter 23 for an account of the history of investigative and reform reporting.) Between the 1890s and 1920, writers such as Ida Tarbell, Upton Sinclair, and Lincoln Steffens combined interviews and public-records searches to unearth neglect or outright villainy in uses of public funding or property. In an 18-part series in *McClure's* magazine beginning in 1902, Tarbell's reporting based on court records exposed not only the Standard Oil Company's monopolistic power abuses under John D. Rockefeller but also the greater problem of trusts within the American economy. In 1909, a writer for *Cosmopolitan* exposed the sugar trust's false-weighting of its products, and political bribery. Sinclair, using a controversial but soon common approach, went undercover to expose corruption in America's meat-packing industry.[28]

NEWS, CAMERAS, AND ACTION

If three words could capture reporting after 1900, they would be speed, doggedness, and ambivalence. For news really to be news, it had to be fast—preferably faster than competing reports. And reporters, backed by ever-faster presses, telegraph- and telephone-driven interviews, and visuals, became all the more powerful as pursuers of facts. But with advancing speed of American news gathering and news distribution—speed bringing ripple-effects across the globe—came questions about speed's implications. It was in this era that news gathering became capable of outpacing daily life itself. Reporters, more and more, were informing sources of news rather than vice-versa. One reporter in the early 20th century told of having to approach the door of a widow who did not know her husband had been killed in a train wreck near Kansas City. The family was celebrating a child's birthday. Reporter William Salisbury rang the doorbell but almost turned away. "I felt like a criminal," he recalled. "For the moment I even regretted that I was a reporter. This was not the kind of work I had dreamed of doing. This was a hellish mission, fit only for one who reveled in slaying joy. I wanted to flee." But rather than escaping the moment, Salisbury gently informed the woman of what few details he had of the wreck—then gave the family a lift to a relative's home. And he got the quotes needed for his story.[29]

Though news over the airwaves began raising the bar on speed of news gathering after the 1920s, print reporters' patterns of old-fashioned digging for facts, documentation, and quotes would remain the bedrock underlying all news—radio and television included— through the end of the century. A uniqueness, moreover, of 20th-century print journalism was its willingness to use varieties of techniques and technologies to get stories. The *New York Times*, in 1912, used a wireless telegraph to get its story about the *Titanic's* sinking to readers before any other newspaper in the world. It also used telephone reports, eyewitness accounts, and traditional telegraph dispatches to pull together not only straight news about the sinking, but sidebar biographies—all for the first edition the day the ship went down. Competing papers missed or bungled the story.[30]

Advances in transportation helped 20th-century reporters much more quickly than in previous centuries. While horses and "iron horse" trains had been chief modes by which reporters could reach news scenes before 1900, the new century allowed them to clamber into their own automobiles, into speedier, safer trans-oceanic ships, and eventually into airplanes and helicopters. The improved transportation would allow them to cover stories with much more regularity and with tighter deadlines.

Reporting on or near battlefields was not new when the United States entered World War I, but the rise of 20th-century war correspondents—as a special class of reporters— bears special note. (See chapter 25 for an account of the history of war reporting.) Ernest Hemingway's European exploits during World War I for the *Kansas City Star* made him a legend of journalism too often overlooked when weighed against his longer literary career. His reporting gave readers the sights, sounds, smells, and tastes of war. An added side-note to the war correspondent phenomenon was the celebrity status some reporters gained. Publishers and publication marketers unashamedly touted their reporters' exploits as marks of press distinction. In one such push, a war reporter told readers, in a splashy, full-page advertising layout, that the biggest story he'd ever covered "was written on top of a crate of tommy-guns in the hold of a cargo plane 6,000 feet above an African jungle."[31] It is arguable that this celebrity status, though at times distracting, helped reporters gain access to sources and locations otherwise inaccessible.

While world war took American reporters to locations rarely, if ever, seen or heard with such vividness, it left a press industry groping for manpower. And lacking men, it chose women—women whose place in newsrooms had been growing steadily for more than a century but who suddenly gained new visibility.[32] Could women dig out the same stories—or better ones—than men? They got their chance to answer this question as they gained access to such formerly male-only bastions as the press box at the New York Polo Grounds, and the White House press room under Eleanor Roosevelt.[33] (See chapter 9 for an account of the history of women in journalism.)

Though reporters, after 1900, could dig faster and deeper for news, they were increasingly hounded by press agents intent on packaging news in ways easily usable by reporters on deadline. This push—amid ever-speedier deadlines—put pressure on reporters to short-cut news gathering and make their stories simple rewordings of official information.[34] Events in the late 1950s and early 1960s changed such automated news gathering. Deep-digging by such reporters as Seymour Hersh, I. F. Stone, Drew Pearson, and George Seldes had an uncommon pointedness. Theirs was news gained by detective work—some so piercing that advertisers winced and mainstream publications declined to give it print. With targets ranging from the U.S. Supreme Court to General Electric, reporters used public documents, posed as workers in allegedly corrupt businesses, and gathered facts no one else knew existed.[35] Such dogged news gathering launched an investigative reporting movement that peaked in publication of the Pentagon Papers by the *New York Times*. Later, investigative reporting by the *Washington Post's* Bob Woodward and Carl Bernstein—aided by others—unearthed dirty tricks and cover-ups by the administration of President Richard Nixon. That reporting, and events surrounding it, led to Nixon's impeachment and resignation.

News gathering would get a final push before century's end. In the 1970s, three movements in information technology merged in ways so culturally explosive for journalism and news gathering as to rival the invention of the telegraph and rotary press. Computer technology, linked with telephone de-regulation and the opening of a global network called the Internet, would make news an instantaneous possibility anywhere in the world that one could find electricity, a telephone line, and a computer-modem hook-up.[36] Newsrooms that in the 1970s clattered with typewriters were, only a decade later, humming with video display terminals (VDTs), later to be replaced by networks of smaller, more versatile machines similar to personal computers sold on department store shelves. By the mid–1990s, print, video, and audio news reporting had merged on computer web sites. Electronic mail, also accessible by telephone or fiber-optic cable through a computer, helped newsroom reporters chat—by means of typewritten text—with news sources on other continents, gain access to databases of information across town or across the planet. It also allowed them to print out breaking-news photos and import graphs or charts needed to illustrate the increasingly-complex news they were gathering.[37] (See chapter 37 for an account of the history of technology used in news gathering.)

As had been true in the era of Pulitzer and Bennett, tenacity for reporting in recent years raised as many questions as answers for journalists. Yet the undying mandate of keeping Americans informed—that satisfying of a hunger American democracy had perhaps always had—today keeps news gatherers unyielding in their pursuit of better stories.

Selected Readings

Barkin, Steve M. "Changes in Business Sections, 1931–1979." *Journalism Quarterly* 59 (1982): 435–39.

Bowers, Thomas A. "'Precision Journalism' in North Carolina in the 1800s." *Journalism Quarvurn* 53 (1976): 738–40.

Copeland, David A. "'A Receipt Against the Plague': Medical Reporting in Colonial America." *American Journalism* 11 (Summer 1994): 204–18.

Corbalis, Kathy J. "'Atomic Bill' Laurence: He Reported the Birth of the A-Bomb." *Media History Digest* 5, 3 (1985): 9–11, 28–30.

Desmond, Robert W. *The Information Process: World News Reporting to the Twentieth Century*. Ames: Iowa State University Press, 1978.

Henry, Susan. "Reporting 'Deeply and at First Hand': Helen Campbell in the 19th-Century Slums." *Journalism History* 11 (1984): 18–25.

Kielbowicz, Richard B. *News in the Mail: The Press, Post Office and Public Information, 1700–1860s*. Westport, Conn.: Greenwood Press, 1989.

Knight, Oliver A. *Following the Indian Wars: The Story of the Newspaper Correspondents Among the Indian Campaigners, 1866–1891*. Norman: University of Oklahoma Press, 1960.

Leonard, Thomas C. *The Power of the Press: The Birth of American Reporting*. New York: Oxford University Press, 1986.

Nilsson, Nils Gunnar. "The Origin of the Interview." *Journalism Quarterly* 48 (1971): 707–13.

Olasky, Marvin. "When World Views Collide: Journalists and the Great Monkey Trial." *American Journalism*. 4 (1987): 133–46.

Pratte, Alf. "The Honolulu *Star-Bulletin* and the 'Day of Infamy.'" *American Journalism* 5 (1988): 5–13.

Schwarzlose, Richard A. "Early Telegraphic News Dispatches: Forerunner of the AP." *Journalism Quarterly* 51 (1974): 595–601.

Schwarzlose, Richard. "The Foreign Connection: Trans-atlantic Newspapers in the 1840s." *Journalism History* 10 (1983): 44–49, 67.

Shaw, Donald L. "News Bias and the Telegraph: A Story of Historical Change." *Journalism Quarterly* 44 (1967): 3–12.

Steele, Ian K. *The English Atlantic 1675–1740: An Exploration of Communication and Community*. New York: Oxford University Press, 1986.

Stein, Harry. "Lincoln Steffens: Interviewer." *Journalism Quarterly* 46 (1969): 727–36.

Stewart, Robert K. "The Exchange System and the Development of American Politics in the 1820s." *American Journalism* 4 (1987): 30–42.

Turnbull, George. "Some Notes on the History of the Interview." *Journalism Quarterly* 13 (1936): 272–79.

Notes

1. Joseph Pulitzer, *New York Evening Post*, 30 October 1911.

2. George S. Johns, "Joseph Pulitzer: Early Life in St. Louis and His Founding and Conduct of the Post-Dispatch up to 1883," Fourth Article, *Missouri Historical Review* 25:2 (January, 1931): 210–11; and Fifth Article, 26:2 (February, 1931): 165–66.

3. *New York Herald*, 19 August 1836.

4. *Boston Gazette*, 18 April 1720, 3.

5. Charles E. Clark, *The Public Prints: The Newspaper in Anglo-American Culture, 1665–1740* (New York: Oxford University Press, 1994), 211.

6. *Connecticut Courant*, 21 October 1783.

7. Thomas C. Leonard, *The Power of the Press: The Birth of American Reporting* (New York: Oxford University Press, 1986), 68–71.

8. Barnett Fine, *Editor & Publisher*, 3 June 1933, 12.

9. Victor Rosewater, *History of Cooperative News-gathering in the United States* (New York: D. Appleton and Company, 1930), 9.

10. Tom L. Walker, *History of the Lexington Post Office, from 1794 to 1901* (Lexington: E. D. Veach, 1901), 12, 15.

11. *New York Herald*, 8 December 1837.

12. *New York Evening Post*, 27 May 1844; *New York Times*, 18 October 1907, 1.

13. Annteresa Lubrano, *The Telegraph: How Technology Innovation Caused Social Change* (New York: Garland Publishing, Inc., 1997), 50–52.

14. Sylvanus Cadwalter, *Three Years with Grant, As Recalled by War Correspondent Sylvanus Cadwalter*, ed. Benjamin P. Thomas (New York: Alfred A. Knopf, 1955), 98.

15. Ford Risley, "Bombastic Yet Insighful: Georgia's Civil War Soldier Correspondents," *Journalism History* 24:3 (1998): 104–08.

16. Ulysses S. Grant to Jesse Root Grant, 3 August 1861; Ulysses S. Grant to Julia Dent Grant, 25 September 1861; Ulysses S Grant to Capt. John C. Ketton, 29 November 1861, *The Papers of Ulysses S. Grant*, vols. 2–3, ed. John Y. Simon (Carbondale: Southern Illinois University Press, 1970), 80, 234–35, 311.

17. Quoted in James W. Markham, *Bovard of the Post-Dispatch* (Baton Rouge: Louisiana State University Press, 1954), 1–2.

18. Willlard G. Bleyer, *Main Currents in the History of American Journalism* (Boston: 1927), 190; Piers Brendon, *The Life and Death of the Press Barons* (New York: Atheneum, 1983), 8–9, 21–25.

19. Oliver Carlson, *The Man Who Made News: James Gordon Bennett* (New York: Duell, Sloan and Pearce, 1942), 383–89; Mark Wahlgren Summers, *The Press Gang: Newspapers and Politics, 1865–1878* (Chapel Hill: University of North Carolina Press, 1994), 16–17, 138, 158; Brendon, ibid., 33–34.

20. Oliver Gramling, *AP: The Story of News* (Port Washington, N.Y.: Kennikat Press, 1940), 231–32. The fight's location was aimed at avoiding legal complications. Boxing was illegal in most states at the time.

21. George Turnbull, "Some Notes on the History of the Interview," *Journalism Quarterly* 13 (1936): 272–79; Harry Stein, "Lincoln Steffens: Interviewer," *Journalism Quarterly* 46 (1969): 727, 734; Nils Gunnar Nilsson, "The Origin of the Interview," *Journalism Quarterly* 48 (1971): 707–13.

22. Thomas A. Bowers, "'Precision Journalism' in North Carolina in the 1800s," *Journalism Quarterly* (1976): 738–40.

23. *The Journalist*, 29 May 1886.

24. U.S. Congress, Senate, Committee on Education and Labor, *Report of the Committee of the Senate upon the Relations between Labor and Capital, and Testimony Taken by Committee*, 48th Congress (1883–1885), vol. 2, 1265–83. For Sherman's planted news, see *New York Herald*, 11, 12, 18, 20 May 1864.

25. *Articles of Association of the New York and Boston Magnetic Telegraph Association, Together with Office Regulations, Records of Meetings of the Trustees, Stockholders, and Directors* (New York: Chatterton and Christ, 1848), 24.

26. Michael Carlebach, *The Origins of Photojournalism in America* (Washington, D.C.: Smithsonian Institution Press, 1992), 64.

27. *New York Daily Graphic*, 4 March 1880; Carlebach, ibid. (Washington, D.C., 1992), 162.

28. Ida M. Tarbell, "History of the Standard Oil Company," *McClure's Magazine*, December 1902, 115–28. Results of Tarbell's newsgathering ran in *McClure's* from

November 1902 to July 1903 and from December 1903 to October 1904. The series eventually became a book. Lincoln Steffens' in-depth reporting on governmental corruption in U.S. cities—also later to become a book—appeared in serial form in *McClure's* during the years Tarbell's Standard Oil reports appeared. cf. Lincoln Steffens, "The Shame of Minneapolis: The Rescue and Redemption of a City that was Sold Out," *McClure's*, January 1903, 227–239; James R. Barrett, "Introduction" to *The Jungle*, reprint ed. (Urbana: University of Illinois Press, 1988), xvi; David L. Protess, et al, *The Journalism of Outrage: Investigative Reporting and Agenda-Building in America* (New York: Guilford Press, 1991), 37–39.

29. William Salisbury, *The Career of a Journalist* (New York: B. W. Dodge & Company, 1908), 51.

30. *New York Times*, 16 April 1912, 1–5. For managing editor Carr Van Anda's newsgathering instincts, see Geoffrey Marcus, *The Maiden Voyage: The Titanic Epic from the Embarkation to the Disaster and the Dramatic Courtroom Aftermath* (New York: Viking Press, 1969), 200–01; David Halberstam, *The Powers that Be* (New York: Alfred A. Knopf, 1979), 212; also, Joshua Harris Prager, "'Is it too late to run a correction?' How this paper bungled the *Titanic* story," *Wall Street Journal*, 26 January 1998, B1.

31. *Editor & Publisher*, 16 January 1943, 17.

32. *Editor & Publisher*, 2 January 1943, 14.

33. Maurine Beasley and Sheila Silver, *Women in Media: A Documentary Sourcebook* (Washington, D.C.: Women's Institute for the Freedom of the Press, 1977); Deborah Davis, *Katharine the Great: Katharine Graham and her Washington Post Empire* (Acacia Press, 1991); Katharine

Graham, *Personal History* (New York: Vintage Press, 1998); Maurine H. Beasley, "The Women's National Press Club: Case Study in the Professionalization of Women Journalists," paper presented at the annual convention of the Association for Education in Journalism and Mass Communication (Norman, Okla., August 3–6, 1986); Julia Edwards, *Women of the World: The Great Foreign Correspondents* (Boston: Houghton-Mifflin Company, 1988); Sherry Ricchiardi and Virginia Young, *Women on Deadline: A Collection of America's Best* (Ames: Iowa State University Press, 1991), 191–201.

34. Kyun-Tae Han, "Composition of Board of Directors of Major Media Corporations," *Journal of Media Economics* 1:2 (Fall 1988): 85–100; Peter Dreier and Steve Weinberg, "Interlocking Directorates," *Columbia Journalism Review*, November/December 1979, 51–68; Lawrence C. Soley and Robert L. Craig, "Advertising Pressures on Newspapers," *Journal of Advertising* 21:4 (1992): 1–10.

35. Edd Applegate, *Journalistic Advocates and Muckrakers: Three Centuries of Contributing Writers* (Jefferson, N.C.: McFarland Publishers, 1997), 145, 158, 172.

36. Brian S. Brooks and Tai-en Yang, "Patterns of Computer Use in Newspaper Newsrooms: A National Study of U.S. Dailies" paper presented at the Association for Education in Journalism and Mass Communication, Kansas City, Mo., August 11–14, 1993.

37. Bruce Garrison, "Online Newsgathering Trends, 1994–1996," paper presented at the Association for Education in Journalism and Mass Communication, Chicago, Ill., July 30–August. 2, 1997.

16

Cooperative News Gathering

RICHARD A. SCHWARZLOSE

Cooperative news gathering historically occurred in three settings: occasional collaborations among individual reporters who were not direct competitors to cover specific news events, among competing editors to produce a daily news report for the common use of all who were cooperating, or among several news organizations to cooperate synergistically in reporting and presenting news on a daily basis.

One historic example of cooperating reporters occurred in the spring of 1961 when, amid persistent rumors that Cuban exiles were being trained in the United States to invade Fidel Castro's Communist Cuba, Tad Szulc of the *New York Times* and Stuart Novins of CBS Radio collaborated by gathering and sharing information about the covert operation. On April 6 each reported in his own news outlet that the U.S. government was training paramilitary forces for the ill-fated Bay of Pigs invasion fiasco 11 days later.

By far the longest-standing cooperative news-gathering effort, however, has been among newspaper publishers who shared the cost of covering news and receiving a daily news report by transportation, and later, by telegraph. In the 1830s news still moved fitfully and unpredictably between towns and from abroad, constantly the victim of daily and seasonal weather conditions and a transportation system designed to move people and goods rather than news. To hasten the arrival of news, editors ran expresses from distant cities, employed correspondents in major news centers, and even rowed out into Eastern harbors to collect news from incoming ships.

News gathering in those days was difficult, even dangerous. Consider the plight of Harry Blake, who gathered news in Boston harbor after 1800 for Boston's *New England Palladium* and later for the *Boston Courier*. He would visit the wharves at midnight, looking for items for next morning's paper, and frequently went out alone in a boat "in darkness, storm, and tempest," said historian Joseph Buckingham, to meet ships. The stresses of harbor duty and problems with his wife, led Blake, as Buckingham delicately put it, "to indulgences not justified by strict requirements of temperance. Seldom, too, when [Blake] found or made acquaintances on ship-board," Buckingham continued, "was he allowed to depart without partaking of a social cup. At length he sank under the pressures of intellectual and physical disorders.... *Alas! poor Harry Blake.*"[1]

Some of the large New York City dailies in the early 1830s ran their own horse expresses from Philadelphia to rush Washington, D.C., news to their newsrooms, until the cost of the enterprise forced the dailies to cooperate. These same dailies individually also sent schooners as far as 200 miles out into the Atlantic Ocean in the 1830s to meet westbound sailing ships in the 1830s, again later forced by the expense to cooperate.

Boston papers cooperated in running a locomotive from Washington to Boston in 1836 at speeds that few people had ever experienced. "In one case, an editor nearly lost his life by excitement," biographer Isaac C. Pray reported, "in riding on the locomotive from Worcester to Boston, about forty miles, in as many minutes."

Having fainted from traveling 60 miles per hour, he was rushed in a carriage to a newspaper office where the news dispatch he was carrying had to be pried from his clenched fingers.[2]

Both the appearance and expansion of cooperative news gathering were driven by new technologies that, in turn, offered both the promise of faster or fuller news reports and the twin perils of the technology's excessive costs and the threat that a competing editor could scoop you by using the new technology. Although naturally drawn to technologies that could move news faster or over longer distances, editors found that they had to cooperate with local competitors to control costs, benefiting from technology only by settling for the same news reports that competitors received.

Technological innovation smiled on U.S. newspapers in the 1840s. First, in 1840 Samuel Cunard established regular twice-monthly steamer service between Liverpool in England and Halifax and then Boston (and later, to New York City). Regardless of the weather in the Atlantic, the original 207-foot "Cunarders," equipped with side paddles, could splash their way across the ocean in from 14 to 16 days, a regular ocean ferry that brought foreign dispatches and newspapers at predictable intervals.[3]

Eastern newspaper editors found that they had to cooperate in transporting these steamers' foreign news down the coast from Halifax to newsrooms in Boston, New York City, Philadelphia, and Baltimore. Before the telegraph reached Halifax, Daniel H. Craig of Boston used homing pigeons to carry brief summaries of European news from the steamer to Boston newspapers and beyond. "I carried my birds by land to Halifax to meet the incoming Cunard steamers, and then took passage [on them] for Boston," he said years late. "After gathering news from London and Liverpool journals, I printed it on tissue paper, with small type, in my stateroom, fastened it to the legs of the birds, and at the proper time flew them from the desks or portholes of the steamers. My birds carried the news to Boston several hours in advance of the steamers."[4]

The telegraph was the earliest technology to harness electricity for moving news and thus was the mother of permanent cooperative news gathering in the United States. Telegraphy arrived in the spring of 1844 with the appearance of Samuel F. B. Morse's first line, erected between Washington, D.C., and Baltimore. Almost immediately after telegraph lines began to creep from town to town along the Atlantic coast, partnerships and cooperatives of newspaper editors sprang up as the only economical way of using this new technology.

The earliest known cooperative news gathering by telegraph appeared early in 1846 along a telegraph line going up between Albany to Buffalo across the middle of New York State. On February 3 after the line from Albany reached Utica, the *Utica Gazette* carried a column of telegraphic news from Albany, suggesting to editors along the proposed route of the line that they, too, could run telegraphic news. When the line was completed to Buffalo on July 4, 1846, the editors had employed an agent in Albany who gathered news and transmitted a daily telegraphic dispatch to all papers along the line that helped pay for the service.[5]

New York City's six circulation-leader dailies in the mid–1840s represented a broad spectrum of political, economic, and sociocultural reading audiences: two political-party papers (the *Courier & Enquirer* and *Express*), a mercantile paper (the *Journal of Commerce*), and three penny papers (the *Sun*, *Herald*, and *Tribune*). Because each had a unique reading audience, cooperation among the newspapers was feasible. By 1848 these six dailies sat in the middle of a rapidly expanding telegraph network that reached north to Boston and was moving toward Halifax; north and west to Albany and Buffalo and was moving toward Chicago; and south to Philadelphia, Baltimore, and Washington, D.C., and was moving toward New Orleans. In 1849 these six dailies formed the Associated Press, a cooperative partnership.

The Associated Press in New York City took several forms: organizing a harbor newsgathering system in the spring of 1848, collecting news from steamers at Halifax via horse expresses until the telegraph reached Halifax, and hiring Alexander Jones as general agent who gathered news and wrote a single one- to two-column daily news dispatch, copies of which were hand delivered to each of the six Associated Press newspaper offices at around midnight. By 1851 Jones had hired news-gathering agents in Baltimore; Buffalo; New Orleans; New Orleans; Boston; Albany; Cincinnati; Norfolk, Va.; and even Montreal and Toronto, Canada.[6]

Craig, who had aggressively gathered European news at Halifax with pigeons and later horse expresses, replaced Jones as general agent in 1851. From then until 1866 when he was fired, Craig controlled U.S. cooperative news gathering, compiling a daily telegraphic dispatch of foreign and domestic news that not only went to the leading New York City dailies (which included the *New York Times* after its founding in 1851) but also to a growing number of Midwestern papers over an expanding telegraphic network.

After subduing a challenger, the Abbot & Winans wire service, in the early 1850s, Craig set out to create a national AP monopoly. "A cool, shrewd, indefatigable man, to whom processes were valuable only as they secured success," said historian James D. Reid, Craig "preserved at all times the placidity of a summer's morning. [But] beneath this calm exterior there was ... an energy and force of will, which, for a time, made him a very prominent factor in the telegraphic enterprise."[7]

"I visited all the leading editors of the country and the managers of the numerous telegraph companies," Craig said 30 years later, "and explained to them my purpose to establish a complete system for reporting the details of all important news by telegraph. I found a large majority of the editors violently opposed to my views, ... their selfish and absurd idea being that each individual editor should telegraph all the news he desired to publish, and thus bring a larger grist to their mill. [But] until I retired [from the AP] every journal in the country and in Canada was compelled to submit to our rules in regard to telegraphic news dispatches."[8]

Craig finally established a cooperative

news gathering monopoly after 1855 because he controlled the gathering of foreign news brought by the Cunard steamers to Halifax and brought by other ships to New York City harbor. Moreover, he and his correspondents aggressively gathered news throughout the nation east of the Mississippi River and especially from Washington, D.C., where AP's Lawrence A. Gobright reported news in a nonpartisan way. "My business is to communicate facts," Gobright once told a congressional committee. "My instructions do not allow me to make any comment upon the facts which I communicate. My dispatches are sent to papers of all manner of politics and the editors say they are able to make their own comments upon the facts which are sent to them.... I ... try to be truthful and impartial."[9]

Craig also constantly negotiated with telegraph companies to get special reduced rates and desirable transmission times for his news reports, and if one company would not cooperate with him, Craig would support another telegraph company's effort to erect lines in competition with the first one.

Meanwhile five other local Associated Presses were forming along the Eastern seaboard to control the local distribution of Craig's news dispatches. The Boston AP appeared in November, 1849,[10] later renamed the New England AP. That first wire service, operating between Albany and Buffalo beginning in 1846, became known as the New York State AP. The Philadelphia AP and the Baltimore AP had close ties to the New York City AP from the start in 1848,[11] and the Southern AP actually predated the New York City AP, organizing in December, 1847, to issue a daily news report from Washington, D.C., and New Orleans.[12]

On June 1, 1861, telegraph company officials cut their trunk line that connected the North and the South on the Long Bridge over the Potomac River at Washington, D.C., severing AP's access to Confederate news and the Southern AP. By this time, Confederates had fired upon Fort Sumter, and Union troops were controlling Union telegraph lines.[13] Craig's settled routine of preparing nightly domestic news dispatches, punctuated fortnightly by arrivals of Cunard steamers with foreign news, was about to be shattered by the onrushing American Civil War. While the war was a tour de force for city newspaper editors and their correspondents, Craig's AP contended with all of war's discomforts and few of its glories. Staffs of New York City papers skimmed the cream of war coverage, leaving Craig to handle official dispatches and brief update bulletins.

In the South William H. Pritchard, editor of the *Augusta Constitutionalist*, took charge of the Southern AP office in Richmond, but by early 1862 Confederate editors were attempting to create a better, more cooperative wire service. Finally on February 4 and 5, 1863, Southern editors organized the Press Association of the Confederate States of America with John S. Thrasher as superintendent.[14] Hemmed in by a restrictive government that was not winning enough battles and by spotty access to the modest Southern telegraph system, Thrasher's wire service rode the gradually diminishing fortunes of the Confederacy to defeat in 1865. After the Civil War, the Southern AP reappeared when the U.S. War Department in September, 1865, consented to AP's transmission of a 100-word daily news report south across the Potomac River.[15]

Midwestern, and especially Chicago, editors complaining about AP's thin war reports throughout the war finally placed their own agent in AP's New York City office in 1864 to transmit more news to Midwestern newspapers. In March, 1865, these Midwestern papers formed the Western Associated Press headquartered in Chicago and occupying the territory from Canada to the Ohio River and from the Appalachian Mountains to Colorado. The appearance of an aggressive Western AP led to years of rancorous bickering between Chicago and New York City, culminating in the 1890s in open warfare between the two agencies on a national scale.[16]

Meanwhile, two other regional APs appeared: the Texas AP, always a pawn in the New York City–Chicago squabbles during the 1860s and 1870s, and the California AP, organized in San Francisco by James W. Simonton who replaced Craig in New York City in 1866. Five "auxiliaries" of the Western AP appeared

over two decades following the Civil War, dependent on Chicago for their news reports. With founding dates and areas represented, they were: the Northwestern AP in 1867 for smaller dailies in Illinois, Iowa, and eastern Nebraska; the Kansas and Missouri AP in 1868 for morning papers in those states; the Trans-Mississippi AP, in 1875 for evening papers in Kansas and Missouri; the Colorado AP in 1875; and the Northern AP in 1882 for papers in Minnesota and the Dakotas.[17]

The Associated Press was poised after the Civil War to create a national monopoly, and once again technology played into AP's hand. In 1866 after years of mergers, Western Union emerged as the leading national telegraph company, and AP's close ally. Moreover, after two failed attempts, Western Union successfully laid a working transatlantic cable between North America and England in the summer of 1866, giving AP same-day European news for the first time in U.S. history. To protect this advantage, AP saw to it that not a bad word was written about Western Union in its news report. In return, Western Union gave AP favorable rates and transmission times.

In spite of this postwar news-gathering prowess, a national news monopoly remained beyond AP's grasp for three reasons. First, a growing number of new postwar dailies were evening newspapers, and AP's main news report was timed for AP's very large number of morning papers. The news needs of these new evening papers opened the way for a series of private, commercial news agents to compete with AP. Second, existing AP newspapers used their membership "franchise," as people in the industry called it, that allowed them to deny AP services to new local competitors, once again creating an opportunity for other wire services to step in. Third, disagreements among the New York City AP's seven partners led to the firing November, 1866, of general agent Craig whose force of personality and constant alertness to detail had forged a strong and widespread AP structure after 1851.[18] Craig's replacement, James W. Simonton, although an excellent journalist who had covered Congress professionally, was a weak administrator, barely able to hold the AP edifice together, let alone build a monopoly.

A movement opposing AP appeared in 1868 when Henry George came east to get an AP membership for his *San Francisco Herald*. Simonton, who owned the competing *San Francisco Evening Bulletin* and the *Morning Call*, refused to give the AP report to George, who then arranged with boyhood friend and former Philadelphia AP agent John Hasson to receive a daily news report. The beginnings of a competitor for AP, Hasson's News Association was reorganized in 1870 as the American Press Association, aided by a rapidly growing new telegraph company, the Atlantic & Pacific.[19] Several large new dailies, unable to get AP memberships because local AP papers exercised their franchise rights excluding them, paid large assessments to support APA.

When one editor acquired a majority of APA stock and began controlling the news it reported, APA dissolved in 1876, replaced by the National Associated Press Company, which, in turn was purchased by a new United Press in December 1882.[20] While its predecessors had limped along, UP under the able and seasoned direction of manager Walter P. Phillips prospered. AP now faced 10 years of grueling, threatening national competition from UP.

Meanwhile within Associated Press, political intrigue was rampant. William Henry Smith became Western AP's general agent in Chicago in 1871. With calculated daring Smith orchestrated an assault on contractual obligations that subordinated his Western AP to New York City's AP. Periodically stirring the caldron with innuendoes and assertions about Simonton and some New York City partners, Smith drew the New York AP into an escalating conflict based on little more than regional jealousies, specious allegations, and exaggerated descriptions of motives. Abruptly Simonton resigned in 1881, and with help from allies in Western Union and the New York AP, Smith became general manager for both the New York City and Western APs.

The 1880s witnessed enormous changes in cooperative news gathering. The wire services began leasing lines from telegraph companies for their own private use, typewriters appeared in newsrooms in 1885 for faster

recording of a news report that was growing in length and diversity. As the pace quickened along the news circuits, AP and UP turned their lights increasingly on disasters, government crises, military adventures, foreign affairs, crimes, and sports events with greater intensity in a news report that was from four to six newspaper columns of copy a day.

Wire services did not use bylines until the 20th century, but in the 1880s were developing a system of bulletins and new leads to update their stories on breaking news events and to serve newspapers with different deadlines in the four time zones established in 1883. More correspondents were sent into remote areas to cover tragedies and violence and could find telegraph lines there to file their stories. Wire service news reports, by the 1890s, while still reasonably nonpartisan, were becoming a more significant part of American life, helping to knit the nation together with the shared experience of daily glimpses of life and death here and abroad.

On a parallel track in the 1880s feature syndicates and cooperatives that sold preprinted and printing-plate pages to country newspapers took off as the number of weeklies surpassed 7,000 nationally. Called "patent insides" and "boiler plate," respectively, these feature services provided small-town dailies and weeklies with copy that they could not have produced on their own. Ansel Nash Kellogg pioneered in Chicago in 1865 offering printing plates to country papers. Among many syndicates, two notable leaders—Western Newspaper Union and the American Press Association (not to be confused with the wire service mentioned above)—appeared in the 1880s and were successful because of the quality of their feature reporting and writing.[21] The news and features from these syndicates arrived as printed on paper, as thin metal printing plates, or as papier-mâché mats from which printing plates could be cast.

Led by the *Chicago Daily News* and beginning in the late 1890s several leading dailies—notably the *New York Times*, *New York Herald Tribune*, and *Chicago Tribune*—provided supplemental foreign news reporting for other dailies. Featuring highly regarded correspondents who were permanently assigned to foreign capitals, these supplementals' reporting and commentary complemented national wire services' reporting. Although the supplemental services emerged from World War II as important news sources, they gradually had to give up their costly foreign news staff, replacing it with copy from their newspapers' name columnists, feature writers, and enterprise reporters on the domestic front. The supplementals gained substantial numbers of newspaper subscribers in the 1960s and 1970s, and by 1989 the supplemental leaders were Los Angeles Times/Washington Post News Service, New York Times News Service, and Scripps-Howard News Service.[22]

Back on the main wire service track, Phillips' United Press succeeded nationally after 1882 in large part because many old AP papers would not share the AP report with new local papers and because Western Union could not halt a steady parade of telegraph competitors. Now managing both the New York and Western APs, Smith, in order to protect AP from UP, agreed to divide the nation into exclusive AP and UP territories and to share news dispatches with UP. Phillips then offered to sell UP stock covertly to AP officials to guarantee the exclusive territories and news sharing. AP's leaders had become entangled in that UP stock pool and it would be their downfall.[23]

Although the nation's two leading, and supposedly competing, wire services had formed a secret trust, such a widespread collusion would inevitably be detected, especially when editors saw the news dispatches they had sent to AP appearing in their UP competitor's paper. And detect it—and attack it—the Western AP did, led by AP members Victor F. Lawson of the *Chicago Daily News* and Frederick Driscoll of the *St. Paul Pioneer Press*, who mounted an investigation of the AP-UP trust in 1891.

"What I want the [investigating] committee to be satisfied about," Smith wrote to Lawson and Driscoll in 1891, "is, that in carrying out [the contract with United Press] on behalf of the Assd. Press, I have faithfully conserved Associated Press interests, and have protected our papers at every point."[24] Smith

and his trust colleagues were an older generation who, having acquired power, did whatever was necessary to keep it. The investigators, second-generation AP editors, relished the power that came from challenging their elders. The revelations led to recriminations by Western AP's young bucks and by stubborn resistance from New York City AP's old guard.

The showdown came in August 1891 when Western AP editors, armed with the investigators' report that included copies of the news exchange and stock pool agreements, voted seven reformers onto their board of directors, throwing out five old-guard directors.[25] The new board replaced the old bylaws with new ones describing a national Associated Press, chartered in Illinois but envisioning a national news-gathering cooperative. On August 1, 1893, this new national AP came into existence.

In the East the old New York City AP, which had operated since 1848, died in December, 1892, its seven newspaper partners joining United Press. A bitter national war for control of news gathering followed, in which newspaper memberships were the prizes. AP's membership totals pulled away from UP's with increasing momentum until, on March 29, 1897, UP ceased operating. AP had won, and the winning "general" was Melville E. Stone, the aggressive general manager who had replaced Smith in 1893.

AP faced another bump in the road when one of its practices forced it to leave Illinois. According to AP bylaws, its board of directors could declare other news services "antagonistic" and prohibit AP members from receiving such services. In 1898 the *Chicago Inter Ocean*, an AP member since 1865, was discovered receiving the antagonistic Laffan News Service. Facing expulsion from AP, the *Inter Ocean* sought to enjoin AP in court. The Illinois Supreme Court in February, 1900, declared AP a public utility. According to the court, AP could not expel the *Inter Ocean*, nor could it exclude any newspaper that applied for an AP membership.[26]

To escape this damaging reading of its bylaws, AP reorganized as a membership cooperative under New York state law in 1900. Although "antagonistic" declarations were eliminated, a "protest right" was granted to over half of AP's morning papers and to over a third of its evening papers. Another form of the franchise, the protest right permitted these AP papers to block AP membership for local newspapers in their city or within a radius of from 60 to 150 miles of the city.[27] AP could not escape the internal tug-of-war between members' self-protectionism and AP's national expansion.

The victory over UP, however, still did not create an AP monopoly. When E. W. Scripps and William Randolph Hearst, both publishers of growing national newspaper chains, could not get AP memberships for some of their papers in 1897, they formed their own wire services. Scripps, who owned five dailies and a piece of another one, in 1897 organized two regional news associations and allied them with a third, the three providing a national news report for Scripps' papers and about 100 other papers across the country. In 1907 Scripps combined these regional wires to form United Press Associations, a private stock corporation and a subsidiary of the Scripps newspaper chain.[28]

Having spent 10 years trying to secure AP memberships for his New York City and Chicago newspapers and realizing that he probably would be barred from AP memberships for some other dailies he expected to start, Hearst set up within his company a modest wire report for his papers. In May 1909, he expanded this service into a national news wire for his papers and any others that wanted to subscribe. At first called the American News Service, it was renamed the International News Service nine months later. Like Scripps' UP, Hearst's INS was a privately owned commercial wire, rather than a membership cooperative on the AP model.[29]

In 1915 AP had 908 members and Scripps' UP had 625 clients, and in 1917-18 INS claimed 400 clients.[30] While president of UP from 1912 to 1920 Roy Howard built the wire's clientele and the news report's quality to become a major competitor for AP. One writer described UP's early challenge to AP as "the belligerent attitude of an intoxicated field mouse squaring off against an elephant."[31] Howard toured the country signing up client newspapers and en-

thusiastically pumping up UP staffers, urging them to write with flair, to use "brilliancy in the narration of the day's events."[32]

World War I was UP's opportunity to gain a foothold in news gathering in two respects. First, an AP contract for international news with Reuters, the British wire service, constrained AP's growth of foreign correspondents. UP had no such limitation and sent dozens of war reporters abroad to cover the carnage in Europe. Second, because Europe was five hours ahead of New York City, the day's war news was complete in time for UP's predominantly afternoon wire for evening dailies. UP and its evening clients could beat AP and its predominantly morning members with a complete report each day from the battlefield—and a more lively report than AP allowed itself to write.

AP was also handicapped by its aging general manager, Melville E. Stone, who ran AP as the stodgy, colorless voice of the establishment. An internal study committee of AP editors back in 1908 had concluded that "there is a lack of responsiveness to suggestions and a disposition to adhere too rigidly to the limitations and restrictions that have become tradition in The Associated Press."[33] Stone retired in 1921; and after four years of little change under Frederick Roy Martin as general manager, Kent Cooper came to the post and began making AP a modern, more competitive wire.

Meanwhile within a few years of its founding, International News Service had acquired a reputation for recklessness and fabrication. A *Harper's Weekly* writer asserted in 1915 that INS's "name" European correspondents did not exist. The foreign staff was "simply a common, ordinary, contemptible Hearst fake." The fact that neither Hearst nor INS editors ever answered these charges hit Hearst newsrooms like a bomb. "Morale in the newsroom," reported a Hearst staffer, "hit rock bottom and stayed there for years."[34]

Another blow hit INS in October, 1916, as World War I was gathering momentum, when French and British authorities refused INS access to their transatlantic cables and mail service because Hearst's newspapers editorially opposed U.S. entry into the war. Finally AP sued INS for copying its war dispatches and sending them to clients as INS's own. The Supreme Court decided against INS in 1918, established a property right for news reports.[35]

The debate between profit-making and membership wire services continued for years in the early 20th century. In 1913, for example, AP President Frank B. Noyes, on the 20th anniversary of the modern AP's founding, said AP membership structure was free of corporate bias and, referring to UP, said that "a powerful, privately owned and controlled news-gathering agency is a menace to the press and people, [one] which dealt at arm's length with newspapers to which they sold news at such profit as might be secured."[36]

On the 20th anniversary of UP's founding, its president Karl A. Bickel described UP as "militantly and aggressively a business institution," which had the same goal as "every great and enduring privately owned American newspaper [which is] to render a service and to make a profit." He called AP a "socialist experiment."[37]

AP's protest right was finally challenged by the *Chicago Sun*, founded in 1941 by Marshall Field, III, as a pro–Democratic alternative to the *Chicago Tribune*'s strident, isolationist conservatism. The *Tribune* blocked AP membership for the *Sun*, which with the help to the U.S. Justice Department brought suit against AP. The U.S. Supreme Court in 1945 instructed AP to eliminate the protest right from its bylaws and to admit all newspapers capable of paying for the service.[38] The *Sun* finally got its AP membership.

After the decision, many papers rushed into AP, making it harder for UP and INS to keep their clients. Finally in 1958 UP with 5,063 clients and INS with 3,000 clients merged into United Press International, a subsidiary of the Scripps company. As newspaper circulations and numbers gradually fell in the 1980s and 1990s, UPI became known as the second wire behind AP. UPI served 54 per cent of U.S. dailies in 1966, 37 per cent in 1985, and only 16 per cent in 1990, while AP's numbers in those years shot up from 68 per cent to 73 per cent, and 87 per cent.[39]

With UPI posting hefty annual deficits by 1982, Scripps sold the wire to the first of three owners all of whom increasingly had difficulty keeping the wire going on the old basis of serving newspapers and broadcast stations. UPI filed for bankruptcy protection in 1985 and 1991, and in the 1990s attempted to reestablish itself as an international business wire and then as an Internet news provider.

The telegraph spawned cooperative news gathering in the 1840s, and wave after wave of new technology subsequently allowed wire services to increase the variety, volume, and speed of their news reports. By 1900 AP's own telegraphers transmitted an average news report of 40,000 words per day at speeds of about 30 words per minute in dot-and-dash Morse code. In the newsrooms the report was received by ear. As the sounder clicked out the news report in Morse code, the receiving telegrapher heard words that he either wrote down or typed.

Teletype appeared in newsrooms in 1915, a typewriter device driven by telegraph impulses that typed the news report at 60 words per minute on a continuous roll of paper. In the 1950s, Teletypesetter machines appeared in many smaller newspaper offices sending the news report at 45 words per minute typed on paper and perforated on paper tape that could drive automatic typesetting machines. Teletype and Teletypesetter machines were replaced by satellite dishes in the 1980s when wire services began sending their news reports via computer at more than a 1,000 words per minute directly into newspapers' computers via communication satellites.

Although UPI in 1962 pioneered with computer delivery of stock market data to a few metropolitan newspapers, AP in 1970 began introducing computers in its bureaus that "talked" to each other, moving stories and the news report digitally. At the beginning of the 21st century, the entire wire service network was computerized, and four-color photos were shot, edited, and transmitted in digital form via satellites. With the broad availability of the Internet in the 1990s, both AP and UPI went online, offering their news reports to the general public. Today, while UPI offers its news at www.upi.com, AP permits its news report to be accessed by the public through AP newspapers' websites at wire.ap.org.

Finally, a third method of cooperative news-gathering, called synergy in the industry, began appearing in the 1990s as media companies merged to form large conglomerates, in most cases involving several kinds of news organizations. By combining print and broadcast resources, for example, to create both joint news broadcasts and published articles on the same subject, corporate officers believed they were using their news units more economically, each enhancing the quality of the other's reporting. *Time* magazine and CNN, both owned by Time Warner, cooperated in January, 2000, on "CNN & Time," a weekly cable news documentary, and on "AllPolitics.com," a combined Internet reporting effort to cover "the U.S. scene."[40]

Meanwhile in the late 1990s unrelated news companies began cooperating on their news coverage. In 1999 the CBS, ABC, and Fox networks, for example, agreed to supply news coverage video to each network's affiliated stations,[41] and NBC News, MSNBC, the *Washington Post*, and *Newsweek* agreed to cooperate on reporting news and promoting their news products online.[42]

Cooperative news-gathering, which dates from the 1830s in the United States, has succeeded as a wire service and among individual reporters, photographers, and producers pursuing news stories. Whether it succeeds as a way for competitors to protect themselves in a rapidly changing news and information marketplace, remains to be seen.

Selected Readings

Baillie, Hugh. *High Tension: The Recollections of Hugh Baillie*. New York: Harper, 1959.

Cooper, Kent. *Kent Cooper and the Associated Press: An Autobiography*. New York: Random House, 1959.

Gordon, Gregory, and Ronald E. Cohen. *Down to the Wire: UPI's Fight for Survival*. New York: McGraw-Hill, 1990.

Gramling, Oliver. *AP: The Story of News*. New York: Farrar & Rinehart, 1940.

Hogan, Lawrence D. *A Black National News Service: The Associated Negro Press and Claude Barnett, 1919–1945*. Rutherford, N.J.: Farleigh Dickinson University Press, 1984.

Knights, Peter R. "The Press Association War of 1866–1867." *Journalism Monographs* 6 (1967).

Koenigsberg, M[oses]. *King News: An Autobiography*. Philadelphia: F. A. Stokes, 1941.

Morris, Joe Alex. *Deadline Every Minute: The Story of the United Press*. Garden City, N.Y.: Doubleday, 1957.

Rosewater, Victor. *History of Cooperative News-Gathering in the United States*. New York: D. Appleton, 1930.

Schwarzlose, Richard A. *The Nation's Newsbrokers: Volume One, The Formative Years: From Pretelegraph to 1865*. Evanston, Ill.: Northwestern University Press, 1989.

Schwarzlose, Richard A. *The Nation's Newsbrokers: Volume Two, The Rush to Institution: From 1820 to 1920*. Evanston, Ill.: Northwestern University Press, 1990.

Shmanske, Stephen. "News as a Public Good: Cooperative Ownership, Price Commitments, and the Success of the Associated Press." *Business History Review* 60 (Spring 1986): 55–80.

Singletary, Michael W. "Newspaper Use of Supplemental Services: 1960–73." *Journalism Quarterly* 52 (1975): 748–51.

Stone, Melville E. *Fifty Years a Journalist*. Garden City, N.Y.: Doubleday, Page, 1921.

Swett, Herbert E. "AP Coverage of the Lincoln Assassination." *Journalism Quarterly* 47 (1970): 157–59.

Watson, Elmo Scott. *A History of Newspaper Syndicates in the United States, 1865–1935*. Chicago, 1936.

Wilson, Quintus C. "The Confederate Press Association: A Pioneer News Agency." *Journalism Quarterly* 26 (1949): 160–66.

Notes

1. Joseph T. Buckingham, *Specimens of Newspaper Literature with Personal Memoirs, Anecdotes, and Reminiscences*, 2 vols. (Boston: Charles C. Little & James Brown, 1850), 2:170–71. Emphasis in original.

2. "By a Journalist "[Isaac C. Pray], *Memoirs of James Gordon Bennett and His Times* (New York: Stringer & Townsend, 1855), 372.

3. F. Lawrence Babcock, *Spanning the Atlantic* (New York: Knopf, 1931), 50–51, and Carl H. Scheele, *A Short History of the Mail Service* (Washington, D.C.: Smithsonian Institution, 1970), 102.

4. Daniel H. Craig, *Answer of Daniel H. Craig ... to the Interrogatories of the U.S. Senate Committee on Education and Labor at the City of New York, 1883* (New York, 1883), 2.

5. Letters and documents in the New York State Associated Press Papers, Oneida Historical Society, Utica, N.Y.

6. Alexander Jones. *Historical Sketch of the Electric Telegraph, Including Its Rise and Progress in the United States* (New York: Putnam, 1852), 136, 148.

7. James D. Reid, *The Telegraph in America, Its Founders, Promoters, and Noted Men* (New York: Derby Brothers, 1879), 362.

8. Craig, *Answer*, 4–5.

9. George H. Manning, "Bennett Fight Opened Senate to Press," *Editor & Publisher*, 21 July 1934, 118, and Ben: Perley Poore, "Washington News," *Harper's Monthly*, 48 (January 1874), 229.

10. Francis O. J. Smith, *An Exposition of the Differences Existing between Different Presses and Different Lines of Telegraph ...* (Boston: Dutton & Wentworth, 1850), 34–35.

11. S. N. D. North, *History and Present Condition of the Newspaper and Periodical Press of the United States ...* (Washington, D.C.: Government Printing Office, 1884), 108.

12. *Niles' National Register*, 25 September 1847, 50.

13. Robert Luther Thompson, *Wiring a Continent: The History of the Telegraph Industry in the United States, 1832–1866* (Princeton, N.J.: Princeton University Press, 1947), 374; David Homer Bates, *Lincoln in the Telegraph Office: Recollections of the United States Military Telegraph Corps during the Civil War* (New York: Century, 1907), 14–37; and J. Cutler Andrews, *The South Reports the Civil War* (Princeton, N.J.: Princeton University Press, 1970), 55.

14. E. Merton Coulter, *The Confederate States of America, 1861–1865*, vol. 7, *A History of the South*, ed. Wendell Holmes Stephenson and E. Merton Coulter (Baton Rouge: Louisiana State University Press, 1950), 496–97; Andrews, *South*, 55–58; and Press Association of the Confederate States of America, *The Press Association of the Confederate States of America* (Griffin, Ga.: Hill & Swayze's, 1863), 5–7.

15. *Telegrapher* 16 (October 1865): 175.

16. Various numbers of the Western Associated Press, *Proceedings* (Detroit, 1867–91).

17. For details and sources on these postwar AP developments and the rise of competitors, see Richard A. Schwarzlose, *The Rush to Institution, from 1865 to 1920*, vol. 2, *The Nation's Newsbrokers* (Evanston, Ill.: Northwestern University Press, 1990), esp. 33–62.

18. For an explanation of Craig's firing, see Schwarzlose, *Rush*, 42–47, and Peter R. Knights, *The Press Association War of 1866–1867* (Austin, Texas: Journalism Monograph, no. 6, 1967), *passim*.

19. U.S. Congress, Senate Committee on Education and Labor, *Report of the Committee of the Senate upon the Relations between Labor and Capital and Testimony Taken by the Committee*, 5 vols. (4 vols. published), 48th Cong., 2nd. sess., 1885, 1:482.

20. Walter P. Phillips, *The United Press: Address upon the Opening of the New Offices of the United Press in "The World" Building, January 1, 1891* (N.p., [1891]), *passim*, and *United Press (1882–97), The United Press* (New York: Evening Post, 1884), *passim*.

21. Elmo Scott Watson, *A History of Newspaper Syndicates in the United States, 1865–1835* (Chicago, 1936), 7–16, and Frank Luther Mott, *American Journalism, A History: 1690–1960*, 3rd ed. (New York: Macmillan, 1962), 479.

22. Nathan Kingsley, "The Supplemental News Services," in *The Future of News: Television-Newspapers-Wire Services-Newsmagazines*, ed. Philip S. Cook, Douglas Gomery, and Lawrence W. Lichty (Baltimore: The Johns Hopkins University Press, 1992), 178.

23. Western Associated Press, Special Committee of Conference. *Report* (Detroit, 1891), *passim*, esp. pp. 2–7, 20–24, and numerous letters between mid–1884 and June 30, 1891, among Whitelaw Reid, William Henry Smith, Richard Smith, Walter Phillips, Walter N. Haldeman, Charles R. Baldwin, Robert S. Davis, and James W. Scott in the Whitelaw Reid Papers, 1861–1912, Library of Congress, Washington, D.C.; William Henry Smith Papers, 1756–1907, Indiana Historical Society, Indianapolis, and 1800–1896, Ohio Historical Society, Columbus; and William W. Clapp Collection, New England Associated Press Papers, 1874–1890, Baker Library, Harvard University Graduate School of Business Administration, Boston. This form of collusion among competitors to form a self-protective trust was common in the 1880s, causing Congress to pass the Sherman Antitrust Act in 1890.

24. Smith to Lawson and Driscoll, Smith Papers, 19 February 1891, Ohio H. S.

25. Western Associated Press, *Proceedings* (1891), 7–8, 12, 15–16.

26. Inter Ocean Publishing Co. v. Associated Press, 184 Ill. 438 (1900) reprinted in Associated Press (Illinois), *Annual Report* (1899), pp. 48–52. The *Chicago Inter Ocean* was called the *Chicago Republican* from its founding in 1865 to 1872 when it changed its name to *Inter Ocean*.

27. Associated Press (New York), *Annual Report* (1901), *passim*, and Associated Press (New York) *Proceedings* (1900), 1–18, 74–144.

28. "The United Press Association," Negley D. Cochran Papers, 1890–1940, Toledo Public Library, Toledo, Ohio, and Joe Alex Morris, *Deadline Every Minute: The Story of the United Press* (Garden City, N.Y.: Doubleday, 1957), 19, 23, 25. This United Press wire service had no relationship to the United Press of 1882 to 1897, discussed earlier.

29. Alfred McClung Lee, *The Daily Newspaper in America: The Evolution of a Social Instrument*, (New York: Macmillan, 1937), 538–39; "I N S," publicity release hand-dated 1938, "Highlights in the History and Development of I.N.S." an undated post–1937 chronology, "International News Service," publicity release dated 30 November 1946, and "From United Press International," publicity release hand-dated 10 July 1958, all from Kenneth Smith Papers, privately held collection, United Press International, New York.

30. AP, *Annual Report*, (1916); Morris, *Deadline*, 76; and Lee, *The Daily Newspaper in America*, 539.

31. Jack Alexander, "Rip-roaring Baillie," *Saturday Evening Post*, 1 June 1946, 39.

32. Lee, *The Daily Newspaper in America*, 537.

33. AP, *Annual Report* (1908), 80.

34. H. D. Wheeler, "At the Front with Willie Hearst," *Harper's Weekly*, 9 October 1915, 340–42, and George Murray, *The Madhouse on Madison Street* (Chicago: Follett, 1965), 150.

35. International News Service v. Associated Press, 248 U.S. 215 (1918).

36. Frank B. Noyes, "The Associated Press," *North American Review* 197 (May 1913): 701–2.

37. Karl A. Bickel, "Bickel Reviews History of United Press," *Editor & Publisher*, 30 April 1927, 31–53.

38. *Associated Press v. United States*, 326 U.S. 1 (1945).

39. Author's tabulations of wire service affiliations as noted in Editor & Publisher *International Year Book*s.

40. "Time's Extended Family," *Time*, 31 January 2000, 21.

41. Bill Carter, "3 TV News Operations Unite To Provide Video to Affiliates," *New York Times*, 21 December 1999, C8.

42. Joe Flint, "Washington Post, NBC Form Alliance To Share Editorial, Internet Resources," *Wall Street Journal*, 18 November 1999, B14.

17

Coverage of Washington

ELLIOT KING

Journalism has always occupied a central role in the national political life of the United States. The founders of the country assumed that the press was essential to inform the public about the work of the national government. George Washington noted in his Fourth Annual Message to the U.S. Congress in 1792, that if for some reason the transmission of newspapers to distant parts of the country was being inhibited, it would undoubtedly be remedied because "the circulation of political intelligence through these vehicles [is] justly reckoned among the surest means of preventing the degeneracy of a free government."[1]

Many factors have shaped Washington correspondence over time. In the 19th century, Congress was the dominant governing institution. In the 20th century, the president became the central focus of politics in Washington. And as news media evolved from small political journals of opinion to broadcast and Internet-based media with instantaneous global reach, Washington corespondents adjusted.

The history of Washington correspondence can be conveniently divided into four periods. From the founding of the republic through the early 1830s, the official relationship between politicians and reporters and the unofficial expectations of both shaped the character of national political reporting. In the period from the mid–1830s until the turn of the century, Washington journalism was defined by the needs of mass newspapers in major urban centers such as New York and the Congressional leadership of the major political parties.

From the beginning of the 20th century, the activist presidency of Theodore Roosevelt and ongoing national crises including two world wars and an economic depression shifted reporters' attention from Congress to the White House. Presidents started to manage the news to further their policies. During this period, reporters and columnists, as opposed to editors and publishers, emerged as the preeminent players in journalism.

The emergence of television as the major national medium ushered in the final period of Washington correspondence. Since the 1960s, the relationship between the press and national politicians has become increasingly antagonistic. Politicians attempted to use news media to bypass journalists and communicate directly to the public. How successfully office holders communicated on television was viewed as a significant political skill.

In response, to some degree Washington reporters came to see it as their responsibility to cut through politicians' efforts to construct favorable images and to debunk politicians' attempts to put a sympathetic spin on events. Often, an adversarial relationship between journalists and national political figures re-emerged, an adversarial relationship not based on policy or ideological differences—as had been the case in the partisan early years of the Republic—but on the question of what information should be presented to the public by whom.

Reporting on national affairs has its roots prior to the adoption of the United States Constitution in 1789. When the Articles of

Confederation proved unworkable, the Congress authorized a convention to correct its shortcomings. The press assumed responsibility to prepare the general population for the new constitution that emerged. The news media were generally so pro–Constitution their activities have been described as the selling of the Constitutional Convention.[2]

The U.S. Constitution reflected the framers' awareness of the need for unfettered reporting for the functioning of a democracy. The First Amendment to the Constitution prohibited the federal government from abridging the freedom of the press. But the founders of the United States saw the role of the press as proactive. Thomas Jefferson, for example, asserted that newspapers were a necessary part of a system in which the basis of the government was the opinion of the people.[3]

With the establishment of the federal government in 1789, two problems immediately surfaced. First, how should Congress communicate its activities including its deliberations and the laws it passed to the public and, second, how free should the press be to present the actions of Congress? These questions have underscored political reporting from Washington, D.C., over time. While politicians need journalists to publicize their activities and journalists need access to politicians to ensure that they have the latest news, the two groups often differ as to what should be reported. Consequently, reporters and politicians frequently have a love-hate relationship and clash over the content and quality of the news.

The uneasy relationship between elected officials and journalists was exacerbated in the early days of the republic because journalists were closely identified with political parties. Although politicians hoped that the press would report on the workings of government favorably for elected officials, as the competition between political parties developed, the Federalists and Republicans supported newspapers allied to the parties. In New York City, the nation's first capital, John Fenno launched the *Gazette of the United States* in 1789, in part, as a mouthpiece for the Federalist party. In response, Benjamin Franklin Bache began publishing the *Aurora* in Philadelphia in 1790 as an

advocate of the Republicans. The following year, Thomas Jefferson helped persuade Philip Freneau to start a mouthpiece, the *National Gazette*, by giving him a $250-a-year clerkship in the State Department.[4] The partisan newspapers hurled fierce rhetoric at both politicians and each other. For example, after George Washington's farewell address was made public, Bache denounced him, writing, "If ever a nation was debauched by a man, the American nation has been debauched by Washington. If ever a nation has suffered from the improper influence of a man, the American nation has suffered from the influence of Washington. If ever a nation was deceived by a man, the American nation has been deceived by Washington."[5]

Moreover, newspapers, particularly newspapers in Washington, D.C., were not economically stable operations. They depended on patronage and printing contracts from the government to sustain their operations. The access reporters should have to Congress' activities was frequently debated starting from the First Congress. On September 28, 1789, Representative Aedanus Burke of South Carolina noted that several newspapers had published accounts of the House debates in newspapers and "misrepresented those debated in the most glaring deviations from the truth; often distorting the arguments of the members from the true meaning...." Those distortions brought ridicule upon the House of Representatives, Burke argued, and the press should be prohibited from publishing the debates.[6]

Although Burke's feelings were widely shared, the majority of the House of Representatives did not agree, and journalists continued to be allowed to report on the debates of the House. The secretary of state was authorized to select newspapers to officially publish the laws.[7]

The effort to allow the public to view the activities of the Senate was led by Philip Freneau, the editor of the *National Gazette*. In 1792, for example, he wrote, "A motion for opening the doors of the senate chamber has again been defeated by a considerable majority—in defiance of instruction, in defiance of your opinion, in defiance of every principle which give security to free men.... Are you freemen who ought to know the individual conduct of your legislators, or are you an inferior order of beings...?"[8] The Senate opened its doors to public observation in 1795 though no special accommodations were made for the press.

When the nation's capital moved to Washington, D.C., in 1801, the need for newspapers to report on the activities of the federal government grew more acute. Washington was a small village far removed from the urban centers of New York and Philadelphia. It could barely support newspapers on its own. Congress was in session for only three to five months a year. The Supreme Court was in session for only a few weeks at a time. Boston, New York, Philadelphia, and New Orleans were centers of American business and culture, and most state capitals were more important to many citizens than the national capital was.[9] Eventually, Congress authorized two reporters from each of the city's three dailies to report on its debates, and the newspapers received official printing contracts as well.[10]

It was partisanship that lay behind the innovation of newspapers outside Washington assigning correspondents to cover the national capital. Until newspapers began using correspondents, they got most of their news from Washington through private letters from acquaintances in the city and from stories in the *National Intelligencer* or other papers such as the *Federalist* located in the capital. The *Federalist*'s accounts, however, were inferior to those of the *National Intelligencer*, and Federalist editors did not like having to rely on the Republican *Intelligencer* for explanations of government proceedings. In 1808, therefore, the *United States Gazette* in New York and then the *Freeman's Journal* in Philadelphia employed individuals of Federalist persuasion to write reports from Washington. Their arrangements ceased prior to the War of 1812, but in the 1820s a number of papers took up the practice of hiring Washington correspondents.[11]

The vitriol from competing newspapers reached a crescendo in the administration of John Adams, when Congress passed the Sedition Act of 1798, which made it a crime to "write, print, utter or publish ... false, scan-dalous and malicious writing against the government of the United States ... with the intent ... to bring [it] into contempt or disrepute."[12] Several Republican editors, including William Duane, editor of the *Aurora* after the death of Bache, were imprisoned under the Sedition Act. The act lapsed when Thomas Jefferson assumed office.

Jefferson, like Adams, was unhappy with the way the press covered his administration. In his second Inaugural Address on March 4, 1805, he noted that "the artillery of the press has been leveled against us, charged with whatsoever its licentiousness could devise or dare." Nevertheless, he argued that since he was able to win reelection despite what he saw as the distortions of the truth by the press, the American experiment in freedom of speech and the press was succeeding.[13]

With the election of Jefferson, the Republicans and then, with the election of Andrew Jackson in 1828, the Democrats dominated the national political arena for nearly 40 years. The *National Intelligencer*, under the leadership of Samuel Harrison Smith and then his successors, Joseph Gales and William Seaton, dominated journalism in Washington. The *National Intelligencer* held official printing contracts from departments of the executive branch and from Congress, becoming the official printers of both Houses of Congress in 1819.

The *National Intelligencer* may have dominated the news from Washington, but editors in general were deeply embedded within the political system. Three of the five closest advisors to President Jackson, his so-called kitchen cabinet, were experienced journalists. Jackson appointed 57 editors to patronage positions, primarily as postmasters or in the customs service.

The relationship between the Washington press and the officials of the federal government that was established in the late 18th and early 19th century was always an uneasy one. Despite their dependence on each other, politicians and journalists often held the other in contempt. John Quincy Adams, who was elected President in 1824, recalled correspondents as "a set of individuals who would disgrace any man who comes into contact with them .... [They are] base, corrupt, penniless scoundrels."[14] And the feelings were reciprocated. As the *New York Express* editorialized on January 8, 1839, "The bitter hostility of [politicians) to a Free Press is easily accounted for as it tears the Lion's Skin from the Jackass, and distinguishes the braying of that stupid beast from the roar of the Nobel Monarch of the Wood."

As newspapers evolved into a dynamic mass medium starting in the middle of the 1830s, the role of Washington correspondence changed as well. James Gordon Bennett, editor of the *New York Herald*, led the change. He had won a national reputation as a Washington correspondent for the *New York Enquirer* in the 1820s. When he established the *Herald* in 1835, he shifted the focus of journalism from commentary to newsgathering. And since newspapers like the *Herald*, the *New York Tribune*, the *Baltimore Sun*, the *Cincinnati Gazette* and others were financially successfully, they no longer needed contracts from the federal government to survive.

From 1835 on, Washington, D.C., emerged as an increasingly important source of news for major newspapers. In the late 1830s and early 1840s, Bennett led the fight to allow journalists representing non–Washington papers into the House and Senate. At the same time, the Congress hired its own printers to record impartial records of its proceedings. With the development of the telegraph in 1844, news from Washington could be transmitted to major centers across the country, breaking the grip of the Washington newspapers. In fact, after Samuel F. B. Morse telegraphed the historic words "What hath God wrought" on May 24, 1844, the telegraph's first day of service, the second transmission was "Have you any news?"[15]

Newspapers competed fiercely to be the first to publish the news from Washington. By the 1850s, there were 50 to 60 correspondents accredited to sit in the Congressional press galleries, including Ben: Perley Poore (his punctuation), who began writing his "Waif in Washington" column in 1853 and eventually came to be seen as the dean of Washington correspondents from this period.[16] Although primarily a male occupation, a few women were also accredited as Washington correspondents at this time. The first major female correspondent of the period was Anne Royall, who won notoriety by securing an interview with John Quincy Adams by sitting on his clothes while he swam in the Potomac River. She refused to get up until he answered her questions. Jane G. Swisshelm was the first woman to sit in the Senate press gallery when she was accredited as the correspondent of the *New York Tribune* on April 17, 1850. She left in an uproar after her first column accused Daniel Webster, a prominent senator from Massachusetts, of fathering a mulatto child.[17]

Although Washington correspondents were creating an independent occupational identity, they remained closely entwined with political parties and government itself. For example, Ben: Perley Poore was on the government payroll for 25 years and wrote speeches for members of Congress while he served as a correspondent. Correspondents worked as clerks for House and Senate committees as well as the executive branch. Patronage was understood as the wages of political journalism.[18]

Journalists were significant players in national politics. Editors and reporters including Horace Greeley, editor of the *New York Tribune*, and Henry Raymond, editor of the *New York Times*, simultaneously held elective office and reported from Washington for their newspapers. Tension between politicians and journalists, however, persisted. Correspondents frequently broke stories or leaked information that government officials hoped to keep from public view. For example, the *New York Herald's* Washington correspondent "Galvienses" published confidential messages that President James Knox Polk had sent to Congress in support of the Treaty of Guadeloupe Hidalgo, which ended the Mexican War.[19]

Following the Civil War, Washington politics was noted for its corruption. Journalists regularly exposed this corruption, particularly when the newspaper with which the correspondent was associated was affiliated with the party out of power. The attack on corruption did not involve investigative reporting in the contemporary sense of the word but repeated editorial attacks. For example, in 1871, the *New*

York Sun published a series of columns calling President Ulysses S. Grant "The Present Taker," and listing the names of his relatives who held public office.[20] The *Sun* broke the Crédit Mobilier scandal in which several members of the House of Representatives received bribes in connection to a construction company organized to help build the Union Pacific railroad in 1872.[21] Ironically, many correspondents were also involved in corrupt activities. An 1875 investigation in the House revealed that four reporters had received between $5,000 and $30,000 to secure a federal subsidy for a steamship line. An observer reflected that journalists were perhaps the most unprincipled and unscrupulous men in Washington.[22]

To gather the news and formulate their views, Washington reporters followed a well-prescribed routine. They generally would stop by the White House, visit major hotels to talk to the visitors, drop by Capitol Hill to question members of Congress, and socialize with the Washington elite to learn the cocktail-party perspective on the events of the day.[23]

During the second administration of Grover Cleveland, that routine began to change. In 1895, William W. Price, a reporter for the *Washington Evening Star*, stationed himself permanently outside the gates of the White House to interview visitors as they left. Other correspondents followed suit, and a coterie of reporters would gather regularly at the White House.[24]

Within 10 years, the locus of power in Washington would began to shift from Congress to the president, a trend that would unfold over several decades. (See chapter 18 for an account of the history of presidents and the press.) The press came to be understood as a powerful tool for the president to wield against Congress in the struggle to lead public opinion.[25] At the same time, leading newspapers were being transformed into large, complex organizations with professional management. Washington correspondents were frequently seen as newspaper's "ambassadors" to the federal government. Consequently, Washington correspondents no longer operated in the shadow of the editors of their newspapers. They were expected to develop their own inside relationships with the president and key members of Congress.

Theodore Roosevelt was the first president to exploit the possibilities presented by the new conditions in Washington. Coming to power after the assassination of President William McKinley, he could not count on the support of leading Republican newspapers. Instead, he met regularly with White House reporters who he believed would support his programs and policies. He provided them both with information intended for public consumption and confidential information that made reporters feel as though they were insiders. He developed a strict set of guidelines governing how reporters could use the material he provided and banished any reporter who violated those guidelines. His approach to managing press relations was so revolutionary that, when he first began meeting with reporters, it made front-page news.[26]

The changes in presidential-press relations set in motion by Roosevelt were institutionalized over the next 40 years. Warren G. Harding, a former newspaper publisher, was the first president to set a fixed schedule for press conferences and created the role of the official presidential "spokesperson," which allowed the president to be quoted without having to assume full responsibility for the remarks.[27]

As interactions between the president and reporters became routine, the stature of the Washington correspondents and Washington columnists was enhanced. Washington bureau chiefs and reporters such as Arthur Krock of the *New York Times*, Mark Sullivan of *Collier's* magazine, who also wrote a syndicated column, David Lawrence of the *New York Evening Post*, who later established *U.S. News and World Report*, and Richard Oulahan of the *New York Sun* became influential figures in their own rights. Columnists such as Walter Lippmann, who became a Washington columnist for the *New York Herald Tribune* after he served as editorial page editor for the *New York World*, became political insiders, influencing policy at the highest levels of government.

The changes in presidential press relations set in motion by Theodore Roosevelt came to a peak in the administration of Franklin Roosevelt. Swept into office during the Great Depression in 1933, under Roosevelt, the executive branch dominated both the federal government and the news from Washington. Roosevelt handled the press masterfully, meeting with reporters twice a week. He charmed Washington reporters and enlisted their aid in the New Deal. As one contemporary reporter put it, "Mr. Roosevelt is a great hit among newspapermen in Washington.... If he fails the craft by any false word or deed, he will break a hundred hearts that have not actually palpitated for any political figure in many a year."[28]

With the close of World War II, television became a major factor in reporting from Washington. The potential impact of television on national politics and news from Washington had been clear from its inception. The Democratic National Convention was broadcast in 1948. In 1950, televised Senate hearings into organized crime had propelled Senator Estes Kefauver of Tennessee into the national limelight as a potential presidential nominee of the Democratic party. In 1954, Senate hearings into allegations made by Senator Joseph McCarthy of Wisconsin against an officer in the United States Army and a subsequent broadcast by CBS correspondent Edward R. Murrow helped to turn public opinion against McCarthyism.

In 1954, President Eisenhower began to allow his press conferences to be filmed by television crews for broadcast later. And in 1961 President John Kennedy allowed the television networks to broadcast press conferences live. From that point, news from Washington was largely shaped by television.[29] White House correspondents such as Dan Rather of CBS News and Sam Donaldson of ABC News became celebrities in their own rights. Television shows such as *Meet the Press, Face the Nation,* and *Washington Week in Review* on which reporters questioned politicians and reflected on the news helped shape the political debate.

With the president as a single, central character, the White House was more suited for television coverage than the constant cacophony of Congress. A president's skills on television — how he "communicated" — came to be seen as essential for political success.[30]

Journalists and politicians came to realize that techniques that were used to sell products on television could be used to sell the politics and personalities of national politicians.[31] Washington correspondents saw it as their responsibility to cut through the efforts of political leaders to manipulate or "spin" the news and report what they saw as the facts. Many media observers, however, felt journalists generally failed in those efforts and allowed their readers and viewers to be manipulated.[32] National politicians, on the other hand, criticized the Washington press for pursuing their own agendas. President Richard Nixon expressed this view to his newly appointed cabinet in 1969. "Always remember, the men and women of the news media approach this as an adversary relationship," he said. "The time will come when they will run lies about you, when the columnists and editorial writers will make you seem to be scoundrels or fools or both and the cartoonists will depict you as ogres."[33]

Image was not the only area of conflict between reporters and national politicians. Starting with the war in Vietnam and a series of scandals including Watergate, the Iran-Contra scandal in the Ronald Reagan administration, and the Lewinsky affair during Bill Clinton's administration, the Washington press corps often doubted pronouncements from Washington officials. In the Johnson administration, journalists spoke openly of the "credibility gap," a shorthand to indicate that news from the White House was not to be believed. The media reported on the discrepancy between what officials in Washington said and what reporters knew to be the facts.

Interestingly, during Vietnam and the Watergate scandal, however, the Washington-based national political press did not take the lead in exposing the activities of the administrations. For example, during the Watergate scandal, the *Washington Post* metro reporters Carl Bernstein and Robert Woodward played lead roles. By the mid–1980s, some media critics felt that the Washington media too often uncritically reported the official perspective on events.[34]

With the widespread emergence of cable television in the 1980s and the Internet and the World Wide Web in the 1990s, the context of Washington correspondence shifted again. News networks such as Cable Network News and news-oriented Web sites have created a need for more reporting about activities in Washington. The impact of the Internet became controversial in 1998, when Matt Drudge, who operated a one-person news and gossip bulletin board on the Internet at the time, learned that *Newsweek* magazine had decided to hold a story by Michael Isikoff, one of its Washington reporters, that alleged that President Bill Clinton had conducted an improper sexual relationship with a White House intern and had urged her to lie about it to a Federal grand jury. Based in Los Angeles, Drudge published his information about the *Newsweek* story on his Web site on Monday, January 19. That week the *Washington Post*, ABC News, the *Los Angeles Times*, the *New York Times*, and *Newsweek* itself on America Online reported the allegations. Over the weekend, the pundits on the Sunday morning news-and-views television shows weighed in. ABC News' White House correspondent Sam Donaldson opined that "if he is not telling the truth, I think his presidency is numbered in days."[35]

Within a week, a scandal of historic proportions involving the president of the United States uncovered by a Washington correspondent had been reported to the public by an Internet gossip columnist based in Los Angeles. By the weekend, the Washington pundits had pronounced their verdict. The story set off a series of events that eventually led to the impeachment of the president. The battle for impeachment was fought as much in the press as in Congress and by the special prosecutor appointed to investigate the president. At one point, special prosecutor Kenneth Starr's office was brought before a U.S. Federal District Court judge after being accused of illegally leaking secret grand jury testimony to reporters.

The public battle for impeachment reached an unprecedented pitch on September 11, 1998, when the report outlining the grounds for the impeachment of the President was posted on the Internet by the U.S. House of Representatives before it was delivered to the White House. In choosing the Internet to release the impeachment report, the members of the House bypassed the Washington-based news media signaling a shift in the way people receive news about America's national leaders.

At the same time that new technology made coverage of politicians more readily available to readers, national politicians had many more channels of communication through which they could communicate directly to the public, bypassing reporters. For example, in 1994, Vice President Al Gore conducted an on-line, live chat with 300 participants on the Compuserve computer network.[36] Some people have speculated that the proliferation of news media reporting on Washington will force politicians to be more open and accessible to reporters as well as to the public.[37]

From the founding of America, reporting from the nation's capitol has been seen as an essential element of democratic governance. The public must be informed about the activities of national leaders to make wise choices during elections. While the precise nature of Washington-based journalists has changed over time, the fundamental role of Washington correspondence—to keep the American public well informed about activities of the federal government—has remained constant.

Selected Readings

Blanchard, Robert O. *Congress and the News Media.* New York: Hastings House, 1974.

Essary, J. Frederick. *Covering Washington: Government Reflected to the Public in the Press.* Boston and New York: Houghton Mifflin Company, 1926.

Grotta, Gerald L. "Phillip Freneau's Crusade for Open Sessions of the U.S. Senate." *Journalism Quarterly* 48 (1971): 667–71.

Hess, Stephen. *Live from Capitol Hill.* Washington, D.C.: The Brookings Institution, 1991.

Kaminski, Thomas H. "Congress, Correspondents and Confidentiality in the 19th Century: A Preliminary Study." *Journalism History* 4 (1977): 83–87, 92.

Marbut, Frederick B. *News from the Capital. The Story of Washington Reporting.* Carbondale and Edwardsville: Southern Illinois Press, 1971.

Ritchie, Donald. *Press Gallery: Congress and the Washington Correspondents.* Cambridge, Mass.: Harvard University Press, 1991.

Rosemont, Victor. "The Constitutional Convention in the Colonial Press." *Journalism Quarterly* 14 (1937): 364–66.

Rosten, Leo C. *The Washington Correspondents.* New York: Harcourt, Brace, 1937.

Weaver, David H., and G. Cleveland Wilhoit. "News Media Coverage of U.S. Senators in Four Congresses, 1953–1974." *Journalism Monographs* 67 (1980).

Notes

1. George Washington, Fourth Annual Message to Congress, November 6, 1792, downloaded from http://ww.yale.edu/lawweb/avalon/presiden/sou/washs04.htm.

2. John Alexander, *The Selling of the Constitutional Convention* (Madison, Wis.: Madison House, 1990), 9.

3. John Boyd, ed., *The Papers of Thomas Jefferson*, 19 vols. (Princeton: Princeton University Press, 1950–1971), 11:49.

4. Wm. David Sloan, "The Party Press, 1783–1833," chapter 5 in Wm. David Sloan and James D. Startt, eds., *The Media in America*, 4th ed (Northport, Ala.: Vision Press, 1999), 74–80.

5. *Aurora* (Philadelphia), 26 December 1796.

6. *Annals of Congress*, 1st Cong., 1st Session (Philadelphia, Pa., 1789–90) 1:953.

7. Culver H. Smith, *The Press, Politics, and Patronage: The American Government's Use of Newspapers 1789–1875* (Athens: University of Georgia Press, 1977), 2.

8. *National Gazette*, 13 February 1793, reprinted in Wm. David Sloan, Cheryl S. Wray, and C. Joanne Sloan, *Great Editorials*, 2nd ed. (Northport, Ala.: Vision Press, 1997), 51.

9. J. Frederick Essary, *Covering Washington: Government Reflected to the Public in the Press 1822–1926* (Boston and New York: Houghton Mifflin Company, 1927), 19.

10. Robert O. Blanchard, ed., *Congress and the News Media* (New York: Hastings House, 1974), 29.

11. Sloan, "The Party Press, 1783–1833," 89.

12. Sedition; An Act in Addition to the Act, Entitled "An Act for the Punishment of Certain Crimes Against the United States," Sec. 2 (July 14, 1798), *U.S. Statutes at Large*, I: 596–97.

13. Thomas Jefferson, Second Inaugural Address, March 4, 1805 downloaded from http://www.yale.edu/lawweb/avalon/presiden/inaug/jefinau2.htm.

14. Charles Francis Adams, ed., *The Memoirs of John Quincy Adams* 12 vols. (New York : AMS Press, 1970), 9: 493–94.

15. *Alfred Vail's Telegraph Journal*, Vail Telegraph Collection quoted in Menaham Blondheim, *News of the Wire: The Telegraph and the Flow of Information in America, 1844–1897* (Cambridge, Mass.: Harvard University Press, 1994), 33–34.

16. Mark Summers, *The Press Gang: Newspapers and Politics 1865–1878* (Chapel Hill: University of North Carolina Press, 1994), 80.

17. Maurine Beasley, *The First Women Washington Correspondents*, vol. 4, GW Washington Studies (Washington D.C.: George Washington University, 1976), 3–4.

18. Donald Ritchie, *Press Gallery: Congress and the Washington Correspondents* (Cambridge, Mass.: Harvard University Press, 1991), 63–65.

19. James Pollard, *The Presidents and the Press* (New York: MacMillan, 1947) 250–51.

20. *New York Sun,* 1 July 1871, 2.

21. *New York Sun,* 4 September 1872, 2.

22. *Many Secrets Revealed; or Ten Years Behind the Scene in Washington City*, quoted in Stephen Hess, *Live from Capitol Hill* (Washington D.C.: Brookings Institution, 1991), 20–21.

23. Summers, *The Press Gang…*, 86.

24. "First White House Reporter Dies," *Editor & Publisher*, 31 October 1931, 38.

25. Elmer Cornwell, *Presidential Leadership of Public Opinion* (1965; reprint ed., Westport, Conn.: Greenwood Press, 1979).

26. George Juergens, *News From the White House* (Chicago: University of Chicago Press, 1981), 65–66.

27. Blaire Atherton French, *The Presidential Press Conference: Its History and Role in the American Political System* (Lanham, Md: University Press of America, 1982), 5.

28. Marlen E. Pew, "Shop Talk at 30," *Editor & Publisher*, 8 April 1933, 36.

29. Stephen Hess, "The Once and Future Worlds of Presidents Communicating," *Presidential Studies Quarterly* 28:4 (1998): 748–54.

30. "Going Public," *Transcript of Online NewsHour: Presidential Communications*, 28 January 1997.

31. Joe McGinnis, *The Selling of the President 1968* (New York: Trident Press 1969), 34.

32. Howard Kurtz, *Spin Cycle: How the White House and the Media Manipulate the News* (New York: Touchstone Books, 1998).

33. Quoted in James Keogh, *President Nixon and the Press* (New York: Funk & Wagnells, 1972), 2–3.

34. Mark Hertzgaard, *On Bended Knee* (New York: Farrar, Straus, Giroux, 1988).

35. Jules Witcover, "Where We Went Wrong," *Columbia Journalism Review*, March/April 1998, 19–25.

36. Randy Reddick and Elliot King, *The Online Journalist*, 2nd ed. (Fort Worth: Harcourt Brace College Publishers, 1997), 11.

37. Alison Mitchell, "McCain Embraces the Press and Open Campaigns of Old," *New York Times*, 15 February 2000, 1.

18

The Press and U.S. Presidents

JAMES D. STARTT

Institutions evolve, and so it is with the press and the presidency. Although it is often referred to as adversarial, the relationship between the president and the press has varied over the course of the last two hundred years. The press, it is true, has made life uncomfortable for every president. Harry Truman spoke for all of them as he reflected, "When the press stops abusing me, I'll know I'm in the wrong pew."[1] On the other hand, presidents have used the press in various ways. To understand the relationship in all of its variety, it is first necessary to grasp its nature through the major stages of its development. Three such stages can be discerned. The first occurred from 1789 to 1833; the second, from 1833 to the 1890s; and the third, from 1900 to 2000.

EMERGENCE OF THE PRESIDENTIAL-PRESS RELATIONSHIP, 1789 TO 1833

Unpredictable and tenuous as the first period of the American republic was, it spanned the time in which the young nation took root and began to grow. During those years the first generation of presidents had to develop the polity and the administrative organization needed to allow the new nation to function. They also had to create an economic basis for the country, to restrain sectional differences, and to resolve domestic disputes. They led the country in an undeclared naval war with France (1798–1800) and a declared war with Britain (1812–1815). Washington's first inauguration also corresponded with the opening of the French Revolution—an event whose repercussions swept across the Western world, leaving divided political loyalties in its wake. The impact that revolution had in the United States, along with disputes over economic policy, hastened the formation of the country's first party system.

The nation's founders took a dim view of political parties. Nevertheless, political parties did emerge. During Washington's first term, two parties, the Federalist (not to be confused with Federalists of 1787-1788 who championed ratification of the new Constitution), and the Republican (not to be confused with the modern Republican party that dates from 1854), coalesced respectively around the figures of Alexander Hamilton and Thomas Jefferson. Like Washington, and every president before Jackson, many newspaper publishers at first professed their nonpartisanship, but they soon assumed a position in support of one of the two parties.[2] Consequently, a political party press emerged that, with little exception, determined the nature of presidential-press relations throughout the first party system and survived the realignment of parties in the late 1820s to reach its pinnacle of influence in the early 1830s. It remained, thereafter, a political force for many years, but its roots can be traced back to the political debates of the 1790s. By the end of that decade, the stalwart Federalist, Fisher Ames, felt compelled to declare, "The newspapers are an overmatch for any government. They will first overawe and then usurp it. This has been done, and the Jacobins [i. e. the Republicans] owe their triumph to the unceasing use of this engine."[3]

Indeed, before Washington concluded his first term, John Fenno, a Bostonian who had assisted the well-known publisher Benjamin Russell on his *Massachusetts Centinel*, founded his own *Gazette of the United States* in New York on April 11, 1789. He intended to produce a national journal devoted to supporting the "Constitution and the Administration."[4] Although he contended that a "printer [who] can be made the tool of a party ... merits universal contempt," his vigorous support of Washington's administration, his endless publicizing of presidential pageantry, and his extolling of Hamilton's financial and economic program in particular, led Thomas Jefferson to perceive Fenno's *Gazette* as "a paper of pure Toryism." "No government ought to be without censors and where the press is free [meaning free from executive influence] no one ever will," Jefferson complained to Washington.[5] His concern about how Fenno was disseminating anti-democratic ideas, led him, along with James Madison to find someone who could publish another newspaper to counter Fenno's influence. They settled on the gifted poet, writer, and journalist, Philip Freneau, who launched the *National Gazette* in October 1791. Now, two newspapers, published in Philadelphia, then the national capital, claimed to be "national" journals, and each advanced the cause of their preferred party. Hostilities ensued between them as each denounced the others' articles and arguments. More important, if Fenno's *Gazette* continued to glorify the government and the Federalists, Freneau's *Gazette* held them both to a different standard and criticized both in the name of Republican principles. The President came to believe that Freneau's attacks injured "the tranquillity of the nation," and in private he became impassioned in his denunciations of Freneau's criticism.[6]

Nevertheless, Fenno and Freneau had anticipated a style of political journalism that, with slight exception, would characterize presidential-press relations for years to come.

Belligerent political journalism flourished as both Federalist and Republican editors and pamphleteers denounced their opponents in spirited terms. One prominent Republican editor attacked Washington for "his own want of merit and that of others whom he has placed in office" and recommended he retire from office or be impeached.[7] Washington considered such attacks "indecent" and said he wished he could depart from government to stop being battered "in public prints by a set of infamous scribblers."[8] Sometimes a scribbler would reverse course and redirect his attacks. Such was the case of the transplanted Englishmen William Cobbett. Although a master of impertinent and sarcastic argument in defense of the Federalists, and although a supporter of President John Adams early in his administration, he turned on him when he seemed to act too conciliatory toward France and labeled him "a precipitate old ass" who had abandoned principle.[9]

No wonder Adams felt opposition editors had vilified him. His successors prior to Andrew Jackson also had reason to complain about how opposing newspapers treated them. For the most part, however, Presidents Madison, Monroe, and John Quincy Adams chose to remain silent about it.[10] The most interesting case by far of a president's reaction to press criticism in these years was that of Thomas Jefferson. Federalist editors were severe in attacking him during the election of 1800 and afterwards. Stalwart Federalist correspondents in newspapers like the *Washington Federalist* berated him as an irreligious Jacobin and a hypocrite who had slandered George Washington, and the skillful magazine editor Joseph Dennie made sure that Jefferson was "pilloried weekly" in his *Port Folio*, the most important magazine in the country.[11]

Despite such attacks, Jefferson often professed his belief in a free press. He led the opposition to the Sedition Act, which the Federalists passed in 1798 at the time of the undeclared naval war with France, in an effort to restrain the Republican newspapers. During the hard-fought election of 1800 and in the years following, when the Federalist press reached its height as did its criticism of him, he rarely responded to those attacks. He held that truth would prevail over falsehood in the press, and his re-election in 1804 seemed to confirm that belief. It is not, however, unusual for commitment to principle, strong though it may be, to fall short of being absolute. In Jefferson's case, while he contended that Congress could not restrict a free press, he allowed that states could do so by imposing libel laws. Moreover, although he never instigated any libel charges himself, even in the cases of his detractors' most abusive and outrageous accusations, he offered tacit approval of those who did so in his behalf.[12] There are, in fact, detectable ironies in Jefferson's press relations. While he conceived of the press in commonwealth or nonpartisan terms, he was instrumental, in the case of Freneau's *National Gazette*, in the emergence of a partisan press. While professing a lofty commitment to the principle of a free press, he wavered from that commitment in practice.[13] Nonetheless, his lifelong conviction that a free press, like public opinion, was integral to the life of democracy remains one of his greatest legacies.

Jefferson also shared with all the presidents of this period a concern about government publicity. How were the views of government to reach the people? It was in an effort to publicize their respective views that Hamilton and Jefferson patronized Fenno and Freneau. The tactic of using a preferred newspaper to publicize official news became the practice of every president until Lincoln's time. These newspapers, though conducted independently and deserving of being considered semiofficial organs, acquired the status of official newspapers. For the first two decades of the 19th century, the *National Intelligencer* was the preferred newspaper of the presidents. Supported by a system of "executive patronage" that included government printing contracts and other lucrative awards, the *Intelligencer* held a privileged position. Until the 1820s, no other newspaper in the capital could give it serious competition. In return for privileges received, the editors of the *Intelligencer* held their treatment of news to a high standard. The fact that other newspapers copied it as a source of government announcements and news from the capital made it a valued means by which the government could reach the wider public. The *Intelligencer's* preeminent position in Washington prevailed throughout the presidencies of Jefferson, Madison, and Monroe.

Nevertheless, during Monroe's second administration, circumstances shifted in a manner that affected the press not only in the capital but also throughout the country. Following the War of 1812, and with the disintegration of the Federalist party at the national level, a period of one party government followed that was characterized, in part, by the nation's newspapers assuming a more temperate tone. But with the debates surrounding the Panic of 1819 and the Missouri Compromise of 1820, political factionalism returned, albeit within the Republican party. Matters reached an impasse in the election of 1824, which failed to produce a majority in the electoral college for any of the five candidates. The House of Representatives had to decide the winner. When it named John Quincy Adams president, Andrew Jackson, who had won more electoral votes than Adams, felt he had lost by means of political maneuvering. Pro-Jackson editors across the country erupted with charges of corruption and foul play as the temperate tone of the press apparent only a few years before gave way to a resurgent partisan journalism.

Jackson's supporters disdained what they considered the "heresy ... of amalgamation" and began to build a new party, the Democratic party.[14] Adams' followers responded by organizing their own National Republican party (subsequently the Whig party). Partisan journalism was a bulwark for both efforts. In 1826 Jackson's friends in Washington brought out the *United States Telegraph* as their own newspaper in the capital. Its editor and proprietor Duff Green demonstrated his mastery of the use of ridicule, cruel humor, and innuendo in his journalistic attacks. He soon won the title of "field general of the Jackson forces."[15] In time, however, Jackson lost confidence in him and turned to Francis P. Blair, a Kentuckian with a bombastic journalistic style, and helped him found the *Washington Globe* as his administrative newspaper. Blair was not only an editor willing to comply with the wishes of the

President but also a close friend and a member of the inner circle of his advisors known as the "Kitchen Cabinet."[16]

President Jackson understood the value of publicity and the importance of the press in achieving it. He made unprecedented use of executive patronage in appointing loyal journalists to official positions and stoutly defended the practice. His State Department redistributed over 70 per cent of press assignments to publish the laws, a practice he condemned as a candidate, to pro–Jackson newspapers.[17] These "patronage newspapers," paid by the government to publish the laws, also received the *Globe*, which they were free to use in any way they chose. When copies of these newspapers containing articles based on the *Globe's* own content were sent to the State Department as a matter of record, Blair would extract items from them to publish in his *Globe* as evidence of public opinion from around the country. The combination of Blair's hard-hitting journalism and the systematic production of sympathetic opinion led even Duff Green to complain about Jackson's "servile press."[18] Nevertheless, pro–Jackson newspapers did not always follow in lockstep behind the *Globe*, and the Whig press refused to grovel before either the President or his press. By the end of Jackson's second term in 1836, the majority of the press opposed him, and four years later neither the *Globe's* nor Jackson's endorsement could save Martin Van Buren in his bid for re-election. The partisan press, in fact, had passed its zenith, and in the years ahead presidential-press relations would change.

CHANGES IN PRESIDENTIAL-
PRESS RELATIONS,
1833–1890S

Guided by the transformation of political culture before and after the Civil War and by developments in journalism, the nature of presidential-press relations fluctuated in the mid and late 19th century. Although partisan newspapers, often in the hands of editors who gave them a competitive edge, continued to flourish throughout the middle decades of the century, two journalism developments came to characterize those relations in the 20 years before the Civil War. The first was the decline of the administrative newspaper. In time, bitter fights surfaced over the distribution of the Congressional contracts for official printing as the amount of that printing grew beyond the capacity of any one newspaper to handle it. Meanwhile, more and more newspapers in other cities began to send their own correspondents to Washington. They were able to speed news to their editors at home by means of special courier, express train, and, after 1844, by telegraph. Just as important was the deep rift, particularly in the Democratic party, that the issues of slavery and sectionalism caused making it impossible for the administrative newspaper to please both sides in the party strife. Finally, in 1860 President Buchanan broke off relations with the *Constitution*, his own "official" newspaper. However, by that time Congress had passed an act creating the Government Printing Office for its own printing needs, thus ending the subsidies that had supported administrative newspapers.[19] The second, and more famous, development to affect presidential-press relations was the advent of the penny press in 1833. Smaller, cheaper, brighter, and more sensational than their larger and more sober metropolitan predecessors, these newspapers soon spread from New York to other major cities. They were popular publishing successes, and while professing independence from political parties, they retained an interest in politics. They enlivened presidential campaigns with their coverage and were effective in supporting the political causes of their choice.[20] Presidents, however, could not depend on their constant support, especially when in the hands of the irreverent James Gordon Bennett, the founder of the *New York Herald* or his great rival, Horace Greeley, the erratic and moralistic founder of the *New York Tribune*.

None of the presidents who served during these two decades can be considered models of success in dealing with the political journalism of their day. Several grew indifferent to the press and tried to distance themselves from it.

Others found it impossible to rouse the press, even that of their own party, to their support—so severe were the political divisions of their time. James K. Polk, the most successful president of the period, despaired of embarrassing leaks to the press, and the stinging criticism of the opposing Whig press angered him. He came to distrust the press in general.[21] Perhaps the overriding conditioning factor of the era was the fact the political culture of the time made effective relations with the press impossible for any president, a fact that did not bode well for Abraham Lincoln when he entered office in 1861.

Nevertheless, few presidents (perhaps none) have matched the finesse Lincoln demonstrated in his press relations. He invited influential editors, even some critical of him, to visit him. Following the practice common at the time, he appointed a number of journalists to diplomatic posts. He welcomed reporters, many of whom he knew by name, to impromptu interviews, a habit that led his secretary of navy to complain, "He permits the little newsmongers to come around him and be intimate.... [He] likes to hear all the political gossip...."[22] Lincoln, in fact, seemed to enjoy the reporters, and tried to help them in various ways. At times he interceded on their behalf with his field commanders. By 1864 Mathew Brady had photographed him no fewer than 30 times. He also carried on an extensive correspondence with editors. It reveals the care he took to thank them for their support and suggestions, and it shows the detailed knowledge he had of his correspondents' opinions, the patience he had when dealing with editors who opposed him, and the considered manner in which he wrote to correct misstatements appearing about himself. A record of his attempts to try to mitigate the wartime suppression of newspapers when he considered such acts questionable or politically unwise can also be found in the letters.[23] Despite these efforts to maintain open lines of communication with the press, more than any of his predecessors, he became the target of some of the most brutal press criticism of any president.[24] The nation, of course, was enduring the most tragic war of its history; emotions ran high; and various acts of wartime news suppression inflamed them even more.

None of the late 19th-century presidents had Lincoln's skill for dealing with journalists. Nor were they able to adjust to the changing nature of the press. Toward the end of his life in 1876, James Watson Webb, an editor who had done his share to enliven the political journalism of the previous generation, lamented to James G. Blaine, "When you and I were editors we did not follow, but made public sentiment; and we also made presidents. But things have changed now."[25] Indeed they had. As the old partisan journalism was becoming an anachronism, a new journalism, prefigured by the earlier penny press, emerged. Most personified by Joseph Pulitzer and his *New York World*, newspapers of this type concentrated on news of general interest, on news that enhanced sales. They sought accounts of crime, scandal, and disaster—news that supplied sensational matter fit for its large headlines, action pictures, and sprightly columns. Presidential news in general also had a place in these newspapers, but the political reporters now became more interested in news that featured human interest aspects of prominent figures as well as scandalous items about them. The long-serving Washington correspondent Richard Oulahan observed that it became journalistic convention to bring "a trace of lightness into the serious presentation of official news."[26]

Gilded Age reporters in Washington were more attracted to Congress, the news center of the time, than to the occupants of the White House, and the latter did little to change the situation. Ironically, among the presidents of these decades only Andrew Johnson went out of his way to engage the press. He granted the first formal presidential interview and frequent less formal ones and generally tried to reach the public through the reporters, but he could not prevail against the onslaught of many of the nation's most influential papers that denounced him.[27] His successors (Presidents Grant, Hayes, Garfield, Arthur, Cleveland, and Harrison) were unable or unwilling to build constructive relations with the press. Like many of their predecessors, they distrusted the press and tried to distance themselves from it. It fell to President

William McKinley to nudge the press away from Congress and toward the White House. He had a secretary brief the press each evening and increased the flow of press releases to reporters, whom he allowed to work inside the White House in the reception room outside his own office. His secretary, George Cortelyou, established good relations with the reporters and did much to make their work more efficient.[28] Although these gestures failed to save McKinley from jingoistic elements in the press attacking him for hesitating to declare war on Spain in 1898, they did open the way for a different type of presidential-press relationship.

THE MODERN PRESIDENTIAL-PRESS RELATIONSHIP, 1900–TODAY

In broad terms, the growth of the commercial orientation of the press and the expansion of the power of the presidency defined the nature of modern presidential-press relations. Internal changes, of course, occurred in both institutions as the century proceeded and as each became more involved with the other. For instance, new media (i.e., film, radio, and television) gave presidents a greater presence in the public mind than ever before, and in some respects, they changed the way the press covered them. In the 20th century, it became commonplace for presidents to hold press conferences and to have groups of reporters follow them as they traveled near and far. Some of out best journalists were assigned to the White House press corps, a group that grew in size to about 60 regularly assigned reporters. Beyond that group, by the end of the century, about 2,000 journalists in Washington had White House credentials and might visit 1600 Pennsylvania Avenue from time to time.[29] Moreover, as the media grew into a numbers-conscious business in quest of the largest possible audience, they became more interested in personalities than in the details of policy, and this celebrity orientation influenced actions and ob-

jectives of reporters covering the presidents. It was natural for the press to focus attention on the presidents, who in the 20th century became world leaders, and the fact that the commercially based press professed political independence did not mean that it would be neutral in politics. In fact, a sprawling media with their own role to play in the national political culture had emerged. How would the presidents deal with them?

Most historians date the modern presidency from the time of Franklin D. Roosevelt, but its identifying roots go back to the early 20th century progressive era. It was then, as reaction set in against the industrial and political abuses associated with the Gilded Age and against Congress that had failed to check them, that many reformers came to believe that the solution for the problems lay in more powerful national government with a more powerful president at its center. The ascendancy of presidential power then became a hallmark of that office, and circumstances associated with World War I, the Great Depression, World War II, and the cold war magnified that power. But to be effective, presidents had to have public support, and they had to be able to mobilize public opinion. Their need to communicate with the public grew as did their need to project a positive image. "If the man who lives in the White House," Richard Oulahan once reflected, "does not constantly appear to be doing something to the peoples' taste, to be prodding the Senate or the House, or both; to be keeping at it so everlastingly that the public eye must be forever focused on him ... do not his fellow citizens gain the impression that he is not working hard enough at attending to their business?"[30] Consequently, the press became a more significant factor in presidential politics than it had been in the late 19th century, but if it were instrumental in disseminating news from the White House, how it reported and interpreted that news could impair a president's effort to reach the public.

Modern presidents, therefore, had to develop a number of tactics for dealing with the reality of an independent press. Although many of them appeared earlier, especially in the presidencies of Theodore Roosevelt and Woodrow

Wilson, or even before then, it was during Franklin Roosevelt's time that they were fused together into a system of presidential publicity. Press conferences, both by the President and by cabinet members, press briefings, handouts and news releases, privileged access to the President, and inspired news stories all became part of the system. His administration also monitored the press to allow him and his associates to be well informed about public opinion. Roosevelt also nurtured relations with friendly journalists, publicized himself as a news source, and had the executive departments conduct public relations campaigns. Under him, government publicity bureaus staffed by competent public information officers increased. The President was masterful at radio communication (like Kennedy and Reagan would later be with the television medium), and he also received "public service" airtime for other government publicists to make "spot" announcements and to air "informational" programs.[31] His advisors exploited the film medium and worked to assure positive coverage of him in newsreels. All modern presidents have employed intermediaries to deal with the press on their behalf, and, in Stephen Early, Roosevelt found one of the best. A former journalist who was sensitive to the needs of newsmen, many of whom he knew personally, Early advised the President about press matters on the one hand while on the other he served as administrative spokesman in a manner that won him the respect of the White House press corps. He also ably handled a number of additional publicity functions for Roosevelt, as did other intermediaries with the public, especially his wife Eleanor and his secretary Louis Howe.[32] Central to it all, of course, was the President whose skills in the art of communication were extraordinary.[33]

Every president since Roosevelt has devised a news and publicity system along these lines. Considering the needs of the modern presidency and the capacity of the modern media to influence the presentation of news, such a system could be credible. However, if presidents used it to close off news sources, to circumvent the press (in either case for unjustified, self-serving reasons) or to intimidate the press, then credibility would be lost. Harry Truman, for instance, who suffered constant attacks from the press and believed we were at risk of having a "one party [Republican] press in a two party country" kept the sources of White House news open and remained on good terms with the correspondents who felt he was being honest with them.[34] Richard Nixon, to the contrary, allowed his press conferences to become staged affairs, in private took steps to intimidate individual media, and led his administration into open warfare with journalists. Like Lyndon Johnson before him, he assumed a "siege mentality" towards the press.[35] Consequently, during their time a credibility gap opened up between the president, indeed, the government, and the press. In the 1980s, President Reagan and his aides made a habit of staging the news and limiting access to the President. Presidential news became less believable as his aides shielded him from reporters, as they tried to explain away his erroneous and misleading answers, and as he derided the press in an effort to deflect adverse criticism from himself.[36] Although practiced long before, the term "spin" dates from 1984, and it came to symbolize the efforts of Reagan's aides to place a favorable interpretation on presidential news. They "achieved a new level of control over the mechanics of modern communication," complained the chief *New York Times* White House correspondent.[37] Subsequent presidents made similar efforts. At the end of the century, for instance, Bill Clinton did not help himself by entering office with the intention to skirt the traditional news outlets by utilizing a variety of alternative media, particularly various Internet avenues, to reach specific audiences without going through the filter of press interpretation.[38]

Nevertheless, the news media were also responsible for the decline of credibility in their relations with the president in the later 20th century. From the 1960s on, the rise of investigative reporting, the tendency toward "infotainment" in television news, the media's fascination with polls and ratings, and their fixation on scandal, on shock journalism, and on beating a story to death, along with the 24-hour news cycle, all affected the shape and content of political news. Moreover, their focusing on leadership and on the character of public figures often meant concentrating on personal failures. Neither "pack journalism" nor the "feeding frenzy" tendency of the news media, nor their fixation on critique and on exposé journalism allowed public figures much respite from the adversarial positioning of the news media.[39] None of these things, however, occurred in a political or cultural vacuum. Just as the Vietnam conflict and the Watergate and Iran-Contra scandals made presidents less believable in the eyes of journalists, so, perhaps in a more intangible way, the end of the cold war, the rise of public cynicism, a general lessening of public civility, and the ascendancy of polarized politics help to explain their more critical attitude toward the president today. Compared to what they had been earlier, presidential-press relations have grown more estranged in our own time.

CONCLUSION

For more than 200 years, the presidential-press relationship has lent vitality to the political life of the nation, and without that vitality democracy can decline. The relationship has been sometimes more effective than at others, and as has been seen, it has changed over time due either to shifts in the political climate or to internal developments in one or the other of the institutions. Another variable in the relationship has been a president's personality and his basic perception of the role the press plays in a democratic society. Some presidents have even been able to interject a refreshing touch of humor into the relationship. For instance, at his press conference on May 9, 1961, Kennedy was asked to comment on the press coverage of his administration. He replied with the now well-known comment that he was reading more but enjoying it less. His answer, however, deserves to be read in full:

Well, I am reading more and enjoying it less, and so on, but I have not complained nor do I plan to make general complaints. I read and talk to myself about it but I don't plan to issue any general statement on the press. I think

they are doing their task, as a critical branch, the Fourth estate [sic]. I am attempting to do mine. And we are going to live together for a period, and go our separate ways.[40]

The wisdom of that statement speaks for itself.

Selected Readings

Best, Gary Dean. *The Critical Press and the New Deal: The Press versus Presidential Power, 1933–1938.* Westport, Conn., 1993.
Blackmon, Robert E. "Noah Brooks: Reporter in the White House." *Journalism Quarterly* 32 (1955): 301–10, 374.
Cornwell, Elmer E., Jr. "The Press Conferences of Woodrow Wilson." *Journalism Quarterly* 39 (1962): 292–300.
Cornwell, Elmer E., Jr. *Presidential Leadership of Public Opinion.* Bloomington: Indiana University Press, 1965.
Jordan, Myron K. "Presidential Health Reporting: The Eisenhower Watershed." *American Journalism* 4 (1987): 147–58.
Juergens, George. *News from the White House: The Presidential-Press Relationship in the Progressive Era.* Chicago: University of Chicago Press, 1981.
Leiter, Kelly. "A President and One Newspaper: U. S. Grant and the Chicago *Tribune.*" *Journalism Quarterly* 47 (1970): 71–80.
Liebovich, Louis W. *The Press and the Modern Presidency: Myths and Mindsets from Kennedy to Clinton.* Westport, Conn.: Praeger, 1998.
Moon, Gordon A., II. "George F. Parker: A 'Near Miss' as First White House Press Chief." *Journalism Quarterly* 41 (1964): 183–90.
Nelson, W. Dale. *Who Speaks for the President? The White House Press Secretary from Cleveland to Clinton.* Syracuse, N.Y.: Syracuse University Press, 1998.
Pollard, James E. *The Presidents and the Press.* New York: Macmillan, 1947.
Pollard, James E. *The Presidents and the Press: Truman to Johnson.* Washington: Public Affairs Press, 1964.
Ponder, Stephen. *Managing the Press: Origins of the Media Presidency, 1897–1933.* New York: St. Martin's, 1998.
Spear, Joseph C. *Presidents and the Press: The Nixon Legacy.* Cambridge, Mass.: MIT Press, 1984.
Tebbel, John, and Sarah Miles Watts. *The Press and the Presidency: From George Washington to Ronald Reagan.* New York: Oxford University Press, 1985.
Turner, Kathleen J. *Lyndon Johnson's Dual War: Vietnam and the Press.* Chicago: University of Chicago Press, 1985.
Winfield, Betty Houchin. *FDR and the News Media.* New York, 1994.

Notes

1. Quoted in Helen Thomas, "Ronald Reagan and the Management of the News," in *The White House Press on the Presidency: News Management and Co-option,* ed. Kenneth Thompson (Lantham, Md.: University Press of America, 1983), 41.
2. "American Newspapers and Editorial Opinion, 1789–93," appendix 2, Douglas Southhall Freeman, *George*

Washington: A Biography, 6 vols. (New York: Charles Scribner's Sons, 1954), 6:393.

3. Quoted in ibid.

4. John Fenno, "An Address," enclosed in the agreement to underwrite the *Gazette* by John Lucas, et. al., 1 January 1789, in "Letters of John Fenno and John Ward Fenno, 1779–1800, Part 1: 1779–1790," *Proceedings of the American Antiquarian Society* 89 (1980): 312–13, and Jeffrey L. Pasley, "The Two National Gazettes: Newspapers and the Embodiment of American Political Parties," *Early American Literature* 35 (2000): 54–57.

5. Quoted in ibid., 64. It was Jefferson's custom at this time to report to Washington about the press and to place the president's announcements in appropriate newspapers. See Jefferson to Washington, 10 April 1791 and 8 May 1791, Dorothy Twohig, ed., *The Papers of George Washington*, 8 vols. (Charlottesville: University Press of Virginia, 1983–1999), 8:78 and 163.

6. Quoted in Freeman, "American Newspapers and Editorial Opinion," 407.

7. Pamphlet, Benjamin Franklin Bache, *Remarks Occasioned by the Late Conduct of Mr. Washington as President of the United States* (Philadelphia: 1796), 3.

8. Washington to Oliver Wolcott, Jr., 6 July 1796 and Washington to Hamilton, 26 June 1796, quoted in James Tagg, *Benjamin Franklin Bache and the Philadelphia "Aurora"* (Philadelphia: University of Pennsylvania Press, 1991), 281.

9. Quoted in *Porcupine's Works*, vol. 9, p. 4, in David A. Wilson, ed., *William Cobbett: Peter Porcupine in America* (Ithaca: Cornell University Press, 1994), 36. Turnabouts of political loyalty could affect presidents in either party. James Callender, one of the hard-hitting Republican editors of the 1790s, became disgruntled with the lack of support Jefferson accorded him in 1802 and published a series of attacks on him that included the first details of the Jefferson relationship with Sally Hemings. See Michael Durey "With the Hammer of Truth," *James Callender and America's Early National Heroes* (Charlottesville: University Press of Virginia, 1999), 145–63, and Charles A. Jellison, "The Scoundrel Callender," *Virginia Magazine of History and Biography*, 67 (1959): 303–5. The Sally Hemings article appeared in the *Richmond Recorder*, 1 September 1802, p. 1.

10. John Tebbel and Sarah Miles Watts, *The Press and the Presidency: From George Washington to Ronald Reagan* (New York: Oxford University Press, 1985), 51 and 57, and Charles Francis Adams, ed., *Memoirs of John Quincy Adams: Comprising Portions of His Diary 1795 to 1848*, 12 vols. (1874–77; reprint, Freeport, N.Y.: Books for Libraries Press, 1969), 5:469.

11. Frank L. Mott, *Jefferson and the Press* (Baton Rouge: Louisiana State University Press, 1943), 39. See also Charles O. Lerche, Jr., "Jefferson and the Election of 1800: A Case Study in the Political Smear," *William and Mary Quarterly*, 3rd Series, 5 (Oct. 1948): 467–91, and Constance B. Schultz, "'Of Bigotry in Politics and Religion:' Jefferson's Religion, The Federalist Press, and the Syllabus," *Virginia Magazine of History and Biography* 91 (1983): 79–82.

12. William Sterne Randall, *Thomas Jefferson: A Life* (New York: Henry Holt & Co., 1993), 572; James E. Pollard, *The Presidents and the Press* (New York, Macmillan, 1947) 76; and Tebbel and Watts, *The Press and the Presidents*, 32–34.

13. For accounts of Jefferson's wavering on press freedom see Bernard Bailyn, "Jefferson and the Ambiguities of Freedom," *Proceedings of the American Philosophical Society* 137 (1993): 509.

14. Quoted in Ralph Ketcham, *Presidents Above Party: The First American Presidency, 1789–1829* (Chapel Hill: University of North Carolina Press, 1984), 144.

15. Culver H. Smith, *The Press, Politics, and Patronage: The American Government's Use of Newspapers 1789–1875* (Athens: University of Georgia Press, 1977), 66, and Gretchen Garst Ewing, "Duff Green, Independent Editor of a Party Press," *Journalism Quarterly* 54 (1977): 734–35.

16. Robert V. Remini, *Andrew Jackson and the Course of American Freedom*, 1822–1832, 3 vols. (New York: Harper and Row, 1981) 2:292–99 and 326, and Tebbel and Watts, *The Press and the Presidency*, 159.

17. Smith, *The Press, Politics and Patronage*, 96 and 199.

18. Ibid., 134–35. Blair actually perfected the newspaper publicity system that Green had initiated. See ibid., 72.

19. Buchanan to William M. Brown, 25 December 1860, quoted in Pollard, *Presidents and Press*, 299. Congress passed the cited act June 23, 1860; however, already in 1848 John C. Rives established the *Daily Globe* (i. e., the *Congressional Globe*) as a nonpolitical publication to carry the congressional debates, and in 1852 Congress designated the *Congressional Globe* its official reporter. The *Globe* continued in this capacity until 1872, but it was not a newspaper. The State Department's practice of paying selected newspapers to publish laws continued until 1875. See Smith, *The Press, Politics and Patronage*, 172–73, 229, and 245. For a general discussion of the decline of administration newspapers, see ibid., 163–73 and 206–45.

20. For example, the support the *New York Herald* provided President Tyler during the stormy debate over his veto of the bill to recharter the national bank in 1841 exceeded even that of Tyler's own "official" paper, the *Madisonian*. Moreover, the *Herald's* reported the news about the veto in a dramatic way geared to attract public interest. See *New York Herald* and the *Madisonian*, 5–25 August 1841.

21. Pollard, *Presidents and Press*, 221, 249, 266, and 293–95, Tebbel and Watts, *The Press and the Presidency*, 103, 144, 155–56, and 165.

22. Quoted in Pollard, ibid., 358–59.

23. For examples of this correspondence, see Roy P. Basler, ed., *The Collected Works of Abraham Lincoln*, 9 vols. (New Brunswick: Rutgers University Press, 1953–55), 4:139–40 and 145–46; 5:152–53, 169, 225, 388–89, and 544; 6:120, 248, 326, 329, and 338; 7:281, 347–50, 360–61, 409–10, 482, 485, 494 and 526; and 8: 87–88. Lincoln also understood the negative repercussions that could result from a president's complaining in public about how a newspaper falsified his position. See Carl Sandburg, *Abraham Lincoln: The War Years*, 4 vols. (New York: Harcourt, Brace, & Co. 1939), 3:249–50.

24. Some of Lincoln's critics labeled him a "half-witted usurper," "the head ghoul at Washington," or worse. See Tebbel and Watts, *The Press and the Presidency*, 191. Even Lincoln's masterful addresses could be made the subject of crude invective. See, for example, the *Chicago Times'* editorial about his now famous Second Inaugural Address on the theme of "with malice toward none." *Chicago Times*, 7 March 1864, 2.

25. Webb to Blaine, n.d., 1876, quoted in Donald A. Ritchie, *Press Gallery: Congress and the Washington Correspondents* (Cambridge: Harvard University Press, 1991), 143.

26. Richard Oulahan, "Presidents and Publicity," unpublished book ms., chap. 11, p. 11, Pre-Commerce Papers, Herbert Hoover Papers, Herbert Hoover Presidential

Library, West Branch, Iowa, box 2. An examination of the *New York Tribune's* and *New York World's* coverage of the 1884 and 1888 presidential elections indicates the "lightness" was quite apparent in news and commentary about national politics already in the 1880s, and an examination of the *Tribune's* indexes for 1876–1895 shows the growth of the human interest factor in presidential news.

27. Tebbel and Watts, *The Press and the Presidency*, 212–14.

28. W. Dole Nelson, *Who Speaks for the President? The White House Press Secretary from Cleveland to Clinton* (Syracuse: Syracuse University Press, 1998), 16, and Ritchie, *Press Gallery*, 202.

29. Stephen Hess, "President Clinton and the White House Press Corps—Year One," *Media Studies Journal* 8 (Spring 1994): 1.

30. Oulahan, "Presidents and Publicity," chap. 1, "The Stage in Washington," p. 7.

31. Richard W. Steele, *Propaganda in an Open Society: The Roosevelt Administration and the Media, 1933–1941* (Westport, Conn.: Greenwood Press, 1985), 22–23.

32. Ibid., 10–11, and Betty Houchin Winfield. *FDR and the News Media* (Urbana: University of Illinois Press, 1990), 79–88.

33. For examples of FDR's communication skills, consult his press conferences, especially his first one on March 8, 1933. *The Press Conferences of Franklin D. Roosevelt*, 12 reels (Hyde Park, N.Y.: Franklin D. Roosevelt Library, 1971), reel 1, pp. 1–3.

34. Quoted in James E. Pollard, *The Presidents and the Press: Truman to Johnson* (Washington: Public Affairs Press, 1964), 54. Truman often complained in private about what he called the "sabotage press." He detested the Hearst newspapers plus a number of the country's leading newspapers, magazines, and columnists. See Robert H. Ferrell, *Off the Record: The Private Papers of Harry S. Truman* (New York: Harper & Row Publishers, 1980), 40, 47, 63, 192, 214, 232–33, 238, 269, and 279.

35. Blair Atherton French, *The Presidential Press Conference: Its History and Role in the American Political System* (Lantham, Md.: University Press of America, 1982), 19;

Joseph C. Spear, *Presidents and the Press: The Nixon Legacy* (Cambridge: MIT Press, 1984), 79–84; and James Deakin, "The Problem of Presidential-Press Relations," in Thompson, *The White House Press on the Presidency*, 9.

36. Tebbel and Watts, *The Press and the Presidency*, 535–53, Louis W. Liebovich, *The Press and the Modern Presidency: Myths and Mindsets from Kennedy to Clinton* (Westport, Conn.: Praeger, 1998) 130–41; Thomas, "Ronald Reagan and the Management of the News," 37; and David Broder, "The Insulation of the Presidents," syndicated column in (Gary) *Post Tribune*, 18 October 1984, A6. A good example of how Reagan's aides attempted to explain one of his ill-informed statements occurred in 1985 when Reagan defended his policy of no sanctions against South Africa by announcing that racial segregation in public places "has all been eliminated." His press spokesman Larry Speakes answered critics by saying that the President was referring to some major South African cities where "there's been a step in that direction to remove apartheid." (Gary) *Post Tribune*, 27 August 1985, A1 and A6.

37. From an article by Steven R. Weisman, quoted in Tebbel and Watts, *The Press and the Presidency*, 549. See also Liebovich, *The Press and the Modern Presidency*, 131, and W. Lance Bennett, News: *The Politics of Illusion*, 3d ed. (White Plains, N.Y.: Longman, 1996), 100.

38. Hess, "President Clinton and the White House Press Corps—Year One," and Mark A. Thalhimer, "Adventures in 'Ideaspace': The Electronic Age Comes to 1600 Pennsylvania Ave.," *Media Studies Journal* 8 (Spring 1994): 4–5 and 139–43. Some students of presidential press relations have cited Clinton's early efforts to circumvent the Washington press corps as one reason for the negative treatment he received later. His administration was clearly abrasive in its early dealings with the press. However, he had excellent media skills, which he displayed from time to time in his dealings with Washington journalists. It is too early to reach a balanced conclusion about his press relations.

39. Thomas E. Patterson, *Out of Order* (New York: Random House, Vintage Books, 1994), 100, 153, and 201.

40. Quoted in Deakin, "Problem of Presidential-Press Relations," 19.

19

Coverage of Political Campaigns

John Allen Hendricks
and Shannon K. McCraw

The role of the press in the political process has always been substantial. However, the manner in which the press covers politics has changed drastically. Initially, the partisan press existed because of its ties to political parties and individual politicians. With the advent of the penny press, those connections were broken, and newspapers were able to generate sufficient revenue through advertising and subscriptions to cover politics independently and without formal allegiance to political parties. After the press established its autonomy from parties, the electronic media appeared and gained popularity. By the 1920s, radio had emerged as a dominant force in the political process. Then in the 1950s, television began altering political coverage.

Although candidates were not actively campaigning during the presidential elections of 1789 through 1820, politicians found they still were not immune to the party press. George Washington was reluctant to serve a second term as president because of the critical and negative press. Partisan papers accused him of misappropriating land that belonged to Lord Fairfax, who was a personal friend. Washington challenged the editors spreading such information to substantiate their accusations. During the election of 1800, John Adams blamed the press for a lack of support for the Federalist party. With the 1824 election, the press became even more active in the political process, and individuals seeking the presidency began to campaign aggressively.

Aside from the campaign in 1800 between Thomas Jefferson and John Adams, presidential campaigns lacked true competitiveness until 1824. That campaign involved several prominent political leaders, including John Quincy Adams, Andrew Jackson, and Henry Clay. They battled for the presidency, and the press covered almost every effort they made. The party newspapers aligned themselves with candidates. The *Intelligencer* of Washington, D.C., supported both Adams and William Crawford. The *Republican* in Washington supported John Calhoun, while Washington's *City Gazette* supported Crawford. The opposition press accused Adams of using a beautiful girl to seduce the Russian Emperor Alexander in an attempt to gain political favors. Newspapers reported the girl was a maid and nurse for the Adams family. The same election brought charges by newspapers that Andrew Jackson's mother was a mulatto and that Adams' wife was not American, but English.[1]

Following Jackson's election, it was not long into his term before the press began discussing and covering issues relating to the 1832 presidential campaign. Speculation was rampant as to whether Jackson would seek re-election and whether his opponent in the next campaign would be Martin Van Buren or John C. Calhoun.

Coverage of the campaigns involving Jackson was entertaining at best and scandalous at worst. The press accused him of being a murderer because of the execution of six militiamen on his orders following their conviction. It reported that he and his wife had lived adulterously before her divorce from her first husband. Jackson harbored a great deal of resentment over this coverage because the couple believed that her divorce had been taken care of properly by the time of their marriage. Once they discovered there was a problem, the Jacksons married for a second time to rectify any problems or inappropriate appearances. Despite these efforts, the opposition press still used the situation against him.

Newspapers covered the adultery story heavily during Jackson's campaigns. The *Cincinnati Gazette* and the *National Journal* (Washington, D.C.), the organs of the Adams administration, both emphasized it. The *United States Telegraph* (Washington, D.C.) devoted 10 columns to the story and provided detailed information with official documents as well as witness testimony relating to the alleged adultery. The publisher of the *Cincinnati Gazette* refused to let the story pass and circulated a pamphlet that asked the question, "Ought a convicted adulteress and her paramour husband to be placed in the highest offices of this free and Christian land?"[2] During the 1828 election, Jackson in a letter to a friend wrote that Charles Hammond, editor of *Truth's Advocate*, had spread false stories about his family, and he was looking forward to the day when he could settle the matter. The "day of retribution," Jackson threatened, "must come...."[3]

The press covered the 1840 presidential campaign with as much vigor as previous campaigns. Similar to prior campaigns, the press devoted attention to scandalous charges and name-calling. Newspapers claimed that William H. Harrison was too old and decrepit to be president. The *Philadelphia Spirit of the Times* called him a coward and an enemy of the people, and another paper called him an abolitionist. The *Ohio Statesman* published a 15-year-old rumor that Harrison had seduced a young and unprotected female. Although untrue, stories surfaced that he had lived in a log cabin, and this legend became fodder for the press. Many papers that came into existence to support Harrison during the campaign adopted names using the log cabin theme. Examples include the *Dayton Log Cabin*, the *Chillicothe Log Cabin Herald*, the *Log Cabin Rifle*, and the *Log Cabin Advocate*. They used the log cabin theme, which began as a sneer, to present a positive image by labeling Harrison as a man of the people.

During the 1844 campaign, newspapers reported that James Polk was a duelist and coward. One paper reported that his grandfather had been a Tory during the American Revolution. The *Albany Evening Journal* reported that a traveler named Roerback had made a trip through the South and saw a group of 43 slaves that Polk owned with the initials "JKP" branded on their backs.[4] Northern opposition newspapers made particular use of the story. Many continued to publish it even after it was proved to be inaccurate.

In the 1852 presidential campaign, Franklin Pierce was labeled a coward, a drunkard, and anti–Catholic. In Baltimore, the *Old Defender* reported a story that a fellow officer had slapped Pierce in the face during the Mexican War. This story was published even though the officer who allegedly slapped Pierce wrote a letter stating the episode never occurred.

The northern press was comparatively generous to Abraham Lincoln during the 1860 and 1864 presidential campaigns. However, coverage of his 1858 U.S. Senate race in Illinois against Stephen A. Douglas had been intense. It changed the manner and approach in which journalists covered campaigns. The election received inordinate amounts of national press coverage and was the first political campaign to be covered in a modern style.[5] Reporters began traveling with the candidates, defended the press' right to cover the campaign, and recorded campaign speeches via shorthand, thus preserving the candidates' thoughts on the important issues of the day.

The campaign initiated a sense of strong competition among journalists. It was common practice for reporters to wait until the following day to transcribe their notes after covering an important campaign speech or event. To scoop their opposition, reporters for the *Chicago Press and Tribune* transcribed their notes late one evening shortly after a Douglas campaign event and beat the pro–Douglas *Chicago*

Times to the story. The *Press and Tribune* provided an accompanying story defending its action by stating, "The publishers of this paper have determined to introduce a style of journalism heretofore unknown in Chicago."[6]

Douglas and Lincoln were leery of the journalists because they felt their speeches were not being accurately quoted and reported. This caused animosity between the reporters and the politicians. Eventually, the candidates realized the journalists were important to their political success. At the beginning of one speech, Lincoln noticed that a certain reporter was not on the stand to take notes and record the speech. His absence prompted Lincoln to turn to the crowd of 15,000 and ask for the reporter. When the reporter responded that he was trapped at the back of the crowd and could not make his way to the podium, members of the crowd lifted the reporter over their heads and passed him to the front so he could reach Lincoln.[7]

Andrew Johnson, the target of much criticism following the assassination of the popular Lincoln, was the target also of many press charges during his campaign for the presidency in 1868. He was accused of being a Catholic, an atheist, an illegitimate child, and a drunkard. He and his opponent, Ulysses S. Grant, tried to limit their direct contact with the press. Like his predecessors, Grant received much abuse during his campaigns for the presidency. He was labeled a drunkard as well as accused of placing his men, while serving as Union commander during the Civil War, in a position of being butchered while in battle.

During the election of 1876, Rutherford B. Hayes had several accusations leveled against him. The main one was that he defrauded the government by cheating on his income taxes. He was also accused of stealing money from a deserter executed in 1864. Hayes declared that the story was false and decided to tell his side and prevent further damage to his chances of being elected. He agreed to be interviewed by B. J. Loomis of the *Cincinnati Commercial*, but the interview never actually occurred. Instead, Hayes wrote a question-and-answer entry in his diary that he submitted to the *Commercial*,[8] although the paper never published it.

After the Civil War, growing financial independence from political parties allowed the press to be critical of politicians and parties. The campaign of 1880 provides an example of newspapers making editorial comments that pointed out the weaknesses of the parties they supported. Charles Dana, editor of the *New York Sun* and a supporter of the Democratic party, wrote a scathing editorial about the Democratic party's attack on James Garfield. A letter, allegedly written by Garfield, was published in the periodical *Truth*, in which Garfield, supposedly, advocated the controversial use of Chinese laborers. Garfield wrote to newspapers and denied writing the letter, declaring under oath that it was a forgery. Although Dana was usually critical of Garfield, a Republican, he criticized the Democratic party for participating in such dirty politics. "If a party requires such infamous aids," he declared, "that party by whatsoever name it may be called, deserves to perish."[9]

During the 1884 campaign, Grover Cleveland was the first candidate to experience the "new" journalism. New journalism later descended into "yellow journalism" and became synonymous with sensationalism. New journalism consisted of aggressive campaign coverage of candidates and their activities. Republican papers published a report that Cleveland had fathered a son while living in Buffalo, New York. In 1884, the child was 10 years old, and readers were bombarded with titillating stories of Cleveland's illegitimate son. To remind readers of Cleveland's peccadillo, opposition papers repeatedly published the verse: "Ma! Ma! Ma! Where's my pa? Gone to the White House, Ha! Ha! Ha!"[10]

By the 20th century, newspapers continued to identify themselves as party adherents, but their news coverage tended to be generally non-partisan. During the 1912 campaign, Woodrow Wilson fell victim to unfounded rumors concerning his association with Mrs. Mary Peck. In general, however, he had positive experiences with the press. During campaign interviews, journalists were amazed with his ability to explain issues and his versatility in discussing the same topic. His close association with George Harvey, *Harper's Weekly* editor;

James Kerney, *Trenton* (N.J.) *Evening Times* publisher; and Joseph P. Tumulty, his secretary, had helped his interaction with the press.[11]

Wilson believed the press played an important role in publicizing the presidency. He, however, abhorred personal publicity for himself and his family. In 1912, the president-elect and his daughter were riding bicycles after a shopping trip on the island of Bermuda. Wilson told photographers they could photograph him but that they should refrain from photographing his daughter because she was wearing "negligent clothes." A cameraman disobeyed the request and photographed Wilson's daughter. An angry Wilson threatened, "I want to give you the worst thrashing you ever had in your life; and what's more, I'm perfectly able to do it."[12]

During the 1916 election, the "hyphen vote" was a hotly contested issue. The "hyphen vote," so called because it identified people by ancestry (e.g., Irish-American, German-American), grew in importance as President Wilson and Congress attempted to remain neutral during World War I. After receiving an offensive letter from Jeremiah O'Leary, an Irish agitator, Wilson had Joseph Tumulty gather reporters to hear his reply. Wilson declared he would "feel deeply mortified to have you [O'Leary] or anybody like you vote for me.... [S]ince you have access to many disloyal Americans and I have not, I will ask you to convey this message to them."[13] Following Wilson's response, the press overwhelmingly provided editorial support for his policies throughout the campaign.

In 1920, the two candidates for the presidential campaign were journalists. James M. Cox, the Democrat's nominee, was the publisher of the *Dayton* (Ohio) *News*, *Springfield* (Ohio) *News*, and *Canton* (Ohio) *News*. Warren G. Harding, the Republican nominee, was the moderately successful publisher of the *Marion* (Ohio) *Star*. The Associated Ohio Dailies deemed it "a rare privilege" to endorse Cox and Harding as "not only practical publishers and brilliant Ohioans but statesmen of national recognition."[14]

Cox traveled the country giving stump speeches, but it became abundantly clear that the United States had grown weary of Democratic leadership in the White House. Harding, on the other hand, remained in Marion, Ohio, during the campaign. Like William McKinley in his 1896 campaign, Harding met with newspapermen on his front porch and campaigned from that location at his Marion residence. He developed relationships with the newspapermen and built a three-room bungalow to simplify their coverage of him during the campaign. The bungalow allowed reporters to stay in closer proximity to the candidate as well as stay for longer periods to cover the campaign. While Harding enjoyed favorable coverage by many members of the press, there were those who sought to discredit him. He was plagued by a rumor that he had "Negro blood in his veins."[15] While his fear about the rumor increased, the Scripps-Howard newspapers assured him that they would not print anything concerning these reports.[16]

Herbert Hoover served as Secretary of Commerce in the Harding and Coolidge cabinets and enjoyed the respect of the Washington correspondents. During the 1928 presidential election, Hoover's press relationships slowly began to erode. Hoover felt the press should be restricted in its ability to print information. Paul Anderson, a reporter for the *Nation*, stated: "[Hoover] refused to answer pertinent questions and openly resented the fact they were asked."[17] During his presidency, press relationships continued to deteriorate. As the Depression worsened, his administration became more insular. During the 1932 campaign, between September 13 and Thanksgiving, Hoover refused to hold scheduled press conferences. This absence from the press greatly inhibited his ability to present himself as a candidate for re-election. Any information concerning domestic or foreign policy and the campaign against Franklin D. Roosevelt was provided in official press handouts issued through the President's office.

In 1932, William Randolph Hearst played a major role in Franklin D. Roosevelt's presidential nomination by supporting his nomination. Despite Hearst's efforts, most newspapers opposed Roosevelt. The *New York Times* reported Al Smith saying, "In Franklin Roosevelt we have another Hoover."[18] Following Roosevelt's nomination, H. L. Mencken wrote in the *Baltimore Sun* that the Democrats had chosen their weakest candidate. Despite the press' negative criticism, Roosevelt won 472 electoral votes. Upon becoming president, he appointed Stephen Early as the first White House "press secretary." While presidential secretaries had always provided the press with important information, before Early there had never been anyone whose duties were entirely devoted to the press.

By the 1936 campaign, Hearst's support of Roosevelt had cooled considerably. In fact, Hearst wrote front-page editorials condemning the "Raw Deal," a spin on Roosevelt's New Deal. He charged that the Democratic campaign was being conducted from the Kremlin. Switchboard operators at Robert McCormick's *Chicago Tribune* answered phones by asking, "Good Morning, do you know you have only [number] days left to save your country?"[19] While his New Deal policies had alienated many newspaper editors, Roosevelt won re-election.

Throughout Roosevelt's second term, the press asked whether he would seek a third term. On one occasion he remarked, "I am too damned busy literally, to be talking about potential events a long, long way off. I have other things I think are more important for the nation at the present time...."[20] On July 19, 1940, Roosevelt was nominated for an unprecedented third term. He won the 1940 election with his closest margin—27 million to 22 million votes. The *Wall Street Journal* printed the election results on page six.

On July 20, 1944, the Democratic National Convention nominated Roosevelt for his fourth term. While there seemed to be no dispute concerning who would be their presidential nominee, there was considerable question surrounding the vice presidency. The national committee decided on Harry S. Truman. The *New York Times* called Truman "the second Missouri compromise."[21] While considerable attention was paid to Truman's selection, the real issue in the campaign was Roosevelt's health. The *New York Daily* made special reference to his age of 62, while Thomas Dewey

was only 42.[22] *Time* reported that Roosevelt's most persistent health problem was sinus trouble.[23] Less than a year after the election, Roosevelt died on April 12, 1945. Truman became president.

The presidential campaign of 1948 saw the "Truman Special," a train that traveled 32,000 miles and afforded Truman the opportunity to deliver 250 speeches around the nation. Despite his campaigning efforts, few thought that he would be elected. *Newsweek* reported, "Fifty political experts unanimously predict a Dewey victory."[24] Two experts, George Gallup and Elmo Roper, agreed that Dewey would win. Metropolitan newspapers around the nation subscribed to the Gallup and Roper polls. In a stunning upset, though, Truman was elected president, and a photograph of next morning's *Chicago Tribune* banner head reading "Dewey Defeats Truman"[25] became embarrassingly famous.

By the 1920s, radio had become a popular medium and a force to be reckoned with in political campaigning. Commercial television appeared on the scene in 1948, and it was to become even more important than radio. During the 1952 campaign, following an interview on the television show *Meet the Press*, reporters asked vice presidential candidate Richard Nixon about a secret fund that California businessmen allegedly raised for him. The *New York Post* printed the headline "Secret Nixon Fund" on its front page.[26] The *New York Herald Tribune* called for Nixon to resign from the Eisenhower ticket. Television, however, saved Nixon's candidacy. On a Tuesday night, he delivered his famous "Checkers" speech declaring that the only gift he had received was for his daughter, a little cocker spaniel from Texas, named "Checkers," and they were keeping it.

Coverage of candidates changed dramatically when President Eisenhower suffered a heart attack September 24, 1955. During the 1956 campaign, the issue of his health emerged as a central issue. Eisenhower informed James C. Hagerty, his press spokesman, to "Tell the truth, the whole truth; don't try to conceal anything."[27] By early September 1956, the health issue subsided, and reporters began to write positive stories emphasizing Eisenhower's good health. The *Seattle Post-Intelligencer* reported, "Notwithstanding the long day which included a flight across the nation, the President looked well and relaxed as he emerged with Mamie at his side from the Columbine."[28] Hagerty's openness about Eisenhower's condition turned health reporting into an everyday event.

During the 1960 campaign, Nixon and John F. Kennedy engaged in the first televised debates. While newspapers continued to provide readers with in-depth reporting, television became crucial to the survival of candidates. Both television and radio shared the responsibility of disseminating the three Kennedy-Nixon debates. There are conflicting reports concerning the winner of the debates. Those who listened to the debates on the radio indicated that Nixon won, while those who watched the debates said that Kennedy gained a decisive victory. The difference of interpretation may be attributed to the candidates' appearance. Nixon refused to wear makeup and experienced weight loss after a recent illness and hospitalization, while Kennedy wore makeup and appeared invigorated and youthful. Those listening to the debates on the radio were left to judge the candidates based on the quality of their comments.[29] Thus, the visual appearance of the candidates outweighed the general commentary offered during the debates.

Lyndon Johnson was very conscious of the news and installed teleprinters in his office that enabled him to stay abreast of each story and notify journalists quickly of his disapproval of certain stories. Despite his attempts to manipulate journalists, in 1964 the press broke its long tradition of supporting Republican candidates. Forty-two per cent of newspapers supported Johnson's candidacy over Barry Goldwater.[30]

In 1968, Hubert Humphrey was the Democratic incumbent who barely emerged as the victor in the nomination process. The Republicans vigorously supported Nixon as their choice for president. Much of the newspaper coverage focused on the "horse-race" aspects of the campaign. Horse-race coverage emphasizes the reporting of how successful candidates are perceived to be, what issues they are winning or losing, and what their next tac-

tical move will be. Forty-nine per cent of paragraphs written about the candidates in 1968 were devoted to "horse-race" coverage, while 45 per cent displayed substantive issues.[31]

Whereas horse-race coverage dominated the 1968 campaign, in 1972, when Nixon ran against George McGovern, the press paid particular attention to the candidates' political philosophy and professional capabilities. Fifty-two per cent of television commentary concerning their qualifications for president was positive, compared to 36 per cent of press commentary.[32]

During the 1970s, candidates became increasingly aware that television news was dominating the political landscape. Televised news was incapable of providing in-depth analysis of political issues as audiences were subject to more narrowly tailored sound bites and political symbols. The 1976 campaign hosted the first televised debates since 1960. Gerald Ford and Jimmy Carter both performed credibly, but Ford seemed confused when asked about the geopolitics of Europe.

The 1980 campaign stood in the shadows of American hostages in Iran. Carter's campaign was damaged by the news media's reporting of an oil shortage, a recession, inflation, and the hostage situation. The Republican nominee, Ronald Reagan, a former television personality and governor of California, was often referred to as "The Great Communicator." Newspapers began to report stories about how the candidates presented themselves to the nation. The *Tulsa World* described Reagan and Carter each as "... a shill whose job is to advertise the electronic image that bears their name."[33] By the early 1980s, as journalists became concerned about the emphasis on image, newspapers had begun to report on televised political advertisements.

During the 1988 campaign, critics charged television news with being preoccupied with photo opportunities and sound bites, manipulated by media experts, and driven by polls to the point that television news lost sight of its journalistic responsibilities. The horse-race aspect of the campaign received acute attention, with 168 televised stories devoted to it.[34] Negative attack advertising proliferated, and Democrats made a point of criticizing George Bush for his ads.[35]

In 1992 , the news media pledged to perform more responsibly in covering the presidential campaign.[36] President George Bush, however, claimed that the news media were biased against him. During the Republican Convention, Bush, to display his frustration, held up bumper stickers announcing "Annoy the Media: Re-elect George Bush." Bill Clinton's campaign team made a similar argument, criticizing the media for giving his record as Arkansas governor too much coverage, while not examining Bush's as thoroughly. One of the unique features of the campaign was the candidates' use of non-traditional media. Clinton emphasized such forums as late night television talk shows and cable outlets such as MTV.

By 1996, the candidates had once again expanded their scope of media use. Both President Clinton and Kansas senator Bob Dole utilized web sites to provide information to supporters, but political advertisements remained the mainstay of each campaign. The campaign was the most expensive campaign in history up to that point.[37] The Democratic National Committee aired more than 40 televised advertisements in 15 months and spent $42.4 million. The campaign was also the most negative one on record.[38]

The press has played an integral role in the development of presidential campaigns. As the press became more independent, newspapers were afforded the opportunity to be more critical as reporters evaluated the candidates. Since the partisan press covered George Washington's campaign, candidates' private lives have been on public display. Newspapers have reported rumors, covered presidents objectively and aggressively, and interpreted campaign events. As new media were introduced to the mass audience, newspapers altered their content to maintain readership. As radio and television increased in popularity and affordability, newspapers maintained an edge in political reporting because of the reporter's ability to provide context and extended analysis. As technology advanced, however, newspapers were unable to compete with the immediacy that the electronic media provided. Still, newspapers reported the events and sometimes critiqued the candidates' usage of the electronic media.

Selected Readings

Batlin, Robert. "San Francisco Newspapers' Campaign Coverage: 1896, 1952." *Journalism Quarterly* 31 (1954): 297–303.

Clarke, Peter, and Susan H. Evans. *Covering Campaigns: Journalism in Congressional Elections.* Stanford, Calif.: Stanford University Press, 1983.

Graber, Doris A. "Press Coverage and Voter Reaction in the 1968 Presidential Election." *Political Science Quarterly* 89:1 (1974): 68–100.

Joslyn, Richard. Chap. 4, "Journalism, News, and the Coverage of Election Campaigns," in *Mass Media and Elections.* Reading, Mass.: Addison-Wesley Publishing Company, 1984.

Leonard, Thomas G. *The Power of the Press: The Birth of American Political Reporting.* New York: Oxford University Press, 1986.

Russonello, John M., and Frank Wolf. "Newspaper Coverage of the 1976 and 1968 Presidential Campaigns." *Journalism Quarterly* 56 (1979): 360–64, 432.

Shaw, Donald L. "The Nature of Campaign News in the Wisconsin Press 1852–1916." *Journalism Quarterly* 45 (1968): 326–29.

Notes

1. John Adams, 30 June 1828, in Charles Francis Adams, *Memoirs of John Quincy Adams,* 12 vols. (Philadelphia: J. B. Lippincott & Co., 1874–1877), 7:536, 10 May 1828; 7:415–16.

2. Originally published in *Truth's Advocate,* a campaign sheet Charles Hammond edited. Hammond was associated with the *Cincinnati Gazette.*

3. Jackson, private letter, 16 August 1828, in John Spencer Bassett, *Correspondence of Andrew Jackson,* 7 vols. (Washington, D.C.: Carnegie Institution of Washington, 1926–35), 3:426–27.

4. Bassett, ibid., 231.

5. Tom Reilly, "Lincoln-Douglas Debates of 1858 Forced New Role on the Press," *Journalism Quarterly* 56 (1979): 734–43.

6. *Chicago Press and Tribune,* 10 July 1858.

7. *New York Herald,* 29 May 1904.

8. Charles Richard Williams, *Diary and Letters of Rutherford B. Hayes,* 5 vols. (Columbus: Ohio Archaeological and Historical Society, 1922–26), 3: 347–51, 19 August 1876.

9. *New York Sun,* 30 October 1880.

10. Allan Nevins, *Letters of Grover Cleveland, 1850–1908* (Boston: Houghton Mifflin Co., 1933), 45.

11. Ray Stannard Baker, *Woodrow Wilson: Life and Letters,* 8 vols. (Garden City, N.Y.: Doubleday, Page, 1927–39), 3:246–52.

12. Charles Willis Thompson, *Presidents I've Known and Two Near Presidents* (Indianapolis: Bobbs-Merrill, 1929), 295.

13. Joseph Patrick Tumulty, *Woodrow Wilson as I Know Him* (Garden City, N.Y.: Doubleday, Page & Co., 1921), 125.

14. Associated Ohio Dailies, *Proceedings,* 1920, quoted

in James E. Pollard, *The Presidents and the Press* (New York: Macmillan Co., 1947), 698.

15. Sherman A. Cuneo, *From Printer to President* (Philadelphia: Dorrance, 1922), 102–04.

16. Samuel Hopkins Adams, *Incredible Era: The Life and Times of Warren Gamaliel Harding* (Boston: Houghton Mifflin Co., 1939), 179.

17. Paul Anderson, *Nation*, 14 October 1931, 383–84.

18. *New York Times*, 10 July 1932.

19. William Raymond Manchester, *The Glory and the Dream: A Narrative History of America, 1932–1972* (Boston: Little, Brown, 1974), 138.

20. Samuel Irving Rosenman, *The Public Papers and Addresses of Franklin D. Roosevelt, with a Special Introduction and Explanatory Notes by President Roosevelt*, 13 vols. (New York: Random House, 1938), 8:604.

21. *New York Times*, 22 July 1944.

22. *New York Daily*, 29 October 1944.

23. *Time*, 23 October 1944.

24. *Newsweek*, 11 October 1948, 20.

25. *Chicago Tribune*, 3 November 1948.

26. *New York Post*, 18 September 1952, 1–2.

27. Dwight D. Eisenhower, *The White House Years: Mandate for Change* (Garden City, N.Y.: Doubleday, 1963–1965), 538.

28. *Seattle Post Intelligencer*, 17 October 1956, 17.

29. Susan Hellweg, Michael Pfau, and Steven Brydon, *Televised Presidential Debates: Advocacy in Contemporary America* (New York: Praeger Publishing, 1992), 3.

30. Anon., "440 for LBJ—359 for Barry," *Editor & Publisher*, 31 October 1964, 9–13.

31. Guido Stempel, "Prestige Press Meets the Third Party Challenge," *Journalism Quarterly* 46 (1969): 701.

32. Doris Graber, "Press and TV as Opinion Resources in Presidential Campaigns," *Public Opinion Quarterly* 40 (1976): 289.

33. T. R. Reid, "Presidential Candidates Packaged in Advertising," *Tulsa World*, 26 February 1980, A7.

34. S. Robert Lichter, Daniel Amundson, and Richard E. Noyes, "Election 88': Media Coverage," *Public Opinion Quarterly* 11 (1989): 19.

35. Judith Trent and Robert Friedenberg, *Political Campaign Communication: Principles and Practices* (New York: Praeger, 1995), 130.

36. Thomas Patterson, *Out of Order* (New York: Vintage, 1994), 35.

37. Patrick Devlin, "Contrast in Presidential Campaign Commercials of 1996," *American Behavioral Scientist* 40 (1997): 1058.

38. Lynda Kaid, "Effects of the Television Spots on the Images of Dole and Clinton," *American Behavioral Scientist* 40 (1997): 1085.

20

Coverage of Crime

EARNEST L. PERRY

It is now known as "The Chase," and many people know where they were when they either heard about or saw the slow pursuit of the sport utility vehicle carrying O. J. Simpson, the NFL Hall of Fame running back and national advertising pitch man. Millions of Americans were glued to television sets watching and wondering what was going to happen to this successful athlete and entertainer. The pictures they watched came from local television news helicopters. News anchors, both local and network, provided whatever information they could, but mostly they speculated.

Five days earlier, the bloody bodies of Simpson's former wife, Nicole Brown Simpson, and her friend Ronald Goldman were discovered outside her home in the Brentwood area of Los Angeles. Not long after the discovery, police detectives began focusing their investigation on O. J. Simpson, and the media followed. It was a crime reporter's dream—covering a high profile murder case. Media from all over the nation and the world set up shop outside Simpson's home. Despite the intense coverage, Simpson and his long-time friend, Al Cowlings, were able to slip out, minutes before he was scheduled to turn himself in to police.[1] Hours later "The Chase" began.

In the days after the murder, the media showed restraint in covering the story. That changed when Simpson became a fugitive from justice. He eventually turned himself in to police, was tried in what has been called the "Trial of the Century" (you will hear this phrase again later in this chapter), and was found not guilty. He was later found liable in civil court for the deaths of Nicole Simpson and Goldman and ordered to pay $33.5 million in actual and punitive damages. Simpson's arrest and the legal battles that followed have had a lasting impact on the way the media covers the American criminal justice system. It fostered a blurring of the line between so-called "real news" and "tabloid journalism." However, it might be seen as the second coming of "yellow journalism" but now instead of ink and paper, it is video cameras and satellite trucks. Whatever kind of journalism you want to call it, today's crime coverage has one undeniable trait—it attracts attention. Readers and viewers are interested, and the bigger the name the more interested they are.

The Simpson case was not the first to have an impact on the way the media covers crime. This chapter will discuss how crime reporting has evolved by looking at several high-profile cases and events that had an impact on American society.

COLONIAL CRIMES

During the colonial period of America, crime coverage consisted of month-old pirate stories. Before that in England and France, crime stories were not too different from the O. J. Simpson story—spousal murders. However, instead of filling the pages of newspapers, the stories were told by word of mouth in the form of ballads that later appeared in pamphlets. However, by the 1730s, American newspapers, though political in nature, did report on various crimes. Murders and property crimes received the most space. When it came to graphic accounts of horror and brutality, colonial crime stories, in most cases, exceed today's standards. Stories in colonial newspapers in Boston, New York, and other towns and cities ran stories using terms such as "...and some of her Brains sticking on said Ax." or "... some of the Neighbours going accidentally in the Room, found the poor Baby eating the Bread sopp'd in his Mother's Blood."[2]

These depictions and others prove that shock journalism, yellow journalism, sensationalism, or whatever the latest name used to describe this kind of crime coverage has been a part of media history since the first printing press arrived in America. Just as it does today, sensationalism, in colonial newspapers drew people to the pages. They were shocked and entertained, but they were also informed.

Outside of the sensational story, routine crime news and the punishment that followed were handled much differently in colonial newspapers. Law enforcement officials and the courts dealt with moral crimes, such as adultery, blasphemy, and idolatry in the same manner as felony crimes, like murder, robbery, and arson. However, colonial newspaper mainly covered the felony crimes. The moral offenses received attention only when they were sensational, such as sodomy, or when it was in conjunction with a felony crime, such as a husband killing his wife. Colonial newspapers ran stories of people being robbed and killed while traveling the back roads of the new nation. The accounts provided information about the crimes as well as informed people of danger in certain areas.

However, compared to today's media, the amount of space devoted to crime in the colonial press was small. Much of the news, especially at the onset of the Revolutionary War, dealt with politics and the war.

CREATING A LONG-LASTING TRADITION

The blood and guts, crime chasing ways associated with modern crime reporting has its roots in the penny press era. The penny press emphasized local news and its mainstay was crime. However, instead of holding the editorializing to the opinion pages, the writers of the penny press era placed it in their stories. It was not unusual to see people involved in crimes being referred to as "vulgar" and "repulsive." Reporters and editors editorialized in stories and convicted suspects before had they had their day in court.

The first police reporters began showing up at police stations in the 1830s. They looked over police reports, much like today's crime reporters, and wrote stories on the strange cases police had to handle. Penny-press era police reporters were a lot less restrained in their accounts of crimes committed in their communities. However, readers were able to venture into the world of domestic violence, burglary and murder in a way they had not been able to before.

Benjamin Day's *New York Sun*, which began in 1833, was the first of the penny newspapers. Day began the modern look of American newsrooms by hiring editors and reporters—and, with time, many of those were hired to gather crime news. However, compared to today's stories, crime news in the 1830s lacked accuracy and responsible reporting. Penny press reporters routinely omitted vital information, such as names, ages, and the specific location of the crime. Sometimes they also neglected to include the decision of the court.

The newly created reporting positions also allowed for the coverage of trials from the courtroom instead of getting second-hand information from spectators. These stories were printed on the front page, sometimes verbatim from the trial transcripts. As with today's local television news, crime news was the meat and potatoes of penny newspapers. The *New York Sun* and the *New York Transcript* had police reporters on duty from 3 a.m. to 8 p.m.

George Wisner, the first police court reporter for the *Sun*, wrote crime stories that were both informative and humorous. He made news of misdemeanors a standard item in the penny papers, but James Gordon Bennett's coverage of the Robinson-Jewett murder case in 1836 opened the floodgates of sensational crime reporting. Ellen Jewett, a beautiful young prostitute, was murdered with a hatchet and her body set on fire in a New York City brothel. Richard P. Robinson, a wealthy frequent visitor of the brothel, was arrested and charged with the murder. Bennett's coverage of the case from day one was sensational.[3]

Bennett's initial stories, flush with vivid on-the-scene description, all but convicted Robinson. However, three days later after visiting the crime scene for a second time, Bennett's articles changed from declaring Robinson's guilt to supporting his innocence.[4] Day after day, even after public interest waned in the weeks before the trial, Bennett kept up his attack against what he called a conspiracy by the police and brothel owner Rosina Townsend. In the end, Robinson was acquitted, but not before Bennett's *Herald* used the sensational case to become the most popular newspaper in New York City. The more conservative newspapers, such as the New *York Evening Post* and the *New York Commercial Advertiser*, treated the case as a normal news story. They published a story when it happened and another when it was over. Bennett won over the masses and went on to use the same sensational, over-hyped reporting on other stories outside of crime, such as the discovery of Mayan ruins in Central America and the annexation of Texas.

The penny press brought newspapers to the masses. They were interested in the trials and tribulations of those that ran afoul with the law. It did not matter to them that the stories were biased and sometimes not very accurate. It was something other than politics and editorials. Crime reporters also broke new ground by forcing police and court officials to change the way they viewed journalists. As reporters started covering court proceedings in the 1830s, states and ultimately the federal government was forced to pass laws forbidding judges from holding reporters in contempt of court for writing stories on the various criminal proceedings. Using these new laws, court reporters began to open court room doors and expose the still young nation to the judicial branch of government.

As the era of the penny press waned and

the Civil War approached, newspaper editors continued to publicize sensational crime stories. Murder seemed to always make the pages: the higher the profile of a person involved, the closer to the front page the story would get.

In 1859, the press set its sights on the murder trial of Congressman Daniel E. Sickles, who was charged with shooting U.S. Attorney for the District of Columbia Philip Barton Key, the son of Francis Scott Key. Sickles accused Key of seducing his wife. Sickles was acquitted, but not until after the New York and Washington press had publicized every scandalous detail of the case.[5]

In 1892, the untimely deaths of Andrew Jackson Borden and his wife, Abbie, gave the country a new villain that would transcend time thanks to the press. Authorities, on largely circumstantial evidence, charged the couple's daughter, Lizzie, with the ax wielding murders. Despite the fact that the jury acquitted her, extensive, unbiased press coverage, especially in the *Boston Globe*, branded Lizzie Borden, then as well as now, as the vicious murderer of her parents.

The early 1900s witnessed a number of sensational murders and trials that received extensive coverage. One of the most notable was Harry Thaw's 1907 trial for murdering the famous architect Stanford White. It captivated the nation and moved even the *New York Times*, which customarily put little time, effort, or space to crime news, to report extensively on it.

Prohibition in the 1920s and 1930s fostered the era of the gangster. Legendary crime figures such as Al Capone, Bonnie and Clyde, and John Dillinger graced the pages of newspapers all over the country. The most infamous crime during this era was the St. Valentine's Day Massacre. On that day in 1929, seven Chicago gangsters working for George "Bugs" Moran were gunned down in the street. It was alleged, but never proven, that Capone ordered the hit in retaliation for hits made against his organization.

One of the men murdered in the massacre was Alfred "Jake" Lingle, a reporter for the *Chicago Tribune*. Colonel Robert McCormick, publisher of the *Tribune*, posted a $25,000 reward and Hearst's *Chicago Herald and Examiner* matched it. The *Chicago Evening Post* added another $5,000. The Chicago press went to war against Capone and the city's underworld. Elliot Ness, of the Untouchables fame, gave the press unprecedented access to his raids on Capone, while IRS officials tracked his income. In the end, Capone was convicted on income tax evasion. He served eight years of the 10-year sentence and was released in 1939 suffering from advanced paresis caused by untreated syphilis.[6]

The 1920s was also known for its tabloid treatment of unusual or high-glamour criminal cases. One case involved two men who some say were falsely convicted because they were seen as radicals during the time of the Red Scare. Bartolomeo Vanzetti and Nicola Sacco were convicted and sentenced to death for the robbery of a paymaster for a large shoe manufacturer in Massachusetts and the murder and robbery of another shoe paymaster several months later. There were protests in the United States and Europe against the convictions. The press' coverage was also confusing. Some newspaper challenged the verdict, stating that the prosecution had not presented enough evidence. Other newspapers said the convictions were part of a conspiracy to eliminate anarchists. In the end, the press agreed that the men had been given every consideration allowed by law.

The sensational coverage continued during the 1920s as newspapers used crime to lure in readers. In 1921, William Randolph Hearst's *Los Angeles Examiner* and *San Francisco Examiner* literally became involved in the murder trial of comedian Roscoe "Fatty" Arbuckle. He was accused of the rape and murder of film actress Virginia Rappe. Hearst used sensational headlines such as "ARBUCKLE HELD FOR MURDER" and doctored photographs in reporting the story. He sold more papers reporting the case than he had since World War I. Arbuckle was acquitted, but the sensational coverage destroyed his career.

About three years later, the country was captivated by another sensational crime. In May 1924, 14-year-old Bobby Franks was kidnapped while walking home. As the family was putting the ransom together the boy was found dead. Richard Loeb and Nathan Leopold, Jr., confessed to the crime. They said they wanted to collect the ransom before the boy's body was found. During the trial both men claimed insanity, and their stories made for sensational headlines. The *Chicago Tribune* ran doctored photographs, and the *Chicago Herald and Examiner* claimed to have sold more newspapers during the investigation and trial than any other time during the year.

The case of Ruth Synder and Judd Gray was sensational not only for the crime that was committed, but also what happened after the sentence was carried out. Snyder and Gray plotted and killed her husband in March 1927. Synder was convicted and sentenced to die. During the execution, a *New York Daily News* photographer, using a camera strapped to his ankle, took a picture. New York prison authorities had requested that no pictures be taken of the event. The *Daily News* ran the photograph and, despite objections after the fact, sold 500,000 extra copies of that edition.

THE FIRST "TRIAL OF THE CENTURY"

Nothing captivates an audience better than a show trial, and the kidnapping and murder of 20-month-old Charles A. Lindbergh, Jr., the son of famous aviator Charles Lindbergh, held the nation spellbound for more than three years. Journalists from all over the nation and the world descended on Hopewell, New Jersey, in March 1932 after the elder Lindbergh phoned the New Jersey State police claiming that his son had been taken from his upstairs nursery.

As police began a four-state search for the boy, no less than four hundred reporters and photographers descended on the secluded, wooded compound near Princeton, New Jersey. The International Press Photo Service retrofitted two ambulances with developing equipment, but kept the sirens as a way of ensuring fast passage back to New York.[7] There was not much news to report, but that did not stop reporters from sending back enough copy on the first day to fill a novel for each publication and the wire services. They searched for every clue they could use to write a story. A *New York Times* reporter wrote a small three-paragraph story on how the Lindberghs were forced to eat dinner in an alcove of the kitchen because the police had taken over most of the space in their home. The story even included a description of how Charles Lindbergh buttered the bread they ate.[8]

As law enforcement authorities, both state and federal, continued their investigation, the Lindberghs paid the ransom. They were given the baby's pajamas as proof that he was still alive, but two months later his body was found in the woods near the Lindbergh estate. There was evidence that several newspaper reporters paid people to plant evidence near the body. It was not unusual for journalists to plant evidence and show up, with photographer in tow, just as the police arrived.

Journalists kept digging for new information. They combed the woods near the home, talked to anyone connected with the family and headline after headline stated that an arrest was imminent. An arrest did not come for another two and a half years.

In September 1934, Bruno Richard Hauptmann, an illegal immigrant from Germany, used a $10 gold note to purchase gas at a service station in the Bronx. The note was traced back to the ransom money and when authorities searched his home they found another $13,750. He was arrested and indicted for kidnapping and murder.

A New York journalist, Tom Cassidy, planted evidence in Hauptmann's apartment. On a closet door jamb he wrote the address and telephone number of the man who delivered the ransom money. He also wrote the serial numbers of $2 bills. He told police about the information on the jamb. During initial questioning Hauptmann did not deny that he wrote it. He just said that he could have, but did not remember. Cassidy bragged to several other reporters about what he had done, and eventually the lie became the truth.

Chicago Daily News editor H. L. Mencken called the Lindbergh trial "the greatest story since the Resurrection." Reporters from around the world were on hand to record it. Hearst sent 50 reporters to cover it for his papers. A makeshift airfield was built on the edge of town to take film back to New York for developing in time for the next day's papers. Just as with the initial stories on the kidnapping, reporters resorted to all sorts of tactics and extremes to get a story. They talked to anyone and everyone, they analyzed and editorialized, they interviewed the celebrities who attended the trial to be seen.[9] Many accused the press of convicting Hauptmann before the trial began and of executing him during it. It was not journalism's finest hour and created a less-than-honest image for crime reporting.

CRIME COVERAGE THAT CHANGED A NATION

The civil rights movement that began in the late 1950s with the Montgomery bus boycott and the U.S. Supreme Court's school desegregation decision opened up a new chapter in crime reporting. During this period, journalists were not just reporting the facts, they were providing the ammunition that leaders needed to change the unequal system African Americans had lived under for more than 100 years. In the past, crime reporting was a staple of newspaper journalism. However, during the 1950s, television began to invade American homes. By the time the civil rights movement reached its zenith in the mid–1960s, television news told the story like no other medium could. Night after night, Americans watched police chase, beat, and arrest blacks protesting in the South. In some instances, mainly in the Southern media, these stories were portrayed only as crime stories. The protesters were violating the law, and the police were doing their jobs in trying to stop them. However, there was a difference. Reporters from the North covering the civil rights movement in the South portrayed law enforcement and the courts as the enemy.

Many of the early civil rights stories chronicled violent acts committed against African Americans by groups such as the Ku Klux

Klan with the full support of the local and state legal establishment. One such incident, the murder of Chicago teenager Emmett Till, showed the impact the media, especially television, would have on reporting violent crime during the civil rights movement. In 1954, Till was visiting his relatives in Mississippi when he whistled at a white woman. It cost him his life. The woman's husband and half brother dragged 14-year-old Till from his uncle's cabin, shot and mutilated him, and dumped his body in the Tallahatchie River.

The ensuing trial of the two men charged in the murder was one of the first trials covered by national television news networks. The cameras were in the courtroom and television reporters interviewed people on camera in front of the courthouse. Much of the type of television trial coverage seen today began during the Till trial. More than 50 reporters covered the trial. Even small local television stations from other parts of Mississippi and Louisiana sent camera crews. The local inhabitants did not welcome all the attention and were not afraid to let the journalists know it. The intimidation got so bad that some white Northern reporters faked Southern accents in an effort to blend in. The local authorities enforced Jim Crow laws by forcing African American reporters to sit at a separate table in the back while white reporters sat in the front. The African American reporters also devised a plan of self-defense and escape in case violence erupted in the courtroom. Their fear was based on an incident two decades earlier in which an African American defendant on trial for raping a white woman was shot and killed in the courtroom.[10]

Despite eyewitness testimony from Till's uncle, an act that forced him to flee the state, and an admission by the defendants that they kidnapped the boy, the two men were acquitted. However, it opened the door for television and print reporters from around the country to take a closer look at the crimes inflicted on African Americans in the South by white terrorists, many backed by local law enforcement.[11]

Two of the most vicious crimes of the civil rights era also received the most media coverage. The first occurred on September 15, 1963,

when four African American girls died when a bomb exploded at the Sixteenth Street Baptist Church in Birmingham, Alabama. The girls were preparing for Youth Day services on that Sunday morning. Twenty-one bombings had occurred in Birmingham in the previous eight years, but the church bombing was the first in which someone died. Eleven days earlier, the home of attorney Arthur Shores had been bombed for a second time. No one was hurt in either bombing. Media from all over the world covered the story, not just because it was an unbelievable crime, but because it showed the depths to which some whites would go to maintain white supremacy. It took more than a decade to bring those involved to trial. In 1977, former Klan member Robert Chambliss was convicted for his role in the crime. He died in prison. In 2001, another Klansman, Thomas E. Blanton, Jr., was convicted and sentenced to life in prison. A judge declared a third defendant, Bobby Frank Cherry, mentally incompetent to stand trial.[12]

The second crime occurred in the summer of 1964 during what was called Freedom Summer. Three young civil rights workers, Michael Schwerner, Andrew Goodman, and James Chaney were arrested for speeding in Philadelphia, Mississippi. They were released, but a group of deputies followed them. They were found a month and a half later buried in an earthen dam. All three had been shot, and Chaney was brutally beaten. Twenty-one white men, including the deputy sheriff, were tried in state court for the crime but were acquitted. The federal government later convicted six of the men on civil rights charges.

The media put the entire state of Mississippi on trial during the search for the missing workers and the subsequent trials. On the day after the workers were reported missing, a mob forced two reporters from the *New York Times* and *Newsweek* to flee Philadelphia, Mississippi. Television news crews also were harassed as they tried to cover the story.[13] Reporters frequently faced hostile crowds as they tried to cover the demonstrations and later the riots that marked the civil rights movement.

During the riots in 1965 and again when Martin Luther King, Jr., was assassinated in

1968, television and newspaper reporters covered the stories in crime reporting mode. News stories told the number of deaths, injuries, and arrest; the amount of damage caused; and whether order had been restored,—all the typical traits of a crime story. However, what was glossed over or in many cases was not mentioned was a thorough examination of why the riots took place. Seldom did the stories delve into the reports of police brutality and the injustices of the criminal justice system.[14]

The photographs and television news clips changed from police beating non-violent protesters to clashes between police and those involved in the disturbances. Even the language changed. Headlines and lead paragraphs that once read "Non-violent protest" changed to "rampaging Negroes." Reporters trying to cover the civil disturbance in the Watts area of Los Angeles were shot at and beaten and two television crew trucks were damaged.[15] A government-sponsored commission concluded that these changes in coverage occurred because the white reporters documenting the events did so from their own biased backgrounds.

The commission, appointed by President Lyndon B. Johnson in 1968 to investigate the civil unrest, concluded that the press had done a good job of giving detailed information, but failed to address the underlying causes that led to the civil disturbances. Part of this was blamed on the fact that very few news organizations had black reporters on staff. In fact, the civil disturbances forced many newspapers to hire blacks if they wanted to adequately cover the unrest in their perspective cities.[16]

Coverage of the civil rights movement along with the protests against the war in Vietnam in some ways changed crime reporting. It ushered in a new player in the news game—television. In the decades to come news would not only be provided instantly, it would become a hot commodity. Crime news became the way to draw viewers to the daily newscasts. Crime reporting was elevated to a new level.

POLITICS AND CRIME: WHAT'S THE DIFFERENCE?

A "third-rate burglary attempt." That is what Ronald Ziegler, President Richard Nixon's press secretary, called one of the most pivotal crimes in U.S. history. On June 17, 1972, five men were arrested while attempting to burglarize and bug a downtown Washington, D.C., office. The story in the *Washington Post* the next day ran longer than most burglary stories, but it did not allude to the bigger stories that were to follow. It appeared to be a routine crime story until two tenacious *Post* reporters, Carl Bernstein and Bob Woodward, linked the burglars to the White House. This was the beginning of a scandal that eventually brought down a president of the United States.

The Watergate scandal began as a crime story. Burglars had attempted to steal documents and plant eavesdropping devices in the office of the Democratic National Committee. Two men, who were part of the team but were not arrested, G. Gordon Liddy and E. Howard Hunt, were later indicted and convicted for the burglary.[17] However, it was not the burglary that captured the limelight and brought the wrath of Congress down on President Richard Nixon—it was the conspiracy to cover up the crime. Liddy and Hunt were former White House aides and worked for Nixon's re-election committee. They were just small links in the chain that included key figures in the White House including Nixon. In the end, the "third-rate" burglary forced Nixon to resign in disgrace. In all, 18 people on his staff either pleaded guilty or were convicted. His successor, Gerald Ford, later pardoned him.

A little more than a decade after Watergate, politicians began focusing their attention and law enforcement resources on a major war. The enemy was, and in some cases still is, illegal narcotics. Federal, state, and local law enforcement officials, along with Latin American countries, have spent millions of dollars to stop the flow of illegal drugs into the United States.

The War on Drugs was a series of battles. The fighting has occurred overseas, in the streets, in the courthouses, jails, and prisons.

There have been casualties on both sides, and the media have covered it all. Nightly newscasts across the country often start with stories on the latest drug murder, huge narcotics confiscation, or the government's latest initiative to win the war. Newspaper headlines read "New Frontier in the war on drugs" or "Tackling the International Drug Lords." The news media cover the use of illegal drugs in America like a full-fledged war, with body counts, money spent, and detailed analysis of wins and losses.[18]

Police are the front-line soldiers, and crime reporters are there right along side them. Covering the war on drugs has brought police reporting back to its roots. Get the information from law enforcement and witnesses, if available, and get it out to the public. However, the difference between recent police reporting and that of the penny press era has been television. The tube, along with its live trucks and ability to broadcast from anywhere at anytime, has brought the action right into American living rooms.

Today's reporters do not have to embellish with words. They can do it with pictures and 30-second sound bites from police officials. Just as the penny press era gave the impression that there was corruption everywhere, the media's coverage of the war on drugs had Americans thinking illegal narcotic use was out of control. Police reporters' use of law enforcement for information kept the media from effectively investigating the root causes of drug use. It also perpetuated the stereotype that drug use only occurred in poor, urban areas populated by ethnic minorities.[19]

The media's coverage of the war on drugs also ushered in the era of reality-based, or "docu-cop," programs. Shows such as *Cops* and *America's Most Wanted* depicted law enforcement officers from around the country chasing down suspects, handling domestic violence complaints, and dispensing justice. In their inception, the shows centered on police officers' battles to stem the tide of drugs into urban neighborhoods. Using hand-held cameras, the shows' producers followed officers through back alleys, over parked cars, and into drug houses in an effort to show the front-line bat-tles in the war on illegal narcotics. Police reporting became entertainment, with all the glitz and music and hype of an MTV video.[20]

Some local television news organizations adopted this type of approach when covering crime in their communities. They wrapped crimes into 60-second packages but provided little substance concerning the root causes of the crime problem. Many inside and outside of law enforcement blamed the media's exaggeration of crime stories for the public's perception that criminal behavior was out of control and that drugs were at the heart of the problem. This, despite the fact that government statistics indicated that during the 1990s incidents of crime decreased.

THE MORE THINGS CHANGE

During the penny press era, publishers and editors used crime stories to entice people to buy the newspaper. Today, some local television news directors use crime stories to attract viewers. It worked in the past and in some cities, it works today. People love a good story and crime stories generally are good stories.

This brings us back to O. J. Simpson. The initial crime, the murders of Nicole Simpson and Ronald Goldman, made for a good crime story: the former wife of a famous football star stabbed to death in front of her home. The story got better when Simpson was questioned about the deaths. The plot thickened when instead of turning himself in to authorities, Simpson led them on a chase through the freeways of Los Angeles. He eventually gave up, hired the best legal team money could buy, and was acquitted of the crime.

If the story had been reported in this fashion it still would have drawn readers and viewers. However, it was not, as was not the Lindbergh case. Reporters conducted their own investigations, dug for every piece of information, analyzed every aspect of the trial, and paid witnesses for interviews. Reporters made names for themselves, and a fledgling cable channel— Court TV—became a household name. Attorneys moved from the courtroom to the broadcast studio. Covering the crime itself went from being the beginning and end of a story to just the beginning.

There was also a blurring of the lines between reporters who covered the criminal justice system, regardless of the defendants and victims, and those who were there only because it was O. J. Reputable news agencies quoted information that tabloid publications or television shows had first reported. One day public polls said there was too much coverage, and the next day they said there was too little. In the end, the media overlooked a profound aspect of the story. They covered the story as the trial of O. J. Simpson or the "Trial of the Century," while many in the black community viewed it as the trial of the criminal justice system. The news media were surprised when blacks cheered the not-guilty verdict. They were not cheering the fact that Simpson was acquitted, but that he—a black man—had beaten the system.

However, some things remain the same in covering crime. The more sensational the crime, the better the story.

Selected Readings

Baskette, Floyd K. "Reporting the Webster Case, America's Classic Murder." *Journalism Quarterly* 24 (1947): 250–56.
Beasley, Maurine. "A 'Front Page Girl' Covers the Lindbergh Kidnaping: An Ethical Dilemma." *American Journalism* 1, 1 (1983): 63–74.
Brazil, John. "Murder Trials, Murder, and Twenties America." *American Quarterly* (1981): 163–84.
Eberhard, Wallace B. "Mr. Bennett Covers a Murder Trial." *Journalism Quarterly* 47 (1970): 457–63.
Kobre, Sidney. "New York Newspapers and the Case of Celia Cooney." *Journalism Quarterly* 14 (1937): 133–43.
Kobre, Sidney. "The Newspapers and the Zangara Case: A Study of American Crime Reporting." *Journalism Quarterly* 13 (1936): 253–71.
Krajicek, David J. *Scooped: Media Miss Real Story on Crime While Chasing Sex, Sleaze, and Celebrities.* New York: Columbia University Press, 1998.
Lofton, John. *Justice and the Press.* Boston: Beacon Press, 1966.
Pfaff, Daniel W. "The Press and the Scottsboro Rape Cases, 1931–32." *Journalism History* 1 (1974): 72–76.
Ropel, Timothy. "Walter Winchell: The Thirteenth Juror."

Media History Digest 5:4 (1985): 56–61.
Sindall, Rob. *Street Violence in the Nineteenth Century: Media Panic or Real Danger?* Leicester, N.Y.: Leicester University Press, 1990.
Thaler, Paul. *The Spectacle: Media and the Making of the O. J. Simpson Story.* Westport, Conn: Praeger, 1997.
Tucher, Andie. *Froth and Scum: Truth, Beauty, Goodness, and the Ax Murder in America's First Mass Medium.* Chapel Hill: University of North Carolina Press, 1994.

Notes

1. Paul Thaler, *The Spectacle: Media and the Making of the O. J. Simpson Story* (Westport, Conn. 1997), 5–9.
2. Quoted in David A. Copeland, *Colonial American Newspapers: Character and Content* (Newark, Del.: University of Delaware Press, 1997), 76–77.
3. *New York Herald*, 11 April 1836.
4. *New York Herald*, 13–15 April 1836.
5. John Lofton, "The Accused in the Press," in John Lofton, ed., *Justice and the Press* (Boston, Beacon Press 1966).
6. Robert Grant and Joseph Katz, "The People vs. Al Capone," in *The Great Trials of the Twenties: The Watershed Decade in America's Courtrooms* (Rockville Center, N.Y.: Sarpedon, 1998).
7. Ludovic Kennedy, *The Airman and the Carpenter: The Lindbergh Kidnapping and the Framing of Richard Hauptmann* (New York: Viking 1985), 84–85.
8. *New York Times*, 7 March 1932.
9. *New York Times*, 3 January 1935.
10. Stephen J. Whitfield, *A Death In The Delta: The Story of Emmett Till* (New York: Collier Macmillan 1988), 33–38.
11. Simeon Booker, "Adventure in Mississippi—A Negro Reporter at the Till Trial," *Nieman Reports* (January 1956): 12–15.
12. Kevin Sack, ["Cherry Ruled Incompetent"}, New York Times News Service, 17 July 2001.
13. Reflections of Claude Sitton and Karl Fleming at the University of Mississippi symposium "Covering the South," April 3–5, 1987.
14. Both television and newspapers covered the Watts riots in 1965 and the Detroit and Newark riots in 1967 and the civil disturbances in cities around the country after the assassination of Dr. Martin Luther King, Jr., on April 4, 1968.
15. *New York Times*, 14 August 1965.
16. U.S. Riot Commission Report, *Report of the National Advisory Commission on Civil Disorders* (New York: Bantam, 1968), 382.
17. *Washington Post*, 18 June 1972.
18. Michael Massing, "Drugs: missing the big story," *Columbia Journalism Review* 37:4 (November/December 1998): 43–46.
19. Robert Elias, "Official Stories: Media Coverage of American Crime Policy," *The Humanist* 54 (January/February 1994): 4–8.
20. Robin Anderson, "'Reality' TV and criminal injustice," *The Humanist* 54 (September/October 1994): 8–13.

21

Coverage of Sports

JON ENRIQUEZ

This is the most famous lead in the history of sports journalism—possibly of all newspaper journalism.

> Outlined against a blue-gray October sky, the Four Horsemen rode again. In dramatic lore they are known as Famine, Pestilence, Destruction and Death. These are only aliases. Their real names are Stuhldreher, Miller, Crowley and Layden. They formed the crest of the South Bend cyclone before which another fighting Army football team was swept over the precipice at the Polo Grounds yesterday afternoon as 55,000 spectators peered down on the bewildering panorama spread on the green plain below.
>
> A cyclone can't be snared. It may be surrounded, but somewhere it breaks through to keep on going. When the cyclone starts from South Bend, where the candle lights still gleam through the Indiana sycamores, those in the way must take to storm cellars at top speed. Yesterday the cyclone struck again as Notre Dame beat the Army, 13 to 7, with a set of backfield stars that ripped and crashed through a strong Army defense with more speed and power than the warring cadets could meet.[1]

The story was no more notable than the other stories about this important game—except for what happened next. A few days later, a Notre Dame student press assistant named George Strickler staged a photograph in which the four players sat on horses—uneasily, for none of them knew how to ride—and sent the photograph to press outlets across the country. The photo was widely reprinted, and the "Four Horsemen"—and the story that gave them the nickname—were immortalized in sport history.

This episode exemplifies the central tension of the history of sports journalism. Virtually all American news media have sought both to inform the public and to produce a product that the public will purchase. Sports journalism has been particularly contested because the sports page has been widely regarded as a key circulation booster. However, sports journalism has consistently faced an additional problem in that it has also served to build an audience for the entertainment industry that it purports to describe truthfully. The result has been an odd mixture of reporting and publicity, feature story and straight news, style and cliché.

Sports and games appeared in the United States during the earliest European settlement. There are isolated examples of reports on sporting events in newspapers during colonial times, but they were often limited to announcements about events rather than descriptions of them. One of the earliest known sports stories appeared in the *Boston Gazette* on March 5, 1733. It was a description of a prize fight held in England, and it was copied from a London newspaper—a practice typical of the day.

Newspapers in the early 1800s covered certain sporting events as general news, and then only when there was some larger social significance to the contest—as when a Northern horse raced a Southern horse, or an American boxed against a Briton. Otherwise, sports enthusiasts generally turned to specialty publications. Horse racing was probably the most popular sport, and racing enthusiasts read one of the national racing magazines, notably John

Stuart Skinner's *American Turf Register and Sporting Magazine* (founded in 1829) and William T. Porter's *Spirit of the Times* (founded in 1831). These two journals did much to standardize thoroughbred racing across the nation by reporting exact weights and times and promulgating standards for betting and other rules. The *Spirit of the Times* became the dominant periodical, and in 1839 Porter purchased and absorbed the *Turf Register*.

In the years after the Civil War, popular interest in sport increased. Sports were closely associated with class identity, reflected in the different periodicals that covered different sports. Boxing, the main pastime of the working class, was most closely associated with the *Police Gazette*.[2] Richard Kyle Fox, an Irish emigrant who assumed ownership of the periodical in 1878 in lieu of wages, remade it as a sensational sheet catering to the pastimes of working class men. The *Police Gazette* traded in stories about crime, romance, sport, scandal, and the theater. It became a target for moralists, and its pink pages were banned by many respectable newsdealers. Nevertheless, it became regular reading for the emerging urban bachelor subculture. It was a staple in barbershops, hotels, and bars, and its circulation topped 150,000 each week. Fox became the most dominant voice in boxing by controlling popular access to the sport, and helped to standardize boxing just as the *Spirit of the Times* had standardized horse racing. The *Police Gazette* also benefited from the emergence of the charismatic heavyweight champion John L. Sullivan. Although Fox and Sullivan detested each other, and Fox continually belittled Sullivan in print even while Sullivan retained the championship for 10 years, their feud boosted circulation of the *Police Gazette*.

Horse racing and foot racing were the major interests of the revitalized *Spirit of the Times*, which also came into new hands in 1878. The new editor was William B. Curtis, a wealthy New Yorker. He was part of an emerging movement wherein social and economic elites created exclusive organizations combining social functions with sports in order to assert their prestige and importance against the emerging social and economic power of the

growing urban working class. Curtis played a key role in the founding of the Amateur Athletic Union, which asserted strict rules about the definition of amateur sport in an effort to privilege the athletic accomplishments of elites over the superior performances of working-class athletes. In the pages of *Spirit of the Times*, he gave the AAU respectability simply by refusing to cover track and field meets not conducted under AAU auspices. The AAU associated the concept of "amateurism" with a rigid code of conduct—most distinctively, the refusal to accept money for participating in a sport—and ideals about "gentlemanly play." This linkage, which found its way into intercollegiate and Olympic sports, privileged the notion of "amateurism" in sport.

Baseball fans enjoyed two specialty magazines. *Sporting Life* was founded in 1883 by Philadelphia publisher Francis Richter, and *The Sporting News* debuted in 1886 under the leadership of St. Louis–based Alfred H. Spink, who turned the paper over to his brother C. C. Spink a year later. Both magazines gave attention to pastimes including boxing, billiards, rowing, and the stage, but baseball was the main, and eventually the only, attraction. The rival publications were soon caught up in the politics of the baseball business, their fortunes waxing and waning depending on their support of various major league interests. *Sporting Life* finally folded in 1917 after one such political row, and *The Sporting News* bragged in print about its status as "Official Organ/National Commission/Authority of Game."[3]

However, the daily newspaper was the most important medium in the growth of baseball. Baseball was a solidly middle class sport with considerable appeal to the working man, a perfect sport for newspapers trying to expand downward across class lines to reach the middle and working classes. One such paper was James Gordon Bennett's *New York Herald*. Bennett's strategy for creating a broad-based, truly popular newspaper centered on the use of news features, including sports news, to attract a wider audience. In 1859 he added Henry Chadwick to his staff. Chadwick was widely regarded as the nation's leading cricket journalist, and his stories about the emerging sport of baseball helped to popularize that sport. In the *Herald* and in a series of popular baseball guides, he instituted standard formats for conveying information about baseball, notably the method of scoring a game and the box score.[4]

The growing urban middle class was the target audience for the great New York City newspaper circulation war of the 1880s and 1890s. When Joseph Pulitzer purchased the *New York World* in 1883, he sought to break out of the city's crowded newspaper field by reaching out to a broader class of readers. He cut the price of the paper from four cents to two, introduced illustrations, and gave greater emphasis to feature stories. Increased sports coverage was a prominent part of his strategy, and the *World* was the first paper to establish a separate department for sports, headed by a sports editor. Other editors soon copied the separate sports department. When William Randolph Hearst purchased the *New York Journal* in 1895, he copied all of Pulitzer's innovations and tried to go them one better, and this held true for sports news. During the 1890s, the *World* and *Journal* both introduced separate pages or sections for sports, and expanded their sports coverage as part of their general circulation-building strategies. Bennett's *Herald*, which was well aware of the value of sports news, followed suit, as did the *Tribune*, *Post*, and other smaller papers. Even the sober *Sun* and *Times*, both of which sought to remain newspapers for "class" rather than "mass" readership, gave more coverage and separate sections to sports news. This growing emphasis on sports was widely copied by papers across the nation, and helped to establish sports as a respectable pastime for the middle classes.

Middle-class newspapers also created a middle-class identity for the elite sport of intercollegiate football. Since colleges enrolled the sons of the well-to-do, intercollegiate matches became elite social events. Most newspapers covered football games with relatively little emphasis on the game itself and significant emphasis on the spectators. In a story on the Yale-Princeton match in 1897, the *New York Times* wrote, "A list of the well-known men and women who went to the football game from this city yesterday would be simply made up of the rolls of the Princeton and Yale Universities, the New York Athletic Club, and The Social Register. No more representative throng of New York college graduates and society men and women ever attended an athletic contest so far from this city."[5] Society events were a staple of newspapers, and football games fit into established tropes for such events. Newspapers competed to give the reader two things: first, a sense of the audience and the spectacle; and, second, a sense of the rules and object of the game itself. Middle-class readers began to follow football as a way of identifying with the elite.[6]

As the 19th century yielded to the 20th, sports pages acquired a new language and a distinctive flavor. The seminal figure in this transformation was Charley Dryden, who began his newspaper career in San Francisco in 1890. He brought wit and humor to sports news and combined a passion for journalism with a talent for entertainment. He introduced lively, slangy language into his stories. He saw no harm in calling a baseball "the old horsehide" or a football "the oblate spheroid." He coined nicknames that stuck. It was he who first called Charles Comiskey "The Old Roman" and Frank Chance "The Peerless Leader," among others. Yet Dryden was also a committed journalist, and for all his distinctive language he made certain to report the details of the game. He was one of the first sportswriters to earn a byline, and that byline regularly appeared on Page 1 as a circulation-builder. He was widely imitated, but his imitators could only copy his style and not his skill.

Following Dryden, no writer did more to influence sports journalism than Grantland Rice, the author of the "Four Horsemen" story that begins this chapter. He was the grandson of a wealthy cotton planter and a member of the social elite in Nashville, Tennessee. After graduating from Vanderbilt University, he played semi-pro baseball, finally joining the nascent *Nashville Daily News* as its sports editor—though his beat also included political and shipping news—and spent the next several years at papers in Atlanta, Washington, and Nashville again. In 1910 he moved to New York and joined the *Evening Mail*, later moving to the

Tribune, the *Sun*, and then back to the *Tribune*. His "Sportlight" column became the most widely syndicated sports column in the nation. He was the leading influence on sportswriting during the 1920s and 1930s. In addition to the "Four Horsemen" story, his most famous work was his poem "Alumnus Football," which ends with this couplet: "For when the One Great Scorer comes to mark against your name,/ He writes—not that you won or lost—but how you played the Game." Rice's style was lush, romantic, lyrical, full of classical and historical allusion, often written in verse. His voice was often imitated and satirized but, as with Dryden before him, never with his skill.[7]

Stanley Walker, Rice's onetime editor at the *New York Tribune*, coined terms for the two leading schools of sportswriting.[8] Rice was the leading exponent of what Walker called the Gee Whiz school, wherein every player was legendary and every contest was immortal. The competing school, which Walker called the Aw Nuts group, argued that most sports (and most sportswriting) were bunk. Exponents in this school included W. O. McGeehan, Damon Runyon, Ring Lardner, and Westbrook Pegler. They wrote with a cynical voice, making fun of the vices of athletes, coaches, and owners, acknowledging the realities of gambling and greed surrounding the noble contests, refusing to call an ordinary game an immortal contest, and suggesting that participants and spectators alike took sports altogether too seriously. But the Aw Nuts school was never as popular as the Gee Whiz school, despite the generally high quality of its writing. Sports fans simply preferred cheerleaders to cynics.

That preference was shared by the teams themselves, who viewed sportswriters as publicists. Teams, especially major league baseball teams, provided journalists with free food at the ballpark and paid all expenses for reporters traveling with the team. The teams saw this as the price of doing business. It was more difficult for sportswriters to write unflattering or muckraking stories when they were well fed, sheltered in good hotels, and on intimate terms with the athletes. One sports editor believed that, for their part, sportswriters accepted these gifts as compensation for their lowly status

within the journalistic profession. Sportswriters were poorly paid and lightly regarded. They were susceptible to such fringe benefits and readily accepted the implicit bargain.[9]

Some editors tried to play both ends against the middle, offsetting fawning stories from one reporter with critical stories by another. Even these editors, however, were complicit. Newspaper editors and reporters guilds did not establish ethical guidelines prohibiting sportswriters from accepting travel expenses and other gifts until the 1970s. Sportswriters turned a blind eye not only to small sins like whoring and drinking but also to serious offenses, such as when members of the Chicago White Sox agreed to lose the 1919 World Series for the benefit of gamblers. This story was ignored by reporters who were well aware of the rumors and the betting odds, hitting the papers only after the Illinois State's Attorney sought indictments against the players involved.[10]

No sportswriter embraced the public relations role more completely and openly than Arch Ward, the longtime sports editor at the *Chicago Tribune*. He founded the major league baseball all-star game, an annual football game matching the National Football League champions against a team of college all-stars, the Golden Gloves amateur boxing tournament, and the All-America Football Conference (a rival to the NFL). All of these events were calculated to promote the *Tribune*, the city, the sport, and Ward himself. He relished his role as a man with influence, exchanging favorable stories in the *Tribune* for access and exclusive information. He was openly partisan to Notre Dame athletics, advising the university's president on its athletics program, lauding it in print, and crying injustice when it was wronged. In 1944, when the wartime Army football team humiliated Notre Dame 59–0, he saluted the courage of Notre Dame's noble teenagers who gamely met the onslaught of the country's finest soldiers and lambasted Army Coach Red Blaik for running up the score, "bent on avenging the years of gridiron humiliations heaped upon it by the Irish."[11] In 1946, Ward gleefully cheered Notre Dame for holding the mighty Army to a scoreless tie.

The newspaperman's role as publicist was

challenged by the emergence of new media. From the 1880s through the 1920s, the newspaper had been the primary means of experiencing a given sporting event. Far more people read about a given game in a newspaper than saw it in person. As new media supplanted the newspaper as the preferred medium of experience, the newspaper had to find new ways to attract readers—and the sportswriter-publicist faced new challenges in hiding the sins of athletes.

The newsreel allowed national audiences to see limited highlights of sporting events that took place in distant cities. However, radio had a far more significant impact on sports journalism. The first broadcast of a major league baseball game was heard on August 5, 1921, over station KDKA in Pittsburgh, the nation's first radio station. In 1923 the World Series was broadcast to an ad hoc network of stations across the country. The first program aired on the NBC radio network was a sporting event, the heavyweight championship fight between Jack Dempsey and Gene Tunney on September 23, 1926. Radio broadcasts of sporting events allowed millions of fans to experience events with an immediacy that newspapers could not match. No longer did fans have to wait to find out who won, or the final score. Now they could know as soon as the game was over—indeed, while the game was going on.[12]

In response to the growth of radio, print journalists placed greater emphasis on the material that radio did not provide, including in-depth discussions of strategy and analysis, personality profiles of great athletes, coaches, and executives, and coverage of off-the-field events. These trends were the backbone of a magazine founded in 1946, called simply *Sport*. It was the first general-circulation magazine devoted entirely to sports. Its main distinction was its full-page color photographs, usually in heroic action poses or in strong close-ups and well suited to being cut out and tacked to a boy's bedroom wall. Neither the newsreels nor the newspapers could provide color photographs. *Sport* hired the nation's leading sportswriters to provide copy.[13]

This increase in game analysis and off-the-field events did not, however, result in an increase in investigative reporting. Three major scandals in sport were exposed during the 1950s—point-shaving scandals in college basketball, a cheating conspiracy among football players at West Point, and the connections between boxing and organized crime. Sports journalists broke none of these stories. The Army revealed its own shame, and local and federal lawyers investigated and exposed the other crimes. Most newspapers reported these stories not as sports stories but as crime stories. The *New York Times*, for instance, played these stories on page one, and assigned city reporters, not sportswriters, to cover them.[14] Significantly, however, a number of newspapers and magazines did detail the scandals after the fact. If the media could not expose the scandals, they were at least explaining them to readers.

Two very different and very influential voices in sports journalism emerged in the postwar period. Red Smith, a native of Green Bay, Wisconsin, and a graduate of Notre Dame, wrote for the *St. Louis Star* and the *Philadelphia Record* before joining the staff of the *New York Herald Tribune* in 1945. His style was erudite, literate, wry, and understated. Jimmy Cannon was a native New Yorker who had never attended college and who wrote for the *New York Post* and then the *New York Journal American*. His style was romantic, world-weary, witty, and passionate. Smith, who liked Cannon, felt his style was sometimes overwrought. Cannon, who liked Smith, felt he took sports too lightly. After the death of Grantland Rice in 1954, Smith became the nation's most widely syndicated sports columnist, followed closely by Cannon. Theirs were the most powerful voices in print journalism, influencing another generation of sportswriters.[15]

However, even their strong voices were virtually drowned out with the emergence of the new medium of television. Television broadcasting affected different sports in different ways. It devastated boxing, had mixed effects on baseball, and proved a boon to college and professional football. But its arrival had two significant effects on sports journalism. It accelerated the postwar transformation of sport into a middle-class entertainment industry, and it became the dominant mode of experiencing sporting events, further marginalizing the role of the daily newspaper in sports journalism.

Just as radio had done, television allowed sports fans to experience the games with greater immediacy and detail than newspapers could possibly provide. In response, newspapers gradually gave greater emphasis to analysis. Thanks to television, fans had already learned what had happened. Newspapers would tell them why it had happened. One of the pioneers in this regard was Dick Young of the *New York Post*. In 1950 he became the first reporter to seek postgame comments from players for the purposes of including in his stories. His success with this technique quickly permeated the profession. He explained, "I thought it was just an integral part of the story. The older writers didn't like that much. It was pretty much a handout era where the guys would sit up in the press box with a release from the ball club and write what they saw.... I don't know why, but nobody did it any differently."[16]

Young's desire to move beyond the publicist role was shared by other newspapermen in the late 1950s and early 1960s. Under the guidance of Larry Merchant, the sports section of the *Philadelphia Daily News* developed an iconoclastic, irreverent voice that suited the paper's appeal to the working man. But the acknowledged center of the new sportswriting style was the sports section of *Long Island Newsday*. It originally focused on local high school sports, leaving national sports to city newspapers. In the 1950s, though, *Newsday* expanded on several fronts. Jack Mann, who became sports editor in 1960, developed a large and talented young staff, headed by columnist Stan Isaacs. *Newsday* covered high school sports with the same intensity with which it handled the World Series, and vice versa, with all reporters covering all levels of sports. *Newsweek* called it "a startlingly fresh approach to sports. Mixing irony, satire, and solid reporting with liberal grains of salt, the sports section seeks to skip past the publicity handout and the pat phrase...." The magazine praised the newspaper for attacking "the myths of sport, the tired jargon, and the vapid generalization"[17] of the standard sports page.

As a matter of policy, *Newsday* reporters refused all of the customary fringe benefits offered to sportswriters by teams and promoters. They received relatively generous salaries and thus were better prepared to maintain their integrity. Mann also directed his writers to avoid the jargon and clichés into which so much sportswriting had lapsed. In an internal memo, he wrote, "Maybe it isn't possible to put out a sports section without this kind of drivel. Certainly it hasn't ever been done. But let's try it, anyway."[18] The *Newsday* reporters, and their adherents at other newspapers, believed themselves to be on a quest to change sports journalism.

Naturally, this led to a certain insularity, and to tension between them and the other reporters of whom they were implicitly and explicitly critical. One day Jimmy Cannon tried to silence a noisy press-box conversation among some members of the new breed by snarling, "You're chattering like a bunch of chipmunks." The "chipmunk" name stuck, a mark of derision among the established writers and a mark of distinction among the new breed.

The signature Chipmunk story involves Stan Isaacs and Yankee pitcher Ralph Terry, who interrupted a group interview to telephone his wife. Terry returned to the interview after a short time, noting that his wife was feeding their infant son. Isaacs asked, "Breast or bottle?"[19] To the Chipmunks, the question represented the desire to leave no stone unturned and to provide the telling detail. To Cannon and his generation, it was an unspeakably rude question intended only to emphasize Isaacs' cleverness. The clash between Cannon and the Chipmunks reflected conflicting generations and educational backgrounds, but above all it meant a change in attitudes about the myths and traditions of sports and sports journalism. Partly because of a move away from the publicist model of sportswriting, and partly because of a move toward in-depth analysis, the Chipmunk style emerged as the distinctive newspaper voice in the television age.

No newspaper responded as effectively to the challenge of television as the magazine *Sports Illustrated*. It debuted in 1954, part of Henry Luce's magazine empire, which included *Time*, *Life*, and *Fortune*. Originally aimed at enthusiasts of upper-class sports like yachting, it became the dominant national news medium for middle-class spectator sport.

Andre Laguerre, managing editor of *Sports Illustrated* from 1960 to 1974, shaped the magazine's distinctive style. He understood that the magazine needed to address the armchair sports fan. Since television had already shown that fan what had happened, *Sports Illustrated* needed to explain the event in more detail. The armchair sports fan was interested in "big time" sports, not in elite pastimes like yachting. Laguerre gave more focus to pro and college football, riding the game's exploding popularity, as well as baseball, basketball, golf, and ice hockey. He also tried to make action photography one of the hallmarks of *Sports Illustrated*, constantly seeking innovative photographic and printing techniques. One example of *Sports Illustrated's* innovations was mounting a camera inside a hockey goal, giving the reader a unique perspective on game action.[20] Neil Leifer and Walter Iooss, Jr., were the most famous and accomplished photographers on a talented staff. Where *Sport* concentrated on posed photographs, *Sports Illustrated* brought readers detailed action photographs, in black and white and in color, of exceptional quality.

Ironically enough for a magazine called *Sports Illustrated*, its most important element was the quality of its writing. It was epitomized by the work of Dan Jenkins, whose sardonic, witty voice combined the ironic detachment of the Aw Nuts school with the passionate delight in sports characteristic of the Gee Whiz school. He covered college football, a sport then rising to new heights of popularity thanks to television, and golf, which was just starting to reach a middle-class audience thanks to the emergence of Arnold Palmer. Jenkins' analysis of a major event became the standard interpretation for sports fans around the country. Perhaps the most famous example of his influence was his story on the 1966 football game between Notre Dame and Michigan State, the nation's top two college teams. Michigan State opened strongly and raced to a 10–0 lead but allowed Notre Dame to come back to tie the score. Neither team was particularly effective, and the final score remained 10–10. Yet Jenkins

excoriated Notre Dame for playing conservatively at the end of the game, when the Irish had the ball in their own territory and chose to run out the clock rather than gambling on a big play that might win the game—or lose it. His story began, "Old Notre Dame will tie over all. Sing it out, guys. That is not exactly what the march says, of course, but that is how the big game ends every time you replay it. And that is how millions of cranky college football fans will remember it."[21] These words were a self-fulfilling prophecy. Jenkins' article shaped the way fans remembered the game—not as a game in which neither team justified its vaunted reputation, not as a game in which the Irish gamely fought back from a significant deficit, but a game in which Notre Dame took the coward's way out.

The magazine had many other gifted writers, including Frank Deford, Curry Kirkpatrick, Tex Maule, Jack Olsen, George Plimpton, Bud Shrake, and John Underwood. But it was Jenkins' prose that set the tone for the magazine and inspired a generation of reporters. In the words of Mike Lupica, a leading newspaper columnist since the 1970s, Jenkins "used wit and skill to revolutionize sportswriting."[22] He lauded games and players that exhibited the glory of sports, raged against those whose actions and attitudes mitigated that glory, and leavened his voice with a sense of humor that implied that he knew that there were more important things in life than sports—which was precisely why he seemed to care so much.

Throughout Laguerre's tenure as managing editor, and for several years afterwards, *Sports Illustrated* was the dominant national medium for sports news and sports issues. It was willing to examine social problems through the lens of sports, most notably in its unflinching reports on the state of race relations in sport and its examination of women in sport and the impact of Title IX. It flourished during the 1960s and 1970s, an era in which a vast number of newspapers and magazines went out of business. Indeed, the emergence of television helped rather than hindered the magazine. Network television newscasts rarely had room for or interest in covering sports, so a newsweekly devoted to sports was not covering ground already covered by television. And while television helped millions of viewers see events—experiencing the events themselves with far more immediacy and far less mediation than before—few television broadcasts provided the kind of analysis supplied by *Sports Illustrated*.

However, televised sport was quickly coming to provide just this kind of added depth, largely thanks to the innovations of Roone Arledge. A producer for ABC Sports, he believed that early television sportscasts were content to record broad overviews of the action, simply bringing the game to the viewer. The next step was to "bring the viewer to the game ... to heighten the viewer's feeling of actually sitting in the stands and participating personally in the excitement and color.... In short—*we are going to add show business to sports!*"[23] Arledge's ideas revolutionized sports television. He placed microphones on the field to pick up noises in the crowd and on the field. He doubled and tripled the standard number of cameras in order to show reaction shots from coaches and participants as well as pretty cheerleaders and interesting-looking spectators. He encouraged a focus on the personalities of the coaches and athletes. He oversaw the development of the instant replay, which allowed broadcasters to provide analysis more rapidly and more visually than any newspaper. Under Arledge, television assumed every role previously played by print media: it served as the primary medium for experiencing events, it provided detailed analysis, and it gave human faces to the participants.

Arledge also employed television's first true sports journalist, Howard Cosell.[24] He had neither a pleasant voice nor a pleasant face, but he worked hard, never flinched from asking tough questions, and utilized his prodigious memory and prodigious vocabulary to great advantage. Like many great journalists, he believed passionately in battling injustices, and to his mind one such injustice was the persecution of heavyweight boxing champion Muhammad Ali. At a time when Ali was a figure of great controversy because of his religious conversion, his name change, his political stances, and his refusal to be inducted into the Army, Cosell stood by him, often alone. Just as Ali was vilified by much of America, so was Cosell. ABC was deluged with hate mail aimed at Cosell and Ali, but Arledge refused to take Cosell off the air. He liked him and respected his judgment, and he knew that controversy meant ratings. Cosell also distinguished himself with his reporting at the 1972 Olympic Games in Munich, covering, among other stories, the Palestinian capture and execution of Israeli athletes.

Cosell became even more controversial starting in 1970 when Arledge assigned him to *Monday Night Football*, the new broadcast of an NFL game in prime time. Arledge knew that Cosell could be a key factor in "add[ing] show business to sports." He was intelligent, insightful, and provocative, utterly unlike the smooth, portentous commentators working NFL games on other networks. He was teamed with Don Meredith, a former quarterback for the Dallas Cowboys. Cosell's sesquipedalian, provocative persona contrasted nicely with Meredith's folksy, regular-guy style. Keith Jackson, a veteran of ABC's college football crew, provided play-by-play, but the main focus was the by-play between Cosell and Meredith. After the first season, Jackson departed and was replaced by Frank Gifford, a much less talented and experienced play-by-play man, but the program's spectacular ratings never suffered. Much of the show's popularity derived from viewers' loathing of Cosell. Viewers were angered when he told them that a player wasn't particularly good or even that the player had made mistakes. Hating Cosell became a national pastime once again. He was at least as much a showman as he was a journalist. He readily played his part on *Monday Night Football*, sent up his own image in the Woody Allen film *Bananas*, hosted an ill-fated prime-time variety show called *Saturday Night Live with Howard Cosell*, and willingly participated in the trivial celebrity sports program *Battle of the Network Stars*. Yet he was more a journalist than anyone else in sports television, willing to connect sports with social and political developments and always ready to ask tough questions and render tough judgments.

On September 7, 1979, the landscape

changed yet again with the debut of the cable television channel ESPN.[25] It aired a variety of unusual, even marginal sporting events with little television exposure, including college soccer and basketball and auto and hydroplane racing. It also aired a nightly news and highlights program originally called *Sports Recap*, promptly renamed *SportsCenter*. In 1988, ESPN hired John Walsh, a veteran editor who had worked at *U.S. News & World Report*, *Rolling Stone*, and *Inside Sports*, to produce *SportsCenter*. He understood that *SportsCenter*, not the various actual sports events airing on the network, was ESPN's signature program and worked to raise its visibility on the schedule. He changed the *SportsCenter* format, covering stories in order of their news importance rather than according to a series of rigid sport-by-sport blocks. Perhaps more significantly, he hired a number of anchors, most prominently Dan Patrick and Keith Olbermann, who teamed up on *SportsCenter* to deliver extensive and exhaustive highlights, a vast storehouse of sports arcana, and a barrage of jokes, catch phrases, and self-referential comments. *SportsCenter* inspired fanatical loyalty in viewers and became the standard for television coverage of sports news. Indeed, by the end of the 1990s many television news directors had made one of two choices about their own sports news—either be overtly derivative of *SportsCenter*, or abandon the field to *SportsCenter* and eliminate sports news altogether. A handful of stations chose to devote themselves to intense coverage of teams in their market, assuming that fans interested in national sports news would turn to national networks like ESPN or competing cable networks like CNN/SI and Fox Sports Net. ESPN in general and *SportsCenter* in particular assumed the role that *Sports Illustrated* had enjoyed in the 1960s. They shaped how sports fans view and remember a sporting event.

For traditional daily newspapers, ESPN represented one of two strong national challenges to sports reporting. The other came from a new national daily newspaper, *USA Today*. When the paper was born in 1982, it was hardly seen as a threat to journalism in general or to sports journalism in particular. Its mission to cover sports in every state led it to give too much attention to high school sports, which were of little interest to readers in other states. Its relentlessly upbeat tone reduced its feature stories to a series of puff pieces about the personalities of athletes. Its only advantage seemed to derive from its unique satellite-based distribution system. Because this system allowed the paper to delay its deadlines, its sports section contained scores and stories about games on the West Coast that ended too late for inclusion in East Coast dailies. However, this was not regarded (internally or externally) as a significant advantage.

For awhile, it seemed that *The National Sports Daily* would be a much more serious threat to traditional newspapers. It was founded by Emilio Azcarraga, a Mexican businessman who thought that the time was right to launch a national newspaper devoted to sports. He recruited top print journalists including Frank Deford and Mike Lupica with the intention of combining coverage of top sporting events, in-depth stories and statistics on the games of the day, pungent columns, and *Sports Illustrated*–style long features. The paper launched in January 1990 and folded in June 1991, victim of a poor advertising and sales climate and several unsuccessful attempts to establish a national distribution system. However, *USA Today* had already solved those infrastructure problems. Now it sought to copy the most successful elements of *The National*, including better coverage of top events and detailed statistics from daily games. In the 1990s *USA Today* moved aggressively to position itself as a reliable and available alternative for travelers, and the paper's improved sports section was a key factor in the success of the strategy. *USA Today* became a major player in sports journalism.

Faced with the emergence of these two major national media, ESPN on cable television and *USA Today* in print, most local newspapers made the strategic decision to retreat from national sports coverage. They expanded their coverage of local sports, trying to combine game reporting, in-depth analysis, and personality reporting. They gave greater emphasis to sports and athletes not often covered by the national media, including sports at high schools and small colleges as well as professional minor league teams. They still covered national events, but often relied on wire services or syndicates for these games, unless local teams were involved. Similarly, they expanded their statistical pages, but often purchased these data from syndicates or even from *USA Today* itself. In national sports news, newspapers—even *USA Today*—are clearly subordinate to ESPN.

Sports journalism today faces a number of overlapping issues that constitute a vastly complex set of challenges to the journalistic mission. Since the mid–1960s, off-the-field stories—including the business of sports, the role of government in sports, and athletes' brushes with the law—have assumed greater importance in sports journalism. Sports editors find themselves seeking reporters who can cover sports, business, law, and public policy. Athletes, coaches, and leagues are increasingly sophisticated in their attempts to manipulate the media for their own ends. Reporters who work for television networks that broadcast sports events are often required to promote telecasts that may have no news significance whatsoever. Some networks, notably ESPN, allow their reporters to make commercial endorsements, a practice that compromises their journalistic integrity. The phenomenon of media convergence adds complexity to the landscape, as the interlocking alliances and antagonisms of print and broadcast media, sports teams and businesses, and entertainment conglomerates threaten to warp news judgments.

Sports journalism remains a contested field. Athletes and owners seek to use the media to gain publicity for themselves and their teams, while resenting journalists who seek to discover information they prefer to keep secret. Fans turn religiously to sports sections and *SportsCenter*, while decrying the news gathering tactics employed by reporters. Journalists cloak themselves in their professional ideals about learning and disseminating the truth, while acknowledging their needs to preserve relationships with teams and athletes and to provide comfortable, appealing stories that result in a large audience. Sports journalists have to work harder than ever to present on- and off-the-field news about the multi-billion-dollar sports entertainment industry to the public whose dollars fuel that industry.

Selected Readings

Barber, Red. *The Broadcasters*. New York: Dial Press, 1970.

Betts, John Rickards. "Sporting Journalism in Nineteenth-Century America." *American Quarterly* 5 (1953): 39–56.

Egan, Betty. "Baseball Meets the Press." *Media History Digest* 5, 2 (1985): 60–64.

Holtzman, Jerome. *No Cheering in the Press Box*. New York: Holt, Rinehart, and Winston, 1974.

Lorenz, Alfred Lawrence. "'In the Wake of the News,': The Beginnings of a Sports Column, by HEK." *American Journalism* 9 (Winter-Spring 1992): 65–86.

McCambridge, Michael. *The Franchise: A History of Sports Illustrated Magazine*. New York: Hyperion, 1997.

Oriard, Michael. *Reading Football*. Chapel Hill: University of North Carolina Press, 1993.

Powers, Ron. *Supertube: The Rise of Television Sports*. New York: Coward-McCann, 1988.

Rader, Benjamin G. *In Its Own Image: How Television Has Transformed Sports*. New York, 1984.

Sperber, Murray. *Onward to Victory: The Crises That Shaped College Sports*. New York: Henry Holt, 1998.

Stephens, Gary B. "The Media Buildup: 'Gentleman Jim' vs. 'Ruby Rob.'" *Media History Digest* 3, 1 (1983): 6–14, 45, 64.

Towers, Wayne M. "World Series Coverage in New York City in the 1920s." *Journalism Monographs* 73 (August 1981).

Notes

1. *New York Tribune*, 19 October 1924, 1.

2. *National Police Gazette*, decried as a scandalous tabloid, is not well preserved and can be difficult to find in archives. See John Rickards Betts, "Sporting Journalism in Nineteenth-Century America," *American Quarterly* 5 (1953): 39–56; Michael Isenberg, *John L. Sullivan and His America* (Urbana: University of Illinois Press, 1988), passim but especially 89–97; Elliott J. Gorn, "The Wicked World: The *National Police Gazette* and Gilded Age America," *Media Studies Journal* 6 (1992): 1–15.

3. *The Sporting News*, 10 October 1910, 1.

4. Chadwick incorporated much of his newspaper writing into his popular guides. See, for instance, *Beadle's Dime Base Ball Player* (New York: Beadle and Co., 1860), *DeWitt's Base Ball Guide* (New York: R. M. DeWitt, 1869), or any of the *Spalding's Official Base Ball Guides* prepared under Chadwick's direction. Albert G. Spalding quotes liberally from Chadwick's reporting in his *America's National Game* (1911; reprint ed., Lincoln: University of Nebraska Press, 1992).

5. "New Yorkers at the Game," *New York Times*, 21 November 1897, 2.

6. See Michael Oriard, *Reading Football* (Chapel Hill: University of North Carolina Press), 1993.

7. In addition to Rice's newspaper and magazine stories, see his autobiography, *The Tumult and the Shouting* (New York: A. S. Barnes, 1954; Dell, 1956).

8. Stanley Walker, *City Editor* (New York: A. S. Barnes, 1934).

9. Stanley Woodward, *Sports Page* (New York: Simon & Schuster, 1949), 39–41.

10. Eliot Asinof, *Eight Men Out* (New York: Holt, Rinehart, and Winston, 1963; Henry Holt, 1987).

11. Arch Ward, *Chicago Tribune*, 12 November 1944.

12. The best print source on the early days of sports radio remains Red Barber, *The Broadcasters* (New York: Dial Press, 1970). Curt Smith, *Voices of the Game* (Arlington: Diamond Communications, 1987) is also useful.

13. An intriguing discussion of the impact of *Sport* can be found in Murray Sperber, *Onward to Victory: The Crises that Shaped College Sports* (New York: Henry Holt, 1998), 195–205.

14. "Two Ex-Stars Held in Basketball 'Fix' at $2,000 a Game," Meyer Berger, *New York Times*, 18 January 1951, 1; "City College Aces and Gambler Held in Basketball 'Fix,'" Alexander Feinberg, *New York Times*, 19 February 1951, 1; "West Point Ousts 90 Cadets for Cheating in Classroom; Football Players Involved," Richard H. Parke, *New York Times*, 4 August 1951, 1.

15. Some of Cannon's columns are collected in *Nobody Asked Me, but…: The World of Jimmy Cannon* (New York: Holt, Rinehart, and Winston, 1978). Smith's work is more widely available. His collections include *Strawberries in the Wintertime* (New York: Quadrangle/New York Times Books, 1974); *The Red Smith Reader* (New York: Random House, 1982); *and Red Smith on Baseball* (Chicago: Ivan R. Dee, 2000). He benefits from a sound biography, Ira Berkow's *Red* (New York: Times Books, 1986). See also interviews with Cannon and Smith in Jerome Holtzman, *No Cheering in the Press Box* (New York: Holt, Rinehart, and Winston, 1974), 243–59, 273–87.

16. Quoted in Kevin Kerrane, ed., *"Batting Cleanup, Bill Conlin"* (Philadelphia: Temple University Press, 1997), 2; ellipsis in original.

17. "Mann in Charge," *Newsweek*, 27 March 1961, 88–97.

18. Jack Mann, memo of April 25, 1960, quoted in George Vecsey, *A Year in the Sun* (New York: Times Books, 1989), 115.

19. Quoted in Vecsey, ibid., 117.

20. John R. Zimmerman, "View from the Hottest Spot," *Sports Illustrated*, 15 January 1962, 30–37.

21. Dan Jenkins, "An Upside-Down Game," *Sports Illustrated*, 28 November 1966, 22.

22. Mike Lupica, *Shooting from the Lip* (Chicago: Bonus Books, 1988), xxii.

23. Roone Arledge to Ed Scherick, 1960, quoted in Marc Gunther, *The House that Roone Built: The Inside Story of ABC News* (Boston: Little, Brown, 1994), 17–18.

24. Cosell wrote three books about himself, all of which are interesting and one-sided: Cosell with Mickey Herskowitz, *Cosell* (Chicago: Playboy Press, 1973); Cosell, *Like It Is* (Chicago: Playboy Press, 1974); Cosell with Peter Bonventre, *I Never Played the Game* (New York: William Morrow, 1985). Gunther and Carter, *Monday Night Mayhem*, is judicious and more useful. There is a vast body of newspaper, magazine, and television reporting about Cosell, and it awaits an energetic and even-handed scholar.

25. Bill Rasmussen, the founder of ESPN, recounts the events leading up to the first broadcast in *Sports Junkies Rejoice! The Birth of ESPN* (Hartsdale, N.Y.: QV Publishing, 1983). John Walsh is discussed in Tim Carvell, "Prime-Time Player," *Fortune*, 2 March 1998, 134–144; Jim Shea, "The King," *Columbia Journalism Review*, January/February 2000, 45–47.

22

Investigative Journalism

JAMES AUCOIN

In September 1972, reporters James Steele and Donald Barlett of the *Philadelphia Inquirer* decided to find out whether the scales of justice were truly balanced in the Philadelphia courts, one of the largest court systems in America. They had heard police officials and lawyers grumble that the outcome of criminal court cases seemed to hinge on which of the city's judges a defendant stood before.

Steele, a young, cultured Midwesterner who specialized in urban affairs, and Barlett, a street-savvy reporter with the looks of a linebacker and a reputation for exposing scandals, had teamed up the year before, investigating why a federal housing program had failed in Philadelphia. For their study of the courts, the odd-couple pair spent four months in a tiny alcove at City Hall, meticulously picking through 19,000 file folders holding the documentation for a quarter-century of Philadelphia criminal cases. They selected 1,034 cases involving violent crimes, then tracked each case from beginning to end. Forty-two items were tabulated for each case. Then they did something rarely done before by journalists: They fed the data into a mainframe IBM computer (a rather exotic technology in the early 1970s), and analyzed the information to obtain scientifically valid comparisons. To complete their reporting, they hit the streets, interviewing lawyers, judges, defendants, crime victims, and other sources, questioning them about what their computer analysis showed—that Philadelphia's Lady Justice was far from blind. In fact, she winked when bias, politics, or other factors routinely tilted the scales. The articles stunned those who cherished a fair and just legal system.

The week-long Barlett-Steele series, published in March 1973 after seven months of investigation, is a classic example of investigative journalism—reporting that digs behind the press releases and photo opportunities to reveal important public stories hidden from the public. During more than 300 years of investigative reporting, American journalists have exposed corrupt officials, freed innocent death-row inmates, documented systemic police brutality, unmasked election-stealing ballot-box stuffing, uncovered consumer fraud, and told of dangerous environmental and health problems. Investigative reporting is journalism that holds public and private officials accountable to the public and opens a door to reform.

The methods of investigative reporting are traditional reporting techniques amplified: Instead of interviewing a handful of sources, investigative reporters talk to dozens, sometimes hundreds. Instead of reading a single city budget or police report and then writing their story, they search through hundreds, even thousands, of public and private records. They use surveillance and hidden cameras. They go undercover, sometimes risking their lives. They use accounting methods to study financial records and computers to analyze data obtained from public agencies. They scientifically collect samples of food, water, air, or soil for testing at licensed laboratories. They dig through trash and into people's private lives.

The definition of investigative reporting has changed over time. There was no name for the genre until the late 19th century, when some editors labeled it "detective journalism." In the early 20th century, President Teddy Roosevelt, disgusted at the poking and prying of the investigative reporters of his day, derisively labeled them "muckrakers." The name stuck, though it became a badge of honor for some journalists. During the 1970s, after the practice had gained renewed energy, reporters settled on the term "investigative journalism." The most widely accepted definition was developed by Investigative Reporters and Editors (IRE), a national service organization established in 1975. Investigative journalism, IRE's members decided, is journalism that exposes information about an important public issue that someone or some organization does not want the general public to know. Moreover, the resulting articles or books must be the product of the journalist's own digging, and not a rehashing of a law enforcement or other government investigation.[1] IRE later expanded its definition to include journalism that does not expose secrets, but instead reveals information not widely known before. Others have defined investigative reporting as reporting that involves considerable time, includes implicit or explicit appeals about what is right and what is wrong, and connects specific facts to larger social issues.

Although "investigative journalism"—as practiced by professional journalists today—began in about the 1920s, there has been an investigative spirit burning in American journalism ever since the colonial period. In fact, the investigative tradition threads its way through the fabric of journalism history, appearing at various times under different names and in different forms, but eventually evolving into a distinct, separate genre within American journalism by the end of the 20th century.

This tradition can first be found in colonial American newspapers and pamphlets that agitated against the British government. Benjamin Harris, a Boston printer, founded *Publick Occurrences, Both Foreign and Domestick* in 1690, but published only one issue before the paper was banned because of Harris' feisty, though biased, reporting of atrocities during the French and Indian War.

In the early 19th century, America's newspaper editors, beholden to one political party or another, routinely dug up scandalous information about their political opponents. Sometimes mean-spirited editors mixed rumor, opinion, and fact to embarrass politicians, including presidents. One of the most scandalous attacks on a president was that by Virginia editor James Callender, who in 1802 first published details of the alleged love affair between President Thomas Jefferson and the much-younger Sally Heming, one of his slaves. Jefferson's biographers still debate whether the allegation was true. Most conclude that the evidence is inconclusive. Doubtless, Callender's motives were impure (a former Jefferson ally, he attacked the president only after Jefferson denied him a government post). In addition, his evidence fell far short of the standard expected of modern investigative journalists. Yet, his instinct to uncover the secrets of an American politician falls within the investigative tradition.

That instinct was shared and enlarged by many American journalists, particularly after the 1830s. The Age of Jackson was the age of the common man, and reformers of various ilks published numerous pamphlets and specialty newspapers to expose the social ills befalling the poor and working classes. Abolitionists, suffragists, labor activists, and advocates for women, children, prisoners, and farmers published detailed investigations of harsh living and working conditions and mistreatment to stir the winds of change.

During the 1830s, the daily papers changed, too. They started reporting news of scandals, corruption, and crime at a price the average person could afford—one penny, which was much cheaper than the usual six-penny price of commercial and party papers. These "penny papers" began reporting news for the working and middle classes, instead of society's elite. Independent of political control, their editors focused on the everyday life of their cities. More interested in fact than opinion, they got their stories by going to the scenes of events, interviewing witnesses, investigating what occurred. Reporting, as it is known today, was rare before the mid–1800s. Nevertheless, it was a technique embraced by James Gordon Bennett at the penny *New York Herald* and by his cross-town rival, Benjamin Day of the *New York Sun*. Frequently, these editors challenged authority, such as when Bennett and Day covered the scandalous ax murder of the young prostitute Ellen Jewett in 1836.

Though hardly as systematic and objective as modern investigative reporters would have been, Bennett and Day pursued the Jewett murder story vigorously, digging for information beyond what police told the public. A young dandy, Richard P. Robinson, celebrated the night of his birthday with his paramour, Ms. Jewett. When he left the brothel early the next morning, she was dead. Bennett and Day ultimately disagreed on Robinson's guilt, but both pursued the story undaunted. By the time Robinson went to trial, Bennett was certain he was being framed. Day wasn't so sure. After the jury declared Robinson innocent, Day and the *Sun* investigated behind the scenes and exposed the miscarriage of justice that had occurred. With meticulous detail and insight, Day revealed that Robinson's acquittal had been a manipulation of the court system by Robinson's rich and powerful friends.[2]

In late 1870 and through most of 1871, *Harper's Weekly* and the *New York Times* took on the rich and powerful of New York as well. Their target was corrupt Tammany Hall politicians. Boss (William M.) Tweed and his gang of thieves controlled New York City for decades and literally stole tens of millions of dollars in public funds. *Harper's Weekly* cartoonist, Thomas Nast, lampooned the Tweed Ring for months, while the *Times* provided editorials and news stories. Using the Ring's "secret ledgers" leaked to the *Times* by one of the Ring's bookkeepers and later verified by a former county sheriff, reporter John Foord and his editors exposed the bribes, extortion, and outright thievery that had become systemic in New York's municipal government.[3]

In the late 19th century and early 20th century, the investigative instinct among journalists swelled as powerful newspaper barons saw the exposure of corruption, vice, and venality as sensational news and a way to attract readers. Press lords Joseph Pulitzer and William

Randolph Hearst turned their New York newspapers, the *World* and the *Journal*, respectively, into screaming, scandal-mongering news sheets. Though exploitative and sensational, these papers changed American journalism forever by emphasizing information, instead of opinion in their news articles, and encouraging exposés of public graft, corruption, and abuse of power. The most popular example is found among the exploits of Nelly Bly (Elizabeth Cochrane) and her fellow girl stunt reporters, who included among their attention-getting repertoire many pieces that were called "detective journalism." Nelly Bly led the way. Posing undercover as the homeless and confused "Nellie Brown," she spent 10 days locked in New York's notorious Blackwell's Island Insane Asylum for Women. The day after her release, on October 16, 1887, she exposed the hospital's inhumane conditions in Pulitzer's *New York World*, becoming the first woman reporter to get a front-page byline in the paper.

While Bly was making headlines in the *World*, Henry Demarest Lloyd was tapping into and expanding the investigative tradition in the Midwest. Spurned by the New York papers, Lloyd had joined the *Chicago Tribune* in 1872. A lawyer by training, social reformer by heart, and journalist by choice, Lloyd burned with indignation at the social ills widespread during America's industrial age. He and others attributed the social problems to the excesses of capitalism and to America's economic domination by corporate monopolies, or "trusts." So he aimed his journalist's ire at business moguls, especially oil tycoon John D. Rockefeller. Lloyd, applying his skills as a lawyer to his work as a journalist, built his case against Rockefeller and the oil trust with prosecutorial thoroughness, accuracy, and extensive documentation. Correctly perceiving that American society in the late 1800s would only be swayed by irrefutable facts, Lloyd carefully backed up his arguments with information from court records, personal interviews, and government and business documents. His meticulously gathered, exhaustive evidence against Rockefeller, laid out in detail across two full pages of the *Journal* and illustrated in graphs and charts, set a milestone in the evolution of modern

American investigative journalism. His work raised the investigative standard for documentation, enhancing the practice's credibility. His reporting about Rockefeller and the trusts also appeared in the *Atlantic Monthly* (already noted for its investigative articles) and a popular book, *Wealth Against Commonwealth* (1894). Furthermore, his work directly influenced the celebrated muckrakers who became the star journalists of the 20th century's first two decades.

America's muckraking age began with publication of the January 1903 issue of *McClure's*, a monthly magazine that sparked a golden age of investigative reporting and solidified the reputations of three of history's most famous journalists, Lincoln Steffens, Ida Tarbell, and Ray Stannard Baker. That single edition of the magazine carried works by all three, and each is now rated among the best investigative articles ever published: the first installment of Tarbell's damning history of the Standard Oil Company; Steffens' "The Shame of Minneapolis" about municipal corruption; and Baker's "The Right to Work," which exposed the violent underbelly of America's labor unions. Muckraking's inaugural issue reached 400,000 readers across the country, a *tour de force* in American journalism. About a dozen magazines of the era delivered to a mass, national audience hundreds of detailed, dramatic reports of political scandals and deplorable social ills. Muckraking reports encouraged numerous progressive reforms, including passage of the Pure Food and Drug Act of 1906, child-labor laws, and anti-trust regulation.

Samuel McClure's magazine, and others like it, was made possible by technological advances in printing, paper-making, and photo reproduction that occurred during the last two decades of the 19th century and opened the path to inexpensive, attractive, mass-audience magazines. McClure and other editors used their popular magazines as an outlet to push for social change, politically aligning themselves with the reformist Progressive party and against the forceful tide of irresponsible industrialization. As an editor, McClure also contributed to the evolution of investigative journalism standards and values. He demanded that the mag-azine's articles be fully documented and backed by passionless fact—in contrast to the typically opinionated exposés published in the mid- to late 19th century. He wanted *McClure's* articles to shock readers through the reporting of cold fact. He also demanded that the articles personify the social conflict by naming names—by identifying and bringing to life the cruel industrialists and their innocent victims. Above all, the articles in his magazine had to tell an absorbing, narrative story. McClure's standards, applied to the exposure of important social and political injustices, have become integral to the character of modern investigative journalism.

Unfortunately, some of the muckraking, which was always infused with a strong reform motive, failed to meet the high standards set by Henry Demarest Lloyd, Samuel McClure, and others. One embarrassing example was David Graham Phillips' exposé of the U.S. Senate in 1906, a sloppy, exaggerated, and extremist attack that earned the disgust of America's politicians, journalists, and the reading public. Phillips, contrary to the example set by McClure, allowed ideology to taint his evidence and his conclusions. The muckraker's ideological motivation, however well it is controlled, is the fundamental characteristic that sets muckraking apart from today's pure investigative reporting. Muckraking journalists were social activists. Some, like Steffens and Upton Sinclair, were committed radicals who flirted with socialism and used their writings to agitate against the capitalist system. Modern investigative journalism, in contrast, is practiced by reporters and editors who, for the most part, blend objective news standards with their fervent desire to improve—not replace—capitalism and representative democracy.

After the muckraking era ended in about 1917, the investigative tradition split along two distinct paths in American journalism—one was practiced by social activists of various hues who embraced the muckraking model, and the other was practiced by reporters and editors who followed the more mainstream, objective investigative reporting model.

Under both models, though, journalism's investigative tradition lost ground immediately after the muckraking era, particularly between 1917 and 1950. The years of America's involvement in successive world wars proved disastrous for investigative reporting. The public's intense patriotism during the war years, and its hopelessness during the Great Depression, all but smothered the reformist zeal in American journalism. While the investigative tradition never completely vanished, reporters usually had trouble finding publishers interested in political and economic exposés.

One exception was Paul Y. Anderson, who worked for press baron Joseph Pulitzer's *St. Louis Post-Dispatch* and its legendary managing editor O. K. Bovard. Anderson is best remembered for his relentless pursuit of the Teapot Dome scandals during Warren G. Harding's presidency in the 1920s. Oil magnates, including the founder of the Sinclair Oil Co., bribed Department of Interior officials to get access to national oil reserves at highly discounted prices. In 1928, Anderson won the Pulitzer Prize for his articles exposing the corruption.

Although few newspapers shared the *Post-Dispatch's* enthusiasm for investigative reporting from the 1920s to the 1960s, some printed occasional exposés, including Anderson's freelance stories. In fact, throughout the United States there were isolated pockets of aggressive news reporting at papers large and small by journalists willing to take on local investigations, primarily into government corruption. One unusual example was a 1921 investigation into the Ku Klux Klan by Pulitzer's *New York World*. The KKK of the Reconstruction era had recently revived into a popular political and social organization, largely through state-of-the-art marketing techniques brought to the organization by professional publicists Edward Y. Clarke and Elizabeth Tyler. The *World* exposed an adulterous affair between Clarke and Mrs. Tyler, whose behavior contradicted the new Klan's strict moral views. More importantly, the *World* provided detailed evidence of the Klan's violence and other crimes. The *World's* crusade forced the resignation of "Colonel" William Simmons, who was the Imperial Wizard of the Fiery Cross living in a million-dollar mansion paid for with Klan funds. For its work, the newspaper won a Pulitzer Prize, but its crusade backfired. The Klan's racism and stern morality were attractive to many white Protestant Americans, and the *World's* articles and editorials provided extensive publicity for the Klan, causing the organization's membership ranks to swell.

Also an exception to the general lack of interest in investigative reporting on national issues between 1917 and 1950 was "Washington Merry-Go-Round," a nationally syndicated column started in 1932 by Washington, D.C., reporters Drew Pearson and Robert S. Allen. The column specialized in investigative scoops, primarily about Washington politics, but its format hindered examination of the issues the column raised.

In addition, investigative journalism flourished in a handful of small-circulation political magazines and newsletters during this time. This was particularly true of the liberal opinion magazines like *The Nation*, under the editorships of Freda Kirchway and Carey McWilliams, and *The New Republic*. Reporter Fred J. Cook, for example, sent investigative articles to *The Nation* that had been rejected by his editors at the *New York World-Telegram*. Other investigative articles by Heywood Broun, McAlister Coleman, Lewis Gannett, and Louis Adamic also appeared in the pages of these out-of-the-mainstream magazines. Independent journalist I. F. Stone created his own outlet, though, by founding a weekly newsletter, *I. F. Stone's Weekly*, which gained a small, but loyal and respected following, particularly among Washington journalists and politicians.

The investigative tradition also was kept alive by a few book publishers. In the early 1930s, Drew Pearson and Robert Allen published two books that generated interest in their syndicated column: *Washington Merry-Go-Round* and *More Washington Merry-Go-Round*. Capitalizing on the success of the Pearson-Allen books, a smattering of Washington and big-business exposés appeared, including William P. Helm's *Washington Swindle Sheet*, which infuriated readers by detailing corruption and extravagances by Washington politicians, and Matthew Josephson's muckraking *The Robber Barons* and *The Politicos*. Carey

McWilliams, a California lawyer, social activist, and freelance muckraker, published books on race relations and other social causes in the 1930s and 1940s before accepting editorial responsibilities at *The Nation*. His book on the national transient farm labor problems, *Ill Fares the Land*, came out in 1942, predating TV reporter Edward R. Murrow's now-classic investigative documentary on the issue, "Harvest of Shame," by nearly two decades.

Though late to the social issues exposed by McWilliams and others, Edward R. Murrow made up for it by expanding the investigative tradition into the new medium of television. Beginning in the 1950s with Murrow's documentaries, television amplified the power of investigative journalism, taking its stories to a national audience, the size of which dwarfed even the massive audiences of the turn-of-the-century muckraking magazines. A native of Greensboro, North Carolina, Murrow began his broadcasting career with CBS radio in 1935. A resonate voice made him a natural for broadcasting. An innate sense of responsibility and social justice drew him to investigative reporting. Broadcasting live reports during World War II, often while bombs fell from German airplanes on London or while flying in Allied bombers over Germany, Murrow became a national celebrity. After the war, he returned to New York, transferred to CBS' television news division, and pioneered the television news documentary on shows such as *See It Now* and *CBS Reports*.

Investigative journalism also made gains in daily newspapers during the 1940s and 1950s. At the *Des Moines Register and Tribune*, a Cowles Publication at the time, reporter Clark Mollenhoff stood out. Trained as a lawyer, he exposed corruption in local law enforcement and politics during the late 1940s and early 1950s. Moving to the papers' Washington bureau, he turned his investigative attention to national issues, uncovering corruption in the Teamster's Union, tax scandals in the Truman Administration, and a myriad of problems in agricultural regulation. While Mollenhoff was churning out investigations for Cowles Publications, reporter Robert Collins gained notice at the *Atlanta Journal* and, later, at the *St. Louis*

Post-Dispatch with exposés of bootleg liquor, prostitution, illegal gambling, and political payoffs. And investigative reporter Jack Nelson was building his reputation at the *Atlanta Constitution*, exposing gambling in Biloxi, Mississippi, and racial violence. Across the country, the *Utica* (New York) *Observer-Dispatch* was doing some political digging of its own, winning a Pulitzer Prize in 1959 for exposing government corruption at City Hall.

Nevertheless, investigative reporting largely went unpublished from the end of the muckraking era in 1917 until the turbulent 1960s, when investigative journalism re-emerged as a dominant journalistic form. After about 1964, exposés were appearing in newspapers and on local and network TV news regularly. Investigations routinely appeared in mass-circulation magazines, including *Life*, *Look*, and *Saturday Evening Post*, and in targeted-audience publications such as *True Magazine*, *Argosy*, and the radical leftist *Ramparts* and *New Times*.

Investigative reporting teams appeared during the 1960s as well. Robert Greene, tough, cigar-smoking, and streetwise, took on organized crime and political corruption as a reporter and editor at *Newsday* on Long Island, New York. In 1967, he established the first permanent investigative reporting team in U.S. history at *Newsday*. Its best-known project was a 1972 investigation into the smuggling and use of heroin in New York City and its suburbs. Team members traveled throughout Europe, posing as travel writers, to get the chance to observe drug manufacturing and smuggling operations first-hand. In a lengthy special section, the team documented the flow of the illegal drug from poppy fields in Turkey, through a French smuggling pipeline, and into the needle-tracked arms of Long Island addicts. Another newspaper noted for its team investigations was the *Chicago Tribune*, where George Bliss and his colleagues sniffed out election rigging, medical fraud, and police brutality of law-abiding citizens.

On network television in 1968, CBS began the pioneering TV newsmagazine *60 Minutes*, attracting a wide audience with a curious, but successful mix of celebrity profiles and aggressive investigative reports.

Muckraking, too, fueled a 1960s–1970s phenomenon of underground and alternative news media. Weeklies like the *Berkeley Barb* and the *Los Angeles Free Press* and grassroots radio, including the Pacifica Network, became outlets for leftist activists. Like the earlier 19th-century reformers, the activists built their audiences by muckraking repressive and unethical policies of government, big business, and other social institutions.

This outpouring of investigative journalism occurred during the 1960s and 1970s for a number of reasons. For one, the press' lackluster performance during the mid–1950s witch hunts for communists by U.S. Senator Joseph McCarthy and his allies embarrassed newspaper editors, making them more favorable to the new aggressiveness toward authority developing among their reporters. In addition, the civil rights movement and political unrest over America's involvement in Vietnam raised questions of social justice and government policies—and of the press' role in responding to America's political and social problems. It was journalism's "unfulfilled responsibility ... to add the why to the what" of events, editor Harry S. Ashmore of the *Arkansas Gazette* argued at the time.[4]

Political and legal events also increased interest in investigative journalism during this period. The U.S. Supreme Court issued several decisions bolstering the press' right to gather information and to report newsworthy matters, making it easier and safer for journalists to poke and probe into government affairs. Among these, the most important was *New York Times v. Sullivan* in 1964, which freed reporters to write responsibly about public officials without fear of losing libel suits.

In addition, investigative journalism gained legitimacy because a series of political events opened a credibility gap between the American people and their government and gained reporters an elevated status in American society. The most significant among these events were the Kennedy and Johnson administrations' lying to the American people about the extent of U.S. military involvement in Vietnam and the scandals of Watergate during Richard Nixon's administration.

Investigative reporters created a niche for themselves within the general practice of journalism during the 1960s and 1970s. This became evident when in the mid–1960s, the Pulitzer Prize Board added a separate category for local investigative reporting. By doing this, America's top journalism prize panel legitimized the practice's unique characteristics and encouraged the news media to embrace investigative reporting. Throughout the 1960s and 1970s, skills peculiar to investigative reporting were identified and nurtured. Many of the methods used, such as team-reporting, surveillance, and undercover work, were adaptations or refinements of methods used in earlier exposé and muckraking journalism. A few of the methods, though, including computer analysis, were introduced because new technologies had became available. At the American Press Institute in Reston, Virginia, reporters and editors developed a systematic investigative methodology that could be passed on to other journalists. Ben Reese, former editor of the *St. Louis Post-Dispatch*; John Seigenthaler of the *Nashville Tennessean*; and Clark Mollenhoff developed checklists for investigative reporters and blueprints for investigative reporting that could be applied to studies of government or private institutions. This system set a high standard for comprehensiveness and thoroughness, and became the basis for training numerous journalists in investigative techniques.

In the early 1970s, investigative journalism reached its apogee in popularity and prestige when reporters for the *Washington Post* exposed the Watergate scandals. Two young reporters for the *Post*, Bob Woodward and Carl Bernstein, won the Pulitzer Prize for their high-profile, dogged pursuit of wrong-doing in the Nixon White House. It was a most unlikely journalistic team, though. Woodward was the son of a Republican Midwestern judge, a graduate of Yale University, and a former U.S. Navy officer. Bernstein, in contrast, was a rebellious, free-spirited, Washington native, who had flunked out of the University of Maryland. Woodward brought cold objectivity to the team and well-placed government sources. Bernstein contributed a superb writing talent, a natural suspicion of the established power structure, and a street-honed ability to relate to the secretaries, clerks, and assistants who provided the bits and pieces of information that led them into the labyrinthine conspiracy. As Woodward and Bernstein dug ever deeper into the morass of corruption and abuse of official power that infused the Nixon administration, Watergate became the biggest political scandal of the century, forcing President Richard Nixon to resign.

Other investigative reporters made important contributions to uncovering the Watergate scandals, notably Seymour Hersh of the *New York Times*, Jack Nelson of the *Los Angeles Times*, and Daniel Schorr of the *CBS Evening News*. Most of the time, though, Woodward and Bernstein led the journalistic pack. Their later book, *All the President's Men*, told an enthralling adventure story about Woodward and Bernstein's relentless pursuit of the Watergate story, interviewing dozens of sources, gathering bank records, and piecing together the complex puzzle of political intrigue and cover-up—despite threatening denials by President Nixon and his minions. The story captivated the general public. A blockbuster film version of the book (two of Hollywood's hottest stars, Robert Redford and Dustin Hoffman, played Woodward and Bernstein, respectively) further romanticized investigative reporting, and elevated investigative reporters to national stardom.

Flush with the public's enthusiasm for investigative reporting, newspapers, radio, TV, book publishers, and magazines offered exposés on a scale unmatched since the heyday of muckraking 70 years earlier. CBS' *60 Minutes*, with exposés as a staple, became the number-one-rated television show in America.

This success both encouraged and concerned the more serious investigative reporters, who feared that standards would crumble as underskilled, ambitious journalists exploited the practice's popularity. In 1975, a group of these concerned journalists founded Investigative Reporters and Editors, a national service organization for investigative journalists. The group formed to create a network among investigative journalists, provide training seminars in investigative techniques, and promote high ethical standards for the practice.[5] Later,

it became the leading proponent of computer-assisted reporting, in which reporters used computers to analyze huge public databases, from national Census data to local arrest records.

IRE made national headlines shortly after it was founded. When a noted Arizona investigative reporter, Don Bolles, was murdered in 1976 by a target of one of his investigations, IRE reacted by sending a signal to gangsters and other criminals that investigative reporting would not be silenced by violence. The result was IRE's Arizona Project.

Newsday editor Robert Greene led IRE's team, made up of nearly 40 journalists from throughout the United States. After a three-month investigation, the unusual team of reporters produced a 23-part series that outlined mobster influence on politicians, government corruption, judicial failures, and officially sanctioned vice in Arizona—finishing their fallen comrade's work. The series earned IRE the national spotlight and the praise of reform-minded Arizonians.[6] It was a defining moment in the history of investigative journalism—a rare instance when normally competitive investigative journalists set aside their egos, stepped outside their news organizations, and cooperated on a dramatic and startling story.

In the ensuing decades, investigative journalism became institutionalized in American newsrooms. Newspapers, broadcast news outlets, and magazines routinely carried investigative stories. Prominent among them were the *Wall Street Journal*, the major municipal dailies, the national newsmagazines, and all the television networks. In addition, the investigative, nonfiction book became a financial and journalistic blockbuster. A prominent example was Bryan Burrough and John Helyar's *Barbarians at the Gate: The Fall of RJR Nabisco*, a best-seller, and one of the first successful modern investigative books about American business.

This period also saw the rise of muckraking and investigative reporting in politically conservative magazines and newspapers, including William F. Buckley, Jr.'s, *National Review* and the *Washington Star*. Liberals and leftists were long known for muckraking and investigative reporting, but increasingly the practice became a venue for conservatives and right-wing radicals as well.

Large metropolitan dailies, though, dominated the practice. The *Washington Post's* heyday with investigative journalism was during the 1970s, and it was the work of the *Philadelphia Inquirer* that best exemplified the possibilities of investigative journalism in the 1980s. It was not any single investigative project at the *Inquirer*—although there were several outstanding examples of individual efforts—but the overall commitment and achievement of the newspaper under the direction of editor Eugene Roberts that accounted for its dominance of the practice during the decade. From 1972 to 1990, the *Inquirer* won 17 Pulitzer Prizes, many for investigative reporting. The work of James Steele and Donald Barlett, among others at the paper, gained national attention and made the *Inquirer* one of the best newspapers in America. Significantly, the *Inquirer* also proved that publishing investigative journalism also proved to be quite profitable, drawing in a larger circulation.

The *Inquirer* was a star among American newspapers, but the concept that investigative reporting is a duty of the American press permeated the news industry by the 1980s. Many editors and TV news producers agreed that investigative journalism was central to a news organization's mission, and the public showed considerable support for the practice as well.[7]

In television, local stations aggressively pursued investigative reporting. WBRZ-TV in Baton Rouge, Louisiana, for example, gave free-rein to its investigative reporter, John Camp, even when his stories caused advertisers to withdraw their accounts. Local stations in Chicago and other major markets set up "I-Teams" and other investigative projects. At the networks, CBS continued strong with *60 Minutes*, ABC countered with *20/20*, NBC started *Exposé*, and CNN hired veteran investigative reporters for its new "Special Assignment" team. The Public Broadcasting System, too, created an investigative TV documentary series, *Frontline*. In magazines, *Mother Jones* (founded as a leftist collective in 1976) led the

field, including a Mark Dowie exposé revealing that Ford Motor Company's popular Pintos had explosive gasoline tanks that could have been made safe inexpensively; and although Ford executives knew about the problem, they decided not to fix it. Other magazines, including *Time, Newsweek, U.S. News and World Report*, and *Washington Monthly* weighed in with frequent in-depth investigations as well.

While times were flush for investigative journalists during the 1980s and 1990s, there was a gathering swell of opposition, too, both within journalism and in society at large. In some communities, advertisers successfully pressured news media to soften their reporting. In addition, reduced newsroom budgets led to a cutback in costly investigations at many news outlets. More importantly, high-profile libel lawsuits, including suits by General Arial Sharon of Israel against *Time* magazine and by U.S. General William Westmorcland against CBS, raised fundamental questions about investigative standards and caused some corporate owners of newspapers, magazines, and broadcast operations to curtail the practice.

On the positive side, high-profile libel cases and growing public criticism led investigative journalists to re-evaluate some of their reporting methods. Ambush TV interviews, selective film editing, hidden cameras, and use of anonymous sources especially were challenged during the 1990s. While investigative reporters still employed these techniques, they generally agreed to do so more selectively, on stories that could not be obtained any other way.

Despite the practice's controversies, investigative journalism had become a national phenomenon. Traditional outlets like network and cable TV, magazines, newspapers, and books were awash with investigative stories, from the sensationalistic to the journalistically sound. In addition, the Internet and its World Wide Web, made possible by advances in personal computer technology and telecommunications in the mid– to late 1990s, provided a new outlet for investigative reports by professional journalists and social activists. Moreover, investigative journalism emerged as a defining characteristic of the American news media in recent years. When done well, it set the standard against which all news reporting was judged. When done poorly, it was a lightning rod for public disgust with the news media.

Journalism's investigative tradition has grown and endured over the course of America's history. It began as the undisciplined fire of indignation among editors during America's formative years. As the role and character of the press changed during the 19th century, the investigative spirit pushed dailies to champion fact over opinion, and led them into factual reporting of events and issues. In the reform press and the muckraking magazines of the late 19th and early 20th centuries, advocacy merged with investigative reporting. During the next half-century, the journalism of exposure became little more than a whisper of social conscience, but it survived, and emerged stronger than ever in the late 1950s and throughout the 1960s to answer the public's concern for racial and political justice. In recent years, it has become an institutionalized, respected tradition in American newsrooms—a yardstick by which much of journalism is measured.

Selected Readings

Armao, Rosemary. "The History of Investigative Reporting," 35–49, in Marilyn Greenwald and Joseph Bernt, eds., *The Big Chill: Investigative Reporting in the Current Media Environment*. Ames: Iowa State University Press, 2000, 35–49.

Aucoin, James L. "The Re-emergence of American Investigative Journalism, 1960–1975." *Journalism History* 21 (1995): 3–15.

Aucoin, James, and Blevens, Frederick, eds. "Special Issue: Exposing Scamps, Scandals, and Scalawags: American Journalism's Investigative Tradition." *American Journalism* 14 (1997): 257–329.

Bent, Silas. *Newspaper Crusaders: A Neglected Story*. Westport, Conn.: Greenwood Press, 1939.

Downie, Leonard, Jr. *The New Muckrakers*. New York: New American, 1976.

Dygert, James H. *The Investigative Journalists: Folk Heroes of a New Era*. Englewood Cliffs, N.J.: Prentice-Hall, 1976.

Notes

1. John Ullmann, memo to IRE board members, May 30, 1979, IRE files, University of Missouri School of Journalism.

2. Benjamin Day's exposés ran daily on the *New York Sun's* front page beginning June 9, 1836, and ending June 20.

3. Copies of the actual ledgers began appearing in the *New York Times* on July 29, 1871. The entire exposé was reprinted in a *Times* pamphlet later that same year, titled "How New York is Governed: Frauds of the Tammany Democrats."

4. Harry S. Ashmore, "The Story Behind Little Rock," in Louis Lyons, ed., *Reporting the News: Selections from Nieman Reports* (New York: Atheneum, 1968), 132–40.

5. Harley R. Bierce, memo to J. Montgomery Curtis, Feb. 6, 1975, IRE files, University of Missouri School of Journalism.

6. The series became available on March 13, 1977. An edited version of the series was distributed to newspapers and broadcast clients throughout the United States by the Associated Press and United Press International wire services, and IRE mailed copies of the complete series to news organizations that had participated in the project.

7. "Investigative Reporting Has Broad Public Support, but Many Criticize Techniques Used to Unearth Controversial Stories," *Gallup Report*, 196 (1982): 31–37.

23

Reform Journalism, Exposés, and Crusading

HELEN ROUNDS

New York City's Mulberry Bend district, in the 1880s and 1890s, was a rancid, dangerous place. Crime ran rampant. Homeless children slept in dark alleys. It was one of the city's worst slums, a smelly, filthy abyss where humanity's discarded untouchables clung to existence in a bleak, harsh, stagnant world that promised only sickness, hunger, and hopelessness.

Jacob Riis, a police reporter for the *New York Tribune*, had been assigned to the district. Appalled by the district's squalid conditions, he instigated a reform crusade and prepared for battle. Armed with a camera, he captured shocking images of poverty and despair. His photos of outcasts grasping at the margins of society resulted in victory—the renovation of Mulberry Bend. For Riis, his crusade stood "as testimony that on the brink of hell itself human nature is not wholly lost."[1]

Over the years, dedicated journalists, like Riis, have gone undercover, endured adversity, and taken life-threatening risks to empower the weak and downtrodden, expose the powerful and corrupt, and relentlessly seek to balance the scales of society. Throughout the history of journalism, the work of reform journalists has had substantial impact on the lives of not only their contemporaries, but subsequent generations as well. These tenacious men and women have boldly used the influence of the press to win victories for various causes. Some crusaders, like Elijah P. Lovejoy, lost their lives.

Others, like Ray Stannard Baker, saw the materialization of important legislation and regulation stem from their exposés. But, regardless of their personal tragedies or successes, these crusaders were committed journalists who served tirelessly as agents of social reform and champions of humanity.

Long before the days of such stalwart crusaders as Joseph Pulitzer and Edward Wyllis Scripps, colonial newspapers were crusading against oppressive measures such as the British-imposed Stamp Act and the Boston Massacre. The first issue of the *Boston News-Letter* was printed in 1704. Published by John Campbell, it was acceptable to the British authorities because of its lack of crusading. However, in 1719, William Brooker established the *Boston Gazette*, and the competition between the two papers led to some controversies. The *Gazette's* pages, Campbell claimed, "smell stronger of beer than of midnight oil. It is not reading fit for people."[2] When James Franklin and his Anglican allies founded the *New-England Courant* in 1721, it and the other two Boston papers engaged in trenchant arguments over the experimental procedure of inoculating against smallpox. Although the *Courant's* opposition to the practice proved to be wrong-headed, it nevertheless is true that it provided one of the first instances of crusading in American journalism.

Although newspapers did not report the proceedings of the Constitutional Convention in Philadelphia, they did take sides in the fight surrounding ratification of the Constitution. Newspapers advocating ratification of the Constitution included the *Mercury* of New York, which featured Noah Webster's editorials written to rally supporters in New York, and the *Centinel* in Boston, which Benjamin Russell edited in an effort to help turn the tide in support of the Constitution in Massachusetts. Opposing the Constitution was Thomas Greenleaf, editor of New York's *Journal and Daily Patriotic Register*. When New York ratified the Constitution and held a parade to celebrate the event, he devoted a column of the *Journal* to ridiculing the festivities. As a result of his remarks, a mob destroyed his office.[3]

Early reform journalism can also be traced to the 18th-century humanitarian endeavors of the Quakers, whose abolitionist efforts consisted of tracts and broadsheets denouncing slavery. Just as other social reform campaigns (such as proper care of the insane, relief for the poor, education, and prison reform, for example) were indebted to the Quakers for their inception, so was the crusade against slavery. By 1770, Quakers had taken the lead in forming antislavery societies; and members of the Anglican, Presbyterian , and Catholic churches joined them in their efforts.

Even though these early efforts of Quakers gave the abolitionist cause momentum, it was not until the 19th century that an established abolitionist press came into existence. Early antislavery newspapers such as the *Manumission Intelligencer*, founded in 1819 by Elihu Embree in Jonesboro, Tennessee, and the *Genius of Universal Emancipation*, founded in 1821 by Benjamin Lundy, a Quaker, represented a concerted and consistent effort to come to the aid of a subjugated people. However, it was William Lloyd Garrison's newspaper, the *Liberator*, founded in 1831 in Boston, that most notably set the wheels of abolitionist activism in motion. His temerity exploded into print when he explained the intent of his newspaper. "...I do not wish to think, to speak, or write, with moderation....," he wrote. "I am in earnest—I will not equivocate—I will not excuse—I will not retreat a single inch—AND I WILL BE HEARD."[4]

By 1835, another abolitionist editor,

Elijah P. Lovejoy, a former Presbyterian minister, was publishing the *St. Louis Observer*. As editor of an antislavery newspaper, his courage was often tested. Protesters invaded his home, and his press was destroyed three times. Nevertheless, for the abolitionist cause, Lovejoy's resolve remained unshakable. "I think I could have gone to the stake and not a nerve have trembled, nor a quivered," he once told his brother.[5] Two years later, his words proved tragically prophetic. A mob, determined to stop his uncompromising crusade for the abolitionist cause, gathered outside a warehouse housing his new press, threatening to burn the building down. When Lovejoy tried to prevent the arsonists from making good their threats, he became the target of five bullets. He staggered into the warehouse and fell lifeless to the ground. His death made him a symbol of martyrdom for advocates of the antislavery movement.

Another leader in the antislavery crusade was Horace Greeley. In 1841, he founded the *New York Tribune*. He used it to crusade against slavery and other ills of society. His fiery editorials against the spread of slavery in the new territories helped to increase the antislavery sentiment in the North. His voice was clearly heard when, on January 4, 1854, free-soil and slavery rivals clashed as a result of the introduction of a bill by Stephen A. Douglas, a Democrat from Illinois. This bill would leave the decision of slavery to the settlers of the Kansas-Nebraska territories.

The bill quickly fueled Greeley's antislavery engine. He met Douglas and slaveholders head-on with a passionate editorial in the *Tribune*. "Slavery is imperious, encroaching, truculent, belligerent," he thundered. "Its own conduct will thus ultimately generate an explosive force that must blow it to atoms.... We denounce every attempt to remove the salutary restriction upon the introduction of slavery into the Northwest."[6] From that time on, he helped organize protest meetings against the Nebraska bill. He had firmly launched his crusade. Greeley continued to be an important crusader, fighting vigorously for the protective tariff and for anti-liquor legislation.

Frederick Douglass, a slave, escaped to

Massachusetts where he, too, joined the fight against slavery. Douglass became a close associate of William Lloyd Garrison and wrote for his *Liberator* as well as the short-lived *Ram's Horn*, a paper that businessman Willis Hodges owned. By 1847, Douglass had decided to start his own newspaper. In one of the last issues of the *Ram's Horn*, he announced his intent to establish a paper that would not only "attack slavery in all its forms and aspects," but would also have as its objective to "advocate universal emancipation; exact the standard of public morality; promote the moral and intellectual improvement of the colored people; and to hasten the day of freedom to our three million enslaved fellow-countrymen."[7]

In 1851, Douglass' paper, the *North Star*, merged with the *Liberty Party Paper* and was renamed the *Frederick Douglass Paper*. It retained its purpose as a public forum in which slavery was adamantly denounced and racial relations strongly encouraged. Despite violence and criticism directed at both his personal and professional property and pursuits, Douglass remained a crusader for the rights of African Americans until his death in 1895.

Still another crusading effort came in the form of a novel published serially in the *National Era*, an abolitionist paper founded by Lewis Tappan. Slave narratives, written by former slaves or sympathizers, had been a staple of the abolitionist press for at least 10 years before Harriet Beecher Stowe submitted her *Uncle Tom's Cabin* to the *National Era*. The novel, published in installments in the paper from 1851 to 1852, ignited virulent criticism from slaveholders and wrung tears from sympathetic abolitionists.

Upon completion of the story, the editor of the *National Era* wrote: "Mrs. Stowe has at last brought her great work to a close. We do not recollect any production of an American writer that has excited more general and profound interest."[8] The novel caused such an uproar that *Bleak House*, running as a serial in *Harper's New Monthly Magazine* at the same time, went almost unnoticed.

Among Stowe's supporters was P. T. Barnum's "Swedish Nightingale," the well-known singer Jenny Lind (Goldschmidt), who sent Stowe a letter praising her work. "You must feel and know," she wrote, "what a deep impression 'Uncle Tom's Cabin' has made upon every heart that can feel for the dignity of human existence...."[9] And, in a "fan letter" to the editor of the *National Era*, one reader wrote: "None of thy various contributions, rich and varied as they have been, have so deeply interested thy female readers of this vicinity as the story of Mrs. Stowe has so far done and promises to do."[10] Stowe's instant success prompted the *Independent*, a magazine in New York, to offer her a position. She was even asked to tour England, where Queen Victoria received her.

Nonetheless, like other crusaders, Stowe met with harsh criticism from opponents. Her name became hated in the South; and, on the streets of Richmond, Virginia, children were chanting:

> *Go, go, go,*
> *Ol' Harriet Beecher Stowe!*
> *We don't want you here in Virginny—*
> *Go, go, go!*

John P. Jewett of Boston issued a finished copy of *Uncle Tom's Cabin* on March 20, 1852. By June of that year, it was selling 10,000 copies a week. Even President Abraham Lincoln, upon meeting Stowe in 1863, greeted her as "the little lady who made this big war."[11]

One of the most celebrated cases of press crusading came in September 1870, when George Jones of the *New York Times* and Thomas Nast, cartoonist for *Harper's Weekly*, waged a spirited campaign against the corrupt regime of political boss William Marcy Tweed. Because Tweed successfully bribed other New York newspapers with city advertising, the *Times* and *Harper's* were left to bring down the ignominious Tweed ring virtually alone. Their campaigns led to a defeat of Tweed's Tammany men in the election of 1871 and his conviction for misappropriation of public funds.

During the 1880s and 1890s, the reform press embraced rural and labor issues. Agrarian activists publicized the situation of distressed farmers whose crops had undergone severe damage due to drought. The Farmers' Alliance was organized in 1877 to provide mainstream newspapers with information on the plight of the farmers, to establish a network for the agrarian reform effort, and to provide a legitimate means of opposing the dominant political and economic structure that was not offering adequate relief to farmers.[12] The Farmers' Alliance represented an attempt to carry the message of reform to the masses. Until this time, much reform journalism had reached principally those already actively involved in, or at least sympathetic to, the targeted causes.

The 1880s also saw the rise of a new style of journalism that Joseph Pulitzer popularized. He began his career as a reporter for a German-language newspaper in St. Louis, Missouri. After buying the struggling *New York World* in 1883, he transformed it into one of the nation's most vigorous, crusading newspapers. His "New Journalism" (which later descended into "yellow" journalism) featured lively copy while mixing crusading and sensationalism. It emphasized scandal, fraud, corruption, and crime to lure readers. Many contemporaries were critical of its excesses. Alden J. Blethen featured a tongue-in-cheek commentary on New Journalism in his newspaper, the *Seattle Times*:

THE NEW JOURNALISM

Ply your muck-rakes, thrust them in to the
fetid bogs of sin;
Lift them dripping with the slime of the
cesspools of our time;
Search through every social sewer, search for
all that's most impure,
Hunt for every deed of shame and for deeds
without a name
Let the eager public see all our moral leprosy.
For it is our daily stint the unprintable to
print;
'Tis the glory of our clique the unspeakable
to speak,
Run we through our printing-press myriad
miles of nastiness;
Smear with slime its league-long rolls—
Food, my master, food for souls.[13]

Because Pulitzer was able to secure a large circulation for his newspaper, he used it to carry the message of social reform to a broad audience. He attempted to educate the masses by printing news stories that were written to create excitement through impact. The news-

paper's use of color comics and sensationalism exemplified yellow journalism. Nevertheless, because stories in the *World* exposed the exploitation of women workers in sweat shops, the mistreatment of immigrants, the inhumane treatment of the insane, and the appalling conditions of city tenements, subsequent reforms followed.

In 1887, Pulitzer hired a relatively unknown newcomer to New York City, Elizabeth Cochrane ("Nellie Bly"), to investigate the conditions and treatment of the insane on Blackwell's Island as her first assignment for the *World*. Pulitzer was aware of complaints about the asylum from patients who had been treated there. Bly convinced him that she could successfully manage the assignment. A gifted actress, she was determined to succeed. She practiced her "madness" before a mirror so that she could enter the asylum undercover. Her talent and commitment paid off, and she was able to feign madness so successfully that four physicians found her insane. She was committed to Blackwell's Island without any difficulty.

After her undercover investigation of Blackwell's Island, Bly wrote two sensational stories that detailed her experiences. Since the *World* was in its crusading heyday, thousands of New Yorkers read her exposés. She described the cold, the poor food, and the inhumane cruelty inflicted upon patients. She claimed the asylum was a "human rat trap, easy to get into, impossible to get out of."[14] She told of a young girl who had been brought in sick and put up a fight against being confined to the asylum. One night, the nurses beat the girl, held her naked in a cold bath, and threw her on her bed. Describing the girl's fate, Bly wrote: "When morning came the girl was dead. The doctors said she died of convulsions, and that was all that was done about it."[15] As a result of Bly's investigative prowess and the sponsorship of Pulitzer's crusading newspaper, a grand jury voted for improvements for the facility as well as changes to its managerial staff.[16]

When William Randolph Hearst bought the *New York Journal*, he matched his paper against Pulitzer's *World* in a great circulation battle. Through the *Journal*, he pioneered color comics, Sunday supplements, and banner headlines; and he put a premium on ostentatious crusading.

Whereas Pulitzer and Hearst appealed to the masses, Edwin Lawrence Godkin, editor of the *Nation*, influenced the educated, sophisticated readers. He masterfully used irony and humor to attack societal evils and political corruption. He believed that the function of the newspaper was to critically analyze important current issues and not simply to cater to the masses. To this end, he denounced woman's suffrage, labor reform, and immigration.[17] In an editorial in the *Nation*, Godkin criticized the bourgeoisie for imposing their *noblesse oblige* "with supreme indifference to what anybody else thinks or has ever thought" and for having their own "trumpery prophets, prophetesses, heroes and heroines, poets, orators, scholars and philosophers, whom they worship with a kind of barbaric fervor."[18]

Another important crusading newspaper owner, Edward Wyllis Scripps, founder of the United Press Associations (later United Press International) and many other newspapers and newspaper services, stuck to his ideals of public service despite his financial success. The reform journalist Lincoln Steffens once said that Scripps "avoided other rich men so as to escape being one; he knew the danger his riches carried for himself, for his papers, and for his seeing."[19]

Cincinnati citizens respected Scripps because his newspaper, the *Post*, emphasized local political reform and tirelessly battled the city's political corruption. Although the *Post* became nationally known for its government crusades and its agenda for social reform, Scripps remained a humble man. He was proud, though, of his newspaper's crusading efforts, about which he wrote: "Of all the reputations I have won, that which pleases me most is the reputation I have won on account of the *Cincinnati Post*."

Scripps used his newspaper to uncover corruption and crusade for an honest municipal government. For a time, he even joined the Progressives, who engineered major political, economic, and social reforms from, roughly, 1900 to 1917. In his disquisition, "Is There an Unearned Increment?" he wrote: "The re-former is trying to construct a political government founded upon the first principles of Christianity. He is trying to produce a social condition based upon the same principle. He is always striving and always failing."[20]

Jacob Riis, a forerunner of the muckrakers of the Progressive era, was particularly instrumental in sparking reforms in New York City's worst tenement sections. Born in 1849 in Denmark, he emigrated to America when he was 21 and worked a number of odd jobs before becoming a police reporter for the *New York Tribune*, a job he held for more than 20 years.

During that time, he documented the squalid conditions of New York City's slums. He exposed graft, vice, crime, and severe poverty through both words and pictures. Often called "America's first photojournalist," he used cumbersome camera equipment to capture powerful images of human suffering and verify his written accounts of the dismal conditions he encountered.

Many of his photographs became part of his book *How the Other Half Lives*. With its shocking photographs of human misery, it helped motivate the massive renovation of Mulberry Bend, one of New York City's worst slums, including the construction of playgrounds and parks. Because his photographs and writings helped abolish horrific tenement sections, Riis became known as the "Emancipator of the Slums." In his honor, the Jacob A. Riis Neighborhood House for social work was established in the Mulberry Bend area in order to promote the spirit of reform he so tirelessly maintained. Theodore Roosevelt credited Riis for urging him in the direction of social reform when he reflected: "Looking back, it seems for me that I made my greatest strides forward while I was police commissioner, and this largely through my intimacy with Jacob Riis, for he opened all kinds of windows into the matter for me."[21]

The last decade of the 19th century and the first two decades of the 20th century were a period ripe with reforms in response to the various social problems that industrialization and urbanization caused. It was the beginning of the Progressive era, and there was a great ferment in American life as the country faced a massive new wave of immigrants as well as myriad social, political, and economic changes. In 1903, Congress established the Department of Commerce and Labor, and the United States obtained the Panama Canal. In 1905, the United States Forest Service was established to discourage the waste of natural resources.

Trusts, also known as monopolies, gained control over various businesses and industries. One of the most famous trusts was the Standard Oil Company, the enterprise that made John D. Rockefeller enormously wealthy and famous. As a result of their unprecedented power, trusts were able to set prices and determine the working conditions and wages of their workers without regard to the welfare of the worker or the demands of the consumer. Thus, as trusts unabashedly vied for power and control in the American economic structure, their harmful effects became increasingly obvious and a reform movement took shape to curb them.

In the political arena, President Theodore Roosevelt carefully cultivated his image as a "trust buster," and in the press, a group of journalists known as the "muckrakers" fought against social, political, and economic ills with stories that seethed with shocking and graphic details of evils in politics and labor. This type of reform journalism, also referred to as exposure journalism, derived its title "muckraking" from Roosevelt's derogatory charge that the writers of exposure articles were not unlike the "man with the muck-rake" in Bunyan's *Pilgrim's Progress*. Roosevelt, believing that exposé journalism was out of hand, explained at a dinner for the Gridiron Club, a group composed of newspaper correspondents, that the "man with the muck-rake" could look only downward and, when offered a "celestial crown" for his muckrake, would "neither look up nor regard the crown he was offered, but continued to rake to himself the filth of the floor."[22] Despite Roosevelt's criticism, whereas he managed only to regulate rather than "bust" trusts, the muckrakers were able to throw a spotlight on unchecked labor practices and corruption and, in turn, help create effective and strong regulatory measures.

The foremost forum for exposé journalists was *McClure's* magazine. Samuel Sidney McClure founded *McClure's* in 1893, and it became a platform for muckrakers and the leader in exposé journalism. The first muckraker to appear in *McClure's* was Josiah Flynt Willard with his series "The World of Graft," published in 1901. Later contributors included Ray Stannard Baker, Ida Tarbell, and Lincoln Steffens. These journalists were particularly adept at exposing the abuses and misdeeds that often came with monopoly ownership and substantial wealth. As for McClure, his early utopian view guided his career. He recalled in his autobiography that he once believed America was the "flower of all the ages—that nothing could possibly corrupt it" thus, he wanted to do his part "to help bring about the realization of the very noble American Ideal, which when [he] was a boy was universally believed in, here [in America] and in Europe."[23]

Ray Stannard Baker served as associate editor of *McClure's* from 1899 to 1905 and as editor of the *American Magazine* from 1906 to 1915. As part of his exposé efforts, he focused on labor abuses and right-to-work laws. His exposé "Railroads on Trial" helped motivate passage of the Hepburn Act of 1906, which gave the Interstate Commerce Commission authority to tighten regulations of railroads.

Ida Tarbell, the most prominent female muckraker, published her biographies of Napoleon Bonaparte and Abraham Lincoln in *McClure's*. Both features boosted the magazine's circulation and established Tarbell as a popular writer. When she set out to write another biography, one of John D. Rockefeller, she uncovered more than simply the usual biographical data. Her thorough research on Rockefeller and Standard Oil culminated in her powerful exposé "The History of the Standard Oil Company," which revealed the corrupt practices of some of the big corporations and strengthened the movement for establishing antitrust laws.

Tarbell's first article began as a passive sketch of an innocent industry but ended with Standard Oil and its allies involved in an attempted take-over. She described the ordeal of smaller companies that found themselves confronted by Rockefeller's organization. "The suddenness and the blackness of the assault on their business," she wrote, "stirred to the bottom their manhood and sense of fair play, and the whole region arose in a revolt."[24]

Lincoln Steffens, another contributor to *McClure's*, began his career with the *New York Commercial Advertiser* but later joined *Mc-Clure's* as managing editor. There, he wrote the articles that made him famous—studies of the conditions of American cities that exposed corruption in government, business, and labor.

"The most brilliant addition to *McClure's* staff in my time was Lincoln Steffens," Tarbell wrote. "He had made himself felt in the journalistic and political life of New York City by a fresh form of reportorial attack."[25] In his article "Tweed Days in St. Louis," which appeared in October 1902, Steffens lived up to Tarbell's initial impression. "St. Louis," he began the article, "the fourth city in size in the United States, is making two announcements to the world: one that it is the worst governed city in the land; the other that it wishes all men to come and see it."[26]

In 1934, two years before his death, Steffens wrote a letter to Sam Darcy of the Communist party of California in which he summed up his lifelong reform efforts as "following the stink of the trail of our so-called political corruption back up from the bad politics we deplored to the good business that bought and owns our bad government." The "makers of muck," he added, "in high jest bade me to report them," especially when they "jeered at me and my colleagues of the muckrake."[27]

One of Steffens' fellow muckrakers was novelist Upton Sinclair. He tirelessly tried to expose the evils in various industries. In his 1906 exposure novel, *The Jungle*, he uncovered the unsanitary conditions of the Chicago meat-packing industry. The book aroused public concern and helped create pure-food laws.

The Jungle was so powerful that meat consumption dropped drastically after its publication. Humorist Finley Peter Dunne, creator of the popular "Mr. Dooley" essays, could not resist poking fun at Sinclair's exposé in his description of the book's effect on President Roosevelt. Writing in his trademark dialect,

Dunne delivered one of his most effective burlesques: "Tiddy was toying with a light breakfast an' idly turnin' over th' pages iv th' new book with both hands. Suddenly he rose fr'm th' table, an' cryin': 'I'm pizened,' begun throwin' sausages out iv th' window."[28]

Concerning *The Jungle*, Sinclair wrote, "I aimed at the public's heart, and by accident I hit it in the stomach." But, he was cognizant of the good that his novel did and he later wrote, "I helped to clean up the yards and improve the country's meat supply. Now the workers have strong unions and, I hope, are able to look out for themselves."[29] But before *The Jungle* helped improve the working conditions in the meat-packing industry, before it helped gain the passage of the 1906 Pure Food and Drug Act, five publishers had declined it as "too shocking."

Jack London, the popular author of *The Sea Wolf*, read *The Jungle* prior to its publication and recognized its potential for raising public ire and launching subsequent reforms. In a 1905 letter to Sinclair, he praised the book. "Here it is at last!" he wrote. "The book we have been waiting for these many years! The *Uncle Tom's Cabin* of wage slavery!" He further compared Sinclair to Stowe when he added, "... [W]hat *Uncle Tom's Cabin* did for black slaves, *The Jungle* has a large chance to do for the white slaves of today."[30]

In 1907, a financial panic swept businesses when prices suddenly slumped on the New York City stock market. Businesses quickly blamed Roosevelt and his progressive legislation. They also focused their anger on the reform journalists, especially muckrakers, who they saw as the lethal enemies of business and industry. The president of the New York State Bankers Association lamented that the endless discussion of reform "in the present state of the public mind, causes unrest and disquiet."[31] In 1908, in a widely circulated letter from the Simmons Hardware Company, the founder of the National Prosperity and Sunshine Association, businessmen were urged to demand an end to reform measures since "[w]hat the country needs more now than anything else is a quiet time—an absolute rest from the agitation of politics, and assaults upon business."[32]

William Howard Taft, who followed Roosevelt as President, serving from 1909 to 1913, soon antagonized Liberal Republicans by firing Gifford Pinchot as chief of the United States Forest Service. Pinchot made sensational claims accusing the Department of the Interior of abandoning the conservation policies of the Roosevelt administration. He took his crusade to the press and fed muckraking journalists information in order to launch a campaign for conservation. He charged the Department of the Interior with selling land concessions too cheaply to water and power companies and with drafting illegal transactions in the sale of Alaskan coal lands. Even though he lost his position as chief forester, he was able to convince Liberal Republicans that the charges were true. Roosevelt ran again for the presidency in 1912, and Taft's dismal loss to Woodrow Wilson reflected his lack of support from both members of his own party as well as from the reform press.

Newspapers continued to crusade during the 1930s, 1940s, and 1950s for reforms that directly affected the middle class. In a 1936 campaign, the San Francisco Examiner won lower telephone rates for local consumers. A Detroit Free Press crusade in 1938 revealed that the Michigan Bell Telephone Company was discriminating against users of in-state telephone service. Subsequently, the Michigan Public Utilities Commission ordered the company to lower its rates.[33]

The turbulent 1960s saw many protests against racial injustice, and newspapers were often the voice of such protests. In Mississippi, Hazel Brannon Smith, a small-town editor, courageously stood up to white pressure as she relentlessly attacked racism in the Lexington Advertiser. When an appeals court overturned a libel verdict against her for criticizing a sheriff who shot a young black man, the White Citizens' Council organized an advertising boycott of her newspaper. Despite financial hardship, she remained steadfast in her crusade for racial justice. As a result of her activism, she won the 1960 Elijah Lovejoy Award for Courage in Journalism, the 1963 Golden Quill Editorial Award from the International Conference of Weekly Editors, and the 1964 Pulitzer

Prize. Upon receiving the Pulitzer, she said, "My interest has been to print the truth and protect and defend the freedom of all Mississippians. It will continue."[34] In addition to her attacks against racists, Smith also crusaded against corrupt politicians, slot machine operators, gamblers, and liquor racketeers.

The New Journalism of the 1960s was sometimes called "modern muckraking." Reporters for newspapers such as the San Francisco Bay Guardian and the Village Voice focused on uncovering corruption and establishment ills in much the same manner as the muckrakers of the Progressive era had done. Advocacy journalism, allowed in mainstream newspapers, called for various social changes and often took sides in political issues. But the underground newspapers and periodicals that sprang up as part of the tide of New Journalism spawned a whole new wave of contempt by the mainstream press. One of the leaders of the underground press, Ray Mungo, defended this limb of New Journalism when he remarked, "Facts are less important than truth and the two are far from equivalent ... for cold facts are nearly always boring and may even distort the truth, but Truth is the highest achievement of human expression."[35]

By keeping a watchful eye on the government, newspapers have often alerted the public to abuses of power in high places—those thought perhaps to be protected from the "watchdog" function of the press. But in 1973, when America was wracked by one of the greatest political scandals in its history, the repeated use of "Watergate" in the press charged Richard Nixon with high level corruption. Moreover, by operating within the code of objectivity, newspapers showed that it was the President who was corrupt, not the presidency.

The concept of objectivity caused many reform journalists in the late 20th century to tie thorough investigative reporting to their crusades in order to "appropriately" inform the public and yet still evoke reform. In 1974, John L. Hess, a reporter with the New York Times, set out to investigate New York City's nursing-home industry, a mammoth industry with a $1-billion-a-year price tag paid mostly by taxpayer money. He discovered "squalid, sometimes inhuman conditions and sinister financial manipulations."[36] His research revealed a scandal that brought the criminal indictment of 200 nursing-home owners for pocketing millions of taxpayer dollars for personal items. Hess' investigation also caused New York to revamp its nursing-home reimbursement system and establish a permanent prosecutor to handle nursing-home violations. Important was the fact that Hess created a crusade by reporting, for the most part, in the neutral and objective manner of contemporary journalists. Throughout his crusade, he never personally advocated solutions. Rather, he presented a problem built out of mounds and mounds of indisputable evidence.

The commercialism of the 1980s dampened some of the zeal for crusading. Reform journalism was a threat to the comfortable middle class. Newspapers like the successful *USA To*day with its "soft" news and short, bright, happy stories left little room for the sad tales of "modern muckrakers." Even so, crusading reporters have maintained the ability to fight their way through the fluff, the bureaucratic red-tape, and the expected standard of journalistic objectivity to aid the mistreated and bring down the corrupt.

Throughout the history of American journalism, crusaders have relentlessly pursued trails of evidence to uncover all manner of social, political, and economic misconduct. These journalists sometimes put their very lives in jeopardy in order to secure information that would help make life better for others. The work of crusaders like Lovejoy, Greeley, Riis, Tarbell, and Sinclair inspired improvements that, in turn, both benefited those who were unable to fend for themselves and brought to justice those who ingloriously abused the very foundations of democracy.

Selected Readings

Baker, Ray Stannard. *American Chronicle*. New York: Scribner's, 1945.

Daniels, Jonathan. *They Will Be Heard: America's Crusading Newspaper Editors*. New York: McGraw-Hill, 1965.

Dillon, Merton L. *Elijah P. Lovejoy, Abolitionist Editor*. Urbana: University of Illinois Press, 1961.

Filler, Louis. *Appointment at Armageddon: Muckraking and Progressivism in the American Tradition*. Westport, Conn.: Greenwood, 1966.

Fuess, Claude M. *Carl Schurz, Reformer (1820–1906)*. New York: Dodd, 1932.

Harrison, John M., and Harry Stein, eds. *Muckraking: Past, Present and Future*. University Park: Pennsylvania Press, 1973.

Howey, Walter, ed. *Fighting Editors*. Philadelphia: David McKey Co., 1948.

Johnson, Abby Arthur, and Ronald M. Johnson. "Away from Accommodation: Radical Editors and Protest Journalism, 1900–1910." *Journal of Negro History* 62 (October 1977): 325–38.

Johnson, David W. "Freesoilers for God: Kansas Newspaper Editors and the Anti-slavery Crusade." *Kansas History* 2 (Summer 1979): 74–85.

Nelson, Harold L. "The Political Reform Press: A Case Study." *Journalism Quarterly* 29 (1952): 294–302.

Nord, David Paul. "The Paradox of Municipal Reform in the Late Nineteenth Century." *Wisconsin Magazine of History* 66 (1982–1983): 128–42.

O'Kelly, Charlotte G. "Black Newspapers and the Black Protest Movement: Their Historical Relationship, 1827–1945." *Phylon* 43 (Spring 1982): 1–14.

Perry, Clay. "John P. Mitchell, Virginia's Journalist of Reform." *Journalism History* 4 (1977): 142–47, 156.

Sageser, A. Bower. *Joseph L. Bristow: Kansas Progressive*. Lawrence: University Press of Kansas, 1968.

Simmons, George E. "Crusading Newspapers in Louisiana." *Journalism Quarterly* 16 (1939): 325–33.

Turnbull, George S. *An Oregon Crusader*. Portland: Binfords & Mort, 1955.

Van Deusen, Glyndon Garlock. *Horace Greeley: Nineteenth Century Crusader*. New York: Hill and Wang, 1953.

Ware, Louise. *Jacob A. Riis. Police Reporter, Reformer, Useful Citizen*. New York: Appleton-Century, 1938.

Weinberg, Arthur, and Lila Weinberg. *The Muckrakers*. New York: Simon & Schuster, 1961.

Wilson, C. Edward. "The Boston Inoculation Controversy: A Revisionist Interpretation." *Journalism History* 7 (1980): 16–9, 40.

Notes

1. Jacob A. Riis, *The Making of an American* (1901, 1929; reprint ed., New York: Macmillan, 1937), 170.

2. John Campbell, quoted in Silas Bent, *Newspaper Crusaders, a Neglected Story* (1939; reprint ed., Freeport, N.Y.: Books for Libraries Press, 1969), 83.

3. Ibid., 105.

4. *Liberator* (Boston), January 1831.

5. Elijah P. Lovejoy, *Memoir*, p. 163, quoted in Merton L. Dillon, *Elijah P. Lovejoy, Abolitionist Editor* (Urbana, Ill.: University of Illinois Press, 1961), 69.

6. Horace Greeley, quoted in William Harlan Hale, *Horace Greeley, Voice of the People* (New York: Harper & Brothers, 1950), 160.

7. *Ram's Horn* (New York), 5 November 1847.

8. *National Era* (Washington, D.C.), quoted in Charles Edward Stowe, *Life of Harriet Beecher Stowe compiled from her letters and journals* (1889; reprint ed., Detroit, Mich.: Gale Research Company, Book Tower), 158.

9. Jenny Lind Goldschmidt to Harriet Beecher Stowe, quoted in ibid., 183.

10. Unsigned letter to editor of the *National Era*, 1 July 1851.

11. Abraham Lincoln, quoted in Ann Douglas, "Introduction: The Art of Controversy," in *Harriet Beecher Stowe, Uncle Tom's Cabin or, Life Among the Lowly* (1852; reprint ed., New York: Penguin Books, 1986), 19.

12. Quoted in Jean Folkers, "Functions of the Reform Press," *Journalism History* 12 (1985): 22–25.

13. Reprinted in the *Seattle Times*, 6 February 1897.

14. Nellie Bly, quoted in *Ishbel Ross, Ladies of the Press, The Story of Women in Journalism by an Insider* (New York: Harper & Brothers, 1936), 51.

15. Nellie Bly, "Inside the Madhouse," *New York World*, 16 October 1887, reprinted in Wm. David Sloan and Cheryl S. Wray, eds., *Masterpieces of Reporting*, vol. 1. (Northport, Ala.: Vision Press, 1997), 318.

16. Cited in Ross, *Ladies of the Press*, 51.

17. Quoted in Wm. David Sloan, Cheryl S. Wray, and C. Joanne Sloan, *Great Editorials*, 2nd ed. (Northport, Ala.: Vision Press, 1997), 115.

18. Ibid., 125.

19. Lincoln Steffens, quoted in George Seldes, *Lords of the Press* (1938; reprint ed., New York: Julian Messner, Inc., 1939), 77.

20. Edward Wyllis Scripps in his disquisition, 18 November 1908, quoted in Oliver Knight, ed., *I Protest, Selected Disquisitions of E. W. Scripps* (Madison: The University of Wisconsin Press, 1966), 377.

21. Theodore Roosevelt, "How I Became a Progressive," *The Outlook*, 12 October 1912, reprinted in *The Works of Theodore Roosevelt* (New York: Charles Scribner's Sons, 1932), XVII, 315–19.

22. Theodore Roosevelt, quote from Bunyan's *Pilgrim's Progress*, to the Gridion Club, April 14, 1906, quoted in Wm. D. Sloan, ed., *The Age of Mass Communication* (Northport, Ala.: Vision Press, 1998), 344.

23. S. S. McClure, *My Autobiography* (New York: Frederick A. Stokes Company, 1914), 265–266.

24. Ida M. Tarbell, quoted in Mary E. Tomkins, *Ida M. Tarbell* (New York: Twayne Publishers, Inc., 1974), 67. Also see Ida Tarbell, *The History of the Standard Oil Company*, I, 36–37.

25. Ida M. Tarbell, *All in a Day's Work* (New York: Macmillan, 1930), 198.

26. Lincoln Steffens, *The Autobiography of Lincoln Steffens* (New York: Harcourt, Brace and Company, 1931), 373.

27. Lincoln Steffens to Sam Darcy, 1934, in Ella Winter and Granville Hicks, eds., *The Letters of Lincoln Steffens*, vol. 2: 1920–1936 (New York: Harcourt, Brace and Company, 1938), 1050.

28. Finley Peter Dunne, "Mr. Dooley" essay, 1906, quoted in Elmer Ellis, *Mr. Dooley's America, A Life of Finley Peter Dunne* (New York: Alfred A. Knopf, 1941), 217.

29. Upton Sinclair, *The Autobiography of Upton Sinclair* (New York: Harcourt, Brace & World, Inc., 1962), 126.

30. Jack London to Upton Sinclair, 1905, quoted in Upton Sinclair, *My Lifetime in Letters* (Columbia: University of Missouri Press, 1960), 20.

31. President of the New York State Bankers Association, quoted in Robert H. Wiebe, *Businessmen and Reform: A Study of The Progressive Movement* (Cambridge, Mass.: Harvard University Press, 1962), 143.

32. Ibid. Letter from Simmons Hardware Company, 1908.

33. Cited in Bent, *Newspaper Crusaders*, 247.

34. Hazel Brannon Smith, quoted in Sloan, Wray, and Sloan, *Great Editorials*, 277.

35. Ray Mungo, quoted in J. Herbert Altschull, *Agents of Power: The Role of the News Media in Human Affairs* (New York: Longman, 1984), 203.

36. Charles J. Hynes, deputy attorney general, *Third Annual Report* (New York, 1978), prologue, quoted in Robert Miraldi, *Muckraking and Objectivity: Journalism's Colliding Traditions* (New York: Greenwood Press, 1990), 124.

24

The Press and War

Debra Reddin van Tuyll

When the United States becomes embroiled in a war, both the press and the military have their jobs to do. The military's job is to fight the battles and defeat the enemy, an undertaking that is—without argument—vital. The press has an important job also: to keep the American people informed about the war and how it is being conducted. Often, press coverage and editorial views have supported the nation's war aims. During the course of America's several wars, however, friction has arisen when the nation's military aims and the press' reporting or editorial actions seemed to have been in conflict.

The first major war involving the American colonies was the French and Indian War (1754–1763). It threatened nearly everything that was important to the colonists, and it became the focus of newspapers. Americans were tied culturally, social, economically, and religiously to Great Britain. Newspaper printers, like other colonists, believed that a French victory would disrupt all those connections and reverse the entire social order. Unlike many journalists in recent years, colonial newspaper publishers believed that their cause was one and the same as that of their country. Believing that France's military actions represented a grave threat, they encouraged the war effort. "*Friends! Countrymen!...,*" warned the *Virginia Gazette* in 1756. "Awake! Arise! When our Country, and all that is included in that important Word, is in most threatening Danger; when our Enemies are busy and unwearied in planning and executing their Schemes of Encroachments and Barbarity ... I need only repeat, *Your Country is in Danger.*"[1]

America's first war as an independent nation was its revolution against Great Britain. The press' role in the Revolutionary War (1775–1783) began even before the actual fighting did. Colonial newspapers were vital in fomenting the dissension that culminated in the Revolution. Newspapers of the day published vitriolic denunciations of the English crown and condemnations of its colonial policies. Tory newspapers, that is, those that remained loyal to the king, were loudly condemned, and many of their publishers were intimidated into silence. Colonists boycotted some Tory papers and hanged their editors in effigy. As the revolutionary spirit inflamed more colonists, they sought out newspapers to read the latest political essays. In this way, not only did the press stimulate the Revolution, the Revolution led to growth of newspapers. Colonists bought more newspapers, and more newspapers came into existence. In 1750, the American colonies had 12 newspapers. By 1775, that number had grown to 48. These 48 newspapers helped to unify 13 diverse colonies into a single nation with a single objective: to throw off the yoke of English rule. Newspapers galvanized opinion against Great Britain by crystallizing colonists' economic and political resentments.

Despite the demand for news about the issues leading up to the war and the war itself, once the shooting began at Lexington and Concord on April 19, 1775, information was difficult to come by. Editors had to wait for news to make its way to town from the battlefield, and this could take days or even weeks since news typically had to travel by horse or ship.[2] Another frustration for Revolutionary editors, and one that would also plague newspapers during the Civil War, was the shortage of raw materials, especially newsprint, that had to be shipped in from Europe.

Because of the slowness with which news was transmitted during the Revolutionary War, censorship was not much of an issue. News traveled too slowly from the front to be much threat to military security. Consequently, there was no need for press censorship, and the opportunities for conflict to arise between journalists and military officials were rare. General George Washington was so sure of the necessity of newspapers to support the Revolutionary effort that he donated some of the army's supply of paper to keep newspapers publishing.

The War of 1812 (1812–1815), America's second war, featured the same enemy, but the issues revolved around international trade, the English propensity for impressing American sailors into their navy, and the interest of some Americans in annexing Canada. The press, due to its politically partisan nature in this period, was divided in its support for the war. Hezekiah Niles, editor of the non-partisan *Niles' Weekly Register*, urged unity for the duration of the war, but most editors turned a deaf ear. This may have been because so many editors believed that the United States could not lose a war with England.

Newspapers sponsored by or loyal to the Republican party essentially favored the war and wrote stories to maintain public support for the conflict. Most Republican editors believed the British intended a bloody war to devastate the American frontier and to divide the country. The Federalist press, on the other hand, generally opposed the war, often even daring to do so openly. This opposition led the government to debate what to do about press criticism, just as the Adams administration had done during fears of a war with France in 1798–1800. That debate had led to the passage of the Alien and Sedition Acts. However, led by President James Madison, who would not countenance censorship, no official action was taken against any newspaper during the War of 1812. Public action, however, was another matter. Throughout the early and mid–1800s, the

public would mob newspapers that took unpopular positions on political issues. The worst example of a mobbing from the War of 1812 was that of the *Federal Republican* in Baltimore. Somewhere between 30 and 40 men completely wrecked the newspaper's office while a gathering of some 400 watched and cheered them on. The editor, Alexander Hanson, tried twice to restart his paper but was unable to do so because of public opposition.[3]

America's first war in which something approaching modern methods of news gathering and dissemination were employed was the Mexican War (1846–1848). Editors, however, continued to filter events through partisan lenses. Some, particularly abolitionist editors such as Benjamin Lundy, one-time business partner of William Lloyd Garrison, maintained that the war was a ploy by slaveholders to expand territory for their "peculiar institution," the South's favorite euphemism for slavery. Other editors depicted the United States as the unwilling victim of Mexican aggression, as having been forced to take up arms, while a few claimed that America had goaded the Mexicans into beginning the war by sending troops into a disputed border area in Texas.

News dissemination technologies sped up in the Mexican War, but the war was fought on such a distant front that it still took a long time for information to reach American readers. As a result, censorship—and the corresponding poor relationship between the press and the military—was not an issue.

This changed, however, during the Civil War (1861–1865). By then, newspaper production technologies, as well as information dissemination technologies, were sufficiently sophisticated and swift that injudicious reporting could influence the outcome of battles or campaigns. By 1861, hundreds of miles of railways and telegraph lines linked American cities, speeding travel and dissemination of information. Not only was the transmission of news faster in the Civil War than in any previous war, publication of war news was literally in the enemy's backyard. Soldiers and newspaper editors from both sides traded newspapers across the lines. It was a rare day that some Confederate paper did not carry stories from the *Cincinnati Enquirer,* the *New York Herald,* or some other Northern journal—and vice versa. Union General William T. Sherman, in a letter to his wife, admitted that he used intelligence gathered from Southern newspapers in planning his campaigns.

The Civil War was the first war in which the press/military conflict became a perceptible component of war. This is not to say, however, that conflict was universal. Some officers, such as General William S. Rosencrans, tried to use the press to promote their careers, and some reporters would "write up" officers—that is, feature their exploits in dispatches—for money.[4] Bad press/military relations, though, were more common, such as those between Sherman and the press. Early in the war, the Union general had predicted that the conflict would be long and bloody. The Northern press scoffed at this idea and called Sherman crazy. The press' accusations incensed the general—not that he had much liking for journalists to start with—and turned his dislike for journalists into an out-and-out loathing.

Sylvanius Cadwallader, a *New York Herald* correspondent who eventually became that paper's chief correspondent with General Ulysses S. Grant's army, agreed with Sherman. In his memoirs, he wrote that Northern correspondents were "generally snubbed everywhere. The fault is their own. They should dress decently, behave like gentlemen, resent bad treatment, never crowd in where they are not wanted." Cadwallader himself set a different standard. He vowed to take no freebies, to keep his interviews at headquarters short and to the point, and never to interrupt official business. He also made a point of not hanging around headquarters to eavesdrop. Consequently, he always found a warm welcome at headquarters and eventually became close to General Grant, which resulted in greater access to military leaders—and longer, more revealing, conversations.[5]

The level of military and governmental censorship during the Civil War is an often-debated topic. Certainly both the Union and the Confederate armies and governments tried, in varying degrees, to prohibit newspapers from publishing information about troop movements, unit strengths, or any other information that would give aid and comfort to the enemy. The need to control those types of military information was especially acute in the Civil War since Northern papers circulated in the South, and Southern newspapers circulated in the North. While both the Confederate and the Union armies technically censored their newspapers, the censorship rules were only spottily enforced.[6] Ulysses Grant, for example, believed he had too much to do to censor journalists. He left it up to reporters to decide what to report, but with the proviso that if they went too far in their reporting, they would be banished from the front. His general rule was that anything about previous operations could be published, but he disapproved of articles predicting future actions.

Where censorship rules were most strictly enforced, as in Sherman's headquarters, enterprising reporters often found ways around the rules. When the military banned the use of the telegraph by the press, the *New York Herald*'s Cadwallader organized a relay system of private messengers who could get dispatches from Virginia to New York in under 36 hours.[7] Until 1863, when the Confederate Press Association was formed, the Southern press usually did not have representatives at battles or even with commanders at their headquarters, the reporting of sensitive military information was less of a problem for them. In 1863, CPA Superintendent John Thrasher met with many of the South's commanding generals and was able to get them to allow correspondents to cover their commands. In the South, the peoples' extreme state rights position even made censorship constitutionally repugnant. At the end of the war, Confederate President Jefferson Davis was able to brag that he had not had to suppress a single newspaper during the entire war. U.S. President Abraham Lincoln could not make a similar claim.

Correspondents from the Spanish-American War (1898), a war allegedly "created" by newspaperman William Randolph Hearst as a means of selling more newspapers, have been criticized for exaggerating and romanticizing the performance of the American soldier. Newspapers outdid themselves in reporting the gallant and brave deeds of soldiers and turning blind eyes to American set-backs. As a result, censorship was lax because so much press coverage was positive. Reporting the war was complicated, however, because so much of the action took place in jungle terrain, making it difficult for reporters to cover it; and the stories that did get through were highly suspect because they were so favorable.

The same criticism can be offered for World War I (1914–1918). News was highly censored and provided mostly favorable coverage of Allied efforts. Censorship was so extensive that an army official even managed to censor a correspondent's expense account. When Daniel Dillon, an International News Service correspondent, tried to send in his expense account report with a $250 bill for entertaining General John Pershing, a press officer deleted the item. He did not want anyone to know the general had been spending time with reporters.[8]

The U.S. War Department set up a complex procedure just to weed out reporters who would be likely not to cooperate with the military in getting out its version of the story. To be accredited to report on the American forces in World War I, a correspondent had to:

1. Appear before the secretary of War or his designate.
2. Swear to report the truth, but not anything that might aid the enemy.
3. Hand write an autobiography, including an account of the correspondent's work, experience, character and health; what he planned to do in Europe; and where he was going.
4. Pay the Army $1,000 to cover his equipment and expenses.
5. Post a $10,000 bond to ensure he would "comport himself as a gentleman of the press."
6. Agree to wear a green armband with a big red "C" on it.
7. Pay the Army $500 if he planned to take along an assistant.[9]

Coverage of World War I tended to be highly patriotic and supportive. The press offered little criticism of official policy because there was general agreement that the war was necessary.

In World War II, though, correspondents often lived with the men about whom they were writing.[10] This led to a new kind of war story: dispatches about the men who were actually fighting the war. These stories fell into step better with military objectives of keeping up morale on the homefront—so long as they did not reveal too much detail about living conditions and troop locations. Some of these "hometown stories" were contributed by a new kind of correspondent—one who worked not for a newspaper or radio network, but for the military services themselves. Dar Levin, who served as a Marine correspondent, recalled, "We were the hands recruited to sing the deeds of the Joe Blows."[11] He and the other Marine correspondents were soldiers first and correspondents second. Their gear different only slightly from that of regular Marines, Levin and his fellow correspondents received a baby Hermes typewriter in addition to the regulation M-1 rifle. Like famed correspondent Ernie Pyle, Levin and his brethren were not at the front to tell the bigger story of the war, but to tell the story of "average Joes." Pyle and the other reporters who focused on this kind of reporting were criticized for not telling Americans the true story of what was happening in the war, but many historians agree that Pyle told the American people as much as he could without making them ill.

During World War II, correspondents generally went along with censorship because they thought it was in the country's best interest to do so. On a practical level, correspondents could only go to the front if they agreed to abide by censorship rules, so there were motives other than patriotism in agreeing to let the military examine dispatches before they were sent off. By and large, though, censorship during World War II was voluntary and based on a gentleman's agreement with the censorship office. A good example of how well the voluntary censorship worked is the atomic bomb story. Some journalists were aware that the bomb was under development, but they wrote little about it until August 6, 1945, the day Hiroshima was bombed. William Laurence, a *New York Times* science writer, had written a secret history of the Manhattan Project, but his editors never knew the nature of the project. As a reward for his discretion, he was allowed to go along when Nagasaki was bombed.[12]

During the Korean Conflict (1950–1953), one of the difficulties that correspondents had in getting out the story was in knowing what they could report and what was prohibited. This was so much of a problem that they eventually asked for censorship rules so they could be assured of consistency. In the early part of the conflict, there were no official rules of censorship, and this resulted in two correspondents being expelled for stories deemed helpful to the enemy. Actually, dispatches from Korea faced double censorship—they were censored at 8th Army Headquarters in Korea and then again in Tokyo. This led to significant delays in transmission and an eventual relaxation of the rules.

The American press and public were immediately supportive of President Truman's decision to send troops to South Korea to resist the Communist North Korean invasion. Soon after hostilities began, the *New York Times* praised Truman's action as "momentous and courageous."[13] Some media critics have complained that reporting from Korea, especially that of American reporters, was superficial and sensationalized. Others, though, have commended much of the reporting, primarily because many of the World War II–trained war correspondents were still on the job when the conflict began.

The Vietnam Conflict (1965–1973) was technically a war without any censorship. This was one reason why the military was so wary of the press.[14] Authorities realized the futility of trying to impose censorship regulations on reporters from so many different countries. In the early years of that conflict, strict censorship was unnecessary since the American people and media paid little attention to the war.

As the war escalated, so did press attention. Many Americans who had previously supported a war they thought their country was winning were suddenly confronted with stories that indicated U.S. forces were bogged down in a civil war somewhere off in Indo-China. Popular support for the war began to falter and

pretty much crumbled altogether as a result of the 1968 Tet Offensive. While that offensive technically ended in victory for America and South Vietnam, it came across on television as a major loss. TV coverage was critical to attitudes about the war effort because a whopping 60 per cent of Americans got their war news from television. The death blow for America's involvement in Vietnam came about a month after the Tet Offensive when CBS news anchor Walter Cronkite went to Southeast Asia to find out what was going on. He studied the situation and then put together a one-hour special in which he concluded America had no chance to win this war.

Since Vietnam, the American military has been involved in several police and peace-keeping actions. The police actions, such as the invasion of Grenada to rescue a group of American medical school students, and Panama, to capture Nicaraguan leader Manuel Noriega, have been of short duration. They were more like spot news stories than sustained war reporting. Consequently, there was little opportunity for much reporting, even if there had not been any censorship.

Although relations between the press and the military began to disintegrate during the Vietnam War, the real watershed, that is, the point at which press/military relations reached the lowest of the low, was during the 1984 invasion of Grenada.[15] The media dissatisfaction with the Pentagon-arranged press pool during the Persian Gulf War in 1991 did little to improve relations between the press and the military.

The military was reluctant to allow coverage of actions like those in Grenada and the Persian Gulf because of new communications technologies that allowed for "real time" reporting. Some scholars believe that the new technologies will lead to new kinds of military reporting—and to new kinds of restrictions on that reporting.[16] Nevertheless, the Persian Gulf War was probably America's best covered *and* worst covered war as a result of the new technologies. On the one hand, instantaneous communication was possible. On the other, it was not allowed because of military censorship. And because the censorship was so restrictive, war coverage devolved into lots of stories about the technology of the Patriot missile and behind-the-lines reporters reporting on their own courage.[17]

In the Persian Gulf War (1991), censorship began only after the war actually began. In fact, Americans knew, thanks to CNN, the war had begun a full 27 minutes before the Pentagon press office announced the firing of the first shots. CNN correspondents Peter Arnett and John Holliman and anchor Bernard Shaw reported live and uncensored throughout that first night of war in January 1991. Arnett was in the interesting position of being able to broadcast live from the enemy capital throughout the short war. His censors were not Americans but Iraqis who were intent on using his reports to gain sympathy for their side.[18]

One of the lessons the military learned in Vietnam—and applied in the Gulf War—was that if reporters don't go to where combat is occurring and don't have a chance to film bodies, they can't show the fighting or the bodies to viewers at home. During the Gulf War, the military completely controlled reporters' movements. They could not travel anywhere in the war zone without a military escort and could not talk to soldiers without military permission. This was particularly true of the pool reporters who got their slots only if they agreed to abide by military regulations. Some reporters took off on their own without military assistance, but they were few.

Pentagon censorship of the Gulf War has been called "unprecedented," and some critics have claimed that the military censors not only wanted to control the information that got relayed home, but also the perceived reality of events. Censorship, according to one critic, was primarily intended to make the reporting of numbers of casualties impossible.[19] Gulf War censorship was different from any other war's. Rather than requiring that completed stories be submitted to censors, as had been done in previous wars, censorship policies gave the Pentagon the power to determine what news people could and could not see.

This tension between what Americans want to know about their wars and what they need to know has continued to be an issue in contemporary conflicts and may offer at least a partial explanation for why Americans today so often favor press censorship. They may agree that a war needs to be fought, but many do not want graphic battle footage or stories brought into their homes. No wars have been fought on American soil for more than 130 years. The American public is used to watching war from a sanitized distance. Certainly during the Persian Gulf War, citizens supported the military action against Saddam Hussein (throughout the conflict, opinion polls showed from 75 to 84 per cent of Americans supported the war[20]), and while they thrilled to hear Peter Arnett, Bernard Shaw, and John Holliman reporting on the bombing of the enemy capital, they were often critical of journalists' attempts to get out of headquarters and report on what was actually happening in the field.

That contrast in the public's attitudes illustrates the dual-faced issue of the press and war. The effect of war reporting on public morale has been an enduring question since the Civil War. The war reporters whom later journalists have thought most highly of, however, are those who went beyond merely giving reports of battlefield action. They asked those troublesome questions that the military, and oftentimes the public, would just as soon not answer—questions dealing with issues such as the performance of U.S. forces, the wisdom of U.S. defense policies, the nature of national interests, and even the qualifications of the commanders in charge.

Selected Readings

Berg, Meredith, and David Berg. "The Rhetoric of War Preparation: The New York Press in 1898." *Journalism Quarterly* 45 (1968): 653–60.

Berger, Carl. *Broadsides and Bayonets: The Propaganda War of the American Revolution.* Philadelphia: University of Pennsylvania Press, 1961.

Braestrap, Peter. *Big Story: How the American Press and Television Reported and Interpreted the Crisis of Tet 1968 in Vietnam and Washington.* Boulder, Colo.: Westview, 1977.

Brown, R. A. "New Hampshire Editors Win the War." *Rhode Island History* (1939): 35–51.

Bussel, Alan. "The Atlanta *Daily Intelligencer* Covers Sherman's March." *Journalism Quarterly* 51 (1974): 405–10.

Cogswell, Andrew C. "The Montana Press and War: 1914 to 1917." *Journalism Quarterly* 21 (1944): 137–47.

Copeland, David. "'Join or Die': America's Press During

the French and Indian War." *Journalism History* 24:3 (Autumn 1998).

Costrell, Edwin. "Newspapers' Attitudes Toward War in Maine 1914–17." *Journalism Quarterly* 16 (1939): 334–44.

Harwell, Richard B. "The Creed of a Propagandist: Letters from a Confederate Editor." *Journalism Quarterly* 28 (1951): 213–18.

Humphrey, Carol Sue. "The Media and Wartime Morale: The Press and the American Revolution." Chap. 4 in Wm. David Sloan and James D. Startt, eds., *The Significance of the Media in American History*. Northport, Ala.: Vision Press, 1994.

Humphrey, Carol Sue. *"This Popular Engine": New England Newspapers During the American Revolution, 1775–1789.* Newark: University of Delaware Press, 1992.

Jones, Lester. "The Editorial Policy of Negro Newspapers of 1917–1918 as Compared with That of 1941–1942." *Journal of Negro History* 29 (January 1944): 24–31.

Knightley, Philip. *The First Casualty: From the Crimea to Vietnam—the War Correspondent as Hero, Propagandist, and Myth Maker* (New York: Harcourt, Brace, Jovanovich, 1975).

Marszalek, John F. *Sherman's Other War: The General and the Civil War Press.* Memphis: Memphis State University Press, 1981.

Nelson, Anna Kasten. "Secret Agents and Security Leaks: President Polk and the Mexican War." *Journalism Quarterly* 52 (1975): 9–14, 98.

Olasky, Marvin N. "Hawks or Doves? Texas Press and the Spanish-American War." *Journalism Quarterly* 64 (1987): 205–08.

Randall, James G. "Federal Generals and a Good Press." *American Historical Review* 39 (1934): 284–97.

Schlesinger, Arthur M. *Prelude to Independence: The Newspaper War on Great Britain, 1764–1776.* New York: Knopf, 1958.

Smith, Jeffery. *War and Press Freedom: The Problem of Prerogative Power.* New York: Oxford University Press, 1999.

Startt, James D. "The Media and Political Culture: The Media and World War I." Chap. 10 in Wm. David Sloan and James D. Startt, eds., *The Significance of the Media in American History*. Northport, Ala.: Vision Press, 1994.

Thompson, Loren. "The Media Versus the Military: A Brief History of War Coverage in the United States," in Loren Thompson, ed., *Defense Beat: The Dilemmas of Defense Coverage.* New York: Lexington Books, 1991.

Washburn, Patrick S. "The *Pittsburgh Courier's* Double V Campaign in 1942." *American Journalism* 3 (1986): 73–86.

Wilson, Quintus C. "Voluntary Press Censorship During the Civil War." *Journalism Quarterly* 19 (1942): 251–61.

Wyatt, Clarence R. "'At the Cannon's Mouth': The American Press and the Vietnam War." *Journalism History* 13 (1986): 104–13.

Yodelis, Mary Ann. "The Press in Wartime: Portable and Penurious." *Journalism History* 3 (1976): 2–6, 10.

Notes

1. *Virginia Gazette* (Williamsburg), 30 April 1756.

2. Wm. David Sloan and Julie Hedgepeth Williams, *The Early American Press, 1690–1783* (Westport, Conn.: Greenwood Press, 1994).

3. Carol Sue Humphrey, *The Press of the Young Republic, 1783–1833,* (Westport, Conn.: Greenwood Press, 1996), 90.

4. Sylvanius Cadwallader, *Three Years With Grant* (Lincoln: University of Nebraska Press, 1996), 3, xxii.

5. Ibid., 237, 12.

6. The Confederate Congress never adopted any censorship legislation and even required generals to rescind some of their censorship orders.

7. Ibid., 11.

8. Philip Knightley, *The First Casualty: From the Crimea to Vietnam. The War Corespondent as Hero, Propagandist and Myth Maker* (New York: Harcourt, Brace, Jovanovich, 1975), 131.

9. Ibid., 124.

10. Jack Stenbuck, ed., *Typewriter Battalion: Dramatic Front Line Dispatches from World War II* (New York: William Morrow and Co., 1995), with an introduction by Walter Cronkite, 4–5.

11. Dar Levin, *From the Battlefield: Dispatches of a World War II Marine* (Annapolis, Md.: Naval Institute Press, 1995), 12.

12. Loren Thompson, "The Media Versus the Military: A Brief History of War Coverage in the United States," in Loren Thompson, ed., *Defense Beat: The Dilemmas of Defense Coverage* (New York: Lexington Books, 1991), 31–32.

13. *New York Times*, 30 June 1950.

14. Miles Hudson and John Stranier, *War and the Media: A Random Searchlight* (New York: New York University Press, 1998), 104.

15. Rune Ottosen, *Media and War Reporting: Public Relations vs. Journalism* (Oslo, Norway: International Peace Research Institute, 1992), 27.

16. Philip M. Taylor, *War and the Media* (Manchester: Manchester University Press, 1998), 265; Major Melissa Wells-Petry, "Reporters as Guardians of Freedom," *Military Review*, February 1993, 31.

17. Robert E. Denton, Jr., *The Media and the Persian Gulf War* (Westport, Conn.: Praeger Series in Political Communication, 1993), 22.

18. Peter Arnett, *Live from the Battlefield: From Vietnam to Baghdad—35 Years in the World's War Zones* (New York: Simon and Schuster, 1994).

19. Margot Norris, "Only the Guns Have Eyes: Military Censorship and the Body Count," In: Susan Jeffords and Lauren Rabinovitz, eds., *Seeing Through the Media* (New Brunswick, N.J.: Rutgers University Press, 1994), 285.

20. Roper Center Review of Public Opinion and Polling, "The American Enterprise," *The Public Perspective* (March/April 1991): 74–77.

25

War Coverage

MANUEL O. TORRES

In February 1917, Floyd Gibbons received a new assignment: covering the Western Front in Europe. The *Chicago Tribune* bought him passage on a ship carrying a recently expelled German diplomat. He suspected German U-boats would not torpedo a vessel carrying one of their own officials and, hoping for a scoop, changed his ticket to the British liner *Laconia*. On a calm ocean on the night of February 25, his bargain paid off. Two German torpedoes sent the *Laconia* to the bottom and Gibbons to journalistic stardom. After his rescue, still wet and chilled to the bone, he cabled one of the most vivid and detailed dispatches of the war. "We watched silently during the next minute," he wrote of the *Laconia's* sinking, "as the tiers of lights dimmed slowly from white to yellow, then to red, and nothing was left but the murky mourning of the night...."[1] The story shocked Americans and provided one of the final acts that drew the United States into World War I.

Gibbons was not an ordinary correspondent, but his case is an example of the dedication and sacrifices of those who have covered wars throughout America's history. Most major developments in journalism can be traced through the history of war correspondence. Many communication technologies used for reporting since colonial times were developed to their maximum potential during wartime. Likewise, wars have stimulated the growth of the press, as when the Spanish-American War carried the sensationalist newspapers to their peak. The coverage of wars has contributed to characteristics that define journalism even today, such as increasing military control over the war press, the development of a critical press, and faster news cycles.

FRENCH AND INDIAN WAR, 1754–1763

News of military developments has appeared in American newspapers since their inception. The single edition of *Publick Occurrences* on September 25, 1690, reported that General Winthrop had led an expedition into French territories to push the French back to Canada during King William's War. Other early American newspapers also carried sporadic reports on the fighting between French and British troops. But public interest in war coverage reached its height during the French and Indian War, from 1754 to 1763.

The result of French and British claims over the disputed territory of the Ohio River Valley, the war captured the attention of American newspapers, for publishers and readers quickly understood that the future expansion of the colonies was in the balance. That understanding was made clear with the publication of Major George Washington's journal, which first appeared in the *Maryland Gazette* in March 1754.[2] The journal revealed the existence of a network of French forts along the Mississippi River, and the alliance the French had forged with Native Americans in preparation for the war. After its publication, public interest in the war rose, and publishers struggled to keep up with developments on the battlefields.

In reporting the war, colonial newspapers faced many difficulties. Communications between the colonies were slow and scarce. News from the battlefield often arrived weeks or even months after they had occurred. Nonetheless, on a few occasions newspapers were able to report on nearby events the day after. Publishers also had to produce their newspapers by themselves. The reporter as we know it today was non-existent in the colonial press, and newspapers were usually a one-man operation, with publishers writing articles and editing the contributions. News came mostly through private letters, personal accounts, other newspapers, and often gossip. Not surprisingly, much of the war coverage was inaccurate. However, accounts of battles also came from letters sent by soldiers and officers. The soldiers' proximity to the battles provided them with a great vantage point to report on the action accurately.

Often reports consisted of only a couple of paragraphs—all the information publishers could gather. When long accounts were available, they usually followed a chronological style, with the writer describing the weather or the terrain before mentioning anything about the battle. Nonetheless, the stories offered readers a glimpse of the carnage. Chronicling the battle at Fort Duquesne on July 1755, an officer wrote how "The General had five Horses killed under him, and at last received a Wound thro' his Right Arm into his Lungs, of which he died the 13th Instant." He continued: "Secretary Shirley was shot thro' the Head; Capt. Morris wounded; Mr. [George] Washington had two horses shot under him, and his Clothes shot thro' in several Places...."[3]

The coverage of the war had plenty of anti–French rhetoric and reports were filled with propaganda. Newspapers often published exaggerated accounts of the cruelty of the French and Native American enemy. A report in the *New York Mercury* told of how French and Indian soldiers took an American prisoner and, after breaking his legs, poured gunpowder into a cut on his back and lit it. Then they scalped him and put hot coals on his skull, finally killing him by crushing his head with rocks.[4]

With all their limitations, colonial newspapers made the war the most important story of the time. They covered all the war scenarios in North America, as well as fighting in Europe and Asia once France and England declared global war. The war coverage fueled the growth of the American press. More importantly, it prepared newspapers for the next big war story, the American Revolution.

WAR OF INDEPENDENCE, 1775–1783

The public's attention to the events of the French and Indian War would prove minimal compared to the demand for news about the Revolutionary War. High literacy levels and a readership genuinely interested in public affairs pushed colonial newspapers to publish as much news about the war as they could.

Newspapers had influenced much of the opinions and public attitudes leading to the growing resistance to British policies, though some publishers supported British rule. The differences increased during the war. Tory newspapers rejoiced with the early victories of the British-paid mercenaries. Patriot newspapers reported with enthusiasm the advances of the revolutionary militia.

Newspapers continued getting their news from soldiers' letters, officials' reports, other newspapers, or just gossip. Reports were often inaccurate or downright false. Newspaper coverage improved somewhat as the war advanced, but it still took days and sometimes weeks to get news from the battlefields to the most remote colonies. However, by the standards of the time news traveled fast enough to keep readers informed. The news of the surrender of British commander Charles Cornwallis at Yorktown, Virginia, on October 19, 1781, reached Providence, Rhode Island less than a week later, and was received in Boston the following day.[5]

As in the French and Indian War, printers faced many challenges in covering the war. Patriot publishers were forced on occasions to move their printers or close their newspapers as British troops overtook their cities. Tory publishers faced constant threats and a few had their printing offices destroyed. A few publishers participated in, or followed, the militia, becoming the precursors of the combat correspondents of future wars. Among those pioneers was Boston printer Isaiah Thomas, who was a member in the militia attacked by British troops at Lexington. "British troops, unmolested and unprovoked, wantonly and in a most unhuman manner, fired upon and killed a number of our countrymen, then robbed, ransacked and burnt their houses!" he wrote.[6]

WAR OF 1812

Newspapers did not change their methods of covering wars during the War of 1812, a conflict over the maritime rights of neutral countries between the young United States and Great Britain. Most reports were provided by letters from soldiers and military officers, and were rich in detail and description, though often dull in style. An American officer, after witnessing the American frigate *Constitution* defeat the British *Guerriere*, described the gruesome scene aboard the English vessel. "Many of the men were employed in throwing the dead overboard," he wrote. "The decks were covered with blood and had the appearance of a butcher's slaughterhouse...."[7]

Despite the irregularity of the letters, historians agree that reports during the War of 1812 were more accurate than during the Revolutionary War. Because some newspapers were close to the battles, they were able to carry first hand reports. These accounts were often reproduced by newspapers across the nation, which now could mail copies to each other for free thanks to the Post Office Act of 1792.

Despite the advances, news cycles were still much longer than they are today. Letters from the battlefields took days or weeks to reach their destination. Communications were so slow that the Battle of New Orleans took place 11 days after a peace treaty had been signed. But entrepreneurial publishers embarked on notable efforts to speed the delivery of news. Some eastern newspapers hired private pony express riders to carry reports faster

than the postal service. News of the end of the war generated a national euphoria. In New York, people launched to the streets to greet the news. "For two hours," wrote the editor of the *Evening Post*, "it was difficult to make one's way through unnumbered crowds of persons who came to see and to hear and to rejoice."[8]

MEXICAN WAR, 1846–1848

The Mexican War marked a major evolution in war coverage. The war coincided with the coming of age of the popular Penny Press, and it became the first war in which press correspondents carried most of the coverage from the fields.

The rise of the correspondent was possible because of recent advances in communications. A full decade earlier the postal service had adopted the pony express, and railroads were rapidly extending their tentacles across the nation. More importantly, the first public telegraphic messages were sent in 1844. All these advances, added to a public demand for news, made the war the first conflict to be reported comprehensively by American journalists.

New Orleans, then the fourth largest city in the nation, became the vortex of the war coverage. The *New Orleans Picayune*, founded in 1837, was the city's first cheap daily, and it became the leader of the war coverage. Co-owner George W. Kendall was one of a group of correspondents who traveled with Gen. Zachary Taylor. Kendall set up an express system to carry his reports to New Orleans and then to New York, where James Gordon Bennett's *Herald* reprinted the news. Riders took Kendall's writings from Mexico's interior to ports in the Gulf of Mexico. Steamships ferried the reports to New Orleans. From there, the news traveled through a relay of 60 riders to the southern tip of the telegraph system at Richmond, Virginia. By the end of the war, this network carried news from Mexico City to Washington in just 17 days, often beating the postal service and the military.[9]

A national public that demanded news of the war received such coverage with enthusiasm. Boats carrying the New Orleans papers north through the Mississippi often displayed special flags and were met at the ports by anxious readers. "The appearance of a boat coming up the river is a signal for a general rush to the Levee," a reporter in St. Louis wrote, "and then such pulling and pushing ... and reading of 'Extras.'"[10]

But the increasing press coverage also brought about military censorship for the first time in the country's history. The military established martial law in the war zones, restricting the movement of correspondents and suppressing some Mexican newspapers. The move received ample support among the mainstream American press, which was not affected. The *Baltimore Sun* wrote: "That the Mexican press must be crushed every reasonable man will at once understand."[11]

In spite of being partial, the coverage of the Mexican War convinced publishers that faster communication and war correspondents were good investments in covering conflicts.

CIVIL WAR, 1861–1865

The coverage of the Mexican War was just a preview of the avalanche of news content that newspapers published during the Civil War. With many of the campaigns taking place close to large cities, the public's demand for news was unprecedented. Growing readership and higher revenues allowed publishers to provide the coverage demanded, and daily newspapers flourished during the war. Improved communication systems sped the delivery of news, and the war correspondents established themselves as a permanent feature of the American press. Newspapers created their own teams of correspondents to cover the biggest news story since the Revolution. Estimates vary, but it is generally accepted that at any given time more than 500 reporters covered the war. The *New York Herald* alone had 60 reporters.

The reporter's job was not easy. Correspondents faced constant dangers, and several died in battles, accidents, or as a consequence of camp diseases. They had to travel far to reach the battlefields. Most were underpaid and overworked, and they were expected to get their stories first. Reporters would bribe railroad and telegraph operators to exclude other reporters or speed the delivery of a particular story. The pressure to be first was best presented in the admonition *Herald's* editors gave their correspondents: "In no instance, under no circumstances, must you be beaten."[12]

Civil War correspondents used a much more developed system of communications than ever before. The pony express and the railroads now extended over most of the nation, particularly in the North. More importantly, the country had expanded the network of telegraphic lines. Reporters telegraphed their stories back to their editors only hours after the battles, and sometimes even before the fighting ceased. Northern newspapers spent lavishly on telegraph bills, with the *Herald* alone doling out $1 million, an enormous sum at the time. Reporters competed for open telegraph lines, and some made operators punch out chapters of the Bible to hold the line while preparing their dispatch. The telegraph allowed newspapers to report the war with an immediacy never before experienced.

The telegraph is also credited with changing the style of war reporting. Because of the telegraph's high cost, reporters had to condense their copy. Civil War reports in general were much shorter and to the point as compared to the stories of earlier wars. The telegraph lines could also be lost or cut by enemy forces, so reporters often sent the outcome of battles first, followed by the details of the event. A larger account was mailed or hand delivered by the reporter. Such practices created the style known today as the inverted pyramid. The *Herald's* report of the surrender of Fort Sumter, published on the same day the action occurred, began: "FORT SUMTER HAS SURRENDERED. The Confederate flag floats over its walls. None of the garrison or Confederate troops are hurt."[13]

But the emphasis on speed and brevity had its drawbacks. Trying to beat the competition, reporters and editors were less concerned with accuracy. Some made up fantastic accounts even though they did not witness the fighting, and artists that missed a battle did not flinch at the idea of creating an "on-the-spot" illustration.

Nonetheless, most reporters tried to report accurately and also to convey a sense of what it was like to be exposed to the dangers and horrors of war beyond the battlefield. A southern correspondent wrote of a hotel turned into a hospital after Shiloh where "Groans fill the air, surgeons are busy at work by candlelight ... and the rain is pouring down upon thousands who yet lie out upon the bloody ground of Shiloh."[14]

Southern reporters faced more difficulties than their northern counterparts. The Southern press languished in a region economically depressed, with inadequate printing materials and many reporters enlisted in the army. Editors often had to explain that they lacked reliable news from the front. "For several days we have had no information of any particular movements, either in advance or otherwise," one wrote.[15] Just like colonial publishers had to escape British troops, some Southern newspapers had to flee from the Northern armies. The *Memphis Daily Appeal* changed location so often that it became known as the "Moving Appeal."[16]

Both Southern and Northern newspapers suffered systematic censorship. The fast reporting of the Civil War led officers from both armies to scan the press for information on the other's troop movements. Both the Union and the Confederacy established censoring policies early in the war, trying to keep military information out of enemy hands. Censors controlled the flow of news mostly by keeping a tight choke over the telegraph lines. Many army generals, particularly in the Confederacy, also excluded reporters from their campaigns or tried to regulate their reporting.

No officer in either army disliked journalists more than Major General William Tecumseh Sherman, who tried to hang *Herald* correspondent Thomas W. Knox for his report of Sherman's defeat at Vicksburg. Knox was court-martialled as a spy, but was found innocent of criminal charges. Still, Sherman expelled him from his campaign. On one occasion, upon hearing incorrect reports that three newspapermen had been killed, Sherman said: "That's good! We'll have dispatches now from hell before breakfast."[17]

By the end of the conflict, the Civil War had changed the expectations of the reading public. No longer was it enough to have the stories a few days after the action. From now on the public would expect to find the latest news in their newspapers the following afternoon.

INDIAN WARS, 1860S–1880S

After the Civil War, newspaper editors needed another story to placate a readership accustomed to the coverage of the war. The Indian Wars, the result of the growing western expansion, provided such a story.

With few exceptions, most newspapers had infrequent coverage of the Indian Wars. Unlike the Civil War, the public did not have much interest in the fighting, in part because it took place far from the cities in the east. Americans also had no great concern about the future of Native Americans. Most eastern newspapers returned to the practice of the Mexican War, covering the campaigns by reprinting accounts from local newspapers and from the Associated Press.

The few correspondents who accompanied the cavalry during the Indian campaigns faced unimaginable conditions. Communications were scarce and unreliable. Reporters had to ride 30 to 40 miles a day, go on half rations, suffer the heat of day and the chill of night, and fight in battles. Several correspondents were killed, including the first photographer who tried to take pictures of the action, *Frank Leslie's* Ridgeway Glover. In a letter to *Frank Leslie's* editor, a cavalry officer wrote that Glover's head was found "completely severed from the trunk, scalped. The body was disemboweled and their fire placed in the cavity."[18] The report was typical of the stories of the Indian Wars, though many of those stories were grossly exaggerated.

The biggest news story of the Indian campaigns was the Battle of the Little Big Horn on June 25, 1876, in what is now Montana. Lieutenant Colonel George Custer led more than 200 of his men to their death in an attack on thousands of Sioux and Cheyenne. The only reporter with Custer's regiment, Mark Kellogg of the weekly *Bismarck Tribune*, died in the battle. In his last report, prepared a few days before his death, he had written to his editors: "By the time this reaches you we will have met and fought the red devils, with what result remains to be seen. I go with Custer and will be at [sic] the death."[19]

The news of Custer's annihilation stunned a nation that until then had lazily followed the Indian campaigns. Public uproar was reflected in a *New York Herald* editorial: "If the Indian will not submit to civilization, let us cage him as we would a tiger or wolf."[20] The press romanticized Custer's attack as the "Custer Massacre" and "Custer's Last Stand." The coverage of the story, which portrayed Indians as savages and demons, galvanized public support for a massive campaign to subdue the Indians of the plains.

SPANISH-AMERICAN WAR, 1898

America's next war, the Spanish-American War, found a sensationalist press hungry and ready for such an event. The two greatest newspaper magnates of the time, William Randolph Hearst of the *New York Journal* and Joseph Pulitzer of the *World*, had been waging a long war of their own for readership. The Spanish-American War offered them the perfect battlefield to display their enterprising and sensational reporting.

The public's growing sympathy for the Cuban independence movement as well as rising imperialism in the United States fueled the demand for news of the war, and both Hearst and Pulitzer were ready to provide it. They received the news they were waiting for on February 15, 1898, when the battleship *Maine* was destroyed by an underwater explosion in Havana harbor, killing 266 American seamen. Both the *Journal* and the *World* trumpeted the story, suggesting that the Spanish government was responsible. The *Journal* even offered a $50,000 reward "For the Detection of the Perpetrator of the Maine Outrage!"[21] The Ameri-

can public received the story with indignation and the phrase "Remember the *Maine*!" became the battle cry of the war.

The sensational press invested heavily in covering the war. Hearst alone spent more than $500,000, and several other organizations spent a quarter of a million or more, in a war that lasted only a few months. The investment paid off handsomely. War coverage catapulted the sensational press to its peak, with circulation soaring. The New York press also sold stories and pictures to hundreds of newspapers across the country that could not afford to send their own correspondents, therefore influencing the national coverage of the war just like the New Orleans press had during the Mexican War.

Military censorship, relaxed during the Indian Wars, returned with force during the conflict in Cuba. Correspondents had their stories held or heavily edited. Weeks before Congress declared war, the military took control of the telegraph lines in Key West, Tampa and New York.[22] To evade censorship, the sensationalist press had already been chartering boats to carry the news back to Key West. The press flotilla became news in itself, with newspapers running merry features about their sea adventures. Hearst himself sailed to the fighting lines aboard his *Commodore* and captured a group of Spanish sailors whose ship had been sunk. The *Journal*, of course, published extensive accounts of the event.

In covering the war, reporters took center stage and many became celebrities. Publishers advertised their star correspondents' assignments, and often the correspondents' every move were as much news as the events they covered. The most renowned and flamboyant war correspondent was the *Journal's* Richard Harding Davis. His reports were full of visual imagery, rich in description and detail. Of the execution of a Cuban rebel, he wrote: "At the report the Cuban's head snapped back almost between his shoulders, but his body fell slowly, as though some one had pushed him gently forward from behind and he had stumbled."[23]

Correspondents also saw little distinction between the roles of reporters and participants of the war. The *Journal's* James Creelman made news by leading a bayonet charge against the Spanish garrison at El Caney, close to Santiago. The attack was successful, although Creelman was shot in an arm. Pinned to a hospital bed with heavy fever, he received a visit from William Randolph Hearst himself. The publisher commended him for his brave reporting and then proceeded to jot down Creelman's testimony for one of the most sensational stories of the war.

Such extraordinary war coverage can only be found during the rise of the "yellow press." But the war also marked the end of the era of the free-willing correspondents. Reporters continued traveling with the troops, but the following war would show that censorship was getting tougher all the time.

WORLD WAR I, 1914–1918

On Sunday, June 28, 1914, *Chicago Daily News* reporter Paul Scott Mowrer was walking down New York's Sixth Avenue when he spotted a newsboy selling an afternoon "extra." The paper had grim news: on a street in the Bosnian town of Sarajevo, Archduke Francis Ferdinand of Austria had been assassinated. Suddenly, Mowrer understood the future of Europe could be at stake.[24] The ensuing war, which eventually involved the largest American military mobilization since the Civil War, was comprehensively reported by hundreds of American correspondents.

Even before the United States entered the war, American reporters covered the action from both sides. The correspondents included more women reporters than ever before. They had to face the regular hardships of war and travel as well as the difficulties of competing in a male-dominated profession.

All correspondents found constant censorship and restrictions of mobility, and had to rely on official reports. The increasing restrictions were the natural result of more immediate reporting and a world linked by fast means of communications. In January 1918, the War Department issued regulations requiring reporters to receive accreditation from the military, and to submit to censors their stories as well as their personal and professional correspondence. The military also prohibited any soldier or officer from acting as a paid correspondent, a practice that had provided many reports in previous wars.[25]

On March 1, 1917, the country was stunned with the news of a secret German message inviting Mexico to join the Central Powers and make war on the United States. Intercepted in transit to the German embassy in Mexico, the message was released to the press. It became one of the biggest news breaks in the early part of the war and it was the final act that sent the United States into the War. When President Wilson asked Congress to declare war on Germany on April 2, 1917, he had the support of the American public.

World War I produced some of the best war reporting ever. Richard Harding Davis again excelled at giving readers back home a real sense of the events in Europe. In August of 1914 he reported on the Germans marching into Brussels as a large "river of steel," that revealed the "lost human quality" of the German army. "At the sight of the first few regiments of the enemy we were thrilled with interest," Davis wrote. "But when hour after hour passed and there was no halt, no breathing time, no open spaces in the ranks, the thing became uncanny, inhuman.... It held the mystery and menace of fog rolling toward you across the sea."[26]

For the first time, Americans were also able to see news of the war through the newsreel. The technology had become a popular media since its introduction in the United States in 1911. But news cameramen had more restriction than their print counterparts and quickly the military took control of the production of newsreels. Most of what Americans watched were carefully edited images intended as much for information as for propaganda.

By the end of the war, a new generation of war correspondents had experienced the biggest story of their lives. Many would remain overseas, bringing news from smaller conflicts in distant fronts in Asia and Europe. But the economic boom of the 1920s and the ensuing Depression of the 1930s attracted most of the attention of the American public. More than

20 years passed before war dominated news in America again.

WORLD WAR II, 1941–1945

December 7, 1941, started like any other drowsy Sunday morning at Pearl Harbor. Church services were under way in some of the battleships anchored there, and it was looking to be a clear and pleasant day. Then, at 7:55 a.m., a wave of Japanese warplanes materialized in the sky and one of the worst attacks suffered by the American military got under way. Two hours later, 18 ships had been sunk and more than 2,400 Americans killed. By the early afternoon, the reporters at the *Honolulu Star-Bulletin* had the day's edition ready. The main headline, in 72-point type, blared: "WAR! OAHU BOMBED BY JAPANESE PLANES."[27] Suddenly, the nation found itself on course to the largest world conflict of modern times.

A massive battery of correspondents covered World War II. The United States alone had more than 1,600 accredited correspondents, including many women correspondents. News of the war dominated the American media throughout the conflict.

For the first time, the nation could also hear the correspondents from Europe through radio. Listening to the news had become a national habit, particularly during the Depression. During the war, the radio broadcasts of correspondents like Edward R. Murrow brought Americans close to the action. Murrow provided "on-the-spot" accounts during the bombing of Great Britain in 1940, opening the broadcast with his well known "This is London." Families gathered every afternoon to listen to the war reports of the day. It was through radio that most Americans had heard of Pearl Harbor.

World War II also brought Americans the first images of television war reporting. Only a few thousand homes across the nation had television at the time, and the medium seldom appears in histories of the war's coverage. But American television stations were active during the war, with live coverage of major events from Pearl Harbor to V-J Day.[28]

News of the war included much more than just the battles on the front. Reporters followed the troops and covered the cities behind the fronts. Syndicated journalist Ernie Pyle earned a national following for his stories of the daily life of ordinary soldiers. An unassuming man, Pyle had an uncanny ability to find stories where others could see none. He wrote about what soldiers missed the most from home, about shaving in a war camp, and about the GIs' letters to their families. Through his column, people at home could sense what it was like to be a soldier. Pyle also wrote about how soldiers faced death. In a report on the death of a captain, Pyle described soldiers approaching the captain's body to pay their last respects. One "reached over and gently straightened the points of the captain's shirt collar, and then he sort of rearranged the tattered edges of the uniform around the wound, and then he got up and walked away down the road in the moonlight, all alone."[29] Pyle won the Pulitzer Prize in 1943. In April 1945, while surveying the post-battle destruction on a beach in Okinawa, he was shot by a sniper and died instantly.

The dropping of the atomic bombs on Japan would ultimately become one the most important stories of the century. At first the American press had little to print. The bomb had been developed in complete secrecy, and its first use was revealed only hours after by President Trumann. In the following weeks hundreds of stories were written about every conceivable aspect of the bomb. However, the military did not allow western reporters into Hiroshima until a month after the bomb was dropped.

The tight military control in Hiroshima reflected the increasing censorship correspondents encountered. President Roosevelt created the Office of Censorship in December 1941, which restricted the content of news. The military, experienced in controlling print media, ran into trouble with radio at first. Live broadcasts, such as Murrow's reports from London, could inadvertently reveal military secrets. The problem was solved by placing a British censor next to Murrow. If the broadcaster started talking about sensitive military information, the censor tapped him and Murrow changed the subject.[30] The government also appealed to the press to use voluntary censorship, and many newspapers collaborated. Journalists up to World War II would often comply with such requests from the military, but that would not last for long.

KOREAN WAR, 1950–1953, AND VIETNAM WAR, 1964–1975

Galvanized by the victory over Germany and Japan, the American press and the public supported the country's involvement in the Korean War and the beginning of the Vietnam War. Both conflicts would prove to be difficult wars for the United States. Vietnam became the greatest defeat of American troops in history.

The Korean War was one of the hardest conflicts to cover for American correspondents. The first reporters were constantly on the run, as North Korean troops overran the South's armies. Even when American troops were advancing, most of the front line reporters were armed. Communications were limited, and reporters had poor working conditions. After initial reports of military defeats, the military established a system of censorship. Although there were critical reports of the war, particularly towards its end, most of the coverage of the Korean War favored the military.

It was the Vietnam War that marked the final separation between the military and the press. Vietnam also divided journalists and public opinion as no other conflict had since the Civil War. Relations between the press and the government strained as the war grew unpopular, for the sympathetic correspondents of World War II were replaced by a cadre of accurate but critical journalists.

As in previous wars, the press coverage grew with American involvement. But unlike previous wars, correspondents quickly started questioning America's involvement. The turning point was the coverage of the 1965 Ia Drang Valley campaign in the central highlands of South Vietnam, the first major encounter between American troops and the North Vietnamese. The press reported the heavy casualties on both sides, quickly creating controversy between correspondents and military officials. The mutual distrust would only increase throughout the war.

At the heart of the controversy was a generational distinction among war correspondents and how they saw themselves in relation to the military.[31] Most World War II correspondents considered themselves to be above all patriotic Americans. Even if they had second thoughts about the war, they were "part of the team" and would not criticize the war effort. On the contrary, younger correspondents, many of whom had just covered the civil rights movement, distanced themselves from the military and the government. Their critical reporting is believed to have contributed to the disenchantment of the American public toward the war in Vietnam and toward the government.

Such coverage was possible in part because the press was able to report extensively in Vietnam. The government tried to control as much of their reporting as possible, keeping a tight lid on the number of casualties. But the military could not use outright censorship because Vietnam was not a declared war and it provided no legal base for censoring reporters. Instead, correspondents received credentials and the military tried to control access to combat areas. Reporters paid highly for such access. Forty-five correspondents died, and 18 were declared missing during the war.

The public's opposition to the war has generally been attributed to a new development in war correspondence: comprehensive television coverage. Television brought into America's living rooms dramatic images of massacres in small Vietnamese villages, and of wounded and dead American soldiers being loaded onto helicopters. The coverage changed the romantic views many Americans had of the conflict in Vietnam.

Despite their critical coverage, one of the biggest stories of the war was not revealed by a war correspondent, but by a dedicated reporter back at home. No other single event surpassed the impact of the news of the My Lai massacre, where American soldiers killed about 100 Vietnamese civilians. Correspondent Seymour Hersh discovered the details of the March 16, 1968 tragedy after months of interviewing dozens of war veterans. My Lai revealed the dehumanization of the military in Vietnam, and increased public opposition to the war.

RECENT CONFLICTS AND THE PERSIAN GULF WAR, 1991

CNN's correspondent Peter Arnett and his crew were too restless to sleep. For weeks they had been one of only two western news organizations left in Baghdad, waiting for the American bombers to start the attacks of Desert Storm. They had set up the cameras at their hotel room's windows in case something happened outside. It was January 17, 1991, and a clear night hung over Baghdad. Then, a sudden flash lit the sky. "The staccato crack of guns firing into the skies confirmed that the war had begun," wrote Arnett. "I looked at my watch for history's sake: 2:32 a.m."[32]

In a couple of minutes, images of the bombing of Baghdad were being televised into millions of homes around the world. For the first time in the history of war correspondence, the public was seeing the main battlefield as the action was taking place. The time lapse between an event and its news story, which reporters throughout history had been trying to reduce, was finally gone.

The Persian Gulf War's instantaneous reporting showed the future of war coverage. But the war also demonstrated a government and military control of the press like never experienced before. Reporters were limited to covering the war through the videos and briefings provided by the Pentagon. When reporters were allowed on military bases, it was as part of a closely watched pool of correspondents. Military censors edited their reports. Those who were offered access to action had to adhere to the strict terms of the military. Correspondent Christopher Hanson, who went into Iraq

with an armored regiment, had to accept the conditions of the regiment's spokesman, Captain Bob Dobson. "I can go only when Dobson goes and must never venture out by myself," Hanson wrote. "Reluctantly I agree to the terms. The alternative is sitting out the war in the rear. Captain Dobson is now my assignment editor."[33]

In spite of the censorship, the press showed remnants of the critical reporting that first appeared during the Vietnam War. As in Vietnam, such reporting came under attack. When CNN's Baghdad crew showed the effects of the American bombing among civilians, critics argued that the reports, which were censored by the Iraqi government, were contributing to Iraqi propaganda. Despite its critics, the press' response to the war showed the dawn of a new era in war coverage dominated by instant communication technologies and an ever more professional war press.

CONCLUSION

Ever since its beginnings, American war correspondence has reflected the major developments of the American press. In many occasions, war has accelerated such developments. A few of them include:

First, war correspondents have always pushed for speeding up reporting and the delivery of news. Publishers during the colonial wars exchanged newspapers to receive news faster. In the 19th century, communication developments such as the telegraph radically accelerated the delivery of news. The process was completed in the 20th century, where breaking news reached the public at the moment they were occurring. The shrinking of the news cycle, from days and weeks during the French and Indian War, to hours during the Civil War, to instantaneous broadcast during the Persian Gulf War, has also added pressure to the job of the war correspondent. Errors have not been eliminated, but modern correspondents have a stronger emphasis on accuracy than ever before.

Second, the effectiveness of war correspondents has motivated the government and the military to increase their censorship of war news. From the earliest efforts at censorship during the Mexican War, to the total control of military scenarios of the post–Vietnam era, the military has become more effective at restricting the news media. The control has not come without criticism, both from the press and the public.

Finally, the war correspondent has risen as one of the most important members of the American press, although the job is still dangerous. The history of the field shows that some of the first American reporters covered wars. As the press evolved, the war correspondent became a celebrity in the Civil War and later conflicts. Today, some correspondents, particularly in television, are household names and their professional stature is among the highest in the profession.

Selected Readings

Andrews, J. Cutler. *The North Reports the Civil War.* Pittsburgh: University of Pittsburgh Press, 1955.

Andrews, J. Cutler. *The South Reports the Civil War.* Princeton, N.J.: Princeton University Press, 1970.

Braestrap, Peter. *Big Story: How the American Press and Television Reported and Interpreted the Crisis of Tet 1968 in Vietnam and Washington.* Boulder, Colo.: Westview, 1977.

Brown, Charles H. *The Correspondents' War.* New York: Scribner's, 1967.

Bullard, Frederic Lauriston. *Famous War Correspondents.* Boston: Little, Brown, 1914.

Corbalis, Kathy J. "'Atomic Bill' Laurence: He Reported the Birth of the A-Bomb." *Media History Digest* 5, 3 (1985): 9–11, 28–30.

Crozier, Emmet. *American Reporters on the Western Front, 1914–1918.* New York: Oxford University Press, 1959.

Crozier, Emmet. *Yankee Reporters, 1861–65.* New York: Oxford University Press, 1956.

Desmond, Robert W. *Tides of War: World News Reporting, 1931–1945.* Iowa City: University of Iowa Press, 1984.

Gilbert, Douglas. *Floyd Gibbons, Knight of the Air.* New York: McBride, 1930.

Goldsmith, Adolph O. "Reporting the Civil War: Union Army Press Relations." *Journalism Quarterly* 33 (1956): 478–87.

Knight, Oliver. *Following the Indian Wars: The Story of the Newspaper Correspondents Among the Indian Campaigns.* Norman: University of Oklahoma Press, 1960.

Mander, Mary S. "American Correspondents During World War II: Common Sense as a View of the World." *American Journalism* 1:1 (1983): 17–30.

Mander, Mary. "Pen and Sword: Problems of Reporting the Spanish-American War." *Journalism History* 9 (1982): 2–9, 28.

Mathews, Joseph J. *Reporting the Wars.* Minneapolis: University of Minnesota Press, 1957.

May, Antoinette. *Witness to War: A Biography of Marguerite Higgins.* New York: Beaufort, 1983.

Mott, Frank Luther. "The Newspaper Coverage of Lexington and Concord." *New England Quarterly* 17 (1944): 489–505.

Pratte, Alf. "The Honolulu Star-Bulletin and the 'Day of Infamy,'" *American Journalism* 5:1 (1988): 5–13.

Reilly, Tom. "The War Press of New Orleans: 1846–1848." *Journalism History* 13:3–4 (1986): 86–95.

Sharp, Eugene W. "Cracking the Media Censorship in 1899 and 1900." *Journalism Quarterly* 20 (1943): 281–85.

Sloan, Wm. David, et. al. *The Great Reporters: An Anthology of News Writing at Its Best.* Northport, Ala.: Vision Press, 1992.

Starr, Louis M. *Bohemian Brigade: Civil War Newspapermen in Action.* New York: Knopf, 1954.

Stein, M. L. *Under Fire: The Story of American War Correspondents.* New York: Julian Messner, 1968.

Stevens, John D. "From the Back of the Foxhole: Black Correspondents in World War II." *Journalism Monographs* 27 (1973).

Villard, Henry. "Army Correspondence: Its History." *The Nation*, 1 (July 20, July 27, Aug. 3, 1865), 79ff, 114ff, 144ff.

Wagner, Lilya. *Women War Correspondents of World War II.* Westport, Conn.: Greenwood, 1989.

Weisberger, Bernard A. *Reporters for the Union.* Boston: Little, Brown, 1953.

Notes

1. *Chicago Tribune*, 26 February 1917.

2. George Washington's Journal, *Maryland Gazette* (Annapolis), 21 and 28 March 1754. Available at earlyamerica.com/earlyamerica/milestones/journal/journaltext.html

3. *New York Mercury*, 9 August 1755.

4. *New York Mercury*, 30 August 1756.

5. "Cornwallis TAKEN!" broadside (Boston) 26 October 1781, reprinted in Wm. David Sloan and James D. Startt, eds., *The Media in America: A History*, 4th ed. (Northport, Ala.: Vision Press, 1999), 63.

6. Isaiah Thomas, *Massachusetts Spy*, 3 May 1775.

7. Report of Captain Orme, reprinted in Henry S. Commager and Allan Nevins, eds., *Witness to America: A Documentary History of the United States from Its Discovery to Modern Times* (New York: Barnes & Noble, 1939), 235–37.

8. Quoted in Commager and Nevins, ibid., 248.

9. Tom Reilly, "The War Press of New Orleans: 1846–1848," *Journalism History* 13:3–4 (1986): 93.

10. *New Orleans Delta*, 3 June 1846.

11. *Baltimore Sun*, 9 October 1847.

12. Albert Richardson to Sidney Gay, 11 April 1863, quoted in Louis M. Starr, *Bohemian Brigade: Civil War Newspapermen in Action* (New York: Knopf, 1954), 61.

13. *New York Herald*, 14 April 1861.

14. *Macon Journal & Messenger*, 23 April 1862, quoted in Cal M. Logue et. al., "The Press under Pressure: How Georgia's Newspapers Responded to the Civil War Constraints," *American Journalism* 15:1 (1998): 22.

15. *Macon Journal & Messenger*, 16 July 1862.

16. M. L. Stein, *Under Fire: The Story of American War Correspondents* (New York: Julian Messner, 1968), 19.

17. Stephen W. Sears, "The First News Blackout," *American Heritage* 36:4 (June-July 1985): 30.

18. Samuel L. Peters to *Frank Leslie's* publisher, printed in *Frank Leslie's Illustrated Newspaper*, 27 October 1866, 94.

19. *Bismarck Tribune*, 12 July 1876.

20. *New York Herald*, 9 July 1876.

21. *New York Journal*, 17 February 1898.

22. Charles H. Brown, "Press Censorship in the Spanish-American War," *Journalism Quarterly* 42:4 (1965): 581.

23. *New York Journal*, 20 January 1897, reprinted in Wm. David Sloan and Cheryl S. Wray, *Masterpieces of Reporting*, 2 vols. (Northport, Ala.: Vision Press, 1997), 1:72–77.

24. Paul Scott Mowrer, *The House of Europe* (Boston: Houghton Mifflin Co., 1945), 217–21.

25. Cedric Larson, "Censorship of Army News During the World War, 1917–1918," *Journalism Quarterly* 17:4 (1940): 314.

26. *London News Chronicle*, 23 August 1914, reprinted in Wm. David Sloan et. al., *The Great Reporters: An Anthology of News Writing at Its Best* (Northport, Ala.: Vision Press, 1992), 73–75.

27. *Honolulu Star-Bulletin*, 7 December 1941.

28. James A. Von Schilling, "Television During World War II: Homefront Service, Military Success," *American Journalism* 12:3 (1995): 290.

29. Ernie Pyle, ["The Death of Captain Henry Waskow"], Scripps Howard Newspaper Alliance, 10 January 1944, reprinted in Sloan and Wray, *Masterpieces of Reporting*, 1:202–04.

30. John Chancellor, "From Normandy to Grenada: A Veteran Reporter Looks Back," *American Heritage* 36:4 (1985): 32.

31. Harry D. Marsh, "The Media in Transition, 1945–1974," chap. 23 in Sloan and Startt, *The Media in America*, 445–46.

32. Peter Arnett, *Live from the Battlefield: From Vietnam to Baghdad, 35 Years in the World's War Zones* (New York: Simon & Schuster, 1994), 365.

33. Christopher Hanson, "What We Saw, What We Learned," *Columbia Journalism Review* (May-June 1991).

26

Foreign Correspondence
CATHERINE CASSARA

From the 1700s, colonial American newspapers carried stories of piracy, diplomacy, crime and the doings of European royalty. Those early stories were not deliberately produced for American audiences, but they nonetheless bear an eerie similarity to world news briefs found in modern newspapers. This chapter surveys the development of American foreign correspondence from the early days of haphazard reporting sent home by genteel travelers, to the days of swashbuckling adventure, to the modern, high-tech profession, providing news of the world to the citizens of the world's last global power.

EARLY FOREIGN NEWS COVERAGE

Colonial editors gladly filled their newspapers with stories lifted verbatim from letters, dispatches, and European newspapers. After the Revolution general interest in events beyond the country's borders was at low ebb. Early Americans were eager for news from elsewhere heightened during periods of diplomatic or military activity, even though the news was often old by the time they got it. It is a familiar story that Americans waited seven weeks to receive word of the signing of the treaty of Ghent, which ended the War of 1812—two weeks before the battle of New Orleans was fought. It took the penny press, news competition among city dailies, and the advent of new technologies to put foreign news back on the American news budgets.

Penny press publisher James Gordon Bennett was the first American editor to make a commitment to expand foreign news coverage. The advent of transatlantic steamers in 1838 meant that voyages could be cut to several weeks. Bennett was among the travelers on the return leg of the first European steamship's transatlantic voyage. While abroad, he sent the *New York Herald* chatty letters, news stories, and editorials.[1] He also retained the services of correspondents in five major cities to keep the paper appraised of events in Europe after his return home.

Foreign correspondence takes its name from the letters that travelers sent home describing the exotic sights and experiences encountered during their foreign travels. The letters sometimes took on more serious subjects, like the letters Margaret Fuller sent Horace Greeley's *New York Tribune* from Britain in 1856. She wrote variously of the conditions of the poor and the British literary scene. She is remembered best as a journalist, however, for her accounts of the Italian struggle for independence. She met Italian activists in London and followed them to Italy. Committed to the cause of Italian independence, she mixed political and journalistic work, and eventually married an Italian involved in the struggle. Events in Italy had particular salience for their American readers because Italy was a popular destination for the British elite and Anglophile Americans. Educated women had opportunities from the beginning to do foreign reporting for newspapers that would not have allowed them to enter their newsrooms.[2]

One of the first conflicts on foreign soil to get notable and timely attention in American newspapers was the Mexican War of 1846–1848, which brought to a head the dispute between the United States and Mexico over who would lay claim to Texas. Coverage of the war was significant for several reasons. First, New Orleans publisher George W. Kendall took great pains to get the story back to his *Picayune*, and from there to the papers on the East Coast. Using a network of couriers and boats, he routinely beat both the competition and the official U.S. military dispatches. Second, it cost the large Eastern dailies a lot of money to bring the news from Mexico over a 4,000-mile route that included express riders, steamboats, railroads, and telegraphs. As a result, the following year the owners of five fiercely competitive New York newspapers formally agreed to share the cost of gathering and transmitting news, which they would use and then sell to other newspapers. The organization that resulted eventually evolved into the Associated Press.

Fuller, Kendall, and others wrote about military action, but British journalist William Howard Russell was the first modern war correspondent. Assigned to go to the Crimea for the *Times* of London in 1855, he provided stark coverage of the conduct of the war, battlefield conditions, and the lack of facilities to treat wounded British soldiers. Use of the telegraph meant that his accounts quickly reached London, where they provoked a public uproar and forced changes in the British government's conduct of the war. Russell was also on hand to cover the U.S. Civil War, but American reporters like George W. Smalley and his team of journalistic veterans of the Civil War introduced the concept of breaking news coverage to Europe.

Smalley traveled to Europe for the *New York Tribune* in 1866 and returned to New York to recommend that the paper establish a London bureau to direct coverage of the continent. His bosses agreed, sending him back across the Atlantic in 1867. As a result, the *Tribune's* European operation was up and running in 1870 in time for the outbreak of the Franco-Prussian War. Smalley's European operation produced coverage that was more streamlined and objective than was generally the norm. Some of the stories his staff produced were shared with an alliance of British newspapers.[3]

In 1870 the European news services signed an agreement with the AP that gave each exclusive access to the products of the others. Each service got exclusive rights to cover the parts of the globe dominated by its country's interests. Thus, the AP would cover the United States, supplying news to the French Havas, the British Reuters, and the German Wolff agencies, while the AP would receive all of its foreign news from those services. The British, who controlled supplies of a critical resource needed to complete international cables, dominated the global cable network. The cartel later expanded to include the Italian and Russian services, dominating international news coverage for the next 50 years.

TRAVELING COMMISSIONERS

The development of formalized foreign correspondence coincided with the rise of the modern nation state and was facilitated by the technological developments of the second industrial revolution. American publishers, recognizing the value of foreign news, now wanted something the wires could not provide—the work of personality journalists who could provide readers with scintillating stories and whose adventures themselves made good copy. For their traveling commissioners, or "specials," they hired well-known writers or college educated men with a literary bent. The reporters who covered the events of the Spanish-American War epitomized this type, and it is important to note that they were not solely foreign correspondents. The New York editors were just as likely to send their star correspondents off to the gold fields of Alaska as they were to send them to Greece, if it sounded like a lively story.

A lot of attention has been paid to the Spanish-American War, in part because of the controversial role in the drama played by New York newspapers, particularly Joseph Pulitzer's *World* and William Randolph Hearst's *Journal*.

Engaged in a circulation war at home, the duo pushed long and hard for American action in Cuba, providing inflammatory coverage calculated to whip up public sentiment against Spain. This sensational campaign epitomized the practice of yellow journalism. The most familiar episode in the tale was the coverage the papers gave to the sinking of the U.S.S. *Maine* in Havana Harbor. Sent south by editors hoping for anti–Spanish stories, the correspondents cooperated by sending home elaborately inflated stories, which were often further embellished in New York.

Coverage of the Spanish-American War was an interesting landmark in foreign coverage for reasons that go beyond yellow journalism. The New York editors invested a lot of time, effort, and talent in covering the story. Young writers attracted by the excitement of the story had the chance to mature in the course of discovering and reporting the conditions faced by Cuban nationals. Writers sent to dig up sensational stories also spent time honing their understanding of military strategies. Star correspondents like Stephen Crane and Richard Harding Davis sent long ardent essays north by mail, and while lesser writers were restricted to what they could get on the cable, their output was nonetheless elaborate by modern standards. Further, the correspondents were openly partisan about the causes they covered and had few qualms about acting as combatants. Sylvester "Harry" Scovel of the *New York World*, one of the most respected journalists covering the war, acted throughout as a spy for the U.S. Navy.[4]

With the end of the Spanish-American War, a corps of hardy individualists struck off to travel around the world to cover the series of wars and revolutions that ran end to end right up to the outbreak of World War I. American newspapers made some deliberate choices of what to cover and what not to (for example, they covered both sides of the Sino-Japanese War but ignored the Italo-Turkish War), but the correspondents made many of these decisions themselves, based on their personal interests.

FOREIGN ADVENTURES GIVE WAY TO SERIOUS REPORTING

Several factors influenced the development of foreign news reporting in the first decades of the new century. The United States had become an imperial power as the result of its victory over Spain. And, while many Americans were slow to recognize it, this new role would demand greater global involvement. At the same time, American businessmen were increasingly involved in foreign markets. As a result, Americans were traveling more and paying more attention to events abroad. American editors and their foreign correspondents spent the first three decades of the century sorting out all these interests and negotiating what should constitute foreign news.

Reporters at home were more than a little suspicious of their paper's staff abroad, who had the alarming tendency to affect "mustaches, spats and canes," wrote Paul Scott Mowrer.[5] Headed to Paris to take over the *Chicago Daily News* bureau in 1910, Mowrer, too, adopted the affectations as a camouflage necessary to deflect the attentions of eager Parisian tour guides. Like others who found their way to the continent over the next several decades, Mowrer was drawn to Europe by literary ambitions and the romance of life in Paris.

Edward Price Bell ran the *Daily News* operations in Europe from London and supervised Mowrer's work. At first that job entailed keeping the newspaper apprised of which wealthy Chicagoans were traveling on the continent and giving wealthy visitors tours of the Parisian night life. With Bell's support, however, Mowrer eventually carved out a broader mandate for himself and started covering Europe. In 1912 he traveled to the Balkans and wrote a book about the national and ethnic forces at work in the region. When Austrian Archduke Ferdinand was assassinated in 1917, Mowrer quickly guessed what was coming and cut short a visit to the United States to return to Europe to cover the growing conflict.

The start of the Great War found correspondents like Richard Harding Davis at the front in Belgium in conditions reminiscent of the Spanish-American War. By the end of the war, however, the nature of war reporting had changed irrevocably. Correspondents were now required to seek military accreditation to get anywhere near the action. They rode in military vehicles with military escorts and were clothed in standard issue uniforms. As a result, the news was no longer shaped by individual exploit as much as it was managed through official military communiqués.

Correspondents for a wide range of American newspapers and magazines arrived in Europe hoping to see action, but their efforts were hampered. American neutrality meant that U.S. correspondents were at the mercy of foreign governments that saw no particular reason to give any journalists access to the front. Now and then they were given group tours of the war zones in Belgium, but even then they were not allowed near the front. Ironically, women journalists had a slight advantage since they often worked as nurses for the Red Cross behind the lines.[6] Correspondents based in Paris like Mowrer had it a little easier if they were creative. They could supplement their own observations with those of expatriates and French friends who were not adverse to trying to cover history as it happened.

The arrival of the American Expeditionary Force in Britain in 1917 eased the access for male correspondents, American and Allied alike, but did not help many women. The only woman accredited to cover the AEF was Peggy Hull, who had covered U.S. Army troops for two years in Mexico. When she finally got formal accreditation in 1918, it only allowed her to cover Allied troops sent to support White Russians in their civil war against the Bolsheviks.[7]

Given the nature of the arrangement the AP had with the international news cartel and the British dominance of cable facilities, it is little wonder that Americans found a pro–British slant to the coverage of the Great War. Publishers and editors who could afford it sent more of their own correspondents abroad, while others turned to wire services such as United Press, the International News Service, and supplemental services such as the North American Newspaper Alliance.

FOREIGN CORRESPONDENCE MATURES

The period between the wars provides a fascinating study in the development of foreign correspondence.[8] Many of the journalists on hand for the war stayed on to cover the peace negotiations and the efforts to establish the League of Nations. They also helped to train a new generation of reporters who fanned out around the world and watched as events unfolding in Europe and Asia brought the world back to the brink of war.[9] The journalists saw the world in a way most Americans could not and were among the first to recognize the importance of United States' role in global politics. At a time when many Americans were isolationists, they began to argue for the resources—financial support, reporting staff, and space in the publications—to do a better job of covering foreign news, as the first step in a larger global role.

Three new types of men and women came to foreign correspondence in the years after the end of the Great War. The first group was in place in Europe for personal reasons or had just arrived as the war ended. Eager to gain seasoning, they worked with or for the veteran correspondents like Paul Scott Mowrer, George Seldes, and others who had covered the war. Others, still teenagers or college students when the war ended, hurried to see the world for themselves. College educated and often trained as journalists, they were often eager to leave a United States struggling to deal with the social high costs of rapid urbanization and industrialization. More interested in the larger world than their parents' generation, they were drawn to Europe, Asia, and other points around the globe intent to witness history in the making. The final group had cut its teeth in radical journalism, working for various American labor and social reform movements. Disillusioned by the failure of reform efforts at home, they left for Italy, Russia, and China, looking for outlets for their zeal.[10]

The landscape of foreign reporting was very different after the war. The changes in foreign reporting that Mowrer, Bell, and others had urged a decade earlier were becoming common place. Correspondents no longer focused on traveling Americans, struggling instead to make sense of the global depression and the social and political turmoil it triggered. As Eugene Lyons observed in the 1930s: "Before the war foreign news had been largely a matter of personalities and spectacles: the rise and fall of politicians and rulers, the doings—and even more so the misdoings—of royal personages, etc. Since the war foreign news had become an ever more intricate business calling for some understanding of history and economic forces; classes had in large measure taken the place of individuals as protagonists in the great show."[11]

While some employers still ordered their correspondents to go off in search of "personal adventures,"[12] wrote Vincent "Jimmy" Sheean, for the most part, the job of the foreign correspondent had evolved to a foreign version of the tasks undertaken by reporters at home. "The foreign correspondent of the legend is a virile swashbuckling fellow who obtains sensational news by the exercise of daring and dexterity.... The unromantic fact, however, is that the average correspondent cribs three-quarters of his news from the local newspaper. The fourth quarter he draws from official handouts, the mendacities of paid tipsters, and his own fertile imagination."[13]

It was a heady time to be a foreign correspondent. Reporting on the rise of Hitler or the progress of the Russian experiment with Communism, correspondents were convinced that the topics they were covering mattered, and journalists and audiences alike at home seemed to agree. Paul Scott Mowrer won the first Pulitzer Prize for foreign correspondence in 1929 for stories on the efforts to create the League of Nations. In following years, Leland Snow, H.R. Knickerbocker, Walter Duranty, and Paul Mowrer's brother, Edgar Ansell Mowrer, all won Pulitzers for their foreign reporting.[14] On visits home correspondents were feted, invited on cross country speaking tours, and the books they wrote often became best-sellers.[15]

Their experiences abroad affected correspondents in vastly different ways. Working as journalists in Russia and China, respectively, Eugene Lyons and Anna Louise Strong both recalled that they hoped to further the cause of world reform by sharing the struggles of the reformers with American readers at home.[16] Lyons worked in the United States for TASS, the Soviet news agency. Once he made the move to Moscow, he worked primarily for United Press and wrote for American magazines, including the *Nation* and the *New Republic*. Strong on the other hand, mixed her work for mainstream media with propaganda efforts for both the Chinese and Russian Communists. She also wrote for English language papers in China and Russia. After years covering Stalinist Russia, Lyons came to believe that the dream of a proletarian revolution had been lost in the construction of a totalitarian state. Strong's faith never wavered.

Sheean had the opposite experience. He began his work as a foreign correspondent without any particular political passions and picked them up along the way. "As I acquired a steadier and more intimate acquaintance with the struggles going on under the surface of the smooth black print on white paper," he explained, "I came in time to 'take sides' and have opinions ... [and] reversed the familiar procedure by which a good many of my colleagues, having begun with beliefs and enthusiasm ended in callous indifference towards all human effort."[17]

The correspondents covering Europe were among the first to realize that the Treaty of Versailles had failed to produce a lasting peace. Correspondents, both men and women, worked hard throughout the 1920s and '30s charting the events in Europe and Asia that would lead to the outbreak of World War II. In Moscow they attempted to make sense of political, economic and social upheaval as Stalin solidified Soviet power. In Berlin and Rome, Dorothy Thompson, Sigrid Schultz, William Shirer, and others charted the rise of the Fascists. By the outbreak of the Spanish Civil War, all of them understood that the outbreak of another war was just a question of time.

The approach of war brought with it a new method of reporting, spearheaded by Edward R. Murrow, based in Europe for CBS Radio. In the early days of radio, commentators had shared their thought with listeners, but there were no radio reporters per se. As an announcer, Murrow's job was to invite other people to come on the air to discuss timely topics, but he himself was not supposed to talk. Chafing at such restrictions, he established a network of people in European capitals. As a result, CBS Radio was able to give listeners a firsthand account as the Nazis moved into Austria and Czechoslovakia.[18] Murrow's first person reports on the Battle of Britain were a highlight of American war coverage. Other networks followed the CBS example, often hiring print journalists who were already in place to provide European reporting.

World War II was thoroughly covered. Even though the United States was late entering the war, correspondents were among the first Americans in Britain. Conditions for journalists were better this time around, but they were also more controlled. Gone were the days when an unaccredited journalist might find some other way to the front. In exchange for the uniforms, transportation, and escorts, the correspondents' work was subject to a great deal more scrutiny, censorship, and supervision. When the United States joined the war, even more correspondents were accredited and sent out to various points around the globe. The complex nature of modern warfare also meant that it became impossible for individual correspondents to see the big picture of any battle. As a result, media organizations hired their own military experts to help piece things together in the newsroom and gave the correspondents very focused assignments. While some correspondent gleaned what they could from the formal communiqués available at military headquarters, others traveled with specific units or, like Ernie Pyle, concentrated not on the progress of the larger war, but rather on the lives of the men fighting in the trenches.

The journalism of the World War II and Korea was similar in outlook and approach. The most significant difference was that the men and women covering the Korean fighting were faced with working conditions far worse that what most had faced during World War II. Early in the war, Army officials threatened to expel Marguerite Higgins from the Korean battlefield because there were "no facilities for women." Higgins, who had shared muddy trenches with the troops, pointed out that there were no facilities for anyone. General Douglas MacArthur allowed her to return to the front, but recalcitrant military officers nonetheless erected artificial obstacles that compounded the grueling. Undaunted, she made a point of covering the U.S. Naval assault at Inchon, a turning point in the war. That coverage won her a Pulitzer Prize.

In the aftermath of military conflicts, extra time and attention are often paid to the conduct of journalism in general and foreign coverage in particular. World War II and Korea were no different. Confronted with the experience of wartime coverage, professional journalists and lay people alike were reminded of the power of international news reporting as well as its inadequacies. The result was the formation of the International Press Institute in Geneva in 1951. Its first efforts were surveys of international news content in newspapers from countries around the world.[19] These studies drew on social-scientific methods and the professional expertise of journalists from many countries. In all, the IPI published six surveys. The first dealt with the "improvement of information," and was the birth of what is now known as international news flow research. Later surveys, published between 1951 and 1962, dealt with coverage of Russia, news of the Middle East, a report of government pressures on the press, the press in authoritarian countries, and professional secrecy and the journalist.[20]

THE COLD WAR AND VIETNAM

Woven throughout the IPI research and other studies of media systems conducted was the growing recognition that media coverage had become a powerful tool—a tool that could be wielded by friend and foe alike. The Soviet Union and its Iron Curtain states became the enemy. As the Cold War stretched its tentacles around the globe, countries in Africa, Latin

America, and Asia became proxies for their super-power allies. Whereas correspondents in the early days of Stalin had wondered how much of the story to tell not wanting to be unfair to a young country, correspondents on both sides were charged with revealing the dangers and inadequacies of the "other side," though sometimes the sides were blurred. One of the nation's most prestigious journalism awards is given in the name of George Polk, a CBS news correspondent murdered in Greece while covering a story that might have brought to light CIA involvement in Greek politics.

For correspondents, Vietnam was a war like no other. For the first time, the American military gave correspondents relatively unlimited access to the battlefield and censorship was minimal. While some correspondents lived a fairly comfortable life in Saigon attending the daily official briefings, others rode helicopters in and out of the war zones to cover American troops in action. Reporters and photographers from newspapers, magazines, and television news operations did their best to make the war real to American audiences half a world away. The presence of television reporters meant that for the first time regular footage of the war appeared on network news, making stars of the reporters and raising insoluble questions about the power of video images of war.

Vietnam became a watershed for both foreign correspondence, in general, and war reporting in particular.[21] As in the past, the end of the war brought questions about both the war and media coverage of it. This time, however, the media were blamed for their role in generating dissent at home, dissent that critics were convinced had "lost" the war. In time, expert analyses from organizations as diverse as the Pentagon and the Twentieth Century Fund would suggest that media coverage was not responsible for America's defeat.[22] But such findings had little power to overcome the popular view about the negative impact of news coverage on American military efforts. Years later, this view led the Reagan administration to send troops into Grenada without even a pool of reporters to cover the action.

In the early 1980s, the mindset led conservatives at home to criticize reporters covering political unrest in Central and South America because their stories implicated American allies and American military advisers in widespread human rights violations. The critics accused reporters of having let supposed liberal biases warp their coverage. For correspondents like Raymond Bonner of the *New York Times* and Alma Guillermoprieto of the *Washington Post* the criticism of their reporting from El Salvador was both personally and professionally damaging. Their critics included Republican politicians and policy makers, as well as reputable members of the mainstream press like the *Wall Street Journal*.[23] A decade later the correspondents' work was vindicated when forensic pathologists found conclusive evidence that their accounts of the massacre of the residents of the village of El Mozote were accurate. In 1990s the declassification of U.S. government documents revealed that American activities involvement in Central and South America had been far more serious than anything that the correspondents reported.

The day of personal adventure reporting was lost in the wilds of time, but an occasional journalist still managed to find the adventure, which he or she usually turned into a book or magazine article if not front page news. Journalists traveled into the highlands of Central American to cover the efforts of left-wing guerrillas, while others traveled under cover with the Afghan rebels as they fought off the Soviet invasion of their country.[24]

By the mid–1970s the media of the United States and Western Europe were the dominant powers in international reporting and not everyone was happy with their work. While the governments and media in developing countries were dependent on Western news organizations for news of the rest of the world, they resented the bias they found in that news, particularly the Western journalism's focus on bad news. That Western preference for news of disaster and crisis particularly upset them because it meant that bad news dominated what little news of their own countries reached the rest of the world. This widespread discontent resulted in the formation of development journalism—an approach to news coverage that focused on successes rather than failures. It also produced discussions at UNESCO, which resulted in the New World Information and Communication Order. While the NWIO was never formally adopted, discussions about its controversial provisions made parties to the global news exchange more aware of each other's concerns.

RECENT YEARS

As Barbara Tuchman wisely noted, it is hard to write history of recent events, for "[t]he contemporary has no perspective; everything is in the foreground and appears the same size."[25] Nevertheless, some of the developments in foreign correspondence over the last several decades of the 20th century seem noteworthy enough that even 50 years from now they should be deemed significant. That they have parallels earlier in this history is hardly surprising.

As the telegraph once revolutionized news gathering and ushered in a new era of foreign correspondence, so CNN irrevocably altered both the gathering and the conduct of international news reporting. First, Ted Turner had the vision to see that there was a market for a 24-hour-a-day, global news network. Then having built the network, he expanded its satellite footprint until it in fact became possible for people in China to watch CNN broadcasts from Atlanta to find out what was happening in Tianamin Square in 1989. At the same time, news is happening so fast that it is often broadcast raw, and sometimes even foreign policy makers find themselves referring to CNN to find out what they should be doing or what their opponent thinks—a phenomenon the *New York Times* dubbed the "CNN" effect.[26]

As American entry into global politics spurred greater need for international news, the role of the United States as the lone super power among the industrialized nations now impacts the shape and content of American foreign correspondence. Journalists and policy makers struggle harder than ever to figure out whether it is news coverage that sets the agenda for policy makers or policy makers who govern what the news covers.[27] Familiar tensions still

shape that coverage. In times of international crisis Americans are glued to their television sets for the latest development—whether it's an earthquake in Mexico or the death of a British princess. At other times, however, observers find less and less news space or airtime devoted to international news. But if mainstream news organizations neglect international news, American financial news organizations have expanded their commitment to international news and have expanded their networks of foreign bureaus.[28]

The advent of the Internet and the World Wide Web has meant that Americans interested in international news have many more sources than ever before. Such access also gives freedom fighters and terrorists direct access to global audiences around the world, bypassing governments, reporters, and editors alike. But even enhanced technological capacities have not resolved the perennial access issues surrounding wartime coverage. In the wake of the Persian Gulf War, critics again scrutinized media coverage of the hostilities, finding plenty to worry about in both the military and the media handling of the story. The questions raised by coverage of conflicts in Bosnia, Somalia, Rwanda, and Kosovo have complicated things even further.

While satellite phones and laptop computers have vastly increased the lone reporter's range, the new technologies have also vastly increased the cost of getting news. There are fewer networks, wires, and newspapers willing to maintain international bureaus. Instead, they retain the services of independent video companies, local journalists, or part-time stringers. They fly in the big-name journalists or news teams when a crisis erupts.[29] It is the rare correspondent who spends enough time anywhere to have a personal adventure, never mind report on it.

Selected Readings

Bassow, Whitman. *The Moscow Correspondents: Reporting on Russia from the Revolution to Glasnost.* New York: William Morrow, 1988.

Bjork, Ulf Jonas. "The Commercial Roots of Foreign Correspondence: The New York Herald and Foreign News, 1835–1839." *American Journalism* 11 (Spring 1994): 102–115.

Crowl, James William. *Angels in Stalin's Paradise*. Washington, D.C.: University Press of America, 1982.

Desmond, Robert W. *Crisis and Conflict: World News Reporting Between Two Wars*. Iowa City: University of Iowa Press, 1982.

Desmond, Robert W. *Windows on the World: World News Reporting 1900–1920*. Ames: Iowa State University Press, 1981.

Edwards, Julia. *Women of the World: The Great Foreign Correspondents*. Boston: Houghton Mifflin, 1988.

Geyer, Georgie Anne. *Buying the Night Flight: The Autobiography of a Woman Foreign Correspondent*. Washington: Brassey's, 1983.

Grierson, Don. "Battling Censors, Chiding Home Office: Harrison Salisbury's Russian Assignment." *Journalism Quarterly* 64 (1987): 313–16, 375.

Hamilton, John Maxwell. "China Reporter Edgar Snow: Forty-Five Years on Back of a Tiger." *Media History Digest* 7, 1 (1987): 55–64.

Heald, Morrell. *Transatlantic Vistas: American Journalists in Europe, 1900–1940*. Kent, Ohio: Kent State University Press, 1988.

Hohenberg, John. *Foreign Correspondence: The Great Reporters and Their Times*, 2nd ed. Syracuse: Syracuse University Press, 1995.

Libbey, James K. "Liberal Journals and the Moscow Trials of 1936–38." *Journalism Quarterly* 52 (1975): 85–92, 137.

MacKinnon, Stephen R., and Oris Friesen. *China Reporting: An Oral History of American Journalism in the 1930s and 1940s*. Berkeley, Calif.: University of California Press, 1987.

Mathews, Joseph F. *George Washburn Smalley: Forty Years a Foreign Correspondent*. Chapel Hill: University of North Carolina Press, 1973.

Milton, Joyce. *The Yellow Kids: Foreign Correspondents in the Heyday of Yellow Journalism*. New York: Harper & Row, 1989.

Mowrer, Paul Scott. *The House of Europe*. Boston: Houghton Mifflin Company, 1945.

Prochnau, William W. *Once Upon a Distant War*. New York: Times Books, 1995.

Rosenblum, Mort. *Coups and Earthquakes: Reporting the World for America*. New York: Harper & Row, 1979.

Schaleban, Joy. "Getting the Story Out of Nazi Germany: Louis P. Lochner." *Journalism Monographs* 11 (1969).

Strong, Tracy B., and Helene Keyssar. *Right in Her Soul: The Life of Anna Louise Strong*. New York: Random House, 1983.

Taylor, S. J. *Stalin's Apologist, Walter Duranty: The New York Times' Man in Moscow*. New York: Oxford University Press, 1990.

Notes

1. Oliver Carlson, *The Man Who Made News, James Gordon Bennett* (New York: Duell, Sloan and Pearce, 1942), 200–02.

2. Anne Sebba, *Battling for News: The Rise of the Woman Reporter* (London: Hodder & Stoughton, 1993).

3. George W. Smalley, *Anglo-American Memories* (London: Duckworth & Co., 1911).

4. Joyce Milton, *The Yellow Kids: Foreign Correspondence in the Heyday of Yellow Journalism* (New York: Harper & Row), passim.

5. Paul Scott Mowrer, *The House of Europe* (Boston: Houghton Mifflin Company, 1945), 129–130, 133.

6. Mary Roberts Rinehart, *My Story* (New York: Rinehart & Co., 1948). See also Julia Edwards, *Women of the World: The Great Foreign Correspondents* (Boston: Houghton Mifflin, 1988).

7. Wilda M. Smith and Eleanor A. Bogart, *The Wars of Peggy Hull: The Life and Times of a War Correspondent* (El Paso: Texas Western Press, 1991).

8. Morrell Heald, *Transatlantic Vistas: American Journalists in Europe, 1900–1940* (Kent, Ohio: Kent State University Press, 1988).

9. Vincent Sheean, *Personal History* (New York: The Modern Library, 1940); Sebba, *Battling for News*; and Mowrer, *The House of Europe*.

10. Sheean, *Personal History*; Eugene Lyons, *Assignment in Utopia* (London: George G. Harrap & Co. Ltd, 1937); Peter Rand, *China Hands: The Adventures and Ordeals of American Journalists Who Joined Forces with the Great Chinese Revolution* (New York: Simon & Schuster, 1995); Anna Louise Strong, *I Change Worlds: The Remaking of an American* (New York: Henry Holt and Company, 1935); Waverly Root, *The Paris Edition, 1927–1934* (San Francisco: North Point Press, 1989).

11. Lyons, *Assignment in Utopia*, 393–394.

12. Sheean, *Personal History*, 210.

13. Lyons, *Assignment in Utopia*, 107.

14. Heinz-Dietrich Fischer, *The Pulitzer Prize Archive, vol. 1. International Reporting, 1928–1985* (Munich: K. G. Saur, 1987).

15. Strong, *I Change Worlds*; Webb Miller, *I Found No Peace: The Journal of a Foreign Correspondent* (New York: Simon and Schuster, 1936); Lyons, *Assignment in Utopia*; Sheean, *Personal History*; Mowrer, 1945; Eric Sevareid, *Not So Wild A Dream* (New York: Knopf, 1946).

16. Lyons, *Assignment in Utopia*; Strong, *I Change Worlds*.

17. Sheean, *Personal History*, 45–46.

18. William Shirer, *The Nightmare Years, 1930–1940* (Boston: Little, Brown, 1984), 303–04.

19. International Press Institute, *International Press Institute Surveys, Numbers 1–6* (New York: Arno Press, 1972 reprint).

20. International Press Institute, *As Others See Us* (Zurich: International Press Institute, 1954); International Press Institute, *The Flow of the News* (New York: Arno Press, 1972).

21. Michael Herr, *Dispatches* (New York: Avon, 1977); William W. Prochnau, *Once Upon a Distant War* (New York: Times Books, 1995).

22. Peter Braestrup, *Battle Lines: Report of the Twentieth Century Fund Task Force on the Military and the Media* (New York: Priority Press Publications, 1985); William M. Hammond, *Reporting Vietnam: Media and Military at War* (Lawrence, Kan.: University Press of Kansas, 1998).

23. Michael Massing, "About-face on El Salvador," *Columbia Journalism Review* 22:4 (1983): 42–49; Leigh Binford, *The El Mozote Massacre: Anthropology and Human Rights* (Tucson: University of Arizona Press, 1996).

24. Georgie Anne Geyer, *Buying the Night Flight: The Autobiography of a Woman Foreign Correspondent* (Washington: Brassey's, 1983); Jan Goodwin, *Caught in the Crossfire: A Woman Journalist's Breathtaking Experiences in War-torn Afghanistan* (London: Macdonald, 1987).

25. Barbara Tuchman, *Practicing History: Selected Essays by Barbara W. Tuchman* (New York: Knopf, 1981).

26. Warren P. Strobel, *Late-Breaking Foreign Policy* (Washington, D.C.: United States Institute of Peace, 1997).

27. Jacqueline E. Sharkey, "When Pictures Drive Foreign Policy: How the Photos of the Dead U.S. Soldiers in Somalia Affected U.S. Policy," *American Journalism Review* (December 1993): 14–19; Nik Gowing, *Real-Time Television Coverage of Armed Conflicts and Diplomatic Crises: Does it Pressure or Distort Foreign Policy Decisions?* (The Joan Shorenstein Barone Center on the Press, Politics and Public Policy, John F. Kennedy School of Government, Harvard University, 1994).

28. Garrick Utley, "The Shrinking of Foreign News: From Broadcast to Narrowcast," *Foreign Affairs* 76:2 (1977): 2–10; Mort Rosenblum, *Who Stole the News? Why We Can't Keep Up With What Happens* (New York: John Wiley & Sons, Inc., 1993); Orvill Schell, "Can Business Reporting Become a Positive Force in Foreign News Coverage?" *Nieman Reports* (Spring 1999): 66.

29. Mark Pedelty, *War Stories: The Culture of Foreign Correspondents* (New York: Routledge, 1995).

27

Objectivity

Bruce J. Evensen

The American press has a long history of self-congratulation. In celebrating the nation's centennial, the country's oldest daily newspaper, the *North American & U.S. Gazette*, then in its 91st year, heralded the record of the press in separating "one fact from ninety-nine lies," while serving the American people with news they needed to know. "Fact-finding" was the principal purpose of the press, 67-year-old publisher Morton McMichael told his readers. The "aim and end of true journalism" had been and remained "a birdseye view of transpiring events." When journalists gathered at Philadelphia's press club on the first day of the centennial year, they celebrated journalism's contribution "to the grandest century in the history of men." The nation's newspapers could claim credit for raising the intelligence and sense of justice of the average American. This, the press saw, as fundamental to "the onward sweep of progress."[1]

Nearly 50 years later, the nation's news editors insisted the same standard of "truthfulness, impartiality, fair play and decency" was threatened by the jazz age press with its fetish for personality reporting and sensational storytelling. The infant American Society of Newspaper Editors, meeting in the nation's capital in 1923, established an ethical code of conduct designed to quarantine the profession from the tall-tale telling of the tabloids. Forty-nine editors signed a constitutional covenant pledging maintenance "of the best ideals of the profession" against "the Typhoid Marys of journalism" who were awash in "a terrific tide of half-truths."[2]

Today the story is still the same. More than 500 top executives, editors, and working reporters still report that they consider fair-minded fact-finding journalism's most important job. Seven in 10 thought the line between news and opinion in the press had "seriously eroded." A lack of objectivity remains the most often cited public criticism of the press. At century's end, the public had no more confidence in the honesty and integrity of its press than in its politicians.[3] Walter Cronkite, the veteran CBS news anchorman, put it starkly. "When people doubt they're getting the truth," he warns, "their cynicism spreads through the nation like a virus, eating away at the confidence in our institutions and threatens the very foundation of democracy."[4]

NEUTRALITY IN COLONIAL AND REVOLUTIONARY AMERICA

Editors in the information age understand that fairness and fact-finding are no less central to journalism's public service responsibility than it was for editors of the newly emerging Republic. Editors then trusted eyewitness accounts of reliable sources in the news they reported. Increase Mather solicited letters from ministerial friends when communicating remarkable occurrences to New England's 17th-century readers.[5] Those early 18th-century newspapers published by the authority of the crown, such as the John Campbell's *Boston*

News-Letter, saw themselves bound to report what official sources told them. Newspapers supported by competing interests saw no such obligation. James Franklin's *New-England Courant*, launched at the height of a smallpox epidemic that would infect more than half of the colony's 10,000 settlers, was a case in point. It claimed neutrality in its coverage of the crisis, but only one of 50 items run by the paper in the fall of 1721 supported a controversial plan to inoculate against the dreaded disease.[6] Anything Cotton Mather and the Puritan authority supported, Franklin and his Anglican backers appeared dedicated to oppose.

There was a lesson to be drawn from Franklin's repeated attacks on Puritan authority and the government's suspension of the *Courant* that was not lost on his younger brother. Benjamin Franklin recognized as did other colonial editors that printing was a public business and that printers violated the legitimate expectation of readers for both sides of an argument at their own peril. His classic articulation of this viewpoint would appear in the June 10, 1731, edition of his *Pennsylvania Gazette* and was widely circulated in Colonial America as an "Apology for Printers." The "Business of Printing," as Franklin saw it, "has chiefly to do with Men's Opinions." Printers, always anxious of "getting a Living," feared alienating any reader with what they published, Franklin reasoned. That was why they defended a press open to all sides of an argument. Everyone "ought equally to have the Advantage of being heard by the Publick," Franklin observed, while making it plain in his autobiography that getting an opinion published was a little like riding a stagecoach. Those who could pay had "a Right to a Place."[7]

Journalistic neutrality in colonial America became a casualty of the Stamp Act of 1765, a tax by Britain on colonial newspapers and other paper products designed to recover some of the cost of fighting the nine-year French and Indian War. Many newspapers folded because they couldn't or wouldn't pay the tax. The Tombstone edition of William Bradford's *Pennsylvania Journal and Weekly Advertiser* was characteristic in its outrage. "Unable to bear the burden" and "unable to escape the insup-

portable Slavery" of the tax, the paper was "expiring, in Hopes of a Resurrection to Life again."[8] Peter Timothy, the editor of the *South-Carolina Gazette*, had hoped to stay out of the political fray. As postmaster for Charles-Town he claimed neutrality in the growing conflict between colonists and Whitehall. Patriots wouldn't hear of it. They launched a competing newspaper sympathetic to their views. Timothy wrote Franklin that only "the most violent opposition" to Parliament's policies would now be permitted in print. He had gone from "the most popular to the most unpopular man in the province." The experience of neutral editors after the Boston massacre was much the same. John and Thomas Fleet, whose family-owned *Boston Evening Post* had developed a reputation for journalistic impartiality over four decades, was forced to cease publishing after the fighting at Lexington and Concord, hoping to resume when "matters are in a more settled State." They never did.[9]

Isaiah Thomas, an historian of the revolutionary press and a celebrated printer himself, observed that "impartiality" was impossible in the "general commotion" of the period.[10] His *Massachusetts Spy*, launched in 1770 as a paper "Open to All Parties and influenced by None," became by May 1775 "an American Oracle of Liberty," when it blamed the British and "three or four traitors born among us" for "first firing upon their countrymen," provoking the conflict.[11] Those newspapers that saw it differently paid for their candor. Characteristic was James Rivington's *New-York Gazetteer and Weekly Advertiser*, an "Open and Uninfluenced Press" closed by vigilantes shortly after its page one printing of the names of loyalists opposed to armed insurrection against the "great George our King."[12] Hugh Gaine, publisher of the *New-York Mercury*, switched sides several times to avoid a similar fate. Thomas urged editors to abandon any pretext of impartiality while "the grand American controversy" lasted. That meant making George Washington into a "great man," despite his many military defeats, while disparaging King George as a "devil" turned "tyrant."[13] The pattern would often be repeated. Fair-minded fact-finding diminished as national crisis grew.

THE PARTISAN PARTY PRESS

There was little impartiality in the press during the 50-year interval following the Peace of Paris and the rise of the penny press. Newly emerging political parties subsidized a press that would shape public opinion and solidify their hold on power. The pattern was set at the Constitutional Convention in June of 1787. The *Pennsylvania Herald* distrusted the deal-making at the meeting and was banned from further coverage by armed guards posted at the entrance of Independence Hall. Three days later the *Independent Gazetteer* was re-published widely when it insisted there were no factions in Philadelphia. Readers were assured that a certain secrecy necessarily surrounded the work of delegates who were "worthy of our complete trust."[14]

When Federalists launched the *Gazette of the United States* in April 1789 its editor, John Fenno, promised to conduct a national newspaper that was "independent" and "impartial." It was neither. The Democratic-Republicans published a competing paper, the *National Gazette*, which made a familiar promise. Philip Freneau told readers "perfect fairness and the greatest latitude" would guide the reporting of political differences. It didn't. Things got appreciably nastier when Benjamin Franklin Bache, the great man's grandson, told Philadelphia's readers Washington had "debauched" the nation. For his trouble, the *Aurora's* offices were ransacked and Fenno gave him a personal public caning. A rival paper, the spiny *Porcupine's Gazette*, heartily approved. Editor William Cobbett wrote that such a fate awaited other editors who were little better than "a Turk, a Jew, a Jacobin, or a dog" and who were little more than "a tool and a hireling." Cobbett departed from the language of fellow editors who claimed neutrality. In his view, the partisan pages of his newspaper greatly aided "the cause of good government." That was why he vigorously endorsed the presidency of Federalist John Adams and aggressively attacked his political opponents. The perils of the early Republic, editors came to believe, and America's perilous experiment in direct democracy required the argument of adamant de-fenders and not feckless "professions of impartiality."[15]

Behind the pretext of non-partisanship stood the reality of political interests, who paid editors to see their views in print. Noah Webster, known for his speller, children's essays, and later a dictionary, was one of those who cashed in. Prominent Federalists, led by Treasury Secretary Alexander Hamilton and Chief Justice of the United States Supreme Court John Jay, persuaded Webster through $1,500 in seed money to give up a Hartford law practice and come to New York to launch a newspaper. Webster called it the *American Minerva*. Minerva had won Rome's wars by might and right; and when the paper debuted on December 9, 1793, Webster promised no less. He would be "chaste and impartial," knowing "no party but that of my country." Republicans responded by creating the *New York Argus* under Thomas Greenleaf, who intensified his attacks on the Adams administration following the passage of the Alien and Sedition Act in 1798, legislation designed, in part, to muzzle the Republican press. Fourteen editors would by tried and convicted under the law, which did little to silence the partisan attacks. Greenleaf wrote, "The Federalists are resolved that if they cannot force the Republicans to admire John Adams, they shall not speak what they think of him."[16]

The election of 1800 was in part a referendum on Federalist press policy and secured Republican dominance during the first third of the 19th century. The *National Intelligencer* was widely reprinted for news out of Washington and was a return to greater impartiality in Congressional reporting after the "turbulent passions" of the previous period. The pattern of the Revolutionary period, however, was repeated when the War of 1812 began and a mob broke in on Alexander Hanson and the offices of Baltimore's *Federal Republican*. First in line was rival editor Thomas Wilson, who wrote death was "too good" for "murderous traitors who provoke the people."[17] The hero of that war, Andrew Jackson, launched another period of the partisan press when he ran unsuccessfully for president in 1824. Old Hickory had been the leading vote getter in that campaign but lost the race when John Quincy Adams cut a deal with Henry Clay. Jackson's paid supporters in the press made much of the "corrupt bargain." Duff Green of the *U.S. Telegraph* and Francis Blair of the *Washington Globe* worked as political chairmen in Jackson's landslide victories of 1828 and 1832. When editors showed too much independence, Jackson used his economic leverage and cut off their source of support. All that was about to change.

THE PENNY PRESS AND THE RISE OF OBJECTIVITY

On the morning of September 3, 1833, the inaugural edition of an unremarkable looking daily sold for the remarkable price of a penny and promised "to lay before the public, at a price within the means of every one, ALL THE NEWS OF THE DAY." The pledge of Benjamin Day's *New York Sun* may have miffed "respectable New Yorkers," the competing *Herald* contemptuously reported, who "viewed the ridiculous little thing with curiosity and contempt." But working class readers and advertisers in urbanizing America appreciated the emphasis on entertainment and the displacement of views with news. Sensational stories sold best. When James Gordon Bennett devoted the front page of the *Herald* to reporting the murder trial of a New York prostitute, extra editions failed to meet the demand and broke his steam press. Providing news "up to the latest hour" was creating a clamor "never before seen in New York," he reported immodestly.[18]

Coverage of the Ellen Jewett murder case may have read like a cheap novel, but it employed techniques of interviewing and fact-finding that would later serve objectivity well. The penny press was not above reprinting the *Sun's* circulation-stimulating account of Batmen and blue unicorns on the moon or supposedly exclusive interviews with the 161-year-old nurse of George Washington. The *Herald*, followed by other penny press papers, advertised itself to a wide readership claiming it was a newspaper "whose veracity can be relied on." Newspapers that expected to survive in a crowded marketplace needed to "avoid mendacity" and be "sustained by what truth and honesty conspire to dictate." The competing *Evening Post* observed that a newspaper's "public duty" was to "advance opinions" informed by "facts" that provided "an adequate foundation" readers could trust.[19]

The penny press period is marked by a growing realization by editors that serving the public with news they needed to know was not only good journalism but good for sales. The way the *Sun* saw it, the arrival of a newspaper the working class could afford marked "the advent of a new era of general intelligence" dedicated to delivering "an impartial history" of the day's events, including the activities of its police and courts. Only by "openly disclaiming all parties" and "all politics," promised the *Herald's* James Gordon Bennett, could the "cause of truth, public faith and science" be served. Charles A. Dana, who was to serve for 15 years as city editor on Horace Greeley's widely circulated *New York Tribune*, put the emerging idea of journalistic fact-finding another way. "Whatever the Divine Providence permitted to occur," he later observed, "I was not too proud to report."

Even if the penny press was not always true to its promised purpose of "giving a correct picture of the world," it did position its reporters on regularly assigned beats, where they cultivated sources through aggressive interviewing under deadline for "the earliest intelligence." Timely reporting of important public events permitted readers to participate in civic life in a growing number of communities across the nation. The new editor of the *New York Times* understood this widening social responsibility of the press when he promised a sober summary of the day's news while pledging "to make it a point to get into a passion as rarely as possible." George Wisner, a police reporter on the *Sun*, said dispassion was at the center of a journalist's civic responsibility. "Deeds of death, of broken bones, heads and hearts" were reported "without a solitary feeling of sorrow" over breakfast to "the morbid appetites of cormorants for news."[20]

STANDARDIZATION
IN THE NEWS

By 1840, the penny press was firmly established in Baltimore and Philadelphia and was spreading to other cities east of the Alleghenies and along the Ohio River Valley. By the spring of 1844 Baltimore newspapers were reporting news out of Washington by telegraph. Within two years telegraph networks spread to the West and included Illinois, Ohio, and Missouri. George W. Kendall's eye witness accounts of the Mexican War, published in the *New Orleans Picayune*, were transmitted throughout the nation by telegraph, pony express, and ship. Raymond organized a cartel of six New York newspapers to expedite news from Europe. It became the Associated Press. The telegraph and press associations tended to accelerate the standardization of news reporting. The wire service became a relatively cheap way for newspapers to get international and national news. Since these newspapers reflected a wide variety of political orthodoxies, wire service reporters and editors found it in their interest to report the news neutrally.[21]

The business of information gathering and the competition to quickly disseminate it had begun to systematize reporting patterns before the Civil War. The conflict would hasten the development of the inverted pyramid with the most important elements of the story placed at the beginning of the article. The Northern appetite for news gave Secretary of War Edwin M. Stanton wide latitude in controlling information from the front. Between the big battles, however, stories filed by special correspondents were often slanted to conform to the editorial policies of each paper. Eyewitness accounts were hastily conceived, turgidly written, and avidly read. More than 300 peace papers in the North deplored the war and their reporting reflected it. Forty-three newspapers in the South were bound by a press association dutiful in their deference to military authority.[22]

Although a great deal of Civil War reporting was strained and hyperbolic with little fidelity to accuracy and impartiality, some of it reflects a new standard of conciseness then coming into view. B. S. Osbon's account of the firing on Fort Sumter is a classic of its kind. "The ball is opened," began his front-page report in the *New York World*. "War is inaugurated. The batteries of Sullivan's Island, Morris Island, and other points were opened on Fort Sumter at four o'clock this morning. Fort Sumter has returned the fire, and a brisk cannonading has been kept up." The spare prose of Ned Spencer, reporting the carnage at Shiloh where 24,000 men were slain in two days fighting, anticipated 20th-century war reporting. "As I sit tonight writing this epistle," he begins, "the dead and wounded are all around me. The knife of the surgeon is busy at work, and amputated legs and arms lie scattered in every direction. The cries of the suffering victim and the groans of those who patiently await medical attention are most distressing." The *Philadelphia Inquirer's* headline might boast that Gettysburg had "Eclipsed Waterloo," but Whitelaw Reid's vivid account of the war's turning point read more literally. "Up to the rifle pits, across them, over the barricades—the momentum" of the rebel charge, "the mere machine strength of their combined action swept them on. They were upon the guns, were bayoneting the gunners, were waving their flags above our pieces. But they had penetrated to the fatal point."[23]

By war's end, the front pages of much of the Northern press had become a repeater service for the war department. Characteristic was the *New York Herald's* reprint of 14 reports, emanating from Secretary Stanton's office, detailing negotiations to end the fighting. The unforeseen consequence of Stanton's control over information was to further the development of the inverted pyramid with its dispassionate promise of giving readers only the most important facts first. Reports of President Lincoln's assassination are a case in point. "This evening at about 9:30 P.M., at Ford's Theatre," Stanton wrote, sitting near Lincoln's bedside, "the President, while sitting in his private box with Mrs. Lincoln, Mrs. Harris and Major Rathburn, was shot by an assassin, who suddenly entered the box and approached behind the president—The wound is mortal."[24] Newspapers nationwide published Stanton's report.

Although Lincoln's critical condition was buried in the fourth sentence, Stanton's fact-based summary of the who, what, when, where, and why of the story would become the narrative strategy of choice for Gilded Age reporters and readers.

Late 19th-century editors liked to think of themselves as careful and conscientious chroniclers of America's romance with industrialization and urbanization. Increasing production costs were making newspapers multi-million-dollar investments, leading to what one veteran journalist described as "a business-like seriousness, stability and impersonality." A leading lecturer and cultural commentator agreed. "Reporters are the hardest working class in the community," Joseph Cook observed. "Our heads are in newspapers and ledgers." Their obligation was "to offer with lightning speed news" that not only "mirrored public sentiment" but, on occasion, inspired it. The work of the reporter was to be "an impartial chronicler of passing events," the *Boston Journal* assured readers. Stories sustained by "speculation" were not "profitable," because they interfered with the reporter's real job to "follow facts" wherever they might lead and to offer "accurate accounts" of what he found. Perceived partisanship in anything other than the people's business cost readers and advertisers, William Cullen Bryant concluded, after 46 years in the newspaper business.[25]

By the end of the 19th century, professional standards of accuracy and truthfulness were widely articulated if not always practiced. E. L. Godkin, editor of *The Nation* and the *New York Evening Post*, called it every reporter's responsibility "to get accurate news." Leading editors like Melville Stone began to describe the "educational force" of the newspaper when it put fact-finding above partisanship. The circulation wars between Joseph Pulitzer and William Randolph Hearst, the yellow boys of the Gilded Age, seemed to belie the suggestion that sensationalism had had its day. In the West, frontier editors puffed their hamlets hoping to attract credulous readers out beyond the Great Divide. One transformed Steamboat Springs, in the northwest corner of Colorado, into "an American Eden," while another claimed that Alamosa on the banks of the Rio Grande would one day command "a vast empire" because the region boasted "the best wheat, oats and barley in the nation." The necessity of civic boosting replaced any pretext of objectivity. In Leadville, financial ruin was described as "a temporary dullness in the markets." A frontier editor's survival, wrote one, rested on the precarious fate of the frontier town. Disasters were muted and occasional successes were overblown. News coverage always "extended the right hand of fellowship to the homeseeker."[26]

INTO THE TWENTIETH CENTURY

By the time Charles Ross, an editor at the *St. Louis Post-Dispatch* and a journalism professor at the University of Missouri, used the term "objectivity" in describing the responsibility of the reporter to be accurate, fair, and balanced in chronicling the day's events, the practice was becoming well established within the profession. Casper Yost, the founding father of the American Society of Newspaper Editors, thought objectivity central to "establishing an ethical standard of professional conduct" that would separate serious-minded journalists from the tabloid press. Charles Dennis, editor of the *Chicago Daily News*, spoke for many of his colleagues when he declared objectivity would "allow newspapers to approximate the best ideals of the profession."[27] Textbooks, academic journals, and journalism schools helped to standardize the teaching to the next generation of journalists. The industry's trade press and statewide press codes reflected how widely objectivity was seized upon as an explanation of professional conduct and the social responsibility of the press. Those critical of the tabloid tendencies of jazz age journalism encouraged the training of students who would labor as scientists in building fact upon fact that would then give readers a picture of the world that could serve as the basis for critical action. By 1926, 50 such schools had 5,500 students.[28]

America's largest selling newspaper during the jazz age and Depression era, the *New York Daily News*, and its widest circulating newspaper chain, the Hearst press, were widely criticized for paying little attention to the profession's slowly evolving paradigm. Instead, their "common pandering to the meretricious taste of the masses" struck some as sacrificing the respect many editors sought for short-term circulation success. Their propensity for self-promoting "exclusives" that could be "told in a flash" seemed to substitute "undiluted entertainment" for fact-finding. They were accused of "gathering garbage from the gutters of life," while leaving in ruin the reputation of the press among serious-minded citizens. The anger was more than jealousy. It reflected a growing determination within journalism to elevate the status of the profession through the application of science-based observation and fact-finding designed to meet the social responsibility of the press.

A tradition of 20th-century muckraking, conducted in the hope of re-moralizing the political and social landscape, has been grounded in the conviction that given trustworthy information the public would do the right thing. Ida Tarbell's path-breaking exposé of John D. Rockefeller and the Standard Oil Trust was crafted through pain-staking detective work largely drawn from original sources. Articles by Lincoln Steffens "followed the facts" in awakening a nation to municipal corruption.[29] Ray Stannard Baker's investigative reporting "let light and air in" as he followed the color line in the segregated South. His job was "to see as straight as it lies in me to do," while offering readers "a picture of conditions as they were."[30] Jacob Riis spoke for 20th-century fact-finders when he argued, "the power of the fact is the mightiest lever of this or any day." Will Irwin's review of early 20th-century investigative reporting found journalists "are coming to recognize the importance of their profession, its usefulness and potential standing" when they "tell the truth in the language of the people."[31]

BY MILLENNIUM'S END

By mid-century objectivity was beginning to get a bad name, and by millennium's end it was no longer fashionable to emphasize fairness, balance, and impartiality as consensus values that shaped journalism. Certain radio reporters joined by the *New York Times* and other elite media saw themselves shaping as well as chronicling public policy.[32] Some journalism textbooks began to reflect the change as did the professional literature. "Objectivity," said Curtis MacDougall, author of the widely circulated *Interpretative Reporting*, "is impossible, and if possible, undesirable."[33] A Commission on the Freedom of the Press took testimony from 275 journalists at mid-century before concluding what the nation needed was more interpretative reporting that made the day's events meaningful.[34] The success of Wisconsin Senator Joseph McCarthy in using the press in his reckless anti–Communist campaign accelerated the trend toward interpretation already underway.[35]

By the end of the century, three quarters of all Americans got all or most of their news from television. This worried veteran newsmen who saw the intense competition for ratings threatening traditional standards of accuracy.[36] The struggle and confusion in newspaper offices to win back lost readers is no more reassuring for the future of objectivity.[37] Many in the profession no longer have a faith in facts and remain unconvinced that the public is intelligent or patient enough to sort through stories in their search for significance. Journalism textbooks and media practice at century's end frequently reflect the uncertainty.[38] The debate within journalism over objectivity parallels a celebration of subjectivity outside the profession at the millennial mark.[39] Survey research suggests Americans may have a better memory than members of the press. They list a lack of objectivity in the news media as the number one reason they are dissatisfied with it and claim a return to impartiality and fairness in reporting would do much to restore their confidence in it.[40]

Selected Readings

Brooker-Gross, Susan. "Nineteenth Century News Defini-tions and Wire Service Usage." *Journalism Quarterly* 60 (1983): 24–27.

Evensen, Bruce J. "The Debate Over Objectivity," 411–28 in Wm. David Sloan and Emily Erickson Hoff, eds., *Contemporary Media Issues*. Northport: Vision Press, 1998.

Mindich, David T. Z. *Just the Facts: How "Objectivity" Came to Define American Journalism*. New York: New York University, 1998.

Miraldi, Robert. *Muckraking and Objectivity: Journalism's Colliding Traditions*. Westport: Greenwood Press, 1990.

Moses, James L. "Journalistic Impartiality on the Eve of the Revolution: The *Boston Evening Post*, 1770–1775." *Journalism History* 20 (Autumn-Winter 1994): 125–130.

Randolph, J. Ralph. "The End of Impartiality: *South Carolina Gazette*, 1763–75." *Journalism Quarterly* 49 (1972): 702–09, 720.

Schiller, Dan. *Objectivity and the News: The Public and the Rise of Commercial Journalism*. Philadelphia: University of Pennsylvania, 1981.

Shaw, Donald L. "News Bias and the Telegraph." *Journalism Quarterly* 44 (1967): 3–12 and 31.

Stensaas, Harlan. *The Objective News Report: A Content Analysis of Selected U.S. Daily Newspapers for 1865 to 1954*. Ann Arbor: University Microfilms International, 1987.

Notes

1. *North American & U.S. Gazette*, 31 December 1875, 1; *Philadelphia Public Ledger*, 1 January 1876, 2.

2. Minutes of the American Society of Newspaper Editors, 25 April 1922, 1–2 and 10–12, ASNE. Archives, Newspaper Center, Reston, Va. *Problems of Journalism* (Washington: American Society of Newspaper Editors, 1923), 14–21; "Our Faith and Action," *Editor & Publisher*, 23 February 1923, 44; and "Editors Mean Business," *Editor & Publisher*, 3 May 1924, 26.

3. "Striking the Balance: Audience Interests, Business Pressures and Journalists' Values," a report by the Pew Research Center for the People and the Press and the Project for Excellence in Journalism, March 1999, 1–5. Results from the *Los Angeles Times-Mirror* Center for the People and the Press are cited in "The Cronkite Report: Headlines & Sound Bites," Discovery Communications, Inc., 1995. Also, Rick Garlick and Bruce J. Evensen, "What the Polls Show," in Bruce J. Evensen, ed., *The Responsible Reporter*, 2nd ed. (Northport, Ala.: Vision Press, 1997), v–vii.

4. Walter Cronkite, remarks at a public forum at Kutztown University, broadcast on the Cable Satellite Public Affairs Network, April 13, 1999.

5. Increase Mather, *An Essay for the Recording of Illus-trious Providences; Wherein an Account is given of many Remarkable and very Memorable Events, which have happened in this last Age, Especially in New England* (Boston: printed by Samuel Green for Joseph Browning and Are to be Sold in his Shop, 1684); see particularly the preface.

6. *Boston News-Letter*, 8 May 1704. Also, Wm. David Sloan, "Neutrality in Colonial Newspapers," in Steven R. Knowlton, ed., "History of Objectivity in American Jour-nalism," unpublished manuscript.

7. *Pennsylvania Gazette*, 10 June 1731, 1; Leonard W. Labaree, ed., *The Autobiography of Benjamin Franklin* (New Haven: Yale University, 1964), 174–75.

8. *Pennsylvania Journal and Weekly Advertiser*, 31 October 1765, 1.

9. Peter Timothy to Benjamin Franklin, September 3, 1768, in Leonard Labaree and W. B. Wilcox, eds., *The Papers of Benjamin Franklin* (New Haven: Yale University, 1959), 202; *Boston Evening Post*, 24 April 1775, 1 and 2.

10. Isaiah Thomas, *The History of Printing in America*, 2 vols. (Worcester, Mass.: From the Press of Isaiah Thomas, Jr., Isaac Sturtevant, Printer, 1810), I:377–80.

11. *Massachusetts Spy*, 3 May 1775, 1 and 3 and 10 May 1775, 1.

12. *Rivington's New-York Gazetteer; or Connecticut, Hudson River's Weekly and the New-Jersey, and Quebec Advertiser*, 20 April 1775, 1.

13. Thomas, *The History of Printing in America*, I:377–80; *Massachusetts Spy*, 3 May 1775, 1 and 3; 10 May 1775, 1, and 28 June 1776, 1 and 3; *Rivington's New-York Gazetteer; or Connecticut, Hudson River's Weekly and the New-Jersey, and Quebec Advertiser*, 20 April 1775, 1; *American Journal* (Providence, R. I.), 16 December 1779, 1; *Boston Gazette*, 11 February 1782, 1.

14. *Pennsylvania Herald*, 13 June 1787, 1 and 2; *Independent Gazetteer*, 17 June 1787, 1.

15. *Gazette of the United States*, 15 April 1789, 1; *National Gazette*, 31 October 1789, 1; *Philadelphia General Advertiser* (the *Aurora*), 23 December 1796, 1; *Porcupine's Gazette and Advertiser*, 5 March 1797, 1; 5 September 1797, 1; and 16 November 1797, 1.

16. *American Minerva*, 9 December 1793, 1; *New York Argus*, 11 May 1795, 1 and 15 October 1799, 1.

17. *National Intelligencer*, 18 February 1801, 1; (Balti-more) *Federal Republican*, 20 June 1812, 1. Wilson's reply is reported in the July 28, 1812, edition of the *Baltimore Whig* that was reprinted in the *New-York Evening Post* of July 31, 1812.

18. *New York Sun*, 3 September 1833, 1; *New York Herald*, 12 April 1836, 1 and 4 June 1836, 1.

19. *New York Sun*, 25 August 1835, 1 and 1 September 1835, 2; *New York Evening Post*, 18 August 1835, 2; *New York Herald*, 3 September 1835, 2 and 9 September 1835, 2; *New York Evening Post*, 10 September 1835, 2.

20. *New York Sun*, 17 April 1834, 2; 4 April 1835, 2; and 12 September 1835, 2; *New York Herald*, 6 May 1835, 2 and 7 May 1835, 2; *New York Times*, 18 September 1851, 1 and 2; Isaac Clark Pray, *Memoirs of James Gordon Bennett and His Times* (New York: Stringer and Townsend, 1855), 266–68 and 374–375; Charles A. Dana, *The Art of News-paper Making* (New York: D. Appleton, 1895), 17–18; Au-gustus Maverick, *Henry J. Raymond and the New York Press* (Hartford: A. S. Hale, 1870), 49–55 and 168–73.

21. Donald L. Shaw, "News Bias and the Telegraph," *Journalism Quarterly* 44 (1967): 3–12 and 31; Susan Brooker-Gross, "Nineteenth Century News Definitions and Wire Service Usage," *Journalism Quarterly* 60 (1983): 24–27; Harlan Stensaas, *The Objective News Report: A Content Analysis of Selected U.S. Daily Newspapers for 1865 to 1954* (Ann Arbor: University Microfilms International, 1987), 23–35.

22. Louis M. Starr, *Bohemian Brigade: Civil War Newsmen in Action* (New York: Knopf, 1954), 232–63; J. Cutler Andrews, *The North Reports the Civil War* (Pitts-burgh: University of Pittsburgh, 1955), 273–286; Joe Skidmore, "The Copperhead Press and the Civil War," *Journalism Quarterly* 16 (1939): 345–55; Quintus C. Wilson, "The Confederate Press Association: A Pioneer News Agency," *Journalism Quarterly* 26 (1949): 160–66.

23. *New York World*, 13 April 1861, 1; *Cincinnati Times*, 10 April 1862, 1; *Philadelphia Inquirer*, 6 July 1863, 1; *Cincinnati Gazette*, 3 July 1863, 1.

24. *New York Herald*, 10 April 1865, 1. Also, David T. Z. Mindich, "Edwin M. Stanton, the Inverted Pyramid, and Information Control," *Journalism Monographs* 140 (1993).

25. *New York Advance*, 19 April 1877; *Boston Journal*, 5 April 1877; *New York Evening Post*, 16 May 1872, 1.

26. Edwin L. Godkin, "Opinion-Moulding," *The Nation* 9 (12 August 1869), 126–27; Melville E. Stone, *Fifty Years a Journalist* (New York: Doubleday, Page, 1923), 53–57; *Steamboat Springs Pilot*, 5 January 1898, 1; *Alamosa Independent-Journal*, 20 February 1902, 1; *Leadville Evening Chronicle*, 3 January 1902, 1; *Routt County* (Colorado) *Courier*, 21 October 1909, 1.

27. Charles G. Ross, *The Writing of News: A Handbook* (New York: Henry Holt, 1911), 17–20. Yost's attitude was first expressed in a letter he wrote to his wife on April 25, 1922, at the founding of the American Society of Newspaper Editors. The letter is in the private collection of his son, Robert W. Yost of Webster Groves, Missouri. It is repeated in the *Problems of Journalism* (1923), 18–19 and 21–22.

28. Ernest Greuning, "Can Journalism Be a Profession? A Study of Conflicting Tendencies," *The Century Magazine* (September 1924), 687–702; Nelson A. Crawford, "Schools of Journalism Today," *American Mercury* 6 (October 1925), 197–200; Charles R. Corbin, *Why News Is News* (New York: Ronald Press, 1928), 3–6 and 101–103; Walter Lippmann, "Two Revolutions in the American Press," *Yale Review* (March 1931), 3–12.

29. Tarbell describes her craft in her autobiography *All in a Day's Work* (New York: Macmillan, 1939), 27–29 and 204–06, and in letters to her employer, S. S. McClure, that are dated from the fall of 1937. See S. S. McClure Papers, Correspondence, Box 8, Folder 54, Lilly Library, Manuscript Department, Indiana University, Bloomington. Her articles for *McClure's* magazine were published as *History of the Standard Oil Company* (New York: McClure, Phillips, 1904). Steffens describes his craft in *The Autobiography of Lincoln Steffens* (New York: Harcourt, Brace, 1931), 433–34, and in his preface to *Lincoln Steffens Speaking* (New York: Harcourt, Brace, 1936).

30. Baker's comments appear in *McClure's* magazine 26 (March 1906), 548–49, and in his Notebook C, 23–24, 36–38, and 142–45; Notebook J, 116–18; and Notebook K, 131–35, written between 1903 and 1908, Ray Stannard Baker Papers, Library of Congress. See also, *American Chronicle: The Autobiography of Ray Stannard Baker* (New York: Charles Scribner's Sons, 1945), 17–19, 57–60, and 192–93.

31. Jacob A. Riis, *The Making of an American* (New York: Macmillan, 1901), 99–100 and 126–28; Will Irwin, *The American Newspaper* (Ames: Iowa State University, 1969), 83–84.

32. H. V. Kaltenborn, America's most listened to broadcaster, thought it his job to "guide public opinion." See H. V. Kaltenborn, *Kaltenborn Edits the News* (New York:

E. P. Dutton, 1942), 2–4, and H. V. Kaltenborn, *Europe Now: A First Hand Report* (New York: Didier, 1945), x–xi. The attitude of the *Times* and others in the elite media is reflected by James Reston, *The Artillery of the Press* (New York: Harper & Row, 1966), 48–59 and 63–76, and Lester Markel, "The Real Sins of the Press," *Harper's* (December 1962), 85–94.

33. Curtis MacDougall, address to American Association of Teachers of Journalism, reprinted as "What Newspaper Publishers Should Know about Professors of Journalism," *Journalism Quarterly* 24 (March 1947): 3. See also, Frederic E. Merwin, "The Journalism Teacher Faces the Atomic Age," *Journalism Quarterly* 23 (March 1946): 1–3.

34. Commission on the Freedom of the Press, *A Free and Responsible Press: A General Report on Mass Communication, Newspapers, Radio, Motion Pictures, Magazines, and Books* (Chicago: University of Chicago, 1947), 19–22.

35. Elmer Davis, "News and the Whole Truth," *Atlantic Monthly* (August 1952), 32 and 35; and Melvin Melcher, "McCarthy: Who Made Him?" *Nieman Reports* (January 1953), 23–32 and 41–47.

36. Walter Cronkite, *A Reporter's Life* (New York: Ballantine Books, 1996), 373–84; Susan and Bill Buzenberg, eds., *Salant, CBS, and the Battle for the Soul of Broadcast Journalism: The Memoirs of Richard S. Salant* (Boulder: Westview Press, 1999), 277–307.

37. Edwin Diamond, *Behind the Times: Inside the New York Times* (New York: Villard Books, 1994), 3–32; Doug Underwood, *When MBAs Rule the Newsroom: How the Marketers and Managers Are Reshaping Today's Media* (New York: Columbia University, 1995), 55–70.

38. Theodore L. Glasser, "Objectivity and News Bias," 174–78, in Elliot D. Cohen, ed., *Philosophical Issues in Journalism* (New York: Oxford University, 1992); Gene Goodwin and Ron F. Smith, *Groping for Ethics in Journalism*, 3d ed. (Ames: Iowa State University, 1994), 7–14; Jack Fuller, *News Values: Ideas for an Information Age* (Chicago: University of Chicago, 1994), 14–22; Henry H. Schulte and Marcel P. Dufresne, *Getting the Story: An Advanced Reporting Guide to Beats, Records and Sources* (New York: Macmillan, 1994), 7–17.

39. Richard Rorty, *Objectivity, Relativism, and Truth* (Cambridge: Cambridge University, 1991), 21–45; Lorraine Datson and Peter Galison, "The Image of Objectivity," *Representations* 40 (Fall 1992), 81–98; Barry Barnes and David Bloor, "Relativism, Rationalism and the Sociology of Knowledge," 21–47, in Martin Hollis and Steven Lukes, eds., *Rationality and Relativism* (Oxford: Blackwell, 1982); Clifford Geertz, "Anti Anti-Relativism," 12–34, in Michael Krausz, ed., *Relativism: Interpretation and Confrontation* (Notre Dame: University of Notre Dame, 1989); and Allan Megill, *Rethinking Objectivity* (Durham: Duke University, 1994), 1–20.

40. This research is summarized in Bruce J. Evensen, "The Debate Over Objectivity," 411–13, in Wm. David Sloan and Emily Erickson Hoff, eds., *Contemporary Media Issues* (Northport, Ala.: Vision Press, 1998).

28

Sensationalism and Tabloidism

Erika J. Pribanic-Smith

"Woman that lately was delivered of a Toad, a Serpent, and a child."[1]

"Body of a Woman Wrapped in a Table Cover and Carpeting Had Been Strangled."[2]

"Madman Cut Up His Date and Put Her Body in the Freezer."[3]

Though the language has changed over the course of 300 years, the idea remains the same: the unusual sells news. Sensationalism by its very nature exploits the unusual. The landscape of American newspaper history is dotted with peaks and valleys of sensationalism. At the crests, newspapers assault readers with stories of scandal and murder. Even in the low points, traces of sensational tactics appear in America's print media.

Historians have long argued the definition of sensationalism in journalism. A consensus of the arguments includes an appeal to baser emotions—excitement, titillation, shock, astonishment, horror, and so forth. Newspapers can elicit such emotions through display, emphasis, illustrations, and writing style, but the content itself plays the largest part. Sensational news typically consists of crime, sex, or some sort of gossip—the more bizarre, the better. This type of news will not only draw an emotional response from the reader, but it will also draw attention to the newspaper.

EARLY DAYS OF SENSATIONALISM

Sensationalism in the news began long before the first American newspaper reached the hands of the colonists. The spread of news dates back to the dawn of humanity, when people primarily used word of mouth to pass along information ... and gossip. Sensational accounts have infested the dissemination of information since then, as newsbearers exaggerated and expanded on the truth to make their stories more interesting and keep the attention of the listener.

It follows that sensationalism crept into each new method of disseminating news. The cylinder printing of the Sumerians over 2,000 years B.C. contained sensationalized accounts, particularly of war. This printing, which entailed rolling a cylinder engraved with pictures over wet clay, portrayed warriors with exaggerated muscular features and relayed tales of graphic physical violence.

By the inception of the printed word, sensationalism in the news had become commonplace. In the 17th century, people received some news by way of broadsides—sheets on which news was printed, usually in the form of rhyming verse.

After attracting the attention of potential readers through titles such as "A True Account How the Wife of John Waterman of Fisherton-Anger Was Delivered of a Monster on October 26, 1664," these broadside ballads relayed sensational stories of murder (often reported in explicit and gory detail), scandal, and curious abnormalities. One story told of a man with an odd physical deformity: another person growing from his side. A verse of this tale read as follows:

Onely one legge with foot and toes
Is to be seene, and some suppose,
      The other is contain'd
Within his brothers body, yet
Nature hath vs'd him so to it
      [he never thus is pain'd.][4]

Early newspapers in Europe followed the precedent set by the broadsides, eliciting reader interest through the inclusion of stories about murder, sex scandals, supernatural occurrences, and monstrosities of nature. Since the publishers of the first newspapers in the American colonies imitated and often lifted material from British newspapers, colonists found their early papers riddled with sensationalism.

In the first colonial newspaper, *Publick Occurrences, Both Foreign and Domestick*, Bostonian Benjamin Harris printed sensational stories of scandal and murder among international and colonial society. *Publick Occurrences* relayed gossip on the sexual indiscretions of a French royal and his son's wife, speculated on the fate of two children who disappeared while "the barbarous Indians were lurking about," and described the suicide of a man who hanged himself in his "Cow-house."[5]

Although *Publick Occurrences* lasted only one issue because Harris failed to gain a license, it served as an example for future colonial newspapers that would emulate its sensational style in an effort to attract readers. Successful colonial newspapers devoted ample space to sensational stories of war, crime, sex, and disasters, paying particular, though not exclusive, attention to events pertaining to the upper class.

As the 18th century drew to a close, the new American government offered a plethora of new targets for newspaper gossip. Partisan readers hungrily consumed scandalous material about political figures from the opposing party while the government scrambled to squelch the sensational writings. In 1803, New York newspaper publisher Harry Croswell stood trial for printing in *The Wasp* numerous sordid details about the personal and political lives of Thomas Jefferson, among them the accusation that Jefferson had committed adultery with and fathered several children by one of his slaves.

SENSATIONALISM IN THE PENNY PRESS

While such political scandal may have appealed to the elite partisans, an audience of commoners existed that did not find the partisan ramblings, however sensational, alluring. Editors of the penny press, beginning in the 1830s, sought to market their newspapers to this broad general audience. In order to attract a mass audience, the penny press lords turned to a more basic strain of sensationalism. Contrasted with the stilted and serious writing of previous newspapers, the sensational stories printed in the penny papers appeared lighter and more readable to the common person, with more colorful wording and shorter sentences. Content also changed in the sensational stories of these new mass newspapers. Unlike previous newspapers, which tended to focus on scandals among the upper classes, the crime and scandal appearing in the penny press centered on the average citizen.

Murders involving otherwise unnotable figures appeared prominently on the front page of penny newspapers, at times drawing more interest to the murder than it might have received without such publicity. In 1836, the *New York Herald* created the first opportunity for an ordinary person to become national news when it reported the murder of 23-year-old prostitute Helen Jewett by a Richard Robinson, a 19-year-old clerk and one of Jewett's regulars. *Herald* editor James Gordon Bennett, often heralded as the father of journalistic sensationalism, lamented in the first of a series of stories on the crime that the city had been disgraced "by one of the most foul and premeditated murders, that ever fell to our lot to record."[6] Bennett's front-page coverage of the case brought the attention of readers and other newspapers alike to the crime and ensuing trial.

While articles such as those about the Robinson-Jewett murder case may have been composed through credible reporting techniques, a story need not have even been true to appear in the penny papers. Writers commonly invented news that drew attention to the newspaper. According to the biographer and critic James Parton, lying was not only the easy route but also the effective one when it came to journalism. He wrote that when men succeed at "purging their conversation of the usual exaggerations and credulities," their conversation tends to become "as dull as it is correct." He continued, "But the journalist lies under an inexorable necessity of *not* being dull. Incorrect he may be, to a certain extent, and live; but if he is dull, he dies."[7]

The penny newspapers were not beneath printing lies in an effort to give vivacity to their pages. The trend that emerged of publishing "hoaxes" as news could be described as anything but dull. Richard Adams Locke of the *New York Sun* offered one of the most famous newspaper hoaxes when he wrote a series of stories in August 1835 referred to thereafter as the Great Moon Hoax. Using fabricated testimony from a real astronomer, he wrote of lunar vegetation and animals the likes of which "would be classed on earth as a monster." One of these animals was described as "a bluish lead color, about the size of a goat, with a head and beard like him."[8] Locke fooled and astounded readers, scientists, and other newspapers with the story, which was only exposed as a fabrication when he revealed the rouse to a friend in a saloon.

Some of the stories created by sensationalist newspaper staffs were not altogether false. Often the news staffs would make news themselves, performing spectacular deeds and writing about them in the newspaper. In 1872, James Gordon Bennett, Jr., hired Henry Morton Stanley to locate the missionary David Livingstone (who didn't know he was lost). Bennett insisted that Stanley find Livingstone no matter the expense for the benefit of his paper, the *New York Herald*. Bennett told him of his aims to make the paper greater than even his infamous father had. "I mean," he explained, "that it shall publish whatever news will be interesting to the world at no matter what cost."[9] Stanley's search through Africa certainly interested readers. Published serially in the *Herald*, the story drew much attention to the newspaper and spawned the phrase "Dr. Livingstone, I presume?"

THE SENSATIONAL FRONTIER

Papers outside of New York created news as well. Mark Twain and Dan De Quille awed readers of the *Territorial Enterprise* in Virginia City, Nevada, with exciting and often fabricated stories about life in the West. One such hoax included the gruesome tale of a family murdered in their log cabin. "The scalpless corpse of Mrs. Hopkins lay across the threshold, with her head split open, and her right hand almost severed from her wrist," Twain wrote. He continued that six children had been found in the bedroom—"[t]heir brains had evidently been dashed out with a club."[10]

Despite the falsity of such items, the stories sold papers. Frontier dwellers and remote readers alike had an unquenchable thirst for such grotesque stories that appeared to embody life in the West. However, most proprietors of frontier newspapers found that reality provided enough material for sensational news reports. Colorful tales of gunfights, bar brawls, and prostitution in western towns thrilled newspaper readers. Particularly in the mining towns, where a sense of lawlessness pervaded, newspapers carried little other than these exciting accounts of crime and scandal. As these astonishing stories spread in newspapers across the nation, legends of the forty-niners, criminals, and heroes of the Wild West were created.

One such legend, Jesse James, owed his fame in part to the newspapers that lauded his heroics as an outlaw who robbed from the rich to give to the poor. Sensational accounts continued to spread after his death, as newspapers relayed the exciting tale of his shooting. These stories served as a eulogy to the hero, as in one Missouri newspaper that claimed, "To look upon that face is to believe that the wonderful deeds of daring ascribed to Jesse James have not been exaggerated."[11]

Just as newspaper readers eagerly followed the shoot-outs in the Wild West, they also were hungry for information on the gunfire between Union and Rebel soldiers. Newspapers found numerous ways to appeal to the baser emotions of readers through Civil War reporting. Tales of inhumanities inflicted upon each side by the other blazed across the pages of the nation's newspapers. Even before the war had commenced on the battlefields, the newspapers on each side of the Mason-Dixon Line engaged in a combat of words. Much of this contest concerned the issue of slavery, with many northern newspapers using sensational tactics to turn readers against the ways of southerners. A *New York Tribune* article described a slave auction in Georgia where "human feelings [were] of no account." "The Negroes were examined with as little consideration as if they had been brutes indeed," the article asserted, depicting the great humiliations to which potential buyers subjected the slaves. Newspapers with southern loyalties expressed their dismay at the reckless disregard with which northern newspapers "horrified" the public "by tales of Southern outrages and Southern barbarity, for the purpose of maddening the people and rendering a peaceful solution of our difficulties impossible." Such writers blamed the Union papers for starting the war with their emotion-eliciting descriptions of such atrocities, many of which the Southern writers labeled as gross exaggerations. One Pennsylvania newspaper warned that the realities of war "will be beyond the inventions of facile imaginations," and "will spare but little room for a continuation of the absurd, and sometimes wicked, exaggerations which have assisted in a great measure to bring the horrible calamity to our doors."[12]

The exaggerations did not cease once the fighting had begun. Skeptical writers cautioned against "newspaper vampyres, who suck their very existence out of the people by taking advantage of their desire for news." These admonitions increased after a Boston newspaper's "imaginative editor" had created a story on "the great fight at Alexandria." Some critics blamed the telegraph for the falsification of news, saying "news agents catch at every floating rumor and without waiting to hear the confirmation, they rush to the telegraph office." These critics had "no doubt that in a majority of cases (news agents) telegraph whatever will sell, without much regard to its truth or falsity." Newspapers

awed readers with the speed with which news from the front could reach their hands. News consumers were delighted with the quick and colorful war reporting, giving the newspapers a captive audience for their false reports.[13]

Another string of battles that provided fascinating reading for consumers of American news were the Indian Wars. From 1867 to 1891, eastern newspapers dispatched correspondents to cover the campaigns in the West. The sensational accounts that appeared in some newspapers riveted readers with descriptions of bloody battles and romanticized Indian warfare. As had become a common practice among sensationalist newspapers, some correspondents fabricated items when no suitably exciting news presented itself. Margaret Irvin Carrington, wife of the commander at Fort Phil Kearney, accused the correspondents of writing "warped and false representations" that "discredited every good thing." She claimed that "a large margin was left for the play of fancy, and the imagination was drawn upon with great freedom and success." The *New York Tribune* offered one fabricated story telling readers of a massacre at Fort Buford where "Colonel Rankin, his wife, one child, and the whole garrison was slaughtered." For added effect, the article claimed that Rankin "shot his wife to save her from falling into the hands of the Indians." Despite the fact that the *Tribune* labeled the story as false four days later, both *Harper's Weekly* and *Leslie's Illustrated Newspaper* lifted the story without apology. True or false, such sensational accounts sold papers.[14]

YELLOW JOURNALISM

New York World managing editor John Cockerill described the practices of 19th-century newspapers as the "constant effort made to secure, by telegraph, by special correspondence, or by indefatigable reporters, at any cost, and to present in the most meretricious form ... occurrences which will catch the curious eye and hold the morbid fancy."[15] The gay '90s ushered in a new era of such sensational journalism as William Randolph Hearst of the *New York Journal* and Joseph Pulitzer of the *World* made New York City a battleground for their journalistic conflict.

Like the New York penny papers earlier in the century, the newspapers of Hearst and Pulitzer contained exciting stories to draw in readers. However, Pulitzer eschewed the tactics of fabrication and scandalous gossip used by his predecessors. He felt that "a newspaper should be scrupulously accurate, it should be clean, it should avoid everything salacious and suggestive, everything that could offend good taste or lower the moral tone of its readers." He did believe that his newspaper had a place for "dramatic accounts of murders, railroad wrecks, fires, lynchings, political corruption, embezzlements, frauds, graft, divorces." The purpose was not to make money, though, but to educate and inform the public. He said, "There is not a crime ... there is not a vice which does not live in secrecy. Get these things out in the open, describe them, attack them, ridicule them in the press, and sooner or later public opinion will sweep them away."[16]

While the sensational journals of the 1890s may not have blatantly fabricated news, they were not beneath creating news to attract attention. *World* reporter Elizabeth Cochrane (AKA "Nellie Bly") circled the globe in an attempt to beat the fictional record of Jules Verne's Phileas Fogg in *Around the World in Eighty Days*. When she returned to New York in "72 days, six hours, ten minutes, and some seconds," she arrived at the railroad station to find "ten thousand eyes on her." The *World* reported policemen "almost at fisticuffs with the crowd there. From the balconies bunches of flowers [were] thrown into the struggling crowd."[17] Bly's sensational exploit had certainly attracted attention.

The two yellow journals, named for the comic strip character "The Yellow Kid" that appeared in both papers, took the creation of news one step further with their involvement in starting the Spanish-American War in 1898. As difficulties arose in Cuba, Hearst sent illustrator Frederic Remington and writer Richard Harding Davis to "describe and depict the atrocities which the cruel Spaniards were inflicting upon the courageous Cubans, struggling for their liberties." According to Hearst, the correspondents "did their work admirably and aroused much indignation among the Americans." Hearst continued to help the impending war along with stories promising battles and reminding President Cleveland of his duty to act on behalf of the people. At one point Remington suggested that war might not occur, but correspondent James Creelman claimed that Hearst sent Remington a cable saying, "You furnish the pictures and I'll furnish the war."[18] Pulitzer joined Hearst's crusade on the Cubans' behalf. When the battleship *Maine* exploded in February 1898, both editors plastered the story complete with large illustrations on the front page of their newspapers. By April, the prominent reports in the *World* and the *Journal* had aided in coercing Congress into a formal declaration of war.

Yellow journalism extended beyond New York into other areas of the country. Texas newspapers displayed the same showy layout techniques as their New York counterparts. The scandalous and often gory content was, however, more reminiscent of the penny papers. In 1895, the *Dallas Morning News* reported the murder of a young woman who had been strangled so that her tongue had been forced "to protrude from her mouth." Additionally, her legs "had been hacked off with a sharp ax or a butcher's cleaver, and pieces of ragged skin and flesh were hanging from the dismembered legs." Often the Texas papers would also report the punishment for such crimes, as when one murderer was hanged in Houston. According to the *Daily Post*, "The body was left hanging eighteen minutes when it was cut down and put into a coffin."[19]

THE BIRTH OF
THE TABLOIDS

The epitome of sensational news appeared in tabloid newspapers. Essentially, tabloids differ from the average newspaper in their size:

12 inches wide, 16–18 inches deep, with four to six columns per page. But while some tabloids steered clear of sensational tactics, the most widely circulated tabloids embraced them.

A successful tabloid formula originated in Great Britain, where Sir Alfred Harmsworth (Lord Northcliffe) found an audience for his half-penny illustrated newspaper called the *London Daily Mirror*. Small in size and full of pictures, the much-imitated *Daily Mirror* contained amusing and sensational stories of interest to the moderately educated middle and lower classes. Joseph Medill Patterson, grandson of the Chicago newspaperman Joseph Medill, became fascinated with Lord Northcliffe's style and brought the formula to America. Thus the *New York Daily News*, the first successful tabloid in the United States, appeared in 1919.

With his cousin Robert McCormick, Patterson aimed his tabloid at those for whom the city's larger, more serious newspapers held no appeal. When the *Daily News* exceeded a million in daily circulation in the mid–1920s to become the highest circulation newspaper in the country, it proved "conclusively that only a sharp lowering of the IQ of a newspaper was necessary to make it attractive to a hitherto unexploited portion of the great metropolitan rank and file." Critics balked at the lack of intellectual stimulation afforded by the *Daily News* and others like it, claiming that the excessive use of pictures "tell the stories in a way that leaves absolutely nothing to the reader. He need not read, he need not think. All he need do is clutch the paper,—and look!"[20]

Like the *Daily Mirror* in England, the *Daily News* spawned many imitators in America. Never one to shy away from competition, William Randolph Hearst entered the tabloid race with his *Daily Mirror*. Despite the decline of his *Journal*, Hearst embarked in a press battle that smacked of yellow journalism. He and Patterson each began running lotteries in their respective newspapers to win each others' readers. Patterson opened the pot with $1,000, and as each man increased his prize the other would raise his promised sum higher. After the prize had been worked up to $20,000, Patterson promised that any further increase by Hearst

would be doubled. Although the lotteries ceased, Hearst and Patterson each made reader contests a staple in their tabloids. Running the gamut from tongue twisters and crossword puzzles to contests for prettiest legs and most popular barber, these games, according to *Daily News* general manager William Field, brought "a lot of sunshine into otherwise dull lives."[21]

A third and more extreme tabloid, Bernarr Macfadden's *Evening Graphic*, also ran reader contests. In one of his more popular competitions, Macfadden endeavored to find the perfect male and perfect female to make a love match. This contest exemplified his obsession with the human physique. Macfadden, whose job titles prior to entering the newspaper field included physical therapist, professional wrestler, athletic director, and exercise machine demonstrator, displayed the human body "religiously" in his newspaper. "If the human form, unfettered by garments, is divine, then every edition of the *Graphic* is a prayer," quipped one critic. Dubbed the "Evening Pornographic," the paper contained some of the most shocking illustrations to date. Macfadden's own daughters were among the models for the photographs of "well-nourished nudes, some in provocative positions," that appeared in each issue of the *Graphic*.[22]

Photographs and other illustrations, however shocking, characterized the sensational tabloids. In addition to the entire front page, the two center pages—known as the double truck—typically contained nothing other than pictures, bold headlines, and witty captions. The content of the pictures themselves mattered little, as long as there was "some attack upon a simple emotion. The true tabloid reader will gape at any picture, whether it means anything or not."[23] Often the picture did not even have to be real to intrigue the reader. In the spirit of their predecessors in sensational news, tabloids carried numerous fabrications, particularly in the area of illustration. The "art" departments of the tabloids frequently doctored old pictures to fit their needs, such as labeling a picture of an Armistice Day parade as "The Funeral of Frank A. Munsey." Reporters would even pose for photographs, called composographs, simulating an actual scene. One

Evening Graphic staffer nearly met his death when he posed as Gerald Chapman for a photograph of the criminal's hanging.

Tabloid or not, the newspapers that fared well in the 1920s were those that emphasized crime news, particularly murders. Individual murder trials reported in the newspapers captured public attention so often that Charles Merz observed in 1927, "A nationally famous trial for homicide is no longer a startling interruption in a more lethargic train of thought. It has become an institution, as periodic in its public appearances and reappearances as the cycle of the seasons." One of these trials also serves to illustrate the tendency for sensational newspapers of the 1920s, like their predecessors, to create news. In 1926, Hearst dug up an unresolved murder case from four years before in which New Jersey minister Edward Hall and Eleanor Mills, a choir singer from his church, had been found dead together. Hearst's *Daily Mirror* proclaimed to have new evidence in the case, which resulted in the minister's widow being prosecuted for the murder. Newspapers from the *Daily News* to the *New York Times* lauded the case as the "Crime of the Century" and dispatched correspondents to set up camp and cover the trial in Somerville, New Jersey. According to one skeptic, "editors, perceiving a case which looks to them like a good standard murder mystery, began by dressing it up attractively in an effort to sell it to their readers." He continued that "they send out reporters who have read plenty of detective fiction and know what is expected." Tabloids and "respectable" newspapers alike devoted enormous amounts of space to the trial. Silas Bent reported that the *New York Times* devoted "more words than Theodore Dreiser needed for the development of his monumental novel 'An American Tragedy.'" Overall, "[e]nough words have been sent out of the Jersey village to fill volumes of the 'Encyclopedia Britannica.'" While newspapers like the *Times* led the way in news stories and editorial comment, the tabloids gleefully contributed the most space in pictures and headlines.[24]

SENSATIONALISM IN THE DEPRESSION

As the stock market crashed, so did the spirit of journalism. The Depression and ensuing war had a sobering impact on sensational newspapers and ended many of the tabloids that had become popular during the roaring '20s. Macfadden's *Evening Graphic* floundered in 1932 due to a loss of financial backing. The *Daily News* survived, but in an altered form. With the sobriety of the Depression, Patterson shifted his tabloid to a more serious, informative tone.

Despite the serious cast that overtook the country and by extension the nation's newspapers, reporters found scandals and murders to relay to the American public. Among the most celebrated stories of the 1930s was the kidnapping of aviator Charles Lindbergh's infant son. For over four years, stories of the search for the missing child, the discovery of the dead baby, and the trial and execution of his murderer saturated the newspapers. "Lindbergh Baby Kidnapped" flashed across the front page of newspapers nationwide the day after the crime. Over two months later, the *Daily News* reported the discovery of the child's body in gruesome detail, including the fact that a "mark resembling a footprint was spread across the tiny form, as if the kidnapper had viciously tried to stamp it into the ground." Even more gruesome were the stories published four years later describing the execution of the killer, Bruno Richard Hauptmann. The *Daily News* covered its front page the following day with an artist's drawing of the execution scene, and sold 450,000 more copies than usual. *Editor & Publisher* depicted the scene of reporters and cameramen crowding for a look at Hauptmann's grief-stricken wife at Fresh Pond Crematory, where "Bruno's electricity-seared body was reduced to ashes." According to the journal, some newspapers "threw practically all journalistic restraint overboard to tell the ghastly story in startling pictures and dramatic news accounts."[25]

In the pattern of newspapers of the 19th century that used sensational journalism to make legends of frontiersmen, newspapers of the Depression era immortalized the mobsters that inhabited major cities across America. Elevating the FBI to hero status, the newspapers relayed the sensational stories of the good guys tracking down the bad guys. Jack Lait of the International News Service vividly described the stakeout and death of the "most wanted" man in America, John Dillinger. "A Federal man, revolver in hand, stepped from behind a telegraph pole at the mouth of the passage," Lait wrote. "'Hello John,' he said, almost whispered, his voice husky with the intensity of the classic melodrama." Later in the story, two bullets "went through the bandit's heart. He staggered, his weapon clattered to the asphalt paving, and as he went three more shots flashed. One bullet hit the back of his head, downward, as he was falling, and came out under his eye."[26]

FOR INQUIRING MINDS

The end of World War II filled the nation with a new economic and social vitality, and a new hunger for the super-sensationalism of the tabloids. Generoso Pope, Jr., offered a feeding frenzy beginning in 1952 with his *National Enquirer*. Filled with well-illustrated stories of sex, murder, and the supernatural, the *Enquirer* began anew the lust for sensational scandal. The *Enquirer* actually originated in the 1920s as an experimental paper funded by William Randolph Hearst. Pope conducted some experiments of his own and eventually turned the *Enquirer* into a crime sheet. "I noticed how auto accidents drew crowds and I decided that if it was blood that interested people, I'd give it to them," Pope said.[27] Pope coupled graphic stories under such headlines as "Mom Boiled Her Baby and Ate Her," "Kills Son and Feeds Corpse to Pigs," and "Digs Up Wife's Rotting Corpse and Rips it Apart" with gory photographs of mutilated bodies and dismembered body parts.

After over a decade of ultra-gore, the *Enquirer* shunned its super-sensational style for a slightly cleaner though still unusual content. *Newsweek* reported in 1969 that the *Enquirer* had reformed. "The steady diet of sex and

sadism has given way to a platter of offbeat pieces, ranging from kooky success stories ... to reports of mischief in the Capital," the magazine announced. *Time* added "gossip by and about celebrities, plus an overdose of the occult and the quasi-scientific" to the list of the *Enquirer*'s new content. The catalyst for this shift was the leveling off of circulation at one million. This stall came in part because of the closing of a large number of newsstands, the *Enquirer*'s main outlets of distribution. Pope looked to the supermarket as a new avenue for disseminating his product, but he had to tone down the smut to appeal to "those women in hair curlers who pass through the checkout lines." The new formula worked. By 1974, the tabloid's circulation had risen to four million. The soaring circulation was Pope's goal from the outset. He claimed he didn't care if the *Enquirer* got respect from other media, stating that a Pulitzer Prize "ain't going to win us two readers."[28]

The *Enquirer* did win the respect of Australian publisher Rupert Murdoch, who followed the model of the *Enquirer* with his *Star*. He seemed cut out for the tabloid business. One writer even compared him to the sensationalism king of the century, calling him a "late nineteenth century Hearstian figure who has seemingly materialized in the New York City of the late 1970s through some curious time warp."[29] After launching successful tabloids in Great Britain and Australia, Murdoch introduced the *Star* to America in 1976. Initially, it was a gory murder sheet in the pattern of the original *Enquirer*. He soon came around to the *Enquirer*'s subdued supermarket style and approached it in circulation.

As the tabloids subdued their content, the mainstream newspapers increased their sensationalism to meet them. Two events served as catalysts for a new surge of sensational reporting in mainstream newspapers: the murder of newspaper giant John S. Knight III and the kidnapping of William Randolph Hearst's granddaughter Patricia. The grandson of John S. Knight, founder of the Knight-Ridder group, Knight met his death at the hands of three young men who also robbed the millionaire of thousands of dollars in jewelry and silverware. Reporters exploited every scandalous detail of the case, particularly allegations of homosexuality. One paper announced that police were questioning "homosexuals, male prostitutes, and homosexual procurers. Police said many of those questioned were known to have frequented Knight's Dorchester apartment." Many papers capitalized on the relationship between Knight and an informant on the case, William Sage. The two supposedly "had a homosexual relationship that extended over five years."[30]

The press' handling of the murder's sexual angle led some to dub the Knight case as most sensational story of the decade. However, Patty Hearst's kidnapping nearly two years earlier spawned "shrill and overblown" press coverage that rivaled the excessive treatment of the Knight story. Both the Hearst and the Knight story suggested that a new era in sensationalism had begun and led one critic to question the ethics of such journalism. "In both the Hearst and the Knight cases, the nation witnessed the spectacle of the press devouring its own young," Jerry Knudson wrote. "This process posed serious ethical questions for the entire profession."[31]

Since the mid–1970s, gossip and scandal-laden stories have masqueraded as news in the pages of dailies across America, telling of the imprudence among celebrities and politicians. Murders still took center stage in the late 20th century as cases involving celebrities such as former football great O. J. Simpson and child beauty JonBenet Ramsey captivated media consumers. Sexual scandal also maintained prominence, particularly when politicians were involved. The sexual indiscretions of such figures as Clarence Thomas, Gary Hart, and Bill Clinton seized headlines of tabloids and mainstream papers alike. With this direct competition between mainstream and tabloid papers, the tabloids resorted to cutthroat tactics in order to out-scoop and out-scandal their new competitors. The extreme measures taken by tabloid photographers (AKA "paparazzi") led to the death of Princess Diana of Wales in 1997.

The timeline of sensationalism began long before the history of American journalism. American newspapers have incorporated sensational tactics from their inception. While some eras in newspaper history have contained more scandal, more gore, and more gossip than others, the newspapers have constantly used sensationalism as a cry for attention. Judging by the circulations of newspapers that have used these tactics well, the cry has been heard.

Selected Readings

Bessie, Simon M. *Jazz Journalism*. New York: Dutton, 1938.

Bird, S. Elizabeth. *For Enquiring Minds: A Cultural Study of Supermarket Tabloids*. Knoxville: University of Tennessee Press, 1992.

Cohen, Lester. *The New York Graphic: The World's Zaniest Newspaper*. Philadelphia: Chilton, 1964.

Crouthamel, James L. "James Gordon Bennett, the *New York Herald*, and the Development of Newspaper Sensationalism." *New York History* 54 (July 1973): 294–316.

Dorwart, Jeffery M. "James Creelman, the *New York World* and the Port Arthur Massacre." *Journalism Quarterly* 50 (1973): 697–701.

Dwyer, Richard A., and Richard E. Lingenfelter. *Lying on the Eastern Slope: James Townsend's Comic Journalism on the Mining Frontier*. Miami: University Presses of Florida, 1984.

Fedler, Fred. *Media Hoaxes*. Ames: Iowa State University Press, 1989.

Francke, Warren. "An Argument in Defense of Sensationalism: Probing the Popular and Historiographical Concept." *Journalism History* 5 (1978): 70–73.

Francke, Warren. "Sensationalism and the Development of 19th-Century Reporting: The Broom Sweeps Sensory Details." *Journalism History* 12 (1985): 80–85.

Meyers, W. Cameron. "The Chicago Newspaper Hoax in the '36 Election Campaign." *Journalism Quarterly* 37 (1960): 356–64.

Nelson, Jack A. "Roommates: Mark Twain and Dan De Quille: Partners in Hoaxes in Old West." *Media History Digest* 6, 1 (1986): 2–7.

Nordin, Kenneth. "The Entertaining Press: Sensationalism in Eighteenth-Century Boston Newspaper." *Communication Research* 6 (1979): 295–320.

Olasky, Marvin. "Late 19th-Century Texas Sensationalism: Hypocrisy or Biblical Morality?" *Journalism History* 12 (1985): 96–100.

Shaw, Donald L. "In the Eye of the Beholder? Sensationalism in American Press News, 1820–1860." *Journalism History* 12 (1985): 86–91.

Stevens, John D. *Sensationalism and the New York Press*. New York: Columbia University Press, 1991.

Notes

1. Laurence White, "True wonders and strange news," 1675, reprinted in *The Pack of Autolycus, or Strange and Terrible News of Ghosts, Apparitions, Monstrous Births, Showers of Wheat, Judgments of God, and Other Prodigious and Fearful Happenings as told in Broadside Ballads of the Years 1624–1693*, ed. Hyder Edward Rollins (Cambridge: Harvard University Press, 1927), 191.

2. *Dallas Morning News*, 1 April 1895.

3. *National Enquirer*, 6 May 1962.

4. Martin Parker, "The two inseparable brothers, or A true and strange description of a Gentleman (an Italian by birth) about seventeen years of age, who hath an imperfect (yet living) Brother, growing out of his side, having a head, two armes, and one leg, all perfectly to be seen," 1637, reprinted in Rollins, *The Pack of Autolycus,* 12.

5. *Publick Occurrences, Both Forreign and Domestick* (Boston), 25 September 1690.

6. *New York Herald*, 11 April 1836.

7. James Parton, "Falsehood in the Daily Press," *Harper's New Monthly Magazine*, July 1874, 273.

8. Richard Adams Locke, "Great Astronomical Discoveries," *New York Sun*, 25 August 1835.

9. Sir Henry Morton Stanley, *How I Found Livingstone: Travels, Adventures and Discoveries in Central Africa* (New York: Scribner, Armstrong & Co., 1872), xviii.

10. Mark Twain, "Empire City Massacre," *Territorial Enterprise* (Virginia City, Nevada), 28 October 1863.

11. *Tribune* (St. Joseph, Mo.), 3 April 1882.

12. *New York Tribune*, 9 March 1859; *Daily Chicago Times*, 14 December 1860; *Lancaster Intelligencer*, 21 May 1861.

13. *Lynn Weekly Reporter*, 1 June 1861; *Daily Dayton Journal*, 29 May 1861.

14. Margaret Irvin Carrington, *Ab-sa-ra-ka, Home of the Crows: Being the Experience of an Officer's Wife on the Plains* (Philadelphia: J. B. Lippincott & Co., 1868), 223 and 219; *New York Tribune*, 5 April 1867.

15. John A. Cockerill, "Some Phases of Contemporary Journalism," *Cosmopolitan* (October 1892), 696.

16. Lecture by Joseph Pulitzer, quoted in Alleyne Ireland, *An Adventure with a Genius: Recollections of Joseph Pulitzer* (New York: E. P. Dutton & Company, Inc., 1920), 113–115.

17. *New York World*, 26 January 1890.

18. William Randolph Hearst, *A Portrait in His Own Words*, ed. Edmond D. Coblentz (New York: Simon & Schuster, 1952), 58; James Creelman, *On the Great Highway* (Boston: Lathrop, 1907), 178.

19. "Mysterious Murder," *Dallas Morning News*, 1 April 1895; "Doran Done For," *Houston Daily Post*, 21 August 1880.

20. Richard G. de Rochemont, "The Tabloids," *American Mercury*, October 1926, 188; Aben Kandel, "A Tabloid a Day," *The Forum*, March 1927, 380.

21. William H. Field, quoted in de Rochemont, ibid., 188.

22. Kandel, "A Tabloid a Day," 383.

23. de Rochemont, "The Tabloids," 189.

24. Charles Merz, "Bigger and Better Murders," *Harper's Monthly Magazine*, August 1927, 341; Bruce Bliven, "The Hall-Press-Mills Case," *The New Republic*, 1 December 1926, 39; Silas Bent, "The Hall-Mills Case in the Newspapers," *The Nation*, 8 December 1926, 580.

25. "Baby Dead," *New York Daily News*, 13 May 1932; John W. Perry, "Execution Story Got Smashing Play," *Editor & Publisher*, 11 April 1936.

26. Jack Lait, International News Service, 23 July 1934, quoted in Calder M. Pickett, *Voices of the Past: Key Documents in the History of American Journalism* (Columbus, Ohio: Grid, Inc., 1977), 295.

27. "Goodbye to Gore," *Time*, 21 February 1972, 64.

28. "From Worse to Bad," *Newsweek*, 8 September 1969, 79; "Goodbye to Gore," 64; Elizabeth Peer, "Up from Smut," *Newsweek*, 21 April 19. Chris Welles, "The Americanization of Rupert Murdoch," *Esquire*, 22 May 1979, 52

30. *Philadelphia Daily News*, 9 December 1975; *Philadelphia Inquirer*, 10 December 1975.

31. Jerry W. Knudson, "Philadelphia Story: The Murder of John S. Knight III," *Mass Communication Review* 6, 2 (Spring 1979): 11.

29

Radio Journalism

GARY W. LARSON

Radio journalism in America, like any other form of mediated communication, has been closely tied to the changing technology of the medium and the changing political whim of the nation. The development of broadcast journalism in America was quickened at several key points when technology, content, and politics intersected. The period from 1922 to 1938 was marked by strife between radio and newspapers. The period of 1938 to 1946 saw rapid expansion of radio journalism, largely driven by World War II. The period of 1946 to 1960 was a transitional period for radio journalism, due to the introduction of format radio and to the expansion of television. From 1960 to 1980, radio journalism was influenced by the greater utilization of the FM band, which forced radio news to redefine itself in the wake of a more fragmented audience. Finally, the period of 1980 to the present witnessed a rebirth of radio journalism, albeit on a smaller scale. These five intersections of politics, technology, and content have defined radio journalism in America.

While the first period didn't begin until the mid–1920s, news on the radio was certainly nothing new by the mid–'20s and early '30s. However, as former journalist Paul White recounted in 1947, "… there were relatively few broadcasts or summaries."[1] That did not mean that America hadn't been listening. One of the earliest radio broadcasts was November 2, 1920, when KDKA in Pittsburgh broadcast the results of the Harding-Cox presidential election. In 1925, WGN in Chicago broadcast from the Scopes Trial, and in 1927 the transatlantic flight of aviator Charles "Lucky" Lindbergh captured the attention of radio listeners all over the world.

Regularly scheduled news broadcasts on the networks didn't start until 1929 or 1930. Floyd Gibbons began "The Headline Hunter" for NBC in 1929, while "Lowell Thomas and the News" premiered in September 1930. H. V. Kaltenborn's regular newscasts began the same year with three-times-per-week broadcasts on CBS. Gibbons, Thomas, and Kaltenborn could be heard on the airwaves of the nation by more people than might ever see a story in a newspaper. In the first two years of the 1930s, coverage of the Lindbergh kidnapping and the subsequent trial of Bruno Hauptman whetted the nation's appetite for more news coverage, and effectively made the reputation of some news reporters, such as Boake Carter for CBS.[2] But the economics of the Great Depression conspired with newspaper publishers, who effectively forced the wire news services to stop making their product available to radio networks. The newspapers feared that news on the radio would siphon off advertising and sales revenue. The networks responded by creating their own news bureaus all over America and in locations throughout the world. By the end of 1933, radio network executives had recognized the expense of setting up the bureaus, while at the same time the established wire services and newspaper publishers had recognized that radio was a force that simply could not be ignored. The period is known as the "Press-Radio War," and at stake was the power to control how news would be distributed.

THE PRESS-RADIO WAR AND BILTMORE AGREEMENT

The opening salvo of the Press-Radio War was fired in 1922 when the Associated Press wire service issued a notice to subscribers that AP news copy was not to be used for broadcasting purposes. This notice went largely ignored, however, since many of the early radio stations were owned by large newspapers. Also, other wire services (United Press and International News Service) said they would continue to provide copy to all their subscribers, especially in light of the 1924 presidential election.[3] For the next 17 years—until 1939—the journalists of America were at war, not as chroniclers of U.S. military action but rather at war within their own ranks. The Press-Radio War changed journalism in this country, molding the future of broadcast journalism for both radio and television. The key event of this period was a meeting in December of 1933 at the Biltmore Hotel in New York.

The meeting of wire service representatives, network executives, and newspaper publishers resulted in a document known as the Biltmore Agreement. This document limited the radio networks to only two, five-minute newscasts per day. The newscasts had to be broadcast in the mornings, but only after 9:30 a.m., and in the evenings, but only after 9:00 p.m. There could be copy only from the established wire services, and no breaking or up-to-the-minute news could be broadcast. Finally, the agreement stipulated that radio news must not have any advertising support, and that listeners were to be encouraged to consult their newspapers for the latest news.[4]

Since shortly after the 1922 Associated Press moratorium on broadcast use of news copy, the radio networks had been putting together their own news gathering organizations. The wire services were afraid that granting access to radio networks would bring down the wrath of their traditional customers, the newspapers. The impetus for the Biltmore Agreement was clear: the publishers recognized that radio could—and probably would—take revenue away from newspapers. The agreement al-lowed the networks access to some wire service content, but restricted the broadcast content to a format that would, first, be long enough only to whet the information appetites of the news-consuming public; second, not interfere in the prime newspaper-selling periods of mornings and evenings; and, third, not compete with newspapers for advertising dollars. T. R. Carskadon, writing in *The New Republic* in 1936, said the Biltmore Conference was held in "smoke and hate-filled rooms" and characterized the agreement as "savage" and "an open invitation to revolt."[5]

When the publishers, wire service executives, and radio network executives met at the Biltmore on December 11 and 12, 1933, the meeting foreshadowed something that would later be called "audience segmentation." In effect, the various media would agree to split up the audience, with newspapers concentrating on news and information, and radio concentrating on entertainment. A representative of independent stations at the meeting said he would not commit to such an agreement. Since three-quarters of the radio stations in the country at this point were independent, the non-network radio stations wielded some power. Broadcasters not affiliated with the large radio networks simply ignored the agreement and set about gathering and broadcasting their own news. Because they were so decentralized they were able to resist pressures from the networks.

In the years following the agreement, broadcasters redefined how they presented news. The agreement stipulated the length and timing of "newscasts" but said nothing about "commentary." Paul White says that "the first thing that happened was an arbitrary decision by the network that Winchell, Thomas, Carter and Kaltenborn weren't news broadcasters but commentators. Hence they could be sponsored."[6] Hadley Cantril, writing for *Public Opinion Quarterly* in 1939, said that the commentator "interprets the news, thereby helping people to give meaning to the scattered news items of the day."[7] It didn't take long for the Biltmore Agreement to crumble under the combined weight of pressure from independent radio stations and all the commentary on the network airwaves. The ending of the Press-

Radio War in 1939 had as much to do with economic reasons as did the beginning, 17 years earlier. Newspapers continued to view radio stations as lucrative, with the number of newspaper-owned or affiliated stations more than doubling in the period of 1933–38. Finally, the Associated Press lifted its ban on radio transmission of wire copy in the spring of 1939, signaling the end of the Radio-Press War.

Of course, other events in the world were gearing up to make radio an even greater force in American society. As economic crises in Europe escalated and saw the rise of National Socialism in Germany, American audiences could follow the news from Europe on a daily basis. Audiences had grown accustomed to the commentary format that radio networks had adopted during the Press-Radio War, ensuring that news on the radio would be more than just a bare reporting of facts. It would be personality-driven and dependent on the prose storytelling abilities of the commentators. Certainly an exemplar of this was coverage of the *Hindenburg* disaster of 1937.

The airship *Hindenburg*, the pride of the burgeoning German society under National Socialism, was to dock at the Lakehurst, New Jersey, airship station on the evening of May 6, 1937. As the *Hindenburg* joined to the docking pole on this stormy evening, broadcast commentator Herb Morrison was recording a description of the events. A broadcaster for WLS in Chicago on "The Dinner Bell Hour," he was at the arrival of the *Hindenburg* on the first anniversary of its transatlantic crossing as part of a publicity stunt for American Airlines. He was using a portable recording device called a "disc-cutter" that allowed him and his engineer to make recordings in the field, even though the rule at the networks during this period was no recordings would be used on the air.

As the *Hindenburg* touched the docking pole and burst into flame, the shock wave of the explosion caused deep grooves to be cut into the lacquer of the disk, but Morrison's eyewitness account of the disaster was faithfully reproduced. He and his engineer flew back to Chicago, where an excerpt of the now-famous recording was played on the air the following morning. It was the first recording ever allowed to be broadcast on NBC.

RADIO GOES TO WAR

In September 1938, tensions in Europe reached a climax as Hitler's Nazi troops invaded the Sudetenland. As this story broke, CBS's H. V. Kaltenborn began one of the landmark broadcasts of this period of radio journalism. For 18 straight days of the Munich Crisis, he took bulletins from the wire services and stories from reporters and turned them into a stream of more than 85 separate broadcasts, some lasting as long as two hours. He and other CBS commentators such as Edward R. Murrow and William Shirer ushered in the era of modern newscasting through their reporting of the international crisis and subsequent events in Europe that presaged the start of the war. World War II began a year after the Munich Crisis, when audiences heard the voice of British Prime Minister Neville Chamberlain read the declaration of war against Germany on September 3, 1939. This began what must be described as one of the greatest and most turbulent periods of radio journalism in the history of the medium.

American audiences were primed for this moment since the inauguration of President Roosevelt in 1933, when he told the nation that the only thing it had to fear "is fear itself." Over the next few years, he used the radio airwaves to bring himself closer to the American people with his Fireside Chats, starting with the first address just a week after his inauguration in 1933. Between 1933 and 1935 he broadcast as many as 40 speeches, with as much as 30 per cent of the American people listening in.[8] By the time war was declared in 1939, Americans were tuning into radio not only for the entertainment it offered every night, but also for continuing news coverage and commentary on world events. Already by 1939, a Roper poll showed that more than a quarter of the population relied on radio for their news and that most of them felt radio news was more objective than what could be found in newspapers.[9]

From the invasion of Sudetenland in

September 1938 to the end of the war in August of 1945, radio journalists brought stories of the conflict into the living rooms of millions of Americans. The war in Europe drove the development of radio journalism, with CBS broadcasting the first overseas News Roundup in March of 1938. By 1940, all of the networks had roundup programs from London, Paris, Berlin, Rome, and Washington on the air—nearly 20 hours weekly of war coverage.

Just as the move to a commentary format drove radio journalism into a culture of personalities, so, too, did coverage of World War II. With millions of Americans tuning in every day to hear the latest news about the war, and with relatively few choices from which to receive that news, it is hardly surprising that recognizable personalities emerged from this period, or that those personalities were intensely personalized by the American listening public. Edward R. Murrow and Charles Collingwood in London, Eric Sevareid in Paris, and William Shirer in Berlin all became household names, comforting voices during the greatest global crisis of the century.

The war effort in America demanded much of its citizens. Sacrifice for the good of the war effort was the watchword of the country during this period. Victory gardens, meatless days, fuel rationing, scrap metal drives, and many other impositions were embraced by a willing population, all eager for their sons, husbands, fathers and brothers to come home from the war. There was sacrifice in broadcasting as well. While the country gave up meat and fuel, the broadcasting industry gave up the material needed for expansion, particularly the copper that was needed in large quantities for transmitter tubes, along with the factories that were converted to wartime materiel production.

TELEVISION ONSLAUGHT

While World War II saw the nation tune in with ever-greater numbers to radio for news as well as entertainment, another technological marvel was being developed and was about ready to burst upon the American consuming public. Television had been introduced most publicly at the World's Fair in New York in 1939, but with the outbreak of the war and the retooling of production lines for military purposes, the medium was relegated, for the most part, to research labs and experimenters. At the end of the war, though, America was still home to over 900 radio stations and more than 31 million families who used radio. In the spring of 1946, a survey showed that about 35 per cent of the American public listed newspapers as their primary news source, while more than 60 per cent listed radio.[10] The immediacy of radio over television in reporting the news from the battle zones had taken its toll on newspaper readership.

After the war, though, television broadcasting was set to be the new rage in America. The trade publication *Variety* even likened the new medium to a movie-house monster, calling television the "Frankenstein" of radio.[11] It is true that television is an extension of radio technology, and that the same people who built commercial radio were also building commercial television. But radio had some new technological enhancements to keep it vital. Television was not on the verge of killing its creator just yet.

In the last years of the 1940s and into the '50s, television networks were siphoning off the talent (and advertisers) that had made radio the powerhouse communication medium during the preceding three decades. Entertainers like Jack Benny, Milton Berle, serialized programs like *Amos 'n' Andy* and *The Guiding Light*, and broadcast journalists like Walter Winchell, Edward R. Murrow, Fred Friendly, and Douglas Edwards all migrated from radio to television. The loss to the radio networks during this period was great and some new form of radio programming was needed to make radio news a viable force in American journalism once again. In 1950, Murrow produced and wrote a new type of program for CBS radio, called *Hear It Now*. A format later to be called a "news magazine" that included interviews with newsmakers along with commentary and lighter stories, *Hear It Now* lasted only 18 months on radio but moved to CBS television as *See It Now* in late 1951.

The technology gleaned from the war

years provided one way for radio to keep an established foothold in broadcast journalism. Smaller, lighter transmitters had been developed for the war effort, and now came into play domestically, allowing broadcast journalists to report live from many places that had been unreachable in the past. The other major technological enhancement that dramatically affected radio journalism in this period was the development of recording tape. Tape technology was a product of the German war effort and was developed quickly in the immediate post-war years by the Ampex Corporation. With high fidelity recording tape bringing the voices of newsmakers quickly to newscasts, radio journalism in the 1950s witnessed an increased immediacy in reporting. "Immediacy" subsequently became a watchword for radio journalism. Television equipment, by comparison, was still very large and bulky and videotape was in its infancy during this period.[12]

So radio journalism in this period reinvented itself, from a format of commentary and even re-enacted news stories, to a format of shorter, immediate reporting of breaking news, coupled with high fidelity "sound bites" that added the voices of actual newsmakers to the immediate coverage. But not only was the format of radio changing, so too was the audience. The introduction of format radio and a better understanding of how audiences were segmented meant that news programming on radio could be targeted to a narrower but more receptive and faithful demographic segment of the audience. The radio networks became providers of news content "feeds" allowing affiliate stations to tape and re-use the voices of newsmakers and the stories done by network correspondents.

In terms of numbers, more and more radio stations were going on the air during this period, particularly smaller, independent stations that were geared to serve primarily rural populations. This was also a period of falling radio audience numbers. Ratings for radio fell from an average of 13 in 1948 to a rating of one in 1956, despite a gain in the use of radio in the mornings. But the AM band was getting crowded with signals, so broadcasters started looking for solutions to the overcrowding.

Once again, a technological shift would change the public face of radio, and with it, American radio journalism.

"Find Me" Radio and Audience Segmentation

FM band radio was certainly not new in 1960: Edwin Armstrong took out the original patents on FM radio in 1933 and with RCA conducted tests from the Empire State Building in 1934. The development of FM was interrupted because of wartime shortages and later the development of television (which used part of the FM band for audio). In 1945, the Federal Communications Commission shifted FM from its prewar location to its present location of 88 to 108 MHz, making obsolete all the FM receivers built prior to the war. AM radio and television broadcasters would joke through the 1950s that "FM" meant "find me."

Audiences were changing as well. The introduction of heavily formatted radio in the 1950s and a greater dependence on music programming created audience segments, each of which had different needs and desires for news and information from the radio. More radios were installed in automobiles as the country moved into outlying suburban areas during the early 1960s, creating "drive times" when captive audiences in their cars turned to their radios for news and entertainment on their way to and from work. Programmers blocked shorter newscasts between blocks of music and commercials, geared to an increasingly mobile workforce. While the recognizable names on radio in previous decades had been the newscasters and commentators, the new personalities of the air were the disc jockeys who entertained commuters. News programming was slowly being reduced in stature.

With a 1961 FCC ruling on technical standards for FM stereo, FM broadcasters were poised to take away from AM radio one of the markets AM had worked so diligently to cultivate from the very beginning: that of entertainment. Up until this time, most FM licenses were held by AM broadcasters, and much of the FM programming was simply a rebroad-casting of the AM signal. In 1965, the FCC ruled that FM stations in markets with popu-lations greater than 100,000 could duplicate no more than 50 per cent of a companion AM sta-tion's programming. The ruling, coupled with the establishment of FM stereo standards, meant that FM could realize its potential as a provider of high fidelity, stereophonic musical programming.

As FM became the band of choice for broadcasters seeking to give their audiences better sounding music over the airwaves, American radio journalism was marked by a further segmenting of the broadcast audience.[13] The smaller, mostly rural independent AM sta-tions that had blossomed during the '50s tar-geted their news coverage to issues that had a direct impact on their primarily agricultural audiences. Newscasts were positioned earlier in the mornings, not only to target people in their cars, but also to target people in their barns. The AM band became heavily talk-oriented, both in rural and urban markets. As early as 1961, programming pioneer Gordon McLen-don started the first all-news AM radio station, XETRA, with a transmitter in Tijuana, Mex-ico. Because Mexican stations were not subject to U.S. regulatory restrictions on transmitter power, XETRA's signal blanketed all of south-ern California, from San Diego to Los Angeles. With the exceptions of a relatively few high-powered "clear channel" stations, the AM band became very localized, preferring to address a limited local market than a wider regional mar-ket. On the FM side of the dial, journalism be-came primarily entertainment, music, and spe-cial topic coverage. Short newsbreaks, headline news, and rapidly-paced stories became the norm for FM radio—with one exception: National Public Radio (NPR).

National Public Radio was the radio side of the Corporation for Public Broadcasting, chartered by Congress in 1967. Broadcast through a network of affiliated NPR stations, many of which were situated at colleges and universities, NPR brought a level of broadcast journalism back to radio that hadn't been seen in quite a while. Programs such as "All Things Considered" raised the standard once again for

the viability of radio journalism. In 1979, as a confirmation of the rapid changes happening in radio, the audience share for FM radio sur-passed the share for AM for the first time.

Between 1960 and 1980, radio went through many changes: from AM to FM and FM stereo, from network-oriented program-ming to highly localized programming, and from being the major provider of broadcast news and information to being a player in a much more diverse arena. The first war to be seen in the living rooms of America—the Vietnam conflict—came and went. Unprece-dented coverage of the war, along with cover-age of a turbulent period civil and political un-rest all across the nation, cemented television as the new provider of the nation's news. The development of videotape cassettes in the late 1960s did for television what recording tape had done for radio 20 years earlier.

As broadcast journalism was changing, so was the nation. Americans heard and saw the assassination of President Kennedy, the chants and marches of the Civil Rights and Free Speech movements, the assassinations of Rob-ert Kennedy and Rev. Martin Luther King, Jr., the resignation of Richard Nixon, and the end of the war in Vietnam. It was a 20-year period of enormous social upheaval, and, through it all, radio journalism managed to adapt to changes, maintaining a presence in the world of broadcast journalism through the 1970s when three-fourths of all radio programming was music.

SATELLITES AND DEREGULATION: RADIO JOURNALISM COMES FULL CIRCLE

With the election of Ronald Reagan to the presidency in 1980, along with the seating of a largely Republican congress, radio in America was on the brink of large-scale changes that would have a great impact on the practice of radio journalism. The early years of the decade were marked by deregulatory legislation, and one of the first industries to be deregulated was broadcasting. The old Public Interest—or PICON—standard (that broadcast licenses were granted in the "Public Interest, Convenience, Or Necessity") that had been a large part of broadcast licensing since the Radio Act of 1927 was thrown out in the 1984 rewrite of the Communications Act, allowing fewer content restrictions and loosening ownership restrictions. The impact on radio journalism was found in fewer and fewer owners, each holding larger numbers of stations, not only nationally but also in the same markets. This meant fewer voices and a homogenization of editorial policies. Journalism had long been the most costly, personnel-intensive part of a local broadcast operation and owners of larger groups of stations sought economies of scale by relying on satellite-delivered national news summaries and greatly reduced local news staffs.

The advent of satellite-delivered programming to radio stations has meant a return to the old days of large networks. Syndicated programming, originating from a single source, may be heard from many stations across the country. With the cost of downlink technology falling, many broadcasters since the early 1980s have found satellite-delivered programming to be a cost-effective way to bring both news and entertainment programming to their listeners, and advertising revenue to their owners. These large, albeit ad hoc, networks of stations recreate the radio climate of the early days of broadcasting, when the large formal networks ruled the airwaves. The majority of stations still making sizable commitments to local radio journalism are AM clear channel stations with long historical roots in their communities. Audience segmentation has reduced the size of potential audiences to a point where maintaining news staffs for individual stations is often seen as a costly, and unnecessary, operating expense.

With loosened content restrictions, this latest period in radio has been marked, at least in part, by a rise in controversial programming that is designed to get and keep listeners. Quasi-journalist personalities such as Paul Harvey and Larry King remind many of the commentators of the 1920s and 1930s, while shock-value personalities such as Howard Stern and Don Imus, partisan commentators such as Rush Limbaugh, and many others use radio in ways no others have ever used it. Tabloid-style talk formats, all-talk formats, and all-news formats have been tried with varying degrees of success. The glue that holds all these different formats together, though, is the shift to a highly segmented radio audience that started in the 1960s. With fewer restrictions on content, coupled with falling prices for stations and equipment, it became financially feasible for station owners and managers to relentlessly pursue smaller but more loyal audience segments.

The technological and political climates at the end of the century brought sweeping change to radio and radio journalism. A continuing deregulatory stance in the 1990s has brought about relaxation of ownership rules. Stations, particularly AM stations, were bought up in a glut of speculative buying as prices plummeted in the 1980s and early 1990s, creating station "groups" and even "supergroups" through mergers. In 1992 the FCC loosened its rules and allowed a single owner to operate two AM and two FM stations in markets with at least 15 stations. The Telecommunications Act of 1996 expanded this policy, lifting the national cap on radio station ownership, and further homogenizing the news and information available on radio.

Young professionals, chiefly the post-war "baby boom" generation, still view radio as a viable source of news and information, even if radio is not their chief source of news. That appellation has now been passed on to television. News on the radio—what's left of it—is designed for delivery to people in their cars and for people in their workplaces. Radio continues to be the most cost-effective medium for the delivery of immediate information, and so enjoys a special status for coverage of fast-breaking news events, and of course for weather emergencies. But within the industry itself, the production of news programming at the local level is a major cost-center for most stations. Following deregulation, many station managers and owners looked to the bottom line, and since deregulation lifted the mandate for public affairs programming, news operations at

many radio stations were cut, or even eliminated.

CONCLUSION

Radio journalism in America has undergone many changes since the Biltmore Agreement of 1933. Some of the changes have been
most influenced by changes in technology,
some by changes in politics, and still others by
changes in ourselves as an audience. What
needs to be understood is that change does not
happen in a vacuum. If one part of an equation
changes, it influences all the other parts: a
change in the political climate changes technology, and vice versa. This has been evident
in the history of American radio journalism.

And yet, through the 70 or so years of
radio journalism, there is sense of commonal-
ity, a thread—or series of threads—that binds
the history together. The Paul Harveys and
Howard Sterns of contemporary talk-format
radio can trace a performance legacy back
through people like Ed Sullivan and even
Walter Winchell. National Public Radio's continuing commitment to quality journalism on
radio can find its own roots in the formation of
the first organized radio news gathering efforts
of CBS and NBC in the years prior to the
Press-Radio Wars. Radio has always attracted
survivors to its ranks: people who wouldn't let
the political, economic, or technological climate of their day slow them down. The threads
in radio journalism continue unbroken from
the Biltmore Agreement and Press-Radio War
through the satellite-delivered programming of
today. Flexibility and a willingness to be out on
the edge has always been the strength of radio.
It has always managed, throughout its entire
existence, to change with the times. To be fluid
and adaptable ... to survive.

Ironically, the changes in politics and
technology that ostensibly weakened radio
journalism in the last couple decades now may
bolster the power of medium. Satellite uplinks
are becoming more affordable, allowing journalists to file audio stories—either complete
audio news packages or sound bites—to the
world for a fraction of the cost of just a decade

ago. The wire services are changing as well.
Associated Press expanded its radio news service
in 1994, launching a 24-hour news network for
stations unable to afford the ever-increasing
cost of producing their own all-news format.

Even more importantly, the digital audio
revolution is maturing at a rapid rate, allowing
greater compression of digital file sizes and allowing the "webcasting" of radio over the
global Internet, a medium of little regulation
and huge potential for both democratization
and capitalist exploitation. So we've come full
circle, from the rapidly expanding and largely
unregulated medium of radio broadcasting in
the third decade of the 20th century, to the
rapidly expanding and largely unregulated
medium of the Internet today. As FCC
Chairman Reed Hundt said in a 1994 interview in *Broadcasting & Cable Magazine*, "The
time has come to ... renew the social compact
between the public and the broadcasting industry."[14] And a prime component of that social compact must be the news and information
that ensures an informed populace.

Selected Readings

Bliss, Edward, Jr. *Now the News: The Story of Broadcast
    Journalism.* New York: Columbia University Press, 1991.
Bohn, Thomas W. "Broadcasting National Election Returns:
    1916–1948." *Journal of Broadcasting* 12 (1968): 267–86.
Ditingo, Vincent M. *The Remaking of Radio.* Boston: Focal
    Press, 1995.
Emery, Michael C. "The Munich Crisis Broadcasts: Radio
    News Comes of Age." *Journalism Quarterly* 42 (1965):
    576–80, 590.
Fang, Irving. *Those Radio Commentators.* Ames: Iowa State
    University Press, 1977.
Jackaway, Gwenyth. *Media at War: Radio's Challenge to the
    Newspapers, 1924–1939.* Westport, Conn.: Praeger, 1995.
Kaltenborn, H. V. *Fifty Fabulous Years: A Personal Review.*
    New York: G. P. Putnam's Sons, 1950.
Lott, George E., Jr. "The Press-Radio War of the 1930s."
    Journal of Broadcasting 14 (1970): 275–86.
Murrow, Edward R. *In Search of Light: The Broadcasts of
    Edward R. Murrow 1938–1961.* New York: Alfred A.
    Knopf, 1967.
Rose, Ernest D. "How the U.S. Heard About Pearl Harbor."
    Journal of Broadcasting 5 (1961): 285–98.
Shirer, William L. *20th Century Journey: A Memoir of a Life
    and the Times.* New York: Little, Brown & Company,
    1984.
Smith, Robert. "The Origins of Radio Network News
    Commentary." *Journal of Broadcasting* 9 (1965): 113–22.
Weeks, Lewis E. "The Radio Election of 1924." *Journal of
    Broadcasting* 8 (1964): 233–43.

Notes

1. Paul White, *News on the Air* (New York: Harcourt, Brace), 1947, 33.

2. "Radio Covers Lindbergh Kidnapping," *Broadcasting*, March 15, 1932.

3. *Editor & Publisher*, "Chicago Tribune Defies Associated Press Rule," October 25, 1924, 1.

4. "Radio-News Program in Final Stage," *Broadcasting*, February 1, 1934, 7.

5. T. R. Carskadon, "The Press Radio War," *The New Republic*, March 11, 1936, 133–34.

6. White, News *On the Air*, 43.

7. Hadley Cantril, "The Role of the Radio Commentator," *Public Opinion Quarterly* 3:4 (October, 1939): 660. Veteran journalist Mitchell Charnley in his 1948 book, *News by Radio* (New York: Macmillan), echoed Cantril, saying that commentary explained a news event "in light of the speaker's personal knowledge and judgment" (308).

8. Reports of the number of Fireside Chats vary, however. J. Fred MacDonald, in *Don't Touch That Dial! Radio Programming in American Life, 1920–1960* (1979), says that Roosevelt broadcast forty speeches between 1933 and 1935. Lichty and Topping, in *American Broadcasting: A Source Book on the History of Radio and Television* (New York: Hastings House), 1975, report twenty-eight such speeches between the first in 1933 and the last in 1944. The confusion rests with exactly what constituted a Fireside Chat.

9. *Variety Radio Directory, 1940–41* (New York, 1941), 107–9.

10. MacDonald, *Don't Touch That Dial!*, 288.

11. *Variety*, 23 October, 1946, 91.

12. Edward Bliss Jr., *Now The News: The Story of Broadcast Journalism* (New York: Columbia University Press), 1991, says that Ampex demonstrated the video recorder in 1956, but it wouldn't be until 1969 that the Sony Corporation would release the first video cassette recorder for broadcast use.

13. Vincent M. Ditingo, *The Remaking of Radio* (Boston: Focal Press), 1995, 5–6.

14. Kim McAvoy, "Hundt's New Deal: FCC Chairman Says It's Time to Revisit Social Compact Between Broadcasting and the Public," *Broadcasting & Cable Magazine*, August 1, 1994, 6–8.

30

Television News

WILLIAM E. HUNTZICKER

Robert Pierpoint felt nervous about appearing on television for his first year-end roundup in 1951 with the men from CBS News in New York. He had covered fighting in Korea, but these men had covered World War II for CBS Radio and invented broadcast journalism in the process. He quickly discovered, however, that his experienced heroes were more nervous about television than he was. As he joined them, he noticed that Edward R. Murrow's face was covered with sweat, Eric Sevareid sat with a white face and drummed his fingers on the table, and David Schoenbrun sat on a pillow to look taller and frantically ran to the men's room at the last minute. To Pierpoint, these men seemed positively ill.[1]

This scene illustrates several key facts about early television: It was illustrated radio, and many radio personalities did not adapt well to television. In addition, the 1951 program provides a dramatic contrast with television now. CBS's annual roundups, called *Years of Crisis*, premiered the idea of verbal sparring in news discussions. Although sometimes personal, their discussions revealed a sense of history, an in-depth knowledge of their subjects and a desire to convey ideas with intellectual depth and sophisticated language. Critics and ratings both smiled on those early CBS talking heads—nervous though they were.

Generations of aspiring television reporters celebrated the Murrow heritage, but Murrow and his colleagues were reluctant recruits to television. As World War II came to a close, radio stations across the nation moved into television but not all moved into news immediately. Many had experimented with television in the 1930s, and RCA demonstrated a television set to President Franklin Roosevelt at the 1939 World's Fair in New York City. By 1949, Americans owned a million television sets. By 1951, the number was 10 million and rising. Neither Murrow nor CBS owner William Paley saw the potential of television at first, however. Paley saw no profit in it and thought it could hurt radio. Murrow and his colleagues were writers and journalists. They saw television as an entertainment medium that would compromise their journalistic principles.

Broadcasters across the nation went into television with varying degrees of enthusiasm, and following no single model. Westinghouse Broadcasting, which had pioneered radio with KDKA in Pittsburgh, moved slowly into television with WDTV, later named KDKA. Its first news reports provided a narrator's voice over purchased film, and the station did not open its own studio until November 1950.[2] In Minnesota's Twin Cities, a radio station owner and newspaper owners started competing television stations, creating an intensely competitive market that continues today. The families that owned the *Minneapolis Tribune* and the *St. Paul Pioneer Press* jointly began WTCN (Twin Cities newspapers) television in July 1949, but they were not first in the market. Radio station owner Stanley E. Hubbard jumped enthusiastically into television, going on the air with KSTP-TV in April 1948. He demonstrated his enthusiasm for hard news by mounting illegal emergency lights on his luxury car and trying to beat the police and fire fighters to big events. Both stations broadcast a regular five-minute news programs, using still pictures and filmed reports from outlets that supplied newsreels to movie theaters. KSTP-TV also took programs and news reports from the NBC network and WTCN chose from the others: ABC, Mutual, and CBS.[3]

Television stations added programs as they got sponsors. WCCO (formerly WTCN) in weather-conscious Minnesota, for example, found a sponsor for the weather before it had a regular news program. Radio announcer Bud Kraehling read the weather, and WCCO recruited local actor Dave Moore to read the news. Demonstrating longevity rare in television, they anchored WCCO news and weather for more than 30 years. Other stations often switched anchors as trends, consultants, and ratings changed. Eventually, news, weather, and sports became a seamless program with the anchors at a single set using informal conversation to pass stories to one another. In some markets, this conversational style became a trivial form the critics called "happy talk."[4]

Early network stars moved into television reluctantly. When Murrow and his CBS colleagues Sevareid, Charles Collingwood, Dick Hottelet, Larry LeSueur, and Howard K. Smith set out to cover the 1948 political conventions in Philadelphia, they developed a radio strategy drawn from their experience on European battlefields. Another reporter, Douglas Edwards, didn't even know he would be the lead television correspondent until he arrived in Philadelphia. To cover the convention, television reporters wore headsets and carried 30-pound voice transmitters on their backs. Operators behind large cameras in booths above the floor scanned the auditorium for reporters waving red-tinted flashlights over their heads. Cameras were connected to coaxial cable, so they could not move far. If the view were clear and the lens long enough, reporters could conduct an interview from the floor. Both conventions met in Philadelphia because the city was wired with enough coaxial cable to televise them.

NBC was even less prepared than CBS to cover the convention, and the network's sponsor, *Life* magazine, stepped into the void. As both a news operation and sponsor, *Life* pub-

lisher Andrew R. Heiskell played a dual role, crossing all the traditional lines between news and advertising. The Democratic convention seemed made for television. Minneapolis Mayor Hubert Humphrey made a dramatic plea for a civil rights plank in the party's platform while Southerners stormed from the convention, vowing to create their own political party. While delegates worked for compromise behind closed doors, the contenders appeared before the cameras to state their positions and wage the fight. Working together, NBC, *Life* magazine and the Young & Rubicam advertising agency persuaded the defecting delegates to stage a dramatic walkout for television by tossing their credentials onto a desk. At a social gathering later, Murrow angrily confronted Heiskell for betraying the integrity of news by staging an event.[5]

By the end of the year, CBS and NBC solicited sponsors for regular daily newscasts. Douglas Edwards read the 15-minute daily CBS broadcast, which employed three writers. Don Hewitt, who had been hired from Acme Newspictures and who had produced CBS' convention coverage, became Edwards' producer within the first year. CBS relied on Telenews, an independent contractor, to provide nearly all of its pictures outside of New York City. In 1949, technological innovations included 16mm film (a concession to television's daily needs by the newsreel companies), sound on film (previously, reporters wrote scripts to read over silent film), and the Tele-PrompTer, a device that scrolled the script so the newscaster could look at the camera while reading his copy.[6]

NBC's first sponsor became directly involved in the news program. The R. J. Reynolds Tobacco Company helped select the staff, the name, and policies of the 15-minute *Camel News Caravan* with John Cameron Swayze. No one presumed to ask what a news caravan was, wrote Reuven Frank, who worked on the program and later headed NBC News. "What Camel wanted Camel got—because they paid so much, because they might have gone to CBS." While CBS built its television news operation on its base of radio talent and reputation, NBC plunged into a stronger use of pictures. "The money from Camel cigarettes supported the entire national and worldwide structure of NBC Television News—salaries, equipment, bureau rents, and overseas allowances to educate reporters' children."[7] Camel paid for the infrastructure for NBC News. As a result, cigarettes were often seen in filmed reports, a cigarette burning in an ashtray was part of the set, and cigars were banished from its pictures.

See It Now, a blend of CBS Radio's news roundup and film documentary style, premiered November 18, 1951, with a mixture of show business glitz and serious content. The series brought together three men who would become giants at CBS—Murrow, Hewitt, and Fred Friendly, who became Murrow's producer and, briefly, president of CBS News. Murrow's first program used a split screen to show pictures of the Brooklyn and Golden Gate bridges taken at the same time, demonstrating television's live coast-to-coast capabilities. The set placed Murrow in a control room with a monitor behind him. Because of his special relationship with CBS owner Paley, Murrow's program was allowed to run grossly over budget and to emphasize substance over style. Nonetheless, Murrow also exploited television's celebrity values with *Person to Person*, a half-hour interview program begun in 1953 with Murrow in a studio and guests speaking from their homes.

Political conventions offered controlled situations in which to create television news. In 1952, CBS stars Murrow and Sevareid again declined offers to host convention coverage and, lacking confidence in Edwards' audience appeal, the network turned to its Washington radio affiliate's political reporter, Walter Cronkite. He proved such a solid, credible reporter that the network coined the term *anchor* to characterize his stability. Four years later, NBC News executives teamed Washington reporter David Brinkley with Chet Huntley, whom they had recruited in 1955 to compete with Murrow, to cover the political conventions. The team worked so well together that NBC put them in Swayze's place on the evening news.

The Huntley-Brinkley Report, which premiered on October 29, 1956, gave NBC News a more professional image and destroyed the CBS monopoly on broadcast news. To provide cues for AT&T technicians switching between Brinkley in Washington and Huntley in New York, they used each other's names. So when David ended a segment, he said, "Chet," giving the technicians a cue to switch to New York. Although the two men hardly knew each other at first, the use of each other's first names gave viewers the sense that they worked together intimately. Their sign-off became so famous that it became part of common language: "Good night, David." "Good night, Chet." "And good night for NBC News." The 15-minute newscast expanded to half an hour in 1963, and it ended with Huntley's retirement July 31, 1970.

Although television created celebrities, it also exposed abuses. Murrow's exposé of Republican Senator Joseph McCarthy's tactics on a series of *See It Now* programs in 1954, and ABC's decision to go live with its broadcast of hearings into McCarthy's attacks on the United States Army undercut the Wisconsin senator's most abusive anti–Communist tactics. Even though newspapers and radio commentators had long criticized McCarthy's abuses, the senator's fall may have come as much from the poor image he projected on television as from his flagrant abuses of civil liberties. Nine months after the broadcasts, the United States Senate censured him for bringing it into dishonor. In 1955, *See It Now* expanded to an hour broadcast but it was aired only eight to ten times a year until its end in 1958. In the spring of 1959, Murrow joined in the creation of *CBS Reports*, an occasional hour-long documentary, which provided some of the best broadcasts, including "Harvest of Shame" on the hardships of migrant workers, in television history. Although Murrow narrated many of the earliest reports, Paley personally rejected him as a regular host for *CBS Reports*. In 1961 Murrow joined the Kennedy administration as head of the United States Information Agency, but in 1965 Murrow, who had often smoked on the air, died of lung cancer after years of illness.

The civil rights movement provided one of television's first ongoing national stories. On September 4, 1957, television cameras watched as 15-year-old Elizabeth Eckford, a nicely dressed African-American girl with books under her left arm, emerged from a school bus at Central High School in Little Rock, Arkansas. National Guardsmen lined the street to enforce Governor Orval Faubus' pledge that black children would never enter the school, despite a court order for integration. "Lynch her!" someone yelled. Others shouted racial slurs, and CBS reporter Robert Schakne ran up to her, stuck a microphone in her face and asked for a comment. She was too frightened to speak. NBC reporter John Chancellor was there, too, taking racial slurs and taunts from the crowd. The mobs threatened reporters, especially television reporters, as well as people seeking to integrate public accommodations, schools, and voting booths throughout the South. Mobs attacked cameramen more often than the reporters, because the bulkiness of their cameras and cables made it difficult for them to escape. But the dramatic television pictures moved the nation as no written report or commentary could.[8]

Television helped an eloquent orator, the Reverend Martin Luther King, Jr., find a national audience and demonstrate the stark contrast between his nonviolence and the violence of white police forces. In 1963, Birmingham, Alabama, gave King and his followers the perfect TV villain, police commissioner Eugene T. (Bull) Connor, who used fire hoses and police dogs to brutalize peaceful marchers. Watching on television, President John Kennedy said the scene made him sick. When he proposed a civil rights bill in 1963, he privately called it "Bull Connor's bill" because the dramatic television pictures had given the issue a sense of urgency.[9]

A few Southern stations, most notoriously WLBT in Jackson, Mississippi, did not welcome civil rights news. Before a civil rights story, a WLBT announcer would say something like, "What you are about to see is an example of biased, managed, Northern news. Be sure to stay tuned at seven twenty-five to hear your local newscast." Once it carried a slide saying, "Sorry, Cable Trouble," rather than a portion of an NBC documentary on the sit-in at the local Woolworth store in Jackson. In

1964 the United Church of Christ challenged the station's license renewal before the Federal Communications Commission; and, in an unprecedented move, the FCC revoked WLBT's license. By contrast, other stations took a lead in civil rights. For example, owners of WLOF-TV in Orlando, Florida, saw televised violence as bad for business and used news reports and editorials to promote peaceful integration.[10]

Meanwhile, CBS and NBC fought for higher ratings. After Huntley and Brinkley became evening news leaders, CBS put Walter Cronkite in the anchor's chair in 1962 and expanded its 15-minute program to half an hour in 1963. The first half-hour network news show debuted with Cronkite's interview of President Kennedy. NBC quickly followed by doubling the length of *The Huntley-Brinkley Report* as well, also with a Kennedy interview. ABC expanded to half an hour in 1967.

When Kennedy was shot in November 1963, the first bulletin came from a United Press International reporter on a car phone in the president's motorcade through Dallas. CBS Texas correspondent Dan Rather told an editor he believed the president was dead, and his comment accidentally went out live on CBS Radio. A few minutes later, Cronkite went on television—his voice cracking and tears in his eyes—to say the president had died, beating the other networks by 17 minutes. Two days later, CBS and ABC took a pool feed from Washington, where the president's coffin was about to be removed from the White House to the Capitol rotunda to lie in state. NBC went to a live report from the Dallas Police Department where suspect Lee Harvey Oswald was being transferred from the city to the county jail. As he approached the camera, a man stepped forward and shot him. Millions watched Oswald collapse in pain, murdered—live on television.[11] More than half of the 93 per cent of American homes with television stayed tuned for 13 consecutive hours while the nation grieved the president's death. Images provided the nation's memory. From Friday to Monday, NBC devoted 71 hours, 36 minutes without commercials to the president's death, funeral and related events. Coverage involved more than 2,000 employees, costing the networks and advertising agencies more than $32 million.[12] Some critics and insiders worried that the media circus had made it impossible for Oswald to get a fair trial, if he had lived.[13]

Another major television story, the Vietnam War, lasted for decades. Like other Americans, television correspondents went to Vietnam with World War II assumptions about war and politics, a traditional sense of the goodness of American fighting men, and the Cold War ideology of a worldwide struggle against Communist-dominated tyranny.

In a war without fronts and clearly defined lines, Liz Trotta, the first female television war correspondent, provided an illustration of how television covered the war. With cameraman Vo Huynh one day in September 1968, she headed for action around Tay Ninh near the Cambodian border. They landed with the troops in helicopters to find that most of the 3,000 villagers had fled under United States air strikes. In the midst of the shooting, Huynh propped a camera on one shoulder and said: "You either get it—or you don't," she recalled. "To this day I don't know if he meant get the picture or get killed, but in either case it holds." Huynh stood up, "trying to entice me to do a standup to camera under fire. 'Good picture. Lots of action.' I hugged my legs closer to my chest." Eventually, she did her stand-up report in a crouched position. Film then had to be rushed to Tokyo for processing and the pictures transmitted from there to New York. Her story and his pictures, with combat footage, led *The Huntley-Brinkley Report* on September 12. Huntley updated the story with news that arrived after the film had left Vietnam: the enemy abandoned the village.[14] Correspondents had to write with the assumption that their stories would be aired several days after the events pictured.

Television news seldom emphasized violence and suffering inflicted by American troops, at least before the 1968 Tet offensive. Nor did the networks show identifiable bodies of American soldiers, in case families watching at home might recognize casualties. Coverage of the air war focused on pilots, technology and professionalism.[15] A film crew, in those days, usually required two or three people—a photographer, reporter and often a sound technician—tied together with cables and a microphone.

Some of the war's most dramatic pictures, such as CBS correspondent Morley Safer's August 5, 1965, report of U.S. Marines burning villages of Cam Ne with cigarette lighters, were memorable but exceptional. His report threw President Johnson into an outrage. He called CBS President Frank Stanton and said he had "shat on the American flag." Johnson, his press staff, and Pentagon officials tried to get Safer recalled by CBS, accusing him of faking the story and calling him a Communist and Soviet agent. CBS managers protected the reporter from pressure. "I was oblivious," Safer recalled, "to the impact of the Cam Ne story until months later, when I returned to New York for a rest and was stunned that people were still talking about it."[16] His report led military officials to consider subjecting television reporters to restrictions not placed on print journalists.[17]

Cronkite believed in objective reporting with a strong middle-of-the-road appeal. So President Johnson became alarmed in early 1968 when he heard Cronkite offer a rare and pessimistic commentary after a trip to Vietnam. Stalemate, Cronkite said, seemed inevitable. "But it is increasingly clear to this reporter that the only rational way out then will be to negotiate, not as victors, but as an honorable people who lived up to their pledge to defend democracy, and did the best they could."[18] Reportedly saying that if he had lost Cronkite, he'd lost the nation, President Johnson announced in March that he would not seek reelection. Cronkite, however, worried about newscasters having such influence.[19]

Violent confrontations between police and antiwar activists at the Democratic National Convention in Chicago where cops attacked 21 reporters as well as demonstrators made dramatic television in 1968. "[B]eating up on kids was just good, clean fun, while we were seen as the bastards who were making a big deal out of it," wrote Reuven Frank, who was in the NBC control booth. Cronkite referred to "thugs" in the convention after someone punched reporter Dan Rather.[20]

Republican Richard Nixon, who had a long-standing love-hate relationship with television, narrowly defeated Vice President Hubert Humphrey for the presidency in 1968. As Eisenhower's running mate in 1952, Nixon had faced allegations of financial improprieties, but he saved his career with a powerful television appeal. In it, he emoted warm tones to defend one donor's gift: a cocker spaniel named "Checkers" that his two young daughters loved. No matter what was decided about his future, Nixon said defiantly, they would keep the dog. Nixon's "Checkers" speech saved his career, and he served two terms as vice president. In 1966, he toured an American exhibit at an industrial exposition in Moscow and had a dramatic argument with Soviet Premier Nikita Khrushchev in a kitchen exhibit. This "kitchen debate" contributed to Nixon's image of strength in foreign policy.

But Nixon also hated television. As vice president, he had tried to succeed Eisenhower in 1960, but his Democratic challenger, Senator John F. Kennedy of Massachusetts, enticed him into a series of televised debates. Nixon, an accomplished college debater, was tired and ill during the first debate on September 26, 1960. Shaken by his tired appearance, director Don Hewitt offered to provide make-up help, but Nixon refused. By contrast, Kennedy looked refreshed. People who saw the debates on television believed Kennedy won, but those who heard them on the radio believed Nixon won. The four televised debates gave Kennedy's campaign a major boost. After a narrow loss to Kennedy in 1960, Nixon ran for governor of California in 1962 and was again defeated. At a famous "last news conference," a despondent Nixon told reporters they would not have Dick Nixon to kick around any more.[21]

After winning in 1968, Nixon demonstrated that he could hold a grudge as strongly as he could stage a comeback. The president kept "enemies lists," which included journalists. He wiretapped their telephones, ordered income-tax audits, and tried to get the FCC to deny license renewals for stations whose news coverage he disliked. In 1969, Vice President Spiro Agnew attacked un-elected television commentators for offering opinions with raised eyebrows and subtle facial expressions and for undermining national security by analyzing presidential speeches.

In 1972, television reporters initiated few stories about the Watergate break-in and Nixon's subsequent efforts to cover it up. *Washington Post* reporters Carl Bernstein and Bob Woodward did nearly all the enterprise reporting on Watergate. Within a month of the 1972 election, however, the *CBS Evening News with Walter Cronkite* promised a two-part report on the break-in and cover-up. On Friday, October 27, Cronkite reported that Watergate began as a minor break-in, but it had grown into "charges of a high-level campaign of political sabotage and espionage unparalleled in American history." In concluding, he promised a second report on "the money behind the Watergate affair." The first report took 22 minutes, and the second one seven minutes.[22] He did not know at the time that his second broadcast had been shortened under White House pressure.[23]

Cronkite and CBS News President Richard Salant resisted temptations toward sensation and entertainment. Tabloids gave people want they wanted. CBS, like the *New York Times*, gave them what they needed. Cronkite, who had been a United Press World War II reporter and international correspondent, steadfastly defended objectivity, signing off each evening with, "And that's the way it is," followed by the date. Salant represented integrity in broadcast journalism by resisting advertisers' pressure and refusing to integrate music, sound effects, or sponsors' logos into the news. He felt no pressure to make news a profit center. Instead, he had Paley's blessing to provide news as a public service.

Ironically, Salant led CBS News when it inaugurated *60 Minutes*, the program that demonstrated that news divisions could produce profitable programs. In fact, it became the most successful television show ever, critically and financially. *60 Minutes* debuted September 24, 1968, with Don Hewitt, a veteran of Edwards' and Murrow's programs, as producer. Borrowing from a critic, Hewitt said *60 Minutes* combined the "high Murrow" of *See It Now*'s serious documentaries with the "low

Murrow" of *Person to Person's* celebrity interviews. From entertainment programs, he took
the idea of a repertory company of several major
players, instead of a single anchor.[24] Salant approved *60 Minutes* only after network executives
agreed to continue occasional hour-long documentaries, like *CBS Reports*, which were more
in-depth, more expensive, and less profitable.

In the early 1980s, ABC, long a poor third
in the ratings, changed the rules for all three
networks and indirectly selected their news anchors. Roone Arledge, who had made ABC
Sports the industry's leader, took charge of
ABC News in 1977. He started a bidding war
for talent. He raided NBC first, hiring Barbara
Walters, a long-time interviewer and co-host of
NBC's *Today Show*, for the first $1 million an-
nual salary in news. She was to be the co-an-
chor with a reluctant Harry Reasoner, who had
joined Howard K. Smith—both earlier refugees
from CBS—as co-anchors of ABC's evening
news. But the Walters-Reasoner chemistry
failed to work. So Arledge began looking for
other anchors. First, he negotiated with Dan
Rather, former White House correspondent,
then working on *60 Minutes* and *CBS Reports*.
He offered him $2 million. CBS panicked and
began negotiating feverishly with Rather,
promising he could replace Cronkite and giving him a $22 million contract over 10 years
beginning in 1980. Arledge then looked to
NBC, where he picked Tom Brokaw, the news
reporter on *Today*. Like CBS, NBC panicked
and hired Brokaw as its evening news anchor
for another multi-year, multi-million contract
beginning in 1982. News anchors had become
increasingly important as living network logos,
and CBS estimated that one news ratings point
was worth $5 million. The highly visible ne-
gotiations made ABC a major player and removed Cronkite, the dominant competitor,
from the scene.[25] ABC then experimented with
a trio of anchors: Frank Reynolds in Washington, Max Robinson in Chicago and Peter Jennings in London. Jennings succeeded Reynolds
and Robinson to become sole anchor in 1983.
He led ABC gradually to the top of the ratings
against Rather and Brokaw. The evening newscasts of the three networks were competing
rather evenly by the end of the century.

As network news divisions fought with
entertainment divisions to get on prime time,
Arledge began eyeing the 11:30 p.m. (Eastern)
time slot, a ratings desert for ABC and CBS.
NBC owned late-night with Johnny Carson's
Tonight Show. After Iranian students took
American officials hostage in the Teheran embassy in late 1979, Arledge began nightly use of
the time with *America Held Hostage*. Satellites
allowed ABC's diplomatic correspondent, Ted
Koppel, to simultaneously interview people in
different parts of the world. Koppel, who
looked at a blank chromakey screen, appeared
as though he were facing his guests on moni-
tors. Nearly five months into the hostage crisis, *Nightline* debuted on March 24, 1980.
Dramatic consequences of the first program,
like so much that happens in journalism, were
neither foreseen nor intended. Koppel had two
guests: Dorothea Morefield, wife of hostage
Richard Morefield, and Ali Agah, Iran's chargé
d'affaires in Washington, who had not been
warned of his impending confrontation. "I
don't see how a letter from my husband to me
or a phone call from my husband to me could
be a threat to your security in any way," she
protested to the ambassador. "Just the look on
Ali Agah's face," a producer said later, made
good television. The time for the program's end
came, and Arledge ordered the producers to
continue with the live confrontation. Critics
panned the program, and Koppel admitted it
was shameless. But half a world away, Morefield began receiving mail for the first time since
being taken hostage.[26]

As competition increased, CBS, long the
most respected broadcast news organization,
began to self-destruct. Van Gordon Sauter,
who became CBS News president in the early
1980s, liked nothing about the Cronkite-Salant
era, which he considered boring. The entertainment values Salant resisted became Sauter's
mantra: stronger theme music and graphics,
more celebrity interviews, fewer hour-long
documentaries. He saw television as an emotional, not informational, medium. The news
should strive for powerful, memorable "moments." Arledge had already instituted lively
production values at ABC News as the network
began increasing in both ratings and credibility.

Sauter's efforts to catch NBC's *Today Show* and ABC's *Good Morning America* became jokes in the industry. The CBS morning anchor positions underwent musical chairs, occupied briefly by some of the most respected people in the business, including Diane Sawyer, Ike Pappas, Robert Pierpoint, and Charles Kuralt, who had achieved phenomenal success with his folksy "On the Road" features on Cronkite's evening news and his subsequent laid-back approach to *Sunday Morning.*[27]

Like the networks, local stations discovered that news could become a profit center in the 1970s. Local newsrooms had fewer resources than the networks, and the limitations forced local news to depend on the anchors' personalities, dramatic video, high story counts, large advertising budgets, and cogent sound bites. Television stressed time-sensitive stories, yielding an imbalance toward events that developed in the evening: crime, traffic, and fires.[28] They got into technological races with their competitors over who had the best weather equipment, helicopter reports, and satellite access. These efforts yielded high production values and little substance. Reports often aired live just to show off equipment and to give a sense of timeliness to stories that would have been stronger with careful editing before broadcast. With vans and satellite dishes, stations used electronic news gathering (ENG) to send edited and live reports to their stations. With this technology, local stations competed with their own networks by putting the faces of their own anchors at major national and international events.[29] Ironically, local stations developed closer ties with their audiences than other media or the networks. A 1997 study found that more than half of all Americans got most of their information from watching local television every day. Similar numbers read the newspaper and listened to the radio, but they trusted local television news most.[30]

While the mainstream networks cut international coverage, the owner of a Southern UHF television station with professional wrestling interests thought the world needed access to news 24 hours a day. Ted Turner, who knew little about the techniques or ethics of news, hired experienced and committed journalists, such as Reese Schonfeld, for the Cable News Network, which went on the air June 1, 1980. Critics called the low-budget, mistake-ridden operation the "Chaos News Network" and the "Chicken Noodle Network." Clearly, they underestimated the impact of live remotes from the world's hot spots. Turner converted CNN to theme programs and opened a second channel, CNN Headline News, on December 31, 1981, providing news summaries and updates every half hour. When the Gulf War began in 1991, CNN's crew, including reporters Peter Arnett, Bernard Shaw, and John Holliman, were the only ones allowed to remain broadcasting live from Baghdad, while American planes bombed the city. The war, followed by other dramatic events covered live, established CNN as a paying proposition.[31]

The first hour-long television network news broadcast (as opposed to cable news) came from the Public Broadcasting Service with *The MacNeil/Lehrer NewsHour* in 1983. It evolved through the 1970s with the team of Jim Lehrer and Robert MacNeil, who had provided PBS's gavel-to-gavel coverage of the Senate Watergate Committee hearings. After MacNeil's retirement in 1995, the program became *The NewsHour with Jim Lehrer* and went online the following year.

An in-depth alternative to the networks came from cable. After negotiating a complex agreement with the House of Representatives, Brian Lamb launched the Cable-Satellite Public Affairs Network on March 19, 1979, with live cable coverage of House floor debates and speeches. In 1986, C-SPAN2 began televising the Senate. Congress controlled the feeds, and C-SPAN promised to carry the live floor debates. The network, on the other hand, made all of its other programming decisions, such as what committees and other events to cover.[32]

Corporate mergers increased the pressure for news to produce profits at less expense. At the same time, television networks began the 21st century facing major competition from one another, from cable and from local stations with satellite technology. Cable stations produced news 24 hours a day with small staffs. The result has often been programs that milk a single story, whether the president's sexual indiscretions or the murder of a child model, with on-air debates rather than reportorial enterprise.

CBS News, once the pride of a corporation owned by a single entrepreneur, has become part of a larger corporation seeking profits from all of its many sectors. Owner Bill Paley was forced to retire in the process. As rivalries built within CBS, outside forces created additional pressure. ABC and NBC positioned themselves to take advantage of the prestigious Cronkite's departure and, at the same time, competition from CNN and other cable programming began to erode all the networks' audiences.

CNN's 24-hour news forced the networks to feed breaking stories to affiliates throughout the day, rather than holding them for the daily half-hour network broadcast. Although CNN's ratings remained small, viewers paid attention during times of crisis, such as the suspenseful 2000 presidential election and the 1991 Persian Gulf War. CNN, in turn, faced an increasing number of competitors, including Fox News, MSNBC, and 24-hour local news channels.[33] With satellite access, local stations themselves began to broadcast live from major events around the world.

Instead of three to five major networks at a White House news conference or camped outside the home of a newsmaker, today hundreds of cameras may show up. During the Clinton scandals and impeachment, the number of reporters and their behavior became scandalous with sources being pushed and shoved by the mobs. Local news broadcasts became more ratings sensitive than the major networks, often resorting to the promotion of on-air anchors and other personalities and higher production and entertainment values within the news.

Selected Readings

Allen, Craig. "Television, 1948–Present: Entertainment or Information?" in Wm. David Sloan, ed., *Perspectives on Mass Communication History*, 334–46. Hillsdale, N.J.: Erlbaum, 1991.

Allen, Craig. *Eisenhower and the Mass Media: Peace, Prosperity, and Prime-Time TV*. Chapel Hill: University of North Carolina Press, 1993.

Ashdown, Paul G. "WTVJ's Miami Crime War: A Tele-

vision Crusade." *Florida Historical Quarterly* 28 (1980): 427–37.

Barnouw, Eric. *The Image Empire*. New York: Oxford University Press, 1970.

Barnouw, Erik. *Tube of Plenty*, 2nd ed. New York: Oxford University Press, 1990.

Bliss, Edward Jr. *Now the News: The Story of Broadcast Journalism*. New York: Columbia University Press, 1991.

Bluem, A. William. *Documentary in American Television*. New York: Hastings House, 1965.

Buzenberg, Susan, and Bill Buzenberg, eds. *Salant, CBS, and the Battle for the Soul of Broadcast Journalism: The Memoirs of Richard S. Salant*. Boulder, Colo.: Westview Press, 1999.

Cloud, Stanley, and Lynne Olson. *The Murrow Boys: Pioneers on the Front Lines of Broadcast Journalism*. Boston: Houghton Mifflin Company, 1996.

Cranston, Pat. "Political Convention Broadcasts: Their History and Influence." *Journalism Quarterly* (1960): 186–94.

Cronkite, Walter. *A Reporter's Life*. New York: 1996.

Donovan, Robert J., and Ray Scherer. *Unsilent Revolution: Television News and American Public Life*. New York: Cambridge University Press, 1992.

Frank, Reuven. *Out of Thin Air: The Brief Wonderful Life of Network News*. New York: Simon & Schuster, 1991.

Friendly, Fred W. *Due to Circumstances Beyond Our Control*. New York: Random House, 1967.

Garay, Ron. "Television and the 1951 Senate Crime Committee Hearings." *Journal of Broadcasting* 22 (1978): 469–90.

Hammond, Charles Montgomery, Jr. *The Image Decade: Television Documentary, 1965–1975*. New York: Hastings House, 1981.

Lashner, Marilyn A. *The Chilling Effect in TV News: Intimidation by the Nixon White House*. New York: Praeger, 1984.

Matusow, Barbara. *The Evening Stars: The Rise of the Network News Anchors*. Boston: Houghton Mifflin, 1983.

Mickelson, Sig. *The Decade That Shaped Television News: CBS in the 1950s*. Westport, Conn.: Greenwood Press, 1998.

Murray, Michael D., and Donald G. Godfrey, eds. *Television in America: Local Station History From Across the Nation*. Ames: Iowa State University Press, 1997.

Powers, Ron. *The Newscasters: The News Business as Show Business*. New York: St. Martin's Press, 1977.

Schaefer, Richard J. "Reconsidering 'Harvest of Shame': The Limitations of a Broadcast Journalism Landmark." *Journalism History* 19 (1994): 121–32.

Yaeger, Murray R. "The Evolution of See It Now." *Journal of Broadcasting* 1 (1956): 337–44.

Notes

1. Stanley Cloud and Lynne Olson. *The Murrow Boys: Pioneers on the Front Lines of Broadcast Journalism* (Boston: Houghton Mifflin Company, 1996), 260–63.

2. Lynn Boyd Hinds, *Broadcasting the Local News: The Early Years of Pittsburgh's KDKA-TV* (University Park: Pennsylvania State University Press, 1995).

3. WTCN soon changed its call letters to WCCO, and the name WTCN was later adopted by an independent station that, in turn, became KARE after Gannett purchased it. Mark Neuzil and David Nimmer, "News Leader:

WCCO-TV, Minneapolis," in Michael D. Murray and Donald G. Godfrey, eds., *Television in America: Local Station History From Across the Nation* (Ames: Iowa State University Press, 1997): 245–67; *Midwest Spirit* 13 (Commemorative Issue; Fall 1998): 7–11; Jim McGovern, *The 50,000 Watt Broadcast Barnum: A Book Noir of Stanley E. Hubbard, His Life and Times* (privately printed, 1996).

4. Bud Kraehling, personal interviews with the author at Minnesota History Center, 30 September 1999, 10 February 2000.

5. Reuven Frank, *Out of Thin Air: The Brief Wonderful Life of Network News* (New York: Simon & Schuster, 1991), 12–27.

6. Sig Mickelson, *The Decade That Shaped Television News: CBS in the 1950s* (Westport, Conn.: Praeger, 1998), 13–25, 27.

7. Frank, *Out of Thin Air*, 33.

8. Reporters' comments are from "Covering the South" symposium at the University of Mississippi, April 3–5, 1987.

9. Robert J. Donovan and Ray Scherer, *Unsilent Revolution: Television News and American Public Life* (New York: Cambridge University Press, 1992), 16–17.

10. Linda M. Perry, "A TV Pioneer's Crusade for Civil Rights in the Segregated South: WFTV, Orlando, Florida," in Murray and Godfrey, *Television in America*, 128–54.

11. Edward Bliss Jr., *Now the News: The Story of Broadcast Journalism* (New York: Columbia University Press, 1991), 337–343.

12. Erik Barnouw, *The Image Empire, Vol. 3: A History of Broadcasting in the United States from 1953* (New York: Oxford University Press, 1970), 227–38. Quotations are from 234 and 235. See also Erik Barnouw, *Tube of Plenty: The Evolution of American Television*, 2nd rev. ed. (New York: Oxford University Press, 1990), 332–38.

13. Barnouw, *The Image Empire*, 231–34.

14. Liz Trotta, *Fighting for Air: In the Trenches with Television News* (New York: Simon & Schuster, 1991), 122–28.

15. Daniel C. Hallin, The *"Uncensored War": The Media and Vietnam* (New York: Oxford University Press, 1986), 105–58.

16. Morley Safer, *Flashbacks on Returning to Vietnam* (New York: St. Martin's Paperbacks, 1991), 133–52; Donovan and Scherer, *Unsilent Revolution*, 79–82.

17. William M. Hammond, *Reporting Vietnam: Media and Military at War* (Lawrence: University Press of Kansas, 1998), 58–62.

18. Walter Cronkite, "We Are Mired in Stalemate," CBS News, 27 February 1968, reprinted in *Reporting Vietnam, Vol. 1: American Journalism 1959–1969* (New York: The Library of America, 1998), 581–82.

19. Jonathan Alter, "Walter Cronkite: Rolling Stone Interview," (1987) reprinted in Thomas Fensch, ed., *Television News Anchors: An Anthology of Profiles of the Major Figures and Issues in United States Network Reporting* (Jefferson, N.C.: McFarland & Company, 1993), 190.

20. Frank, *Out of Thin Air*, 270–71; Ron Powers, "Playboy Interview: Walter Cronkite," *Playboy* June 1973 reprinted in Fensch, *Televison News Anchors*, 70–90. Quote is from p. 81.

21. Herbert G. Klein, *Making It Perfectly Clear: An Inside Account of Nixon's Love-Hate Relationship with the Media* (Garden City, N.Y.: Doubleday & Company, 1980), 20.

22. Susan and Bill Buzenberg, eds., *Salant, CBS, and the Battle for the Soul of Broadcast Journalism: The Memoirs of Richard S. Salant* (Boulder, Colo.: Westview Press, 1999), 101–03.

23. Walter Cronkite, *A Reporter's Life* (New York: Alfred A. Knopf, 1996), 310–12, 362–63.

24. Don Hewitt, *Tell Me a Story: Fifty Years and 60 Minutes in Television* (New York: Public Affairs, 2001), 104–08.

25. The dollar amounts come from Bill Leonard, *In the Storm of the Eye: A Lifetime at CBS* (New York: G. P. Putnam's Sons, 1987), 24, 31–33; Marc Gunther, *The House that Roone Built: The Inside Story of ABC News* (Boston: Little, Brown and Company, 1994), 142–47; and Cronkite, *A Reporter's Life*, 352.

26. Ted Koppel and Kyle Gibson, *Nightline: History in the Making and the Making of Television* (New York: Times Books, 1996), 13, 21–46.

27. Peter J. Boyer, *Who Killed CBS? The Undoing of America's Number One News Network* (New York: Random House, 1988). The story of the *CBS Morning News* is entertainingly told by Peter McCabe, *Bad News at Black Rock: The Sell-Out of CBS News* (New York: Arbor House, 1987).

28. Phyllis Kaniss, *Making Local News* (Chicago: University of Chicago Press, 1991), 101–32.

29. Michael D. Murray, "The Contemporary Media, 1974–Present," in Wm David Sloan and James D. Startt, eds, *The Media in America: A History*, 4th ed. (Northport: Ala.: Vision Press, 1999), 459–78; and Sydney W. Head, Christopher H. Sterling, Lemuel B. Schofield, *Broadcasting in America: A Survey of Electronic Media*, 7th ed. (Boston: Houghton Mifflin, 1994), 362–65.

30. Based on a national survey of 1,500 people, commissioned by the Newseum and developed by the Roper Center for Public Opinion Research. The telephone survey was conducted in January 1997. Accessed online at the Newseum Web site, http://www.mediastudies.org/tvsur.html, in January 2000.

31. Hank Whittemore, *CNN: The Inside Story: How a Band of Mavericks Changed the Face of Television News* (Boston: Little, Brown and Company, 1990); Robert Goldberg and Gerald Jay Goldberg, *Citizen Turner: The Wild Rise of an American Tycoon* (New York: Harcourt Brace and Company, 1995); and Perry M. Smith, *How CNN Fought the War: A View from the Inside* (New York: Birch Lane Press, 1991). For the Murdoch-Turner feud and merger finances, see Frank Rich, "More Mogul Madness," *New York Times*, 13 November 1996; Mark Landler, "In Cable TV, More Is Less," *New York Times*, 10 November 1996; Geraldine Fabrikant, "Talking Money with Ted Turner," *New York Times*, 24 November 1996.

32. Stephen Frantzich and John Sullivan, *The C-SPAN Revolution* (Norman: University of Oklahoma Press, 1996), 23–73; Janette Kenner Muir, "Video Verité: C-SPAN Covers the Candidates," in Robert E. Denton Jr., ed., *The 1992 Presidential Campaign: A Communication Perspective* (Westport, Conn.: Praeger, 1994), 227–45.

33. Ree Schonfeld, *Me and Ted Against he World: The Unauthorized Story of the Founding of CNN* (New York: Cliff Street of HarperCollins, 2001), xiii–xx, 375–81.

31

News Writing Structure and Style
TIM P. VOS

When Boston postmaster John Campbell published the first successful newspaper in New England, the paper's news writing was far from original. The structure and style of the news were literally lifted from newspapers across the Atlantic. The first issue of the *Boston News-Letter*, published in April 1704, began, "Letters from Scotland bring us the Copy of a Sheet lately Printed there. In a letter from a Gentleman in the City, to his Friend in the Country concerning the present Danger of the Kingdom and of the Protestant Religion."[1]

This "news" was reprinted from a *London Flying Post* published more than four months before, and the *Flying Post* had reprinted it from a Scottish "sheet." While the news form and structure were deeply rooted in European tradition, American journalism would eventually develop its own ways of casting the news. But it would be a mistake to jump ahead to new developments too quickly—the cast of this first news story in the *Boston News-Letter* leaves an imprint that tells us something about what shapes news structure and style.

These early issues of colonial newspapers bore the imprint of the literary media and conventions of the day, of the implicit purpose of the newspaper, of contemporary events and circumstances, and of the broader cultural spirit of the age.

Two forms of early 18th-century communication were in evidence in this *News-Letter* story: letters and military communiqués. Colonial papers included other forms of communication, such as, lists, sermons, and essays. The purpose of the *News-Letter* in this piece ap-peared to be surveillance—to keep local colonists apprised of developments back home. Thus the form of a communiqué or letter was a suitable choice. A variety of circumstances also left their mark on the structure of news. For example, the need to publish "by authority" led to a reliance on official letters, speeches, and other sanctioned newspapers or newsletters. This first item in the *Boston News-Letter* also bore the mark of its age. Protestant Christianity contributed to a writing style that attributed the events of human history to divine causation. Meanwhile, a mercantile mentality formed the basis for many social interactions and also shaped news structure, for example, lists of items in shipping news.

As literary conventions, newspaper purpose, circumstances, and world views changed during the 300-year history of American newspapers, so too did news structure and style. It took a conscious embrace of objectivity for the inverted pyramid to become a dogma of journalism and a common tool of the journalist. It will likely take a conscious break with modernism for corresponding changes in news structures to occur in the 21st century.

COLONIAL PRESS

Newsletters and newspapers of this era were closely tied to the colonial authority structure. John Campbell published the *Boston News-Letter*, at least initially, because it was an extension of his official position as postmaster. Campbell, when he was not reprinting news from overseas, printed official letters, proceedings, and proclamations. An example of an official letter appeared in the second installment of the *News-Letter*. An item titled "South Carolina Via New York" began, "An Account of what the Army from there had done, under the Command of Colonel Moore in his Expedition last Winter against the Spaniards and Spanish Indians. In a letter from him to the Governor of Carolina. May it please your Honour to accept this short Narrative of what I with my Army under my command have been doing."[2] What followed was a chronological account of events of the expedition. Chronology was used regularly as a news form in the pages of colonial newsletters and newspapers.

At times chronology expanded to something closer to story. In a 1729 issue of the *Weekly News-Letter*, the following short piece related the details of a single event: "We have a very melancholy Relation from Ballybogh, in the County of Dublin, viz: That on Saturday last late in the Night a Fire broke out in a Cabbin belonging to a laboring Man, who had a Wife and 7 children, and he and his Wife and Children being in bed and fast asleep, were in a very deplorable Manner burnt to Death."[3] Another brief item in the same issue tied together a number of events and identified a few characters to tell a story. The story was told for humorous effect, much as a fictional story might be told to amuse an audience. These chronological articles were almost always very brief—details were related in a few sentences or even in a single sentence, like the Ballybogh fire story. Story-like pieces also found a place in newspapers. A 1751 issue of the *Boston Weekly News-Letter* reprinted an item that told a fairly detailed and sensational story of the murder of a man in Jamaica.[4]

A question-and-answer or dialogue form was another structure for news. A 1740 issue of the *Boston Weekly News-Letter* printed a nearly three column piece, "Extracts from the Votes of the Honourable House of Representatives."[5] The item recorded an exchange regarding taxes between the Governor and a House committee and was organized in an order-answer argumentative style. The form was obviously fit the event being described, but the style was also fa-

miliar to the readers. The format was used frequently in English sheets like the *Tatler* and *Spectator*, which were both popular and regularly copied in the American colonies. The style was also familiar from the catechisms used for religious instruction (in fact, imprints of catechisms were for sale in the very same issues of these newsletters).

Lists were a common news structure in newsletters of this time. The newsletters attempted to meet some of the information needs of the merchant class. Thus, shipping news was a regular feature. Lists of names and goods appeared under such headings as "Entered Inwards" "Cleared Out" and "Outward Bound."[6] But lists were also used within a larger piece to tell the news. For example, in an article titled "His Majesty This Day assumed his Royal Stall as Sovereign of the Most Noble Order of the Garter, and made his offering in the Chapel of St. George," a detailed description is given of an important event.[7] The piece includes a list, arranged spatially in a column, of those who were present.

While items for papers and letters were edited to fit the length of a two-page sheet, there is little evidence that Campbell or others added much of their own original writing. To be sure, brief introductions and headings were added; but Campbell and his contemporaries were not journalists in the modern sense. They did not craft their own stories. News story structure was generally imported into the newspaper from the items reprinted from other papers and from the text of official speeches and proclamations.

Perhaps the most notable change in news structures and style during the colonial period was the emergence of a more detailed telling of the news. For example, in the piece on the royal installation mentioned above, the article described what was worn ("Mantles of blue Velvet"), how the party entered, and what the organ played. This sort of detail made for a short step to a more self-conscious story telling style later.

REVOLUTIONARY ERA PRESS

A number of changes left a mark on news forms in the second half of the 18th century. The defining moments of this era were clearly the events and actions surrounding the Revolutionary War. As the colonists became dissatisfied with British rule, they turned to the presses to have their voices heard. Eventually the social role of newspapers changed. John Campbell lost his position as postmaster in late 1719 but had continued to publish his newsletter. Thus, the tie to official authority was already tenuous. The masthead of the *Massachusetts Gazette and Boston News-Letter* told the difference in 1767—while the first *Boston News-Letter* had been printed "By Authority," the 1767 paper was "Published by Desire."[8] However, the form and content of the newspaper changed slowly. Important letters and items clipped from other papers continued to fill much of the newspapers.

While initially it had little impact on news forms and structures, one subtle change was that letters from ordinary colonists more commonly made it into the newspaper. Eventually this practice expanded to include publishing parts of political pamphlets.[9] The pamphlets had a more developed essay style, i.e., ideas were explored, problems were analyzed, and the writer attempted to persuade the reader to see things differently. As the purpose of the newspaper began to change, the essay, introduced via pamphlets published by citizens, became a major structure for news. Newspapers and newsletters took up the cause of justice, as they saw it—particularly, the cause of righting injustices forced on the colonies.[10] The closer the colonies came to the fateful year of 1776, the more strident and confrontational the essays became, such as a January 1776 article titled "My Fellow Citizens" that urged countrymen to prepare to become soldiers.[11]

The essay form was also married with a dialogue form in many pieces. For example, a January 1773 essay began, "Mr. Draper [the editor], Please insert the following Dialogue, between an high Patriotic Bostonian, and a plain honest Countryman, if haply it may contribute a mite to the saving of this endangered Pro-vince, not from foreign Enemies, but from its more Mortal Foes, ourselves."[12] The pedagogical possibilities of the question-and-answer form served well the didactic purposes of the essay. This form also fit well with the continuing popularity of the Enlightenment mindset—it fit the goal of exposing problems and articulating ideas through a process of rational discourse.

On a few rare occasions verse was even used to tell news, such as "The Soliloquy of the Boston TREE OF LIBERTY" in 1776.[13] "The Genius of America" was similar to an essay but written in verse.[14]

Other forms carried over largely unaltered from the colonial press. Chronological pieces were used frequently, especially to relate the details of notable events. For example, a general's letter reprinted from the *London Gazette* was a very thorough chronology of the "siege and surrender of Quebeck."[15] Since newsletters were often four pages instead of two, as they were earlier in the century, publishers could give more room for news items, permitting a more detailed telling of events. Nevertheless, papers contained an "Anecdotes" section, with short items written in a story-like style. The stories, like items of an earlier time, were told to humor the readers. However, these anecdotes displayed many of the formal characteristics of a story, including dialogue.

The newsletters and newspapers continued to serve the merchant class. Shipping news continued as a regular feature—thus lists and eventually tables of data appeared in the columns of the papers. For example, a 1766 paper contained a chart in four small columns arranging data on lots and taxes.[16] Lists appeared in other contexts as well. In an item titled "South Carolina—In the Commons House of Assembly" a list of resolutions of rights and grievances were printed.[17]

The primary innovation in news structure during the Revolutionary period was the introduction of and, at times, reliance on the essay. The circumstances surrounding the war transformed the newspaper into a forum for political discussion and debate. The essay form continued after the war—sometimes for political and partisan purposes (such as, an essay on the new constitution[18]) and sometimes for other ends. The *Massachusetts Gazette* ran a series of essays on diverse issues, "Observations on the Government of the Passions," "Observations on Revenge," and "Observations on the Passion of Love."[19] At the close of the century another innovation took root. The editors of newspapers began to craft their own essays. This led to a new news structure in the following decade—the editorial.

PARTY PRESS AND PENNY PRESS

The first half of the 19th century produced notable changes in news forms and structures—which is no surprise given the dramatic changes in newspapers during this period. At the beginning of the century, newspapers continued to serve political and partisan purposes. Thus, the essay remained a common ingredient in the newspaper. However, changes were brewing. The editor of a newspaper was frequently attached to a partisan cause or political party—in part, his role was to write essays for the cause or party. The editor became a writer and the essay became the editorial. The editorial eventually replaced the pamphlet-style essay. Brief editorials were a common feature of newspapers by 1810.

The political purpose of papers led to another innovation. Newspapers, instead of relying on private letters for news, hired men to send correspondence with news from the nation's capitol. Since large urban newspapers were going to daily publication, a regular and reliable source of news was needed. Thus, the new role of editors and the introduction of correspondents meant news written by employees of the newspaper began to fill the newspaper. This, in turn, eventually affected news structures and style, although the changes occurred slowly.

The introduction of the penny papers in the 1830s also had a significant impact on news forms and structures. Again, radical changes did not occur overnight. The printing of letters and proclamations persisted, but these became increasingly rare. Essay content also did not disappear entirely. While much has been made of the political independence of the penny press, political comment was still present—it was simply woven into new forms. An item in James Gordon Bennett's first issue of *New York Herald* exhibited such a form. It used description and dialogue to tell of an overheard plot to kidnap a prominent abolitionist. "We verily believe that there is an organized *corps* in this city determined to carry off one of the leading abolitionists to the south, and there hang him up like a Vicksburgh gambler. We dont like the abolitionists, but we give them a fair warning."[20] While this item started as a story, it concluded as an essay. This news form was common in Bennett's early papers.

The story form was also used to tell simple stories without significant comment. News from the police courts was a mainstay of penny papers and cases were frequently written in story form. The stories usually contained some dialogue and the writing style included a liberal use of metaphors. Brief stories were also told to amuse readers—for example, a story might end with, "The spree has excited considerable merriment." On occasion, long involved stories were also told in the papers—sometimes spread over more than one issue.[21]

Meanwhile, some news was written in straightforward chronology without the embellishments of a story. A news story about a meeting would likely be written in such a form. Newspapers also made frequent use of lists to relay mundane information, such as, a list of letter bags in the Exchange Reading Room. The paper also listed various directories, for example, columns of officers in the local banks. Stock exchange tables also became a regular feature of the papers.

The penny papers highlighted a number of changes in the culture of the time. America was becoming more urban and commercial interests were becoming more prominent. Newspapers, if not news stories, were becoming commodities. While the papers attempted to serve the growing commercial class, the penny papers also attempted to attract the growing lower income urban residents. For whatever reason, the story structure appeared to appeal to these readers. The newspapers' social role was also changing—the paper was valued for its ability to simultaneously inform and entertain—this was another factor that valued the story structure.

By mid-century essay content was either relegated to an opinion page or coupled with stories to tell moral tales. Story content was a regular and prominent way to tell news, and writers frequently employed chronology. The structure of news in the partisan newspapers of 1800 looked much different than the story structure of the penny papers of 1850. But the changes set in motion by the penny press led to even more pronounced changes in news form and structure in the latter half of the 19th century.

THE CIVIL WAR AND INDUSTRIAL ERA PRESS

The second half of the century witnessed some of the most lasting changes in the structure and form of news. A growing reliance on the telegraph, the outbreak of the Civil War, the drive toward industrialization, and the rise of modernism combined to reshape news and to produce tensions in journalism that would not easily be resolved. The changes in news structure, as with many developments in journalism, were not immediate.

Telegraph lines began to appear in the 1840s and by 1850 newspapers made regular use of the telegraph wires to send news. The case has been made that summary leads appeared during the Civil War because telegraph wires could be easily cut and if a chronological form was used to tell news, the climax of a story might not be transmitted before wires were cut.[22] However, few news stories during the time surrounding the Civil War were written in this summary lead form.

The industrial revolution, which brought mass production to the newspaper industry, also created a climate for the routine production of news stories. The rise of modernism, particularly positivism with its presumption that values could be separated from facts, paved

the way for the press to embrace the notion of objectivity. All this shaped news structure and style.

Bennett's *New York Herald* put the telegraph to use to report on the actions of Congress. Correspondents provided both brief summaries of congressional action and lengthy, detailed reports on congressional debate. Some 1850 reports were little more than a transcript of debates. By 1860 the papers took more effort to print introductions, summaries, and reactions to congressional action and debate. The newspapers continued to print entire speeches, but only after the major events of the congressional day had been summarized and commented upon. However, other news stories of speeches were told in strict chronological order with little attempt at summary. For example, the *New York Herald* used this kind of news structure in an 1860 story on a meeting of the United Cartmen's Protective Association.[23] While the mayor's appearance before the association received disproportionately more space in the article, each detail of the evening's business, including songs sung, was meticulously recounted in chronological order. In sum, different forms were in use: some news items relied more heavily on the structure of a speech or proclamation, while other news articles bore more the imprint of reporters' choices in summary and structure.

The imprint of the reporter most directly affected the structure of a news story when the reporter's questions were inserted into the story. While a question-and-answer format was used frequently in the 1700s, reporters' questions rarely appeared in news stories. The following 1870 article, "The Social Evil," in the *New York Herald* was an exception. It read in part:

> Reporter—I am here from the Herald and wish to procure what statistics you have touching the social evil....
> Mr. Kennedy—I have nothing to give. You are engaged in a work of damnation. You ought to know better. You insult me....[24]

Reporters were clearly using the interview as a news-gathering device. The fact that the reporter then typically arranged that information in some other form is significant—it demonstrated that reporters were actively engaged in constructing the news by structuring the news story. What was obtained in an interview might appear in a news article that was written as story or as chronicle.

The most significant event of this period to make a mark on news structure was the Civil War. The war crystallized the evolution of the press from a role of social comment and political argument to a role of information provider. Readers were eager to pay for information on the war, such as, battle outcomes, battle locations, and legislative and executive actions. The emphasis on information resulted in a news story such as "The Social Evil." It wove together statistics, quotes, and summary in a structured way to explore the "social evil" of prostitution. The reporter claimed to be looking for statistics in his exchange with Mr. Kennedy. And the story was, indeed, crammed with statistics—sometimes summarized and sometimes in graphical, table form. Tucked in the text, columns and rows of numbers told the story of the groups who cared for "reclaimed prostitutes." Clearly there was a focus on information. However, the social and political purposes of the newspaper were not absent. One of the decks over the piece read, "The Evil in This City—Statistics and Facts for the Legislature." Thus, even though there were signs of "objectivity," the voice of the editor still appeared in the pages of the newspaper.

By 1870 newspapers could contain news articles that were written as stories or as chronology—either could be accompanied by summaries, tables, or lists. The articles might also have contained some opinion. From this mix of elements eventually came the "inverted pyramid" form of news organization. While the Civil War was fertile ground for the emergence of the inverted pyramid, newspapers seldom contained stories in this form during the war.

By the early 1880s only a crude form of the inverted pyramid was in evidence, and newspapers still regularly used other forms of news organization. News stories contained an introduction that established the general topic of the news, but the introduction often gave little sense of the direction or essential details of the story. For example an article in an 1881 *New York Tribune* began, "General Grant was received by both houses of the Legislature in the Assembly Chamber to-day, and interesting ceremonies followed."[25] The piece then was written in a chronological arrangement, beginning with the plans made for Grant's arrival, the procession into the chamber, description of the chamber, the entire official introduction of Grant, and then the entire speech by Grant. Meanwhile, chronological organization without introduction or summary was also still in use at this time.

By the 1890s, newspapers contained much less chronology, more story-like structure, and a still somewhat crude form of inverted pyramid. While elements of chronology were woven into news articles, the strict chronological structure was largely absent from newspapers. Meanwhile, a well-developed story structure was more in evidence. An article in an 1892 issue of the *New York Herald* was a clear example of this story structure. Although the news story began with some introduction and summary, most of the piece was told in story form. The article emerged from the *Herald's* investigation of the murder of a New York police officer and filled four columns with description, dialogue, and even some graphical illustrations. Attention was given to setting, well-developed characters, and plot development.

The inverted pyramid-type news article continued its slow development in the 1890s. The opening paragraph of these news stories had changed little in a decade—the articles each included an introduction, but only a few news items included an opening that summarized the main thrust of the story. Though not in regular use, what was beginning to emerge was the declining interest pattern of story organization—the most prominent details were included high in the story column and the less significant details were near the end of the article.

At the end of the century the wide variety of news forms had begun to narrow. A form recognizable as an inverted pyramid had taken shape and the story-form had been refined. While different papers emphasized one of these two forms in the 1890s, it is also true that papers included both news structures. News stories with lengthy verbatim accounts of speeches and strict chronological description of an event were becoming rare.

By the end of the century, newspaper publishing had become a big business, newspapers were mass-produced and news stories were, in a sense, a commodity. However, the structure, or structures, of news stories were too anomalous to maintain that news story production had also become industrialized or routinized. Nevertheless, news story production was being pushed in that direction by the industrial, business climate. It would take a conscious embrace of modernism and the self-conscious embrace of journalistic objectivity, before news forms and structures would become a dogma of the journalism profession and a common tool of the news writer.

THE TWENTIETH CENTURY

The inverted pyramid became the most common news form during the first half of the 20th century. For the majority of news the inverted pyramid was the news form. One of the early books to explain newspaper reporting, published in 1912, included a chapter titled, "The News Story Form." The chapter described what journalists today would call an inverted pyramid. "In the old days news stories were written in the logical order of events just like any other narrative, but constant change has brought about a new form as different and individual as any other form of expression." Grant Milnor Hyde concluded the news story "does not lead the reader up to a startling bit of news by a tantalizing suspense in an effort to build up a surprise for him; it tells its most thrilling content first and trusts to his interest to lead him on through the details that should logically precede the real news."[26]

Similar instruction to prospective news writers could be found in *The Editor*—a publication that called itself "The Journal of Information for Literary Workers." The journal was geared to creative and fiction writers, but as early as 1911 offered advice on newspaper work.

For example, a 1913 article advised on "Starting a Home News Bureau." In 1914 *The Editor* described the "Essentials of News Writing." "The news-story must be 'organized' in its proportioning and handling of material.... Let the first paragraph of a news-story tell all the tale in a brief digest. Expansion can come later as space and time for writing permit. But 'get the story' in the first paragraph. That is perhaps the fundamental rule of news writing."[27]

Newspapers were indeed using such a form to cast much of their news. Stories were written in the declining interest form with tightly formulated summary leads. For example, a 1903 issue of the *New York Herald* had page after page of news stories written in this structure. The summary lead of a news story on a railroad strike began, "After three unsuccessful conferences with Horace G. Burt, president of the Union Pacific, representatives of that railroad's striking machinists decided yesterday that no agreement could be reached in New York, and arranged with Mr. Burt to move the conference headquarters to Omaha."[28]

However, some news articles also had stretches of story-like structure. For example, on the same page of the same 1903 issue of the *New York Herald* a news article told the story of a fight in a Broadway hotel. The story began with a summary lead that revealed the story's climax, but then developed as story with dialogue, rising tension, and (a retelling of the) climax. Newspapers in the early decades of the century included a variety of other narrative structures. Lists and tables were still used for specific purposes; for example, tables structured financial information and lists were used under such headings as "Amusement To-Day and Evening" and "Transatlantic Travellers." Lists, arranged graphically, were also included in a variety of news stories. However, for most news on most newspaper pages, two news forms were in use—most news was written in the inverted pyramid, the remainder was structured as story.

A 1916 book, *Types of News Writing*, also reduced the options for structuring news to two basic forms: the "common" news form with summary lead and the story form. The book's author, Willard Grosvenor Bleyer, identified the first form with common news of the day and the second form with "human interest" or "feature" stories. "The popular demand for novelty and variety," he wrote, "prevents any form of newspaper writing from becoming fixed, and results from time to time in the development of new forms and new styles of news writing." He continued, "To make some news stories entertaining rather than purely informative, a number of newspapers abandon the conventional summary beginning, or lead, and use unconventional ones like the beginnings worked up into so-called 'human interest' or 'feature' stories, because in that form they make entertaining reading."[29]

Nearly every subsequent journalism textbook of the 20th century echoed Bleyer's description of the two news writing forms. What would later be called the inverted pyramid was considered conventional, and a story-form was unconventional and to be used for a specific, less-serious kinds of news. Bleyer's description, for the most part, appeared to be accurate—however, anomalies persisted and neat categories were not always maintained. The front page of a 1921 *New York Herald*, for example, contained two stories of shootings—one was written in the standard form, but the other was written in a story form, without a summary lead.[30] Thus, some timely, significant news was still occasionally being written as story.

The origin of the term "inverted pyramid" is uncertain, but it was used by name in a 1934 textbook written by Carl Warren. "The figure of the equilateral pyramid," Warren explained, "set with broad base upward, serves in a general way to visualize the makeup of the standard news story...."[31]

The arrival of textbooks on news writing accompanied a conventionalizing of news forms and structures. Granted that such early books would have been scarce in journalism classrooms or in newsrooms, the textbooks represented a movement to professionalize and codify journalism practice. The American Society of Newspaper Editors established the first code of journalism ethics in the early 1920s and several textbooks on newspapers and news writing followed. In the spirit of industrialism and modernism, journalism moved into an age of professionalism. Even though both Hyde and Bleyer's books portrayed news forms as evolving and dynamic, the publishing of these and other books helped give normative force to contemporary practice and created fixed forms of news writing.

Hyde's book reached a third edition by 1941. Renamed *Newspaper Handbook*, it no longer portrayed news forms as evolving. Rather, Hyde reified the inverted pyramid: news "'tells itself' in that form, and such should be the case when the news is so vital that the method of presentation should not obtrude itself."[32] In other words, the inverted pyramid was no longer seen as historically and socially situated, but as part of the natural world of journalism.

The naturalization of the inverted pyramid tied closely with the rising ideology of objectivity. As journalism was professionalized, it embraced objectivity as a philosophical foundation. For the ideal of objectivity to be maintained, news forms and structures had to lend themselves to the accurate and unbiased reporting of reality. News forms could not be formative. This is exactly what Hyde and his contemporaries argued, that news told itself in the form of the inverted pyramid. The push toward professionalization and the ideal of objectivity were also held out as an antidote to darker commercial impulses. Juicy stories sold papers and thus there was constant incentive for "exaggeration, sentimentality, or falsehood"—sins that had been recently committed in a period of "yellow journalism."

But there were conflicting impulses that shaped how news forms were perceived and used. One the one hand, modernism gave rise to journalistic professionalism that valued the journalist as a "literary craftsman," a skilled professional capable of vivid, compelling writing. On the other hand, modernism gave rise to an industrial revolution that shifted skill and craftsmanship to the designer of the tools and machines and away from the user of the tools and machines. The inverted pyramid had become a tool in the "modern" sense. Reporters used the inverted pyramid as a tool to cast consistent, uniform news stories out of the confusing chaos of reality. The use of news forms meant news stories could be standardized and could be produced by an interchangeable work force.

The first half of the 20th century saw few significant changes in literary conventions, newspaper purpose, circumstances, and cultural spirit of the age. Nonetheless, changes set in motion during the first 200 years of the North American newspaper matured and intersected to produce the inverted pyramid as the primary news form of the 20th century. Meanwhile, journalistic professionalization, itself a product of the spirit of modernism, contributed to the reification of the inverted pyramid, thereby turning a historical description into a universal prescription. That prescription would not be seriously challenged for the remainder of the century.

The inverted pyramid remained the standard form for casting news and the story form remained an accepted deviation under various circumstances during the last half of the century. Nevertheless, the tensions inherent in the evolution of news forms would move the pendulum a time or two. A renewed push for professionalism led to "precision journalism" in the early 1970s and later to computer-assisted reporting. The emphasis was on using social scientific research techniques to quantify data and therein introduce more precise description to news articles. The quantification also encouraged renewed use of tables, graphs, and lists to organize some information within or along side news stories.

One area of change in news forms and structures was the relative value placed on story structures and story-telling techniques to present the news. Carl Warren, in a 1951 edition of his news writing text, concluded that news written in story form is "usually brief, seldom of consequence and always strong in human interest and suspense."[33] This story form was called "suspended interest." Instead of summarizing the climax in the lead of the news article, readers would have to read to the end to see the climax presented and the story resolved. However, the ideology of objectivity had created distrust of story-telling methods, limiting the use of story structures to "human interest" or "feature" news stories. In his 1960 text John Hohenberg argued, "Those who advocate the

adaptation of the familiar techniques of belles-lettres to journalism tend to forget that the purpose of news writing is to inform, not to entertain." Hohenberg warned that story telling style could lead to "distortions and worse."[34]

However, the romantic notion of the journalist as "literary craftsman" had not been lost. Romanticism fundamentally contradicted the rationalist, modernist assumptions of objective journalism. Romanticism led to a movement in the 1960s and '70s known as "new journalism." Writers composed stories using traditional fiction-writing techniques, at times using quotes of what people were thinking. This form of writing largely appeared in book form or in magazines, seldom in newspapers. Nevertheless, it represented a movement that valued the story form and this in turn appeared to influence the value of story forms in newspapers. In 1977 Melvin Mencher encouraged the student journalist to learn from fiction writers.[35] The increased use of story in newspapers was clear in subsequent years. The suspended interest form gained some popularity, but the most significant shift came in the use of some story elements within larger inverted pyramid stories.

Thus, news writing was being pulled in two directions during the last decades of the 20th century—toward a logically structured form like the inverted pyramid but also toward the story structure. The philosophy of objectivity, which favored the inverted pyramid form of news organization, had not given up its grip even though the broader spirit of the age was turning against the assumptions of modernism and rationalism. The rise of post-modernism in recent years did not make changes in news forms and structures. That may have been because changes in structures have been slow to occur, as they were in the 19th century. It may also have been the case that the institutions of journalism were among the last holdouts of modernist faith.

CONCLUSION

Presentation of the inverted pyramid news structure over the last several decades has led to a reification of the form as the natural way to tell and organize news. The present has become the standard for evaluating and judging the past—past deviations from this form, like chronological structure or an essay form, have been relegated to the pre-scientific past. But all news forms, even the inverted pyramid, were products of a nexus of inherited literary forms, the evolving purpose of the newspaper, past events, and circumstances and the spirit of the age.

Selected Readings

Barkin, Steve M. "The Journalist as Storyteller: An Interdisciplinary Perspective." *American Journalism* 1:2 (1984): 27–34.

Connery, Thomas. "Julian Ralph: Forgotten Master of Descriptive Detail." *American Journalism* 2 (1985): 165–73.

Dicken-Garcia, Hazel. "Changes in the News during the Nineteenth Century." Chap. 3 in *Journalistic Standards in Nineteenth-Century America*. Madison: University of Wisconsin Press, 1989.

Francke, Warren T. "W. T. Stead: The First New Journalist?" *Journalism History* 1 (1974): 36, 63–66.

Mindich, David T. Z. "The Inverted Pyramid: Edwin M. Stanton and Information Control." Chap. 3 in *Just the Facts: How "Objectivity" Came to Define American Journalism*. New York: New York University Press, 1998.

Miraldi, Robert. "Fictional Techniques in the Journalism of David Graham Phillips." *American Journalism* 4 (1987): 181–90.

Mott, Frank Luther. "Facetious News Writing, 1833–1883." *Mississippi Valley Historical Review* 29 (June 1942): 35–54.

Pomerantz, Sidney I. "Newspaper Humor in the War for Independence." *Journalism Quarterly* 21 (1944): 311–17.

Schudson, Michael. "Stories and Information: Two Journalisms in the 1890s." Chap. 3 in *Discovering the News: A Social History of American Newspapers*. New York: Basic Books Inc., Publishers, 1978.

Shaber, Sarah R. "Hemingway's Literary Journalism: The Spanish Civil War Dispatches." *Journalism Quarterly* 57 (1980): 420–24, 535.

Sloan, Wm. David. "Scurrility and the Party Press, 1789–1816." *American Journalism* 5 (1988): 97–112.

Sloan, Wm. David, and Cheryl S. Wray. *Masterpieces of Reporting*. Northport, Ala.: Vision Press, 1997.

Sloan, Wm. David, Julie Hedgepeth, Patricia Place, and Kevin Stoker. *The Great Reporters: An Anthology of News Writing at Its Best*. Northport, Ala.: Vision Press, 1992.

Stevenson, Robert L. "Readability of Conservative and Sensational Papers Since 1872." *Journalism Quarterly* 41 (1964): 201–06.

Terrell, Russell F. *A Study of the Early Journalistic Writings of Henry W. Grady*. Nashville, Tenn.: George Peabody College, 1927.

Webb, Joseph M. "Historical Perspective on the New Journalism." *Journalism History* 1 (1974): 38–42, 60, 62.

Whitby, Gary L. "Tough Talk and Bad News: Satire and the New York *Herald*, 1835–1860." *American Journalism* 9 (Winter-Spring 1992): 35–52.

Winfield, Betty Houchin, and Janice Hume. "The American Hero and the Evolution of the Human Interest Story." *American Journalism* 15:2 (1998): 79–100.

Notes

1. *Boston News-Letter*, 17 April–24 April 1704, 1.
2. Ibid., 24 April–1 May 1704, 1.
3. *Weekly News-Letter*, 26 December–2 January 1729, 1.
4. *Boston Weekly News-Letter*, 3 January 1751, 1.
5. Ibid., 27 December–3 January 1740, 1.
6. *Weekly News-Letter*, 2 January–9 January 1729, 2.
7. Ibid., 13 February–20 February 1729, 1.
8. *Massachusetts Gazette and Boston News-Letter*, 4 December 1767, 1.
9. For example, see ibid. The issue included a pamphlet that pleaded to reduce imports and increase liberty.
10. *Massachusetts Gazette and Boston News-Letter*, 4 December 1767. This issue included excerpts from a pamphlet on the appropriateness of taxing the colonies.
11. Ibid., 11 January 1776, 2–3.
12. Ibid., 14 January 1773, 1.
13. Ibid., 22 February 1776, 1.
14. *Massachusetts Gazette*, 8 July 1788, 1.
15. *Boston News-Letter*, 7 February 1760, 1.
16. *Massachusetts Gazette and Boston News-Letter*, 19 June 1766, 1.
17. *Massachusetts Gazette*, 9 January 1766, 1.
18. Ibid., 28 October 1788, 1.
19. Ibid., 1 July 1788 to 11 July 1788.
20. *New York Herald*, 31 August 1835, 2.
21. For example, the *New York Herald*, 1 September 1835, 1, began a series of articles, "Two Yards of Jaconet, or a Husband—A Virginia Tale." It read as fiction, replete with dialogue, characters, and plot conflict.
22. David T. Z. Mindich, *Just the Facts: How "Objectivity" Came to Define American Journalism* (New York: New York University Press, 1998), 68.
23. *New York Herald*, 1 March 1860, 5.
24. Ibid., 7 February 1870, 5.
25. *New York Tribune*, 20 January 1881, 1.
26. Grant Milnor Hyde, *Newspaper Reporting and Correspondence* (New York: D. Appleton and Co., 1912), 36.
27. William R. Murphy, "Essentials in News-Writing," *The Editor* 38 (1914): 420–21. Advice on writing for newspapers could be found in a handful of other issues of this journal; e.g., J.V.R., "The Journalistic Wedge," *The Editor* 34 (1911): 111–12; W. H. Sheridan McGlumphy, *The Editor* 35 (1912): 264; "Starting a Home News Bureau," *The Editor* 37 (1913): 38–39.
28. *New York Herald*, 7 January 1903, 5.
29. Willard Grosvenor Bleyer, *Types of News Writing* (Cambridge, Mass.: Riverside Press, 1916), 4–5.
30. *New York Herald*, 8 July 1921, 1.
31. Carl N. Warren, *Modern News Reporting* (New York: Harper & Bros. Publishers, 1934), 88.
32. Grant Milnor Hyde, *Newspaper Handbook*, 3rd ed. (New York: Appleton-Century, 1941), 94.
33. Carl N. Warren, *Modern News Reporting*, 2nd ed. (New York: Harper, 1951), 87–88.
34. John Hohenberg, John, *The Professional Journalist* (New York: Holt, Rinehart & Winston, 1960), 126 and 81.
35. Melvin Mencher, *News Reporting and Writing* (Dubuque, Iowa: Brown, 1977), 140–41, 112.

32

Editorial Writing

W. DAVID SLOAN

Although American newspapers have almost always carried news, for most of their history editors believed that their most important function was to express opinion. In the beginning, some colonial newspapers were intended principally as a means of publishing opinion rather than news, and those publishers who wished mainly to publish news invariably sprinkled observations throughout news reports and filled much of their space with essays. In the 19th century, newspaper owners and editors devoted most of their attention to the editorial page, and most of the leading journalists of that century gained their reputation from their editorial writing. Today, even though editorials occupy a place that is much less important than in the past, they remain a staple of newspapers.

Before editorials developed their modern form, 18th-century newspapers published most of their opinion pieces in the form of essays. Publishers actively solicited contributors from the public, for having such help was the only way that a printer could get all the work done that was necessary for publishing a newspaper on a weekly basis. In beginning publication of the *Pennsylvania Gazette* in 1729, for example, Benjamin Franklin told readers that "[t]here are many who have long desired to see a good Newspaper in Pennsylvania; and we hope those Gentlemen who are able, will contribute towards the making This such." He asked for assistance from readers, he explained, because publishing a newspaper required a wide range of knowledge. It was "not so easy an Undertaking as many People imagine it to be," for the

"Author of a Gazette (in the Opinion of the Learned) ought to be qualified with an extensive Acquaintance with Languages, a great Easiness and Command of Writing and Relating Things clearly and intelligibly, and in few words; he should be able to speak of War both by Land and Sea; be well acquainted with Geography, with the History of the Time, with the several Interests of Princes and States, the Secrets of Courts, and the Manners and Customs of all Nations. Men thus accomplish'd," he declared, "are very rare in this remote Part of the World; and it would be well if the Writer of these Papers could make up among his Friends what is wanting in himself...."[1] Because the columns were open to contributors, one thus finds that outsiders wrote many of the early statements of opinions that newspapers published. These essays served as the equivalent of today's editorials.

Occasionally, owner-editors themselves wrote opinion material for their newspapers. For the first century and more after the founding of America's first newspaper in 1690, however, "editors" were usually only printers and had little time—or, frequently, ability—to pen editorial opinion. Contributors writing under pen names usually submitted what opinions the papers carried, although occasionally enterprising printer-editors would write letters to themselves, signing the pieces "from a correspondent" or with some other such identification. Seldom did the printer-editor or another member of the staff actually write the material that appeared as the opinion of the newspaper. In some instances, a group of like-minded individuals would devise a plan to publish a newspaper, contract with a printer-publisher, and agree to provide written contributions.

More frequently, writers not officially associated with the newspaper contributed its opinion pieces. A contributor might be a sponsor who occasionally provided financing for the paper but who did not actually work for it (such as Alexander Hamilton in his relation with the *Gazette of the United States* around the turn of the 19th century) or a writer with no connections to a paper but who sometimes presented material for publication (such as Thomas Paine in his association with the *Pennsylvania Journal* in the Revolutionary era). In either case, the writer was at most loosely connected with the publishing of the newspaper.

Because newspapers, along with pamphlets, were the favored medium for writers wishing to publish their views, we find in newspapers some of the most important works in early American history, including such classics as John Dickinson's "Letters from a Farmer in Pennsylvania,"[2] a series of essays that were published in the *Pennsylvania Chronicle and Universal Advertiser* in 1767 and were instrumental in the American colonies' opposition to British parliamentary power; Thomas Paine's "Crisis" essays,[3] which helped rally colonists' morale during the American Revolution; and the "Federalist Papers,"[4] which argued for adoption of the U.S. Constitution and today are recognized as the greatest work on political science ever produced in the United States.

The Revolutionary crisis brought an increase in the activity of contributors, mostly agitators and political philosophers. Their writings frequently resembled the form of pamphlets and were published a section at a time in successive issues of newspapers.

THE PARTISAN ERA, 1783–1833

The colonies' victory in the Revolution did little to change the characteristics of newspaper opinion. In the decade after independence, it remained the domain primarily of the contributor and its nature that of the pamphlet. A significant event in the development of the editorial occurred, however, during the 1780s. It was at that time that the editorial in its modern form appeared. During the Revolution, a few isolated printers began to italicize their opinions to differentiate them from other parts of news accounts in which the opinions appeared, and others began to print the news they gathered themselves or their brief comments on the news under a hometown heading. Whereas earlier opinion had been dispersed throughout the pages of newspapers, in the early 1780s some newspapers began to separate their opinion statements from the news and to reserve a specific place for them. The editors Noah Webster and James Cheetham began publishing a separate section of short paragraphs they had written. Other editors began to place a specific caption over the opinion, indicating that the opinion was that of the editor rather than of a contributor.

These two practices—opinion separated from news, and a typographical designation of an opinion to indicate that it was the newspaper's—came together for the first time in Hartford's *Connecticut Courant* in 1783, comprising the form that today we consider that of the editorial. During the early part of the Revolution, the *Courant's* George Goodwin had begun to place local material beneath a "Hartford" heading. In the 1780s, he and his partner, Barzalai Hudson, began to reserve that space for their own writing and reporting. Whenever they wished to express themselves and have it known that a particular opinion in the *Courant* was that of the paper's ownership, they printed it in the Hartford column.

In the October 28, 1783, issue of the *Courant*, Goodwin and Hudson printed for the first time a synopsis and *comment* on action the state assembly had taken and published the piece under the local column heading. Previously, the paper had included only titles of laws. The author of the column was Noah Webster, the *Courant's* "official" contributor. That essay was the first editorial, in the modern definition of the term, ever to appear in an American newspaper. For their innovation of summarizing legislative action and then adding a comment on it in the Hartford column, Goodwin and Hudson were widely criticized. In response, they argued forcefully for the right of the public to be informed about the conduct of their representatives.[5]

With the rise of strong partisan feeling during the presidency of George Washington, the nature of editorializing began to change. During the Revolutionary crisis, publicists had recognized the growing importance of the newspaper in influencing public opinion. In the early Constitutional period, party leaders such as the Federalist Alexander Hamilton and Republican Thomas Jefferson saw fit to establish organs to espouse their party sentiments. The group that controlled a paper had none of the characteristics, however, of a modern corporation. Few of its members invested in the paper with the main goal—or even an expectation—of making a profit. Their main purpose was to have a forum to promote their party's views and, they hoped, to win elections, control the machinery of government, and thus determine the nature that the political system was to take.

Although politicians still contributed essays to the papers, journalists with the essential features of the modern editor, who did their own writing, began to appear. Previously, most newspapers were conducted by owners who were printers only and who thought of themselves primarily as craftsmen and publishers. They did little in the way of imaginatively selecting news to be published or composing their own writings. However, as the newspaper in the new Republic came to play a critical role in the political process, there was a growing need for individuals who could voice their faction's views in an effective manner. By the time the first parties developed from factions in the 1790s, the position of editor already was well-established, and newspapers were viewed no longer as simply the mechanical product of their printer-conductors but the expression of the editors' views. Noteworthy were such Federalists as John Fenno of the *Gazette of the United States*, William Cobbett of *Porcupine's Gazette*, Noah Webster of the *American Minerva*, and William Coleman of the *New York Evening Post*. Leading Republicans included Benjamin Franklin Bache and William Duane of Philadelphia's *Aurora*, Philip Freneau of the *National Gazette*, and James Cheetham of the *American Citizen*. The most talented writer of the group was Cobbett. A master of satirical invective, he adopted the pen name "Peter Porcupine." A fellow Federalist editor, Benjamin Russell of the *Columbian Centinel* in Boston, described his role harshly but probably accurately. Cobbett, Russell said, "was never encouraged and supported by the Federalists as a solid, judicious writer in their cause; but was kept merely to hunt Jacobinic [i.e., Republican] foxes, skunks, and serpents."[6]

By the early 1800s, the editorial had been accorded an established position in many newspapers, but several conditions—especially the harsh tone of writing—handicapped its effectiveness as a literary form. Throughout the entire period of the party press' dominance of American journalism, which ended around 1860, the hallmarks of newspaper opinion were extreme vituperation, personal abuse, and domination by political subjects. These features frequently repel the modern reader, but partisan editorial writers, on the other hand, exhibited a number of enviable strengths. Many of them held key posts in local, state, and national politics and thus possessed an intimate and detailed knowledge of political issues. As a result, their editorials often revealed a keen understanding of the intricacies involved in public affairs. Because newspapers and editors were so closely tied to politics, it can be argued that at no other time in the history of editorial writing in the United States has the newspaper's editorial role been of such critical importance to the functioning of the nation's political system.

THE POPULAR ERA, 1833–1900

During the period of the penny press, the editorial came to full flower. The revolution was not, however, effected instantaneously with the appearance of the first penny papers in the 1830s. It was not until 1853, for example, when

S. S. Cox published "A Great Old Sunset" in the *Ohio Statesman*,[7] that editorials began their liberation from domination by political subjects. That editorial had no reference to politics and instead simply described the scene following a thunderstorm. Newspapers nationwide picked up the editorial and reprinted it. It became so famous that its author thereafter was referred to as "Sunset" Cox. The sudden popularity of human interest subjects did not, however, mean that political editorials suddenly vanished. Even today they are the staple of editorial pages. After the 1850s, however, editorials on non-political subjects appeared more and more frequently.

The years from the advent of the penny press in 1833 until the Civil War often have been referred to as the "Golden Age" of editorial writing. During these years the editorial gained a generally recognized importance. Emphasis on news gave papers a financial freedom they had not experienced during the partisan era. Political independence grew. Yet editors, gaining their political freedom, did not become slaves of the newspaper dollar. Although many made their living at journalism, they did not view their papers simply as a business. Tied to neither political control nor the profit motive, editorial writers enjoyed full freedom to express themselves. As a result, the prestige of the editorial writer grew.

Conditions were ideal for editorial writing. Newspapers were, many people believed, the preeminent forum for the improvement of humankind and civilization. "The brilliant mission of the newspaper," wrote the journalist Samuel Bowles II, "...is, and is to be, the high priest of History, the vitalizer of Society, the world's great informer, the earth's high censor, the medium of public thought and opinion, and the circulating life blood of the whole human mind. It is the great enemy of tyrants, and the right arm of liberty, and is destined, more than any other agency, to melt and mold the jarring and contending nations of the world into that one great brotherhood which, through long centuries, has been the ideal of the Christian and the philophropist."[8]

With such respect accorded to newspapers, editors were ideally positioned to play a leading role in society. Many were intricately involved in public affairs but were not under the direction of politicians or parties. Although the function of newspapers as journals of news had increased in importance, editors still considered the editorial to be the heart of the newspaper. Since most editors owned their own newspapers, the leading ones spent only a small proportion of their time dealing with business affairs. Consequently, they exercised complete editorial control without deference to employers, and they focused their attention and energy on their newspaper's editorial operations. Under these conditions, the public thought of the editorial not simply as the policy statement of a newspaper institution, but as the voice of its editor. In the hands of the great personal editors of the age, editorials as a result enjoyed a greater prestige than at any other time during their history.

The legend of editorial writing of this "Golden Age" is in large part the shadow of one man, Horace Greeley. As editor of the *New York Tribune* from 1841 to 1872, he consistently fought for the causes he felt would aid humankind. He became one of the most influential figures of his age and perhaps the most influential journalist ever. He was one of the leading proponents of many of the most important movements in American society in the mid–1800s. The *Tribune* was the most visible advocate of the great westward migration of the nation, and it stood as the preeminent journalistic voice on slavery for the generation that wrestled with the issue prior to the Civil War. It was said that thousands of readers would wait to decide where they stood on issues until they heard what "Uncle Horace" had to say.

His effectiveness came not only from his command of the language, but also from the firmness of his belief that he was right. "He was thoroughly in earnest," explained Beman Brockway, a life-long journalist and *Tribune* writer. "He was not always right—he was human, like the rest of us—but he sincerely believed in the truthfulness of whatever he wrote at the time of writing. Very often he saw only one side of the question; he was therefore only partly right. Unlike Henry J. Raymond, who, according to Mr. Greeley, saw both sides to such an extent as to be troubled to distinguish the one from the other, Mr. Greeley saw but one side. That to his vision was the right one...."[9]

If Greeley could be criticized, it would be for his naïveté and eccentricity on some causes and for his passion when he believed he was right. Such was not true of Henry Raymond. Founder of the *New York Times* in 1851 and its editor until 1869, he was Greeley's temperamental opposite. In the *Times'* opening statement, he wrote that he did not intend to "write as if we were in a passion, unless that shall really be the case; and we shall make it a point to get in a passion as rarely as possible."[10] He lived up to his promise. His editorials were temperate, objective, rational, cautious. Partially because of his moderation, he exercised less power than Greeley and contemporaries such as William Cullen Bryant of the *New York Evening Post* and Samuel Bowles II and his son of the *Springfield* (Mass.) *Republican*. His writing had neither the force of Greeley's nor the stylistic appeal of Bryant's, but it was he who set the tone for the rational, dispassionate, impersonal editorial style of today.

With the departure of several of the great names—such as Greeley, Raymond, Bryant, and the senior James Gordon Bennett of the *New York Herald*—around 1872, many observers noted the passing of the "Golden Age" of journalism. The dirges, however, were premature. Under such editors as Charles Dana, E. L. Godkin, and Joseph Pulitzer, editorial pages by 1900 were to achieve a freshness, a depth, and a practical influence greater than ever.

Dana, editor of the *New York Sun* from 1868 to 1897, brought to editorial writing a liveliness, a freshness, and a sparkle it had never exhibited. Human-interest, brief literary essays, humor, and biting phrases became the hallmark of the *Sun's* editorial page. Its attention to writing came to be symbolized by its famous "office cat." Describing the cat, Dana wrote: "When a piece of stale news or a long-winded, prosy article comes into the office, his remarkable sense of smell instantly detects it, and it is impossible to keep it from him. He always assists with great interest at the opening of the office mail,

and he files several hundred letters a day in his interior department. The favorite diversion of the office-boys is to make him jump for twelve-column articles on the restoration of the American merchant marine.

"He takes a keen delight in hunting for essays on civil-service reform, and will play with them, if he has time, for hours. They are so pretty that he hates to kill them, but duty is duty. Clumsy and awkward English he springs at with indescribable quickness and ferocity; but he won't eat it. He simply tears it up. He can't stand everything...."[11]

Despite his nimble style, Dana was a cynic, and he encouraged levity and perversity on the editorial page. In the 1880 presidential campaign, for example, the *Sun* endorsed Democrat Winfield Scott Hancock as "a good man, weighing 250 pounds."[12] As a result, editorially he was never as effective as he might have been otherwise. Still, he created a model of pungency, lightness, and wit in editorial writing, and the *Sun's* casual editorial essays remain the best examples of sensitivity to fundamental human concerns combined with sophisticated tongue-in-cheek humor. The most famous editorial ever written, containing Francis Church's declaration that "Yes, Virginia, there is a Santa Claus,"[13] exemplified the *Sun's* felicity.

Dana's chief rival for editorial fame was E. L. Godkin, editor of the *Nation* from 1865 to 1899 and of the *New York Evening Post* from 1883 to 1899. He was the foremost leader of public opinion in his day. The philosopher William James wrote of him: "To my generation, his was certainly the towering influence in all thought concerning public affairs, and indirectly his influence has assuredly been more pervasive than that of any other writer of the generation, for he influenced other writers who never quoted him, and determined the whole current of discussion."[14] Godkin's readership was not large, as the circulation of the *Nation* and the *Evening Post* never exceeded 35,000; but it was composed of the leaders of public opinion—teachers, ministers, and judges, for example—and they disseminated his ideas.

Two factors accounted for Godkin's influence: his intellect and his writing style. Possessing an analytical and critical mind, he was concerned with the underlying principles of issues rather than their superficial surfaces. He thus offered penetrating insight into public questions. As for his writing, it exhibited versatility of style, lightness of touch, and pungency. Witty and ironic, it also could be devastatingly cold and cutting. Of Godkin's style, Wendell Phillips Garrison, the *Nation*'s literary editor, observed: "His pen was fluent and ready, but his diction was never careless; rather it bore at all times the marks of training and culture of a high order. While able to develop a subject at any length, he had extraordinary aptitude for paragraph writing; his touch in either case was always light, his matter always pithy. His expression was very direct, vigorous, and trenchant; and he had an exceptional gift for descriptive narration."[15] Godkin's only real handicap as an editorial writer, later liberal critics claimed, was his disdain for the common man. Even his admirers remarked that his critical analysis and biting writing style occasionally were too much for even his intellectual, upper-class readers.

Of a different bent was Joseph Pulitzer. He made his fortune and journalistic fame by his *New York World's* outright appeal to the lower classes. Although catering to less sophisticated readers through sensational news, he considered a respected editorial page to be the heart of his paper. Upon purchasing the *World* in 1883, he declared his purposes in a prospectus on the front page. "The entire WORLD ... will, from this day on, be under different management—different in men, measures and methods—different in purpose, policy and principle—different in objects and interests—different in sympathies and convictions—different in head and heart...." He explained that the paper would be "truly Democratic—dedicated to the cause of the people rather than that of purse-potentates—devoted more to the news of the New than the Old World—... will expose all fraud and sham, fight all public evils and abuses—[and] will serve and battle for the people with earnest sincerity...."[16] He made the *World* into a constructive, accurate, crusading instrument against social and governmental ills.

Despite the fact that the nature of the *World's* readership probably limited the paper's editorial influence, no other newspaper has matched its record for observable editorial accomplishments, from presidential elections to insurance reform to foreign policy to civic improvement. The *World* took the lead in these and other causes for what Pulitzer conceived to be the public good.[17] Once Pulitzer determined the issue, he and the World's editorial writers pounded at it day after day in a writing style marked by clear, forceful language.

THE PROFESSIONAL ERA, 1900–PRESENT

With the beginning of the 20th century, two trends of paramount importance to editorial writing could be seen taking shape. The first and more important was the growth of newspapers as big business. The second—which seemed to some people to be a counterpoising force but which in reality was an outgrowth of the first—was the professionalization of journalism.

Attending the growth of newspapers as business enterprises was—and continues to be—an emphasis on profit as the primary motive of newspaper owners. Even while the preeminent editors such as Dana, Godkin, and Pulitzer practiced their art in the late 1800s, huge new forces were closing in on journalism. The changes had begun with the penny press. When partisanship ceased to be the primary purpose of the newspaper, a means of economic support was cut from under the editorial writer. Even while the great personal editors were at the height of their glory in the 1800s, the news and business departments were becoming the real supporters of their papers. Here and there throughout the latter part of the 19th century a shining name in journalism stands out, but the motive of profit—sustained by the concepts of readership through news and of business efficiency—was already taking over the newspaper profession. By the 20th century it dominated.

For those looking for dates, we might

name 1896 as the conspicuous year of the victory of business over expression as the prime purpose of journalism. That was the year Pulitzer, in the name of financial health for his *World*, was swept fully into a circulation war with William Randolph Hearst. Responsible expression gave way to frenzied sensationalism. But even more important in the history of journalism's change to big business was Adolph Ochs' assumption in 1896 of the management of the foundering *New York Times*. Reacting against the sensationalism and boisterous editorial policies of Pulitzer and Hearst, Ochs revitalized the *Times* on the basis of thorough news coverage, objectivity, sound business practices, and a strong financial base. In these, the *Times* became the model for America's 20th-century newspapers.

The potential benefits of such an approach to the newspaper profession are obvious. Partisanship is reduced, readers are given the unbiased information necessary to make well-founded decisions, newspapers can afford to hire qualified personnel, financially stable newspapers can resist efforts by advertisers to influence editorial policy, and so forth.

On the other hand, as ideas of business efficiency took over, competition was reduced, newspaper content became standardized, chain ownership multiplied, the corporate structure of papers became commonplace, the value of newspapers increased, and the newspaper became in most cases primarily a business investment. These changes had several effects on editorials.

As news received greater emphasis, the eminence of the editorial faded. The news report replaced the editorial as the heart of the paper. The direct persuasive impact of editorials may have suffered consequently. Illustrating the changed attitude about the nature of newspaper influence, the chain publisher E. W. Scripps declared frankly, "Our headlines are our editorials."

Because the editorial page came to be viewed as secondary, publishers placed little importance or money in it. On most papers, the page came to be understaffed, editorial writers had inadequate time to devote to writing editorials, and the general quality of editorials suffered. As a counterpoint to those trends, many, mostly larger newspapers continued to place considerable emphasis on the editorial page, allotting it substantial resources and staff members. The professional concerns of individual writers and of writers' organizations also provided evidence of a widespread commitment to editorial writing. The professional activities of many writers indicate that in some ways editorial writing today exhibits more talent and commitment than at any time in the past.

Despite such healthy signs in the field, however, the tone and tenor of the editorial changed under the influence of corporate journalism and professional attitudes. Editorials became less passionate and more reasoned.

One could point to a number of reasons for the change, but one factor was the disappearance of competing papers. When partisan competition and vigorous expression were the rule, newspapers attempted to appeal to limited groups of readers. When profit emerged as a paper's motive, newspapers attempted to broaden their appeal by presenting both sides of issues and even-tempered opinion. When a city's one newspaper was its only one, and the paper's readership was composed of liberals and conservatives, Republicans and Democrats, poor and rich, the newspaper ownership found it incumbent to be circumspect in its editorial comment. Pulitzer Prize winner W. W. Waymack in 1942 pointed out this principle: "Both the economic pressure (what constitutes 'good business') and a fair recognition of social obligation reinforce the principle of news objectivity, divorced from editorial bias. They also dictate less of passion and more of reason in editorials."[18]

In some regards, this attitude made sense. When a city had only one daily, it could be a disservice to readers if the paper became the opinionated mouthpiece of one faction or cause. Although corporate newspapers strove to appear nonpartisan, some tended, on the other hand, to adhere to the conservative line and to take stands that benefited business interests. That editorial position was a natural result of the fact that newspaper owners themselves were businessmen. On the other hand, working journalists in the 20th century tended to be ideologically liberal. Thus, many editorial writers imparted a liberal perspective to their writing.

Editorial writing in the 20th century came to be marked also by a noticeable absence of boldness. Circumspection engendered by business concerns sometimes gave way to timidity. "American journalism," *Editor & Publisher* editorialized in 1937, "...is officed by too many people intent upon balance sheets, and content with a product that holds circulation and causes no complaints from advertisers and articulate readers." At another time, an editor of *Editor & Publisher* told the American Society of Newspaper Editors: "Reader confidence has been impaired because too many newspapers seem, on their face, to be cautious to the point of cowardice, morbidly expedient, slyly illiberal, holding back from any forthright part in the great controversies that are sweeping the country, and many people deduce that they are hogtied by managements in league with special interests."[19]

The business character of newspapers also changed the position and nature of the person who wrote editorials. "Personal editors" disappeared, employees with the function only of writing editorials emerged, and much of the editorial page was given over to syndicated columnists. These changes in personnel duties resulted from changes in the complexity, size, and motives of newspapers. As the size of the newspaper operation grew, the owner no longer was capable of performing all its functions. With increased complexity and operating expenses, owners, concerned about financial health, had to devote their attention more and more to the business end of their papers. They had little time to write editorials. "Certainly when [the personal editor] and his office departed," wrote an observer in 1911, "something warm, something humanly tangible, something directly and conspicuously responsible, passed out of the relation between the reader and the editorial, the first effect of which was to rob this department of a considerable part of the reader's confidence, to raise doubts or even suspicions in his mind, and—what was still more disastrous—to chill the sense of personal relation which formerly had existed."[20]

Often, the editor was no longer the boss. In the 19th century, a paper's editor had also been its owner. Editorials were known to be the voice of the editor. In the 20th century, the editor often was simply the employee of a corporation and the editorial the anonymous, amalgamated voice of an institution. The *New York Tribune* was considered Greeley's paper; the *Times*, Raymond's; the *Sun*, Dana's; the *Evening Post*, Bryant's and later Godkin's. Hardly any major paper in the last 50 years was identified as the voice and property of its editorial writer. Few readers could even name the editor of the local paper, much less that of the editorial writer.

As the newspaper grew in size, its functions were divided into the hands of departments. Specialization became the rule. The successor to the personal editor was the editorial writer, often multiplied into the editorial staff. Being an employee, the editorial writer did not speak with the authority of ownership. The effect this change had on editorial writing was pointed out in the 1930s by Eric Allen, a professor of journalism at the University of Oregon. "Now this subordinate," he wrote, "being a subordinate, and being known to be a subordinate, began to be more or less kicked around. Among his worst critics were his fellow subordinates. The circulation crew wanted him for heaven's sake to lay off editorials that caused opinionated people to stop the paper. The advertising crew wanted to know why in God's name did he always pick on the biggest advertiser to excoriate when the woods were so completely filled with other and worse malefactors of great wealth who didn't advertise. The news staff, perhaps the most critical of all, sneered at his sesquipedalian sentences, full of semicolons and with the periods three inches apart.... It was all very discouraging."[21]

The opinion function began to fall more and more not on a staff writer but on an outsider, the syndicated columnist. Columnists frequently provided better, more informed writing at a cheaper price than editorial writers could. Because columnists were clearly identified, the public could more often recognize them than a newspaper's anonymous editorial writer. They filled, in some fashion, the void left by the demise of the personal editor—except, of course, that they were distant, not local, voices.

Liberal critics in the 1930s and '40s charged that editorial writers' views shifted with whatever opinion their employers ordered or thought would increase circulation for the corporate newspaper. They could point to Arthur Brisbane, chief editorial writer for the Hearst newspapers for more than 30 years, for proof. Even though he popularized the editorial page in the early 1900s, his published views could change from issue to issue depending on the political and social ideological peregrinations of his boss. The late Pulitzer Prize winning editor of the *Richmond* (Va.) *Times-Dispatch,* Virginius Dabney, writing in 1945, summed up what he saw as the effect that the newspaper's evolution into big business had had on the ideology of editorial writing. "Today," he said, "newspapers are Big Business and they are run in that tradition. The publisher, who often knows little about the editorial side of the operation, usually is one of the leading business men in his community, and his editorial page, under normal circumstances, strongly reflects that point of view. Sometimes he gives his editor a free hand, but far oftener he does not. He looks upon the paper primarily as a 'property,' rather than as an instrument for public service.... The fact that the average American publisher ... often imposes his views upon his editor, is the greatest single reason why the American editorial page has declined so sharply in influence."[22]

The state of editorial writing in recent years was not as politically bleak as Virginius Dabney painted it at the middle of the 20th century. The influence that the business character of newspapers exerted on editorial writing was balanced by the professionalization of the field. Alongside conservative editorial pages there was a proliferation of liberal ones. By the end of the 20th century, the standardization of journalism ideology, with the result that editorial pages took predictable stands on politics and a variety of other issues, came to pose a greater threat to open inquiry than political ideology did. Personal editors did not vanish in the 20th century, and at no other time in history have there been more polished editorial

writers than today. William Allen White, owner and editor of the *Emporia* (Kan.) *Gazette* from 1895 to 1944, and Henry Watterson, part-owner and editor of the *Louisville* (Ky.) *Courier-Journal* from 1868 to 1921, were outstanding examples of editorial writers who spoke with the power of ownership. Frank Cobb and Walter Lippmann, both employee-editors of the *New York World,* wrote with a force and depth seldom matched. Perhaps no editorial writer ever matched the *Portland Oregonian's* Ben Hur Lampman's mastery of language. More recently, Ralph McGill and Eugene Patterson of the *Atlanta Constitution* proved that editors of a major newspaper need not be anonymous editorial writers. Despite subjugating himself to Hearst, Arthur Brisbane showed that even an employed writer could gain fame in the editorial field.

Editorial writing in recent years also has had substantial talent practicing the craft. Paul Greenberg of the *Arkansas Democrat* and James Kilpatrick, who went from editorial writing in Richmond, Virginia, to become a nationally syndicated columnist, were prime examples. In reading the winning editorials in such national contests as those sponsored by the American Society of Newspaper Editors and the Pulitzer Prizes, one cannot help but admire the work of many of today's editorial writers. While it is true that even some contest winners are dull and superficial and that many newspapers' editorials are less interesting than readers' letters to their editors, it nevertheless is true that there is a substantial group of editorial writers who do a fine job. They recognize the weaknesses of the field, and they work hard at their own writing. They have their own organization, the National Conference of Editorial Writers, which does not hesitate to illuminate the problems in the field and sponsors a number of activities aimed at improving the craft. Among the entire body of working journalists today, no group is more critical of its own work or more committed to quality than are editorial writers.

Selected Readings

Hart, Jim Allee. *Views on the News: The Developing Editorial Syndrome, 1500–1800.* Carbondale: Southern Illinois University Press, 1970.

Nevins, Allan. *American Press Opinion, Washington to Coolidge.* New York: Heath, 1928.

Peterson, Wilbur, and Robert Thorp. "Weeklies' Editorial Effort Less Than 30 Years Ago." *Journalism Quarterly* 30 (1962): 53–56.

Rystrom, Kenneth. "The Editorial Page That Used To Be." Chap. 1 in *The Why, Who and How of the Editorial Page,* 2nd ed. State College, Pa.: Strata Publishing Company, 1994.

Sloan, Wm. David, and Laird B. Anderson, eds. *Pulitzer Prize Editorials: America's Best Editorial Writing 1917–1993,* 2nd ed. Ames: Iowa State University Press, 1994.

Sloan, Wm. David, Cheryl S. Wray, and C. Joanne Sloan. *Great Editorials: Masterpieces of Opinion Writing,* 2nd ed. Northport, Ala.: Vision Press, 1997.

Stonecipher, Harry. "Editorial Role-Playing in History." *Grassroots Editor* 16 (March-April 1975): 18–24; 16 (May-June 1975): 18–22.

Windhauser, John W., Will Norton Jr., and Sonny Rhodes. "Editorial Patterns of the Tribune Under Three Editors." *Journalism Quarterly* 60 (1983): 524–28.

Notes

1. *Preface to the Pennsylvania Gazette,* 2 October 1729.
2. The first essay in the 12-part series was published in the *Pennsylvania Chronicle and Universal Advertiser* on 30 November 1767.
3. The first essay in the series began with the now-famous introduction "These are the times that try men's souls" and was published in the *Pennsylvania Journal* on 19 December 1776.
4. The "Federalist Papers"—a joint effort by Alexander Hamilton, James Madison, and John Jay—consisted of 85 essays that were published in the *New York Independent Journal* during 1787 and 1788.
5. For a history of the *Courant's* development of the editorial form, see Wm. David Sloan, Cheryl S. Wray, and C. Joanne Sloan, *Great Editorials: Masterpieces of Opinion*

Writing, 2nd ed. (Northport, Ala.: Vision Press, 1997), 41–42.
6. Benjamin Russell quoted in Frederic Hudson, *Journalism in the United States, From 1690 to 1872* (New York: Harper and Row, 1873), 154.
7. S. S. Cox, "A Great Old Sunset," *Ohio Statesman,* 19 May 1853.
8. *Springfield Republican,* 4 January 1851.
9. Beman Brockway, *Fifty Years in Journalism: Embracing Recollections and Personal Experiences with an Autobiography* (Watertown, N.Y.: Daily Times Printing and Publishing House, 1891), 152.
10. *New York Times,* 18 September 1851.
11. *New York Sun,* 12 January 1885.
12. *New York Sun,* 19 October 1880.
13. "Is There a Santa Claus?" *New York Sun,* 21 September 1897.
14. Quoted in Kenneth Stewart and John Tebbel, *Makers of Modern Journalism* (Englewood Cliffs, N.J.: Prentice-Hall, 1952), 79.
15. Wendell Phillips Garrison, "E. L. Godkin" (an editorial written upon Godkin's death), *The Nation,* 22 May 1902.
16. *New York World,* 11 May 1883.
17. The *World,* for example, led the efforts to raise funds to build a pedestal for the Statue of Liberty with its editorial "An Appeal" on March 16, 1885. Pulitzer considered the statue the embodiment of liberty, which was one of his paramount lifetime concerns.
18. W. W. Waymack, "Editorial Pages in Wartime—Their Techniques and Ideology," *Journalism Quarterly* 19 (March 1942): 34–39.
19. Quoted in Gayle Waldrop, *Editor and Editorial Writer* (New York: Rinehard & Co., 1948), 42.
20. Tiffany Blake, "The Editorial," *Collier's,* 23 September 1911.
21. Eric W. Allen, "Economic Changes and Editorial Influence," *Journalism Quarterly* 8 (Fall 1931): 352.
22. Virginius Dabney, *Saturday Review of Literature* (February 24, 1945).

33

Newspaper Design

SALLY I. MORANO

Over the years of the American newspaper, design has changed dramatically. How a newspaper looks has gone from being a seemingly unimportant issue to a controlling force and consideration in the development of the newspaper. These changes cannot be attributed to any single factor, but rather a combination of varying changes over time. Technology, societal influences, economic pressures, and commercialization predominantly have worked interactively to play the most influential roles in changing the face of newspapers.

Benjamin Harris published the first colonial newspaper, *Publick Occurrences, Both Foreign and Domestick*, in 1690. It was patterned after the standard book page of the times, sized at 6" × 9½". However, Harris did attempt to differentiate its design from that of the traditional book. News filled three pages, and a fourth page was left blank so that readers could add additional news by hand before passing the paper on to the next reader.

Although Harris used a book printing press, which belonged to a Boston colleague, he carefully chose a typographic display that would distinguish his newspaper visually. It included text set in two columns. The body copy was 12-point type, which was notably large compared to contemporary British newspapers. The point was (and still is) the standard unit of type size, equaling .01383 inches, or approximately 72 points to the inch. *Publick Occurrences'* design consisted of lines of type with no obtrusive headlines, the only exceptions being the all-capital-letter nameplate and some large drop capital letters at the beginnings of paragraphs.[1] This appearance supports the notion that while Harris was concerned with the content and function of the paper, he did not attempt to distinguish it visually. This is not to say that design was ignored, but simply that printers made sure to keep within the accepted British standards that were already in place. Harris' paper accordingly mimicked the contemporary unornamented British style.

While *Publick Occurrences* had a life span of only one issue before the government suppressed it, in 1704 the second American newspaper, the *Boston News-Letter*, was the first to be successfully sustained. Its success was primarily due to the fact that its publisher, postmaster John Campbell of Boston, first obtained official approval, which he proudly displayed in large letters below the nameplate of the newspaper.[2]

The paper was a single sheet 8" × 12¾", also known as a "half-sheet." The *News-Letter* looked almost identical to the *London Gazette*.[3] Like the *Gazette*, it consisted of a solid two-column design of 11-point type and filled both the front and back of the sheet of paper. In a box at the left of the title was a sailing ship signifying that most of the news came from abroad, and to the right was the figure of the galloping post-boy, who became a familiar symbol on colonial newspapers. Within the body copy, the *News-Letter* included small column labels the same size as the body copy, functioning somewhat like the headlines of today. During the years Campbell controlled the newspaper (until 1721) he showed little interest in any unusual graphic presentation.[4] The page size or format and typographic style of the *News-Letter* became the often repeated standard in the emerging newspaper marketplace in America.

One of the first notable changes in the makeup of the American newspaper was the inclusion of an illustration. Though newspapers included some etched woodblock pictures in their nameplates, such as the British ships, post-boys, and flags, the body of the papers consisted only of gray columns of type. In the May 9, 1754, issue of his *Pennsylvania Gazette*, Benjamin Franklin included on the second page a wood-cut illustration of a dismembered snake, each section labeled with initials for New England, New York, New Jersey, Pennsylvania, Virginia, North Carolina, and South Carolina, and below it a caption in large type stating "Join, or Die."[5] This first cartoon was one of earliest to appear in an American paper and laid the groundwork for grandiose illustrations, information graphics, pictures, and cartoons of future newspapers.

In colonial newspapers, advertising did not occupy any great amount of space, but as newspapers grew, advertising flooded into them. Although a few editors saw advertising as an intrusion on the space dedicated to the readers,[6] most made open efforts to attract advertisers and even included ads on the front page. John Campbell included one paragraph in the original issue of the *Boston News-Letter* stating that "all persons who have any Houses, Lands, Tenements, Farms, Ships, Vessels, Goods, Wares, or Merchandise, etc. to be Sold … may have same inserted at a Reasonable Rate.…" This advertisement, announcing that advertisers could negotiate the appropriate rate for their advertisements, appeared in type within the columns, adding no form of unusual deviation to the eye.[7] Throughout the 18th century, advertising in newspapers consisted largely of official notices, ship-sailings, articles for sale, and rewards, all displayed in the form of the same type as the rest of the paper and without illustration. As early as 1743, John Zenger (probably better known for his trial concerning seditious libel) included the first double-column advertisement in his *New York Journal*, but other than the additional width, the advertisement was essentially as unobtrusive as its single-column counterparts.[8]

Among the first outside factors to affect the format of newspapers were government taxes on printing supplies, particularly the Stamp Act.[9] The Stamp Act, passed by the House of Commons on February 27, 1765, taxed, among other things, the sheets of paper or parchment that had to be used by printers. The tax fell most heavily upon those who dealt with newspapers, almanacs, and legal documents in their daily affairs.

On February 14, 1765, Benjamin Franklin, living in London, wrote to his *Pennsylvania Gazette* partner, David Hall, and told him of his plan to avoid some of the proposed tax. He explained that he learned that colonial papers printed on full sheets (which were folded) would be taxed one penny per sheet, while those printed on half-sheets would be taxed one-half penny. With this knowledge, the ever-thrifty Franklin purchased 48,000 half sheets in London and shipped the paper to his partner in Philadelphia for the future printing of the *Pennsylvania Gazette*.[10]

Like Franklin, other printers found ways to minimize the effects of the taxes. The main effect of the taxes on the format of newspapers was a noticeable increase in page size. Publishers began to economize by using a large sheet instead of several smaller ones. The less expensive half-sheet was even more economical when its actual size was increased.

These pages continued to increase in size throughout the 18th century, up to the limits of handmade paper and the capacity of hand-operated presses. Also affecting the growing page size was an increase in the quantity of news and advertising.

Overall, the design of a newspaper was simply not something to which colonists gave much new thought. Instead, printers were careful not to violate the accepted standards. They followed the form of British newspapers without hesitation or question.

In colonial times, the printer was also the publisher, which left little room for serving as designer. In "To Publish a Good News-Paper," Benjamin Franklin listed qualities such as "…extensive Acquaintance with Languages, a great Easiness and Command of Writing and Relating things cleanly and intelligibly" and being

"...able to speak of War" and "well acquainted with Geography, with the History of the Time..." as desirable qualities in an accomplished printer. However, he never mentioned anything relating to the visual presentation of the newspaper.[11]

This was due largely to a lack of need to draw readers in with inviting visuals. If a colonial reader obtained a newspaper, because of the scarcity of printed material, he would most likely read it from beginning to end. Douglas McMurtrie, director of typography for Ludlow Typography Company, presented an excellent example of this at the 1940 American Society of Newspaper Editors convention. He referred to a July 2, 1776, newspaper in which "the middle of one of the columns on the back page is printed a three-line item in 10-point, without a head. The item reads: 'This day the Continental Congress declared the United Colonies free and independent states.'" While this was clearly a news item of great importance, in the colonial newspaper, it was given the exact same amount of space attention as an adjoining column labeled "A quantity of white and brown buckram to be sold by Mary Flanagan, the corner of Front and Spruce Streets." [12]

Another cause for the general lack of change in colonial newspaper design was the unchanging technology in printing throughout the period up until the 19th century. Newspapers were printed as they had been in England before American newspapers existed, with type composed by hand. Eighteenth-century printers used printing technology not that much different than the procedures established by Gutenberg with his invention of movable type. While effective for the needs of the colonists, this early form of printing did not even allow for any great extent of embellishment in design.

With the turn of the century came many changes in the design of the newspaper, made possible by new technology. Newspaper format changes were for the most part dictated by the sway of technology. The first of these new technologies in the 19th century was the art of mechanized papermaking, which was sponsored by the Fourdrinier family and put into operation in 1803 in Hartfordshire, England,

by the ingenious engineer Bryan Donkin.[13] This process was aided by Lord Stanhope's invention of the iron press in 1800 that allowed for a larger impression than could be made on existing wooden presses. This process of mechanical papermaking allowed for larger sheets than could be made by hand. Though they were introduced in England in 1803, the first Fourdrinier machine was not set up in the United States until 1827. The introduction led to the development of even larger newspaper formats, up to "blanket sheets" of 30 inches or more in length and 24 inches in width. For a period of time, these blanket sheets were highly in vogue for newspaper printers who wished to boast of their success and technological superiority. Despite the increasing page size, the design of tightly packed columns of print with minimal headlining continued.

Social pressures also contributed to the urgent need for new printing methods. The public needed a more affordable paper that could truly serve the common man, while printers, publishers, and advertisers sought to increase sales. This idea of publishing an expensive newspaper occurred to a medical student by the name of Horatio David Sheppard as an excellent way to provide newspapers for those of a meager salary, while profiting the publisher by increasing sales. The idea came to him as a result of frequently walking along Chatham Street in New York City, which was known for its "penny a piece" sales. He was stricken by the realization that people generally were quick to purchase items that cost only a penny.

Sheppard concluded that in order to make a fortune, "one has nothing more to do than to produce a tempting article ... and place it where everybody can see it...." [14] Despite his good intentions and innovative thoughts concerning a penny press, Sheppard failed in his attempt to activate this plan. However, on September 3, 1833, Benjamin Day's *New York Sun* became the first successful penny daily.[15]

The success of these emerging penny papers, which began to take on a new look, was the result of the ever-improving printing technology. Through a series of constantly improving developments, printers adequately perfected the cylinder press, which led to significant change in the face and composition of newspapers. The invention and use of the cylinder press was the first major alteration of the Gutenberg style of printing that had been used for almost four centuries. Impression speed increased from about 200 to nearly 1,000 per hour. A speedier version of this original Koenig press was first installed in the United States at the *New York Daily Advertiser* in 1825. These cylinder presses were further improved by the application of steam power in later models, which led to their widespread use.

Another change in format that came with the penny press was a shrinking of page size. Because penny papers were usually sold on the streets, they were much easier to handle and carry around at a smaller size. The penny newspapers were generally half-sheets, similar to today's tabloid size, a stark contrast to the large blanket sheets that had been popular with the party press. The page makeup was usually three-column.

By 1847, the Hoe Company, the leading American press manufacturer, developed the first high-speed rotary press and mechanized production began to play a role in design. In this process, the type, which was held in place by V-shaped column rules, was locked onto the large cylinder that rolled over the paper. This column rule actually printed as a thin hairline between each column of type, which allowed for the type within the columns to be moved even closer together. Only about 6 points, or .08 inches, of space (which was occupied by the hairline) generally separated columns in contrast to the 12 to 24 points of space between hand-printed columns. Using the newer "lightning" rotary presses, newspapers could print up to 20,000 sheets per hour.

The greatest effect the rotary press had on the appearance of the newspaper was creating the necessity of one-column headlines. The column rules running the height of the page wedged the type in place, but because of the hairline column division, headlines of more than one column were not possible. The result was the use of "decker" headlines: a series of stacked titles running vertically down the column. The number of decks varied anywhere from one up to a dozen headlines, based upon the amount and weight of the news.[16] The outbreak of the Civil War led to the extensive use of deckers, such as the April 13, 1861, issue of the *New York Sun's* seven-decker declaration of the war's beginning.[17] Most papers tended to favor slab-seriffed Egyptian or 'Antique' typefaces either bold or bold condensed, though some sans-serif types did begin to appear.

Around the same time period, another crucial design change came about: illustrations. Newspapers had been using some very modest forms of illustration such as the carvings of ships or the galloping post-boy, but illustration was generally disregarded because publishers were too busy trying to get the type on the page.

James Gordon Bennett, editor of the *New York Herald*, pioneered many newspaper practices that became widely used in the industry. One of these practices aimed at attracting readers was the extensive use of illustrations. Bennett hoped to reach the reader in part with the newspaper's visual appeal. The *Herald's* June 25, 1845, issue displayed a first for American newspapers: a full page news illustration that was published on the occasion of the death of former President Andrew Jackson.[18] In the climate of competition between newspapers, illustrations became an important part of reaching readers, and publishers began to pay attention to the newspapers' visual appeal.[19]

In 1861, just as the Civil War was beginning, another printing innovation called stereotyping came about, solving the problems of the rotary press. The practice of stereotyping began well before the 19th century, but not in a practical form. The printer Charles Brightly discussed his method of stereotyping "in its present imperfect state" as early as 1809 in the book *Method of Casting Stereotype with a Stereotype Metal Plate*.[20] Thomas Hodgson went even further in an essay by detailing the history and founding of the art of stereotyping, concluding that it had "conferred such inestimable benefit on society."[21] Newspapers in America began to use stereotype printing by 1861, abolishing any mechanical need for the continuance of the rigid vertical makeup with divided columns. Vertical makeup continued, however, without any mechanical justification, probably out of habit or a preference developed over the years. Makeup remained vertical for many years; and during the Civil War, headlines were still one column with six to twelve decks descending from them, consisting of several different type faces.

Further press developments came only two years later when the first web-perfecting press was installed in an American newspaper in 1863. The paper was fed onto the press from a roll rather than in sheets. As far as design changes were concerned, the web-perfecting press allowed for the paper to be printed on both sides simultaneously as it passed through the press. This process dramatically sped up printing.

The abundance of news growing out of the Civil War led to several design innovations. Instead of one-line labels, wordier action headlines were introduced. Sub-heads were used to break up the gray columns of type and allow more white space. Column widths went through experimentation until the page size settled down to a standard of about 20 inches in length by five or six columns in width.

With the Civil War came more of a demand for newspaper illustrations. Photography, although in its early stages, was sufficiently developed to the point of practical use. Photographers traveled to battle sites to capture still photographs of the scenes, although action shots were not yet possible. While newspapers did not yet have the technology to reproduce photographs, they used photographs in the process of making woodcuts. These real-life illustrations became important to readers. Reproduction quality was continuously improved; and by March 4, 1880, the New York Daily Graphic included the first photograph to appear in a newspaper.[22]

The period from the end of the Civil War to the turn of the century was a time of intense development in American newspapers. The pressures of mass circulation and competition fueled the sensationalism of the "Yellow Press." This term arose from a cartoon in an 1893 issue of Joseph Pulitzer's New York World, titled "The Yellow Kid," which was the first printing of color in a newspaper. Further in the tradi-

tion of yellow journalism, Pulitzer ran up to four columns of advertising on his seven-column broadsheet front page and stories about subject matter that was considered unfit for printing up until that time.

Yellow journalism brought with it big black Gothic headlines. It also brought about the first consistent use of headlines wider than one column. Horizontal display was introduced as a design technique in the 1890s and became widely used by sensational papers such as the World and the Sun of New York. They included often jumbled masses of large banner headlines, spreads, and illustrations designed to aggressively draw in the eyes of potential readers.[23] Placement of stories on the page also became an issue. Newsworthiness was considered, and the display of the stories reflected their importance. By the end of the 19th century, the design of newspapers was generally driven by attempts to attract readers more than anything else. The techniques started by yellow journalism led the newspaper industry into the era of modern design.

The newspaper entered the 20th century as a much changed product from that of its humble beginnings in 1690. At the turn of the century, the effects of yellow journalism and sensationalism were still greatly impacting the design of newspapers. Notable publishers such as William Randolph Hearst and Joseph Pulitzer, though often criticized for sensationalizing the content of the news in their papers, certainly made an impact on design.

Just as these publishers were changing the design of their newspapers for reasons based on circulation and competition, another printing innovation came along to further contribute to change, while also making it easier. Several people, including Mark Twain, had been repeatedly attempting to produce some sort of machine that could speed up the process of hand setting the type.

Finally, on July 3, 1886, Ottmar Mergenthaler succeeded in inventing the Linotype machine, which Thomas Edison hailed as the "eighth wonder of the world." Mergenthaler claimed that "we are going to have full success for the reason that we have attacked the problem in an entirely different way than did those who failed." He solved the problem of how to set type without using individual pieces by realizing that the answer was to combine the casting and composition processes into one machine.[24] The machine used a keyboard to assemble brass character matrices against which hot lead was poured into mold. By doing so, Mergenthaler vastly improved the speed, cost, and quality of composition. Those changes in turn led to an improvement of the typography used in newspapers, as well as the development of many new typefaces.

The Linotype was first adopted by the *New York Tribune* and was quickly incorporated into the production of many newspapers around the world by the 20th century. By the 1930s, nearly all papers, including the small papers that were slow to change, had converted to some form of hot-metal composition inspired by the Linotype.

Other new 20th-century advances came in the area of illustration, due to developments that made photograph reproduction more effective. The first real news photography developed during the Spanish-American War in 1898, but it was still widely considered to be a sensational fad. Melville Stone, editor of the *Chicago Daily News*, discarded newspaper photographs as "just a temporary fad, but we're going to get the benefit of the fad while it lasts."[25] The development of the halftone process and other photographic innovations such as rotary photogravure caused photo illustrations to become a permanent fixture in American newspapers. Halftone, the most influential of these methods, was the process by which the original image was rephotographed through a screen that broke the continuous lines of the image into a matrix of tiny dots. This process mechanically transferred photographs with text to the printed page.

The First World War had a revolutionizing effect on newspapers, particularly in the area of typographic changes and headlining. As a result of the war, a constant in most American dailies became the banner headline, which consisted of one or two lines of large-size bold condensed sans serif capitals of 72 up to 96 points spanning the full width of the page.[26] By the end of the war, competition was at its height

with most cities having many daily newspapers. Americans developed a strong desire for visually active and appealing design, which led to changes in both format and typography.

The post-war period from 1919 to the 1929 stock market crash, known as the "jazz era," had a characteristic newspaper by-product that emerged: the tabloid. Tabloids were half-sheet papers that extensively used the relatively new halftone process, along with other conspicuous design techniques, such as dramatic sans serif headlines in the heaviest condensed gothic fonts. New illustrated newspapers such as Joseph Medill Patterson's and Robert McCormick's *Illustrated Daily News* arose, emphasizing the power of photography, flashy design, and poster-like front page design.[27] The *New York Illustrated Daily News*[28] was another popular tabloid that had a front page that often looked more like a poster than a newspaper.

Amid this chaos, the genesis of modern design came when in 1917 the *New York Tribune* hired a notable New York typographer, Ben Sherbow, to redesign the newspaper. He used his skills of design and typography to measure the readability of various headlines through a series of experiments timing the speed at which the eye moved to certain words and fonts. He used these findings to radically simplify the *Tribune*. The redesign involved restricting type to only one family, Bodoni, and also changing the headlines to "downstyle," in which only the first word and proper nouns were capitalized. The effect was the creation of more striking and quickly readable headlines. Sherbow's work was the first systematic application of modern design to newspapers and was considered a radical change for newspapers. A 1937 issue of the *New York Tribune* observed that until 1916 "the notion that news printing could be a thing of practical beauty, far removed from the brashness of a screaming headline, had not dawned in America."[29]

Furthering the tradition of Sherbow was one of his younger followers, John Allen. While an employee of Mergenthaler Linotype Company, the young Allen watched Sherbow's experiments done to measure the readability of the *New York Herald Tribune*. Allen furthered the cause of modern design by both redesigning issues of the *Linotype News* and writing a series of books detailing the precepts of modern design. In 1936, in his first book, *Newspaper Makeup*, he pointed out examples of design techniques that worked against attractiveness and legibility and techniques that worked in favor of those things. He also presented a history of the physical evolution of newspapers and the factors that caused those changes.[30] He then updated the propositions in later books, such as *The Modern Newspaper*, which included significant changes from the first book.[31]

He referred to his design technique as "streamlining," which has generally come to refer to the popular commercial design style of the 1930s. At the 1940 American Society of Newspaper Editors convention, Douglas McMurtrie referred to streamlining as the structural design "that will remove or reduce as much as possible their conflict with the innumerable interests and distractions of modern life that claim the attention of the readers." He summed this up explaining that this design technique simply meant "making the newspaper more useful to its readers, more easily and quickly read."[32] Certainly the top newspaper editors in the country at the time were paying attention to the design changes.

Other newspaper designers including Allen Hutt, Gilbert Farrar, Heyworth Campbell, and Edmund Arnold paid attention to Allen's suggestions. These modernists attacked the traditional Victorian style of the newspaper in favor of the clean, simplified modern look that utilized space as a tool for creating emphasis. They also strongly moved away from vertical makeup and became more aware of the importance of this modernist philosophy of design.[33]

An important development in printing technology came again in 1939 with the invention of offset printing, a method in which the ink was transferred from the plate to a rubber blanket and then to the paper. This method produced a higher quality of printing and became popular with small newspapers. They usually also employed cold type composition, a photographic process that did not require metal type. As manufacturers increased press speed, papers with larger circulation slowly

went from hot-metal type to offset. Though the technology was available in 1939, the move to offset printing occurred slowly. The method was adopted by smaller newspapers before larger papers, but was not widely used overall until the late 1960s. Even as late as the 1990s, a few papers were still making the change.

With this improved printing quality, papers began to show off. This showed up in the form of increased size and number of photographs. The practice of photojournalism was refined in the 1960s and 1970s as photographers began to be incorporated into the newsroom. Offset printing also allowed for an unlimited variety in type sizing and fonts. With offset, type was composed with a photographic strip of a font, rather than an entire metal set of letters. Because these photographic strips were considerably cheaper than metal type sets, a newspaper could own a much wider variety of fonts in a variety of sizes, which could be incorporated into page design.

In the 1970s, the *Minneapolis Tribune* changed to employ a method of modular packaging of the news. With the trend set, the vast majority of American newspapers began to follow. Newspapers grouped elements of news stories, including text, headline, and any illustration or graphic, into well-defined rectangular spaces on the page.

Along with this organizing of the elements on the page came a desire for more orderly and legible typefaces. Generally throughout previous times, the goal of typographers was to create attractive fonts that would be pleasing aesthetically. In an attempt to achieve orderliness and simplicity much like the goals of modular design, typographic designers began to create more effective and legible types stripped of unnecessary embellishment. This led to the development of many new sans serifs fonts, such as the Swiss type family Helvetica, which became the standard for headlines of newspapers using the modular design.

On June 7, 1939, the Associated Press distributed a color news picture to the daily press for the first time. Though color pictures were much more difficult to process and print, they were used on special occasions and in special sections before they became common in the

1960s. In the 1970s more advanced technology allowed for ease in color processing, and computers were used to further enhance the product.[34] In the 1980s and 1990s the development of a filmless digital camera led to quicker processing, decreased costs and improved quality. The use of color photographs was also improved by the industry's move to offset printing.

In 1982, *USA Today* emerged, revealing a new and noticeable design deviation. Along with the compacting of stories by using a tight writing style, *USA Today* included a bright and colorful display filled with photographs, maps, charts, graphs and other such informational graphics. While upholding modular design, *USA Today* did away with the spaciousness and simplicity many newspapers had adopted. Though newspapers such as the *Wall Street Journal* and the *New York Times* clung to their simple and classic design, many newspapers began to imitate in varying degrees the effective use of color, photographs, graphics, and varied typography *USA Today* employed.

Well known design consultant Edmund Arnold spoke out against this movement toward "disturbing" design, explaining that newspapers of the *USA Today* format "have become too superficial." He hoped that in the future newspapers would move away from the color-splashed, busy pages to a simpler and more traditional style.[35] At the 1990 meeting of the American Society of Newspaper Editors, design expert Mario Garcia suggested limiting the use of color.[36]

Over the more than 300 years of the American newspaper, design has drastically evolved to suit the needs of the changing times and readers. It has been influenced by a number of outside forces including technological advances, societal demands, economic pressures, and political influences. As a result of these various influences, newspapers have gone from book-like gray masses to often colorful and highly commercial beacons. Whether intentional or not, a newspaper's design influences its ability to attract readers and relay information effectively. Because of the impact that it can have, newspaper design has become increasingly important to newspaper production since its beginning in 1690.

Selected Readings

Hutt, Allen. *The Changing Newspaper: Typographic Trends in Britain and America 1622–1972*. London: Gordon Fraser, 1973.

Notes

1. *Publick Occurrences, Both Forreign and Domestick*, 25 September 1690.

2. *Boston News-Letter*, April 1704.

3. *London Gazette*, 1 February 1665.

4. Allen Hutt, *The Changing Newspaper: Typographic Trends in Britain and America 1622–1972* (London: Gordon Fraser, 1973), 41–46.

5. *Pennsylvania Gazette*, 9 May 1754.

6. Jason Rogers, *Building Newspaper Advertising* (New York: Garland Publishing, Inc., 1986), 3–8.

7. *Boston News-Letter*, 24 April 1704.

8. *New York Journal*, 1743.

9. Stephen Hopkins, *The Rights of the Colonists Examined* (1764; reprinted ed., Providence, R.I.: Rhode Island Bicentennial Foundation, 1974).

10. Benjamin Franklin to David Hall cited in C. A. Weslager, *The Stamp Act Congress with an Exact copy of the Complete Journal* (Newark, N.J.: University of Delaware Press, 1976), 34–43.

11. Benjamin Franklin, "The Papers of Benjamin Franklin," quoted in Charles Clark, *The Public Prints* (New York: Oxford University Press, 1994), 193–94.

12. Douglas McMurtrie's address in the *Proceedings of the Eighteenth Annual Convention of American Society of Newspaper Editors, April 18–19, 1940* (Washington D.C.: National Press Club, 1940), 69–70.

13. Hutt, *The Changing Newspaper*, 43.

14. Horatio Sheppard to James Parton, cited in James Parton, *The Life of Horace Greeley, Editor of the New York Tribune* (1855; reprint, New York, 1970), 140.

15. Wm. David Sloan and James D. Startt, eds., *The Media in America: A History*, 4th ed. (Northport, Ala.: Vision Press, 1999), 121.

16. Kevin Barnhurst, *Seeing the Newspaper* (New York: St. Martin's Press, 1994), 163–67.

17. *New York Sun*, 13 April 1861.

18. *New York Herald*, 25 June 1845.

19. Sloan and Startt, *The Media in America*, 129.

20. Charles Brightly, *Method of Casting Stereotype with a Stereotype Metal Plate* (1809; reprint ed., New York: Garland Publishing, 1982).

21. Thomas Hodgson, *An Essay on the Origin and Progress of Stereotype Printing* (1820; reprint ed., New York: Garland Publishing, 1982).

22. *New York Daily Graphic*, 4 March 1880.

23. Carl Schlesinger, *The Biography of Ottmar Mergenthaler: Inventor of Linotype* (New Castle, Del.: Oak Knoll Books, 1989).

24. Wolfgang Kummer to Carl Schlesinger quoted in ibid., vii–viii.

25. Melville Stone quoted in Daryl R. Moen, *Newspaper Layout and Design* (Ames: University of Iowa Press, 1984), 9.

26. Hutt, *The Changing Newspaper*, 97.

27. John Tebbel, *An American Dynasty: The Story of the McCormicks, Medills and Pattersons* (Garden City, N.Y.: Doubleday and Company, 1947). See also John Allen, *Newspaper Makeup* (New York: Harper and Brothers, 1936).

28. *New York Illustrated Daily News*, 26 June 1919.

29. *New York Herald Tribune*, 28 February 1937.

30. Allen, *Newspaper Makeup*.

31. John Allen, *The Modern Newspaper: Its Typography and Methods of News Presentation* (New York: Harper and Brothers, 1940).

32. Douglas McMurtrie's address in the *Proceedings of the Eighteenth Annual Convention of American Society of Newspaper Editors*, 69–70.

33. Allen, *Newspaper Makeup*.

34. Moen, *Newspaper Layout and Design*, 10.

35. Edmund Arnold quoted in Howard Finburg, *Visual Editing: A Graphic Guide for Journalists* (Belmont, Calif.: Wadsworth, 1990).

36. Mario Garcia, "Graphics, Design and Color: What's New for 1990?" address to American Society of Newspaper Editors 1990 convention (Washington D.C.: National Press Club, 1990).

34

Newspaper Illustrations

LISA MULLIKIN PARCELL

"This is the age of experiment, and ... of revolution also. You can afford a great many pictures, and some of the most important newspapers of the country devote themselves to fancy pictures," said *New York Sun* editor Charles A. Dana speaking at the end of the 1800s. "There are lots of pictures of men dancing on tight ropes, for instance, and ladies dancing without any tight ropes. These are supposed to be very popular. I dare say they are," Dana explained. "Now, I am an old-fashioned expert. I don't believe so many pictures are going to be required for any great portion of the next century. It is a passing fashion. It seems to me that it has gone by already to a considerable extent."[1]

Dana's prophecy could not have been more wrong. Beginning with the first newspapers printed in America, illustrations have gradually increased in number and importance. From woodblock prints in colonial newspapers to full-page color graphic and photograph packages today, newspapers have changed their use of illustrations dramatically over the last 300 years.

On April 24, 1704, the first regularly printed newspaper arrived at the homes and taverns of colonial Americans. John Campbell, a printer by trade, decided the people of Boston needed a newspaper. The resulting *Boston News-Letter* closely resembled in design the English *London Gazette*, which began publication in 1665. The *News-Letter* carried no illustrations or other artwork to attract the eye of the people of Boston. In fact, it ran its first illustrations approximately three years later in its January 19–26, 1707–08,[2] issue. A small wood-cut reproduction of the new flag adopted by the United Kingdom of England and Scotland gave colonists a better idea of the design of the flag now flying over their homeland.[3]

Small illustrations to either side of the title became common with early American newspapers. In 1719 the *Boston Gazette* added a detailed illustration of a ship to the left of the title and an illustration of a postman with a trumpet riding a running horse to the right.[4] William Bradford's *New-York Gazette* ran a woodblock of the arms of the province to the left of the masthead and on the right, as fellow printer Isaiah Thomas sarcastically described it, "a postman, on an animal somewhat resembling a horse."[5] The *Boston Gazette* later added small woodblocks of a pine tree and a news carrier holding a copy of the paper in his hand. The publisher of the *New Hampshire Gazette* was lucky enough to acquire a series of cuts used to illustrate *Aesop's Fables*. He used these to enliven his paper by printing them one by one.

At the same time, very small illustrations began to appear in advertisements. The first advertisement pictures were small stock cuts of ships, cargoes, and passenger accommodations. For example, a clock-face represented the watchmaker, scythes and sickles identified the hardware dealer, pictures of a hand holding an open book ran in a bookseller's advertisement, and an illustration of a running Negro was placed with an announcement of a runaway slave.

Few illustrations appeared elsewhere in

the early newspapers. Only rarely did a larger piece of artwork illustrate the news. Not until Britain's war with Spain and its broadening into the War of the Austrian Succession in the 1740s did the *Pennsylvania Gazette* print a large woodcut to illustrate the action. It used a drawing of the fortress at Louisbourg then under siege to help readers understand the accompanying news story. The map, found on an inside page of the June 6, 1745, issue, included a key and a description of the scene. The first sentence of the page, placed right over the map, included an explanation of the map's purpose. "As the CAPE-BRETON expedition is at present the Subject of most conversations," explained the *Gazette*, "we hope the following Draught (rough as it is, for want of good Engravers here) will be acceptable to our Readers; as it may serve to give them an Idea of the Strength and Situation of the Town now besieged by our Forces, and render the News we receive from thence more intelligible."[6]

The beginning of the political and social unrest preceding and during the Revolutionary War ushered in a new wave of newspaper illustrations, this time in the form of political cartoons. These cartoons were designed to stir emotion either for or against England. The most famous of these, Benjamin Franklin's "JOIN, or DIE" cartoon, ran in the *Pennsylvania Gazette* in the summer of 1754 when the representatives from the colonies were called to a meeting in Albany to discuss the upcoming French and Indian War. This illustration bore a snake divided into eight parts, each labeled with the initials of one of the colonies along the eastern shore beginning with N. E. for New England at the snake's head to S. C. for South Carolina at the tail. The label "JOIN, or DIE" ran with the illustration.[7] The meaning was clear to the colonists—the British colonies on North America's eastern seaboard should unite against the threat of French aggression from the western interior. Newspapers in other colonies soon created similar snake cartoons to run in their papers.[8] The same snake would come to life again in the Stamp Act crisis in 1765[9] and during the Revolutionary War.[10]

While this was the first political cartoon published in a newspaper, it was not the first

political cartoon used in the colonies. Benjamin Franklin had learned the importance and power of political cartoons back in 1747 when he printed and distributed a pamphlet encouraging Pennsylvanians to prepare for their own defense as the war between Spain and Britain heated up. On the frontispiece sat an illustration of a kneeling wagon driver praying, while his team of three horses pulled a heavily laden wagon out of the mud. Latin text at the bottom explained that "Divine assistance and protection are not to be obtained by timorous prayers, and womanish supplications."[11] According to Franklin, this illustration and pamphlet worked: subscribers to his plan of defense amounted to upwards of 10,000.[12] Clearly the success of this illustrated pamphlet encouraged Franklin to draw the "JOIN, or DIE" cartoon a few years later.

The Boston Massacre in 1770 sparked the *Boston Gazette and Country Journal* to rapidly produce another set of woodblocks to illustrate the news. A full-page story told of the murder of four men, while directly below the story sat four cuts of tombstones side by side across the column. The engraver carved, in order, the initials of each man killed. A heavy black border running down the column rules on the two inside pages further added to the graveyard look.[13]

Creating these early "woodblock" illustrations took both time and talent. Printers, who called themselves "mere mechanicks" or "leather apron men,"[14] carved each illustration out of small blocks of wood. The printer, or hired engraver, first sketched the design on a block of wood and then carefully scraped around the lines of the drawing. The printer then clamped in the woodblock along with the moveable type to create the page.

Illustrations were kept small and few in number for several reasons. Using woodblocks took a great deal of time and made the press more difficult to operate. In addition, a paper shortage following the Revolutionary War forced practically all the illustrations out of newspapers until later in the 1800s. The first woodblock cuts to reappear were the small advertising illustrations and later the larger news-related illustrations. While these woodblock illustrations predated movable type, American newspaper printers continued to use them until near the end of the 19th century.

The party press period also increased the use of political cartoons. These woodblock cartoons used satire to comment on the political issues of the day. The "Gerry-Mander" from the *Boston Weekly Messenger* ranks as one of the most famous of these cartoons. Just before the Massachusetts election in 1812, Governor Elbridge Gerry drew new political districts for Essex County to assure election of the Republicans. One of these districts resembled a salamander in shape, sparking the *Weekly Messenger* to run a cartoon with head, wings, and claws added to the amphibian.

The advent of the penny press and the growing rivalry between these papers forced editors to look for new ways to attract readers. One of the ideas they hit upon was the use of a few scattered pictures in the paper. While the majority of these penny newspapers remained gray with a few small woodblock illustrations, particularly in advertisements, a few editors discovered the selling value of pictures. Large pictures illustrating the news of the day occasionally attracted the eyes of the working class as they headed to and from their jobs. For example, in May of 1835, the *New York Herald* ran a two-column picture of a disastrous fire at the Merchant's Exchange along with a map of the same size showing the area destroyed by the blaze.[15]

Many new inventions made these cheap dailies possible. The paper shortage at the turn of the century was relieved by the invention of the Fourdrinier machine making newspaper plentiful and allowing space for more pictures by 1830. New presses and new engraving techniques also made it practical for these newspapers to use more illustrations. Richard Hoe's invention of his high-speed rotary press in the 1840s was inspired by the need of the penny press to increase circulation while producing cheaper and faster newspapers.

The type of press used also affected the kind of engraving method adopted. Since wood-engraving blocks were type-high and could be locked into a letterpress and printed with other type, they were popular with newspapers. Copperplate and steel engraving or lithographs, on the other hand, had to be printed as a separate press run and were less practical for newspapers.

The high cost of time and money to produce woodblock prints, however, encouraged inventors to devise an economical and reliable photoengraving process for printing plates. The first breakthrough came in 1826 when Joseph Nicphore Niepce, a French technician, made his first photographic print. By 1842, Fox Talbot began experimenting in England with a process to break up photographic images to make gravure printing plates. The resulting method was adapted to acid etching and the making of relief printing plates. That same year, the *Illustrated London News* used these plates to run a spot news picture of an assassination attempt on Queen Victoria.[16] This method evolved into the photoengraving method used in letterpress printing with plates of copper, zinc, magnesium, and, later, plastic.

Engravers also began to experiment with these various types of metal plates. One experiment that became cheap and popular for years was the use of chalk plates. The plates were formed by coating smooth, flat, steel plates about one-sixteenth of an inch deep with a clay-like substance. The artist then sketched the design on the chalky surface, which was cut through to the plate beneath. These chalk plates were then used as molds to cast metal plates.

In the 1850s, Charles Wells invented a new way to speed up the process of woodblock engraving. His compounding system joined together several small blocks into one large one. These smaller pieces were held together in the back by a series of brass bolts and nuts. Artists could carve each piece separately and then bolt the whole block back together. This made it possible for woodblock illustrations of any size to be made quickly and cheaply.

Newspapers adopted these new sectional woodblocks immediately. To make better use of this new method, editors expanded their staffs to include more artists and wood engravers. The engraving process began when an editor sent an artist, known as an "artist-on-the-spot," out to make a hasty drawing of the latest fire, brawl, or other newsworthy event.

Once back in the office, the artist first assembled the blocks and then transferred his thumbnail drawing by sketching on the blocks. He then disassembled the compounded block and passed the pieces out to other engravers. Each craftsman carefully carved his block, making sure to follow the drawn lines to ensure that the picture would not be disjointed. This was painstaking work. One mistake by an engraver would make the whole woodblock useless. The reassembled block was then added to the press. This process made larger pictures possible under deadline pressure.[17]

The first American illustrated weekly newspaper began in the 1820s and was designed specifically to take advantage of new technology that made using numerous illustrations possible. The *New York Mirror* began publication in July of 1823, but it was not until the 1850s that the more well-known illustrated weekly newspapers like *Frank Leslie's Illustrated Newspaper* and *Harper's Weekly* made their come-out. These papers followed the successful example of the *Illustrated London News*, founded in 1842. Full pages of illustrations mixed in with text told the news stories through both visuals and copy. Leslie alone employed more than 100 artists, engravers, and printers to create elaborate pictorial displays. The Civil War provided these illustrated newspapers with the perfect opportunity to do what they did best: provide the public with an ongoing pictorial account of the most gripping story of the day.

Political cartoons blasting the "Northern Aggressors" or the "Rebellious Southerners" incited fury in readers on both sides of the conflict. Newspapers ran large illustrations of battle scenes, men in camp, and military leaders. Editors made extensive use of hand-carved maps, allowing readers to track troop movements and strength. Most of these illustrations began in the field where "traveling artists" like Winslow Homer and Thomas Nast[18] sketched the action as they saw it. These rough sketches were then rushed back to the cities where the engraving process would begin. If the artist had any special instructions for the engravers, he sketched them in the margins of the drawings. The invention of the telegraph in 1844 allowed artists in the field pinched for time to quickly "call in" a picture and attempt to describe the scene before them.

Photography became a powerful tool for illustration during the Civil War. While photographs could not be printed directly into the newspapers, engravers back at the office could use a photograph to sketch out a drawing on woodblocks. Photographers Matthew Brady and Andrew Gardner along with others followed troops and endured the hardships of military life in their quest for documenting the war on film. They even traveled with their own darkroom wagon, designed to allow them to develop pictures in the field.

Just after the Civil War, the methods of wood engraving improved rapidly. Engravers switched from using the popular intricate pencil drawings to black ink-wash paintings on the woodblock. This method gave them more control on delicate shading. Artists also became experts in one area of illustration, specializing in political cartooning, news illustrations, fashion illustrations, decorative boarders, or copies of photographs.[19] Later, a new specialty was required as engravers discovered how to transfer the photographs directly on to the blocks for carving.

Lithograph illustrations began to appear in American newspapers during the 1870s, with the first appearing in the *New York Daily Graphic* on December 2, 1873. Newspapers, however, did not adopt the use of lithography for picture reproduction at that time since the illustrations had to be printed separately on special presses, making two press runs necessary. Only the most prosperous publications could afford the extra time and money needed for this process.

The *New York Daily Graphic* was the first illustrated daily newspaper in the United States and one of the few newspapers dedicated to spending the time and money to research and develop new technologies and methods for improving reproduction of illustrations. It began publication on March 4, 1873, and during the next few years pioneered costly and important experiments in an effort to improve the photomechanical methods of reproducing pictures in newspapers. On March 4, 1880, it was able to report success. The *Daily Graphic* published the first halftone in a newspaper. The picture, titled "A Scene in Shantytown, New York, " by Stephen H. Horgan ran with text explaining that the photograph was taken from nature, not redrawn, and the transfer print was obtained directly from the original negative. "…We are still experimenting with it," wrote the *Daily Graphic*, "and feel confident that our experiments will, in the long run, result in success, and that pictures will eventually be regularly printed in our page direct from photographs without the intervention of drawing."[20]

The circulation wars between the yellow journalism papers of Pulitzer, Hearst, and others helped to speed this prophecy along. Within 10 years, newspapers were printing photographs directly onto the page. Now photographs and engravings vied for space in the papers. Editors realized that readers were no longer content with "gray" newspapers and that graphics were needed to spice up the pages. In a speech before the American Social Science Association in 1881, writing expert Charles Dudley Warner explained the importance of producing an eye-catching paper. "Scarcely less important than promptly seizing and printing the news is the attractive arrangement of it, its effective presentation to the eye," he said. "Two papers may have exactly the same important intelligence, identically the same despatches: the one will be called bright, attractive, 'newsy,' the other, dull and stupid."[21]

When Joseph Pulitzer began running sketches of important local citizens in the *New York World* in 1884, New Yorkers were thrilled. Years later when the growing cost of illustrations began to bother the penny-pincher in him, he decided to cut back on the number of pictures in the paper. Readers were not pleased. Circulation plummeted, and Pulitzer hurried to quickly restore the sketches and photographs into the paper. He had realized what Warner did, that even pictures of ordinary people could sell newspapers. He began running photographs of teachers, actors, and political figures. A display of women titled "Ladies Who Grace and Adorn the Social Circle" attracted many female readers looking for friends or even themselves in the paper. The managing editor re-

marked that after the addition of these photographs, circulation had commenced rising like "a thermometer on a hot summer day."[22] Other editors soon followed by adding more and more illustrations as it became technically and financially possible to do so.

Some newspapers even used illustrations to advertise themselves. Alden Blethen's *The Penny Press*, for example, ran a line drawing over the top of the classified page advertising the advertisements. The picture showed a man seated at a desk perusing a newspaper on the left and a woman standing in the doorstep of her home holding a copy of the paper and looking at a long line of perspective female employees. A bubble over her head read, "Just look at the girls." Two telephone lines on either side with lines running between them tied together the illustration, while piles of money falling from the sky accumulated at the man's feet. The words, "Penny press promptly fills all wants" stretched across the bottom pulling the reader into the section and advertising for new classified clients.[23]

New mechanical ways of reproducing photographs during the 1880s and 1890s began to eliminate the need for the highly skilled craftsmen who transferred the artists' designs into handmade printing plates. These men were forced into early retirement or new occupations. Others continued employment as "back-up" for photographs, following the photographer to the scene and making sketches just in case the photo did not turn out. The camera had replaced up to a week's work in preparing a complex wood engraving. This much cheaper camera method took only one or two hours to complete and made it possible for newspapers to add an almost infinite number of pictures.

Along with photographs, more graphics began to creep into the newspapers, giving readers a better understanding of the accompanying news stories. During the years of the Klondike gold rush in the late 1890s, for example, the *Seattle Times* printed dozens of guides to the gold fields in special supplements and editions. The newspaper ran information on how to get to the Yukon, how to prospect for a gold claim, what supplies to bring, and where to buy them. These supplements were well illustrated with maps and pictures of the men working and living in the camps. For example, in the July 24, 1897, edition of the *Seattle Times*, a map drawn exclusively for the *Times* by a "Klondyke" prospector told gold hunters exactly where to pan for gold. (This was one of the very first maps for the region.)[24]

By the turn of the century, editors had become increasingly aware of the selling value of illustrations. Pictures were "news of the first magnitude," according to George Bastian in his 1927 textbook, *Editing the Day's News: An Introduction to Newspaper Copyreading, Headline Writing, Illustration, Makeup, and General Newspaper Methods*. "The old time editor had it as his set principle that no picture should be used that was not more valuable than the reading matter it displaced," explained Bastian. "Then came the age of 'art,' when the watchword was 'pictures for art's sake'; that is, the pictures had to be artistic as well as of news importance…. Now the situation has taken a new turn, and the watchword is 'pictures for pictures' sake.' The newspaper editor today will use every picture susceptible of news treatment. He will illustrate every possible unit of text with either maps, drawings, diagrams, or photographs, and sometimes with all four."[25]

With increases in circulation providing the financial support, editors were now more willing to experiment with illustrations. Pictures throughout the newspaper grew in size and importance, particularly on the front page where editors tried to place either a line drawing or a photograph above the fold. By the end of the 1920s, newspaper editors recognized the ability of photographs to help the reader better understand the accompanying article.[26] Editors especially desired photographs of important people in the news, action shots, entertaining or instructional photos, and photographs with some sort of artistic value or other beauty. In fact they often went to great lengths to get these pictures in the paper quickly and in number. In a rush to provide *Seattle Times* readers with images of the 1906 San Francisco earthquake, managing editor C. B. Blethen offered $50 for each photograph that arrived in Seattle by train from the scene.

A four-page photo-supplement featured these images, with a full-page photograph filling the front page below the headline "First Photographs of Fire and Earthquake!"[27]

It wasn't long after newspapers printed the first halftones that they began to find new uses for the art. Newspapers like the *New York Tribune* printed series or page spreads of pictures on one topic designed to capture reality and feed it to the readers. The *Tribune*, for example, printed a photographic series exposing the slums New York City's poor called home. Photographers no longer simply tried to capture one shot of an event for a record, now the goal was to tell the whole story with photographs. Other photographers ran contests for the most beautiful woman in the town or became famous for series of shots on one subject that ran in the Sunday sections. The era of photojournalism had begun.

While photographers and editors were eager to fill the papers with exciting photos, one technological hurdle remained. The presses used in the early part of the 20th century made it difficult to print both the halftones and the type on the same page. To solve the problem, printers produced photograph sections in advance on a rotogravure printing press and then inserted the sections into the middle of the paper. In the rotogravure process, the pictures and the text are engraved directly on the surfaces of huge copper cylinders and from these the printer makes an impression. While this practice was the only feasible way to print photographs, it was more expensive than letterpress and could not be used daily. To make the best use of this technology and to ride the wave of the photo frenzy, the *New York Times* started a picture section in 1915 using the rotogravure method. It was a hit. New Yorkers snapped up copies and convinced the paper to run a second pictorial section in the middle of the week.[28]

Sunday feature sections had many advantages over the regular press runs in that they had more time and money to produce quality work. These sections occasionally showed off the paper's technical capabilities by running full-page hand-tinted photographs or color illustrations to the delight of readers and artists alike. The Sunday supplements were set up and even printed ahead of time, giving artists, lay-out designers, and color printers extra time to do quality work.

The invention of photograph transmission by wire allowed newspapers to tell the world's news by both word and picture. To use this method, a transparent sheet was fitted over the picture at the sending end and then the positions and lines of the photograph are wired to the destination according to a grid. This grid came from sheets of tiny numbered squares at each end of the wire. In addition, the photographer could send additional information about lighting and shading to help the receiving artist fill in the picture. This method, for example, allowed newspapers across the country to print the first pictures of the Japanese earthquake of September 1923. The photographs were transmitted from Seattle to Los Angeles, Chicago, New York, and other cities after the photographic plates had been thrown off a Pacific liner to a waiting messenger. The success of Wirephoto beginning in 1935 opened the way for even more spot pictures alongside spot news coming from other cities.

The use of color printing added new flair to the art of photographs and other illustrations. The *Chicago Daily Tribune,* a leading pioneer in the use of color, printed its first four-page color section on news presses in 1901. Experiments began around the same time by other large papers, including the *New York Journal, New York World, New York Herald,* and *Boston Post.* The *San Francisco Examiner* made spectacular use of this new method at the end of World War I. The message "Peace on Earth/Germany Surrenders" ran below a dramatic picture of a red, white, and blue giant eagle with American flag wings on November 11, 1918.[29] By the end of the 1930s, the *Tribune,* as well as many other newspapers, printed three- and four-color news pictures, maps, fashion illustrations, and advertisements.

While many newspaper artists had lost their jobs by this time, a few remained up until 1960 to prepare photographs for publication and create line drawings like cartoons and Sunday section borders. Artists armed with paints and airbrushes also created photo sections and layouts to show off the art of pho-tography. In the more sensational papers, these designs often called for cutting a person out of one photograph and adding him or her to another. The artist blended the two images together with paint to create an image that fooled the reader into thinking it was reality. Other early photograph artists simply "touched up" the appearance of their subjects. A combination of ethics and the everyday use of photographs restrained most newspaper artists, however, from doing more than using paint to create a mono-color background to help in reproduction. Photographs could also be trimmed into different shapes and given a fancy border to add spice to the page, although this practice waned as the photo-engraving process improved.

For the most part, the bulk of the paper relied on line drawings or etchings through the 1920s. Editorial cartoons remained on the front page during the first part of the century and lured in readers at the newsstands. Artists continued to sketch the unfolding drama during court trials where judges forbid photography. Maps were still drawn and labeled by hand. Editors occasionally requested symbols or other drawings placed over photographs to create an informational graphic. Small graphic elements throughout the paper, for example initial letters, a row of stars between the masthead and the first headline, or designs in the masthead itself, continued to be the handiwork of a staff artist.

World War II created a new demand for informational graphics to accompany the confusing political and military strategies in progress throughout Europe. In 1941, the *Chicago Daily Tribune,* for example, printed a full page of maps the day after the bombing of Pearl Harbor showing in detail the Hawaiian Island of Oahu and the Philippines. The headline over the maps read, "Maps with Which to Follow Developments in the War Between Japan and the United States." That same issue also included an informational graphic that used photographs and type boxes to outline details about the Japanese warships, including the location of their weapons and the kinds of armor on the ships.[30] Also during the war, many newspapers began adding "at a glance" boxes that gave brief

war news and detailed map battles and diagrams. Other graphics included descriptions
and plans of ships, planes, and other military
equipment.

By the middle of the century with public
demand for photographs rising and improved
technology making photo reproduction easier,
newsrooms instituted changes in each section
of the paper. Sunday magazine sections printed
with the rotogravure method continued to be
popular as each newspaper added more color
pictures. The women's and society pages in
particular included more illustrations, especially drawings of dress styles and accessories
and photographs of society women. Feature
pages used photographs and other illustrations
as dramatic elements that were artistic and
often bold. Sports pages often prominently featured the stars of the day. Sports editors were
also allowed to use more "art" in their pages
than in the general news pages. Financial pages
often included mug-shots of the movers and
shakers in the business world as well as stock
and bond tables. While these tables ran in
wider columns and smaller type size than the
rest of the paper, editors did not consider this
a problem for readers since they would probably only want to read a few lines. In many
newspapers, a two-column weather map was
placed below the fold and above the weather
forecast on the financial page. This was an
effort to catch some readers who would otherwise skip that page and was of interest to stockholders whose stock might be effected by
weather changes. Larger newspapers with radio
pages ran the programs of several radio stations
in tables much like the financial and classified
pages. These ran as information charts or list-
ings with headlines like, "Today's Programs" or
"The News Radio Time Table."

In the summer of 1939, Basil L. Walters,
editor of the *Minneapolis Star*, explained his
successful plan in redesigning his highly illustrated paper. "We went in heavily for pictures,
and, instead of using pictures as filler material,
we set up a picture copy desk and scheduled
them into the paper exactly as we scheduled
news stories into the paper. In the case of
doubt, we would kick out what we regarded as
a five-per-cent-news-reader-interest picture,"

explained Walters. "As a result of our experience here I have the feeling that the greatest
opportunity for development of American
newspapers, both in holding the reader interest and in getting results for advertisers, lies in
a more intelligent use of photographs in conjunction with better written, better edited and
better displayed news stories."[31] Walters' intu-
ition was right, yet it took over 30 years for
newspapers to adopt this style.

Various trade and popular magazines further convinced editors of the need for more illustrations. One publication that pioneered design and illustration change was the trade
magazine *The Linotype News*. The magazine
was designed to show other newspaper editors
ways to design and illustrate newspapers using
examples from successful papers. It ran thousands of pictures throughout the years. Even at
the beginning it was known as "the paper with
so many pictures." Some issues carried more
than a hundred reproductions, mostly of people. The November-December 1939, issue, for
example, ran approximately 400 people pictures and included an assortment of articles
touting the importance of pictures in newspapers.[32] Even popular magazines influenced
newspaper make-up. The first issue of *Life*
came out on November 23, 1938, and *Look* in
January 1937. Immediately successful, these
magazines attracted readers in droves to the
beautiful and detailed photographs filling the
pages. Newspaper editors quickly saw which
way the wind was blowing and hired more photographers.

The age of the computer in the 1970s dramatically changed newsroom operations and
indirectly affected illustrations. Informational
graphics were now easier to create. Not only
could graphics editors design elaborate charts
and diagrams, they could also now label maps
by computer. Sandra White, graphics editor of
the *Detroit Free Press*, told George Tuck in
APME News that newspapers were going through
a transition phase in the 1970s and '80s. "We're
in a period of stretching the limits of what can
be done graphically," she said. "It may seem to
some people at times that the emphasis in
newsroom has shifted to graphics, but what's
really happening is that the emphasis is shifting

to include graphics."[33] Some newspapers, in an effort to create a link between the article and the art, originated in the 1980s the position of "assistant managing editor for graphics" or "designer." Former news editorial reporters became "graphic journalists," trained to work with both a spatial design sense and news judgment. In the ideal situation, their offices were between the art and news department, with the department heads being equal. Maureen Decker, assistant managing editor for graphics at the *Allentown* (Pa.) *Morning Call*, declared, "I cannot emphasize enough the importance of people working together well. Designers at the *Morning Call* work with reporters, editors and photographers as early as possible to determine the best means of communicating the information at hand."[34]

Traditional use of colorful informational graphics and large photos soon received an overhaul when *USA Today* rolled off the presses on September 15, 1982. Newspaper designers either called the new paper "McPaper" or "innovative," depending on how willing they were to try new designs themselves. Yet the paper became a huge success, giving readers short, easy to comprehend articles along with colorful and informative graphics and photos. Newspapers across the United States quickly adopted elements of the *USA Today* style, feeding readers more condensed news and visual elements.

CONCLUSION

Beginning with the early colonial newspapers, editors began a gradual process of adding more and more illustrations in the form of drawings, etchings, maps, informational graphics, and photographs. A combination of technological inventions and a gradual interest in graphic elements to add spice to the gray pages allowed for an increase in illustrations through the years. New newspaper styles like the yellow journalism papers of the late 1800s and the graphic-heavy *USA Today* of the 1980s used illustrations to sell newspapers and attract readers. Times of confusion beginning with the Revolutionary War through the Civil War and the World Wars created an immediate need for illustrations, pictures, and other informational graphics to help readers understand the political and social upheaval of the time. A combination of all these factors allowed for the difference between the completely gray first issue of *Boston News-Letter* and the colorful and eye-catching newspapers of today.

Selected Readings

Allen, John E. *Newspaper Makeup*: New York: Harper & Brothers, 1936.

Cook, Karen Severud. "Benjamin Franklin and the Snake That Would Not Die." *British Library Journal* 22 (1996): 88–112.

Hawkes, Elizabeth H. "John Sloan's Newspaper Career: An Alternative to Art School," *Proceedings of the American Antiquarian Society* 105 (1995): 193–209.

Jensen, Oliver. "War Correspondent: 1864. The Sketchbooks of James E. Taylor." *American Heritage* 31 (August/September 1980): 48–64.

Long, Robert P. *Wood Type and Printing Collectibles*: New York: Robert P. Long, 1980.

Meggs, Phillip B. *A History of Graphic Design*: New York: Van Nostrand Reinhold, 1983.

Shilobod, Marlene. "Winslow Homer: Illustrator of Sea and War." *Media History Digest* 5, 4 (1985): 52–55.

Sutton, Albert A. *Design and Makeup of the Newspaper*: New York: Prentice-Hall, 1948.

Notes

1. Charles A. Dana. *The Art of Newspaper Making: Three Lectures* (New York: D. Appleton, 1895, 1970), 95–98.

2. Because of the change in calculating calendar years, these early newspapers were dated one year earlier than the date we would use to describe that time today. In other words, the date on the newspaper was 1707, but we would consider that year to be 1708 today.

3. *Boston News-Letter*, 19–20 January 1707–08.

4. *Boston Gazette*, 14 March 1719/20.

5. Isaiah Thomas, *The History of Printing in America* (Worcester, Mass., 1810), 486.

6. *Pennsylvania Gazette*, 6 June 1745.

7. *Pennsylvania Gazette*, 9 May 1754.

8. *New-York Gazette*, 13 May 1754; *New-York Mercury*, 13 May 1754; *Boston Gazette*, 21 May 1754; *Boston News-Letter*, 23 May 1754.

9. The *Constitutional Courant*, 21 September 1765. The *Constitutional Courant* was an opposition paper against the upcoming Stamp Act on November 1. The masthead of the paper included the snake cartoon with the words "JOIN or DIE" as a central feature. The imprint of the paper read: "Printed by ANDREW MARVEL, at the Sign of the Bribe refused, on Constitutional Hill, North America." "Andrew Marvel" was the pseudonym of William Goddard, a printer who had recently left Providence, Rhode Island, for New York City.

10. *New-York Journal*, 23 June 1774 and *Pennsylvania Journal*, 27 July 1774. The snake illustration again appeared

in three mastheads during the American Revolution. John Holt, the publisher of The *New-York Journal*, changed the masthead design on June 23, 1774, from the former British Royal Arms to a new version of the snake illustration thereby proclaiming the paper's anti–British sympathies. William and Thomas Bradford picked up the illustration in the *Pennsylvania Journal* on July 27, 1774.

11. PLAIN TRUTH, quoted in William Murrell, *A History of American Graphic Humor, Vol. I* (New York, 1933), II. The Latin text only ran in the first edition of Plain Truth, while a second edition translated the Latin into English.

12. Benjamin Franklin, quoted in *Benjamin Franklin's Memoirs,* Max Farrand, ed. (Berkeley and Los Angeles: 1949), 278–9.

13. *Boston Gazette and Country Journal,* 12 March 1770.

14. Benjamin Franklin, cited in Stephen Booties, "'Meer American Printers," *Perspectives in American History* 9 (1975): 127–225.

15. *New York Herald,* 1 May 1835.

16. *Illustrated London News,* 30 May 1842.

17. Frank Leslie, *Frank Leslie's Illustrated Newspaper,* 2 (1856): 124–25.

18. Fletcher Harper of *Harper's Magazine* hired Thomas Nast when he was only fifteen years old to make battlefield sketches during the Civil War. Lincoln said of Nast, he was "the best recruiting sergeant…" and General Ulysses S. Grant said that Nast had done as much as anyone to bring the war to an end. After the war, Nast stayed at *Harper's* and drew his images in reverse directly on the woodblock for the craftsmen to cut. He has been called the "Father of American Political Cartooning" and is the creator of many of the symbols we know today: Santa Claus, John Bull (as a symbol for England), the Democratic donkey, the Republican elephant, Uncle Sam, and Columbia (a symbolic female signifying democracy that became the prototype for the Statue of Liberty.

19. *Philadelphia Inquirer,* 16 December 1894, 39, 10, 43. Cited in Elizabeth H. Hawkes. "John Sloan's Newspaper Career: An Alternative to Art School," *Proceedings of the*

American Antiquarian Society 105 (1995): 196. A special section of the *Philadelphia Inquirer* introduced the reading audience the art department and included illustrations and descriptions of the work of the staff.

20. *New York Daily Graphic,* 4 March 1880.

21. Charles Dudley Warner, 6 September 1881, "The American Newspaper," in *Fashions in Literature: And other literary and social essays & addresses* (New York: Dodd, Mead, 1902), 43.

22. Quoted in Albert A. Sutton. *Design and Makeup of the Newspaper* (New York: Prentice-Hall, 1948), 347.

23. *The Penny Press,* 17 August 1895. The same issue also included small illustrations throughout the classifieds of people both looking for help and work.

24. *Seattle Times,* 21 August 1897 and 24 July 1897.

25. George C. Bastian, *Editing the Day's News: An Introduction to Newspaper Copyreading, Headline Writing, Illustration, Makeup, and General Newspaper Methods* (New York: Macmillan, 1927), 193.

26. Walter E. Mattson, "What Do We Do Next in the Newspaper Business?" address to the Southern Newspaper Publishers Association annual convention in 1930. Quoted in Allen Hutt, *Newspaper Design* (London: Oxford University Press, 1960), 155. Mattson, the president of the New York Times Co., told the audience that he believed "[i]llustrations will be used extensively to help the reader better understand the accompanying article."

27. *Seattle Times,* 23 April 1906.

28. *New York Times,* 5 April 1915.

29. *San Francisco Examiner,* 11 November 1918.

30. *Chicago Daily Tribune,* 8 December 1941.

31. Basil L. Walters, quoted in John E. Allen, *The Modern Newspaper: Its Typography and Methods of News Presentation* (New York: Harper & Brothers Publishers, 1940), 82.

32. *The Linotype News,* November-December 1939, cited in Allen, ibid., 88.

33. Sandra White, *APME News,* quoted in Hutt, *Newspaper Design,* 157.

34. Maureen Decker, *APME News,* quoted in Hutt, ibid., 154.

35

Photojournalism

KEN SEXTON

Photojournalism is the profession of recording and reporting news by means of photographs. As this book is being written, the first major era of photojournalism is coming to a close—thanks to the development of computers and digital imaging—and a new and exciting age is just beginning. Those who read this book may well become the pioneers and Pulitzer Prize winners in a new age of reporting-through-pictures. Photojournalism, according to Wilson Hicks, who directed *Life* magazine's photo department from 1937 to 1950, is the "particular coming together of the verbal and visual mediums of communication...." He added, "In journalistic print, the firsthand account which comes closest to reproducing the actuality of an event is the picture story: good headlines plus good photographs plus good captions."[1]

Photojournalism could not have developed had there been no cameras, or photographs. In 1839, inventors in Paris and London independently announced two of the fundamental photographic processes. In Paris, Louis Jacques Mande Daguerre, a stage designer, announced to the French Academy of Sciences the realization of an age-old dream, to make permanent the image projected by a "camera-obscura," a pin-hole projector. His product was a unique, left-to-right-reversed, single-color image on a silver-coated copper plate—the "daguerreotype."[2] In London, scholar William Henry Fox Talbot had created a paper negative. When he placed his paper negative over another piece of light-sensitive paper and illuminated it, a single-color positive image was created. Thus, each image Daguerre made was unreproducible (thus unique) while Talbot's paper negative could be used again and again.[3] Though Daguerre won the world's admiration and lasting fame, it was Talbot's process that led to photography as we know it.

There were Americans at both the Paris and London announcements in 1839, and the visitors brought back the photographic process (and the necessary equipment and chemicals) to the United States. Visionaries like Samuel F. B. Morse, inventor of the telegraph in 1844, trumpeted the novelty and potential usefulness of photography. Demand for photographs swept the nation during the 1840s, '50s, and '60s, creating a large and profitable industry. A Louisville correspondent in 1855 wrote to a national magazine, "There is not a place of one hundred inhabitants in any of the southern or western states that have [sic] not been visited by from one to any number of [picture-taking] itinerants."[4] But it would be decades before photographs could be "imported" directly into printed news.

Americans, always on the lookout for new, helpful, and profitable technology, took photography to their hearts. Photography quickly became both a social phenomenon and the key to a good living for young men (but few women) who otherwise faced drudgery in grimy factories or behind plow teams in the dusty farm fields. Self-employed photographers scattered out across the nation in the 1840s and 1850s to "take the likenesses" of citizens, usually charging a dollar or two. As early as 1840, dental-equipment manufacturer Alexander Wolcott sold American-made cameras.[5]

In the larger cities, portrait studios sprang up. In New York and Washington, D.C., a skilled photographer named Mathew Brady (a student of Morse) started a career that would earn him a fortune and lead eventually into a work of mammoth proportions: photographing the U.S. Civil War (1861–1865). Some of the products of Brady and other photographers found their way to publication in some aspect. The daguerreotypes of national leaders, generals, admirals, and other famous people were sought by the picture magazines popular at the time, Frank Leslie's publications, *Harper's Weekly*, and *Ballou's Pictorial Drawing-Room Companion*. However, in the composing rooms of the magazines, the photographs had to be copied by skilled artists onto blocks of wood, soft stone, or linoleum. These intermediate pictures could then be used on the printing presses, but not the photographs themselves. By the mid–1850s, photography studios were established in every good-sized city of the United States and Canada.

If one early, major event established photography as a means of reporting the news, it was the War Between the States. Brady was already prosperous with his studios in New York and Washington. But as war clouds gathered over the issues of states' rights and slavery, he considered how to photograph the coming conflict between the North and the South. Thus, Brady and one of his most talented employees, Alexander Gardner, were ready with cameras when Federal forces moved into northern Virginia in July, 1861, to meet the Confederate army at the first Battle of Bull Run. All of Washington was betting on a quick, decisive Federal victory, and the throngs of civilians who came by carriage to watch the battle from the hills above thought they would celebrate in a captured Richmond, the Confederate capital. But the Confederates, with artillery in quantity, blew Federal hopes for a short war to smithereens. Lost in the rout of the Union forces, as troops and civilians fled back to Washington, were many of Brady's first wartime photographs.

Brady was undeterred: he trained a squad of photographers, replaced his cameras and supplies, and sent employees like Gardner,

Timothy O'Sullivan, and George Barnard to photograph as many scenes as possible. By late 1862, soldiers or home folks could purchase by mail order any of 570 Brady-produced views of soldiers, encampments, forts, cannons, ships, or other implements of war.[6] Photographers followed the armies of both the North and the South. There may have been more than a thousand photographers snapping pictures sometime during the four years of the war.[7]

After the Civil War, the business of photography continued much as it had before the war, and some photographers, like Gardner, O'Sullivan, and federal officer Andrew Joseph Russell went out west to capture the images of cowboys, native Americans, railroad construction projects, and the grand landscapes of the frontier. Russell and William H. Jackson, in particular, were among the frontier photographers whose magnificent photos made them legends.

It has been said that "there is no news like war news," and the development of the halftone screening process gave newspapers a valuable tool with which to report the Spanish-American War of 1898. That war started when a still-unexplained explosion in February 1898 sank the U.S. battleship *Maine* in Havana Harbor. Spain at the time controlled both Cuba and the Philippines, and the loss of the American battleship and most of its crew (272 men) ignited tensions between Spain and the United States. Newspapers and wire services sent hundreds of correspondents, some with cameras, to cover the simultaneous U.S. military actions in Cuba, the West Indies, and the Philippines.

Photographs taken before the 1890s couldn't find their way directly to newspaper or book publication because the process of screen printing hadn't been invented. Screen printing is the process whereby an image with a wide range of tones (a wide range of blacks and whites) is converted into dots of either black or white. The inventor of the screen printing (or "halftone") process was Stephen H. Horgan, who eventually enriched the *New York Tribune* newspaper with his invention. Horgan, and his competitor, Frederick Ives, worked for decades to translate the diverse tones of a photograph into something graphic that could be printed along with newspaper text. Horgan came up with a glass screen with fine lines on it, which, when placed between a negative and a light-sensitive metal plate, translated all those gradations of blacks and whites into a metal picture made up of clusters of black dots surrounded by total white.

When Horgan, then working for the *New York Herald* newspaper, saw that he had the means to convert the tones of a photograph to printable dots and white spaces, he carried the news to his employer, James Gordon Bennett, Jr., the publishing tycoon. Bennett fired Horgan for his ridiculous idea. So Horgan went over to the *New York Tribune*, a newspaper with management more open to invention. Horgan's halftone process allowed his new employer, the *Tribune*, to be the first newspaper to make regular use of halftone screening and the first to use black-and-white photographs on a daily basis. The public was thrilled with this photographic novelty. By 1904, another paper, the *New York Daily Mirror*, announced that its pages, too, would be delivering photographs. Soon, urban newspapers everywhere employed the photographer to capture human interest and newsworthy scenes and employed the halftone process to convert photographs directly to newspaper images.

The enthusiasm of newspapers for photographs coincided with the development of practical, fast-shooting, hand-held cameras. George Eastman, who founded the Eastman Kodak Company in 1880, was determined that his firm was going to equip America with small, practical cameras and photographic supplies. Soon Kodak and other firms offered small, film-loading cameras named, as a class, "detective" cameras, because they were so small and unobtrusive compared to the boxy Graflex cameras of the turn of the century. Eastman's first successful camera, the "Kodak Number One," was a small box camera, about seven inches by three-and-a-half inches in size. It came in a leather case with a shoulder strap and loaded with 100 exposures of paper roll film. The loaded camera cost $25.

Although Stephen Horgan had developed the halftone screen to print photographs directly into newspapers, magazines also caught the fever for illustration. The *Illustrated American* lived up to its name. Other magazines, of course, soon caught on to the appeal of the realistic halftone: *Harper's*, *The Century*, and *Collier's* among them. By 1902, a swell of demand for photographs spurred publishers to embrace halftone prints.[8]

The increasing use of photos opened up opportunities for women photographers. Frances Benjamin Johnson was one of the pioneers with a camera in her hands. Johnson shot portraits, but she also carefully documented industry scenes and workers in a wide range of places. Her photos found publication in *Demorest's Family Magazine*, *Harper's*, *Cosmopolitan*, and *Ladies' Home Journal*. Another early female practitioner was Sarah Kneller Miller, who worked for *Leslie's Illustrated Weekly*. The first woman known to have worked with a camera full time was Jessie Tarbox Beals, a Canadian hired in 1901 by the *Buffalo Inquirer*. Beals eventually became a schoolteacher who, with her husband along, was also a life-long traveling photographer. Early in her career, her Buffalo employer sent her by train to photograph the destruction of a large part of Rochester, New York, by fire. "…I thought I had never seen anything that so reminded me of Dante's Inferno as the smoking acres of burned over blocks at that fire…," she remembered. "When I came out of the fire space I would not have known myself. Icicles were frozen all over my wraps and it took me literally hours to get thawed out so I could finish up my negatives."[9] Between the years 1880 and 1910, women photographers rose in number from under 300 nationwide to perhaps 5,000 by 1910.

By the first part of the 20th century, disasters, military conflicts, demonstrations of any new, dramatic technology, and the faces of the rich and the famous (and the infamous) all made ready targets for the increasing numbers of photographers at work. The San Francisco earthquake of April 18, 1906, was not reported in page-one photographs in New York newspapers until April 24. But photos taken as the quake ignited the city had already been published in San Francisco printing houses (those that survived) within hours of the disaster.

Not all the photography done at the turn

of the century was sensational or designed to sell. There was a reform urge in the land. One of the early reformist photographers was Lewis Hine. He was born in Oshkosh, Wisconsin, in 1874 but moved to New York City in 1901. There, he found an industrial landscape crowded by thousands of immigrants arriving each year, and by the in-migration of previously rural people who left their farm-fields (or who left the dying industries of the Northeastern states).

In New York, Hine studied sociology and by 1908 he was a photographer for the National Child Labor Committee, an organization fighting the exploitation of children in industry. There was plenty of exploitation (some called it "child slavery") to uncover. Between 1908 and 1916, he crisscrossed the nation to document the abuse of children in the workplace. When the Child Labor Act finally passed, it was said that his photographs had clinched it.

A *New York Herald* police reporter, Jacob Riis, also used realistic, hard-hitting photographs of poor working people to illustrate articles calling for social reform. His "beat" was a particularly vicious slum named "Mulberry Bend." In a memorable book, *How the Other Half Lives: Studies Among the Tenements of New York* (1890), he documented the extreme hardships of people on the bottom of the city's economy and their lack of social services. The book carried 40 plates, 17 of which were half-tone reproductions of Riis photographs.[10]

What Hine, Riis, and others began—using black-and-white photography to dramatically portray social conditions—matured in two ways. First, the self-styled street photographers of the nation's large cities, men whose names are now legendary among photographers, set out to capture the "soul" of the city. They were often living and working out of their automobiles, often paying informants or doing favors for police, often making nuisances of themselves. Worse, many broke the codes of personal privacy or decency in mad pursuit of newsworthy or sensational photos. But these men produced remarkable photos of crime, lust, drunkenness, greed, disaster, and other misfortunes of a dizzying variety.

A second major campaign to use photos to comment on social or economic conditions was launched and paid for by the United States Government. During the Roosevelt administration of the 1930s, photographers under the guidance of bureaucrat Roy Stryker, of the Farm Security Administration (F.S.A.), set out to capture the heart-wrenching scenes of farmers and other workers beset by the evils of economic depression, droughts, and storms of historic proportions. While the original purpose of the photographic campaign may have been to help justify federal money spent in numerous aid programs, the eventual collection of 270,000 photos became a national "photo-album" of Depression-era life.

Among Stryker's photographers were Ben Shahn, said to value the human interest in particular as the source of emotional appeal; Dorothea Lange, who carefully photographed the plight of women and their children displaced by the Depression; and Arthur Rothstein, who shot a famous image of a farmer and his two sons, bent against the wind and heading for shelter as a vague, ominous cloud of dirt approached. Rothstein's "Dust Storm, Cimarron County," 1937, remains a lasting, haunting image representing the entire American economy blown away. Stryker also hired an especially talented young African-American photographer, Gordon Parks, Sr. Born in 1912, Parks spent his early life earning his living in a segregated America. He was a brick-carrier, played piano in a honky-tonk, toured with a semi-pro basketball team, and waited on tables in railroad dining cars. In 1937 he saw a newsreel about the sinking of the river gunboat *Panay* in China and decided to become a photographer. In 1942–43 he won a fellowship to study with Roy Stryker at the Farm Security Administration. He joined *Life* magazine in 1948. His photo essays on street gangs, civil protests, and other social subjects received awards and vast public attention. As a filmmaker, he would later add to his fame with the movies *The Learning Tree* (1969), *Shaft*, and *Shaft's Big Score* (1972), and others.[11]

Kentucky-born twins transplanted to Harlem helped document the exciting New York life in the decades following the Harlem Renaissance of the 1920s. Morgan Smith and his brother Marvin were born in 1910 to sharecropper parents. After the family moved into the city of Lexington, the twins attended Dunbar High, the only high school open to black pupils. There they discovered their own raw artistic talent. After graduation, the twins headed for Cincinnati, but found only limited opportunities. Harlem was the next stop. Later they said that they had "learned" Harlem at "The Cotton Club, Connie's Inn, Small's Paradise, the Alhambra, and the Apollo. It was most exciting."[12]

Morgan Smith bought himself a good camera with a side-flash, and the brothers began their street photography career in the heart of New York. Their freelanced images went to newspapers such as the *Pittsburgh Courier*, the *Baltimore Afro-American*, and the *New York Amsterdam News*. Morgan soon got a staff job on the *Amsterdam News*. The two Smith brothers also rented rooms next to the Apollo Theater, a vaudeville house famous then as now, and there they photographed passersby, Apollo theatergoers, music and entertainment stars, showgirls, fashion models, and local politicians. The Smiths used their camera to make a good living, but they also preserved the images of Harlem people striving, prospering, and thriving in the midst of the Depression and surrounded by segregation. The Smiths' Harlem studio closed in 1968. They retired in 1975.

No one typified urban street photography like the freelancer who called himself "Weegee." He was born Usher Fellig in Austria, immigrated with his large family to New York City in 1909 and grew up on the tough Lower East Side. By age 24 he was a darkroom man for Acme News Services. Weegee later recalled, "Over the developing trays in the dark room at Acme, history passed through my hands. Fires, explosions, railroad wrecks, ship collisions, prohibition gang wars, murders, kings, presidents, everybody famous and everything exciting turned up in the Twenties."[13]

In the 1930s, Weegee left Acme and became a legend among photographers and newspapermen for his cleverness and aggressive pursuit of news photos. He made friends with police so he could photograph inside precinct headquarters. He lurked in the dark for the arrival of police paddy wagons. Then he shoved his Speed Graphic camera into the faces of unsuspecting suspects and blasted away with flash bulbs. Weegee bragged that he had photographed "a murder a night for ten years." The best of his 5,000 photos are to be found in his first book, *Naked City*, 1946. That book and its immediate sequel, *WeeGee's People*, also 1946, led Weegee to Hollywood—and decline. He died in 1968.

The first decades of the 20th century brought yet another medium that advertised itself, uppermost, as entertainment, often masqueraded as news, but was, primarily, for profit. This medium was the movie newsreel. The newsreel business was important from the teens of the century through the 1960s. The first successful motion pictures were shown in the United States to paying audiences in 1896 by Thomas Armat and Thomas Edison, inventor of the "Kinetograph." As the 19th century came to a close, Edison improved his movie cameras, and two competing "news film" companies, Vitagraph and Biograph, sprang up.

The first war involving Americans and shown in news films was the Spanish-American War of 1898. However, much of what American audiences paid to see was faked. Smith and Blackton, of Vitagraph, for example, bought prints of American and Spanish warships mounted on cardboard, clipped out the ships, floated them on blocks of wood in a pool, painted a backdrop, set off little charges of gunpowder behind the cutouts, and filmed their commercial success at a total cost of $1.98. When the San Francisco earthquake of 1906 shattered that city, one of the most successful (and convincing) newsreels actually showed a little cardboard city burning on top of a table.

In 1919, Fox Studios joined with the United Press syndicate to form one of the most productive and successful newsreel producers. It would last until 1963. In its first year of operation, the Fox organization reached an estimated 30,000,000 viewers. By 1922, more than 1,000 cameramen fed news to Fox.[14] One unexpected and especially horrifying event that several still and newsreel cameras captured simultaneously was the crash of the German Zeppelin *Hindenburg* at Lakehurst, New Jersey, on May 6, 1937. Press photographers on the scene included men from the big daily news-papers. Newsreel men there represented Fox Movietone, Pathe, the Hearst firm, and others. NBC Radio announcer Herb Morrison was doing a diskrecording to collect, of all things, background sound for the NBC library. The huge Zeppelin, 803 feet long, arrived over the field, at 7:20 p.m. Suddenly, in front of stunned onlookers, an explosion sent a geyser of fire up through the fabric skin of the great, hydrogen-filled airship near her stern. As flames blew up-ward like a volcano, the hulk settled quickly toward the ground. Dozens of sailors, who had been waiting to tie her to her mooring, fled the huge, ominous, burning shape above them. In about 30 seconds, the entire cigar-shaped craft was aflame, and the newsreel films show tiny dark figures leaping from her windows and doors, and sliding down ropes. The flaming wreck collapsed in front of the cameras. NBC's Morrison is remembered for his emotional, recorded report: "The flames are 500 feet into the sky! It's a terrific crash, ladies and gentle-men, the smoke and the flames now ... crash-ing to the ground, not quite to the mooring mast. Oh the humanity! These passengers! I can't talk, ladies and gentlemen. Honest, it is a mass of smoking wreckage."[15]

Between 1900 and World War II, there developed a vast market for photo-rich maga-zines, which published images of the wealthy, the famous, the important, and (just as signifi-cantly) pictures of the everyday citizen or worker. In the United States in 1919, the *Daily News, New York's Picture Newspaper*, had been launched. The same year also saw the forma-tion of photo syndicates: International News Pictures (founded by Hearst), and Wide World Photos (founded by the *New York Times*). Later in starting were Acme Newspictures (1923) and the Associated Press News Photo Service (1927).

Reporting and photojournalism reached a peak—in both volume and quality—during World War II. As conflict spread over Europe, the United States had pursued a policy of iso-lationism and a detached-though-watchful eye toward the hostile intentions of Nazi Germany and Imperial Japan. But that aloofness came to a shocking end in the early hours of Sunday,

December 7, 1941, when some 350 Japanese aircraft, launched off the decks of aircraft car-riers, struck Pearl Harbor and other military facilities in Hawaii.

Even while 2,400 servicemen and civil-ians perished in the attack, movie and still cam-eras were shooting the preemptive strike upon the U.S. Pacific Fleet. Within one week news magazines carried the heartbreaking images of the American ships parked along Battleship Row exploding under a hail of bombs and tor-pedoes.

Of all the photographers who shot the war, among the most adventurous was Robert Capa. He was only 25 years old when named, in 1938, "The Greatest War Photographer in the World." *Life* magazine hired him, and he earned lasting fame for the memorable photos of American infantrymen under heavy fire at the water's edge during the June 1944 Nor-mandy landings in France. Those photos are a story unto themselves. Of 106 frames Capa shot as he and the troops came ashore, a clumsy technician destroyed all but 11. Capa survived World War II to become the co-founder of the Magnum photo service agency but was killed on assignment in 1954, the first photojournal-ist casualty of the Vietnam conflict.

In contrast to the small number of corre-spondents who had reported on U.S. military activities from the front in Europe during World War I, were the more than 700 reporters and photographers made ready for World War II by civilian and military publishers. Of those hundreds of news people ready at the start of World War II, and those who would join in be-fore the war was ended in 1945, 37 would be killed and 112 wounded.

Of all the reporting and camera activity, no photograph of the Second World War had an impact like the one Joe Rosenthal shot on Mount Suribachi, the high ground of the small Pacific island of Iwo Jima. Rosenthal worked for the Associated Press. The Japanese garrison on Iwo Jima (sworn to defend its stronghold to the death) bitterly contested a U.S. Marine landing in February of 1945, and Marine losses were heavy. When a squad of leathernecks finally took the top of Mount Suribachi and raised an American flag, Rosenthal shot one particular frame that was a standout: a cluster of four Marines and a Navy corpsman, their faces hidden by their arms and helmets, lifting the flag on a pole that had just reached a 45-degree diagonal. Back home, hundreds of newspapers and magazines saw in the photo the spirit of American fighting men, and published it. Rosenthal won a Pulitzer Prize, and the photo was used as the model for a huge bronze sculpture raised at Arlington Cemetery near Washington, D.C. Perhaps the photo is made more poignant because three of the five men pictured in it died during the next 31 days of bitter combat on the volcanic soil of Iwo Jima.

As the Second World War came to a close, some press photographers saw a need for greater professionalism for themselves and their colleagues, and a better public image. Two such shooters were Burt Williams and Joe Costa. Williams began his career recording the scenes of a Dayton, Ohio, flood in 1913 and then worked for Cleveland and Pittsburgh newspapers. Costa was the son of a Sicilian Lower West Side, New York, immigrant shoemaker. He became an office boy in Pulitzer's *Morning World* and an artist, then at age 15 he became a photographer in 1919. "The press photographer of that day," Costa recalled, "had come up through the school of hard knocks. It was the most competitive, dog-eat-dog world you can imagine."[16]

But he and Williams had higher aspirations for postwar press photographers. They envisioned photographers sharing improved craftsmanship, raising ethical standards, improving press credentials, and winning greater respect from their employers and the public at large. The National Press Photographers Association was formed in 1945 and soon had 300 members. The hard-working Costa was its first president.

The range of approaches to postwar photojournalism is portrayed in the work of the several photographers who started the photo-cooperative Magnum. Robert Capa, George Rodger, David Seymour, and Bill Vandivert began it in 1947. Its formation was intended to allow photographers to remain in control of the images they shot. Thus, Magnum is a non-profit cooperative in which 50 photographer-members own equal shares. While the best of the photographic images of years past are collected in ever-increasing numbers of yearbooks and anthologies, some critics say that the satellite-linked cameras of Ted Turner's Cable News Network, CNN, have already proven the value of instantaneous coverage with real-time photography. The 1960s saw some of the best markets for photojournalists lost on account of declining circulations. The magazines *Look*, *Life*, and the *Saturday Evening Post* were all casualties. Both *Life* and the *Saturday Evening Post* were resurrected in nostalgia-based modern versions issued far less frequently than their namesakes, but they continue to demonstrate the value of newsworthy photo images.

Today, several photo agencies continue to supply the market: International agencies include Agence France-Presse (AFP), Associated Press (US), Reuters, (Great Britain), and Tass (based in the former Soviet Union). American-based agencies in addition to the AP include Black Star, Contact Press Images, and Magnum. French-based agencies that also work in the United States are Syma, Gamma, and Sipa Press. Increasing in importance are hundreds of small, independent firms that offer photos over the Internet, the new medium that is sure to "democratize" the news photo business.

Selected Readings

Brennen, Bonnie. "Strategic Competition and the Photographer's Work: Photojournalism in Gannett Newspapers, 1937–1947." *American Journalism* 15:2 (1998): 59–78.

Carlebach, Michael L. *American Photojournalism Comes of Age*. Washington and London: Smithsonian Institution Press, 1997.

Cookman, Claude. *A Voice is Born: The Founding and Early Years of the National Press Photographers Association*. Durham, N.C.: NPPA, 1985.

Fielding, Raymond. *The American Newsreel, 1911–1967*. Norman: University of Oklahoma Press, 1972.

Foresta, Merry. *American Photographs: The First Century*. Washington, D.C.: National Museum of American Art, Smithsonian Institution, 1996.

Fulton, Marianna. *Eyes of Time: Photojournalism in America*. Boston: Little, Brown and Company, 1988.

Gardner, Alexander. *Gardner's Photographic Sketch Book of the War*. Washington, D.C.: Philip & Solomons, 1866.

Garver, Thomas H. *Just Before the War: Urban America from 1935 to 1941 As Seen by the Photographers of the Farm Service Administration*. New York: October House, 1968.

Gould, Lewis L., and Richard Greffe. *Photojournalist: The Career of Jimmy Hare*. Austin: University of Texas Press, 1978.

Horan, James D. *Matthew Brady: Historian with a Camera.* New York: Crown, 1955.

Leslie, Larry Z. "Newspaper Photo Coverage of the Censure of McCarthy." *Journalism Quarterly* 63 (1986): 850–53.

McGivena, Leo E. *The News: The First 50 Years of New York's Picture Newspaper.* New York: News Syndicate Co., 1969.

Moutoussamy-Ashe, Jeanne. *Viewfinders: Black Women Photographers.* New York and London: Writers & Readers Publishing, Inc., 1993.

Rosenblum, Naomi. *A History of Women Photographers.* New York: Abbeville Press, 1994.

Schuneman, R. Smith. "A Question for Newspaper Editors of the 1890s." *Journalism Quarterly* 42 (1965): 43–52.

Smith, C. Zoe. "Fritz Goro: Emigre Photojournalist." *American Journalism* 3 (1986): 206–21.

Stettner, Louis, ed. *WeeGee.* New York: Alfred A. Knopf, 1977.

Notes

1. Wilson Hicks, *Words and Pictures: An Introduction to Photojournalism* (New York: Harper & Brothers, 1952), 3.

2. Louis Jacque Mande Daguerre, *An Historical and Descriptive Account of the Various Processes of the Daguerreotype and the Diorama* (London: McLeon, 1839; reprint ed., New York: Kraus Reprint, 1969), 63, 79.

3. William Henry Fox Talbot, *The Pencil of Nature* (London: Longman, Brown, Green and Longmans, 1844; reprint ed., New York: Da Capo Press, 1969).

4. [Anonymous] *The Photographic Art-Journal* 8: 185, 70.

5. *New York Sun*, 4 March 1840. Wolcott's Camera was patented 8 May 1840, U.S. Patent #1,582.

6. Mathew Brady, *"War Views" Catalogue*, 1862.

7. The *U.S. Census* of 1860 reported 3,154 working photographers.

8. For the story of the impact of halftone illustration on American newspapers, see generally, Harry W. Baehr, Jr., *The New York Tribune Since the Civil War* (New York: New York Tribune, 1936), 235–37; and Elmer Davis, *History of the New York Times, 1851–1921* (New York: The New York Times, 1921), 212, 213.

9. [Anonymous] "Ever Meet Jessie Tarbox Beals?" *St. Louis Republic*, 20 February 1910.

10. Jacob A. Riis, *How the Other Half Lives: Studies Among the Tenements of New York* (New York: Hill & Wang, 1890; reprint ed, 1957).

11. See generally, Gordon Parks, *The Photographs of Gordon Parks* (Wichita, Kan.: Wichita State University, 1983).

12. Quoted in Mellissa Rachleff, *Images of Harlem, 1935–1952: A Brief Biography of Marvin and Morgan Smith* (Lexington: University of Kentucky Art Museum, 1983), 7.

13. Quoted in Louis Stettner, ed., *Weegee* (New York: Alfred A. Knopf, 1977), 7.

14. Raymond Fielding, *The American Newsreel, 1911–1967* (Norman: University of Oklahoma Press, 1972), 107.

15. Quoted in "Oh the Humanity," *Time*, 17 May 1937, 35, 37.

16. Joe Costa, quoted in Claude Cookman, *A Voice is Born* (Durham, N.C.: National Press Photographers Association, 1985), 17.

36

Cartoons, Comics, and Caricature
MICHAEL R. SMITH

Political lampoons made cartoons what they are today. The challenge to an unfair law, the questioning of an illogical standard, or attention to silly behavior is fair game for the talents of a cartoonist. While politics remain a favorite topic for a cartoonist, the attention to elaborate backgrounds and foregrounds has changed over the years to concentrate attention on the central character and a singular, main point. In addition, as the work of cartoonists became more accessible to ordinary readers, cartoonists experimented with greater variety including fantasy themes, talking animals, speech balloons, and other innovations. Despite the changes, the ability of the artist to impact an audience with an economy of sketch lines and a few well-chosen words makes cartoons and comics among the best read material in contemporary newspapers.

DEVELOPMENTS IN CARTOONS

Modern cartooning descended from a fine art tradition of Europe, where accomplished artists abandoned devotion to eternal truths of art to concentrate on the momentary truth of class inequities and the challenge of survival in the city. The figure who did the most to establish this new style of drawing was the 18th-century British artist William Hogarth (1697–1764). Along with James Gillray (1757–1815), he presented his world in realistic drawings that derided society. In 1735, for instance, he de-picted a wedding scene where an attractive groom took an unattractive wife to gain access to her wealth while a bitter quarrel played in the background. The hypocrisy of the loveless marriage was amplified with the verse that accompanied the cartoon: "Gold can the charms of youth bestow, and mask the deformity with shew; gold can avert ye sting of shame, in winter's arms create a flame...."

In the United States, Benjamin Franklin (1706–1790) is credited with publishing the first editorial cartoon, titled "The Waggoner and Hercules" in the pamphlet *Plain Truth* in 1747. It depicted a wagon driver praying to the mighty Hercules with the caption "Non Votis, ["God helps those who help themselves"]. Franklin used the illustration to persuade Pennsylvanians to fight for pacifist Quakers. He also produced another first, the first cartoon in an American daily of a severed snake captioned "Join or Die," published in the *Pennsylvania Gazette* on May 9, 1754. The cartoon was based on a folk idea that an injured snake can come back to life if the pieces were put together before sunset. Franklin used the image to galvanize the colonies to unity during the French and Indian War, the revolt over the Stamp Act in 1765, the Intolerable Acts in 1774, and the American Revolution in 1776.

Engraver Paul Revere (1735–1818) adapted the snake cartoon to the masthead of Isaiah Thomas' *Massachusetts Spy* in 1774, but he was an editorial cartoonists in his own right for the creation of an engraving called "Boston Massacre" or the "Bloody Massacre" March 5, 1770. The political cartoon, purloined from artist Henry Pelham (1749–1806), was altered to portray the British as butchers to enhance its propaganda value.[1]

William Charles (1776–1820) was the first major American cartoonist. Among his best cartoons is one called the "The Tory editor and his apes giving their pitiful advice to American sailors," printed in 1808 when most of his cartoons concerned the coming War of 1812.[2] The Tory-apes cartoon depicted a British sympathizer urging three American sailors to resist the federal embargo that President Thomas Jefferson ordered. One of Jefferson's last actions before leaving office was to repeal the hated embargo. Charles's contemporary, Elkanah Tisdale, saw the way a new political district was shaped; added a head, wing, and claws; and named it a Gerrymander from the name of Massachusetts governor Elbridge Gerry. He published it in the *Boston Gazette* on March 26, 1812.

While cartooning matured in the United States, the first cartoon panel began July 1843 with a British periodical, *Punch*. It ridiculed the government for its exhibition of art sketches that could be made into art for the houses of Parliament. *Punch* showed the display with a ragged crowd examining them with commentary that read, "The poor ask for bread and the philanthropy of the State accords an exhibition."

In the United States cartoonists of this same period focused on politics and presidential candidates, particularly during the mid–1800s. From 1848 until the Civil War, Currier and Ives lithographs were a chief source of cartoons, mostly depictions of horse races, steamboats, and trains, before publications such as *Harper's Weekly* began running cartoons using woodcuts. Among the most notable cartoonists during this period were Thomas Nast (1840–1902) and Joseph Keppler (1838–1894). They appeared just before the Civil War when the *New York Daily Graphic*, *Frank Leslie's Illustrated Weekly*, *Vanity Fair*, and *Harper's Weekly* began profuse use of pictorial journalism.

Nast burned his name into the consciousness of America with his work for several of these publications. He drew cartoons of squalid conditions where polluted milk from diseased cows was sold under the protection of corrupt city officials. This work appeared in *Frank Leslie's Illustrated Weekly*, a 16-page weekly that sold for 10 cents. In *Harper's*, Nast exposed civil corruption and lobbied for President Abraham Lincoln and the Union cause. Among his brilliant innovations was the creation of symbols such as Uncle Sam, the Democratic donkey, the Republican elephant, the Tammany Tiger, and the image of Santa Claus, now accepted as standard. He once depicted Santa as a new Union recruit and showed him presenting soldiers with gifts. This use of symbols, which became part of American iconography, allowed later cartoonists to simplify backgrounds in their drawings and concentrate on fewer characters.

Joseph Keppler (1837–1894), Nast's contemporary, founded *Puck* magazine in 1877 with the motto "What fools we mortals be." Its rival was *Judge*, an offshoot of *Puck*, founded by one of Keppler's artists, James Wales (1852–1886). While Nast focused on black-and-white messages using the kind of medium to emphasize his reforms, Keppler's work was colorful and elaborate. For instance, in 1877 *Puck* published one of Keppler's cartoons about Brigham Young and a recent court case that required the Mormon leader to abandon the practice of polygamy as part of his faith. The cartoon featured 12 women in bed crying into handkerchiefs. Young's top hat rested at the center of the headboard, his empty boots sat at the foot of the bed, and his presence among the women was marked by a conspicuous absence. The caption read, "In memoriam Brigham Young. And the place which knew him once shall know him no more." Concerned with social issues, Keppler's other work lobbied for hard-working Americans, particularly immigrants such as himself. In addition, he criticized big business, cheap overseas labor, and inflation.

The work of Nast and Keppler helped spread reform, demonstrating the power of pen-and-ink and, later, the grease pencil to make an impact on society. When cartoons work, their power can topple the powerful, making the cartoonist a king-maker. That's the suspicion of a drawing by Walt McDougall (1884–1952), who may have created the most influential political cartoon in United States history. As voting day neared for the 1884 presidential election, Joseph Pulitzer's *New York World* printed McDougall's cartoon on page one under the headline "The royal feast of Belshazzar Blaine and the money kings."[3] The cartoon became known as "Belshazzar's Feast" and was reproduced on New York state billboards by Democrats to deride Republican presidential candidate James G. Blaine. The cartoon took up six columns and depicted a plutocratic dinner that was held the night before at Delmonico's. Reminiscent of the Last Supper, candidate Blaine sat at a sumptuous dinner of "lobby pudding," "monopoly soup," and other dishes while a needy family dwarfed by the aristocrats implored some help. The cartoon is credited with Blaine losing votes in the key state of New York and advancing Grover Cleveland to the White House.

McDougall may serve as an example of the political cartoonist's influence during the zenith of cartooning, where readers were literate and sophisticated enough to understand the axioms and puns with a minimum of explanation. Issues of class and wealth could be represented with simplicity. The work of this period, sometimes called the period of New Journalism, created characters who are no longer in print but remain part of the lexicon. Harold Tucker Webster (1885–1952) invented Caspar Milquetoast, the epitome of timidity personified. The Yellow Kid, the first successful comic strip, examined the exploits of a street urchin wearing an oversized T-shirt printed in yellow when color comics were first introduced in the *World* in 1894. The Yellow Kid, created by Richard Outcault (1863–1928), established reckless newspapering in the phrase "yellow journalism." The competition by William Randolph Hearst (1863–1951) and Joseph Pulitzer (1847–1911) not only for the Yellow Kid strip but for readers at any cost was summed up in that derisive phrase. Outcault's humor appealed to a burgeoning reading public, particularly immigrants who inundated the shores at the turn of the century. The popularity of Outcault's Yellow Kid in the *World* led Pulitzer to hire a second Yellow Kid cartoonist when Outcault left for Hearst's *Journal*. George Luks

(1867–1933) drew the Yellow Kid comic for Hearst, but maintained a reputation as a master American easel painter. Competition that led to the newspaper circulation wars between rivals Hearst and Pulitzer gave Outcault and Luks a place in comic history.

These drawings helped newspapers increase readership during the days when metropolitan newspapers needed an edge to build circulation at a rival's expense. During the 1880s, urban newspapers used cartoons in Sunday newspapers to attract readers interested in entertaining content.

One of Hearst's best known cartoonists was Homer Davenport (1867–1912), who drew for the *New York Evening Journal*, among other publications. He was an idealist and a moralist who joined in the ridicule of New York's Boss Tweed by rendering the corrupt figure as a smug, overweight man wearing suits spotted with dollar signs. In one of his 1896 cartoons, Davenport showed the paunchy Tweed introducing his friend the "Trusts," depicted by a Goliath holding a club. Davenport's early work was his best. By 1904, his cartoons were less spirited. A good example is one that glorified Republican candidate Teddy Roosevelt in 1904 in which Uncle Sam laid a hand on Roosevelt's shoulders and said, "He's good enough for me."

Brutal caricatures can establish a political cartoonist, but whimsical humor also works well. A cartoonist famous for his gentle humor was John T. McCutcheon (1870–1949), who drew for the *Chicago Tribune* in 1903 after serving on the *Chicago Record*. His 1904 cartoon in the *Tribune* used gentle cheerleading to note that Missouri, the last of the old-guard Southern states, joined the Republicans. The caption read, "The mysterious stranger," and suggested that the bitterness from the Civil War might have been over. McCutcheon also pioneered the nostalgia panel where he celebrated the values associated with the good in life. His cartoon titled "Injun Summer," first published in 1907 in the *Tribune*, is his most famous. It depicted an old man and a boy studying the teepee formation of corn stalks under a full moon. The next panel showed the ghostly forms of Native Americans dancing in the moonlight around the teepees. The old man suggested that this scene represented the term "Injun Summer."[4] In 1932 McCutcheon won a Pulitzer Prize.

Another light-hearted cartoonist was Rube Goldberg (1883–1970), who won a 1948 Pulitzer Prize for an atypical work in the *New York Sun*. It showed a black atom bomb teetering on the edge of a cliff labeled "world control." The abyss was marked "world destruction," and a cozy house with a family enjoying the day under a patio umbrella sat on the bomb. Goldberg called this cartoon "Peace today."[5]

If a first family of editorial cartoonists exist, it may be the Berrymans. Clifford K. Berryman (1869–1949) worked for the *Washington Post* in 1889 then the *Washington Star* after 1906. He won a Pulitzer Prize in 1944, 22 years after the awards began for editorial cartoons. Berryman gave the world TR's Teddy Bear in the *Post*. His son, James T. Berryman (1902–1976), won a Pulitzer Prize in 1950. Awards notwithstanding, the junior Berryman said he received his share of grief for his criticism of FDR and Truman. "Both of them summoned me to the White House to give me hell," he said.[6]

Between the world wars, editorial cartoonists tended to be conservative, which made Arthur "Art" Henry Young (1866–1943) a bit of a exception. He was left-wing, especially during World War I. Although he drew a daily panel for the *Chicago Inter Ocean*, his best work was in *The Masses*, a militantly Socialist magazine.

Another liberal voice was cartoonist Rollin Kirby (1875–1952) of the *New York World*, the first editorial cartoonist to win three Pulitzers, in 1922, 1925, and 1931. He began cartooning in 1911 and hit his peak on the *World* in the 1920s.[7] He also worked for the *New York Post*. He advocated tolerance but used his own brand of intolerance to ideas he despised to portray them as foolish. For instance, his "Mr. Dry," a gaunt, black-frocked, blue-nose bigot, challenged prohibitionists and may have helped lead to Prohibition being repealed. In a typical cartoon, he showed President Herbert Hoover praising the old man with his unshaven face and an odd top hat. The caption read, "Buck up, you're a noble fellow."[8]

Edmund Duffy (1899–1962) of the *Baltimore Sun* also won three Pulitzers, in 1931, 1934, and 1940. At the *Sun* for 25 years, he worked at the *Saturday Evening Post* and later *Newsday*. He was particularly known for skewering the KKK. For instance, a 1925 cartoon about a Klan parade in Washington, D.C., depicted the Klan putting a hood over the Washington monument with the approval of the president, symbolized by a hood over the Capitol seen in the distant background of the cartoon.

A two-time Pulitzer winner was Daniel R. "Fitz" Fitzpatrick (1881–1969), who worked at the *St. Louis Post-Dispatch* from 1913 to 1958. He won Pulitzers in 1926 and 1955. The 1926 cartoon depicted a man wearing a ball and chain standing in front of a 10-story high stack of laws. The two tablets with the Ten Commandments rested in the foreground. The man was bent over with the weight of the laws, and the caption read "The laws of Moses and the laws of today."

Cartoonist and artist J. Norwood "Ding" Darling (1876–1962) began drawing for the *Des Moines Register* in 1906 and then worked for the *New York Herald Tribune* and won two Pulitzers. He signed his cartoons "D'ing" as an abbreviation of "Darling." In addition to his art, he was a leading conservationist and urged Iowans to respect natural beauty. As a tribute to his friend President Teddy Roosevelt, he drew a cartoon titled "The Long, Long Trial," now considered a classic. It ran in the *Register* the day after Roosevelt died in 1919.[9] It also ran on page one of the *Chicago Post* that day. The drawing showed Roosevelt on a horse, his cowboy hat lifted in triumph and farewell, making his way into the clouds, which included the outline of a wagon train winding its way through the heavenly mountains.

Darling's 1924 Pulitzer Prize was for a four-panel series that ran in the *New York Tribune* with the heading "In good old U.S.A." It showed the dramatic transitions a person can make in the United States, from an orphan who trains to be an engineer or economist with the goal of eliminating the cycle of depression. The final panel underlined this potential if society helps children avoid wasting their time and ambition by congregating on street corners without a goal. In addition to his work in Des

Moines, Darling worked for the *New York Herald* two years and later went into syndication.

Among the other giants in editorial cartooning are Herbert "Herblock" Block (1909–), who won Pulitzer Prizes in 1942, 1954, and 1978, and Bill Mauldin (1921–), who won in 1945 and 1958. Mauldin created the characters Willie and Joe for the Army newspaper, *Stars and Stripes*. These foot soldiers presented a human face to the tragedy of war. His Pulitzer Prize–winning cartoon showed American soldiers with prisoners trudging through an European town in a rainfall. The caption read, "Fresh, spirited American troops, flushed with victory, are bringing in thousands of hungry, ragged, battle-weary prisoners."

Paul Conrad (1924–) of the *Los Angles Times*, Garry Trudeau (1948–) of Universal Press Syndicate, Patrick B. Oliphant (1935–) of the *Denver Post*, Jeff MacNelly (1947–2000) of the Richmond newspapers, and Mike Peters (1943–) of the *Dayton Daily News* are among the popular editorial cartoonists in the late 20th century. Wayne Stayskal (1931–) is one of the few well-known conservative editorial cartoonists today. Ollie Harrington (1912–1995) was a pioneering black editorial cartoonist and well known for his comic character Bootsie.

Signe Wilkinson (1959–) was one of the few female editorial cartoonists, and the first female editorial cartoonist to win a Pulitzer, winning in 1992. *Philadelphia Daily News* editorial page editor Richard Aregood called her an "attack Quaker" for her acerbic wit.

Anne Mergen of the Cox newspapers is another female editorial cartoonist best known for her work on Franklin D. Roosevelt while working for the *Atlanta Journal*. Her work never won a Pulitzer. *Journal* editors, however, cited her cartoons for helping the newspaper win its "most meritorious" public service award in 1939.[10] She sold her first free-lance cartoon in 1934, which concerned Florida's voting repeal of Prohibition. She used a frothy head of beer to make her point. Her cartoon of President Roosevelt's death, titled "The supreme sacrifice," played on the idea of Roosevelt's work to end the war and depicted FDR as a war casualty. Eleanor Roosevelt received the original drawings and hung them in the Roosevelt Library Museum in Hyde Park.

The importance of editorial cartoons gained increasing recognition with the founding of the National Cartoonists Society in 1946. It was followed with the founding in 1957 of the Association of American Editorial Cartoonists. Today, they have a combined membership of almost 900.

COMICS

Editorial cartoons may provoke, but the comics delight. While the trend today can include adult-oriented material—edgy topics such as deviance and drug use—the comics most Americans think of appear as black-and-white strips in the daily newspaper and in color on Sundays. Despite a protest movement in the 1950s over the crime and horror content of comic books, the comic format used by newspapers is as strong as ever. The earliest comics included a series known as "The Little Bears and Tigers" about funny animals that ran in the *San Francisco Examiner* as early as 1892. The list also included the antics of Buster Brown, another Richard F. Outcault (1863–1928) creation that originated in the *New York Herald* in 1902.

James Swinnerton (1875–1974), the creator of "The Little Bears" and "Little Jimmy," and Rudolph Dirks (1877–1968), creator of Katzenjammer Kids on December 12, 1897, were among the earliest comic strip artists. Dirks pioneered two innovations: a sequence of pictures seen in the comic narrative and frame lines along with speech balloons to help tell the reader who was speaking. Both Outcault of Yellow Kid fame and Swinnerton pioneered the idea of a continuing character. Dirks was the first cartoonist to successfully use a sequence of pictures, while Outcault was the first to inject speech into his drawings.

Another change in the development of comics was the use of a progression of frames, from left to right, to produce a comic strip. Although Clare Briggs (1875–1930) of the *Chicago American* experimented with the form in 1904, it took Harry Conway Fisher (1885–

1954), better known as "Bud," to create the first successful comic strip, "A. Mutt," and later "Mutt and Jeff." Cartoon panels were common on sports pages during this era, making it easier for Fisher, who was at work on the sports page, to tinker with a new form, borrowing from horse racing for his inspiration.

With the popularity of the comics came criticism and an organized attempt to suppress these drawings. They were linked to the newspaper bids for greater and greater circulation and sensationalism, and critics considered the content intellectually shallow and lacking artistic merit. A comic that proved to be enormously popular and a challenger to the criticism was Winsor McCay's (1869–1934) "Little Nemo in Slumberland," which began in 1905 in a dream sequence as a fairy-tale adventure in the *New York Herald*. The cartoon used delightful fantasies, realistic renderings, and a fine art perspective to create a fairy tale narrative.[11] McCay's most famous panel, published in 1908, showed Nemo in a bed that sprouted legs and took a stroll. As the bed legs grew, the panels elongated. When the bed finally tripped, Nemo awakened and found himself twisted in his bed sheets but unscathed.[12] As was the case with so many fine cartoonists, McCay also drew editorial cartoons that appeared in Hearst's newspaper.

Another cartoon strip given to a lighthearted touch was George McManus' (1884–1954) "Bringing Up Father," which featured Jiggs and Maggie. It first appeared in 1913 in the *American*. While McManus penned other strips, this one is most often linked to his name. It was the antecedent for the husband-wife strips that followed, including "Blondie." The plot concerned the *nouveau riche* and the tension to fit into the affluent class while longing to return to a modest beginning.

Another humorous cartoonist was Billy De Beck (1890–1942). His Barney Google, a pint-sized man, endured the indignities of life and managed to survive. In one strip, for instance, Barney lived in an apartment where the sun blinded him every morning. The management refused to help. So Barney painted his window black. After a good night's sleep, he went to work, where the manager greeted him,

"You're fired for not showing up for two days!" The strip inspired a popular novelty song, "Barney Google with the goo goo googly eyes."

In 1950 Charles Schultz (1922–1999) was syndicated with the strip "Peanuts." Schultz sold his first comic in 1948 to the *Saturday Evening Post*. "Peanuts" inspired a musical, television specials, and a zeitgeist about life's reversals and the indomitable human spirit. It focused on Charlie Brown and his friends, who endured the angst of the adult condition, and a beagle who endured the angst of knowing how to cope with this adult world.

Some comics have entertained more than one generation. Among them are George Herriman's (1880–1944) "Krazy Kat" (a favorite of President Woodrow Wilson), Frank King's (1883–1969) "Gasoline Alley," Harold Gray's (1894–1968) "Little Orphan Annie," Chester Gould's (1900–1985) "Dick Tracy," Chic Young's (1901–1973) "Blondie," and Walt Kelly's (1913–1973) satirical strip "Pogo," which featured animals commenting on life from Georgia's Okefenokee Swamp.

CONCLUSION

Rather than going from simple to complex, the history of cartooning is the reverse. The older political cartoon messages are the most elaborate with rich detail in the foregrounds and backgrounds and a tendency to use the techniques of fine artists. Over the decades, the cartoonist dropped the sophisticated literary references and complicated art in favor of a minimum of figures and a tendency to highlight national and international issues.

Changes notwithstanding, cartoons, comics, and caricatures continue to show no signs of losing appeal. Part of the fun is the ability of a good cartoon to allow a reader to use his own imagination to provide the missing elements. At times the drawings demand very little intellectually; at other times, cartoons require a knowledge of culture, custom, convention, and current events to provide the greatest impact. Motion lines, use of exaggeration, and regular displays of the impossible—talking animals, injuries that aren't permanent, and supernatural occurrences—all allow the reader to willingly suspend belief to enjoy the action and commentary, regardless of how absurd. For readers who must endure a heavy dose of grim reality each time the newspaper is opened, cartoons, comics, and caricatures provide welcome relief. The humor can make a point, but it's the playfulness that makes the work entertaining. When the cartoons are bad, they can be amusing still; but when they are good, they are saved, copied, and mounted in places of honor to be shared with others who enjoy a lighter look at life.

Selected Readings

Barker, Martin. *Comics: Ideology, Power and the Critics.* Manchester: Manchester University Press, 1989.

Brakeman, Mark. "Thomas Nast: Pen With Power." *Media History Digest* 5, 4 (1985): 23–27, 48–49.

Darden, Robert F. *Drawing Power: Knott, Ficklen, and McClanahan, Editorial Cartoonists of the Dallas Morning News.* Waco, Tex.: Markham Press Fund, 1983.

Dennis, Everette E., and Melvin L. Dennis. "Political Cartoonists: Honing a Fine Edge." *Media History Digest* 5, 4 (1985): 17–22, 49.

Harvey, Robert C. *The Art of the Funnies, An Aesthetic History.* Jackson: University of Mississippi, 1994.

Hess, Stephen, and Milton Kaplan. *The Ungentlemanly Art: A History of American Political Cartoons.* New York: Macmillan Publishing Co., Inc., 1975.

Hoff, Syn. *Editorial and Political Cartooning.* New York: Stravon Educational Press, 1876.

Keller, Morton. *The Art and Politics of Thomas Nast.* New York: Oxford University Press, 1968.

Lendt, David L. *DING: The Life of Jay Norwood Darling.* Ames: Iowa State University Press, 1979.

Matthews, Albert. "The Snake Devices, 1754–1776, and the Constitutional Courant, 1765." *Colonial Society of Massachusetts Publications* 11 (1906–07).

Murrell, William. "Nast, Gladiator of the Political Pencil." *American Scholar* 5 (1936): 472–85.

Nevins, Alan, and Frank Weitenkampf. *A Century of Political Cartoons: Caricature in the United States from 1800 to 1900.* New York: Octagon Books, 1975.

Parton, James. *Caricature and Other Comic Art in All Times and Many Lands.* New York: Harper & Brothers, 1878.

Perry, George, and Alan Aldridge. *The Penguin Book of Comics.* Middlesex, England: Penguin, 1967.

Press, Charles. *The Political Cartoon.* London and Toronto: Associated University, 1981

Robinson, Jerry. *The Comics: An Illustrated History of Comic Strip Art.* New York: G.P. Putnam's Sons, 1974.

Spencer III, Dick. *Editorial Cartooning.* Ames: Iowa State College Press, 1949.

Stevens, John D. "Reflections in a Dark Mirror: Comic Strips in Black Newspapers." *Journal of Popular Culture* 10 (Summer 1976): 239–48.

Sullivan, Julie. "Another Voice: The Black Cartoonists." *Media History Digest* 5, 4 (1985): 28–31, 46–48.

Vinson, J. Chal. *Thomas Nast, Political Cartoonist.* Athens: University of Georgia Press, 1967.

Waugh, Coulton. *The Comics.* New York: Macmillan, 1947.

Notes

1. Stephen Hess and Milton Kaplan, *The Ungentlemanly Art, A History of American Political Cartoons* (New York: Macmillan, 1975), 55.

2. Allan Nevins and Frank Weitenkampf, *A Century of Political Cartoons, Caricature in the United States from 1800 to 1900* (New York: Octagon Books, 1975), 24–25.

3. *New York World*, 30 October 1884.

4. *Chicago Tribune*, 30 September 1907.

5. *New York Sun*, 22 July 1947.

6. Charles Press, *The Political Cartoon* (London and Toronto: Associated University, 1981), 190.

7. S. L. Harrison, "Cartoons as a teaching tool in journalism history," *Journalism & Mass Communication Educator* 75 (Spring 1998): 100.

8. *New York Post*, 23 February 1928.

9. *Des Moines Register*, 7 January 1919.

10. Dick Spencer III, *Editorial Cartooning* (Ames: Iowa State College Press, 1949), 82.

11. *New York Herald*, 15 October 1905.

12. Ibid., 26 July 1908.

37

Technologies of News Gathering and Transmission

JOHN SLATER

If you had visited an American newspaper office anytime during the 18th century, you would have found it a very different place from today's newsroom. Naturally, there would have been no telephones ringing, computers clacking, or electric lights burning 200 years ago. But you also would have found no reporters, and not much sense of urgency to discover the news and rush it on to eager readers. In those days "news" wasn't something you went off to find. It was something that came to you in its own good time. Even the printers who wanted to hurry things up found little opportunity to do so. Information had to be carried by people, which meant that it could move no faster than a person on foot, on horseback, or in a boat.

Technology—the application of scientific discovery to specific, practical situations—is what changed all that. It was technology, after all, that led to the creation of the mass media. There could be no newspapers without printing presses, no radio or television stations without transmitters and receivers, no Internet without computers. Over the years media professionals—printers, publishers, editors, reporters, journalists—adopted and adapted new technologies to speed the process of news gathering and transmission. It would be a mistake, however, to think that journalists always embraced new technology as soon as it became available. Journalism is inherently conservative, and over the years many journalists resisted change. Ultimately, though, advances in tech-

nology created new media, changed the definition of news, and revolutionized the way news is gathered, processed, and presented to the public.

SHIPS AND THE MAIL

For three-quarters of a century after the first regularly published American newspaper appeared in 1704, journalists used only two technologies for gathering and disseminating the news—ships and the mail. These technologies were so important that newspapers sometimes arranged their publication dates to coincide with the schedule of ships and post riders.

Ships played an important role in early America. This country was settled by sea, and the earliest settlements were located on waterways. Not only was this new world a maritime world, but its settlers maintained their connections with the old world. The colonists regarded ships as a lifeline to wherever they had come from. They were interested in what was happening overseas. The arrival of a ship, particularly one from abroad, was an event of considerable interest, and early newspapers commonly reported ship arrivals and departures. America was a British colony. Its settlers thought of themselves as British people. A ship from England would bring a wealth of information to the community. The captain would report what he knew of current events. The ship would almost certainly be carrying letters to people in the colony, and the recipients would read them and share their contents. The ship also would be carrying English newspapers, which might provide transcripts or official accounts. Foreign news was important to the colonies, and it arrived by ship.

The "news" that ships brought would not have seemed very new to us. Crossing the Atlantic under sail from England took anywhere from four to eight weeks, and sometimes longer. If the news the ships carried had come to London from other parts of Europe, or if the ships had called at other colonies in the West Indies before arriving on this continent, it would be older still. But it was information not yet known on this side of the ocean, which made it news to the colonists.

The other major news gathering technology was the mail. If it hadn't been for the postal service, newspapers might never have come into being in this country. The mail not only allowed printers to distribute their newspapers, but it also provided them with more information to put in their papers. Since everyone in America's small settlements knew most everything that happened locally, newspapers tended to favor news from other places. As the population grew and new settlements were established inland, most of the non-local news stories that newspapers carried came from other newspapers. Those other newspapers usually arrived by mail.

Copying stories from other newspapers was a common practice and was not regarded as plagiarism. Some stories and even some advertisements ended with the instruction to other editors to "please copy." To facilitate the practice of copying from other newspapers, printers were allowed to exchange their newspapers by mail without paying any postage. This custom originated in the early 1700s, when most postmasters were also printers. Congress endorsed the practice after the revolution, when the Post Office Act of 1792 expressly provided that every printer of newspapers could send one copy of each paper to every other newspaper printer in the country, free of postage. This practice continued until Congress ended the privilege in 1873.

Initially, post-riders—people on horse-back—carried the mail between cities. Later, as volume increased and the roads improved, coaches carried the mail. A "stage-coach" carried the mail in stages, stopping to replace tired horses with fresh ones between each stage of the journey.

EXPRESSES

Despite the widespread sleepiness of the newspaper business in early America, some printers were not content to sit back and wait for the mail to arrive. Samuel Hall, who published the *Salem Gazette* from 1781 to 1785, sent a messenger by horseback to bring back the news from Boston, fifteen miles away, before each edition. A considerable proportion of the news was concerned with shipping.

Boston, a major port, was also an early news center. It was home to the country's first commercial newsroom, a business that collected and posted information from a variety of sources and allowed subscribers to read it. In 1811 a young man named Samuel Topliff, Jr., began working there as a clerk. Topliff implemented his own method of news gathering. Instead of waiting for incoming ships to dock, Topliff rowed out to them in a small boat, collected whatever information they were carrying, and rushed it back to the newsroom. The technique caught on, and by the 1820s newspaper owners in New York and Charleston were using small boats to meet arriving vessels. In 1828 David Hale of the *New York Journal of Commerce* hired a fast schooner to meet the ships 20 or 30 miles offshore. Soon everyone was doing the same.

As populations grew and the amount of available news increased, more newspapers began publishing on a daily basis. Competition among big-city newspapers fueled the desire for faster communication. The publishers adopted other technologies—special express riders that could cut the regular mail time in half, the railroad, even carrier pigeons—to move the news faster. Often they combined these technologies to get the news ahead of their competitors. In December 1830, when President Jackson delivered an important message about the United States Bank and the tariff to Congress, New York newspapers made special arrangements to get the story. The *Courier and Enquirer* and the *Journal of Commerce* each had their own "pony" expresses, and several other papers banded together and hired a third. The news traveled from Washington to Baltimore by horseback, from Baltimore to Philadelphia by steamboat, and from Philadelphia to New York by horseback again, using eight changes of horses. Publishers in Boston arranged to have the news forwarded to Providence by steamer and on to Boston by horseback.

In the 1830s, when printing presses became capable of vastly larger press runs, the competition created by the penny press movement spurred publishers to ever-more-creative innovations. A regular express was established between New York and Boston, using the Providence steamboat and the Boston and Providence Railroad. The *New York Herald* installed a dovecote on its roof and used carrier pigeons to carry news from the state capital at Albany.[1]

News from overseas still traveled slowly. Sailing ships took anywhere from 16 to 83 days to cross the Atlantic from Europe, averaging between 30 and 39 days for the crossing. The arrival of steam reduced the transatlantic crossing to a more predictable 16–17 days. The first two steamships to make the journey, the *Sirius* and the *Great Western*, arrived in New York on the same day, April 23, 1838. James Gordon Bennett, founder of the *New York Herald*, sailed aboard the *Sirius* on her return journey to establish a string of correspondents for the *Herald* in the major cities of Europe, a clear example of technology's influence on news gathering. The British Admiralty awarded a contract for regular steamer mail and passenger service to a Nova Scotian named Samuel Cunard. His British and North American Royal Mail Steam Ship Company would remain the newspapers' chief provider of foreign news for a quarter of a century.[2]

THE TELEGRAPH

On May 24, 1844, Samuel Morse demonstrated the utility of his electromagnetic tele-graph by sending the famous message "What hath God wrought!" from Baltimore to Washington. Morse's invention, which ranks in importance with the invention of movable type, separated transportation and communication and freed messages to go faster than men could transport them. The introduction of telegraphy had far-reaching consequences for journalism, changing the way news was defined, gathered, and written.

Within two years the *New York Herald* bragged that its Washington news came by telegraph to Baltimore, by special steam and horse express to Wilmington, and by telegraph again to Jersey City. Soon the telegraph extended from Washington to New York without interruption. At the start of the Mexican War in 1846, there were 130 miles of telegraph wire in the country. The war created such a market for news that by 1852 there were about 15,000 miles of lines in the United States and Canada, running from Quebec to New Orleans.[3] The telegraph was spreading inexorably across the national landscape.

Telegraph rates were high, and having to pay them increased the cost of running a newspaper. In an effort to control rising prices, six New York newspapers agreed in May 1848 to share the total expense of news brought into the city. They formed the New York Associated Press, another example of technology changing news gathering. This modest cooperative went on to become the worldwide news service we know today as the Associated Press.

The telegraph was revolutionizing communication in the United States, creating new media outlets everywhere it went. Soon it would extend beyond the national borders. In 1856 the Atlantic Telegraph Company began laying the first submarine cable from England to the United States. After two failures, the company finally succeeded in August 1858. The cable carried 730 messages its first week of operation, and then went dead, a victim of the dense water pressure encountered at the bottom of the ocean. The outbreak of the American Civil War would delay its replacement.

But if war slowed transatlantic communication, it had the opposite effect on communication between the East Coast and the West

Coast. Transcontinental communication had always been agonizingly slow. In 1841 the news of President Harrison's death took three months and twenty days to reach Los Angeles. But on April 3, 1860, the Western Pony Express began offering thirteen-day letter service between St. Joseph, Mo., and Sacramento, Calif., for $5 per half-ounce. The company used more than 200 riders and 500 horses, dividing the distance into 190 stages. On October 20, 1861, the Overland Telegraph was completed, eliminating the need for the Western Pony Express and driving it into bankruptcy.

The Civil War changed the newspaper business, which had remained largely a leisurely profession, into one that emphasized speed. Reporters and, for the first time, photographers followed the armies into the field, sending reports back by telegraph. This new technology led to the first real attempts at military censorship. When the war ended in 1865, work began again on the effort to span the Atlantic by cable. By 1866 there were not one, but two such cables. The cost of using the cable was high, however. Fees were set at $5 a word, in gold.[4] One reaction to the high cost was the development of "cablese," a sort of code the press used exclusively for cable transmission. In cablese, correspondents would write, for example, "smorning" for "this morning," "ungo" for "will not go," and "protreaty" for "favored the treaty."

There were more than 180,000 miles of wire in the United States by 1872,[5] and in 1874 telegraph lines and cables linked all the continents. The *New York Herald* and the *New York Times* were devoting up to two full pages to wire and cable dispatches.

Newspaper offices had Morse receiving sets and qualified operators around the clock, and large papers could have as many as a dozen telegraph operators on their payrolls. Most important non-local news came straight from the wire. The 1880 Census reported that 11 per cent of all telegraphic messages sent that year were sent by the press.[6] One way to assess the importance of the telegraph to the newspaper industry is to consider the number of newspapers that have the word "telegraph" in their names.[7]

TELETYPE AND THE TYPEWRITER

For about 75 years the telegraph was a major presence in American newsrooms, but gradually the teletypewriter replaced the Morse key. At the sending end, teletype operators used a typewriter keyboard to punch holes in a paper tape, which they then fed into a telegraphic sending device. The signal activated a special typewriter at the receiving end, typing out copy automatically. The teletype operated at speeds that went from 40 words a minute when the process was introduced to 60 and even 80 words a minute some years later. The Associated Press adopted the teletype for its New York service in 1914, and teletype machines gradually replaced Morse-code telegraphy. By 1935 the AP and most newspapers had phased out the last of their telegraphers. The old Morsemen disappeared, rendered unnecessary by the advent of the telephone and the supremacy of the teletypewriter.[8]

The first practical typewriter was produced in 1867 by three men, one of whom, Christopher Latham Sholes, was a former city editor of the *Milwaukee Daily Sentinel*. Commercial production began in 1873 by E. Remington and Sons, the small-arms manufacturer. Newspapers were slow to accept the new machines, but telegraph operators embraced them. A good telegrapher could copy about 45 words a minute, using a stylus on a pad of carbon copies. Using a typewriter increased the speed to about 65 words per minute. John Payne, a telegrapher for the Western Associated Press at Nashville, began experimenting with a typewriter in 1883, and in July 1885 the AP made the use of typewriters mandatory. In many newsrooms, the first typewriter to appear was the one used by the AP telegrapher. Eventually, reporters began using them, too.[9]

The *Washington Post* bought its first two Remington typewriters in 1893 after publisher Frank Hatton, using a pen, lost a speed contest to editor Harry West, using the "hunt and peck" system.[10]

Legibility and speed were the principal arguments in favor of typewriters. The arguments on the other side included the difficulty of learning to type and the fear that the use of typewriters would discourage good writing. Charles Edward Russell, city editor of the *New York World* from 1894 to 1897, wrote, "...few men can compose on the typewriter in terse, compact, vigorous English—the facility afforded by the machine is too great."[11] Chester Lord, managing editor of the *New York Sun*, agreed, and the *Sun's* reporters continued to write their copy in pencil long after other newspapers had gone to typewriters.[12] The news industry offered no consensus about using the typewriter for about 30 years. Some papers required it, while others left the decision up to the individual reporter. Newsrooms sometimes converted to typewriters overnight. Charles Carpenter, a cub reporter at the City News Bureau of Chicago in 1892–93, remembered his experience: "One day a notice was posted on the wall that typewriters were to be installed and that after a certain date all reporters would have to hand in typewritten copy. We all got very busy picking out our stories on the machine and it sure was tough for some of the boys."[13]

But the typewriter's eventual adoption was never in doubt. Reporters could double their speed, and many thought that the ability to put the words down more rapidly made for better writing. By 1917 a news writing textbook could say, "The first requirement in preparing copy is a knowledge of how to handle a typewriter dexterously. In all offices the reporters are furnished with typewriters, and one is helpless until one learns how to use a machine."[14] The typewriter had become a favorite among newspapermen, and the cacophony of a room full of noisy typewriters became emblematic of the newsroom.

THE TELEPHONE

The telephone, patented by Alexander Graham Bell in 1876, is another device that has become a symbol of modern journalism. It wasn't created for that purpose, though. Even Bell thought of it as an instrument for transmitting entertainment, and he tried initially to develop

a market for this purpose. The first use of the telephone to transmit a news story came on Feb. 12, 1877, when Henry Batchelder, a reporter for the *Boston Globe*, telephoned an account of one of Alexander Graham Bell's telephone lecture-demonstrations from Salem, Massachusetts, to A. B. Fletcher in the newspaper office in Boston. The account ran in the *Globe* February 13 under the headline, "Sent by Telephone: The First Newspaper Dispatch Sent by a Human Voice Over the Wire." Some newspapers began to use telephones. The *Washington Star* strung a wire to the Capitol and thereby gained an hour over its competitors.[15] The *Washington Post* installed a telephone in 1878, number 28 of the original 140 in the city.[16]

Other newspapers were slower to respond. The first New York telephone directory, a single sheet listing fewer than 300 subscribers, included no newspapers. The *New York Sun* had no telephone until 1880, the *Chicago Tribune* not until 1883. In 1884 the *St. Louis Globe-Democrat* had two telephones—one for its reporters and editors, and one for its business department.[17]

The simple fact of a telephone's presence in the newsroom didn't guarantee that it would be used, and resistance to the new technology was pronounced. Some of this resistance was based on the fact that many of the people that journalists needed to talk to did not have telephones. In the early 1890s New York had only 9,000 telephones serving a population of more than 1.5 million. In addition, many reporters believed the only good interview was a face-to-face interview. Charles Rosebault, who started reporting for the *New York Sun* in the 1880s, recalled later that his generation of reporters regarded using the telephone for interviews as "a rank evasion of duty."[18] One measure of newspapers' slow, grudging acceptance of the telephone can be found in the advice published in journalism textbooks. As late as 1917 a journalism text warned reporters not to trust the telephone on important stories, since it was impossible to see a person's gestures and facial expressions.[19]

If newspapers were slow to accept the telephone as a news-gathering device, they had no such reluctance about using it to disseminate news already gathered. Adoption of the telephone for this purpose led to the redistribution of labor and the wholesale reorganization of many newsrooms. Charles E. Chapin, city editor of the *New York Evening World,* created the modern rewriteman. He drew a checkerboard chart of the city and put a reporter in each square. Reporters were responsible for gathering all the news in their squares and telephoning the details back to their offices, often from a drug-store pay telephone. The reporters came to be referred to as legmen, while the people in the newsroom who took down their information were called rewritemen. As soon as a reporter finished telephoning in one story, the city editor would give him his next assignment. In some establishments, it was said, reporters never returned to the office except to pick up their pay.

Telephone technology offered journalism several additional advantages that the inventor never envisioned. Editors needed fewer reporters to cover local news. The telephone directory became a convenient source for verifying names and addresses. Reporters sometimes took advantage of the telephone's anonymity to impersonate someone else—usually city detectives or Federal agents[20]—to get a story. And finally, telephone wires, once installed, could be used for other technologies.

Transcontinental telephone service began January 25, 1915, but long-distance telephony was both more expensive and less reliable than the telegraph, which continued to operate profitably for many years after the introduction of the telephone. Newspaper correspondents were advised in 1917 to use the telephone when the mails were too slow or a telegraph office was not convenient.

By the 1920s the *New York World* was placing 200,000 calls a year and receiving 300,000, using 20 trunk lines and 80 telephones. In 1928 the switchboard at the *Chicago Tribune* was handling six million calls a year, incoming, outgoing, and internal.[21] The telephone had become so much a part of journalism that the 1928 Broadway hit play, "The Front Page," by Ben Hecht and Charles Mac-Arthur, featured seven telephones on stage in the press room of the Chicago Criminal Court Building. Today's cellular telephones allow reporters to call in their stories from almost anywhere.

BROADCAST TECHNOLOGY

In 1896 Guglielmo Marconi patented a system of wireless telegraphy. The invention offered freedom from telegraph lines and the expense of cable. It also offered new possibilities for news gathering. In 1899 the *New York Herald* hired Marconi to provide wireless coverage of the America's Cup race off Sandy Hook. The experiment failed because of radio interference from a second transmitter providing coverage for The Associated Press of Illinois. Marconi's company was more successful with daily transmission of news between Europe and America, which it started in 1903 and continued until World War I.

It wasn't just news that radio carried between Europe and the United States. Transatlantic telephone calls were carried by radio from 1927 until 1956, when the first transatlantic telephone cable was laid.

But radio's biggest use in news gathering probably involved using the technology to listen in on newsmakers. When city police began using radio communication, reporters bought radios and began tuning in to learn the location of crimes and fires. It became commonplace for copy boys to monitor local emergency communications and alert the newsroom to important events.

Radio station KDKA in Pittsburgh was licensed in 1919, and the advent of commercial radio created broadcast journalists. Throughout the early years of radio and then of television, which came a generation later, broadcast journalists gathered and transmitted the news in much the same ways as their print-journalism counterparts.

The advent of recording devices was a boon for broadcast journalists, freeing them to venture further into the field in search of actualities and sound bites. Audio tape recorders were introduced in Germany in the mid–1930s. In 1945, at the end of World War II, U.S.

soldiers found German-built Magnetophones in the studios at Radio Frankfurt. They brought them back to this country, where engineers began working on a U.S.–made version. The result, the Ampex Model 200 tape recorder, became available in 1948.

Television reporters received a similar boost in the late 1960s when magnetic recording equipment was adapted for field use. Until then television camera crews usually used 16mm film cameras for field coverage. Sony began introducing portable video recording equipment in the 1970s. The age of ENG, or electronic news gathering, arrived when CBS-TV sent a video camera and recorder to cover President Nixon's 1972 trip to Moscow. ENG meant more pictures from the scene of breaking news events. Within a few years, TV cameras were combined with portable microwave transmitting equipment, which meant that TV crews no longer had to drive back to the station with their pictures.

SATELLITES AND COMPUTERS

In 1984 ENG was supplanted by satellite news gathering, SNG, which utilized specially equipped trucks for the satellite uplinks. Much as the telegraph led to the creation of the Associated Press, SNG technology spawned satellite news-gathering organizations such as CONUS and Worldwide Television News, which fed news stories to member stations.[22] Communication satellites have made distant coverage cheaper and more available, changing television news coverage in the process. Satellite distribution of news also replaced the teletypewriter.

The electronic computer dates to the 1940s, and the first models became available commercially in the 1950s. The floppy disc was invented in 1970, and Intel built its first microprocessor in 1971, the same year that word processors became available. The microcomputer is a product of the mid–1970s. By 1983 *Time* magazine had named the computer as its "Man of the Year."

Most journalistic interest in the computer was driven by the fact that computers could provide direct input into photocomposition machines, that is, an operator could type on a computer and drive a machine that produced camera-ready type. Until that technology became available, everything in newspapers had to be typed twice—once by the reporter, on a typewriter, and once by a compositor, on a Linotype machine. The computer eventually won out in a competition among optical character reading scanners, electric typewriters, and minicomputers because it allowed journalists to take advantage of computer-assisted reporting.

The news-gathering tool of recent years was computer-assisted reporting (CAR), a term that encompasses both online research and database reporting. Online research includes the use of online commercial services like Lexis/Nexis, Dialog, and CompuServe as well as the Internet. Database reporting involves the use of computers to analyze original databases from other sources, which can lead to stories that otherwise might never be reported. Although CAR really began with general use of desktop computers in the late 1980s, there was a groundbreaking example in the late 1960s. Philip Meyer, a member of the *Detroit Free Press* Washington bureau, used computers and social science methodology to analyze the causes of the 1967 Detroit riots. He exploded the myth that the rioters were Southern immigrants unable to adjust to big city life. The rioters cut across all education and income levels, Meyer found, and the cause of the rioting was alienation.[23]

CONCLUSION

Each of the technologies we have looked at has changed the way journalists do their jobs. Journalism has a history of changing to meet new demands, new expectations, and new technologies. And what of the future? There is no way to predict what new technology may come along next to change the course of journalism. As of this writing, the computer is in the driver's seat. With computer access to the

World Wide Web, any writer can gather his or her own news, create his or her own "publication," and exchange it with other like-minded people, just like the printer/postmasters of two centuries ago. Only faster, and more easily.

Selected Readings

Blondeim, Menaheim. "The Click: Telegraphic Technology, Journalism, and the Transformation of the New York Associated Press." *American Journalism* 17 (Fall 2000): 27–52.

Carey, Arthur C. "Effects of the Pony Express and the Transcontinental Telegraph Upon Selected California Newspapers." *Journalism Quarterly* 51 (1974): 320–22.

Schwarzlose, Richard A. "Newspapers and Technology," 269–86 in *Newspapers: A Reference Guide*. New York: Greenwood Press, 1987.

Shaw, Donald L. "News Bias and the Telegraph: A Story of Historical Change." *Journalism Quarterly* 44 (1967): 3–12.

Steele, Ian K. *The English Atlantic, 1675–1740: An Exploration of Communication and Community*. New York: Oxford University Press, 1986.

Notes

1. Alvin F. Harlow, *Old Wires and New Waves* (1936; reprint ed., New York: Arno Press and the New York Times, 1971), 172–73.

2. Richard A. Schwarzlose, *The Nation's Newsbrokers, vol. 1, The Formative Years, from Pretelegraph to 1865* (Evanston, Ill.: Northwestern University Press, 1989), 37.

3. Isaac C. Pray, *Memoirs of James Gordon Bennett and His Times* (1855; reprint ed., New York: Arno Press, 1970), 377.

4. W. F. S. Shanks, "How We Get Our News," *Harper's New Monthly Magazine*, May 1867, 517.

5. Frederic Hudson, *Journalism in the United States* (New York: Harper & Brothers, 1873), 603.

6. Cited in Alfred McClung Lee, *The Daily Newspaper: The Evolution of a Social Instrument* (1937; reprint ed., New York: Octagon Books, 1973), 512.

7. Peter Young, *Person to Person: The International Impact of the Telephone* (Cambridge, England: Granta, 1991), 51.

8. Frank Luther Mott, *The News in America* (Cambridge, Mass.: Harvard University Press, 1962), 98–99.

9. Richard A. Schwarzlose, *The Nation's Newsbrokers, vol. 2, The Rush to Institution, from 1865 to 1920* (Evanston, Ill.: Northwestern University Press, 1990), 116.

10. Chalmers M. Roberts, *The Washington Post: The First 100 Years* (Boston: Houghton Mifflin, 1977), 82.

11. Charles Edward Russell, *These Shifting Scenes* (New York: Hodder and Stoughton, 1914), 308–09.

12. Cited in Paul Lancaster, *Gentlemen of the Press: The Life and Times of an Early Reporter, Julian Ralph of the Sun* (Syracuse, N.Y.: Syracuse University Press, 1992), 186.

13. Tom Vickerman, unpublished manuscript, cited in A. A. Dornfeld, *Behind the Front Page: The Story of the City News Bureau of Chicago* (Chicago: Academy Chicago, 1983), 49.

14. M. Lyle Spencer, *News Writing: The Gathering, Handling and Writing of News Stories* (Boston: D. C. Heath, 1917), 250.

15. Herbert N. Casson, *The History of the Telephone* (Chicago: A. C. McClurg, 1922 [c. 1910], 210.

16. Roberts, *The Washington Post*, 38.

17. Jim Allee Hart, *A History of the St. Louis Globe-Democrat* (Columbia: University of Missouri Press, 1961), 165.

18. Charles J. Rosebault, *When Dana Was the Sun* (New York: Robert M. McBride and Co., 1931), 246.

19. Spencer, *News Writing*, 42–43.

20. Allen Churchill, *Park Row* (Westport, Conn.: Greenwood Press, 1958), 88.

21. Chicago Tribune, *Picture Encyclopedia of the World's Greatest Newspaper; a Handbook of the Newspaper as Exemplified by the Chicago Tribune—Issued to Commemorate its Eightieth Birthday* (Chicago: Chicago Tribune, 1928), 720.

22. August E. Grant and Kenton T. Wilkinson, eds., *Communication Technology Update* (Austin, Tex.: Technology Futures Inc., 1993), 252.

23. James L. Aucoin, "The Re-emergence of American Investigative Journalism 1960–1975," *Journalism History* 21 (Spring 1995): 11.

38

Printing Technologies

SUSAN THOMPSON

In the mid–15th century, Johann Gutenberg, a German goldsmith in the city of Mainz, conducted work that would revolutionize the world. He manufactured type by pouring molten metal into matrices that formed the shapes of the 24 letters of the European alphabet. He experimented and developed viscous, oil-varnished ink suitable for presswork, fine ink that would not discolor significantly over time. He then arranged the letter types to form words, sentences, and paragraphs by securing them within a specially designed frame. He used opaque, sturdy paper made from cloth, and his special ink that spread evenly across the metal typefaces. He then adapted a printing press based on screw presses that were used at the time to press linen, paper, and other items, to apply enough pressure between the inked types and paper so that a clear impression would result.

It is quite possible that Gutenberg did not invent any of the items he used, but only pulled together existing knowledge, including the manufacture of type, the mixing of ink, and the alteration of a screw press for use in printing. Evidence shows that individual types, for example, were also being made in Holland and France at the same time or even before Gutenberg's work in Mainz. Regardless of the origin of the technologies, the fine products of the Gutenberg press survive to this day as testaments to the printer whose name would forever be associated with the origins of printing. Gutenberg himself died in 1468, blind and deep in debt. His partner, Johann Fust, subsequently became a wealthy man as book printing became more popular and his printing business thrived.[1]

The history of print-related technologies shares some characteristics with the story of the printer from Mainz who purportedly used movable type for the first time in Western civilization. As with the Gutenberg press, most advances in print-related technologies have resulted from the contributions of several people rather than a single individual, but historical evidence usually favors particular individuals upon whom credit is bestowed. Most technological advances have not been the result of revolutionary change, but slow improvements that finally attracted commercial interests. As with Gutenberg, these individuals may or may not have originated particular technological developments, but ample evidence indicates that they were certainly among the first to make use of them. Also, as with the Gutenberg press, new printing technologies through the years have often revolutionized the industry and created new industries.

Major advances in printing technologies have occurred through the centuries from about 1450 all the way to today. The history of printing technology is very much the story of printers' efforts to produce a clearer, more accurate, and more beautiful, finished product, one more appealing to readers, at a cost affordable to the printer and insuring a profit. After the advent of steam power and more sophisticated presses in the early 1800s, mass production became an additional goal of many printers. The craft of printing has always involved the use of supplies and the employment of particular processes, and the chapter addresses these as well.

ADVANCES IN PRINT TECHNOLOGIES, 1450–1800

The methods, tools, and processes that Gutenberg employed would not change for more than three centuries, but social and cultural change resulting from the spread of printing came much sooner. Protestantism owed its development to the power of the printed word. During the 1500s, the sermons and discourses that explained Martin Luther's views and fueled the Reformation movement ran on presses throughout Europe and ignited the passions of readers. Luther's New Testament translation in 1522 constituted one of the earliest best sellers in history, as the Bible began to reach the hands of the common people for the first time. Also in the 1500s, scholar-printers produced fine printed works in major cultural centers such as Paris and Venice. Their literary, scholarly, and religious works kept the early presses busy, but popular printing soon found a market as well. In the 16th century, practical, everyday books, romances and adventures expressly for the entertainment of readers began to find an audience among the ever-growing middling masses. The proliferation and availability of inexpensive reading material to the more common sorts as opposed to the clerical and secular elite encouraged the spread of literacy, and vice versa.

EARLY TYPEFOUNDING AND PIONEER TYPOGRAPHERS

The first written descriptions of the hand-manufacture of metal types can be found in a 1567 work by Christopher Plantin[2] and in Joseph Moxon's *Mechanick Exercises* in the 1680s.[3] The process of typecasting or typefounding by hand was tedious, involved multiple steps, and required specialized skills. The process did not change in any notable way until the 19th century. First, letters were engraved in relief on hard metal. The relief letter was then struck against copper to form a matrix, which was then filed and prepared to attach to a metal mould. The mould had two halves that fit together, and these were covered with wood to allow the typefounder to handle it after the hot metal had been poured inside. With molten metal inside the secured mould, the typefounder shook the contraption to make sure the metal had filled the matrix. After the metal cooled, the mold was opened and a fresh piece of shiny new type emerged from the matrix.

Once early typefounders learned their methods, they spread the knowledge throughout Europe.[4] About 25 years after Gutenberg introduced the printing press, William Caxton took the art of printing with movable type to London. He was not especially talented as a printer, but viewed the press as a practical means of disseminating information. He translated into English and printed about 100 different books, almost all of them in his shop at Westminster Abbey, and made a decent living even though his market was limited to the elite, literate few in 15th-century England. One of the most famous books that he printed was Chaucer's *Canterbury Tales*, printed soon after Caxton set up his press outside London.

Another early typographer, William Caslon, an English engraver, began one of the first type foundries in England. He cut "punches" (or the molds for letters) for a new Arabic font he called "Caslon," and became famous for his craftsmanship and success. Another Englishman, John Baskerville, is remembered for the typeface he developed that carries his name, and for the fine quality of his printing. One of the books issued from his press was Milton's *Paradise Lost*.[5]

William Ged of Edinburgh is credited with the invention of a process now known as stereotyping around 1725. Pages of type could be reproduced using this method, but established printers and letter cutters obstructed widespread use of the new method in order to protect their jobs and business interests. Stereotyping would be rediscovered in another century.

ADVANCES IN OTHER PRINT-RELATED TECHNOLOGIES

From the days of Gutenberg to the start of the 19th century, many of the processes and instruments remained the same or very similar. The printing press, especially, did not change significantly. Other print-related technologies, however, such as ink making and papermaking, made rather significant improvements. Still, major changes would not occur until the 19th century, when mechanization changed everything.

PAPERMAKING

The first watermark, shaped like a cross, appeared on paper made by Italians in the late-thirteenth century. Papermakers produced watermarks by bending larger wire to form the desired shape and then sewing this design into the wire mold, so that the watermark design appeared readily on each finished sheet.[6]

In the 1500s, papermakers began using different methods to produce sheets of paper with various types of finishes. They found that if they separated the pressed sheets from the felts and pressed the sheets again, this produced a smoother final product. Another method involved the rubbing of a smooth stone over the completed sheet of paper. At the beginning of the 1600s, a glazing hammer replaced the stone, and at the start of the next century, paper sheets pressed beneath glazing cylinders of smooth wood produced similar finishes. All these processes occurred prior to the complete drying of the paper. Once the paper achieved the desired finish, the papermaker hung the sheets in a loft, using a t-shaped, wooden device to lift the damp sheets onto wax-coated ropes made from the hair of horses or cows. Usually four or five sheets hung together (such bunches were called spurs) to help retain their smooth surfaces.

In 1670, the Dutch invented a papermaking device and process that became known as the Hollander. Inside a wooden tub, sharp knives mounted on cylinders cut and ground the beaten, watery rags like the blades of a blender, resulting in far more pulp production in far less time.

Nicolas-Louis Robert received the first patent for a papermaking machine in 1798, but the Frenchman's ideas did not find practical use in his own country. British inventors and investors would develop a practical machine in the 19th century.

TYPE COMPOSING AND INKMAKING

Even from the earliest days of composing type, compositors used "cases" or boxes with frames to hold the types. Two cases, one above the other, were mounted in front of the compositor. The upper case held capital letters, and the one directly in front of the compositor held the smaller, non-capital letters—thus the designations "upper case" and "lower case." The quest to create a compositing machine to replace compositors at their cases would occupy the minds and talents of many inventors during the 1800s.

The development of inks suitable for movable-type printing presses came after the development of the presses, but other types of inks had been in use since the first days of block-printing and papermaking. The Chinese produced water-based inks suitable for handwriting and block printing but altogether inadequate for printing from movable type and presses. The thin, watery ink did not spread evenly and smoothly over metal typefaces, but remained in large drops or globules.[7]

Problems in printing with water-based inks were solved with the use of oil-based inks. Paint made from oils dates to the days of the Roman Empire, but a great improvement in the quality of oil paints came in the 15th century. The Flemish painter Jan Van Eyck experimented with oil-based paints and produced products of superior quality and clarity, and his techniques soon spread throughout Europe. His paints used resins as well as oils to produce oleo-resinous products, or varnished oils, the same type of method required for a superior, oil-based, printer's ink.

In addition to using available knowledge such as that advanced by Van Eyck and other fine artists, early printers simply experimented with oils and turpentine and a variety of organic substances to perfect the quality of their printing. Gutenberg produced inks of exceptional quality. Rather than common linseed oil, he most likely used aged nut oil to obtain a superior final blend. After cooking the oil and ridding it of excess grease, he heated and purified turpentine and reduced it to resin, then added the warm resin to the warm, oily ink. The ink colors in the Gutenberg Bible and other products of his press are still noted for their rich, permanent clarity.

From the days of Gutenberg until the arrival of mechanized printing in the 19th century, printers applied ink to the form of type with devices known as inking balls. These hand-held instruments were made from treated leather, sheepskin, dogskin, or the skin of some other animal. Printers alternated soaking the skins and pressing them in the press in order to rid them of their greasiness and prepare them for use. Once the proper texture was achieved, the skins were dried completely, then stuffed with wool or hair to a diameter of about seven inches and nailed to wooden handles. The balls had to be completely dry and non-greasy in order to pick up ink and apply it properly to the form.

Sellers of ink, independent from printers, began to appear in Paris in the early 16th century, and by the start of the 18th century the new industry was well established. By 1701, printers associated with the Cambridge University Press in England had begun purchasing their inks from manufacturers in London and Antwerp. In 1754, Blackwell's began its long and prosperous business as a manufacturer of inks. A number of competitors arrived on the scene in the 1800s as the industry boomed along with the mechanization of the printing press.

LITHOGRAPHY

In the late 1700s in Germany, Alois Senefelder could not afford to purchase the expensive typefaces needed to set himself up as a printer. So he sought to produce his own. A poor man and inexperienced type-maker, he practiced carving his letters on the smooth surface of a printer's stone (traditionally used as a surface for mixing inks for presswork) rather than on the costly copper plates needed for the final product. He simply polished the stone to erase his practice efforts.

Senefelder soon discovered that the stone etchings could be inked and paper pressed against them to transfer the image. The only problem (not to be solved until the advent of "offset" printing many years later) was that all writing had to be done backwards. He also discovered a process of putting letters in relief on the stone by simply writing with erosion-resistant ink and then pouring acid over the stone. In 1798, quite by accident, he discovered that certain mixtures of chemicals would not allow ink to adhere to the stone, while lines drawn with linseed oil soap held the ink perfectly. Only the image held ink, and no carved relief of any kind was needed. The process, called lithography, was purely a chemical one, based on the natural repulsion of grease and water.

NEW PRESSES OF THE 19TH CENTURY

The 19th century brought revolutionary changes to all print-related technologies and processes. In the 1830s, the age of daily mass communication began with the appearance of the first successful penny daily in the United States, the *New York Sun*. The appearance of mass circulation urban dailies, a mid-century boom in book production, and mass demands for more and more printed matter, all contributed to improvements in printing press capabilities and new processes designed to speed up production and improve quality.

One of the most stunning examples of change in the 19th century occurred with relation to the printing press. The basic design for printing presses had not changed since the days of Gutenberg, until 19th-century technologies inspired inventors and manufacturers to experiment with new designs and concepts. By 1800, improvements in the methods of casting iron marked the dawn of an industrial revolution that would transform the world during the 19th century. In 1800, Earl James Stanhope of England, a man of wealth who devoted his time to inventions and scientific pursuits, devised the first all-iron press, which used a system of compound levers to control the pressure of the platen, replacing the old wooden screw method. The Stanhope press featured a large platen that, due to the system of levers, could be lowered in one pull. Only about 250 sheets could be printed in an hour, but the quality of printing and the labor-saving aspects of the iron press over the wooden press were considerable. Iron presses were also remarkably durable. Later in the century, iron hand-presses such as the Stanhope were still being used as proof presses in many printing shops and newspaper offices. Until mid-century, Stanhope presses were still being manufactured and operated around the world.

Soon, as steam power became harnessed in this age of great discovery and invention, innovative printing press makers replaced their hand-cranked designs with mechanized models that operated from steam power.

Cylinder and Rotary Presses

In 1790, an Englishman named William Nicholson patented his idea for using rolling cylinders in printing. He proposed the casting of types into multi-letter molds that could be shaped and inserted upon a cylinder. A corresponding cylinder would be covered with leather and used to distribute ink. Paper would be passed between the two cylinders. The patent lacked specifics and design practicality, and therefore the press was never constructed.

Frederick Koenig invented the first, practical cylinder press. It looked much like the handpresses of the day, only including a pulley to move the form and a self-inking system. In 1810 he produced the first iron mechanized press that included inking rollers rather than old inking balls. This machine produced 400 sheets per hour. He then modified the machine to include a cylinder to replace the platen.

Koenig's first practical, flatbed cylinder press worked by first wrapping paper around the cylinder, then pressing it against the ink bed of type that moved back and forth. Iron frames attached to the cylinder held the sheets of paper in place. Steam was used to power the press; and more than 800 sheets per hour could be printed, with one pressman placing the paper and another removing it after it had been printed.

By 1811, Koenig had plans to develop a double-feeding printing machine that would increase production, and the publisher of The Times in London ordered two of the double-feeder machines to be built. A great amount of secrecy was necessary during the building of the machines and the first night of their use. Mechanization and automation threatened the livelihoods of many people, not only in printing but in other industries as well. Had Koenig's work been discovered he would no doubt have been threatened and harassed and possibly forced to stop. Precautions were taken in setting up the machine. The Times obtained a nearby building to house the monstrous machine and protect it from sabotage. The first issue of The Times printed on the machine, November 29, 1814, was conducted without the knowledge of the pressmen in the other building, who were told the paper was being held up for news on the Napoleonic wars. The publisher of The Times appeared in the old pressroom the next morning with copies of the paper that had been printed on the steam-powered press. He promised to pay each man full wages until employment could be obtained elsewhere, and thus he avoided any violence.

Four types of cylinder presses became popular during the 19th century: the stop-cylinder, the two-revolution, the continuous revolution, and the oscillating or reversing cylinder. The stop-cylinder was so named because the cylinder stopped after each impression and stayed in place as the form returned to position. The two-revolution cylinder allowed an impression to be made with each second revolution of the cylinder. The continuous revolution cylinder continued revolving as the bed returned to its position (with only half the large drum-cylinder blanketed thick enough to come in contact with the inked bed). With the oscillating or reversing cylinder, the cylinder itself was raised and returned to its original position.

Rotary printing also appeared in the 1800s. Paper was passed between two cylinders. One was engraved with the printing surface, and the other served as a pressing cylinder. By mid-century, curved, stereotyped plates were attached to the one cylinder to replace the more tedious, earlier method of adjusting and securing specially cast, individual pieces of type on the cylinder. In 1848, Augustus Applegath built a vertical "type-revolving" rotary press for *The Times*. The type cylinder was 200 inches in diameter, and the ordinary type surfaces were held in such a way to form a polygon. Eight smaller cylinders surrounded the central cylinder, and the paper passed through each. Also at mid-century, Richard Hoe's company in the United States began manufacturing horizontal, type-revolving rotary presses. The Hoe name became synonymous with rotary printing machines. The *New York Tribune*, *Philadelphia Times*, and many other newspapers in the United States and Europe used his presses. In 1863, William Bullock of Philadelphia patented the first rotary press fed automatically by rolls (called "webs") of paper and made use of stereotype plates to print both sides of the paper at once. His press was constructed for the *Philadelphia Inquirer* in 1865 and produced about 8,000 to 10,000 sheets each hour.[8]

Rotary presses continued to be used in newspaper offices until the early 1970s. They produced broadsheet newspapers at a speed of about 70,000 per hour.

ADVANCES IN OTHER PRINT-RELATED TECHNOLOGIES

Many other aspects of print-related technologies and processes experienced development during the 19th century. Among these were the introduction of automated inking systems for the swift, new presses, new methods in typefounding, the commercial use of lithography, mechanization in papermaking, the switch to wood pulp as the base for paper, and the introduction of halftone reproductions of photographs. Additionally, the quest for a practical and affordable composing machine intrigued inventors throughout most of the century, until successful, mechanized composition devices came into practical use.

The new printing presses required proper inking systems to replace the old-style inking process that used animal-skin inking balls. Early presses tried leather-covered rollers, but they proved inadequate. In the early 1820s, printers realized that the same process used to transfer images on pottery might be adapted for press use. It made use of a special glue-and-molasses-based "composition" that held and distributed ink, and the resulting tools adapted for press use became known as "composition balls" and "composition rollers." The printer heated the gluey composition until it melted and then coated the inking cylinders with it. The resulting inking system proved far superior to the leather-covered devices.

In 1811, a Scottish immigrant in the United States patented the trigger mould, the first big improvement in hand moulds since the days of Gutenberg. The trigger device doubled the production speed of typecasting for experienced typefounders.

One of the first patents for a typecasting machine was issued in 1806, but the first machine that came into practical use did not appear until 1838. David Bruce, a New Yorker, improved on the efforts of two Bostonians, M. D. Mann and Stephen Sturdevant, who had patented a machine that produced inferior, porous types that could not withstand the pressure from printing presses. Bruce's invention used a pump to force the molten metal into the mould, and produced about 40 individual types or "sorts" each minute. The types that came from the Bruce machines required additional handwork before they could be used. The first ready-to-use types came from the Johnson and Atkinson machine, patented two years prior to the American Civil War. These machines found a market in the United States and abroad, especially in Great Britain.

MECHANIZED PAPERMAKING

The Fourdrinier papermaking machine, patented early in the 19th century, allowed the production of paper on continuous reels rather than single sheets. By mid-century, the mass-production presses required paper from these large rolls.

In the 19th century, papermakers switched from rags to wood chips as the basic material for pulp. The process did not enjoy commercial success overnight, however, as many obstacles had to be surmounted in the manufacture of a suitable pulp. Impurities in the wood, such as resins, inhibited the process and caused an inferior paper product. In the 1870s, the introduction of chemical techniques to rid the wood of impurities vastly improved the finished product, and the industry was firmly established. By the 1890s, most papers being manufactured came from chemically treated wood pulp.

COMPOSING MACHINES

The setting of type did not change throughout the first 400 or so years after Gutenberg's invention. In the 19th century, however, with the beginning of the age of daily mass communication and the popularity of mass circulation books and periodicals, and the rise of mechanization, the 400-year-old process of composing type by hand suddenly seemed especially antiquated. As the mechanical deficiency became more and more obvious to people, inventors throughout the world sought to build an efficient and practical machine to set type. The

machine would have to receive commands to select and correctly arrange many characters—upper and lower case letters in regular and bold typefaces, punctuation marks, signs, and symbols.

Many inventors patented machines, but newspaper and publishing offices adopted only a select few of them, as none of them solved all the problems associated with type composition. Kastenbein typesetting machines found popularity, especially in newspaper offices, but these did not perform justification. Line justification remained a serious problem for a number of years. Machines could only produce copy set in one continuous line without spaces. Therefore, compositors had to take the machine-produced lines and carefully space the words by hand.[9]

In the late 1800s, two young inventors—Ottmar Mergenthaler with his Linotype, and Tolbert Lanston with his Monotype—solved many of the problems associated with composing machine construction.[10] The Linotype and Monotype enjoyed much commercial success, and the composing machine became a permanent fixture in major newspaper and publishing offices.

HALFTONE REPRODUCTIONS

Development of the halftone in the 1880s allowed for the first time the reproduction of photographs in print media such as books, magazines, and newspapers. Prior to the halftone, printers reproduced drawings or artwork using engravings on wood or metal, or lithographic drawings that repelled ink from particular areas and attracted it to others, forming an image. Such reproductions were time-consuming, costly, and non-realistic.

The principle of halftone reproduction lies in the ability of the human eye to perceive different shades from variously spaced and sized dots. The optical illusion causes the eye to read very small black dots, with white spaces between them, as more grayish in tone than larger black dots more closely spaced. The reproduction process involves taking a picture of the continuous-tone photograph to be reproduced, using a special camera with a ruled halftone screen. The screen causes the exposure to appear within thousands of small black and white dots, and this resulting image is known as the halftone.[11]

The first known halftone in a United States newspaper, produced by Stephen H. Horgan in 1880, depicted a photograph called Shantytown. He used a crude screen that broke the photographic image into dots, but the result resembled a drawing more than a photograph.

THE 20TH CENTURY

Many technologies and processes developed during the 1800s continued to be used throughout much of the 20th century. For example, Linotype machines continued to be used until the printing industry switched to photographic typesetting. While the Linotype benefited from many improvements through the years, the basic design introduced by Mergenthaler remained fundamentally the same. Ink products also remained virtually unchanged until pronounced improvements in ink colors produced more vivid printed products in the latter half of the 20th century.

Major advances in the 20th century came primarily in the areas of photomechanical processes, such as improvements in halftone reproductions and especially the reproduction of color pictures, the widespread use of offset printing, and the rise of phototypesetting. Improvements in the typewriter at the first of the century led to its widespread use. The phenomenal effects of computerization revolutionized the printing industry in the last decades of the 20th century, and continue to do so today.

The typewriter, invented in the 1800s, became popular in the early decades of the 20th century. The great demand for typewriters led to the establishment of a number of manufacturing firms. During the 1930s, manufacturers made several improvements to the typewriter, including the ability to change typefaces, automatic justification, and use of the carbon ribbon. The North Eastern Appliances Co. began manufacturing electric typewriters in 1923, and IBM began research in the 1940s to improve the typewriter. In 1944, the research efforts paid off when IBM introduced a typewriter with proportional spacing that made typed pages appear to have been issued from a printing press.

Offset printing is based on the chemical principle of repulsion between water and grease. The flat offset plate has a photosensitive layer, and the parts containing print are exposed and therefore attract ink, while the other, unexposed part attracts only water. The process is called "offset" because the paper never actually touches the litho plate, but comes in contact with a "blanket" roller that transfers the image to the paper.

In 1904, a New York lithographer, Ira W. Rubel, designed a printing press for offset lithography. The press transferred the litho image to a rubber roller that contacted the paper. At about the same time that Rubel constructed his offset press, Caspar Hermann, an Ohio lithographer of German descent, built one as well. During the 1930s, the *Peninsular Mirror*, a daily newspaper in Palo Alto, pioneered the use of offset printing in the newspaper business. The process did not gain widespread acceptance until the 1960s, but during the 1970s and 1980s it became the foremost method of printing reproductions.

The setting of metal type by hand continued in most publishing firms until after World War I, and printing from metal type and plates continued throughout the first half of the century. In the 1920s, many involved in the printing trade made the move to mechanized typesetting machines, either the Linotype, the Monotype, or something similar. In 1957, the first book to be phototypeset in its entirety hit the market in Great Britain. The process allowed the production of offset-litho plates from film with phototypeset letters rather than from metal composing. Phototypesetting gained widespread use in the 1960s, 1970s, and 1980s. Today, metal type composition is practically obsolete.

The Teletypesetter, another invention that made use of photographic methods of reproduction, went on display in New York in the late 1920s, and found practical application thereafter. The electromagnetic device operated typesetting machines via electrical impulses pulsated through telegraphy. It allowed typesetting via remote control from a distance and brought wire reports into newspaper offices. Teletypesetting came into widespread use in the 1950s and thereafter.

Facsimile, usually shortened to "fax," is the transmission of graphic matter, usually over telephone lines. Although facsimile is often thought of as a modern technology, it originated in Britain in the 1840s. Its first commercial application came in 1907, when newspaper wirephotos were sent across the English channel.

In 1924 New York newspapers published photographs of the Republican National Convention that had been transmitted from Cleveland over telephone wires, using a new piece of facsimile equipment. The process had become so effective that each 5x7 photograph took just four and a half minutes to transmit. One of the photographs was received in New York just 44 minutes after it was taken.[12] The Associated Press began regular wirephoto service to member newspapers in 1934. Digital fax machines now are used to transmit newspaper photographs.

Facsimile also has been used to transmit typescript copy from one location to another. In 1966 Xerox marketed a device called the telecopier, which used telephone lines to transmit pages of copy.

In 1973 the *Wall Street Journal* tested the feasibility of using a communications satellite to transmit facsimiles of full-size newspaper pages to a distant printing plant. The test was a success, and two years later the *Journal* built the world's first newspaper production plant to be operated through a communications satellite, in Orlando, Florida.[13] The plant was the first in a series of similar facilities that have enabled the *Wall Street Journal*, the *New York Times*, and *USA Today* to become national newspapers, offering same-day delivery across the country.

COMPUTERIZATION

The computer age brought immense changes to the newspaper and publishing industries, changes that were necessary for survival in a world served instantly by television and radio broadcasts. During the last 30 years, newsrooms across the country replaced their old-fashioned typewriters and typesetting machines with video display terminals and modern computer systems. Almost all aspects of newspaper operations, including production, layout and composition, circulation, and even morgue (newspaper library) operations, are now computerized. Reporters use the Internet to access records online for use in their stories.

In addition to those who work in the printing industry, individuals now have the opportunity to experience the satisfaction of perusing fresh, printed pages of their own creation. Scanners and affordable desktop publishing software have made it possible for almost anyone to produce high-quality printed work. Computer tools even allow manipulation of photographs, drawings, and etchings, to improve the quality of the final product—or to alter images.

In book publishing, digital printing presses (introduced in 1993) and computer-to-plate (CTP) integrated systems are offering new methods of printing and changing the industry. Printing plates can be made from imagesetters for use on offset presses. In a more recent development, the contents of publications can be sent, via computer, to digital, electronic presses that receive images directly and do not use plates.

The social and cultural changes wrought by new printing technologies and the digital age may prove to be as far-reaching as those produced by the introduction of the Gutenberg press or the mass production presses of the 1800s. Only time will tell. For the present, however, newspapers continue to appear as usual, as do books and magazines. Major revolutions in technological change do not occur overnight, but take much time to develop and spread. In the meantime, the presses—whether digital, offset, or antique hand-cranked—continue to roll.

Selected Readings

Carter, Thomas Francis. The Invention of Printing in China and Its Spread Westward, 2nd ed., revised by L. Carrington Goodrich. New York: Ronald Press, 1955.

Goble, Corban. "Mark Twain's Nemesis: The Paige Compositor." Printing History 36:2 (1988): 2–16.

Hoe & Co., R. A Short History of the Printing Press and of the Improvements in Printing Machinery from the Time of Gutenburg up to the Present Day. New York: R. Hoe, 1902.

Isaacs, George A. The Story of the Newspaper Printing Press. London: Co-operative Printing Society, 1931.

Mooradian, Karlen. "The Dawn of Printing." Journalism Monographs 23 (1972).

Oswald, John Clyde. A History of Printing: Its Development Through Five Hundred Years. New York: Appleton, 1928.

Pickett, Calder M. "Technology and the New York Press in the 19th Century." Journalism Quarterly 37 (1960): 398–407.

Sloan, Wm. David, and Frank Krompak. "The Origins of Mass Communication," chap. 1 in Wm. David Sloan, ed., The Age of Mass Communication. Northport, Ala.: Vision Press, 1998.

Steinberg, S. H. Five Hundred Years of Printing. London and New Castle: British Library and Oak Knoll Press, 1996.

Williams, Trevor I, Charles Singer, E. J. Holmyard, and A. R. Hall, eds. A History of Technology. Oxford: Oxford at the Clarendon Press, 1958. See especially W. Turner Berry, "Printing and Related Trades," vol. 5: 683–715; and James Moran, "Printing." vol. 7: 1268–80.

Wroth, Lawrence. The Colonial Printer. Portland, Me.: Southworth-Anthoensen Press, 1938.

Notes

1. A good recent biography of Gutenberg is Albert Kaper, *Johann Gutenberg: The Man and His Invention*, trans. by Douglas Martin (Aldershot, Hants: Scholar Press, 1996).

2. See Ray Nash, ed., and Stanley Morison, trans., *An Account of Calligraphy and Printing in the Sixteenth Century from Dialogues Attributed to Christopher Plantin, printed and published by him at Antwerp, 1567* (New York: Liturgical Arts Society, 1949).

3. Joseph Moxon, *Mechanick Exercises on the Whole Art of Printing (1683–4)*, 2nd ed., Herbert Davis and Harry Carter, eds. (New York: Dover Publications, 1978).

4. Elizabeth I. Eisenstein, *The Printing Press as an Agent of Change: Communication and Cultural Transformations in Early-Modern Europe* (Cambridge: Cambridge University Press, 1980), explains the social impact of the printing press as it spread throughout Europe, especially its influences on movements such as the Reformation and the Renaissance.

5. Sean Jennett, *Pioneers in Printing* (London: Routledge & Kegan Paul Limited, 1958), contains biographical chapters on various European pioneers in early printing and typefounding.

6. For a detailed examination of technological changes in paper production from 1500 to 1750, see John Overton, "A Note on Technical Advances in the Manufacture of Paper before the Nineteenth Century," in Charles Singer, E. J. Holmyard, A. R. Hall, and Trevor I. Williams, *A History of Technology*, 3 vols. (Oxford: Oxford at the Clarendon Press, 1957), 3: 411–16.

7. C. H. Bloy, *A History of Printing Ink, Balls and Rollers, 1440–1850*, 2nd ed. (London: Wynkyn De Worde Society, 1972), provides a detailed history of ink making and includes a number of old ink recipes reprinted from primary source material.

8. Horace Greeley, Leon Case, et al, *The Great Industries of the United States: being an historical summary of the origin, growth, and perfection of the chief industrial arts of this country* (Hartford: J. B. Burr & Hyde, 1872). This large volume describes state-of-the-art technologies and industries in 1872. Includes chapters on printing, lithography, steel and copper plate engraving, newspapers, and much more.

9. James Moran, *The Composition of Reading Matter* (London: Wace, 1965), provides a readable history of developments in typographical composition from the days of Gutenberg and the compositor's case to the advent of composing machines, and finally to the emergence of computers.

10. Basil Charles Kahan, *Ottmar Mergenthaler: the man and his machine: a biographical appreciation of the inventor on his centennial* (New Castle, Del: Oak Knoll Press, 2000), provides an admiring work with pertinent information on the inventor and his Linotype machine.

11. A. J. Lockrey, *Halftone Processes*, 2nd ed. (New York: J. J. Tepper, 1941). This treatise, if read carefully, provides understandable descriptions of the process for those who have never worked in a print shop.

12. *New York Times*, 20 May 1924, 1.

13. "Wall Street Journal Publishes by Satellite," *Editor & Publisher*, 22 November 1975, 15.

Contributors

James Aucoin (Ph.D., University of Missouri), a former newspaper reporter and editor, is an associate professor of communication at the University of South Alabama, where he teaches the history and ethics of mass communication. He has published articles on the history of investigative journalism in *American Journalism* and *Journalism History*.

Margaret A. Blanchard (Ph.D., University of North Carolina) is the author of *Revolutionary Sparks: Freedom of Expression in Modern America* and *Exporting the First Amendment: The Press-Government Crusade of 1945-52* and of numerous articles on the history of freedom of expression in the United States. She served as editor of the *History of the Mass Media in the United States: An Encyclopedia* and is associate editor for history and law for *Journalism & Mass Communication Quarterly*. A former president of the American Journalism Historians Association, she is William Rand Kenan Jr. Professor of Journalism and Mass Communication at the University of North Carolina.

Frederick Blevens (Ph.D., University of Missouri) is an associate professor of journalism at Southwest Texas State University. He was a journalist on metropolitan daily newspapers for 17 years. His work has appeared in the *Journal of Mass Media Ethics, Quill, Chronicle of Higher Education*, and *American Journalism*. He co-authored *Twilight of Press Freedom* and has served as editor of the *Intelligencer*, the newsletter of the American Journalism Historians Association. In 2001 he was selected Teacher of the Year by the Freedom Forum.

William J. Brown (Ph.D., University of South-ern California) is Dean of the College of Communication and the Arts at Regent University. His research interests include media effects and social influence, particularly through entertainment-education media and celebrities.

Catherine Cassara (Ph.D., Michigan State University) is an associate professor at Bowling Green State University in Ohio. She writes about U. S. international coverage and is past head of the International Communication Division of the Association for Education in Journalism and Mass Communication. She was a Knight Fellow in 1996.

Dane S. Claussen (Ph.D., University of Georgia) is associate professor and director of the graduate program in journalism and mass communication at Point Park College. A former newspaper editor and publisher, he is writing two books: a newspaper management textbook and a history of newspaper industry marketing. He has edited three books, including works on the Promise Keepers and on sex, religion, and the media.

Jon Enriquez (Ph.D., Georgetown University) is assistant professor of history and Associate Dean of Academic Affairs at Hanover College. His research includes journalistic practices in presidential elections in the 20th century.

Bruce J. Evensen (Ph.D., University of Wisconsin) is a professor of communication at DePaul University. His books include *Truman, Palestine and the Press: Shaping Conventional Wisdom at the Beginning of the Cold War; When Dempsey Fought Tunney: Heroes, Hokum, and Storytelling in the Jazz Age*; and *The Responsible Reporter*.

Norma Fay Green (Ph.D., Michigan State University) has been Graduate Journalism Director since 1993 at Columbia College Chicago. She is the author of 12 journalism history articles and book chapters. With more than 30 years in newspaper, magazine, and book publishing, she continues as a freelance journalist. She was a 2000 Fulbright lecturer in Denmark.

John Allen Hendricks (Ph.D., University of Southern Mississippi) is department chair and an associate professor of communication at Southeastern Oklahoma State University. He is the author of numerous journal articles, chapters, and published essays on the history of broadcast journalism.

William E. Huntzicker (Ph.D., University of Minnesota), a Minneapolis writer, has taught journalism at several campuses, including the University of Minnesota. He is the author of *The Popular Press 1833-65* and articles on journalism history. He has been a reporter for the Associated Press and the *Miles City Star* in Montana.

John D. Keeler (Ph.D., University of Texas) serves as professor and director of doctoral studies in Communication and the Arts at Regent University. His research and experience have crossed the fields of journalism, radio, television, film, advertising, public relations, marketing, and organizational communication and leadership.

Paulette D. Kilmer (Ph.D., University of Illinois) is an assistant professor of communication at the University of Toledo. She is the author of *The Fear of Sinking: The American Success Formula in the Gilded Age* as well as journal articles.

Elliot King (Ph.D. University of California, San Diego) is an associate professor of communication at Loyola College in Maryland. He is the co-author of *The Online Journalist* and four other books about the use of new communications technologies. He has served as an officer in the history, magazine, and communications technology and policy divisions of the Association for Education in Journalism and Mass Communication.

Carolyn Kitch (Ph.D., Temple University) is the director of the magazine sequence in the Department of Journalism, Public Relations and Advertising at Temple University, where she also serves as affiliated faculty in women's studies and American studies. She is the author of *The Girl on the Magazine Cover: The Emergence of Visual Stereotypes in American Mass Media* and articles in several communications journals. She is a former writer and editor for *McCall's, Good Housekeeping,* and *Reader's Digest.*

Gary W. Larson (Ph.D., University of Minnesota) is an assistant professor of media studies and broadcast journalism at the University of Nevada, Las Vegas. He is the author of book chapters on the Internet and globalization, as well as numerous national convention papers on visual literacy, synchronous mediated communication on the Internet, and media criticism.

Greg Lisby (Ph.D., University of Tennessee) is an associate professor of journalism at Georgia State University. He is the author of *Mass Communication Law in Georgia,* in addition to 25 articles on legal and historical topics published in *Communication Law & Policy, Journalism Monographs, Journalism Quarterly, Communication & the Law, Journal of Communication Inquiry, Newspaper Research Journal,* and *Georgia Historical Quarterly.*

Michael A. Longinow (Ph.D., University of Kentucky), journalism coordinator at Asbury College, is a former newspaper reporter and photojournalist. He has written numerous magazine pieces for religious and secular publications. He has contributed chapters to books on journalism history and on the culture of religion.

Linda J. Lumsden (Ph.D., University of North Carolina) is an associate professor at Western Kentucky University. She is the author of *Rampant Women: Suffragists and the Right of Assembly* and *Adirondack Artists and Craftspeople* as well as numerous articles on suffragists and the press.

Shannon K. McCraw (doctoral candidate, University of Oklahoma) is an instructor of communication and director of forensics at Southeastern Oklahoma State University. He is the author of numerous journal articles and conference presentations.

Jim McPherson (Ph.D., Washington State University) is an assistant professor of communication studies at Whitworth College. He is a former award-winning newspaper journalist and has written for books, magazines, and academic journals. He is editor of the *Intelligencer*, the newsletter of the American Journalism Historians Association.

Joe Mirando (Ph.D., University of Southern Mississippi) is a professor of communication at Southeastern Louisiana University. A former newspaper reporter and copy editor, he has studied at the American Press Institute and taught classes at Millsaps College.

Sally I. Morano (M.A., University of Alabama) has presented research papers on the history of newspaper design.

Lisa Mullikin Parcell (Ph.D., University of Alabama) is the author of several book chapters and research papers on the history of journalistic writing, the mass media between 1900 and 1945, and children and television. She is a grant writer for WSU-LINK at Wichita State University.

Earnest L. Perry Jr. (Ph.D., University of Missouri) is an assistant professor of journalism at Texas Christian University. His doctoral dissertation won an Honorable Mention in the 1999 American Journalism Historians Association Dissertation Award competition. He has presented numerous papers on the African-American press. He worked 15 years as a reporter and editor at newspapers in Texas and Missouri.

Erika J. Pribanic-Smith (M.A., University of Alabama) is a reporter for *Sun Newspapers* in Cleveland, Ohio. She is the author of several articles and papers on 18th- and 19th-century newspaper reporting and advertising.

Ford Risley (Ph.D., University of Florida) is a former newspaper reporter and an assistant professor at Penn State University. His research focuses on Antebellum and Civil War journalism. He has published articles in *American Journalism, Journalism History, Georgia Historical Quarterly*, and *Civil War History*.

Helen Rounds (M.A., University of Alabama) has presented research papers on the history of newspaper crusading and reform efforts. She is a public school teacher in Nevada.

Dick Schwarzlose (Ph.D., University of Illinois) is a professor of journalism at Northwestern University. He is the author of the two-volume *The Nation's Newsbrokers* and *Newspapers: A Reference Guide*. He received the Northwestern Alumni Association award for undergraduate teaching in 1991.

Ken Sexton (Ph.D., University of Georgia) is an assistant professor of journalism at Morehead State University. He previously worked as a teacher, reporter, photographer, and public relations specialist. He is working on a project to list and publicize the nation's photographic history collections.

John Slater (Ph.D., University of North Carolina) is associate professor of communication at Western Carolina University. A former reporter at the City News Bureau of Chicago, he is the author of numerous articles on the history of mass communication and media technology.

W. David Sloan (Ph.D., University of Texas) is the founder of the American Journalism Historians Association and served a five-year term as editor of its research journal, *American Journalism*. He has published 21 other books, among them *The Media in America: A History; Historical Methods in Mass Communication*; and *The Significance of the Media in American History* (all with James D. Startt); *American Journalism History: An Annotated Bibliography; Perspectives on Mass Communication History; The Early American Press, 1690-1783; The Age of Mass Communication; Great Editorials*; and *Masterpieces of Reporting*. He is co-editor of the seven-volume series "History of American Journalism," a work in progress. He has authored more than eighty articles and papers on history and journalistic writing and has been recognized with several research awards for his work in media history. In 1998 he received the AJHA's Kobre Award for lifetime achievements. He has served as national president (1998-2000) of Kappa Tau Alpha, the mass communication honor society. On its 90th anniversary, KTA selected him as one of the five most important members in its history. He is a professor of journalism at the University of Alabama.

Michael R. Smith (Ph.D., Regent University) is associate professor and chair of journalism at Regent University. He is the author of *The Jesus Newspaper* and the author of eight journal research articles and more than 2,500 articles for newspapers and magazines. He has contributed chapters to books on religion and the press and on people with disabilities.

James D. Startt (Ph.D., University Maryland), senior research professor of history at Valparaiso University, is the author of *Journalism's Unofficial Ambassador: A Biography of Edward Price Bell, 1869-1943* and *Journalists for Empire: the Imperial Debate In the Edwardian Stately Press, 1903-1913* and of numerous articles in journalism history. He has co-authored and co-edited various other works in field and in 2000 received the American Journalism Historians Association's Sidney Kobre Award for lifetime achievement.

Doug Tarpley (Ph.D., Southern Illinois University) is director of Regent University's Washington Graduate Journalism Center. He has worked as a newspaper reporter and section editor and as a magazine managing editor, editor, and design editor. He has served on the governing boards and as an elected officer in a number of national journalism education associations and has received numerous awards for his scholastic work. He has authored many scholarly articles, book chapters, and academic papers in the journalism field.

Susan Thompson (Ph.D., University of Alabama) has authored or co-authored several books, including *Reinventing Media* and *Intro-*

duction to Media Communication (5th ed.), written several book chapters related to media history, and presented papers at national and international conferences.

Manuel Torres (M.A., University of Alabama) is a reporter at the *New Orleans Times-Picayune* and a former Fulbright scholar.

Jim Upshaw (B.A., San Diego State University) is distinguished professor of broadcast journalism at the University of Oregon. He is an award-winning veteran of print and broadcast journalism and worked as a television reporter in Denver, Tokyo, and Washington, D. C., before going into teaching. He has written a number of articles on journalism practice and ethics.

Debra Reddin van Tuyll (Ph.D., University of South Carolina) is an assistant professor of journalism at Augusta State University. She is co-editor of *The Civil War and The Press* and author of several articles on the southern press during the Civil War. She has won awards for her professional work from the Associated Press and Council for the Advancement and Support of Education (CASE), and in 1999 the College Media Advisers named her Magazine Adviser of the Year at four-year colleges.

Tim P. Vos (M.A., University of Iowa) is an instructor of Communication at Dordt College and a doctoral student at Syracuse University. He has 12 years of professional journalism experience.

Julie Hedgepeth Williams (Ph.D., University of Alabama) is the author of *The Significance of the Printed Word in Early America* and co-author of *The Early American Press, 1690-1783*, as well as *The Great Reporters: An Anthology of News Writing at Its Best*. She also has authored chapters on colonial journalism, media and religion, and women in the media for several other books. She has served as a member of the Board of Directors of the American Journalism Historians Association and chair of its Publications Committee. She teaches journalism at Samford University.

Index